HOUSEHOLDS

HOUSEHOLDS

Comparative and Historical Studies of the Domestic Group

Edited by

ROBERT McC. NETTING
RICHARD R. WILK
ERIC J. ARNOULD

UNIVERSITY OF CALIFORNIA PRESS
Berkeley Los Angeles London

UNIVERSITY OF CALIFORNIA PRESS
Berkeley and Los Angeles, California

UNIVERSITY OF CALIFORNIA PRESS, LTD.
London, England

Library of Congress Cataloging in Publication Data

Main entry under title:

Households : comparative and historical studies of the
domestic group.

Includes index.
1. Households—Congresses. 2. Family—Congresses.
3. Social change—Congresses. 4. Culture—Congresses.
I. Netting, Robert McC. II. Wilk, Richard R.
III. Arnould, Eric J.
HQ7.H68 1984 306.8'5 83-17975
ISBN 0-520-04996-9
ISBN 0-520-04997-7 (pbk.)

1 2 3 4 5 6 7 8 9

Contents

Acknowledgments

The Wenner-Gren Foundation for Anthropological Research generously supported Symposium Number 87, *Households: Changing Form and Function,* that met October 9–15, 1981, at the Seven Springs Conference Center, Mt. Kisco, N.Y. In this gracious and comfortable setting, the twenty participants from the fields of anthropology and history enjoyed the satisfactions of intellectual exercise and debate in lively discussions that were genuinely cross-disciplinary but never cross. A preliminary account of the proceedings appeared during 1982 in *Current Anthropology* 23:571–75. An additional grant from the Foundation aided editorial work and publication of this volume. As conference organizers and editors, we want to express our gratitude to the Board of Trustees of the Wenner-Gren Foundation. We also owe a great deal to the unparalleled experience, tact, and continued encouragement of the Foundation's Director of Research, Lita Osmundsen—it was a pleasure and an education to work with her and her helpful staff. Thanks are owing as well to Stanley Holwitz and the people of the University of California Press for the professional and efficient manner in which they brought out this book.

Contributors

Eric J. Arnould
U.S. Embassy
Niamey, Niger

Anthony T. Carter
Dept. of Anthropology
University of Rochester

Brian L. Foster
Dept. of Anthropology
Arizona State University

William A. Douglass
Basque Studies Program
University of Nevada, Reno

Robert Hackenberg
Dept. of Anthropology
University of Colorado

Eugene A. Hammel
Dept. of Anthropology
University of California, Berkeley

David Herlihy
Dept. of History
Harvard University

Peter Kunstadter
East-West Center
Honolulu

Peter Laslett
Cambridge Group for the History of Population and Social Structure
Cambridge, UK

Olga F. Linares
Smithsonian Tropical Research Institute
Balboa, Panama

Orvar Löfgren
Institute of Ethnology
Lund University, Sweden

Arthur D. Murphy
Dept. of Anthropology
University of Georgia

Robert McC. Netting
Dept. of Anthropology
University of Arizona

Andrejs Plakans
Dept. of History
Iowa State University

Martine Segalen
Centre d'Ethnologie Française
Musée national des arts et traditions populaires
Paris, France

Henry A. Selby
Dept. of Anthropology
University of Texas

Richard R. Wilk
Anthropology Board
University of California, Santa Cruz

Arthur P. Wolf
Dept. of Anthropology
Stanford University

Sylvia Junko Yanagisako
Dept. of Anthropology
Stanford University

Introduction

Robert McC. Netting, Richard R. Wilk, and Eric J. Arnould

NOTES ON THE HISTORY OF THE HOUSEHOLD CONCEPT

Is *household* a significant unit in the description, comparison, and analysis of human societies? Social historians and anthropologists in recent years have responded to this question in a strongly positive manner.

> The household is society's most commonplace and basic socioeconomic unit. (Rathje 1981)
>
> I believe that a convincing case can be made out in favour of the household as the fundamental unit in pre-industrial European society for social, economic, even educational and political purposes. . . . The relationship between parents, children, servants and kin within the English household, and the interplay of its size and structure with economic and demographic development, make up an intricate adaptive mechanism which we are only now beginning to understand. (Laslett 1969)
>
> [In a peasant agrarian economy] the household was perhaps the most flexible and responsive social grouping. . . . The family household is an institution sensitive to minor, short-term fluctuations in the socioeconomic environment and a prime means by which individuals adapt to the subtle shifts in opportunities and constraints that confront them. (Netting 1979)

Why the sudden surge of interest in a seemingly obvious and omnipresent social grouping? Why was the household not a focus of interest for preceding generations of social scientists? There are two possible explanations. First, the household or family, as it was more frequently termed, had supposedly evolved from a primitive, large, relatively undifferentiated, extended kin group into the small, specialized, nuclear groups familiar in the modern West. This progressive change was considered so self-evident and cross-culturally valid that little further investigation was warranted. Second, the household was judged to be a transitory group that precipitated in each society from the action of culturally specific systems of kinship, marriage customs, and rules of residence. It was a by-product of socially persistent norms such as those labeled patrilineal descent, polygyny, or matrilocality.

Household was not a designation used by the evolutionists, and it is found infrequently in the indexes of more recent comprehensive treatments of social organization (Lowie 1947, Murdock 1949, Fox 1967). Nineteenth-century evolutionary scenarios of domestic group change envisioned unstructured primal hordes giving way to matrilineal descent groups and eventually to patriarchal families with recognized marriage, primogeniture, and a subsidiary position for women. The nuclear conjugal unit with monogamous marriage and neolocal residence was the inevitable result of "progress," but earlier stages or survivals of larger, extended families were preserved among primitive contemporaries. Even when social scientists discarded the rigid, hypothetical evolutionary stages, they retained a typological and conceptual distinction between the traditional family with multiple conjugal units linked by kinship and the isolated nuclear family of the West. For example, from the time of Sir Henry Maine, the family in India was thought to be a joint, patriarchal, three-generation descent group with common property, a house with a common kitchen, and the common worship of a family idol (Shah 1974: 123–28). Movement toward an elementary family form would only come about through industrialization and urbanization, and the high frequency of small, nonextended family households in censuses from 1825 to 1955 was explained by the disintegration of the ancient joint family system (Shah 1974:90, 127).

Engels perpetuated the typological and unilineal evolutionary view of the family found in the nineteenth-century theories of Morgan, Bachofen, and McLennan, but he sharpened Morgan's emphasis on the role of productive tasks and inheritance in defining marriage and family forms. He saw the monogamous nuclear family as the inevitable product of the development of property rights and one that mirrored the encompassing social structure. According to Engels (1970:123), the nuclear family emerged from the transitional patriarchal joint family or "house community" similar to the Balkan *zadruga*, the French *parconneries*, the Indian joint family, and the Mexican *calpulli*. With the rise of private property and monogamous marriage, the nuclear family became for the first time in history the "economic unit of society" (Engels 1970:138). The modern family is based on the "supremacy of the man . . . to produce children of undisputed paternity because the children are later to come into their father's property" (Engels 1970:125). With the separation of the family from the clan and with the devolution of property rights on the male family head, "household management lost its public character. It no longer concerned society. It became a *private service*: the wife became the servant . . . " (Engels 1970:137). Thus the class conflicts peculiar to capitalism and inherent in the progressive separation of labor from the means of production penetrated to the core of the family system and were mirrored there in relations between husband and wife.

A residue of evolutionary presumptions continued to influence social theorists for some time. The sociological functionalists who followed Talcott Parsons saw the isolated conjugal family as peculiarly appropriate to the needs of industrial urban society. The neolocal nuclear family could be geographically and socially mobile, and its members could take up specialized occupational roles in a fluid labor market (Goode 1963). Households have reputedly been shrinking in size for "ten thousand years or more," right up to the present, and this is a result of an evolving technology that requires fewer cooperating people to secure food, rear children, and look after the sick (Cohen 1981). Yet the romantic critics of modern society, such as Le Play and Tönnies, mourned the passing of the peasant patriarchal or stem family and the rise of the working class *famille instable* with its poverty and fragmentation of property (Laslett 1972:17). Whether positively or negatively evaluated, the trend was seen as global, while the primeval dominance of large family households with enduring kin ties and communal property remained unquestioned.

The anthropologist who confronted speculative reconstructions of evolutionary change with the empirical results of fieldwork had first to document the universality of the family (Malinowski 1913) and the presence of bilateral kin links in all known cases where "husband and wife live together with at least their younger children" (Lowie 1947:65). While traditional concerns with kinship systems, descent groups, and marriage patterns remained central, change in these features and in the resulting family household was recognized, and causes were sought in economic factors. Lowie (1947:66) traced the primary motive for marriage to the founding of a self-sufficient economic aggregate providing for the division of labor, shelter, and cooking. Following Tylor's suggestions (1889),

Murdock in *Social Structure* (1949) emphasized postmarital residence rules as the major interface between material production and kinship (cf. also Lowie 1947:70).

> It is in respect to residence that changes in economy, technology, property, government, or religion first alter the structural relationships of related individuals to each other, giving an impetus to subsequent modifications in forms of family, in consanguineal and compromise kin groups, and in kinship terminology. (1949:202)

Lamenting the lack of data to test his speculations, Murdock nevertheless suggested (1) that the division of labor by sex in a particular economic setting partly determined the preferred form of marriage and residence (1949:36); (2) that abundance of capital resources such as land or other immovables have the effect of creating large extended family groups that can have some of the features of a lineage (1949:37–38); (3) that individual economic enterprises, cash economies, pioneer situations, poverty, and the lack of capital goods all favor neolocal residence and monogamy and sometimes cognatic kinship groups (1949:302–304); and (4) that the relative contribution of the two sexes to subsistence determines the residence system, modified by factors like slavery and warfare (1949: 205–6), a theme that has seen a recent revival (Brown 1970; Sanday 1974).

A major problem with this deductive approach was that household forms became the characteristic outcomes of systems of rules of marriage and residence rather than the reflections of variable patterns of behavior. Explaining culture change became a matter of how *rules* change, moving the inquiry into an essentially ideological realm. Murdock's cross-cultural comparisons had to rely on gross typologies of subsistence systems and labor organization with four variations in residence rules and no quantitative data whatsoever on frequencies of household types or sizes within a single society. It is little wonder then that the household was not a relevant category in his scheme and that the causal link between economies and social structure could be postulated but never demonstrated (Barnes 1971).

Continued fieldwork made it evident that matrilocal and patrilocal were nothing more than "classificatory catchwords" imposed on a society by an outside observer (Lowie 1947:72). Residence rules might be followed, ignored, or temporarily observed. They did not necessarily reflect relations of authority in the family, control of labor, ownership of goods, or rights of inheritance. Indeed two ethnographers censusing the same Trukese population arrived at different frequencies of household types. This led Goodenough to contend that residence required an understanding of both rules and options confronting individual decision makers in a single society. The native's point of view, the actual behavior of household formation, and the factors that alter the form of individual coresident groups through time should take precedence over universal ethnological categories (Goodenough 1956).

A parallel and more explicit concern with intrasocietal household variation (Fortes 1949) and the sequence of forms through which such a group may pass resulted in Goody's (1958) influential model of the developmental cycle in domestic groups. Residence did not arise from marriage rules but was determined by the "economic, affective, and jural relations" that spring from the primary social structural factors of kinship, descent, marriage, and citizenship (Fortes 1958:3). What was called the domestic group underwent a regular series of changes comparable to the growth cycle of a living organism. The developmental cycle had a single general form for each society, and residence patterns were the crystallization, at a given time, of the developmental process. This approach has proved fruitful in ordering the range of household types present in any society (Berkner 1972), but its time-depth and statistical frequencies are still rendered intelligible by reference to *norms* of household composition. Conscious norms are present in statements of ideal household composition to which individuals aspire or which they consider appropriate to their age and status.

According to the normative view, mode of production and demographic differences may influence household size within narrow limits (Goody 1972:115, 117), but the more important determinants are social rules, especially those governing inheritance and household fission. With the characteristic emphasis of British social anthropology, the contrast of matrilineal versus patrilineal norms in two groups decisively influences property rights, though farming system and household economy may be the same (Fortes 1958:7). The timing of joint family fission accounts for the relatively large size of LoWiili farming units as opposed to the economically similar LoDagaba and Tallensi (Goody 1958). "When brothers stand in expectation of inheriting goods or movables from one another, it seems reasonable to suggest that they will farm together for a longer period than when their property goes directly to their sons" (Goody 1972:121). It is true that Goody (1976) has recently come to view household form as a result of property-holding and inheritance systems that depend in turn on the general type of agricultural production. Yet the categories correlated with contrasting lateral or lineal transmission (for example, shifting versus "advanced" agriculture, hoe versus plow technology, African farmers versus herders, Africa versus Eurasia) are so broad that the correlations are uninformative. Like evolutionary stages, these gross categories cannot provide convincing causal chains accounting for variation in household form within one society or between groups at the same technoeconomic level.

In reaction to lingering evolutionary stereotypes and to the large range of seemingly fortuitous household variability found in the quantitative study of any society, modern scholars have often been content to describe and classify households with a minimum of functional analysis (E. C. Smith 1977). Internal variation was a result of the developmental cycle, and regional or continental contrasts were credited to the cultural persistence or transmission of fundamental cognitive structures that were unresponsive to short-term economic perturbations (see Goldschmidt and Kunkel 1971). The household was akin to the kinship system—and just as resistant to change. "Fortes' developmental cycles take no account of history; they are conceived of as sequences within a total system that is static and 'integrated' in Malinowski's sense of the term" (Leach 1964:xii).

Even where there are good data with time-depth, factors such as mean household size in one country may remain fairly constant for centuries (Laslett 1969). Large-scale cross-cultural analyses of household size often seem dedicated to proving that the household is an irrelevant unit for social analysis. It *is* plausible that widespread African practices, such as polygyny and unilineal descent groups, produce a greater frequency of extended or multiple family households while Europe's long tradition of deferred marriage and its high rates of celibacy, monogamy, and neolocal residence should have a nuclearizing effect (Wheaton 1980). Early and universal marriage and strong patrilocality were obviously related to the large, complex households of eastern Europe (Wrigley 1977), Hindu India (Shah 1974), and rural Japan (T. C. Smith 1959). But if the stability of household types and the formal limitation of options in household formation is real, then we are left with a few mere cultural artifacts, as dull as they are repetitive. The opposing view of the household as remarkably fluid in structure and impermanent in boundaries (Wheaton 1975), a "process" rather than an institution (Hammel 1972), a task-group rather than just a product of cultural rules (Carter and Merrill 1979:iii), with a history of adaptive consolidation and nuclearization (Herlihy 1969), returns the discussion to objective cases and potentially solvable problems.

Broad evolutionary syntheses of family change are linear, too simplistic, and rooted in ideological preconceptions. "Theories produce a sense of order, structure, and meaning, while empirical discoveries frequently bring disorder to customary views or models" (Elder 1981:492). Research has shown the lack of any natural evolutionary stages through which family structure, economic conditions, and urbanization change together and in the same direction (Guyer 1981).

Our historical and anthropological knowledge is now adequate to assess the validity and persistence of culture area stereotypes of the family, to discard the universal schemes of large complicated primitive households yielding to nuclear units with the rise of individualism and industrialism (Laslett 1972:ix), and to measure the relative effect of norms and material factors on residential choice. Rather than asking whether Sanskritic law or agricultural labor requirements perpetuate the Indian joint family household, we should investigate how these and other relevant variables interact (Shah 1974). We need not credit family nuclearization on a Caribbean island either to the spread of a mainstream international ideal or to poverty alone, but we can speak of the way ideals and material facts are systemically related (S. E. Brown 1977). We can ask whether the flow of wealth from child to parent in traditional Yoruba multiple families has already reversed direction or whether the beginnings of a trend to nuclear and less fertile families is the result of the educational diffusion of a Western standard of household composition (Caldwell 1977). The richness and diversity of change in an important social grouping can then be comprehensively glossed rather than being glossed over and ignored.

HOUSEHOLD VERSUS FAMILY: THE SEARCH FOR A COMMON FRAME OF DISCOURSE

The Wenner-Gren Foundation symposium, Households: Changing Form and Function, that gave rise to this volume was an effort to bring together anthropologists and social historians who shared a common interest in what the household does and how it works. We all had collected descriptive and quantitative information on household size and composition from one or more contemporary communities or from written historical sources. We used controlled comparison or periodic recensus of the same population to demonstrate the ways in which households change and to seek some of the reasons for change or stability. We believed that the household is sufficiently universal and recognizable for use in cross-cultural and historical comparison. We selected the household for attention from an awareness of its past neglect and because it appeared to represent a "multitude of roles and tasks encompassed within a relatively limited repertoire of shapes and sizes." As organizers, we proposed that "household organization responds sensitively to changes in the environment while preserving certain formal similarities for long periods."

Our group's concerns were not primarily typological. While recognizing the serviceable familiarity and wide applicability of the Hammel-Laslett terminology for simple, extended, and multiple family households (Laslett 1972, Hammel and Laslett 1974), we did not argue about Wolf's use of "grand family" for the Chinese case or Wilk's Kekchi "household clusters." As might be expected, however, questions of definition were both absorbing and critical. From the beginning the household/family distinction was emphasized. While both households and families are culturally defined, the former are task-oriented residence units and the latter are conceived of as kinship groupings that need not be localized (see Linton 1936:152–59). Nonrelatives who live together, as well as servants and lodgers who cooperate in some common activities, are household members, whereas nonresident kin are usually (but not always) affiliated principally with other households. As one of us remarked, "My dog is a member of my household but not of my family." This is not to say that criteria of location (sleeping habitually under one roof), function (sharing a number of activities), and kinship (relationship by blood or marriage) do not frequently occur together (Laslett 1972). The point to be made is that physical location, shared activities, and kinship need not be empirically or logically overlapping (Bender 1967; Rudie 1969/70). An exclusive focus on the composition of comparable units rather than on the household as one locus of activities and interactions "leads to formal and sociologically decontentualized, if empirical, conclusions" (Sanjek 1982:58).

The seeming opposition between a functional, economic view focusing on householding—the common productive, consumptive, and reproductive activities directed toward the satisfaction of needs (Spijkers-Zwart 1980)—and an emphasis on the symbols, values, and meanings that characterize the family brought a creative tension to our discussions. The difference between our approach and that in the diverse literature of family history and psychology was that we avoided the topic of the quality of personal interaction and affective behavior within the family. We eschewed literary evidence on changes in parent-child or husband-wife emotional relationships over time (Shorter 1975; Stone 1977), confining ourselves to the observable and often quantitatively verifiable behavior of individuals in households. Yet we were reminded by Herlihy (this volume) that the Greek notion of *economics* referred to the science of administering the household (*oikos*) and its property and that *family* originally designated a Roman property holder and his slaves. Although many of the conference papers dealt with functional economic issues, the household cannot be divorced from ideas that people have of the domestic group and from symbolic concepts like *family* and *home* (Löfgren, Yanagisako, this volume) that influence decisions and guide actions.

> It is through their commitment to the concept of family that people are recruited to the material relations of households. Because people accept the meaningfulness of family, they enter into relations of production, reproduction, and consumption with one another. They marry, beget children, work to support dependents, accumulate, transmit, and inherit cultural and material resources. In all these activities the concept of family both reflects and masks the realities of household formation and sustenance. (Rapp 1979:177)

IS THE HOUSEHOLD A SIGNIFICANT UNIT OF SOCIAL ANALYSIS?

Selecting the household as a common focus for social scientific research and analysis has both practical and theoretical justifications. Because almost everyone grew up in a household and continues to live in such a unit, there is a pervasive recognition of the reality and relevance of this group. We also have the decided impression that we can easily discern comparable units in literally any human society where an observer might alight. As Peter Kunstadter (this volume) points out, "most people in most societies at most times live in households, membership in which is usually based on kin relationships of marriage and descent, which are simultaneously a combination of dwelling unit, a unit of economic cooperation (at least in distribution and consumption), and the unit within which most reproduction and early childhood socialization takes place." It is not necessary to claim that the household is a universal or categorically distinct social unit in order to recognize that we are not likely to mistake a hunting band (but cf. Cohen 1981), a lineage, a secret society, a commune, an orphanage, or a prison for a household. Though the finer points of definition may cause disagreement, it is difficult to imagine that a student attempting to do a household census in the field should report that there was no such grouping to be found. Generations of headmen and priests and tax collectors have talked about or enumerated their populations as if households were important (though even here there are exceptions, as Herlihy mentions in this volume). Perhaps it is this mundane, repetitive, cross-culturally obvious appearance of households that has led observers to think of them as unproblematic and lacking in interest.

Just the opposite may be true. If households are indeed readily identifiable, countable in a relatively simple and replicable manner, and logically comparable in size and type to one another, we have a social unit that is well suited to understanding through scientific method. The variations among households in one community, in two contemporary societies, or in any group through time are straightforward and unambiguous enough to be specified, classified, and statistically analyzed. This is possible but a good deal harder to do if our units are villages, tribes, or nation states. In such large and complex groups the link between structure and function is proportionately more difficult to draw.

The household is a fundamental social unit. Households are more than groups of dyadic pairs. They have an emergent character that makes them more than the sum of their parts. They are a primary arena for the expression of age and sex roles, kinship, socialization, and economic cooperation where the very stuff of culture is mediated and transformed into action. Here, individual motives and activities must be coordinated and rendered mutually intelligible. The household is "the next biggest thing on a social map after the individual" (Hammel, this volume). Decisions emerge from households through negotiation, disagreement, conflict, and bargaining. Decisions to marry, to build a house, to take in a relative, to hire a maid, or to migrate are seldom made or acted on by isolated individuals, because such decisions necessarily affect household morphology and activities. Statistical patterns of behavior in the course of household histories (Mitterauer and Sieder 1979; Carter, this volume) provide solid evidence of decision making and the factors that influence it, allowing us to speak of household strategies without the dangers of reification.

Pooling and sharing of resources, food processing, cooking, eating, and sheltering from the elements tend to take place in the household, which has therefore become a standard unit of analysis for ecological and economic purposes. Nutrition is characteristically measured there, the division of labor by age, sex, and status can be directly observed, and budgets can be charted. Commonalities are visible in large samples, and the significance of variability can be statistically tested. Governments continue to collect basic census data at the household level, and models of development, both socialist and capitalist, are targeted at households. Farm systems and other studies by agricultural economists use labor expenditure and detailed production registers of rural family households. Any primary group that has become so ubiquitous in social surveys must necessarily be used in further research if we have any hope that our interdisciplinary understandings can become cumulative. A further reason for the study of the household is that when descent groups break down, as ethnic groups and cities coalesce, the household neither disintegrates nor completely transforms itself. The intense controversy about the changes in household patterning that do appear (single-person households, cohabitation by unmarried pairs, the matrifocal household, elderly parents in the households of their married children) should warn us of the cultural and emotional values that surround this grouping. Given both popular and scholarly concern about the household and the accessibility of this unit to existing research methods, it is remarkable that we know so little about household composition and functions and about the symbols and images we use to think about it.

The social salience of the household and its practical ease of definition have not gone unchallenged. Groups are seldom as uncomplicated and stable as they appear, and there are dangers in selecting and reifying those forms that we find familiar in our own culture. Perhaps the frustrating search for simplicity and focus among the "unmanageable particularities" of social life should move from the comparative study of groups to a more basic level of individual decision making or specific limited relationships (Guyer 1981). Rather than concentrating on the household with all of its unpredictable, stochastic fluctuations, Hammel (this volume) suggests we could more appropriately observe the important behaviors and norms of people interacting by virtue of household comembership.

Even intelligible and seemingly accurate surveys or censuses may not produce unambiguous quantitative information. In our discussions Hammel noted that no methods exist for deciding how large a proportion of a sample of households, taken at an undefined point in the domestic cycle of each, from a sample population whose size is unknown, is large enough to allow us to conclude that the population as a whole conforms to a certain household system. A 15 percent difference in the proportions of one household type at two points in time might be a result of mere chance. Wolf pointed out that sampling household size in China after the great periodic natural disasters would produce very different pictures of the household system from the multiple family system that in fact prevailed there. Merrill added that chance demographic fluctuations will compromise any household system at some point unless multiple strategies of recruitment are brought into play. African ethnographic data provide particularly rich examples of the variety of recruitment and distribution strategies available which are not necessarily revealed in census data (see Linares, Arnould, this volume). These factors and others compound sampling error in census data, usually in unpredictable ways. Resolution of the sampling problem requires collection of a large number of cases at several points in time, a solution not often available either to historians or anthropologists. Merrill and Hammel hoped that computer simulation will provide a partial resolution of this sort of problem.

The mere physical propinquity of related conjugal families may be an inadequate indicator of their integration in a household organization. Only by microlevel observations of cooperative work, shared meals, ownership of livestock, financial exchanges, and types of reciprocity could Wilk (this volume) determine whether a Kekchi household cluster was tight or loose. Arnould (this volume) showed that some Nigerien Hausa employ an implicit multivariate definition of household membership in which the tasks of social reproduction are the most fundamental elements. Only when junior household members cease contributing to the marriage, birth, and tax payments of the multiple family household are these individuals, including emigrants, considered to have a domestic unit separate from the parental household. Although there is considerable variation in the degree of cooperation among agnatically related family clusters in the performance of household tasks, the ideology of the traditional multiple family *gida* is maintained unless cooperation in reproductive tasks is broken off.

A different definitional issue was taken up by Foster (this volume). Drawing on graph theoretical models and recent network research, he constructed suprahousehold structures from household units by representing aid relationships in graph form. This mode of analysis of Thai village society also throws light on the division of labor in the performance of household tasks by several related households, a topic also taken up by Segalen. Laslett (this volume) has been concerned to show that the household has never been an autonomous and self-contained unit in English society. Demographic mischance and economic hardship resulting in orphans, widows, and paupers have been handled by local community welfare organizations, national poor laws, and public charities.

If the boundaries and functions of households cannot be delineated on a priori grounds but must be empirically determined in every case, how is it possible to account for changes in household size and composition? One of the major concerns of the symposium was to go beyond static structural studies to a better understanding of the processes that transform the household. Anthropological analysis by synchronic, cross-sectional methods is not an adequate substitute for a detailed longitudinal reconstruction of household change, a method used successfully by historians where annual censuses exist (Mitterauer and Sieder 1979). Carter (this volume) advocated the collection of specific household histories including the temporal movements of people in and out of residence, household positions, and kinship statuses. Such a chronology would also contain information on the changing size of the household, its control and allocation of resources, and changing producer/consumer ratios. Yanagisako (this volume) warned that use of the coresidence criterion tends to draw a functional boundary around groups of people, which in the case of Japanese Americans is not confirmed by emic concepts of household organization. Mutual help and authority patterns persisted beyond the breakup of stem families. She argued that empirical study of households must be preceded by cultural analysis. As Hammel suggested, households may in some instances be statistical outcomes of the action of other powerful cultural values such as gender constructs.

The current focus on household form, function, and meaning has been criticized. The most coherent and incisive arguments have come from anthropologists and sociologists with a Marxist-feminist perspective and from West African ethnographic material. Though realizing the convenience of a social unit with a locus, resources, and a labor force for modeling basic economic and demographic processes, Guyer (1981) is wary of typologies used to classify descent groups which emphasize rules and norms while neglecting variability and behavior. She sees the practical problems of continuously recording household membership when people move about a great deal. The relatively high divorce rate and extensive fostering of children in many West African societies make it difficult to correlate worker/consumer ratios with production patterns. There may be no common budget of husband and wife among the Yoruba, and their families do not form unified production units (Guyer 1981:23). Decisions on fertility and subsistence production are made by individuals, though western demographers and economists continue to use the household as the unit of analysis (Oppong 1981). They also presuppose a male household head and breadwinner in the public domain with the woman as housewife occupied with consumption, reproduction, and child care (Oppong and Haavia-Mannila 1979; see also Löfgren, this volume). The stereotype is both ethnocentric and capitalist as Morgan and Engels long ago pointed out (Rapp 1979). *Household* should remain an "unresolved, multidimensional concept" rather than an analytical heading that tends to submerge women and their work within undifferentiated, closed household organizational systems (Woodford-Berger 1981).

Though these recent criticisms of the household as a unit of analysis are by no means antithetical to our approach, the wide range of ethnographic cases and historical periods studied by the participants required us to seek a broader and more processual definition of the household. The need to shed "preconceptions about the congruence of coresidence, commensality, joint ownership, pooling of income, shared consumption, etc." (Oppong 1981) was the cornerstone of our discussions. Our position was similar to that recently put forward by Sanjek (1982), emphasizing that the degree to which universal activities of production, social reproduction, consumption, sexual union, and socialization of children are household-based varies cross-culturally and intraculturally. Variety and contrast in division of labor and authority, especially in the African examples (Linares, Arnould, this volume) were obvious. Though recognizing the practical problems of data gathering and the theoretical difficulties of applying the designation *household*, our participants continued to regard the household domestic group as a part of our social scientific conceptual vocabulary that can be effectively used. At the very least, the household is more universal and more cross-culturally comparable than many more frequently studied institutions.

CORESIDENCE: HISTORICAL AND ANTHROPOLOGICAL PERSPECTIVES ON HOUSEHOLD BOUNDARIES

If modern studies of the family have often shown a genealogical bias, household studies have been equally slanted toward coresidential criteria. As Hammel pointed out in our discussions, the sharing of a domicile is one of several features of the household that depend on the viewpoint of the investigator. Arriving at a clear-cut, cross-culturally valid definition of the household is as problematic as the blind men's description of the elephant. Coresidence is a particularly slippery standard when applied to guests and transients. It is also difficult to apply to dwellers under one roof who use separate hearths and food stores, adjoining rooms around a compound courtyard, or clustered dwellings. Historians may have no choice but to accept the blocks of names in a census list as reflecting coresidential units, but these may represent the stereotypes of the governmental functionaries for the purposes of tax collection and estate administration (Plakans, Löfgren, this volume) rather than the existing domestic units. It is also obvious that contemporary survey and census design has been influenced by the ideology of a nuclear family model taken as the often implicit prototype for the regulation of kin, sexual, and living relationships (Lenero-Otero 1977). Fortes has pointed out the ethnocentrism of demographers, economists, and most sociologists who write of the family as if it were the monogamous, coresidential, nuclear form that has been the legal, modal, and social norm in Western Europe since at least the sixteenth century (cited in Oppong and Haavia-Mannila 1979).

Hammel (this volume) illustrated a number of problems with the coresidence criterion for users of archival census materials. For medieval Balkan tax lists, for example, household boundaries must be inferred from minimal indications of male kinship ties. Slight changes in assumptions about boundary placement produce massive variation in the inferred incidence of *zadruga*-type joint households. Douglass, in remarks about Basque and Sicilian censuses, added evidence showing how secular and ecclesiastical authorities employed different criteria of coresidence in counting long-term migrants. It became obvious that historians who are necessarily limited to the coresidents listed in census documents may reach different conclusions on household structure than do anthropologists who can take into account emigrants whose economic contributions and eventual return maintain a household in their absence. Carter, Douglass, Wilk, Kunstadter, and Segalen (this volume) provided ethnographic examples of the inappropriateness of coresidence as the single defining characteristic of household membership. In India, North America, Belize, Thailand, and France, long-term or temporary migrants continue to participate in pooling of finances, distribution of goods and services, reproduction, and inheritance. Their emigrant status is not often accurately reflected in census records; nor are the other tasks they perform as members of households. In assessing household functioning and continuing viability, anthropologists must be particularly aware of the absent members who often escape the net of historical inquiry.

A prime example of the limitations of *household* as a means of classifying and analyzing the domestic group concerns the absence of coresidence in Ghanaian Akan society (Woodford-Berger 1981; see also Sanjek 1982 on an urban neighborhood). A woman and her children in a room form a "matricentral cell" of a compound housing matrilateral relatives and others. The husband/father may live elsewhere, receiving food and visits from his wife. Food production and processing, housework, market activities, and transfer of cash are not confined to a single house but are carried out in a number of houses and in relation to different groups of people in a single day. "This obscures the spatial, social, and conceptual boundaries of an analytically isolatable 'household' productive locus, and makes it impossible to attempt to analyze any given house unit as though it were a single and final set of social and economic roles and statuses, or house organization as a uniform system which is the same for everyone in the village" (Woodford-Berger 1981:4). Rescuing a household definition from a welter of overlapping activity spheres is a task addressed by Wilk and Netting (this volume). The physical or spatial dimension of a building where people live should not be conflated with social and demographic or with conceptual dimensions, especially if this uncritically perpetuates the single model of the Euramerican household.

THE PAPERS

Our desire, when planning the conference, was to focus the discussion and papers on what we considered a basic issue—how and why households vary within and between societies or over time within the same society. We wanted to minimize the amount of time spent discussing definitional issues or debating the merits of different methodologies. To further these goals we laid out a programmatic and methodological plan in a paper circulated to conference participants well in advance of our meeting date (Wilk and Netting, this volume). We asked those planning to attend to focus their papers and debate on the interplay between household form and function (which we relabeled "morphology and activity") and we expressed our hope that each participant would address these issues using his or her own unique body of historical or ethnographic data.

These preconference briefings accomplished some of their goals; the papers are indeed focused on household variation over time or between cases. Only three are explicitly concerned with definitional, theoretical, or methodological issues (Hammel, Carter, Foster), and all of these take up quite important topics that were not addressed in our programmatic preconference paper.

We were initially disconcerted, however, by the great number of approaches to household variation which were taken in the other 13 papers. The analytical scheme presented in our preconference paper defined two dimensions of variation for households—morphology and activity—but only about half of the papers dealt explicitly with the interrelations between these two. The rest did not fit our proposed format so neatly (though none contradict it directly), and our postconference reassessment has led us to recognize that the fault lies with our original analysis rather than with recalcitrant conferees.

The proposal in the Wilk and Netting paper is a simple one. Households had previously been assumed to perform certain universal functions or activities—they were units that shared in some combination of production, coresidence, consumption, or reproductive tasks. At the same time households were usually described and enumerated on the basis of structural characteristics—their size and kinship composition or generational extension. We feel that some of the confusion about household variation and change derives from conflating those two dimensions, from not differentiating what households *look like* (morphology) from what they *do* (activity).

The two dimensions are linked to each other, but they are by no means isomorphic. Form may follow function, or vice versa, but neither can or should be reduced to the other. There are a number of cases in the literature in which drastic changes in household activities are not directly reflected by transformations in morphology, and there are cases of the converse as well. A number of the papers in this volume do take up the relationship between activity and morphology in an explicit way, and the authors seem to find it a useful distinction that helps make sense out of cases where households are changing or adapting their functions to new economic, political, or ecological circumstances.

It is clear from other papers, however, that the dimensions of morphology and activity do not include another extremely important aspect of households as social units. To complete our analytical scheme we must recognize that households are also *conceptual units*. While a household can be defined by the activities it performs or by its shape and size, it can also be defined as a symbolic entity—a cognitive model within the minds of the members of a society (Yanagisako, this volume). Within this cognitive realm lie the cultural systems of rules and strategies, which are called the "household system" by Carter (this volume). Carter convincingly demonstrates that rules and strategies of household systems can be separated analytically, and sometimes in practice, from the rules and strategies of kinship systems. Household relationships are ordered by principles of ownership, gender, and seniority rather than by specific rules of kinship. Carter also proposes that the link between economic activities of households and their morphological structure is to be found in the household system; household rules are culturally defined and set limits on the possible structural solutions to instrumental problems.

The separation of the household as a normative or cognized system from its behavioral aspects has already been the topic of some research. It is evident that there are differences between observable household morphology and the ideal models of households that can be elicited as normative statements by an ethnographer (for example, Shah 1974; Berkner 1975). Using Carter's notion of the "household system," we can define and classify a constellation of native concepts that relate to and affect domestic life. Sex roles and cultural gender constructs can define or constrain household forms (Linares, this volume). Symbolic criteria, sometimes codified as systems of rights and duties, are often important in setting cultural boundaries around households (Hammel, conference discussion). Households can be political symbols, as witnessed by the current national controversy over the "decline of the American family," which seems to have its symbolic origins in the political struggle for dominance by the Victorian middle class (Löfgren, this volume). A similar use of the household concept as a political weapon and a tool of exploitation and domination can be found in the controversy over the Afro-American family and household (see Moynihan 1965 and discussion in Staples 1974).

One aspect of the household as a concept and symbol was most prominent in conference discussions and papers. Households, we find, can serve as potent symbols of ethnic identity and historical continuity. To paraphrase Glassie (1975:116), households function within the cognitive structure that relates one person to the other members of a community and one community to others with which it has contact. Whether on the scale of Kunstadter's closely interacting ethnic groups in Thailand (this volume) or Laslett's "noumenal norms" of continuity in accepted standards for household formation over large parts of Europe (this volume), it is clear that people's concepts of households have important and vital effects on their behavior. The continued presence and power of regional cultural traditions is exemplified by the historical continuity of the nuclear family household in England, the multiple family household in China, and the stem family household among the Japanese. The persistence of household norms and structures through time and over large areas and the ways in which people manage to perpetuate them despite changing economic and political situations seem to be important emergent themes in the conference papers.

Many questions about the conceptual dimension of the household group have yet to be answered. Some of the most intriguing questions grow from observations of the contradictions between cognitive models of households and their morphology or activities. What will happen in the case studied by Yanagisako (this volume) where the gulf between Issei concepts of the household and household activities and morphology seems to be growing? How can a cultural model of the household like that of the Chinese be maintained for hundreds of years during which large numbers of people never attain the ideal? How is it that a relatively small group can impose its own concept of the household on the majority of society (see Löfgren, this volume)?

When we add the ideational aspect of *household* to our original analytical scheme, we find that any causative or explanatory scheme must be considerably more complex and sophisticated. As long as we limited our enterprise to activity and morphology alone, there were only two possible directions of causation:

morphology	→	activity
activity	→	morphology

With the addition of that complex of concepts, values, norms, ideals, rights, duties, and rules which Carter calls the "household system" we find that there are four additional causal interactions:

household systems	→	activity
activity	→	household systems
household systems	→	morphology
morphology	→	household systems

Drawing causal arrows in this way is in itself a crude analytical substitute for the great complexities of interaction that occur in every real-world case that comes under study. Yet the task is by no means hopeless—the evidence follows in the chapters of this book. Each author tackles a part of the problem, and several weave together all three of the dimensions we have defined.

We have organized the revised conference essays into groups according to the particular dimensions of the household with which they are concerned. Part I contains theoretical and methodological papers aimed at the household concept itself and proposing appropriate methods of study. The Wilk and Netting paper points out inconsistencies between functional definitions and structural descriptions of the household and proposes some ways of building descriptions of household functions as a solution. The authors include some specific hypotheses on the ways in which household form and function (or morphology and activity in their terms) are interrelated. Hammel also takes up the issue of household definitions, dealing with the problem that units that are culturally specific and accurate may not be cross-culturally comparable. Even when the analytical units are comparable, he raises questions about the degree to which we can make reliable judgments about their similarity or difference on the basis of census material. Carter's article presents a refined model of household systems, using illustrative material from his work on household histories in India to show the interplay between household rules and strategies in the individual decisions that lead to particular household forms. The final paper in this group, by Foster, reverses the traditional direction of analysis of households. Instead of "working down," defining large social groups like clans and lineages and then specifying the place of households within these systems, Foster uses his Thai data to work upward from the household. By means of graph theory, he demonstrates how suprahousehold groups ("global structures") can be generated from the interrelations between households.

Part II includes those papers that stick fairly closely to our original program, exploring the interrelations between the morphology and activities of households. Within this section we find different approaches to dealing with the ideational aspect of households. Some authors consider this realm important but make an attempt to separate it from matters of morphology and activity (Arnould, Douglass, Segalen). Arnould documents pronounced differences in the morphology of Hausa households in three different economic settings in Niger, demonstrating how modes of integration to the capitalist marketplace have affected household economies. Douglass compares Basque households in Spain, the American Southwest, and Australia to demonstrate permutations of an original cultural form in new circumstances. The Breton households studied by Segalen have also changed their economic activities, though not necessarily their structural characteristics, in response to recent economic trends. Paradoxically, both the valued independence of physical residence and increased cooperation between the domestic units of close kin have developed together in the contemporary rural situation. In all three papers the changes in household morphology and/or activity are counterposed to norms associated with traditional household forms that seem to be relatively unaltered.

The other three papers in this section focus more completely on the economic functions and morphological changes in households, with less attention given to their ideational aspects. Hackenberg, Murphy, and Selby use census and survey data on urban Mexican and Philippine households to illuminate economic survival strategies—which are primarily household strategies—among the very poor. Increasing household size by adding adult workers or having children is shown to have positive effects on group income. A comparison of three Kekchi Maya villages in Belize allows Wilk to show how changing agricultural patterns lead to new economic bargains between kin, altered postmarital residence patterns, and different kinds of households. Plakans's careful analysis portrays eighteenth-century Latvian farmers on German estates before and after the abolition of serfdom. He documents a change in residence patterns, mobility, and household form during this social transition, though the historical records are mostly silent on the ideological changes that may also have taken place.

The papers in part III are not greatly concerned with the activities of daily life in households. Instead, the three authors approach the interrelations between the cognized model of households and their morphology. Wolf's paper on Taiwanese households during nearly a hundred years relates the individual life cycle to household cycles. He aims at the question of how people's experience of households affect their thinking about them. The answer to this question is central to explaining the historical continuity and the power of cultural traditions of household form. Yanagisako's paper on Japanese immigrants to the United States approaches this problem by explaining the ways in which a cultural model of the household is conceived, passed on, and transmuted as a system of meanings largely independent of drastic social and economic discontinuities. The ethos of the household can become a metaphor as well as a focus for many other values that seem endangered. Laslett takes the macrolevel approach to the question of continuity in household form. The norm of English simple family households was perpetuated for centuries, while the contrasting stern family form of central Europe and the multiple family household of eastern Europe showed similar historical continuity.

Part IV brings us to the most ambitious group. These papers consider all three analytical dimensions of the household on an equal footing. All use rich sources of data, dealing with synchronic variability and/or historical change. The truly dynamic nature of households as units of change as well as continuity is most clearly expressed in this group. Löfgren's historical study of the morphology, activity, and ideology of the Swedish household makes clear the interplay of macroeconomics and class formation. The yielding of the egalitarian farm household of family and servants to a Victorian urban ideal of hierarchy, privacy, and home reflects an ideological current whose power is still apparent. The idea that household systems can be used as a weapon or a tool of social control is a stimulating one which ties Löfgren's work to the literature on the effect of government policy on domestic groups (see Winch 1975).

Linares compares three Diola villages in Senegambia. Though she finds ecological differences, she attributes household variation to historical and ideological factors. Herlihy's paper provides an interesting counterpoint to other historical treatments of the household. Instead of using census listings, he extracts information from early medieval hagiography bearing on patterns of marriage, kinship, property ownership, and authority that often contrasted with those of a later feudal aristocracy.

By organizing the papers in this way we do not mean to compartmentalize them or convey judgments about their limitations. They could indeed be grouped in a number of other ways to express their similarities and differences. Some are historical, others ethnographic and synchronic. In all there is a stimulating interplay between empirical evidence on households and the theoretical issues we have summarized in this introduction. In both the papers and the conference discussions we find little that adopts polemical attitudes or postures on unproductive and divisive issues. Mentalist/materialist or historical/anthropological dichotomies are subdued here, perhaps because the rich ethnographic and historical material does not allow such simplistic formulations. In pursuing more sophisticated theoretical models of the household, dogma and preconceived notions of causality seem to be more of a hindrance than a help. Many participants found that the analysis of their empirical evidence carried them far from their original theoretical positions. We see this as a sign of an active and growing field of inquiry, where social scientists can produce, distribute, and transmit knowledge instead of just reproducing received wisdom.

REFERENCES

Barnes, J. A.
1971 Three Styles in the Study of Kinship. Berkeley, Los Angeles, London: University of California Press.

Barnum, Howard, and Lyn Squire
1979 A Model of an Agricultural Household: Theory and Evidence. World Bank Staff Occasional Papers, no. 27. Baltimore: Johns Hopkins University Press.

Bender, Donald
1967 A Redefinement of the Concept of Household: Families, Coresidence, and Domestic Functions. American Anthropologist 70:309–20.

Berkner, Lutz K.
1972 The Stem Family and the Developmental Cycle of the Peasant Household: An Eighteenth-century Austrian Example. American Historical Review 77:398–418.
1975 The Use and Misuse of Census Data for the Historical Analysis of Family Structure. Journal of Interdisciplinary History 7:721–38.

Brown, Judith K.
1970 A Note on the Division of Labor by Sex. American Anthropologist 72 (5):1073–78.

Brown, Susan E.
1977 Household Composition and Variation in a Rural Dominican Village. Journal of Comparative Family Studies 3:257–67.
Caldwell, John C.
1977 The Persistence of High Fertility: Population Prospects in the Third World. Changing African Family Series: Family and Fertility Change, no. 1. Canberra: Department of Demography, Australian National University.
Carter, Anthony T., and Robert S. Merrill
1979 Household Institutions and Populations Dynamics. Report prepared for the Bureau for Program and Policy Coordination, USAID, Washington, D.C.
Cohen, Yehudi A.
1981 Shrinking Households. Society 48–52.
Elder, Glen H., Jr.
1981 History and the Family: The Discovery of Complexity. Journal of Marriage and the Family 43:489–519.
Engels, F.
1972 The Origin of the Family, Private Property, and the State. Ed. E. B. Leacock. New York: International Publishers.
Fortes, M.
1958 Introduction. *In* The Developmental Cycle in Domestic Groups, ed. Jack Goody. London: Cambridge University Press.
Fox, Robin
1967 Kinship and Marriage. Baltimore: Penguin.
Glassie, Henry
1975 Folk Housing in Middle Virginia. Knoxville: University of Tennessee Press.
Goldschmidt, Walter, and Evelyn J. Kunkel
1971 The Structure of the Peasant Family. American Anthropologist 73: 1058–76.
Goode, W. J.
1963 World Revolution and Family Patterns. New York: John Wiley.
Goodenough, Ward H.
1956 Residence Rules. Southwestern Journal of Anthropology 12:22–37.
Goody, Jack
1958 The Fission of Domestic Groups among the LoDagaba. *In* The Developmental Cycle in Domestic Groups, ed. Jack Goody, pp. 53–91. Cambridge: Cambridge University Press.
1972 The Evolution of the Family. *In* Household and Family in Past Time, ed. Peter Laslett and Richard Wall, pp. 103–24. Cambridge: Cambridge University Press.
1976 Production and Reproduction. Cambridge: Cambridge University Press.

Guyer, Jane I.
1981 Household and Community in African Studies. African Studies Review 24:87–137.
Hammel, E. A.
1972 The Zadruga as Process. *In* Household and Family in Past Time, ed. Peter Laslett and Richard Wall, pp. 335–74. Cambridge: Cambridge University Press.
Hammel, E. A., and Peter Laslett
1974 Comparing Household Structure over Time and between Cultures. Comparative Studies in Society and History 16:73–109.
Herlihy, David
1969 Family Solidarity in Medieval Italian History. *In* Economy, Society, and Government in Medieval Italy: Essays in Memory of Robert L. Reynolds, ed. David Herlihy, R. S. Lopez, and V. Slessarev. Kent, Ohio: Kent State University Press.
Laslett, Peter
1969 Size and Structure of the Household in England over Three Centuries. Population Studies 23:199–223.
1972 Introduction: The History of the Family. *In* Household and Family in Past Time, ed. Peter Laslett and Richard Wall, pp. 1–89. Cambridge: Cambridge University Press.
Leach, E. R.
1964 Political Systems of Highland Burma. Boston: Beacon.
Lenero-Otero, Luis
1977 Beyond the Nuclear Family Model: Cross-cultural Perspectives. Beverly Hills, Calif.: Sage.
Linton, Ralph
1936 The Study of Man. New York: Appleton-Century-Crofts.
Lowie, Robert H.
1947 Primitive Society (orig. ed. 1920). New York: Liveright.
Malinowski, B.
1913 The Family among the Australian Aborigines: A Sociological Study. London: University of London Press.
Mitterauer, Michael, and Reinhard Sieder
1979 The Developmental Process of Domestic Groups: Problems of Reconstruction and Possibilities of Interpretation. Journal of Family History 4:257–84.
Moynihan, Daniel P.
1965 The Negro Family—The Case for National Action. Office of Policy Planning and Research, United States Department of Labor. U.S. Government Printing Office: Washington, D.C.
Murdock, G. P.
1949 Social Structure. New York: Macmillan.
Netting, Robert McC.
1979 Household Dynamics in a Nineteenth-century Swiss Village. Journal of Family History 4:39–58.

Oppong, Christine
1981 A Note on Some Aspects of Anthropological Contributions to the Study of Fertility. Paper on Population and Demography, National Research Council.

Oppong, Christine, and Elina Haavia-Mannila
1979 Women, Population, and Development. *In* World Population and Development: Challenges and Prospects, ed. P. Hauser, pp. 440–85. Syracuse: Syracuse University Press.

Rapp, Rayna
1979 Examining Family History: Household and Family. Feminist Studies 5:175–81.

Rathje, William
1981 *Quoted in* From Tikal to Tucson, Today's Garbage Is Tomorrow's Artifact (interview). Anthropology Newsletter 22 (3):6.

Rudie, Ingrid
1969/70 Household Organization: Adaptive Process and Restrictive Form: A Viewpoint on Economic Change. Folk 11–12:185–200.

Sanday, Peggy
1974 Female Status in the Public Domain. *In* Woman, Culture, and Society, ed. M. Rosaldo and L. Lamphere. Stanford: Stanford University Press. pp. 189–206.

Sanjek, Roger
1982 The Organization of Households in Adabraka: Toward a Wider Comparative Perspective. Comparative Studies in Society and History 24: 57–103.

Shah, A. M.
1974 The Household Dimension of the Family in India. Berkeley, Los Angeles, London: University of California Press.

Shorter, E.
1975 The Making of the Modern Family. New York: Basic Books.

Smith, Elizabeth C.
1977 Family Structure and Complexity. Journal of Comparative Family Studies 8 (2):299–320.

Smith, Thomas C.
1959 The Agrarian Origins of Modern Japan. Stanford: Stanford University Press.

Spijkers-Zwart, S. I.
1980 The Household and "Householding": Some Conceptual Considerations. *In* The Household, Women and Agricultural Development, ed. Clio Presvelou and Saskia Spijkers-Zwart, pp. 69–73. Wageningen: Veenman and Zonen.

Staples, Robert
1974 The Black Family Revisited. Journal of Social and Behavioral Sciences 20:65–78.

Stone, Lawrence
1977 The Family, Sex, and Marriage in England, 1500–1800. New York: Harper and Row.
Tylor, E. G.
1889 On a Method of Investigating the Development of Institutions, Applied to Laws of Marriage and Descent. Journal of the Royal Anthropological Institute 18:245–69.
Wheaton, Robert
1975 Family and Kinship in Western Europe: The Problem of the Joint Family Household. Journal of Interdisciplinary History 4:601–28.
Wheaton, Robert
1980 Introduction: Recent Trends in the Historical Study of the French Family. *In* Family and Sexuality in French History, ed. R. Wheaton and T. K. Hareven. Philadelphia: University of Pennsylvania Press.
Winch, Robert
1975 Inferring Minimum Structure from Function: Or Did the Bureaucracy Create the Mother-child Family. Paper presented for the Fourteenth Seminar of Committee for Family Research, International Sociological Association, Curaçao.
Woodford-Berger, Prudence
1981 Women in Houses: The Organization of Residence and Work in Rural Ghana. Antropologiska Studier 30–31:3–35.
Wrigley, E. A.
1977 Reflections on the History of the Family. Daedalus 106:71–85.

PART I

Studying the Household: Method and Theory

1

Households: Changing Forms and Functions

Richard R. Wilk and Robert McC. Netting

The word *household* is polysemic, glossing often conflicting concepts at many different conceptual levels. The word is part of both our folk and analytic vocabularies, which leads us to allow a certain vagueness in our definitions, since so much of the concept is a part of our cultural competence. Beneath this seeming consensus we find some serious difficulties concealed. As Hammel (this volume) points out, the household can have different meanings, as a native unit, among different strata of society—as with the census taker who filters what he observes through his own concept of what constitutes a household. Herlihy (this volume) gives an example of the way in which a culturally defined concept of the household emerges where there was no precedent, and Löfgren (this volume) shows how the household as a cultural construct can be changed, dispersed, and replaced by the ideal of the family. Social scientists have often been guilty of imposing their own value-laden folk category of household or family on what they observe (see Moynihan 1965).

The very impetus to separate the concept *household* from *family* can be seen as an attempt to replace a culturally defined unit with one that is more based on observation and can be more readily compared across cultures (Laslett 1972). This goal, while laudable, is unreachable as long as our criteria for finding, defining, and counting households remain vague or inconsistent, grounded in yet more folk categories like "domestic functions" or based on our own intuitive ideas of what a household should look like. A typical example is the insistence of most enumerators that a person cannot belong to more than one household simultaneously, despite excellent ethnographic evidence that this is not an unusual occurrence (see Stack 1974; Douglass, this volume).

As a culturally defined emic unit, the household is certainly of analytic value. People's ideas, norms, and values concerning their domestic life are an important constraint on their behavior, and the household concept often carries a heavy symbolic load. But the household is also a bounded, corporate social group in many societies, and it is always an important nexus of visible behavior. This paper focuses on these structural and behavioral aspects of the household. Our first task will be to seek an objective, cross-culturally useful definition of the household. We will then propose some specific hypotheses about the relationship between household structure and behavior.

LEVELS OF CLASSIFICATION AND ANALYSIS

There has been a tendency in anthropology to confuse or fail to differentiate between what households look like as structural units and what they do and how they function. We argue that observation, classification, and analysis of household variation must rest on a clear distinction between morphology and function. We note that there is a continuing contradiction in household analysis, because morphological classification of household structure (kinship composition or size) is proving a clumsy tool in trying to answer questions about variation in function (see Woodford-Berger 1981; Medick 1976). Before proposing some solutions to this problem, we will briefly consider the way the contradiction is related to traditions of defining and classifying households.

Anthropologists first began to use the word *household* as a residual term to take up the slack between ideal family types and the actual groups of people observed in ethnographic situations. Murdock (1949:23) was obviously much more concerned with the kinship relations that generated families than with the actual coresiding groups he termed households. Kinship relations were logically prior to households, and household composition was generated by the operation of rules of residence which lay within the realm of kinship. The use of the term *household* only acknowledged that sometimes there was a difference between kinship structures and the actual groups of people who lived together.

The contradiction between the concept *kinship*, which is essentially structural, and the concept *residence*, which relates to what people actually do (behavior), became more evident in the definitions and discussions of Keesing (1958), Gonzalez (1961), and Bohannan (1963).[1] The unit labeled *household* gained added weight as further functional elements were added to the definition: "common residence, economic cooperation, and socialization of children" in Gonzalez's words (1969:106). Goody's (1972) domestic group could be viewed as a dwelling unit, a reproductive unit including sexual and socialization functions, or an economic unit of production and consumption. Yet households were still classified in practice by the kinds of kinship relations that "generated" them (Bohannan 1963:95–96).

Bohannan, drawing on the Goodenough-Fischer debate on Trukese residence, also noted that differences in household organization were not *just* a product of residence rules and that household organization lay at least partly outside the realm of kinship analysis. We still live with this contradiction; household organization is widely acknowledged to be separable from the concept of kinship (see Bender 1967), yet when it comes to classifying households into types, we group them on the basis of what kind of family lies at the core. Compounding the contradiction, explicit definitions of the household have been increasingly couched in functional rather than structural terms.

By *morphology* we refer to these structural classifications of the household. Terms like *stem, joint,* and *multiple family* refer to the morphological composition of households in terms of kinship relationships. Morphological descriptions can be highly explicit (Laslett 1972), elaborate (Harter and Bertrand 1977), or mathematically complex (R. Smith 1977), but they all lead to some confusion between household and family. This is because they forsake the functional element, that is, what households do, for the tangible and observable enumeration of personnel. But as the household is in fact defined as a group sharing certain activities (residence, consumption, and the like), we can argue that the elucidation of what it is that households *do* is logically prior to describing their size or composition.

Several authors have argued that use of existing morphological classifications of households can obscure important functional changes (for example, Medick 1976:295–96; Löfgren 1974:22–23; Creighton 1980: 137–38; Hammel 1980:250; Rubenstein 1975:311). All agree that there is a relationship between the functions of households and their size and composition and that this relationship should be a subject of investigation. Yet we must be able to explicitly describe cases in which the morphology of households changes but the functional group remains the same (for example, Brown 1977),[2] and the converse, where the morphology stays the same but the functions of the group vary (for example, Medick 1980).[3] What is needed is a classificatory scheme that considers the activities that household groups perform with the same explicitness as existing morphological classifications. Such a scheme can be based on the existing functional definitions of the household group.

Early functional definitions of the household were purposefully vague; a loose list of "domestic functions" such as those cited above for Gonzalez was considered sufficient. But as Yanagisako argues (1979:166), such an approach begs the question of why these are specifically "domestic" functions. No single functional criterion can be found which exactly and in all situations will specify what are households and what are not in a way that satisfies our intuitive sense of the "domestic." Even the most explicit multifunctional definition must use "sliding" criteria. Laslett (1972:27), for example, excludes members who cooperate economically and eat with the household if they do not share the same roof, but he also excludes "inmates" who *do* share the same roof if they do *not* cooperate economically and eat with the household. Such an inflexible, limited definition can have little cross-cultural utility in answering questions about why people sometimes eat or work together and why they don't at other times and places.

Anthropologists have access to data from many different societies, and one collection of information is sure to contradict any single defining attribute of the household. One solution researchers have taken is to define ethnographically specific groups that are labeled "domestic groups" (Ashcraft 1966; Goody 1972), "production-consumption units" (Cleveland 1980), or "budget units" (Seddon 1976). Such an approach has the advantage of being descriptively specific of just what a particular group is doing, yet it provides problems for a comparative approach (Hammel 1980:251). Worse, it begs the question of why we should use a definition of the household which excludes such basic economic groups in many societies.

Rethinking the problem of definition requires us to follow Löfgren (1974:23) in changing the question from one grounded in structure ("How do we place limits around a group?") to one grounded in activity ("What types of primary groups fulfilled the basic functions of production, consumption, socialization, etc., in . . . society?"). Our definition and classification "should serve to analyze the changing function of household and family in the social context of production, reproduction, as well as power relationships, and in addition to determine the repercussions of social and economic changes on family structure" (Medick 1976:295).

In this perspective we see that our questions involve relating both the morphology *and* the functions of household groups to each other and to wider social, economic, and cultural realms.

WHAT DO HOUSEHOLDS DO?

As a first step in redefining the household in functional terms, we propose to eliminate the troublesome term *function*, which carries a heavy burden of causative and teleological connotations. We do not in fact see people or groups function: we see them act. If we observe some people regularly acting in a patterned association with other people, we can then speak of *activity groups*. Some activity groups operate more frequently and in a more patterned manner than others. Borrowing a term from network theory (Niemeijer 1973), we can speak of the relative *density* of activity groups, based on the frequency of their operation.

Given activity groups of varying density, we can begin to visualize households as groups in which there is a high density of activity. Based on many years of cross-cultural observation, we know that there are certain *kinds* of activities that are consistently associated with the small, numerous, corporate social units observers generally agree in calling households. We can classify these activities into general *spheres* corresponding to what have been termed the basic domestic functions of production, reproduction, and inheritance among others. None of these spheres, however, is necessarily inherent in the household's bundle of activities. By the same token, there are many spheres of activity—marketing, banking, and political action, for instance—that are sometimes part of the household but more often are not. Below we group five categories of the activities most often performed by households—*production, distribution, transmission, reproduction* and *coresidence*—and discuss their separate ramifications. First, however, we should consider the general question of how we can rescue the concept of the household from this welter of optional defining activities.

If we visualize the activity groups within a society as composing spheres of activity, we see that these spheres overlap considerably. A group that shares a living space (coresidence), a group that shares in the activity of food preparation and consumption, and a group that socializes children often overlap completely; they are one and the same. Defining the household in a particular social setting does not require that each household have the same overlapping spheres of activity but that in each case we find, as Hammel so succinctly puts it, "the smallest grouping with the maximum corporate function" (1980:251). Venn diagrams, as suggested by Wrigley (1977), can be used to map the individual activity spheres in relation to one another and to existing human groups. Such a procedure ensures that the household will be placed in a wider context of activities; it specifies which activity spheres lie within the bounds of the household and which activities link households to one another and to other groups. The method can also be used to differentiate male and female activity groups, a distinction that can be of great importance in relating a household's activities to its genealogical organization (as demonstrated by Helms 1975).[4]

This mode of defining and analyzing household groups does not restrict the contributions of historians; it merely requires the historian, like the anthropologist, to distinguish morphological information (that is, size and composition of household units) from information on household activities (which often comes in the form of noncensus documents).[5] Where we have no data on household activities, historians, like archaeologists, must make inferences about activities based on what they know of morphology (Wilk and Rathje 1982). Such inferences require that we be explicit in formulating general, testable hypotheses about the relationships between household morphology, household activities, and the economic, social, and ideological components of social systems. We already possess a rich body of data and analysis from which we can draw material for these hypotheses, and some limited tests are possible at present. The rest of this essay will define the common spheres of domestic activity and will then propose some causal hypotheses about how morphology and activity are linked.

We would like to emphasize that in posing these hypotheses we make no assumptions about the direction of causal interaction between activity and morphology or about the household and other forces within a society. Questions about how ideology constrains morphology or how morphology restricts activity can only be settled empirically. But they must be discussed and clarified using an explicit framework that recognizes their separate but interdependent nature on the analytical level. The relationship between household activity and morphology is complex and diachronic. Households are multifunctional, and different causal factors can easily cancel or augment morphological consequences. Household groups are compromises, always imperfect, between often conflicting functional imperatives, preexisting structures, social norms, and cultural standards.

PRODUCTION

For this discussion we define production as human activity that procures or increases the value of resources. We include housekeeping and domestic labor of the kind stereotyped as nonproductive in our society

(Berk and Berk 1979). There is no question that the organization of production is affected by cultural rules, codes, and the division of labor within a society (Linares, this volume). We also have to recognize that these rules are flexible and changeable and that people will adapt their task-groups and social spheres of production to the specific labor requirements of particular tasks.

This view implies that at any one time in a society people have a definite understanding of what productive tasks should be done by households and how household labor is to be mobilized. In a longer perspective, however, we see that households can alter their size and composition in order to meet the labor needs of productive tasks.

The most important kind of variation in productive tasks which households respond to is variation in *scheduling*. By this we mean the absolute *timing* (in the yearly cycle) of productive tasks and the *sequencing* (the order) of the tasks themselves and the individual operations within a task. Within the category of timing, labor needs vary widely during a productive year, depending on specific local technical and environmental factors. At some times little labor is needed while at other times, called "bottlenecks," a great deal of labor is needed at once. Households try to balance their productive capacity so they will not have surplus labor during most of the productive year, but this usually means that nonhousehold labor must be obtained during bottlenecks.[6]

We can also speak of production systems as being either *diverse*, requiring many different tasks at the same time, or *simple*, meaning that major productive tasks can be ordered one after another. The yearly fluctuation in labor needs will have a strong effect on the optimal labor group size.

Sequencing of labor within a productive task has a great effect on the efficiency of that labor. Some tasks are more efficiently performed in a simultaneous manner, by the application of many hands at the same time. This efficiency arises through economies of scale or through specialization and differentiation. Other tasks, however, can be performed in a linear fashion, one person doing each operation in sequence. Different kinds of sequencing in major productive tasks require different activity groups and determine whether these groups can be part of the household.

From this perspective we can generate some testable hypotheses about the direction and nature of household adaptation to particular differences in scheduling. We expect that the more simultaneous the labor requirements of major productive tasks, and the more diverse the productive tasks within a yearly cycle, the more tendency we will see for larger household groups. Unless there is some other reason for large households to exist, we expect that linear tasks arranged in a simple yearly cycle favor the small household as a productive group. This is the gist of the "incompatibility theory" proposed by Pasternak, Ember, and Ember (1976), though they focus specifically on the diversity of female productive and reproductive tasks. Their cross-cultural test of the hypothesis lends it some support, though the data and method of categorization leave a lot to be desired.

Stronger support for this hypothesis comes from specific cases in which the ethnographer considered labor demands of productive tasks. Befu (1968*a*, 1968*b*) found the large duolocal households of the Nakagiri area of Japan were a response to the complexity and diversity of swidden agricultural production where many plots were cultivated at the same time by a single household. Similarly, Sahlins (1957) claimed that large households on Moala were constituted to pursue diverse productive tasks in widely separated geographical areas. The large medieval Genoese households described by Hughes (1975) also pursued diverse productive and commercial activities in different cities and benefited from task specialization and differentiation.

A related hypothesis is that households will keep their labor group to a minimum size when the productive tasks they perform show decreasing marginal returns.[7] When economies of scale are within the range households can reach, larger groups will be found. An excellent example is provided by Loucky (1979), who found that Guatemalan intensive agriculturalists marry later and have smaller households than rope makers in an adjacent village. He ascribes the difference to the decreasing marginal return in subsistence agriculture and the increasing returns from larger groups in craft production. Similar situations existed in historic European cottage industry (Levine 1974; Medick 1976).

A more general hypothesis relates to the *elasticity* in the labor demands of production. If the size and scale of production is elastic, it can be adjusted to household resources as they vary during the developmental cycle (as Chayanov 1966 proposed). If production cannot be scaled down or expanded as household labor resources vary (this tends to happen with increasing diversity and complexity), extending strategies must be adopted to attract labor—related or nonrelated—into the household (see Reyna 1976; Löfgren 1974).

Together these hypotheses can account for the differences observed between the small households of Kofyar intensive hoe farmers, whose tasks are linear, simple, elastic, and show decreasing returns to scale, and the larger households of Kofyar swidden farmers, whose work is more complex, simultaneous, and inelastic (Netting 1965). These hypotheses also promise to explain why households respond in such diverse ways to new economic opportunities such as cash cropping or wage labor. The response of the household will depend on specific aspects of each cash crop or opportunity; the diversity of household commercial activities may lead to larger households (Singer 1968; Douglass 1980; Shah 1974; Geertz 1961) while simple, linear, and occasional cash cropping or wage labor may cause households to fragment (Rubenstein 1975; Clarke 1953).

In more general terms production itself varies in importance as an organizing principle of households. Few researchers have explicitly taken up the issue of how and why productive activities of households change in relation to other household activities, though there is a general feeling that this is one of the defining characteristics of "modernization" (for exceptions, see Helms 1975 and Medick 1977). Clearly a larger body of relevant data is needed.

DISTRIBUTION

Distribution consists of moving material from producers to consumers. For our purposes distribution includes consumption. The term *distribution* leads us to focus on exchanges and transactions within and between households which tend to be ignored if we merely oppose production and consumption. Distribution is often a convenient boundary marker for the household because social rules for exchange within the household are often different from those in operation between households.

Households are generally characterized by *pooling*, that is, a common fund is created through the practice of generalized rather than balanced reciprocity. Other corporate entities within a society may also have funds pooled by members, but balanced reciprocity is the rule in these cases. This is not to imply that there cannot be distributive subunits within the household. We often find that household members have their own productive resources and retain rights to dispose of part of their income from those resources in any way they like.

It is often hard to separate production and distribution in ethnographic situations, and it is even harder to decide which factor is affecting household morphology. Diverse production within the household seems to require pooling and redistribution of the products while less differentiated production may or may not.

A generalization that seems to apply is that pooling within a larger group (which may be a household) is an effective strategy when sources of income are diverse, seasonal, variable, or unpredictable. The variability can be short-term, as among the Bajau Laut of Borneo who pool fish on a daily basis within a household cluster to even out the variation in daily catches (Sather 1976). Longer term variation in the productivity of a nuclear family during the developmental cycle may also be evened out by pooling within a larger extended unit, as with the Barma of Chad (Reyna 1976).

Where capital rather than income is the most important resource, corporate control and pooling for investment may give a large household unit a competitive advantage, as Hunt (1965) noted among Mexican merchants. Often this advantage is countered by administrative problems and the necessity for a powerful leadership to make decisions for the whole group (Sahlins 1957).

These generalizations can be tied to several more specific hypotheses. Poor households in a market economy do not generally cooperate in production, but they do sometimes pool in distribution for consumption (though rarely for investment) as a form of social insurance—spreading the poverty around. While such "distributive" households tend to be fragile, we propose that they will tend to be large if wage labor or other income opportunities are irregular but relatively uniform in quality and accessibility. When income opportunities are accessible to a limited part of the population or variable in their remuneration and their location, smaller households rather than large pooling units will predominate. This explains the variation between the large households of poor Blackfoot Indians (Robbins 1968), Mexican urban migrants (Hackenberg, Murphy, and Selby, this volume), or Lancashire factory workers (Anderson 1971) and the small households of impoverished Antillean peasants (Rubenstein 1975; Clarke 1953) or the rural English medieval poor (Laslett 1965). When income opportunities are unequal and widely spaced, contributing to a household fund becomes a poor strategy (Stack 1974). The degree to which resources are spatially clustered or temporally variable will determine whether pooling can be effective on the household level or whether it must be done within a larger social group such as a cooperative, a clan, or a regional market system.

A general rule that ties production and distribution together seems evident in cross-cultural data. Large households that pool in production *and* in distribution tend to be stable and have generational continuity. Households that only cooperate in scheduling labor *or* in pooling for distribution tend to be less stable and fragment often. The fragility of the urban Javanese extended households studied by Hildred Geertz (1961) results from little or no cooperation in scheduling labor, accompanied by pooling of products, with all the attendant arguments and resentments engendered by inequities.

We still lack the comparative literature we need if we are to comment on different kinds of pooling within households. Few have reported the details of economic transactions within households or the ways in which household budgets are managed and apportioned (for an interesting exception, see Gonzalez 1978). We expect that some significant variation in allocation methods will eventually come to light.

TRANSMISSION

Where resources are not scarce and where the major contribution to the production of subsistence or goods is labor, the household group may be structured in part by its role in mobilizing and coordinating that labor. But when necessary resources are restricted, when rights to valuable goods, property, and tools become increasingly jural and individual instead of communal and loosely defined, and when families have unequal access to the means of production, the household may begin to function as the social unit that holds, defends, and transmits these rights. The timing and mode of transmitting scarce goods among household members, especially in the form of inheritance, may influence the kinship composition, age structure, size, and patterns of authority in the household.

An hypothesis growing from these generalizations might well be based on the well-known association between density of population, competition for land, agricultural intensification, and individual or family ownership of land (Boserup 1965). We might postulate that with increasing personal rights in productive property there is a tendency to define heirs to property more narrowly, reducing those with a claim on it from community to descent group and then to household members, nuclear family members, and finally a single heir, as in primogeniture. Goody (1976) contrasts lateral inheritance under conditions of African extensive cultivation and joint exploitation by siblings in larger extended households with the "diverging devolution" of more intensive Eurasian agriculture in smaller households. Where the land will support only a single elementary family, the number of potential heirs must be rigidly limited by reducing births, keeping all children but the heir unmarried, or sending surplus children away as servants or laborers (Goody 1976:95). It is worth testing the proposition that transmission of property will increasingly affect household morphology under conditions of growing scarcity, higher costs of goods, and unequal distribution of property used, held, or administered within the household. To the degree that land, livestock, houses, and other resources necessary to sustain a household at some customary economic level are limited and acquired principally through inheritance, there will be a tendency for transgenerational transmission to be restricted and formalized. Legal or customary stipulations of who will be heirs, of the size and type of property in their shares, and of when the inheritance will take place may increasingly dictate household composition and extension.

Where land is relatively plentiful and cheap, such as on the settlement frontier, individuals can acquire temporary usufruct from kin group or community membership, or partible inheritance can assign each offspring equal rights. Households might include large numbers of children, but young adults marry early, take an adequate share of land, and split off from the parental household. Limitations on available farms and livestock, however, might delay inheritance and marriage, leading to households of parents with adult single offspring or celibate siblings (Netting 1979). With further shrinkage of the land base and overpopulation impartible inheritance might be adopted to preserve family estates by passing them on to one heir, as in thirteenth-century England (Homans 1960) or nineteenth-century Ireland (Wolf 1966:75). The stem family in Austria followed from an inheritance system that allowed only one conjugal family to succeed that of the parents while noninheriting heirs became cottagers (Berkner 1972), landless laborers, or industrial workers (Khera 1972). Where agricultural resources are barely adequate to support a family or where estates are fragmented and recombined in each generation through partible inheritance, the simple nuclear family household may be the most frequent adaptation. Under conditions of population pressure and land hunger, such as in Chamula, patrilocal clusters of kin have little incentive to remain together (Collier 1976). Often, however, though inheritance systems may correlate with household type (Berkner 1976), the availability of land may be an unrelated variable, or the inheritance laws may not be followed in practice (Cole and Wolf 1974).

Where impartible inheritance is the rule, marriage (as Löfgren 1974 convincingly demonstrates) becomes a strategy for transmitting and accumulating property and comes under the control of parental authority. Stratified marriage emerges, as heirs have much better prospects than those who have no chance of inheriting. Löfgren also shows that the advent of impartible inheritance coincides with the beginnings of a landless class, a rural proletariat; this is a possible avenue toward social stratification. Such detached persons can also provide the base of urban society and form a ready labor pool for craft specialization or armies.

Legal aspects of land tenure and transmission may also be preserved for centuries or suddenly altered by nation states regardless of changes in land use that may affect the household production unit. The Napoleonic law decreeing partible inheritance did not necessarily result in fragmenting the parental estate or the household in those parts of France where it violated local custom (Berkner 1977: 55; Wheaton 1980:19). Where primogeniture or other forms of impartible inheritance are the rule, stem family households may be encouraged by further testamentary regulations making the heir legally responsible for the food, housing, and care of retired parents as well as for celibate siblings who remain household members. The nature and amount of property transmitted, its value as an undivided versus a divided resource, and the customary or legal rules for inheritance often condition the form assumed by the household. And the importance of economic as against normative factors must be empirically determined in every case.

Intergenerational transmission of property merely represents a node in the household life history, whereas the pooling and consumption of goods may go on continuously. Both these processes make wealth a major determinant of household size in many societies. The rich can afford to support more children, kin, and servants in a single household than can the poor, and the promise of assured future income can keep such a group together longer (Wheaton 1975). Size of household and the frequency of multiple family organization correlated directly with prosperity in medieval Florence (Klapisch 1972). The households of wealthy landowners, tenants, craftsmen, and laborers were of successively smaller size in rural England (Laslett 1965:64). Japanese main families had more members and resident retainers than their poorer relatives in the cadet branches (T. C. Smith 1959), and household size correlated closely with agricultural land holdings in five local censuses spanning more than a century (T. C. Smith 1977). Extensive surveys of late eighteenth- and early nineteenth-century Russian peasants show household size increasing with amount of land sown and number of draft horses owned. Larger average household populations were evidently advantageous because the bigger units had not merely more total productive wealth but also greater wealth per capita (Shanin 1972:64). Corporate control of property or capital by the wealthier classes is associated with greater incidence of the joint family household in India, but this adherence may be a result less of economic factors than of a higher caste ritual status and degree of Sanskritization (Shah 1974: 171–72). Indeed religious learning, ceremonial prerogatives, and social status are often transmitted in the context of ongoing households.

In general socioeconomic stratification appears to be directly reflected in average household size because of the advantages of a larger coordinated labor force and because of the higher fertility that accompanies relative affluence (Netting 1982). Wealth and prestige attract and hold the members of large households while the poor can usually sustain only smaller groups of coresidents. The correlation appears within communities and over time and it is cross-culturally valid (Netting 1982). Where immaterial or material goods in a society are limited and where rights to them are ascribed and inherited, the formal, restrictive rules and practices of transmission may directly influence the size and composition of the household.

REPRODUCTION

Although the household group is intimately related to reproduction, it is obviously not just sexual relationships that bind members together. Indeed, most of the people living together in a household may be neither married nor cohabiting. Incest prohibitions forbid sex between parents and their children, between siblings, and often between other classes of affines. Anthropologists countered Murdock's emphasis on the centrality of the nuclear family as a reproductive unit (Murdock 1949:5) by citing contrary cases. Married spouses or sexual partners were not coresident among the Nayar (Gough 1952) or in a wide variety of matrifocal Caribbean societies (R. T. Smith 1973, 1978). Ashanti married males live separately from their wives during certain stages of the developmental cycle (Fortes 1949), Japanese swidden farmers maintain "duolocal" households (Befu 1968*b*), and Irish Tory Islanders may remain for years as residents of their parental households though they are married and bearing children (Fox 1978). Significant reproduction should therefore be thought of in terms of the mandatory socialization and enculturation of subadult humans that usually goes on in a family-household context rather than the sexual pairing of two or more household members. Socialization generally necessitates coresidence while simple reproduction obviously does not.

The tasks engendered by reproduction, that is, the care, feeding, education, and emotional support of infants and children, must add to and modify the demands for production, distribution, and transmission in the household. Indeed requirements for child raising and other activities such as female agricultural labor may conflict. Reproduction is a stage in a process whereby time and effort are invested in offspring who may later increase the household labor pool and tend the aged parents when they become physically dependent. It would be useful to test the assertion that when women's productive tasks outside the home are incompatible with a reproductive strategy requiring high fertility, the household will be expanded to include nursemaids or surrogate mothers (Pasternak, Ember, and Ember 1976). The timing and rate of reproduction affecting household size and composition are contingent on a variety of external factors (infant death rate and adult life span as linked to food supply, disease, and warfare) and on such internal variables as age at marriage and decisions on family limitation practices.

The "new home economics" and the growing literature on the economic value of children (Nag, White, and Peet 1978) suggests that fertility may increase or be maintained at high levels if children's net economic contribution exceeds their costs when they are still relatively young. A reversal of this wealth flow occurs when children's entry into the labor force is delayed by need for education or lack of necessary adult skills, and this could lead eventually to a conscious reduction in fertility (Caldwell 1977). In situations where high fertility is encouraged by frequent child deaths and enjoined by the high value of children for production and parental security in later life, household kinship composition often reflects individual efforts to increase, restore, or substitute for fertility. Sterility is a major contributor to divorce among the Barma of Chad (Reyna 1977), and the Nigerian Kofyar (Netting 1969) may seek additional wives in polygynous marriage if a spouse is childless. Rapid remarriage of both widowed men and women in eighteenth-century France was made necessary by the sexual division of labor and child care, but it frequently resulted in households with several kinds of half-siblings, scattered sibling groups, and conflicts over inheritance (Baulant 1976). Widespread adoption or fosterage can even out the access to children among differentially reproducing families as in Polynesia (Carroll 1970), and alternate generation households can be created when grandchildren are sent to live with and help grandparents (Gonzalez 1969).

Though increased fertility and survival of children may allow some enlargement of mean household size, it is the initiation of reproduction by marriage, its timing, its absence among celibates, and its association with household fission, that produce significant variations in household form. We might hypothesize that it is through explicit marriage rules and preferences that cultural norms most directly influence family demography and household morphology. Contrasting household types among different classes or occupational groups in the same community may be traced to well-defined marital strategies (Löfgren 1974) that are themselves contingent on the control and transmission of property. "Owing to the typically high mortality before the demographic transition, a five-year reduction in the mean age of parenthood could double the frequency of extended family households (couples with one or more widowed parents) within a society of nuclear family organization" (Mendels 1979). Nineteenth-century Russian landlords required women on their estates to be married by age 17 and fined their fathers if they were not. Early and universal marriage produced not only the expectable rapid population growth but a frequency of multiple family households of over 75 percent

(Czap 1978:118). Marriage under such circumstances could precede physiological maturity and economic independence. Evidently the teenage couples were incorporated in existing economic units under patriarchal authority and an imposed junior status. It is possible to initiate a multiple family household even before children are of reproductive age by bringing in and raising a child bride for the heir, as is the custom in parts of China (A. Wolf 1968). In contrast, the lower fertility of late-marrying Irish rural people was compounded by high celibacy, childless marriages, and migration of offspring from the farm, resulting in a 40 percent rate of "family failure" in all households in a 1969 sample (Symes 1972). It is probable that in most societies most of the time individuals manage to physiologically reproduce themselves. The question of whether household residential groups reproduce themselves *in place* by incorporating kin from outside the nuclear family or retaining adult married children as members requires information on fertility, mortality, and patterns of marriage as well as on the costs and benefits of production, distribution, and transmission.

The desirability of perpetuating a household as a continuing corporate entity is based in part on the cultural values held by members of the society. An ideal such as the Indian joint family hallowed by Sanskrit scripture and popular esteem may persist for centuries, even when few households of brothers ever remain together after their father's death (Shah 1974:92–93). Laslett (1972:67–68) has suggested that the stem family environment may effectively socialize children to recreate such a unit in later life. By looking at the coresidential consequences of individual choice making during a particular life course (Wolf, this volume; Vinovskis 1977; Elder 1977) we may better gauge the relative effects of culturally valued family forms and economic forces. From contemporary American social commentary it would seem axiomatic that many of our emotional ills and inadequacies of child raising can be traced to the lack of an extended family, especially the lack of resident grandparents. In fact, extended and multiple family households have been neither frequent nor preferred. It is clear that in certain rural situations, such as in southern France, the prevailing model of the *oustal* farm requires an indivisible, continuous unit of land, a house, and a resident owner with his married son/heir. Though poverty in the past frequently prevented realization of this cycle, the greater prosperity of the interwar period in Aveyron allowed *oustals* to conform more closely to the rule of succession, and the proportion of three-generation families actually increased from 10 to 15 percent before World War I to 45 percent in the period 1962–75 (Rogers 1979:153, 192). Though adult life expectancy increased and the average marriage age decreased, changes in the household were less a product of the demography of reproduction than of economic improvement in agriculture combined with traditional beliefs about the practices of inheritance. Among townsmen and the rural landless the proportion of three-generation households has declined in line with opportunities for wage labor and the dominant cultural values of the larger French society (Rogers 1979:167). Both the learning and the experience on which reproduction of the parental family form might be based are not consistent within a single community, much less over even a short period of time.

CORESIDENCE

Household membership is so often synonymous with coresidence that most scholarly attention has been devoted to the cases in which the two categories are not perfectly congruent. Where evidence of individuals' actually dwelling under one roof or sharing a common hearth is lacking, as in the manuscript household lists of historians, it must be assumed that the unit singled out by the census taker was coresident (Laslett 1969; Anderson 1972). A building internally partitioned or divided into apartments may provide the premises for what Laslett (1972:36) calls a "houseful," whereas a complex of adjacent structures or a compound of free-standing huts or rooms may shelter a single household. In such cases the size and arrangement of the building may depend more on the permanence of materials and the costs of construction than on the social and economic relations of the inhabitants. Using such additional criteria as the frequency of food sharing and common cooking, separation of sleeping quarters, the presence or absence of common granaries, and the degree of cooperation in production, anthropologists have had little difficulty in isolating household units, such as the *bilek* families inhabiting a single Iban longhouse (Freeman 1955; Sutlive 1978:39). A Kekchi Maya house cluster may represent a single cohesive household or a number of semi-autonomous units, depending on the stage in the domestic cycle of a continuously present set of individuals (Wilk, this volume). The actual distance between Kekchi houses is related to the quantity and quality of economic relations between members, but dwelling location is also a symbolic social statement. The mere physical presence of a dwelling or of several houses does not allow the inference of a particular type of household.

Physical confines and availability of dwelling space do, however, condition the size and composition of the household unit. It may indeed be possible to test the relationship of the permanence, capital investment, and high acquisition costs of housing to extended and multiple family household forms. If house sites are plentiful, materials are obtainable mainly through the expenditure of labor, construction skills are widely shared, and buildings decay rapidly, as in the tropics, structures can be erected, moved, or abandoned to accommodate the social and economic needs of the moment (Wilk 1982). Mbuti pygmies of Zaire can easily put up a shelter of poles and leaves, which allows them to change camps freely yet represents the temporary closeness or hostility felt by family groups toward one another (Turnbull 1962). A similar practice has been observed among Australian aborigines (Gould 1980). When more substantial houses were scarce and costly, as in rural England, adult children might have to remain at home or pool their earnings with parents or siblings to pay the rent. According to Malthus, "one of the most salutary and least pernicious checks to the frequency of early marriage in this country is the difficulty of procuring a cottage" (quoted by Macfarlane 1976:223). A capacious house, in contrast, could fill a profitable demand for housing. Lodgers occupying a bedroom might interact minimally with the household while boarders might be the functional equivalent of resident kin. Where a crowded village environment and the difficulty of enlarging old dwellings or building new ones is compelling, even simple family households may divide sleeping and other activities among a number of noncontiguous structures. Adolescent children in a Swiss alpine village may sleep in separate apartments and use scattered cellars, storehouses, and workshops belonging to their families. Most Iranian households in one particular village are close-knit production and distribution units, but members do not live in self-contained courtyard compounds. Because of partible inheritance of building units, households have one or more rooms at a distance from the main living quarters (Horne 1981).

Cultural expectations about desirable household composition may well be imposed as outside agencies plan and assign new housing. Tuscan landlords encouraged large families by their control over domestic architecture on the estate (McArdle 1978:152). Clearing the slums of Lagos with their maze of compounds and replacing them with single family apartments in suburban blocks destroyed the advantages of multiple family households for the urban poor (Marris 1961). Farm families relocated following construction of a Ghanaian reservoir refused to live in the "modern," two-room masonry dwellings provided by the state (Brokensha, personal communication). American houses may not easily accommodate elderly kin until the children of the owning couple are old enough to move out. Even powerful norms of household structure such as the American ideal of an independent nuclear family in a freestanding, owner-occupied dwelling can be modified by economic necessity. Just as the Great Depression delayed marriage and forced the "doubling up" of several related married couples in the same house, today's real estate market may return grown children unwillingly to the parental nest and send multiple families in search of large, old-fashioned homes.

Under similar conditions of economic stringency perhaps the most important members of many households are those who are not in residence at all (Vinovskis 1977:265). Migratory laborers, craftsmen absent during the slack agricultural season, itinerant merchants, and students away at school may claim to be members of a household and supply it with vital remittances, goods, and services, yet a de facto census may not enumerate them. A major support of the rural joint family of China (Yang 1965:236) or India (Kessinger 1974:196) may be the sons or brothers employed in the cities and sending cash home. Such a division of labor can prevent the competition and friction that causes many coresident households to fragment. Until recently unmarried wage-earning offspring were one of the most valuable assets of a Swiss peasant family. All money beyond a bare subsistence minimum was sent home and used by the parents to support themselves and add to the family estate. South African and Mexican emigrants perform similar roles and provide one of the few existing avenues for economic mobility within their villages of origin. That a household can operate effectively with some members who are not coresident for extended periods of time is a tribute to the moral imperatives of kinship and reciprocal obligation that flourish in the household context (Bloch 1973). Those emigrants who return to their natal households for key tasks of the agricultural cycle (Lewis 1981), who marry and leave wives and children there, or who send back more money than they expend on maintaining themselves at the work place often consider themselves members of the household and expect eventually to return for full-time residence there. In the meantime an extended or multiple family, pooling subsistence goods and cash earnings, may be the most secure household arrangement. In those peripheral parts of the world system where labor migration is appreciable, households must be examined for the presence of *intermittent coresidents* whose economic contributions adapt local productive and reproductive units to the demands of larger, money-based exchange systems.

CONCLUSION

We have discussed some of the many ways in which the organization of activities within households can affect the structure and morphology of the household group. Though we have not discussed household activities that fall outside our five spheres—such as defense or political action—we acknowledge that these activities can be of overriding importance in some cases, such as in large Balkan households banded together for defense. This omission will not be addressed here, but the larger issue it raises must be. For analytical purposes we have discussed household activities one by one, in isolation from one another, without discussing the ways in which household activities interrelate. Two aspects of the interaction deserve comment.

The first is that the morphology of a household is a compromise between often contradictory functional imperatives. If producing groups are large and transmission takes place within a small group of heirs, the group that actually coresides and that creates some corporate self-identification as a household cannot be both large and small. The Venn diagrams of different activity spheres never overlap perfectly, and it is perhaps this constant tension between different activity groups and their corporate morphology which provides the dynamism and adaptability seen in the variety of coexisting households and which results in structured change through time. The ways in which conflicts between functional exigencies are mediated and negotiated clearly deserve further research.

Second, we must recognize that different activities vary in their importance in this process of morphological compromise. At times the household's morphology is congruent with and dependent on a limited range of activities while other activities are performed outside the context of the household group. Furthermore, the activities that dominate household form vary in a way that follows a broadly evolutionary path. The households of hunters and gatherers perform mostly distributive and reproductive tasks and activities, and their morphology responds to variation in these activities. Horticulturalist households, in contrast, seem to be organized principally as productive groups. In fact, the transition from hunting and gathering to early agriculture may be profitably envisioned as a process of transition from band or individual production and household pooling, to a system of household production and exchange among households.

As agriculture becomes more intensive, the importance of households in production and distribution tends to decline. At the same time the role of the household in transmitting goods and land increases, and often the two effects cancel each other out and large households continue to exist, though the structure and organization of the "inheritance" household is different from that of the "production-distribution" household. The industrial revolution seems to have led back to households that are mainly reproductive and distributive units. In this perspective the process of "modernization" is not a transition from one type or form of household to another, but it is more basically a change in the activity spheres that underlie household form. In essence the material flows of labor, goods, and cash in household production, distribution, and transmission are negotiated anew in each generation according to the historical circumstances of the moment but always also with respect to culturally approved options of coresidence and patterns of authority, duty, and affection socially reproduced in the home. The actual form households take during the transition may or may not change. We cannot predict these forms without the specifics of each case and without knowledge of the cultural context of rules and norms by which household form and function are mediated and reconciled.

NOTES

1. These authors all classified households on a genealogical basis and then went on to discuss why households were often constituted for nongenealogical and nonkinship reasons.

2. Brown describes a Caribbean situation in which clusters of nuclear family households perform the same activities as larger multiple family households.

3. Medick discusses the functional differences between the extended family households of land-owning peasants and landless rural proletarians.

4. Helms's comparative study of three Caribbean societies mapped male and female spheres of production, distribution, and reproduction to concisely explain variation in the morphology and developmental cycles of what had been previously lumped together as "matrifocal" households.

5. The first comparative studies of English communities made little effort to consider variation over time caused by exogenous factors or to deal with differences between types of communities. "In order to invest a census study with more significance, one has to stop outside the listings themselves and consider other historical evidence which can be used to add some flesh and blood to the bare bones of statistical analysis" (Goose 1980:347).

6. This balance was of course partially addressed by Chayanov (1966) but more recently has been considered solely as a balance of producers and consumers against each other (e.g., Reyna 1976, Lewis 1981).

7. These are usually simple, linear tasks that do not increase in yield when performed in a simultaneous fashion by more than one or two people.

REFERENCES

Anderson, M.
1971 Family Structure in Nineteenth-century Lancashire. Cambridge: Cambridge University Press.

1972 Standard Tabulation Procedures for Houses, Households, and Other Groups of Residents, in the Enumeration Books of the Censuses of 1851 to 1891. *In* Nineteenth-century Society: Essays in the Use of Quantitative Methods for the Study of Social Data, ed. E. A. Wrigley. Cambridge: Cambridge University Press.

Ashcraft, Norman

1966 The Domestic Group in Mahogany, British Honduras. Social and Economic Studies 15 (3):266–74.

Baulant, Micheline

1976 The Scattered Family: Another Aspect of Seventeenth-century Demography. *In* Family and Society, eds. R. Forster and O. Ranum, pp. 104–16. Baltimore: Johns Hopkins University Press.

Befu, Harumi

1968*a* Ecology, Residence, and Authority: The Corporate Household in Central Japan. Ethnology 7:25–42.

1968*b* Origin of Large Households and Duolocal Residence in Central Japan. American Anthropologist 70 (2):309–20.

Bender, Donald

1967 A Redefinement of the Concept of Household: Families, Coresidence, and Domestic Functions. American Anthropologist 69:493–504.

Berk, Sarah F. and Richard A. Berk

1979 Labor and Leisure at Home: Content and Organization of the Household Day. Beverly Hills: Sage.

Berkner, Lutz K.

1972 The Stem Family and the Developmental Cycle of the Peasant Household: An Eighteenth-century Austrian Example. American Historical Review 77:398–418.

1976 Inheritance, Land Tenure, and Peasant Family Structure: A German Regional Comparison. *In* Family and Inheritance: Rural Society in Western Europe, 1200–1800, ed. J. R. Goody, J. Thirsk, and E. P. Thompson. Cambridge: Cambridge University Press.

1977 Peasant Household Organization and Demographic Change in Lower Saxony (1689–1766). *In* Population Patterns in the Past, ed. R. D. Lee, pp. 53–69. New York: Academic Press.

Bloch, Maurice

1973 The Long Term and the Short Term: The Economic and Political Significance of the Morality of Kinship. *In* The Character of Kinship, ed. J. Goody, pp. 78–87. London: Cambridge University Press.

Bohannan, Paul

1963 Social Anthropology. Holt, Rinehart, and Winston: New York.

Boserup, Ester

1965 The Conditions of Agricultural Growth. Chicago: Aldine.

Brown, Susan E.

1977 Household Composition and Variation in a Rural Dominican Village. Journal of Comparative Family Studies 3:257–67.

Caldwell, John C.
1977 The Persistence of High Fertility: Population Prospects in the Third World. Changing African Family Series: Family and Fertility Change, no. 1. Canberra: Department of Demography, Australian National University.

Carroll, Vern, ed.
1970 Adoption in Eastern Oceania. Honolulu: University Press of Hawaii.

Chayanov, A. V.
1966 The Theory of the Peasant Economy. Ed. D. Thorner, B. Kerblay, and R. Smith. Richard D. Irwin: Homewood, Ill.

Clarke, Edith
1953 Land Tenure and the Family in Four Selected Communities in Jamaica. Social and Economic Studies 1:81–118.

Cleveland, David A.
1980 The Population Dynamics of Subsistence Agriculture in the West African Savanna: A Village in Northeast Ghana. Ph.D. Dissertation, University of Arizona.

Cole, John W., and Eric R. Wolf
1974 The Hidden Frontier: Ecology and Ethnicity in an Alpine Valley. New York: Academic Press.

Collier, G.
1976 Fields of the Tzotzil: The Ecological Bases of Tradition in Highland Chiapas. Austin: University of Texas Press.

Creighton, Colin
1980 Family, Property, and the Relations of Production in Western Europe. Economy and Society 9:128–67.

Czap, Peter
1978 Marriage and the Peasant Joint Family in the Era of Serfdom. *In* The Family in Imperial Russia, ed. David L. Ransel, pp. 103–23. Urbana: University of Illinois Press.

Douglass, William A.
1980 The South Italian Family: A Critique. Journal of Family History 5:338–59.

Elder, G.
1977 Family History and the Life Course. Journal of Family History 2:279–304.

Fortes, M.
1949 The Web of Kinship among the Tallensi. London: Oxford University Press.

Fox, Robin
1978 The Tory Islanders: A People of the Celtic Fringe. Cambridge: Cambridge University Press.

Freeman, J. D.
1955 Iban Agriculture. London: Her Majesty's Stationery Office.

Geertz, Hildred
1961 The Javanese Family. Glencoe, Ill.: Free Press of Glencoe.
Gonzalez, Nancie L. Solien
1961 The Structure of the Peasant Family. American Anthropologist 73:1058–76.
1969 Black Carib Household Structure. Monograph 48, American Ethnological Society. Seattle: University of Washington Press.
1978 Estrategias socioeconómicas del campesinado frente la expansión de la agricultura comercial: Ejido de Loma Tendida, Valle de Santiago, Guanajuato. Tesis de licenciado en antropología social, Universidad Iberoamericana, Mexico.
Goody, Jack
1972 The Evolution of the Family. *In* Household and Family in Past Time, ed. Peter Laslett and Richard Wall, pp. 103–24. Cambridge: Cambridge University Press.
1976 Production and Reproduction. Cambridge: Cambridge University Press.
Goose, Nigel
1980 Household Size and Structure in Early Stuart Cambridge. Social History 5:347–87.
Gough, E. K.
1952 The Nayars and the Definition of Marriage. Journal of the Royal Anthropological Institute 89:23–34.
Gould, Richard
1980 Living Archaeology. Cambridge: Cambridge University Press.
Hammel, E. A.
1980 Household Structure in Fourteenth-century Macedonia. Journal of Family History 5:242–73.
Harter, Carl L., and William E. Bertrand
1977 A Methodology for Classifying Household Family Structures. Journal of Comparative Family Studies 8:403–13.
Helms, Mary
1975 Household Organization in Eastern Central America: A Comparative Study. Paper presented at the 74th annual meeting of the American Anthropological Association.
Homans, George C.
1960 English Villagers of the Thirteenth Century (orig. ed. 1941). New York: Russell and Russell.
Horne, Lee
1981 The Household in Space: Dispersed Holdings in an Iranian Village. American Behavioral Scientist 7:677–87.
Hughes, Diane
1975 Urban Growth and Family Structure in Medieval Genoa. Past and Present 66:13–17.

Hunt, Robert
1965 The Developmental Cycle of the Family Business in Rural Mexico. *In* Essays in Economic Anthropology, ed. J. Helm, pp. 54–80. Seattle: University of Washington Press.

Keesing, Felix
1958 Cultural Anthropology. New York: Holt, Rinehart and Winston.

Kessinger, Tom G.
1974 Vilyatpur, 1848–1968. Berkeley, Los Angeles, London: University of California Press.

Khera, Sigrid
1972 An Austrian Peasant Village under Rural Industrialization. Behavior Science Notes 7:29–36.

Klapisch, Christine
1972 Houschold and Family in Tuscany in 1427. *In* Household and Family in Past Time, ed. Peter Laslett and Richard Wall, pp. 267–82. London: Cambridge University Press.

Laslett, Peter
1965 The World We Have Lost. New York: Scribner's.
1969 Size and Structure of the Household in England over Three Centuries. Population Studies 23:199–223.
1972 Introduction: The History of the Family. *In* Household and Family in Past Time, ed. Peter Laslett and Richard Wall, pp. 1–89. Cambridge: Cambridge University Press.

Levine, David
1974 The Demographic Implications of Rural Industrialization: A Family Reconstruction Study of Two Leicestershire Villages, 1600–1851. Ph.D. Dissertation, Cambridge University.

Lewis, John Van D.
1981 Domestic Labor Intensity and the Incorporation of Malian Peasant Farmers into Localized Descent Groups. American Ethnologist 8:53–73.

Löfgren, Orvar
1974 Family and Household among Scandinavian Peasants: An Exploratory Essay. Ethnologia Scandinavica 74:1–52.

Loucky, James
1979 Production and Patterning of Social Relations and Values in Two Guatemalan Villages. American Ethnologist 6:702–23.

McArdle, Frank
1978 Altopascio: A Study in Tuscan Rural Society, 1587–1784. Cambridge: Cambridge University Press.

Macfarlane, Alan
1976 Resources and Population: A Study of the Gurungs of Nepal. Cambridge: Cambridge University Press.

Marris, Peter
1961 Family and Social Change in an African City: A Study of Rehousing in Lagos. London: Routledge and Kegan Paul.
Medick, H.
1976 The Proto-industrial Family Economy: The Structural Function of the Household during the Transition from Peasant Society to Industrial Capitalism. Social History 3:291–315.
Mendels, Franklin F.
1979 Notes on the Age of Maternity, Population Growth, and Family Structure in the Past. Journal of Family History 4:236–50.
Moynihan, Daniel P.
1965 The Negro Family—The Case for National Action. Office of Policy Planning and Research, United States Department of Labor. Washington, D.C.: U.S. Government Printing Office.
Murdock, G. P.
1949 Social Structure. New York: Macmillan.
Nag, Moni, B. White, and R. C. Peet
1978 An Anthropological Approach to the Study of the Economic Value of Children in Java and Nepal. Current Anthropology 19:293–306.
Netting, Robert McC.
1965 Household Organization and Intensive Agriculture: The Kofyar Case. Africa 35:422–29.
1969 Women's Weapons: The Politics of Domesticity among the Kofyar. American Anthropologist 71:1037–46.
1979 Household Dynamics in a Nineteenth-century Swiss Village. Journal of Family History 4:39–58.
1982 Some Home Truths on Household Size and Wealth. American Behavioral Scientist 25:641–61.
Niemeijer, R.
1973 Some Applications of the Notion of Density to Network Analysis. *In* Network Analysis, ed. J. Boissevain and J. Mitchell. The Hague: Mouton.
Pasternak, Burton, C. Ember, and M. Ember
1976 On the Conditions Favoring Extended Family Households. Journal of Anthropological Research 32:109–24.
Reyna, S.
1976 The Extending Strategy: Regulation of Household Dependency Ratio. Journal of Anthropological Research 32:182–99.
1977 The Rationality of Divorce: Marital Instability among the Barma of Chad. Journal of Comparative Family Studies 2:269–88.
Robbins, Lynn A.
1968 Economics, Household Composition, and the Family Cycle: The Blackfoot Case. *In* Spanish-Speaking People in the United States, ed. June Helm. Proceedings of the 1968 annual spring meeting of the American Ethnological Society. Seattle: University of Washington Press.

Rogers, Susan C.
1979 Sexual Stratification in Rural France: Variations on a Theme of Social Order. Ph.D. Dissertation, Northwestern University.

Rubenstein, Hymie
1975 The Family as a Non-group: Domestic Organization in an Eastern Caribbean Village. *In* Proceedings of the Congress of the Canadian Ethnology Society II, pp. 311–23. Ottawa: National Museum of Canada.

Sahlins, Marshall
1957 Land Use and the Extended Family in Moala, Fiji. American Anthropologist 59:499–62.

Sather, Clifford
1976 Kinship and Contiguity: Variation in Social Alignments among the Semporna Bajau Laut. *In* The Societies of Borneo, ed. G. N. Appell. Special Publication of the American Anthropological Association, no. 6, pp. 40–65.

Seddon, D.
1976 Aspects of Kinship and Family Structure among the Ulad Stut of Zaio Rural Commune, Nador Province, Morocco. *In* Mediterranean Family Structure, ed. J. G. Peristiany, pp. 173–94. Cambridge: Cambridge University Press.

Shah, A. M.
1974 The Household Dimension of the Family in India. Berkeley, Los Angeles, London: University of California Press.

Shanin, T.
1972 The Awkward Class. London: Oxford University Press.

Singer, Milton
1968 The Indian Joint Family in Modern Industry. *In* Structure and Change in Indian Society, ed. M. Singer and B. Cohen. Viking Fund Publication, no. 47. Chicago: Viking Fund.

Smith, Elizabeth C.
1977 Family Structure and Complexity. Journal of Comparative Family Studies 8 (2):299–310.

Smith, R. T.
1973 The Matrifocal Family. *In* The Character of Kinship, ed. J. R. Goody. London: Cambridge University Press.
1978 The Family and the Modern World System: Some Observations from the Caribbean. Journal of Family History 3:337–60.

Smith, Robert
1977 The Domestic Cycle in Selected Commoner Households in Urban Japan, 1757–1858. Paper prepared for a Davis Center Seminar, Princeton University.

Smith, Thomas C.
1959 The Agrarian Origins of Modern Japan. Stanford: Stanford University Press.

1977 Nakahara: Family Farming and Population in a Japanese Village, 1717–1830. Stanford: Stanford University Press.

Stack, Carol B.
1974 All Our Kin: Strategies for Survival in a Black Community. New York: Harper and Row.

Sutlive, Vinson H., Jr.
1978 The Iban of Sarawak. Arlington Heights: AHM.

Symes, David G.
1972 Farm Household and Farm Performance: A Study of Twentieth-century Changes in Ballyferriter, Southwest Ireland. Ethnology 11:25–38.

Turnbull, Colin M.
1962 The Forest People. Garden City, N.Y.: Anchor.

Vinovskis, M.
1977 From Household Size to the Life-course. American Behavioral Scientist 21:263–87.

Wheaton, Robert
1975 Family and Kinship in Western Europe: The Problem of the Joint Family Household. Journal of Interdisciplinary History 4:601–28.
1980 Introduction: Recent Trends in the Historical Study of the French Family. *In* Family and Sexuality in French History, ed. R. Wheaton and T. K. Hareven. Philadelphia: University of Pennsylvania Press.

Wilk, Richard R.
1982 Little House in the Jungle: Causes of Variation in House Size among the Kekchi Maya of Belize. Paper presented at the 47th annual meeting of the Society for American Archaeology, Minneapolis.

Wilk, Richard, and William L. Rathje
1982 Towards an Archaeology of the Household. American Behavioral Scientist 7:617–41.

Wolf, Arthur
1968 Adopt a Daughter, Marry a Sister: A Chinese Solution to the Problem of the Incest Taboo. American Anthropologist 70:864–74.

Wolf, Eric R.
1966 Peasants. Englewood Cliffs, N.J.: Prentice-Hall.

Woodford-Berger, Prudence
1981 Women in Houses: The Organization of Residence and Work in Rural Ghana. Antropologiska Studier 30–31:3–35.

Wrigley, E. A.
1977 Reflections on the History of the Family. Daedalus 106:71–85.

Yanagisako, Sylvia J.
1979 Family and Household: The Analysis of Domestic Groups. Annual Review of Anthropology 8:161–205.

Yang, Martin C.
1965 A Chinese Village. New York: Columbia University Press.

2

On the *** of Studying Household Form and Function

E. A. Hammel

This is an intentionally downbeat essay, but my uncertainty about how downbeat is suggested in the title. Originally I thought of "impossibility" for the missing word. But so many people (including me) have studied the subject that it is impossible to say it is impossible to do so. Later I thought of "futility," in the sense that although one could study the subject no one could properly believe the results. Nevertheless, it is clear that many have and will continue to believe the results of such studies, so it would be futile to say it was futile. Finally I considered using "difficulty" or "problems," but those are such lackluster words that I gave up. All of these prefatory remarks should make it clear that I view the past of this subject with distrust, its present with perplexity, and its future with a resigned foreboding. I therefore leave it to the reader to fill in the missing word after having read the essay.

PROBLEMS OF DEFINITION

Anthropologists and historians study households for two reasons. First, they believe that households are important social units for analysis within and between societies. Second, the people who live in households or the people who count them for various purposes of social control think they are important in the conduct of their own affairs. From the first of these reasons comes an analytic category, from the second a folk category. In our scholarly use the two kinds of categories are mixed. Our own folk category of household has strongly influenced the nature of our analytic category (particularly with respect to notions of ownership, usufruct, commonality of production and consumption, kinship, and coresidence). The epistemological status of household is thus much in doubt and causes some discontent. In addition, because of this discontent, especially among anthropologists, there is a strong tendency to adopt the folk, or "native," category of the society studied. (Some particularly useful critiques of the concept *household* are Yanagisako 1979, Guyer 1981, Rapp 1979, and Oppong 1981.) This annoying unit of social structure, recognizable by anyone but a caviling social scientist, continues, like a metaphysical Cataline, to live through the debate.

From these distinctions and their mixture flow several consequences. First, the more strictly that analyses of different data bases adhere to a particular scheme of analytic categories, the more likely those analyses are to be comparable one with another and the less likely they are to adhere closely either to the appropriate folk categories or to actual behavior in the societies concerned. Second, and conversely, the more strictly analyses of particular data bases adhere to the folk categories appropriate to each such data base, the less likely they are to be comparable. This difficulty has been long recognized in the study of households as well as in other areas; the intrusion of particular European folk categories into analysis plagues social science (Fischer 1958; Goodenough 1956; Hammel 1965, 1978). We have not yet taken the initial step achieved in other fields of endeavor, where, for example, the innumerable local medieval measures of length, weight, area, and time were long ago standardized in the appropriately named "metric" system (but see Hammel and Laslett 1974, where a household typology is proposed). But this is not a plea for new yardsticks, only an observation that the yardsticks we use are all quite flexible. (I should observe that the paper just cited has been both praised and maligned unnecessarily. It was intended to provide a system of ready communication, particularly across languages, where convenient and appropriate, not to offer a theory of household structure or function. It is difficult to see the utility of "testing" the system, as has sometimes been done, particularly with the glee attendant on finding a household that will not "fit." There are no good or bad fits to beds not intended as procrustean.)

Particular care needs to be taken in espousing folk categories, however, for the folk categories in a particular society may not be universally applicable even within it, regardless of our naive assumptions of homogeneity. (Douglass's paper in this volume shows clearly how varying cultural assumptions violate these assumptions.) Certainly, in stratified societies of the kind that leave records of households for historians, we would not be surprised to find differences of view on the definition of households between inhabitants and census takers. Reflection and consideration of the ethnographic record (usually richer than the historical) might also lead us to question the homogeneity of classificatory viewpoints for the rich and the poor, for the adult and the child, for males and for females, for the newly married and the long established, for persons in one ecological zone as opposed to another or at one season of the year and at another. Construction of a concept of household that will accommodate such diversity, in a kind of algorithm of operationalization, is no small task. One would hope that for every society (and who knows what that is?) one might be able to construct a locally appropriate analytic notion of *household* which would show itself ethnographically reliable under different social and environmental conditions surrounding that society and from different social and personal points of view within it. One would hope, to take an analogy from linguistics, to find a deep structure with reliably predictable surface manifestations.

Beginning with that point of view we might hope to extend locally applicable analytic conceptions of the household toward one or a set of globally analytic ones. Initially, the differentiating factor that would allow us to translate a global analytic concept into a local analytic one would be the identity of the society in which the global concept was to be applied. Thus, for example, the concept *house* becomes *Nuerhouse* when applied to the Nuer. Not much is really gained by this, for there is no analytical profit in nominal variables that point only to themselves. One would hope, however, in a finished theory of household structure to reduce the number of such trivialities to a minimum. We might find household structures or recruitment strategies to vary by type of local economy, by position in a hierarchy of political or economic domination, or by other "ecological" conditions. Indeed, many of the current critiques of *household* simply argue for a shift in definition of these independent variables, usually in the direction of materialist infrastructural causation (for example, Guyer, 1981; but compare Linares's use of ideology in this volume). It is possible, but not likely, that some consistent set of independent variables might be found (or agreed on).

Given such luck, we would not find ourselves out of the philosophical thicket. We would still have to contend, at all levels, between the concept of the household as an element in some cognitive system (external or native, male or female, married or unmarried, rich or poor) and the household as a behavioral network (again, young or old, spring or fall, and so on). As noted, households share this annoying briar patch with other members of the spectrum of sociological concepts. Any angelic phenomenologist would retreat in quiet wisdom, but I plunge ahead with cheerful disdain, swinging what I hope is Occam's machete.

THEORETICAL REFERENTS AND LEVELS OF ANALYSIS: THINKING DOWNWARD

I address first the nature of this object, *household*, with which anthropologists and historians deal in the sense of particular households being representatives or exemplifications of something. The question in a way is statistical. What is the nature of the population from which an empirical sample of households is drawn? Very often the population is a metaphorical or ideal one, a "type" population defined in theory, like the "extended family household." Very often we ask a question like "Does village X have the extended family household?" That question means, "Is the proportion of households that are extended in village X within some reasonable distance of the proportion one might expect in a sample randomly drawn from a population felt to 'have the extended household'?" Notice how badly this question is put. The frequency of extendedness in the parent population is undefined. If we insisted that every household had to be extended to qualify for the inclusion of a sample in the parent population, no known empirical sample would suffice. We can be saved from this absurdity by introducing the notion of the developmental cycle of domestic groups, thinking of a parent population in which, ideally, each household passes through an extended stage at some point in its cycle; and by asking whether our sample comes close to the proportion of extendedness expectable at some instant in time as households move through various stages. The empirically observed ages at marriage and births of children, the duration of household stages, and so on can be used to construct some expectation of extendedness in the observed sample of households, based on a cycle of domestic development thought to apply in the parent population. Much of the advance in the study of domestic structures has come from this simple device (Goody 1958; Hammel 1961, 1972).

Even if we adopt the device, we still cannot answer the question on the basis of the single samples with which we often work. Even when a cultural rule of household formation is strictly followed, variation in demographic rates will induce variability in achievement of household forms. Only a multiplicity of samples from some notional population that strictly observes some cycle of extension and that is governed by some general set of demographic rates, but samples that are subject to stochastic (chance) variation, can give us information on inherent variability. We require such information to judge the accuracy of the expectation that a sample is drawn from such a population, or more properly, to determine the range of error we would be willing to tolerate in approaching the expectation. As empirical studies become more numerous, we gain such knowledge, but most often these studies are conducted in differing societies or subsocieties. The variability that these studies manifest thus has an additional component of undetermined strength in underlying cultural differences—differences between parent populations. To my knowledge only computer simulation studies thus far have been able to give us a feeling for the purely stochastic variability we can expect to encounter even if the central expectation is constant and if the underlying demographic rates are centrally constant but vary by chance (Hammel and Gilbert 1966; Hammel and Hutchinson 1973; Hammel, McDaniel, and Wachter 1979, 1980; Hammel, Hutchinson, and Wachter 1976; Hammel and Wachter 1977; Wachter, Hammel, and Laslett 1978; Howell and Lehotay 1978). The absence of reliable information on expectable stochastic variability suggests "futile" for the missing word in the title of this essay; it is futile to discuss differences between samples in the absence of an expectation of variability, although that it is possible to do so is demonstrated by an extensive and sometimes acrimonious literature.

Our difficulty is not solved by resorting to the clever trick of using proportions of kinds of households, for example, the proportion extended versus the proportion not extended, and computing an expected variability in the usual way for proportions, based on the properties of the binomial distribution (standard error of proportion = SQRT((p)(1-p)/n). The proportions of households of type X and of type not-X in a community are not the result of independent random flips of a coin. The events are dependent, for to incorporate a person as extension into one household means that that person cannot be incorporated as extension into another. This situation is *not* like that of coin flipping. Because a coin lands "heads" means *it* cannot have landed "tails," but that event does not constrain any other coin in the sample to land "heads" or "tails." With households in a community, however, if one lands "heads," the outcome for another may be severely constrained, because the households may share potential members.

Nothing will help us besides multiplicity of observation, either empirical or through careful simulation, because any whole community characterized only by a proportion of some household type is but a single observation, like a single coin. When we do make use of multiplicity we may find the amount of purely random (thus theoretically meaningless) difference between samples to be staggering. For village-sized populations of about 500–1,000 persons we should be prepared under quite ordinary conditions to find differences of 5 percent in proportions of particular kinds of households by chance alone between a quarter and a third of the time—that is, in one out of three or four comparisons of communities. We would reach the traditional 5 percent level of statistical significance (the risk of believing a difference to be meaningful when in fact it was not) only by believing differences of 15 percent or more (Wachter, Hammel, and Laslett 1978:55ff). The standard errors of proportions that underlie these figures are based on samples of 64 "villages" for each combination of demographic rates—vastly greater than the usual pairwise comparisons. It is always possible to pick a contrasting pair, even out of a large sample; when we pick (or get) pairs without knowledge of sampling error, we run a risk of fooling ourselves about differences.

But there is another trick, that of forcing events to a lower scale, so that they are multiple rather than single. Instead of looking at households as objects, or even as whole processes through time, we might look at them as samples of decisions. Each household has available to it a potential field of members, under some set of cultural rules. For example, each married son may live in his parental home or not, each widowed parent may rejoin each married child, and so on. If a community consists then not of households as end products but of a history of decisions about a finite field of potential members, analysis of a community examines a multiplicity of trials. If we knew the density of potential recruits to individual families, we could compute *rates* of recruitment for households, groups of households, and communities. This kind of analysis is difficult—it requires fine-grained data and care regarding notions of statistical independence—but at least it is possible and not futile. Few investigators have worked in this way, the best example being Geoghegan's on Samal residence (1970), and life-course analysis has taken a small (but usually very nonquantitative) step in the same direction (Hareven 1978).

THINKING UPWARD

All of these problems are only part of our coin as anthropologists and historians; they have to do with questions of membership or comembership in sets. Is village X "peasant" in its household organization, are villages X and Y sufficiently similar to be considered comembers of some basic form of social structure? Statisticians would recognize these problems as belonging to the area of "hypothesis testing." The questions are deductive.

Our intent is often simpler and different. We come into posession of a document, or we pick a community to work (more often it picks us), and then from our study of it we seek to generalize. Surely few of us study particular communities to describe only them; these communities are examples of something. Of what? This question is inductive, like point and interval estimation in statistics.

Where the definition of the general population to which a community belongs is drawn in terms of place and period, we are on reasonably firm ground. If we have a fifteenth-century Tuscan village, we can try to generalize to all such. If we have ethnographic data on the !Kung, we can try to generalize to all of the San peoples. Place and time are matters on which agreement is generally good. But if we try to generalize to theoretical types, we are in trouble. To generalize from our Tuscan village to Renaissance peasant villages demands that we first classify our village as one of the broader type—not so easy an undertaking unless the classification is only a substitute for less general labels of time and space. We must be quite sure about the applicability of the label to the data in question.

Given one data base, our best estimate of household form in the type population that is the target of our induction is simply what we find in the data base. Of course, our estimate is more likely to be accurate if it rests on a large number of observations. As before, a statement of proportions of households of different types in a data base is but a single observation. Although we would trust a proportion based on a large number of households more than we would a proportion based on a few, we cannot use mathematical knowledge of the properties of the binomial distribution to estimate the variability of observations. As before, only multiplicity of observations will help us. Multiplicity can be achieved in two ways: by finding more than one data base or by driving the level of analysis downward to decisions on household formation rather than considering households as end products.

If we do find other data bases, we must decide whether to estimate household form in the population of our induction as a weighted or as an unweighted average. Is it "one village, one vote," or will large communities overwhelm small ones in the averaging? Some judgment must be made about cultural heterogeneity and the consequences for analysis of different kinds of averages. If we drive the level of analysis downward to the decision level, we have a much finer view of household form, but the data required for such work are very rare.

SENSITIVITY TESTING: TWO EXAMPLES

The decisions we make in analysis on all of these issues are not necessarily irrevocable. Indeed, the very fact that there are choices to be made in analysis suggests that alternative analyses are possible and can themselves be compared. We can, for example, compute weighted averages across a set of communities and compare them to unweighted averages. We may not know whether intercommunity differences in household form are sufficiently conditioned by cultural prescriptions contingent on size to make one or the other kind of average misleading by itself, but we can compute both and consider the importance of their differences. An average, after all, like any other measure, is an answer to a question. We must have the question first.

Similarly, we can examine the consequences of adopting different definitions of the household. For example, it is not clear, or at least not agreed, whether members of complex family households must coreside in the same structure or whether coresidence on the same property but in different structures qualifies them as members of a single household. Even if members coreside in a single structure, to what degree may their apartments be separate? Must they cook and eat together? We rarely have the kind of data that would permit us to carry out alternative analyses and examine their effects. But sometimes we do, as shown by Segalen, Linares, Wilk, Foster, and others in this volume.

The first example of sensitivity testing concerns the definition of household boundaries when the evidence for the boundaries is ambiguous. In the extensive chrysobulls of the monastery of Dečani, in Serbia of A.D. 1330, the census takers enumerated persons and noted their kinship links. The undamaged portions of the text include more than 5,000 persons (all males) in 71 villages or other social units (sometimes occupational groupings). The number of social units within villages—that is, what we might be inclined to call households—can be specified only on the basis of some assumptions. My purpose here is to indicate what these assumptions might be and the effect that they have on the outcome of the usual analysis, in which households are classified by type.

Within any village or similar unit, the census gives a list of personal (Christian) names, with rare occupational designations or patronymics. The names are often joined by coordinating conjunctions, possessive pronouns, and kinship terms. Sets of names are delimited by punctuation marks, but such a delimiter may be followed by a coordinating conjunction that appears to link two name-sets across the delimiter. Schematically, these variations may look as follows, using capital letters to indicate names of persons. An interpretation is given for each.

.A.	Just person A, living alone
.A and his brother B.	A and B in a fraternal joint household
.A and his son B.	A and B in a lineally extended or multiple household
.A. and his brother B.	Here we have a choice. We can consider that A lives in one household and his brother B in another, or that they coreside.
.A and his brother B. and his son C.	Whose son is C? We can decide that he is A's son or B's son.
.A and his brother B. and his brother C and his son D.	If we consider this as two households, the first consists of two brothers and the second of a man and his son. If we consider this as one household, it could consist of three brothers and the son of A or of three brothers and the son of B or of C.

The number and kind of combinations actually encountered in the censuses are more numerous and complex than these examples reveal.

Interpretive difficulties are compounded by uncertainty about the marital status of the males listed. A household of a man and two sons may be classified as nuclear if the sons are unmarried, lineally multiple if one son is married, and both lineally and laterally multiple if both sons are married.

Both issues of interpretation were examined by applying different assumptions, in combination, and assessing the consequences. The assumptions about household boundaries were five in number:

1. The boundary between households was defined by a punctuation mark in the manuscript. This interpretation divides the list of persons into the largest number of units above the level of individuals.

2. Households separated as in assumption 1 but linked by an explicit kinship reference were merged, but kinship links were not rephrased to reflect the fact that the head of the merged household was the head of the first household in the set of those merged.
3. Households separated as under assumption 1 but linked by a coordinating conjunction were merged, but kinship links were not rephrased.
4. As in assumption 2 but with rephrasing of kinship links.
5. As in assumption 3 but with rephrasing of kinship links.

The assumptions about marital status were four in number:

1. Only heads of households (those appearing first in a list of males) and persons explicitly noted as parents were considered married.
2. As in assumption 1 but with the addition of persons estimated to be married on the basis of their generational position in the household and probabilities of married status of persons by generational position derived from the Serbian census of 1948 (for want of reliable earlier material).
3. As in assumption 2 but using the 1948 census for Montenegro.
4. All males married (the usual assumption of most Serbian scholars using these data).

Detailed analyses appear elsewhere (Hammel 1979, 1980); here I simply summarize. Under the weakest assumptions about household boundaries and thus maximum disaggregation of the sets of males and under the weakest assumptions about nuptiality, 50 percent of the households are nuclear. Under the strongest assumptions about household boundaries and nuptiality, 20 percent are nuclear. The proportion of simple families is cut by more than half. For any level of assumption about household boundaries, nuptiality assumptions make as much as a 22 percent difference. For any level of nuptiality assumptions, assumptions about household boundaries make as much as a 9 percent difference. Combined, the strongest assumptions make as much as a 30 percent difference.

That interpretive assumptions are important to the outcome of research is no news. That they can be this important is startling. Analyses of household form seldom examine the results of assumptions; they simply make them, often intransigently. What the busybodies of the past or present give us as data are sets of persons, explicitly or implicitly divided and delimited. Our assumptions about the boundaries of households and the status of persons in them can have effects greater than actual trends in the data, in this instance drastically changing our view of south Slavic social organization in its presumably "classic" period from one in which the touted *zadruga* was present almost universally (80 percent) to one in which it was present half the time, no less than in the sixteenth century or even the nineteenth. Failure to achieve complete universality could be explained easily by reference to arguments about demographic factors and the cycle of family development, while achievement of only 50 percent has caused some scholars to fear for the maintenance of a traditional way of life. Creating the evidence for decision between the vigor of tradition and its impending demise simply by making a few different assumptions gives some pause to the debate.

A second example of sensitivity testing deals with the effects of differences in demographic variation and of cultural prescriptions for household formation. Demographic variability of a random kind, as in the timing of births to individual women, can create random differences between the patterning of household structure of communities, as already noted. But systematic differences between demographic regimes should create systematic differences in household patterns. Similarly, and as all historians and anthropologists would be predisposed to admit, systematic differences in cultural rules should create systematic differences in observed household forms.

Which of the forces affecting patterns of household formation—differences in demography, differences in cultural rules, and randomness—have the greatest weight? An extensive project using historically reasonable demographic rates for seventeenth-and eighteenth-century England and plausible cultural prescriptions throws some light on the question (Hammel and Wachter 1977; Wachter, Hammel, and Laslett 1978). As already noted, randomness can be ignored only at the peril of absurdity. Demographic differences, with one exception, have an effect modest by comparison with that of alteration in cultural prescription (a welcome victory for cultural idealists). Under a given set of cultural rules, changes in population growth rate and even drastic changes in mortality level account for no more than changes of 5 percent in the proportion of households of any type. Changes of about ten years in average age of brides at first marriage, however, will produce as much as a 10 percent change in such proportions. Bride's age at first marriage, of course, is a demographic fact strongly conditioned by cultural prescriptions. The most drastic changes in proportions of households of different types are achieved by rather simple alteration of cultural rules. Under a stem family regime, for example, establishing coresidence of parents and a married child when the first child marries, as against when the last child marries, changes the proportion of stem family households by as much as 40 percent.

Thus, of the three factors that might affect proportions of households by type, an unambiguous and strictly followed cultural rule system has the greatest effect, followed by randomness, followed by actual differences in central demographic rates. Of course, these conclusions could easily differ for different "experiments." The differences in central demographic rates could be larger, creating a larger effect. The cultural rule systems could be less rigid, creating a lesser effect. One could also devise other independent variables. The point is not the specific result but that the results can be examined and that the relative weight of influences can be discussed.

RUBBER YARDSTICKS AND RIVERS OF INK

One can imagine a special part of Hades occupied by scientists whose measuring rods expand and contract in unpredictable ways while their users argue interminably about their observations. (Theories of relativity give no analogical comfort, since their great contribution is precisely to make the changes in the measuring system predictable.) Can we hope, or have we abandoned that emotion on entry?

A major reason why talk goes on forever is often that those engaged in conversation do not know what they are talking about. That is the real source of our trouble. The household is simply not a very good unit of observation. If it is a good analytic category, we would do well to observe not households but the important behaviors and norms of persons interacting by virtue of comembership. But the identity of those behaviors comes out of our own folk category, leading us to miss behaviors important to households in some societies and to demand behavioral evidence not important to households in some others. If *household* is a good folk category, its functional content is again specific, giving us little guide for comparative work. What we really study most of the time in investigating households (particularly as historians) is the classificatory habits of census takers but without any Linnaean system of our own against which to measure their decisions.

Yet in this very dilemma we may find a solution. What does a census taker look for in listing households, that is, in a general sense? He (or indeed sometimes she) looks for a social unit larger than a person and smaller than the limits of his commission, be that village or census tract. A household, in fact, is the next bigger thing on the social map after an individual. It is a level in a taxonomy of social inclusion, more or less finely graded, according to the society. One can think of no society in which there is no level intermediate between the individual and the total society (despite many totalitarian efforts in that direction); thus the family is never the society, and the individual is never (by expectation) the household. Most often there is a range of social groups, more or less institutionalized, between the individual and the community. Groups along this range differ, simultaneously increasing in their inclusion of persons or social roles and losing the multiplicity of their functions. They are numerically and organizationally larger and functionally poorer as one ascends above the level of the individual and conversely smaller and richer as one descends.

The household in any society, I suggest, is that social group larger than the individual that does not fail to control for its members all those resources that any (adult) member could expect to control for himself. It maximizes size and corporacy simultaneously. This may be the formal definition to which census takers respond, the formal unit that one might translate (with luck and very careful ethnography) into units of people recognizing themselves in our analytical descriptions. Indeed, it is the very fact that census takers have recorded households *as such* that saves our investigations from the complete confusion that characterizes much of the rest of social science observation in which fixed native facts are measured with elastic analytical bands. Here, at least, we often deal with categories shared by at least some members of the community studied.

The editors of this volume asked at the conference why, in view of some of my earlier work, I had indulged in such a jeremiad against the homely concept *household*. This essay is no more than the same kind of rebellion others have displayed against rigid categories, sometimes against the newly rigid categories emerging from these same critiques and sometimes against the particular analytical variables on which categories test. My critique stems not from any commitment to idealism or materialism but from a struggle to deal statistically with my own data in comparative terms. I believe that the way to useful comparative analysis is to propose a category so formal, abstract, and devoid of specific cultural content as to rid it of bias. Thus I suggest that in studying households we select in each society or subsociety the largest supraindividual (and perhaps named) group with the greatest multifunctional corporacy and that we compare these formally selected units. Given these units, one may then properly inquire into their variation in function, recruitment, and cycle and their articulation with larger social fields. In this way the ontological horse may finally come to precede the empirical cart. Yet even in this endeavor one is reminded that Plato once defined man as an erect featherless biped, only to be confronted by an empirical Socrates, who plucked a chicken and brought it to the Academy, saying, "Here is Plato's man." It is not clear even now that I have rid *household* of all its feathers.

REFERENCES

Fischer, Jack
1958 The Classification of Residence in Censuses. American Anthropologist 60:508–17.

Geoghegan, William
1970 Residential Decision Making among the Eastern Samal. Paper presented to the Symposium on Mathematical Anthropology, Annual Meeting of the American Anthropological Association, San Diego.

Goodenough, Ward
1956 Residence Rules. Southwestern Journal of Anthropology 12:22–37.

Goody, Jack, ed.
1958 The Developmental Cycle in Domestic Groups. Cambridge: Cambridge University Press.

Guyer, Jane I.
1981 Household and Community in African Studies. African Studies Review 24:87–137.

Hammel, E. A.
1961 The Family Cycle in a Coastal Peruvian Slum and Village. American Anthropologist 63:989–1005.
1965 Introduction. Formal Semantic Analysis. Special Issue of the American Anthropologist 67 (5:2):1–8.
1972 The *Zadruga* as Process. *In* Household and Family in Past Time, ed. P. Laslett and R. Wall, pp. 335–74. Cambridge: Cambridge University Press.
1978 Household Structure in Fourteenth-century Macedonia. Journal of Family History (Fall):242–73.
1979 The Chrysobulls of Decani. Manuscript.
1980 Sensitivity Analysis of Household Structure in Mediaeval Serbian Censuses. Historical Methods 13:105–18.

Hammel, E. A., and John P. Gilbert
1966 Computer Analysis of Problems in Kinship and Social Structure. American Anthropologist 68:71–93.

Hammel, E. A., and David Hutchinson
1973 Two Tests of Computer Microsimulation: The Effect of an Incest Tabu on Population Viability, and the Effect of Age Differences between Spouses on the Skewing of Consanguineal Relationships between Them. *In* Computer Simulation in Human Population Studies, ed. B. Dyke and J. W. MacCluer, pp. 1–14. New York: Academic Press.

Hammel, E. A., and Peter Laslett
1974 Comparing Household Structure over Time and between Cultures. Comparative Studies in Society and History 16:73–109.

Hammel, E. A., and K. W. Wachter
1977 Primonuptiality and Ultimonuptiality: Their Effects on Stem-family-household Frequencies. *In* Population Patterns in the Past, ed. R. D. Lee, pp. 113–34. New York: Academic Press.

Hammel, E. A., David Hutchinson, and K. W. Wachter
1976 A Stochastic Simulation and Numerical Test of the Deterministic Model. Appendix to The Matrilateral Implications of Structural Cross-cousin Marriage. *In* Demographic Anthropology, ed. E. Zubrow, pp. 161–68. Albuquerque: University of New Mexico Press.

Hammel, E. A., Chad K. McDaniel, and K. W. Wachter
1979 Demographic Consequences of Incest Tabus: A Microsimulation Analysis. Science 205:972–77.
1980 Vice in the Villefranchian: A Microsimulation Analysis of the Demographic Effects of Incest Prohibitions. *In* Genealogical Demography, ed. B. Dyke and W. T. Morrill, pp. 209–34. New York: Academic Press.

Hareven, Tamara K., ed.
1978 Transitions: The Family and Life Course in Historical Perspective. New York: Academic Press.

Howell, Nancy, and V. A. Lehotay
1978 AMBUSH: A Computer Program for Stochastic Microsimulation of Small Human Populations. American Anthropologist 80:905–22.

Oppong, Christine
1981 A Note on Some Aspects of Anthropological Contributions to the Study of Fertility. Paper on Population and Demography, National Research Council.

Rapp, Rayna
1979 Examining Family History: Household and Family. Feminist Studies 5:175–81.

Yanagisako, Sylvia J.
1979 Family and Household: The Analysis of Domestic Groups. Annual Review of Anthropology 8:161–205.

3

Household Histories

Anthony T. Carter

Though anthropologists have been aware at least since Fortes's (1949*a*, 1949*b*) pioneering work on the Ashanti and the Tallensi that time is an important dimension of domestic institutions, our methods for the analysis of this dimension remain limited. To all intents and purposes we are able to do little more than study successive cross-sections of ahistorical household types or, on occasion, the contemporary domestic situations of persons belonging to different age groups. The aim of this paper is to outline an assemblage of concepts and measures for describing and analyzing longitudinal aspects of particular household units. These concepts and measures, few of which are themselves original but which are combined with others here in a new way, are intended to capture events that occur in households and the consequences of those events for the state of the household unit and for the lives of its members. The methods are designed to be applicable to a variety of data sources and to provide a cross-cultural framework within which policy-relevant as well as anthropological and historical questions may be posed and answered.[1]

THE HOUSEHOLD DIMENSION OF DOMESTIC GROUPS[2]

Definitions

The term *household* must be defined as precisely as possible since the domestic group is not one thing but several. That is to say, domestic groups, like other conceptually concrete social arrangements, are informed by a number of analytically distinct cultural principles.[3] It is for this reason Gray (1964:4) concluded that "the concept of 'family' as now employed in social anthropology cannot be encompassed in a simple definition" but must be regarded instead as a "nexus of certain processes." In what follows, therefore, the familial dimension of the domestic group is distinguished from the household dimension. The former is defined by the origin of the links between its members, links that have their source in culturally defined relations of birth, adoption, and marriage, regardless of whether those who are so linked live together or engage in any shared tasks. The household dimension of the domestic group, on the contrary, is defined by shared tasks of production and/or consumption, regardless of whether its members are linked by kinship or marriage or are coresident.[4]

The Household in Maharashtra: Tasks, Personnel, and Resources

Household units per se, then, are defined in terms of the culturally recognized tasks for which they are responsible. They perform these tasks on behalf of and by assigning duties to their personnel and by deploying their resources. In the rural Maharashtrian communities where I have done fieldwork, for example, a household generally is referred to by the term *kutumb*. Asked to define *kutumb*, informants are likely to reply with a phrase such as "jointly living relatives" (*ekətryə rahanare natevaik*) and may explain further that "jointly living" has to do with eating from and contributing to the support of a single hearth (*chula*) or set of linked hearths, all under the direction of a single head (*prəmukh*). Often, but by no means universally, the *kutumb* or household is made up of one or more nuclear families, and if there are multiple nuclear families the several husband/fathers tend to be close agnates. A group of related persons maintaining separate residences, however, may continue to comprise a single household if each member has unrestricted access to all of the group's hearths and if resources are undivided and used as a single fund under the authority of the household head. Two or more unrelated persons, two widows, for example, or a *guru* and his or her disciples, also may comprise a household if they possess a single hearth, again with its attendant fund or budget.

Though the personnel who cooperate to perform the tasks associated with the domestic hearth in Maharashtra commonly are kin, the rights and duties entailed by kinship are distinct from those entailed by household membership. A man whose children all are married, for example, may retire from the household headship, turning the office over to one of his sons. In these circumstances a man ceases to exercise the rights and duties of household head but continues to exercise those appropriate to a father, such as performing the annual ancestral sacrifices. This is not to say that ties of kinship do not constrain the actions of household members. But though kinship may be a factor in the action of household personnel, the role of husband/father is distinguished clearly from that of household head.

The rights and duties of siblingship are similarly distinguished from those of household member. Differences of age and sex aside, all members of a household have equal claims to support from household resources and corresponding obligations to contribute to housekeeping tasks and resource management. This equality of resource use prevails regardless of the manner in which household members are related to the household head and applies as much to nonrelatives, if they have been admitted to the household, as it does to relatives. Rights of inheritance and the power to demand household partition, however, are a function of particular kinship relations. In western Maharashtra and elsewhere in India where traditional law conformed to the Mitakshara school, only agnatic relatives of the household head and their wives have rights of inheritance and partition, male agnates to a *per stirpes* share in ancestral property, female agnates to their marriage expenses and dowry, and wives to maintenance. Where brothers who share a joint household have unequal numbers of surviving children, as often happens, the disparities between their per capita claims to resource use and their *per stirpes* claims to resource inheritance are among the pressures leading to household partition.

In Maharashtra, in short, categories of household personnel are distinguished not so much by their kinship relations as by the dimensions of ownership, sex, and seniority. Owners (sing. *malək*) include the household founder or current head and, if the head is a man, those of his agnatic relatives or, if the head is a widow, those of her husband's agnates who have not given up their membership by marrying out or by demanding partition. Wives of male owners are owners as well. Owners contrast with guests (*pahune*), including all other household members whether relatives or nonrelatives. While owners have a legal claim to household resources, guests have only a moral claim to short- or long-term care.

Male owners, whose sphere of responsibility includes the management of productive resources and relations with the wider community, are senior to female owners, whose sphere of responsibility includes housekeeping and child care, but in addition each category of owners is internally graded. Male owners and their female agnates are ranked according to generation and age, while the wives of male owners are ranked according to the seniority of their husbands without regard to their own ages. The senior woman in the household is the wife of the household head or his mother. She may direct the activities of her daughter- and sisters-in-law, taking to herself the less arduous tasks connected with child care and giving to the other women the more arduous tasks connected with food preparation. Among agnatic owners the rule of seniority produces queues that for females govern access to the resources required for marriage and for males govern access to marriage and also to household headship.[5]

Household property in Maharashtra is transmitted from one generation to the next according to what Goody (1976) calls a rule of diverging devolution in which children of both sexes receive a share of ancestral property. This rule is qualified by a subsidiary rule according to which male agnatic descendants are preferred heirs of immovable property while females are, in the first instance, limited to cash and other movables. Within this framework of devolution rules, however, households differ widely in the nature of the resources they possess. Those households that possess productive assets and that are units of production as well as consumption may be subdivided according to both the kind and the amount of the resources they possess. Many households in rural areas are dependent on their land, though many of these are unable to produce enough to live on. A few households possess small businesses such as general merchandise shops or flour mills, and these households more readily lend themselves to diversification and subdivision in hard times (see Carter 1976). A considerable number of households possess no productive assets at all or such a small amount that they are dependent almost entirely on the labor of their members, operating what Tilly and Scott (1978) call a "family wage economy." These households, too, vary in terms of their investment in education and other forms of human capital and the wages and salaries their members can command.

Systems and Structure: Generative Models of Household Institutions

If we are to define the household dimension of domestic groups in terms of culturally recognized tasks, it will be useful as well to distinguish between household structure and household systems and to regard the former as generated by the latter in conjunction with other cultural systems and in response to variable circumstances. Household structure in this limited sense has to do with patterns of observable social arrangements, including household size, composition, and development. Household systems, in contrast, have to do with cultural principles of household formation and management.

On a rough analogy with game theory, the elements of household systems may be divided into two kinds: rules and strategies. Where household rules specify the manner in which culturally defined resources and personnel properly may be combined to form household units, household strategies are concerned with the optimal use of available personnel and resources to achieve individual goals and group tasks.

Household rules also are of two kinds: recruitment rules and rules of devolution. The first class of rules concerns the manner in which persons may succeed to positions within households, each position with its own characteristic rights and duties. The second concerns the kinds of resources available to households and the manner in which resources may be transferred from one holder to another.

Household strategies are more diverse. One set has to do with family formation, that is, the acquisition of children by birth, adoption, or fosterage. Another set has to do with marriage—who will be married, when, and to whom—and with postmarital residence and divorce. Where households may consist of more than one adult of each sex, strategies of partition also are important. Many discussions of households focus on what might be called "the optimistic pattern of development" that may be expected when household units are not rendered incomplete by premature death or divorce. Such expectations are all too rarely fulfilled, however, especially in regimes of high mortality. Household systems thus also require strategies of amalgamation determining which household fragments get combined with which other households and how. More general are strategies of economic management: choice of productive activities, the allocation of resources for consumption, and so on (see Rheubottom 1971 and Cohen 1976).

All of these strategies, of course, are highly interdependent. Household partition may alter the conditions of economic management by producing new units with different producer/consumer and land/labor ratios as well as different amounts of resources and personnel. The quality of economic management, in turn, influences the resources that are available for marriage, inheritance, and so on. Completed family size and the sex ratio of surviving offspring are influenced by the expenditure of household resources on medical care and food, including breast milk, for male and female children as well as by strategies of family formation per se.

THE CROSS-CULTURAL UTILITY OF THE HOUSEHOLD CONCEPT

I have argued that in Maharashtra the household dimension of domestic groups may be distinguished from the familial or kinship dimension and that household structure within the former may be regarded as generated by underlying systems of rules and strategies. The question remains, however, whether these distinctions have any validity in other cultural settings.

Household and Kinship

The distinction between household and familial aspects of domestic groups perhaps is accepted most readily in those societies where households routinely consist of more than one nuclear family and such roles as husband/father cannot universally correspond to particular household positions. It is accepted least readily in societies like our own where the household and the nuclear family routinely coincide.

In several recent historical studies of European populations it is thus assumed that varieties of domestic groups and the positions of persons within such groups may be adequately defined in terms of kinship alone and the term *household* is introduced solely because some few members of the coresident group—servants, lodgers, and so on—are not kin. As Laslett put it,

> The word *household* particularly indicates the fact of shared location, kinship and activity. Hence all solitarities have to be taken to be households, for they are living with themselves, and this is the case when they have servants with them, since servants are taken as household members. In fact because servants always modify the membership of households, we allot all domestic groups to one of two classes, those with and those without servants. *Nevertheless servants can hardly be said to affect the final structure of households, and when it comes to the significant types of domestic groups, the form of description is by the title of the composition of the family in question, followed by the word household.* Hence the descriptions "simple family household," "extended family household," "multiple family household." (1972:28–29; latter emphasis is mine; see also Berkner 1972:410)

The point I am making, however, is that all relationships within the domestic group—those among kin as well as those among nonkin—have a household or task-oriented component. In the European context some of the newest historical studies have taken note of this fact in two ways: as an aspect of composition and as an aspect of native definition. As Plakans notes in this volume, identifiable relatives of the household head who also were counted as farmhands (for example, *Sohn als Knecht*) comprised as much as a quarter of farmhand population in some nineteenth-century Baltic estates. Similarly, an important study of household registers from eighteenth- and nineteenth-century Austria notes, in addition to the now familiar instances of servants' becoming members of the family by marriage or adoption, numerous cases in which children became servants within their natal households (Mitterauer and Sieder 1979). As the authors of this study conclude, "kinship was not the only and certainly not the most decisive basis of interaction" (1979:278; see also Flandrin 1976:4–9).

My point also is substantiated by recent ethnography in the United States, most pertinently Plume's (1974) study of 91 black households in Rochester, New York. The households in Plume's sample are extremely diverse in kinship composition (see figure 3.1). It is difficult, indeed, to see how they could be accommodated within any such typology as Laslett's. Plume convincingly argues, however, that in household terms these seemingly diverse domestic groups may be understood within a single, relatively simple pattern. This household dimension consists of

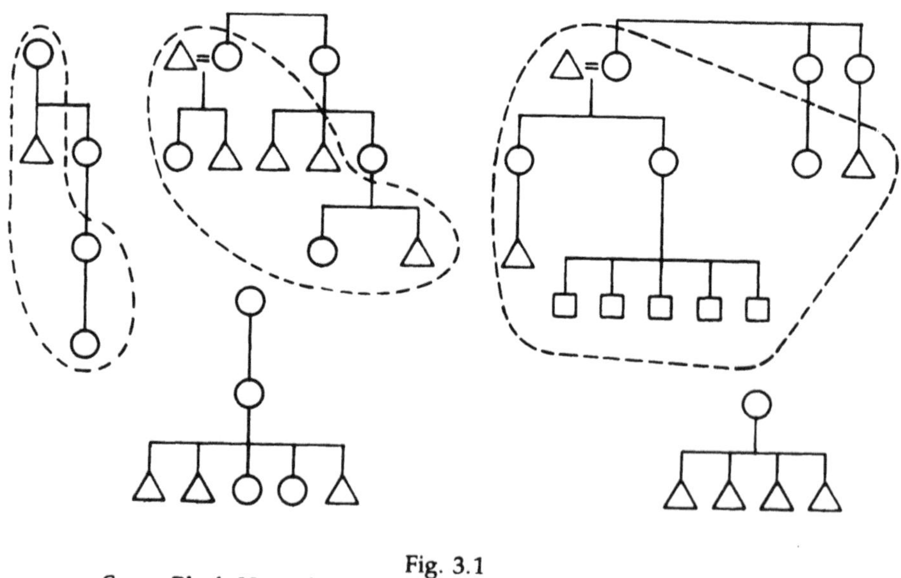

Fig. 3.1
Some Black Households in Rochester, New York (Plume 1974)

the following positions, the first two of which are verbally articulated while the others are implicit in a variety of behavioral distinctions.

1. Head of household: the woman in charge of child care and task allocation
2. Child: all household members who are not adults
3. Woman in the household: adult females other than the head
4. Man in the household: adult males. These may be divided into four subgroups according to two distinctions: junior or senior to the household head; linked to the household by kinship or marriage.

It is significant that these household positions are almost entirely distinct from kinship relations. Thus,

> The head of the household refers to boys and girls of her household as "my child." . . . mothers never say "my child" but rather "my daughter" or "my son." Children refer to themselves as X's child where X is the name of their household head. . . . A household head says of children she raised "He used to be my child." (Plume 1974:165–66)

Though the members of the domestic groups in Plume's sample are related to one another in a large variety of ways, they all may be assigned to one or another of the above household positions and it is in terms of these positions, not their kinship relations, that their task-oriented household activities are organized and carried forward.

One Household or Many

If it is difficult to perceive the household dimension of the domestic group where the nuclear family and the household tend to coincide, the problem in some other societies is that there appear to be all too many task-oriented units. Among the LoDagaba and LoWiili of northern Ghana, for example, several matrifocal cooking groups composed of a woman and her younger children may be contained within a single polygynous farm family or unit of production, while several such farm families in turn may comprise a single homestead or dwelling unit (Goody 1958). Among the Ashanti the picture is even more complex. There, Fortes reports,

> The dwelling group does not, as a rule, have a common food supply nor do its members pool their incomes for the common support. But the norm is for the dwelling group to consist of a single household in the

> social sense, that is, a group in which the rule holds that food and assistance are freely asked and given between members. (1949a:64)

In these cases it may be difficult to imagine that any particular variety of household has much significance, and the household concept in general therefore may not be regarded as of much use (see Oppong 1976, 1978; Linares, this volume).

Such complexities are general in West Africa, but it should be pointed out that the activities of consumption and production among the LoDagaba and LoWiili at least are coordinated by the male heads of farm households. As Goody himself observes,

> The male in a polygamous household will receive a bowl of food from his wives each time they cook. The adolescent boys automatically share his food and some he may give to any children he thinks are not getting as much as others. In this manner he evens out the inequalities in the distribution of grain. (1958:75)

The problem with the West African material is not that there are no task-oriented units, or even that there are so many as to render the household concept meaningless, but rather that the rights and duties of male and female household members are quite unlike those found in Eurasian households (see Forde 1951:99–116; Hill 1975; Goody 1976).

Common Elements of Household Systems

Most studies of domestic groups have so emphasized the familial dimension that we know relatively little about cross-cultural variations in the tasks, personnel, and resources that make up the household dimension. It does appear, however, that some of the factors outlined above for Maharashtrian households are applicable generally, if not universally.

In general, a household is a collection of persons who work together to provide mutual care, including the provision of food, shelter, clothing, and health care as well as socialization. But though households everywhere may be defined as task-oriented social units, the precise pattern of task allocation is variable. In protoindustrial economies (see Braun 1978 and Medick 1976) as well as in agrarian communities, households generally function both as units of production and as units of consumption, while in industrial economies households tend to lose their role as productive units (see Tilly and Scott 1978). As Wilk and Netting observe in their contribution to this volume, "Defining the household in a particular social setting does not require that each household have the same overlapping spheres of activity but that in each case we find, as Hammel so succinctly puts it, 'the smallest grouping with the maximum corporate function' (1980:251)."

The most general task concerning households and the one on which the fulfillment of other tasks depends is the maintenance and enhancement of household viability. Household viability, as defined by Stenning, has to do with the relationship between a domestic group and its resources or means of subsistence. A household or "domestic unit is viable when the labour it can provide is suitable for the exploitation of its means of subsistence, while the latter is adequate for the support of the domestic unit" (Stenning 1958:92). Viability is, of course, a crucial household variable that may and indeed must be studied over the course of household histories where adequate data are available.

In many societies, if not all, households may seek to confine their membership to particular constellations of relatives, but maximizing preferred constellations of kin can never be the sole or even a principal aim of household management. Given the magnitude of stochastic fluctuations of birth and death in small groups, such a goal would come into frequent conflict with other household tasks, including the maintenance of viability. In particularly harsh conditions, as among the urban poor of mid-nineteenth-century São Paulo, Brazil, the organization of the household may become almost entirely separated from that of the nuclear family (Kuznesof 1980:98–105).

Nor can households universally be identified in terms of physical coresidence. It is true that a household commonly has a home and that household members typically have the right to reside there, but for a variety of reasons they do not always choose or are not always allowed to exercise this right. In many developing countries substantial numbers of households send one or more members out in temporary emigration to urban areas and other employment centers (see Cohen 1976:12, 99–148; Sharma 1977, 1980; Arnould, this volume; Foster, this volume). As Sharma observes, migration of this sort, resulting in dispersed households, is

> common where an agriculturally undeveloped region lies within reach of an industrially advanced area (as in many parts of Southern Africa). Where the returns of peasant agricultural production are low and industrial wages are also low in relation to the urban cost of living this pattern of interdependence is necessary for the survival of the poorer family. (1980:81)

In a great many ethnographic settings it cannot be assumed therefore that each residential unit corresponds to an independent household or that a household contains only those persons resident in its principal domicile at any particular moment.

If households everywhere may be defined as task-oriented units, the distinction between kinship roles and household positions also is widely applicable. To say that household positions may be distinguished from kinship is not to deny, however, that household systems vary in terms of restrictions on composition. At one extreme is what Gudeman calls "the co-residential couples prohibition." Among Panamanian countrymen Gudeman reports, and this appears to be widespread in Euro-American cultures,

> No two couples may occupy the same bedroom or even the same house, although single offspring and, for short intervals, widowed parents may share a bedroom with a couple. . . . This proscription is not a norm of kinship. . . . the rule is that no two couples, regardless of their kinship connection, may reside together. (1976:118)

A somewhat weaker restriction is found in Japan and in other areas where so-called stem families are reported. In Japan two or more couples may coreside in a single household but only if each couple contains a person who is or who was married to the household head, the retired head, or the heir (on Japan see Kitaoji 1971 and T. C. Smith 1977; for Ireland and Germany see Arensberg 1937 and Berkner 1976, 1977; for Thailand see Foster 1975*a*, 1975*b*, 1976, and 1977). As in the case of the coresidential couples prohibition, these are not kinship rules, for the relationship between head and heir need not coincide with that between parent and child or between spouse's parent and child's spouse. At the opposite extreme, in India (see Shah 1974), China (Cohen 1976), Yugoslavia (Halpern and Halpern 1972), and much of sub-Saharan Africa (see, for example, Gray and Gulliver 1964), there are no limits on the number of coresidential couples.

In many of the latter systems principles of seniority similar to those found in Maharashtra are used to form queues that, cutting across ties of kinship, govern succession to headship and other household positions and also the order in which household members may have access to household resources for such major expenses as marriage. Among the Jie of northern Uganda, for example, seniority in complex polygynous households is governed by the following rules (Gulliver 1955:64).

1. Within households yards are ranked according to the chronological order of the marriage of the wives of the founding brothers of the household.

2. Within yards sons are ranked according to their birth order.
3. Where the intervals between their births are great (more than five years) the seniority of sons within the household also is a function of birth order. This may result in a disproportionate number of marriages within a single yard, but it apparently is not regarded as proper to require any man to delay his marriage too long just to equalize the opportunities of yards.
4. Where the intervals between their births are small a man is ranked senior to older agnates (1) in senior yards whose intrayard position is lower than his own and (2) in junior yards whose intrayard position is equivalent to his own.

It is as a result of this latter rule that in the household depicted in figure 3.2 son 7 is senior to son 6 and son 13 is senior to son 10. As with other seniority rules, the aim of the Jie system seems to be to equalize the opportunities for marriage of household members while at the same time preserving at least a rough balance among those units, in this case the yards, that ultimately will break away to form independent households. As elsewhere, too, the attempt to achieve equality and balance constantly is threatened by the vagaries of birth and death.

At a minimum, then, it appears that the distinction between the household and the familial dimensions of domestic groups is of quite general, if not universal, cross-cultural utility and that coherent household institutions with significant demographic and economic functions are widely distributed in human sociocultural systems. Though these institutions are diverse, such broad principles as household headship, equal sharing, seniority, viability and so on are sufficiently general as to

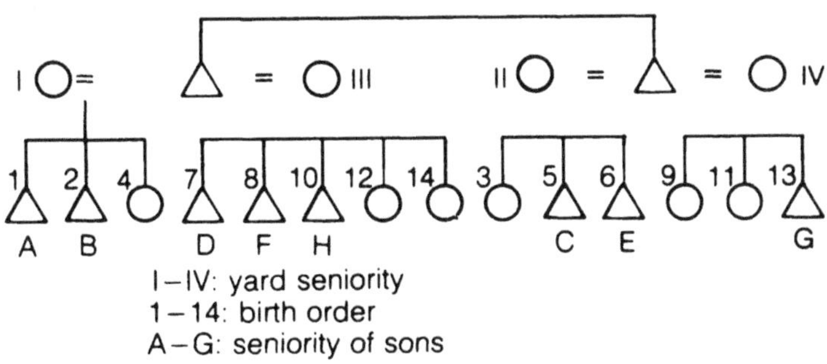

Fig. 3.2
Seniority in a Jie Household (Gulliver 1955:65)

suggest that a single model of household institutions may not be beyond our grasp.

HOUSEHOLD HISTORIES

The distinction between household system and household structure together with the notion that the latter is generated in part by the former draws our attention to regularities in sequences of household decisions, which, though not goals in themselves, are clues to underlying rules and strategies of household management. These regularities also raise the possibility that decisions concerning marriage, fertility, and mortality may be affected by the individual's position within as well as the overall condition of the household unit. As an aid to the discovery of household rule systems, as a clue to changes in exogenous factors influencing household management, and as an index of the circumstances in which demographic decisions are made, therefore, it is essential to have information on longitudinal or historical aspects of household structure.

The Limitations of Cross-sectional Analysis

Longitudinal information will, of course, be difficult to obtain with the usual methods of anthropological fieldwork. It is therefore important to insist that available methods of synchronic, cross-sectional analysis do not provide an adequate substitute for the longitudinal approach. It is extremely difficult if not impossible to infer the elements of household rule systems from statistics concerning household composition at a particular point in time, even with a large sample. One reason is that household forms are ambiguous. They may occur as the result of more than one developmental sequence generated by more than one set of household decisions. A classic stem family household, for example, consisting of a couple together with their married child and the child's spouse, may occur either because the child remains in his or her parent's household after marriage, because the child rejoins the parents' household after a period of residence elsewhere, or because the parents themselves join the previously independent household of the married child (see also Carter 1971; R. J. Smith 1978; Medick 1976).

In addition, such is the impact of random variations in birth and death that the occurrence within different components of a single sociocultural system of different frequencies of household forms may be the result of a single household rule system, while different rule systems may result, depending on demographic and other conditions, in identical frequencies of household forms, though this point cannot yet be regarded as beyond doubt. On the basis of SOCSIM household simulation experiments, Wachter and his colleagues argue that within certain limits household rule systems are not effectively disguised either by systematic differences in demographic regimes or by random demographic fluctuations (Wachter, Hammel, and Laslett 1978:4–11, 13–27, 46–64). Bradley and Mendels (1978), however, have attempted a mathematical analysis of the same problem and obtain much more discouraging results. Wachter, Hammel, and Laslett (1978:10) discount Bradley and Mendels's results, attributing them to oversimplifications in their model of household systems and to ambiguities in their classification of household forms, but it is possible that the SOCSIM experiments themselves fail to reproduce the full extent of random demographic variation found in the real world. Kunstadter (1972), for example, stresses the magnitude of random variation in the sex ratio at birth among sibling sets in small communities and, more particularly, in individual households. This is a component of variance that must have enormous consequences for household formation, but Wachter and his colleagues do not comment on its contribution to their experimental results.

Beginning with Fortes's (1949*a*) work on Ashanti domestic groups, there has been an important series of efforts to reconstruct the longitudinal aspects of household structure from synchronic, cross-sectional data by tabulating information on household size and composition as a function of the age of the household head or of other categories of personnel (see Tait 1956; Hammel 1961; Berkner 1972; Vatuk 1972; Wolf, this volume). Though they are of much interest, such studies are circumscribed by their inability to distinguish the current situation of successive cohorts from the consequences of secular changes either in household rule systems or in the exogenous conditions of household management. This point is all the more important for studies of contemporary households, for it is certainly not impossible that either rule systems or exogenous conditions or both are currently changing with bewildering rapidity.

Household Types and Type Sequences

Several students of household institutions have attempted to analyze the longitudinal aspects of household structure by defining types of households and tracing the manner in which particular households have changed from one type to another (see Otterbein 1970; Segalen 1977; R. J. Smith 1978). Where the available data consist of a series of censuses or household lists and especially where the items in the series are separated by irregular or greater than one-year intervals, then the type sequence approach may be the only one possible. But this approach also has been adopted where the data permit richer analysis.[6] Because analysis in terms of household type sequences is not forced on us by all forms of data, it is well to remember that such analyses suffer from severe limitations.

Household types generally are defined in terms of the number of nuclear families in a household, their completeness (whether they contain widowed or divorced persons), the manner in which one nuclear family is connected to another (for example, by a sibling or a parent/child bond), and the degree to which they are extended by having attached to them persons who currently belong to no nuclear family (see Kolenda 1968:346–47 and Laslett 1972:28–32). Often such schemes treat the essential relations between household members as if they were ties of kinship and marriage. In other schemes an element of household status per se is included as, for example, when R. J. Smith (1978:222) distinguishes among stem family households according to the generational position of the head.

In general, however, no matter how existing classifications of household types handle the family/household distinction, they fail to take account of changes in household composition that may influence the subsequent actions of household members and they give significance to changes that do not so influence the conduct of household members. Most particularly, such classifications ignore differences in the size and sex ratio of component nuclear families and the effects of household seniority. They also treat as distinct types household forms that in fact do not necessarily influence their members' nuptiality, fertility, mortality, or decisions to demand partition. In Maharashtra, for example, a variety of household types may contain two or more component nuclear families headed by a man whose father is dead or by that man's widow. In some types the heads of these component nuclear families are brothers while in others they may be cousins or uncle and nephew. Any of these component units legally may demand partition, however, and the diverse types may therefore be collapsed into a single partitionable household form without regard to the kinship relations between their legally independent components. In order to keep track of these and other factors, proper household histories must pay much closer attention to births, adoptions, and deaths that leave the number of component nuclear families and the kinship relations between them unchanged.

If an attempt is made to apply type sequence analysis to much of Africa, still more modifications are required. In a great many African societies women have personal incomes that vary independently from those of their husbands, in part because where hoe agriculture is practiced women are often the principal farmers (see Goody and Buckley

1973; Hill 1975; Guyer 1980). In these societies the undifferentiated nuclear family cannot be regarded as the unit from which households are constructed (Oppong 1976). Instead the relationships between (1) matrifocal units consisting of women and the immature children for which they are responsible (not necessarily their own) and (2) adult men must be subjected to careful analysis comparable to that given to the relationships between nuclear families.

And finally no form of household type analysis can tell us by and of itself anything about the resource component of household structure.

The Minimum Elements of a Household History

For a set of households in a given community we require records of all movements of persons and resources into and out of household units and into and out of positions within households. Movement of personnel may result from birth, marriage, and death, but in addition to these events social maturation or aging, retirement and succession, fosterage and adoption plus partition and amalgamation must be considered. At the risk of repetition I stress that in order to chart all significant aspects of a household history we need to know not only the kinship relation, if any, between any given person and his or her household head but also his or her position in the household personnel system. Where the person concerned is one of several occupants of a single position, such as, in the Maharashtrian case, an unmarried male owner or unmarried female owner, we also need to know his or her place in the queue of such persons that results from the operation of the rule of household seniority. Finally, we must keep track of the manner in which these events affect the viability of the household unit and the opportunities of its members to pursue their personal goals. This means calculating such measures as:

1. The size of the household
2. The amount or value of resources and the technological requirements of their management
3. The producer/consumer ratio
4. The ratio of resources to personnel
5. The difference between a potentially independent unit's position within an existing household and its position as a separate household. Such units may include matrifocal families and primary individuals as well as nuclear families.

This list is by no means exhaustive, but it does suggest those measures that are likely to be generally applicable and for which the necessary data are more rather than less likely to be available.

An Example from Maharashtra, India

Some of the central elements of a household history are illustrated by the example outlined in figure 3.3. This example concerns the households of a man and his two sons, whose surname I have given as More, resident in Alandi, a small municipality (population about 5,000) some ten miles north of Poona in Maharashtra, India.[7]

The history of the More household is abstracted from the following official records: registers of births and deaths maintained by the Alandi municipality; a register of marriages in the charge of the Registrar of Marriage in Khed, the *taluka* headquarters; land records kept by the Talathi, a local official of the Revenue Department; and a census prepared in connection with the issuance of ration cards to household heads. All of these records, particularly those listing births and marriages, have a number of weaknesses peculiar to the Indian registration system, but taken as a whole the records have two substantial advantages.[8] First, the ration card census reports current household composition while the land records either report directly changes in household composition during the previous 20 years, as when the division of land among heirs is noted, or allow one to infer such changes, as when persons first take out agricultural loans on their own behalf. In these records, then, as with the Japanese household registers, household histories can be distinguished from the family histories of European family reconstitution (Wrigley 1966). It is possible, moreover, to follow the resource component of household histories, primarily through the land records but also through the listing of occupations in the ration card forms.

I have selected the More household for presentation here because it experienced a partition during the period covered by my records and also because all the relevant entries could be located easily. The Mores belong to the Maratha caste, the dominant agricultural caste of the region, though not to either of the two important Maratha lineages in Alandi. Throughout the period for which I have data they owned an acre of unirrigated land divided between two fields. In 1976 the elder of the two More brothers (3) was employed solely as a farmer, but his three eldest children (10–12) were working as day laborers. The younger brother (6) farmed his own land and also worked as a laborer for others.

Several features of the More household histories deserve comment. Beginning on 12 January 1955 the initial undivided More household experienced four deaths in less than two years, cutting its size in half, raising its producer/consumer ratio from .76 to .92 and establishing virtual equality between the conjugal units of the two brothers.

A. Genealogy of the persons involved

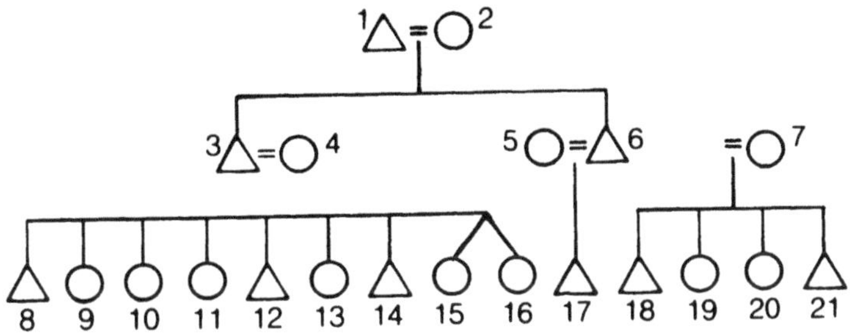

B. Initial state of the More household on 1 January 1955

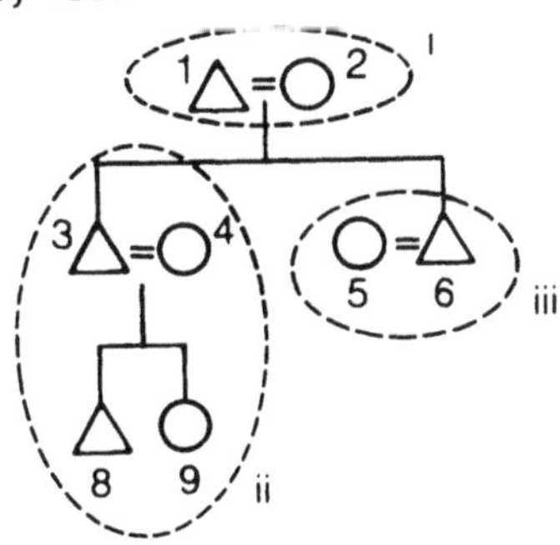

Personnel:

ID No.	Born	Married
1	c 1 Jan 1895	?
2	c 1 Jan 1895	?
3	c 1 Jan 1921	?
4	c 1 Jan 1926	?
5	c 1 Jan 1938	?
6	20 Mar 1942	?
8	c 1 Jan 1949	
9	14 Oct 1952	

Resources:

Survey no.	Area (acres)
72	0.78
38	0.22

Size = 8
Producer/consumer ratio = 5.43/7.12 = 0.76[a]
Resources(acres)/consumer ratio
= 1/7.12 = 0.14
Headship queue = 1(S), 3(S), 6, 2, 4
5, 8(S), 9[b]
Marriage queues:[b]
Male = 8(S)
Female = 9(S)

Conjugal units:[c]

ID no.	IC[d]	Com[e]	P/C	R/C	Marriage queues[f] M	Marriage queues[f] F	Conjugal unit differentials[g] C	Conjugal unit differentials[g] P
i	+	+	0.76	0.17	0	0	−14.9	−15.2
ii	−	+	0.71	0.11	1	1	+32.8	+23.9
iii	−	+	0.85	0.17	0	0	−14.9	− 5.7

Fig. 3.3
History of the More Household

C. Events affecting household composition: 12 Jan 55 through 10 June 67

12 Jan 55	death of 2	1 Jan 60	birth of 11
22 Oct 55	death of 8	29 Jan 62	birth of 18
29 Oct 55	death of 9	10 Mar 62	birth of 12
12 Nov 56	death of 1, 3 becomes head	29 Apr 64	birth of 13
		20 Dec 66	death of 13
8 Jun 57	birth of 10	28 Dec 66	birth of 14
7 Jan 59	birth of 17	10 Jun 67	partition of conjugal units ii and iii
7 Jan 59	death of 5		
21 Jun 59	6 marries 7 (born c 1 Jan 43)		

D. State of the More household on 1 February 1959

Size = 5
P/C = 2.89/3.66 = 0.79
R/C = 1/3.72 = 0.27
Headship queue = 3(S), 6, 4, 17, 10
Marriage queues:
Male = 17
Female = 10

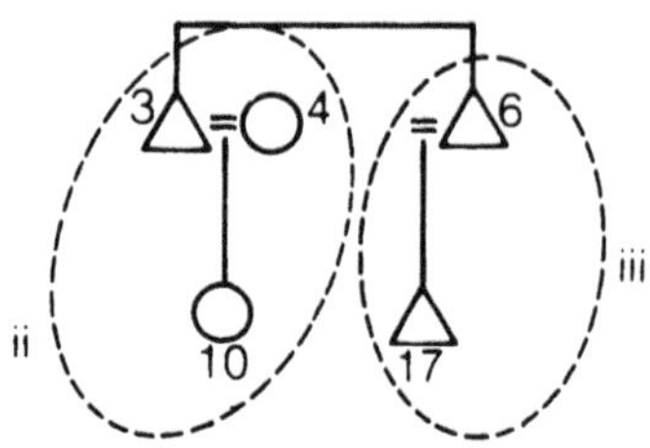

Conjugal units:[c]

ID no.	IC[d]	Com[e]	P/C	R/C	Marriage queues[f] M	Marriage queues[f] F	Conjugal unit differentials[g] C	Conjugal unit differentials[g] P
ii	+	+	0.81	0.21	0	1	+30.6	+38.4
iii	+	−	0.70	0.39	1	0	−30.6	−38.4

E. State of the More household on 1 January 1967

Size = 10
P/C = 4.85/7.62 = 0.64
R/C = 1/7.62 = 0.13
Headship queue = 3(S), 6, 4, 7, 17, 18, 12(S), 14, 10, 11
Marriage queues:
Male = 17, 18, 12(S), 14
Female = 10, 11

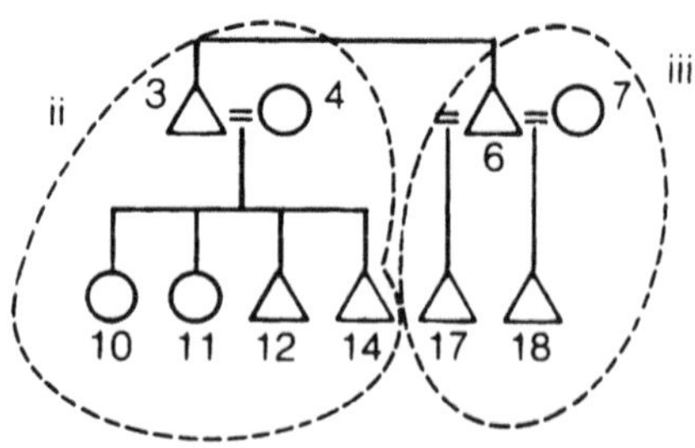

Conjugal units:[c]

ID no.	IC[d]	Com[e]	P/C	R/C	Marriage queues[f] M	Marriage queues[f] F	Conjugal unit differentials[g] C	Conjugal unit differentials[g] P
ii	+	+	0.61	0.12	2	2	+13.9	+8.5
iii	+	+	0.68	0.15	2	0	−13.9	−8.5

Fig. 3.3 cont.

F. State of successor More household on 1 January 1968

Resources:

Survey no.	Area (acres)
72	0.78

Size = 6
P/C = 2.63/4.59 = 0.57
R/C = 0.78/4.59 = 0.17
Headship queue = 3(S), 4, 12(S), 14, 10, 11
Marriage queues:
Male = 12(S), 14
Female = 10, 11

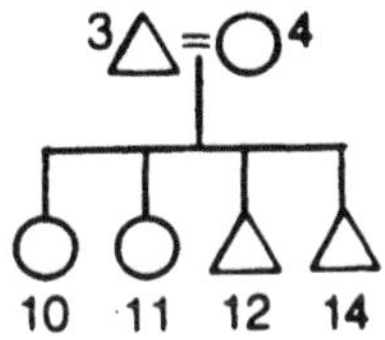

G. State of the new More household on 1 January 1968

Resources:

Survey no.	Area (acres)
38	0.22

Size = 4
P/C = 2.22/3.33 = 0.67
R/C = 0.22/3.33 = 0.07
Headship queue: 6(S), 7, 17(S), 18
Marriage queues:
Male = 17, 18

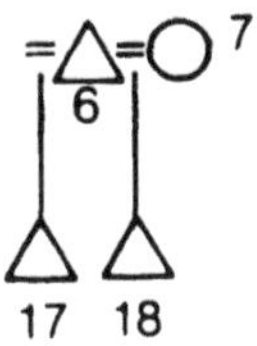

H. Events in the successor More household: 10 Jun 67 through 1 Jun 76

c 1 Jan 69 birth of 15 and 16

I. State of the successor More household on 1 June 1976

Size = 8
P/C = 4.98/7.18 = 0.69
R/C = 0.78/7.18 = 0.11
Headship queue = 3(S), 4, 12(S), 14, 10, 11, 15, 16
Marriage queues:
Male = 12(S), 14
Female = 10, 11, 15, 16

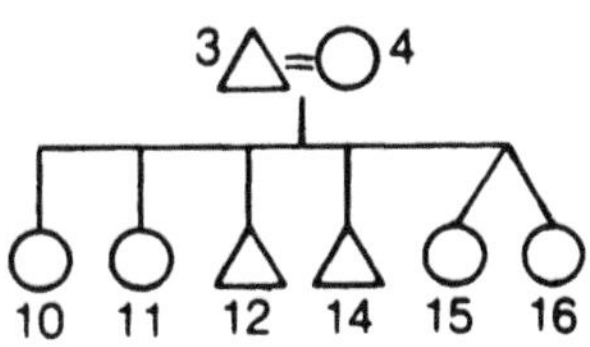

J. Events in the new More household: 10 Jun 67 through 1 Jun 76

2 Feb 68	birth of 19
15 Aug 69	death of 19
c 1 Jan 70	birth of 20
c 1 Jan 72	birth of 21

Fig. 3.3 cont.

Fig. 3.3 cont.

K. State of the new More household on 1 June 76

Resources:

Survey no.	Area (acres)
38	0.22

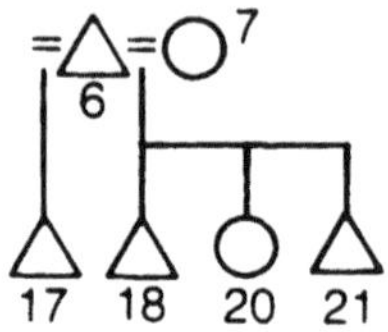

Size = 6
P/C = 3.67/5.24 = 0.70
R/C = 0.22/5.24 = 0.04
Headship queue = 6(S), 17(S), 7, 18, 21, 20
Marriage queues:
Male = 17(S), 18, 21
Female = 20

[a]Household members are regarded as contributing units of production and consumption weighted by age as follows:

Age	Consumption	Production
0	.27	.0
1	.39	.0
2	.45	.0
3	.52	.0
4	.57	.0
5	.62	.0
6	.67	.33
7	.71	.33
8	.75	.33
9	.79	.54
10	.83	.54
11	.87	.54
12	.9	.66
13	.93	.66
14	.97	.66
15–19	1.0	.8
20–29	1.0	.89
30–39	1.0	1.0
40–49	1.0	.88
50+	1.0	.76

The estimates of relative consumption are based on FAO./WHO. estimates of calorie requirements quoted in Cassen (1978:64).

The estimates of relative production are derived from Nag, White, and Peet (1978). I have calculated the average number of hours worked ("household maintenance" as well as "directly productive" work) as a function of age for their four populations (males and females in Java and Nepal) combined. The figures given here indicate the fraction of the highest number of hours work contributed by the age group.

[b]Headship and marriage queues are a function of the rules of seniority described above. The headship queue shows the order in which persons may succeed to the household headship. Marriage queues show the order in which males and females may use household resources for marriage. Those designated by an S are the eldest children of the household head and eldest children of the eldest son's child.

[c]Conjugal units are the potentially independent units out of which more complex households are constructed. Each consists of a man and his wife or wives and their unmarried children. They are indicated on genealogical diagrams by dotted circles and lower case roman numerals. A series of tables labeled "Conjugal units" depict the relationships between conjugal units in multiple unit households.

Fig. 3.3 cont.

[d]IC = independent coparcener. Is the unit legally entitled to demand partition? That is, is the father of the man whose marriage founded the unit dead?

[e]Com = complete. Is the unit complete? That is, does it contain a married couple? Most incomplete conjugal units are inviable.

[f]The number of males and females from each conjugal unit on the household marriage queue.

[g]The percentage difference between the unit's *per stirpes* household share and its weighted per capita contribution. The value of P for any conjugal unit, for example, is given by the formula

$$([(P_{cu}/P_{hh})/SHARE_{cu}]100) - 100$$

where P_{cu} equals the number of production units contributed by the conjugal unit, P_{hh} equals the number of production units in the household as a whole, and $SHARE_{cu}$ equals the conjugal unit's *per stirpes* share of household resources. Male agnates inherit ancestral resources on a *per stirpes* basis so this figure indicates the inequalities introduced among the conjugal units of agnatic coparceners by the random effects of birth and death and by age at marriage.

Each brother then had a child (10 and 17), but the younger brother's wife (5) died in childbirth. At this point (see figure 3.3D) the household consisted of two conjugal units each of which was legally competent to demand partition, but the younger brother's unit was now incomplete and unable to form a viable household on its own. Note, however, that 6 did not return to the household marriage queue. Having been married once, he was not entitled as of right to be remarried from the undivided ancestral resources of the household. Nevertheless, just six months after the death of his first wife, 6 remarried, his older brother playing the role that their father would have taken had he still been living. As the subsequent details of the household partition recorded in the land records make clear (see information on resources in figure 3.3F and G), the expenses of this marriage were regarded as an advance on 6's own *per stirpes* share of his father's estate.

The two brothers maintained a joint household for more than ten years after the death of their father even though despite the fact that during these years 6 appeared to be subsidizing his elder brother's higher fertility. That is, if their estate were divided into two equal shares, as the inheritance rules imply and as one would assume if one did not know that the marriage on 21 June 1959 was 6's second, then 6 could increase the resources and producer units per consumer unit available to his own conjugal unit by requesting partition. When partition finally did occur, however, it became clear that 6 was not in fact subsidizing his brother but had received an advance on his inheritance that was repaid by subsequent unequal division of land. It seems likely therefore that the younger brother initiated partition and that he did so, even though he thereby finally lost access to the larger of the two fields comprising his father's estate, because of the demands that he knew would ultimately have been placed on their resources by the marriages of his brother's four children, especially the two girls who would require dowries (see marriage queues, figure 3.3).[9]

Note, too, that on establishing his own household the fertility of 6 and his wife seems to have undergone a substantial spurt. Though no more than anecdotal, this accords well with suggestions by Taeuber (1970) and Burch (1967:360) that junior household positions are associated with reduced fertility.[10]

Modes of Analysis

We have here then some suggestions for recording events that occur in households and for calculating their consequences for the well-being of the household and for the actions of its members. The question remains, How we are to analyze such longitudinal records? What are we to do with them?

One possibility is to model household histories as Markov processes, that is, as a set of states that over time are maintained or altered, one into another, according to a set of stable transition probabilities. This mode of analysis has been explored in theoretical terms by Buchler and Selby (1968) and White (1973), while empirical studies of the domestic cycle using Markov process models have been carried out by Otterbein and Otterbein (1977) for southern Andros in the Bahamas and by Fjellman (1977) for the Akamba in Kenya. As White notes, such models have an important mathematical property that permits them to be used to assess conditions of stability and change: "it can be proved that the expected frequencies in successive states of the system, as computed by the transition probabilities, approach a limiting set of values or an equilbrium vector. Regardless of the initial set of frequencies of the system, the limiting vector will be reached for a given matrix of transition probabilities" (White 1973:374). In addition to stable transition probabilities, however, such models require that the probability that an element of the system move from a current state to any next state *not be influenced* by the manner in which that element arrived at its current state, that is, by its previous history.

To date, all of the work along these lines has focused on the kind of household type sequences discussed above. Such work therefore suffers from the same ambiguities as do household types themselves. Positions in a household are equated with kinship relations to household head, and such factors as seniority queues or the economic relationships between potentially independent household components are ignored. As regards fertility or infant mortality, household types so constructed ignore the fact that persons with the same kinship status may be distributed over a variety of household positions while persons occupying a single household position may be related to the household head in a variety of ways.

Whether a more adequate set of household types suitable for Markov process models can be constructed using the materials sketched in the preceding two sections remains to be seen. Any such effort, however, is probably doomed to failure. In the first place, how could one define household types in such a way that their transition probabilities would be uninfluenced by their previous histories? Consider, for example, a joint household such as that maintained by the More brothers from 12 November 1956 to 10 June 1967, that is, one consisting of two or more conjugal units each of which has independent coparcener status. The probability of such a household remaining in this state from one time period to the next probably varies inversely with duration of coresidence as well as with inequalities among component units. As a result, even if the units are relatively equal they are more likely to separate the longer they remain together. But duration is a historical characteristic, one that requires a knowledge of when a household arrived at its present condition. And it is a historical condition that cannot be rewritten as an ahistorical condition, by subdividing the original household types into subtypes distinguished by duration of maintenance, without greatly increasing the number of distinct types. Other major historical characteristics of households are age at marriage and mean ages of maternity and paternity, all of which have substantial effects on family and household formation long after the fact (see Mendels 1978).

Nor is it clear if one were to construct a set of household types or states meeting the requirements of a Markov process, that the effort would be repaid. More interesting than the successive states of a household history are the events or decisions that give rise to those states. Those events, however, are extraordinarily diverse. To take another example, consider births, a crucial event if we are to understand the interactions between household institutions and demographic regimes. Here it is important to examine the probability of a woman giving birth as a function of such factors as the following:

1. The woman's current age and age at marriage
2. Her marital status
3. Parity
4. The sex ratio among her previous offspring and their mortality

5. The woman's position in household as defined by rules of seniority and as affected by the presence or absence of a mother-in-law or daughter-in-law
6. The viability of her household as a function of the fertility and mortality experience of other household members

This list does not exhaust the considerations surrounding birth that have been mentioned in the literature, but already it should be clear that household types or states cannot be defined in such a way that transitions from one state to another usefully correspond to significant household events without enormously increasing the number of household types. And to increase significantly the number of household types is to render virtually meaningless frequency distributions among them.

Markov process analysis is thus not a very promising line to pursue. The materials contained in household histories cannot be readily conceptualized as sequences of ahistorical states, and a focus on states in any case obscures the more important underlying events. This negative conclusion does not, however, leave us without alternatives, for we do have the means to examine household events and event sequences.

The best example of the kind of analysis to which I am referring is T. C. Smith's (1977) elegant study, *Nakahara: Family Farming and Population in a Japanese Village, 1717–1830*. One theme running through Smith's analysis concerns the risk of household demise in Nakahara and the ways in which householders managed marriage and fertility to avoid this risk.

Demise is a terminal event in a household history that occurs when a household is unable to renew itself by recruiting new members before the old members die or move out. As T. C. Smith puts it,

> [Households] went out of existence in a variety of ways. Most often they died out biologically; occasionally they were reabsorbed into the main family [i.e., household]; and sometimes they simply moved away from Nakahara. But never did any of these things happen so long as the family had property. It was the loss of property that made continuation as a group in the village impossible. This was the real reason for a demise, even when a family died out biologically; for heirs could always be adopted or appointed posthumously by relatives when there was property to inherit. (1977:37–38).

Of the 100 households that Smith was able to observe between 1717 and 1830, 42 had died out by the end of the period. Keeping track of the duration of households and dividing the number of demises by the number of years of exposure to demise, Smith is able to calculate rates of demise as a function of the amount of household land (see figure 3.4).

Size of first recorded land holding (*koku*)	No. of households	Demises	Demises per 1,000 household-years
0–2	24	16	17.60
2–5	8	5	16.03
5–12	10	6	10.95
12–15	11	4	6.63
15–18	9	3	4.26
18–24	9	2	2.41
24–30	7	1	1.64
30+	7	0	0

Fig. 3.4
Rate of Household Demise by Initial Landholding Size
(T. C. Smith 1977:128)

Of greater interest than Smith's ability to calculate such simple rates for single events is his ability to examine the connections among separate classes of events. Here we begin to understand why Nakahara households experienced demise.

Persons enter households as a result of birth, adoption, marriage, and so on while they exit from households as a result of adoption, marriage, death, and separation. If transactions in land and decisions concerning exits and entrances are manipulated to enhance household viability, then one would expect to see significant correlations among these classes of events. Smith is unable to calculate these correlations precisely, in part because the Japanese records permit him to observe land holdings only at intervals of 8 to 18 years. Nevertheless, he was able to calculate exit and entrance rates during intervals when registered land holdings in individual households were rising, declining, or staying relatively level (see figure 3.5). Contrary to expectations, households with declining holdings have higher entry rates than those with growing or stable holdings. Nevertheless, the net growth rate and the exit rate, especially that part of it attributable to voluntary exits other than deaths, do behave as one would expect if holdings and personnel are mutually adjusted in the interests of viability.

T. C. Smith's analysis of marriage permits further insights into the factors that might cause a Nakahara household to begin to slide toward demise. The Japanese household system provides room in any one generation for only one married couple. As a result marriage involved not only a substantial household expense but also a significant reorganization of the household labor force. Departures of unmarried sons and the out-marriages of daughters tended to cluster in the years immediately before and after the marriage into the household of the heir's spouse

Entrance and exit rates	Change in holding size Increasing	Stable	Decreasing
Exits per 1,000 household-years			
All exits	168.8	219.3	243.5
All exits except deaths	63.1	119.8	144.4
Deaths	105.7	99.5	99.1
Entries per 1,000 household years	205.9	233.3	237.1
Net growth rate	37.1	14.0	– 6.4

Fig. 3.5
Entries and Exits from Households with Increasing, Decreasing, and Stable Holdings (Smith 1977:126)

(T. C. Smith 1977:142-43), helping to produce in the following years a pronounced decline in the ratio of household producer units to household size (see figure 3.6). While household size increased following the heir's marriage and the birth of his or her children, the household labor force "declined steadily from six years prior to the marriage until nine years after, at which time it was about two-thirds starting size and still shrinking" (T. C. Smith 1977:136). Though poor households had difficulty retaining members, they apparently tried to delay the onset of this viability crisis by putting off the marriage of the heir (Smith 1977:90–92, 139). But this strategy risked a still more serious crisis later on. For as the age of the heir at first marriage increased, the chances that he or she would die before his or her own child could marry and take over direction of the household also increased (T. C. Smith 1977:138–39). Caught on the horns of this dilemma, Japanese householders attempted to avoid both kinds of risk by sharply curtailing their fertility, often by means of infanticide (T. C. Smith 1977:59–85).

That these connections among household events in eighteenth-century Nakahara probably are shaped to a significant degree by recruitment rules in Japan's so-called stem family households can be seen by looking at the implications of marriage for producer/size ratios in joint households like those found in much of India and in parts of China. The More household histories presented in figure 3.3 cannot be used for this purpose, for the only in-marriage for which I have a date was the second marriage of the household member concerned. T. C. Smith's calculations can be applied to the carefully detailed sample of Taiwanese household histories appended to Wolf and Huang's (1980) *Marriage and Adoption in*

China, 1845–1945. The results of these calculations, though again they are no more than anecdotal, are shown in figure 3.6. The lower overall level of the producer/size ratio in the Taiwanese example perhaps results from the higher fertility of that population relative to the Japanese. The more important point is that in Taiwan, where any number of children, female as well as male, adopted as well as biological, may marry and bring their spouses into their own household, in-marriages do not seem to precipitate pronounced movements in the household producer/size ratio.

Finally, beyond these descriptive approaches to household events and event interaction, there are available to us a number of more powerful modeling techniques. Geogheghan (1969) and Keesing (1970) have shown that decision trees may be used to represent information-processing models of the factors that enter into and in effect generate household events. More important, such decision trees may be rewritten as computer programs that will simulate household histories, and such simulation programs may be used, through artificial experiments, to test the reality of underlying information-processing or rule system models and to measure the effects of variations in rule systems as well as in demographic and economic conditions. To date, however, the only existing household simulation program is SOCSIM (see Hammel et al. 1976 and Wachter, Hammel, and Laslett 1978). Though it has been used to do some interesting exploratory work, SOCSIM has two notable weaknesses in connection with the household concept. It equates household rules and household positions with family and kinship and it observes the results of its simulation runs solely by accumulating synchronic cross-sections of household types. If progress is to be made in this area more realistic household rule systems will have to be designed as well as subroutines that preserve longitudinal household event records.

CONCLUSION

Domestic institutions long have been a favorite topic in anthropology, though in the beginning the focus was not the household but rather the family. Thus Raymond Firth, one of the first students to join Malinowski's seminar at the London School of Economics, devoted a substantial part of *We, the Tikopia* (1936) to detailed descriptions of household composition and the daily round of housekeeping activities. Indeed, in this early monograph Firth anticipated by 36 years the concern of Laslett and his colleagues with the impact of variable experience during childhood of kinship relations within the household (see also Wolf, this volume). In a subsequent restudy of Tikopia, moreover, Firth was among the first to

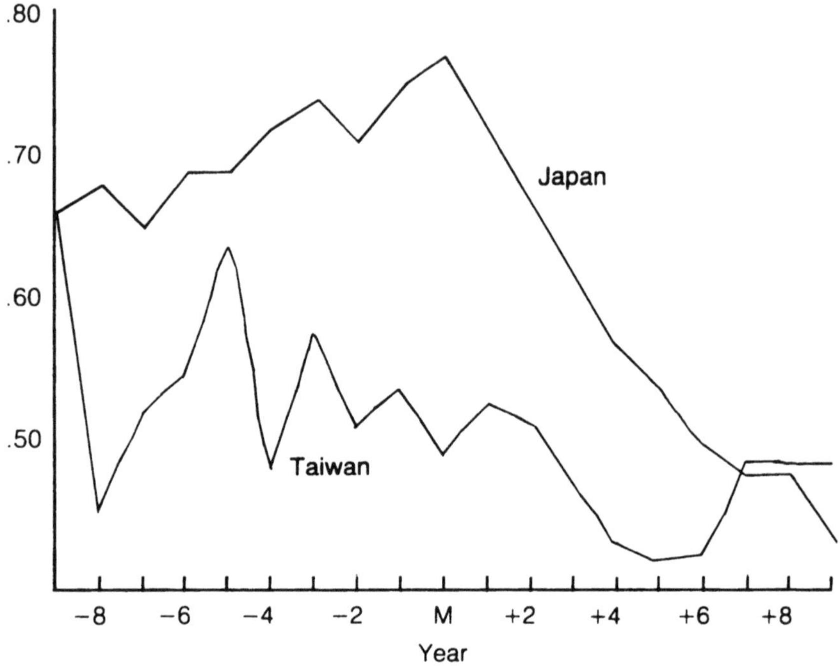

SOURCE: The ratio for Japan was calculated by combining T. C. Smith's figures 8.1 and 8.2 (1977:136–37). The Taiwan ratio is calculated from the first 24 years (3 in-marriages) of the Tan household history presented in Wolf and Huang (1980:357–60).

Fig. 3.6
The Ratio of Household Producer Units to Household Size in Relation to the Time of Marriages into Households in Two Populations

describe changes in household composition and size over a considerable period of time and to attempt to show how these characteristics responded to demographic and economic influences (1959:183–203). As early as 1943 Rosemary Firth was able to observe, "In almost all societies, the household, whatever its composition, is an important unit in the distribution and utilization of wealth. In many societies it is the one unit through which almost the whole of the economy can be studied as a connected and functioning whole." (1966:1).

In the decades since World War II there has been a remarkable flowering of monographic reports on domestic institutions.[11] One cannot quarrel with the ethnographic detail in these studies. In fact, as we have turned in recent years to censuses and other more extensive numerical data sources it is just this kind of ethnographic detail, the actor's point of view, that most often has been sacrificed. Nevertheless, much of the household literature has been organized around a series of broad comparative issues that, as we have now learned, entangle us in the kind of futile exercises castigated in this volume by Hammel.

Though the functional importance of the household was recognized clearly enough, it was assumed that households could be defined as kinship groups delimited by coresidence. As a distinguished committee of the Royal Anthropological Institute put it in the sixth edition of *Notes and Queries*, the household consists of the occupants of a homestead. Though it was to be distinguished from the elementary family—"whether they are living together or not"—the household was nevertheless assumed to be composed of a collection of relatives or the "domestic family." Genealogical inquiries therefore "often yield" information on the "determining factors" of household composition (Royal Anthropological Institute 1959:64, 70–72). It was widely assumed, too, that the principles of kinship and residence rules that shape household size and composition take the form of norms so that a failure to achieve the normative family type is a deviation or falling away from the ideal.

It is against this background that two major approaches to the study of intrasocietal variation in household composition may be understood. Deviations from ideal domestic family composition typically are seen as forced or induced by economic factors. Disadvantaged sections of the population are too ill-equipped to sustain the ideal and may even in time lose sight of it altogether.[12] Those sections of the population experiencing economic development and "modernization," however, are thought to abandon their traditional ideals as these come into conflict with new economic opportunities and western individualism (cf. Arnould, this volume).[13]

Much ink has been spilled on interpretations of this sort without producing any adequate results. Indeed, as Hammel convincingly argues (this volume) such exercises are inherently unproductive in the form in which they generally are cast, that is, in terms of the incidence of various household types in community samples. A more satisfactory approach to these and other important issues must involve both a more complex conception of household norms and a more microscopic level of analysis.

It is first essential to distinguish between the household or task-oriented dimension of domestic groups and the familial or kinship dimension. Increasingly recognized by anthropologists, this distinction is forced on us in fact by informant statements and semantic distinctions in a considerable variety of cultures. Given the flexibility of residential arrangements, it is impossible, moreover, to regard coresidence as a determinant household task or function. We must be content instead to identify households in terms of the density of activity spheres (see Hammel 1980:251 and Wilk and Netting in this volume) or perhaps by the presence of a coordinating head.

It also is essential to distinguish between statistical aspects of household structure and underlying household systems comprised of rules and strategies.[14] Though kinship relations are a significant component of household structure or morphology, they do not exhaust it, not even in conjunction with measures of size and age/sex structure. We must also keep track of culturally recognized aspects of structure that are more directly linked to household activities or tasks. The Latvian concepts of household head and his dependents (*saimnieks* and *saime*) and the notion of a son or brother in the role of farmhand (Plakans, this volume) are excellent exemplars of this feature of structure as are the seniority queues found in Maharashtra and elsewhere. As consideration of the various ambiguities inherent in household types shows, the nonfamilial aspects of household structure have the greatest import for household viability. These features of morphology or structure, moreover, are not limited to such apparently straightforward phenomena as size but instead are subject to precisely the same sort of cultural definition that makes kinship such a beguilingly diverse field of study.

Household rules and strategies in turn give cultural definition to the means with which households are managed and to the environments within which they must exist. Rules and strategies thus mediate the manner in which, to borrow the terminology of Wilk and Netting (this volume), household functions interact with household morphology. Such household systems, not fixed ideals but rather adaptive frameworks within which action may be experienced as meaningful and purposive, are a critical element of any attempt to understand how domestic groups cope with and endure in the face of the dispersive effects of demographic fluctuation.[15] These systems also are essential to an understanding of mixed ethnic situations like that in northwestern Thailand described by Kunstadter (this volume). How otherwise are we to account for the quite different responses of Lua' and Karen highland farmers to similar environmental pressures and functional changes?

Going beyond modes of definition, the study of household institutions would benefit from what Hammel (this volume), calls a more fine-grained level of analysis, a shift of focus to the individual decisions that give rise to particular household forms. As I have argued in this paper, such a shift in the level of analysis is equivalent to a concern with household histories based on accurately dated longitudinal materials. Fortunately, such data and the means to interpret them are available. Few anthropologists will be able to undertake a substantial prospective study of household dynamics, emulating *The Khanna Study* (Wyon and Gordon 1971) or the University of Michigan study *Five Thousand American Families* (Duncan and Morgan 1976), but following the lead of historians we now are aware of vital event and other official records that will enable us to follow event sequences in a variety of historical and contemporary populations. Indeed, if sufficient records are available for rural India, as I have shown, searches for similar materials in other developing countries are likely to meet with success. And even if such records are not available, the work of Forde (1951:100–116) on a Yako household history indicates that useful retrospective studies are not beyond our grasp. In any case neither successive synchronic cross-sections nor age cohort analysis are fully adequate substitutes.

Once household event records are in hand we are for the first time in a position to tackle a variety of questions of practical as well as theoretical import. We can trace the impact of changing socioeconomic systems and of declining mortality on household rule systems as well as the manner in which household strategies adapt to such changes within the framework of unchanging or slowly changing rule systems. A number of observers have suggested, for example, that persistent high fertility in contemporary developing nations, rather than being an outmoded response to formerly high, pretransition mortality, is a rational response of households to changing patterns of resource distribution or to particular kinds of economic environments. Mamdani (1972) argues that households with very small holdings deliberately have as many sons as possible, partly to avoid the costs of hiring labor and partly in the hope of earning enough to increase their holdings. The landless do the same, but in their case because children are seen as the only form of saving and old-age insurance available to them (see also C. Tilly 1978). Cain (1981), however, recognizes that the net income from bearing and rearing children may in fact be less than that which might be earned by other forms of saving (see also Cassen 1978:63–76). Children may be "priceless" and reproduction justifiably unconstrained, nevertheless, in environments in which the probabilities of events that threaten normal household consumption streams are high and in which other forms of insurance are unavailable (Cain 1981). Such microlevel explanations of high fertility appear to accord well with macrolevel fertility differentials and thus lend support to what has been called the distributive justice hypothesis, according to which societal fertility levels are responsive to patterns of economic distribution (see Murdock 1980 and Hackenberg, Murphy, and Selby, this volume). The microlevel explanations, however, rest on rather insubstantial data bases and, though plausible, are only just so. That some informants believe a high fertility strategy makes sense in a high-risk environment or in the absence of other resources is entirely likely, but that the strategy actually can be made to work is somewhat less so (again see Cassen 1978:63–76). There are few if any longitudinal studies that attempt to show that households experiencing proletarianization or increased risk actually switch to a high-fertility strategy or that document the consequences of such strategies over a period of years for the households engaging in them.

The longitudinal approach also will enable us to follow the manner in which features of demographic regimes characteristic of particular societies are generated by household systems themselves. As Burch and Gendell note in a review of the earlier literature on household types and fertility, for example, "Field studies that collect information on current residence and current fertility, or that relate cumulative fertility to the woman's residential family histories are needed" (1971:100).

Nor need the reconstruction of household histories from official records be the end product of anthropological work in this area. Where suitable records can be obtained for a contemporary population a wide range of informants, male as well as female, junior as well as senior, may be asked to review and comment on their own household histories. Such a field procedure holds the promise of a wealth of cultural material tantalizingly lacking from work in historical demography. In addition to culturally variable routine decision norms and logics (Leibenstein 1981), such a procedure will enable the investigator to identify crucial household decision points (see Ortiz 1973), moments that actors themselves regard as times of uncertainty and choice, when routine decision procedures must be set aside in favor of conscious evaluation of culturally defined goals and means and of surrounding conditions.

NOTES

1. This paper is a product of a study of household institutions and demography in rural India supported by a grant from the National Science Foundation (BNS 79-06854). Robert S. Merrill made a number of comments on an earlier draft which helped to clarify my thinking, and indeed many of the ideas in this paper are the fruit of a collaboration with him that began in 1975. I am indebted to him for his intellectual generosity.

2. Much of this section is adapted from Carter and Merrill (1979).

3. The echoes here of Parsons's (1949a:27–41) discussion of analysis are deliberate.

4. For a similar definition of the household dimension of domestic groups see Sharma (1980). For a review of the distinction between kinship and coresidence, including the work of Bender (1967), see Yanagisako (1979). Unlike Yanagisako, I

think it is important to distinguish as well between coresidence and task responsibility. As a general rule, I believe coresidence is a by-product of task-related activities rather than a goal in itself. A contrary view of coresidence is expressed by Verdon (1980) but without either significant supporting ethnographic detail or an informed awareness of the kind of difficulties in determining coresidence which are described by the contributors to this volume.

5. Seniority and other aspects of household position are not merely observers' constructs. Informants refer to them in accounting for the timing of marriages, partition disputes, aspects of address terminology, and so on.

6. Compare the approaches to Japanese population registers of T. C. Smith (1977) and R. J. Smith (1978). Where the latter focuses on type sequences, the former focuses on the dynamics of household management.

7. Fieldwork was conducted in Alandi in 1976 with support from the National Science Foundation (SOC74-19108).

8. For a fuller description of these records see Carter (1976).

9. On the dynamics of household partition in India see Carter (1971) and Parry (1979:150–94).

10. Additional examples of household event records, presented in different formats and lacking information on resources, may be found in Mitterauer and Sieder (1979) and in Wolf and Huang (1980).

11. Recent examples include Cohen (1976), Gudeman (1976), and Parry (1979).

12. See, for example, Freedman (1958:28ff and 1966:47ff) and Moynihan (1965).

13. See Parsons (1949*b*), Bailey (1957), and Epstein (1962).

14. Approaches of this sort have recently been criticized by Verdon (1980) on the specious grounds that no combination of rules and strategies can ever predict behavior. Verdon apparently confuses the statistical test of decision models with predictions of the behavior of particular individuals. As the simulation work of Wachter, Hammel, and Laslett (1978) demonstrates, our inability to do the latter has no bearing on the former. Verdon's alternative is the study of "criteria" of household membership discerned through the study of "pictograms" representing the links between each resident household member and the head, defined as the "person who is not there because of somebody else" (1980:125–28). Were he to stick to it, Verdon's alternative would be inadequate in almost every respect: assuming physical coresidence always to be determinant, equating household relations with the kinship links displayed in "pictograms," and ignoring cultural definitions of headship. But he does not stick to it, choosing instead to bring in through the back door such rules as "laws of devolution."

15. I owe my awareness of the latter point to Robert S. Merrill, but it also is stressed by Weiss (1976), Fallers (1965), Howell (1979), and Wachter, Hammel, and Laslett (1978:113–36).

REFERENCES

Arensberg, Conrad
1937 The Irish Countryman. New York: Peter Smith.

Bailey, F. G.
1957 Caste and the Economic Frontier. Manchester: Manchester University Press.

Bender, Donald R.
1967 A Refinement of the Concept of Household: Families, Co-residence, and Domestic Functions. American Anthropologist 69:493–504.

Berkner, Lutz
1972 The Stem-family and the Developmental Cycle of the Peasant Household: An Eighteenth-century Austrian Example. American Historical Review 77:398–418.
1976 Inheritance, Land Tenure, and Peasant Family Structure: A German Regional Comparison. *In* Family and Inheritance in Rural Western Europe 1200–1700, ed. J. Goody, J. Thirsk, and E. P. Thompson. Cambridge: Cambridge University Press.
1977 Peasant Household Organization and Demographic Change in Lower Saxony (1689–1766). *In* Population Patterns in the Past, ed. Ronald D. Lee. New York: Academic Press.

Bradley, Brian, and Franklin F. Mendels
1978 Can the Hypothesis of a Nuclear Family Organization Be Tested Statistically? Population Studies 32:381–94.

Braun, R.
1978 Protoindustrialization and Demographic Change in the Canton of Zurich. *In* Historical Studies of Changing Fertility, ed. C. Tilly. Princeton: Princeton University Press.

Buchler, I. R., and H. A. Selby
1968 Kinship and Social Organization. New York: Macmillan.

Burch, T. K.
1967 The Size and Structure of Families. American Sociological Review 32:347–63.

Burch, T. K., and M. Gendell
1971 Extended Family Structure and Fertility: Some Conceptual and Methodological Issues. *In* Culture and Population, ed. S. Polgar. Cambridge, Mass.: Schenkman.

Cain, Mead
1981 Risk and Fertility in India and Bangladesh. Population and Development Review 7:435–74.

Carter, Anthony T.
1971 Household Partition in Rural Western Maharashtra. Paper presented at the 70th Annual Meeting of the American Anthropological Association.
1976 Household and Demography: An Indian Case Study. Paper presented at the 75th Annual Meeting of the American Anthropological Association.

Carter, Anthony T., and Robert S. Merrill
1979 Household Institutions and Population Dynamics. Washington, D.C.: Agency for International Development.

Cassen, R. H.
1978 India: Population, Economy, Society. London: Macmillan.
Cohen, Myron
1976 House United, House Divided: The Chinese Family in Taiwan. New York: Columbia University Press.
Duncan, Greg J., and James N. Morgan, eds.
1976 Five Thousand American Families. Ann Arbor: Institute for Social Research, University of Michigan.
Epstein, T. Scarlett
1962 Economic Development and Social Change in South India. Manchester: Manchester University Press.
Fallers, Lloyd A.
1965 The Range of Variation in Actual Family Size: A Critique of Marion J. Levy, Jr.'s Argument. *In* Aspects of the Analysis of Family Structure, ed. A. Coale et al. Princeton: Princeton University Press.
Firth, Raymond
1936 We, the Tikopia. London: George Allen and Unwin.
1959 Social Change in Tikopia. London: George Allen and Unwin.
Firth, Rosemary
1966 Housekeeping among Malay Peasant (orig. ed. 1943). London: The Athlone Press.
Fjellman, Stephen M.
1977 The Akamba Domestic Cycle as Markovian Process. American Ethnologist 4:699–713.
Flandrin, Jean-Louis
1976 Families in Former Times. Translated by R. Southern. Cambridge: Cambridge University Press.
Forde, Daryll
1951 Marriage and the Family among the Yako in South-eastern Nigeria. London: The International African Institute.
Fortes, Meyer
1949*a* Time and Social Structure: An Ashanti Case Study. *In* Social Structure, ed. M. Fortes. Oxford: Oxford University Press.
1949*b* The Web of Kinship among the Tallensi. London: Oxford University Press.
Foster, Brian L.
1975*a* Continuity and Change in Rural Thai Family Structure. Journal of Anthropological Research 31:34–50.
1975*b* Domestic Developmental Cycles as a Link between Population Processes and Other Social Processes. Paper presented at the 74th Annual Meeting of the American Anthropological Association.
1976 Socio-economic Determinants of Stem Family Composition as Mediated by Population Processes. Paper presented at the 75th Annual Meeting of the American Anthropological Association.
1977 Variation in Thai Family Composition. Paper presented at the 76th Annual Meeting of the American Anthropological Association.

Freedman, Maurice
1958 Lineage Organization in Southeastern China. London: The Athlone Press.
1966 Chinese Lineage and Society: Fukien and Kwangtung. London: The Athlone Press.
Geogheghan, W. H.
1969 Decision-making and Residence on Tagtabon Island. Language Behavior Research Laboratory; Working Paper no. 17. Berkeley: University of California.
Goody, Jack
1958 The Fission of Domestic Groups among the LoDagaba. *In* The Domestic Cycle in Domestic Groups, ed. J. Goody. Cambridge Papers in Social Anthropology, no. 1. Cambridge: Cambridge University Press.
1976 Production and Reproduction. Cambridge: Cambridge University Press.
Goody, Jack, and J. Buckley
1973 Inheritance and Women's Labour in Africa. Africa 73:108–21.
Gray, Robert F.
1964 Introduction. *In* The Family Estate in Africa, ed. R. F. Gray and P. H. Gulliver. London: Routledge and Kegan Paul.
Gray, Robert F., and P. H. Gulliver, eds.
1964 The Family Estate in Africa. London: Routledge and Kegan Paul.
Gudeman, Steven
1976 Relationships, Residence, and the Individual: A Rural Panamanian Community. Minneapolis: University of Minnesota Press.
Gulliver, P. H.
1955 The Family Herds. London: Routledge and Kegan Paul.
Guyer, Jane I.
1980 Food, Cocoa, and the Division of Labor by Sex in Two West African Societies. Comparative Studies in Society and History 22:355–73.
Halpern, Joel M., and Barbara K. Halpern
1972 A Serbian Village in Historical Perspective. New York: Holt, Rinehart and Winston.
Hammel, E. A.
1961 The family cycle in a coastal Peruvian Slum and Village. American Anthropologist 63:989–1005.
1980 Household Structure in Fourteenth-century Macedonia. Journal of Family History 5:242–73.
Hammel, E. A., D. W. Hutchinson, K. W. Wachter, R. T. Lundy, and R. T. Deuel
1976 The SOCSIM Demographic-Sociological Microsimulation Program. Institute for International Studies Research Series, no. 27. Berkeley: University of California.
Hill, Polly
1975 The West African Farming Household. *In* Changing Social Structure in Ghana, ed. J. Goody. London: International African Institute.

Howell, Nancy
1979 Demography of the Dobe !Kung. New York: Academic Press.
Keesing, R. M.
1970 Kwaio Fosterage. American Anthropologist 72:991–1019.
Kitaoji, H.
1971 The Structure of the Japanese Family. American Anthropologist 73: 1036–57.
Kolenda, Pauline
1968 Region, Caste, and Family Structure: A Comparative Study of the Indian "Joint" Family. *In* Structure and Change in Indian Society, ed. M. Singer and B. S. Cohn. Viking Fund Publication, no. 47. Chicago: Aldine.
Kunstadter, Peter
1972 Demography, Ecology, Social Structure, and Settlement Patterns. *In* The Structure of Human Populations, ed. G. A. Harrison and A. J. Boyce. Oxford: Claredon Press.
Kuznesof, Elizabeth Anne
1980 Household Composition and Headship as Related to Changes in Modes of Production: São Paulo 1765 to 1836. Comparative Studies in Society and History 22:78–107.
Laslett, Peter
1972 Introduction. *In* Household and Family in Past Time, ed. P. Laslett and R. Wall. Cambridge: Cambridge University Press.
Leibenstein, H.
1981 Economic Decision Theory and Fertility Behavior. Population and Development Review 7:381–400.
Mamdani, M.
1972 The Myth of Population Control. New York: Monthly Review Press.
Medick, H.
1976 The Proto-industrial Family Economy. Social History 3:291–315.
Mendels, Franklin F.
1978 Notes on the Age of Maternity. Journal of Family History 3:236–50.
Mitterauer, Michael, and Reinhard Sieder
1979 The Developmental Process of Domestic Groups: Problems of Reconstruction and Possibilities of Interpretation. Journal of Family History 4:257–84.
Moynihan, Daniel P.
1965 The Negro Family: The Case for National Action. Washington, D.C.: U.S. Government Printing Office.
Murdock, William
1980 The Poverty of Nations. Baltimore: Johns Hopkins University Press.
Nag, Moni, B. N. F. White, and R. C. Peet
1978 An Anthropological Approach to the Study of the Economic Value of Children in Java and Nepal. Current Anthropology 19:293–306.

Oppong, Christine
1976 Ghanaian Household Models: Data for Processing by the New Home Economists of the Developing World. Paper read at the seminar Household Models of Economic and Demographic Decision-Making, Mexico City, IUSSP Committee on Economics.
1978 Household Economic and Demographic Decision-making: Introductory Statement. IUSSP Conference Proceedings, Helsinki.
Ortiz, S. R.
1973 Uncertainties in Peasant Farming. London: The Athlone Press.
Otterbein, K. F.
1970 The Developmental Cycle of the Andros Household: A Diachronic Analysis. American Anthropologist 72:1412–1419.
Otterbein, K. F., and Charlotte S. Otterbein
1977 A Stochastic Process Analysis of the Developmental Cycle of the Andros Household. Ethnology 16:415–26.
Parry, J. P.
1979 Caste and Kinship in Kangra. London: Routledge and Kegan Paul.
Parsons, T.
1949*a* The Structure of Social Action. New York: The Free Press.
1949*b* The Social Structure of the Family. *In* The Family, ed. R. Anshen. New York: Harper and Row.
Plume, Maguerite M.
1974 The Structure of Household. Ph.D. Dissertation, University of Rochester.
Rheubottom, David
1971 A Structural Analysis of Conflict and Cleavage in Macedonian Domestic Groups. Ph.D. Dissertation, University of Rochester.
Royal Anthropological Institute of Great Britain and Ireland
1959 Notes and Queries in Anthropology. 6th ed. London: Routledge and Kegan Paul.
Segalen, Martine
1977 The Family Cycle and Household Structure: Five Generations in a French Village. Journal of Family History 2:223–36.
Shah, A. M.
1974 The Household Dimension of the Family in India. Berkeley, Los Angeles, London: University of California Press.
Sharma, Ursula M.
1977 Migration from an Indian Village: An Anthropological Study. Sociologia Ruralis 17:282–304.
1980 Women, Work, and Property in North-west India. London: Tavistock.
Smith, R. J.
1978 The Domestic Cycle in Japan. Journal of Family History 3:219–35.
Smith, T. C.
1977 Nakahara. Stanford: Stanford University Press
Stenning, D. J.
1958 Household Viability among the Pastoral Fulani. *In* The Developmental

Cycle in Domestic Groups, ed. J. Goody. Cambridge Papers in Social Anthropology, no. 1. Cambridge: Cambridge University Press.

Taeuber, Irene B.
1970 The Families of Chinese Farmers. *In* Family and Kinship in Chinese Society, ed. M. Feedman. Stanford: Stanford University Press.

Tait, David
1956 The Family, Household and Minor Lineage of the Konkomba. Africa 26:219–49, 332–41.

Tilly, Charles
1978 The Historical Study of Vital Processes. *In* Historical Studies of Changing Fertility, ed. C. Tilly. Princeton: Princeton University Press.

Tilly, Louise A., and Joan W. Scott
1978 Women, Work and Family. New York: Holt, Rinehart and Winston.

Vatuk, Sylvia
1972 Kinship and Urbanization. Berkeley, Los Angeles, London: University of California Press.

Verdon, Michel
1980 Shaking Off the Domestic Yoke, or the Sociological Significance of Residence. Comparative Studies in Society and History 22:109–32.

Wachter, K. W., E. A. Hammel, and P. Laslett
1978 Statistical Studies of Historical Social Structure. New York: Academic Press.

Weiss, Kenneth M.
1976 Demographic Theory and Anthropological Inference. Annual Reviews of Anthropology 5:351–82.

White, Douglas R.
1973 Mathematical Anthropology. *In* Handbook of Social and Cultural Anthropology, ed. J. Honigman. Chicago: Rand McNally.

Wolf, Arthur P., and Chieh-shan Huang
1980 Marriage and Adoption in China, 1845–1945. Stanford: Stanford University Press.

Wrigley, E. A.
1966 Family Reconstitution. *In* An Introduction to Historical Demography, ed. D. E. C. Eversley et al. London: Weidenfeld and Nicolson.

Wyon, John B., and John E. Gordon
1971 The Khanna Study. Cambridge, Mass.: Harvard University Press.

Yanagisako, Sylvia J.
1979 Family and Household: The Analysis of Domestic Groups. Annual Reviews of Anthropology 8:161–206.

4

Family Structure and the Generation of Thai Social Exchange Networks

Brian L. Foster

A common approach to studying household composition is to examine different ways in which nuclear families are tied together or truncated to form households. The close analytical relationship between family structure, demographic processes, and postmarital residence rules provides a natural reference point for studying change and variation in household composition or household structure, in some cases leading to a very detailed understanding of the social mechanisms by which changes occur. Just as families can be combined to study the structure of larger domestic units, families and/or households might be combined to form still larger social units. In a general way this kind of procedure is not unusual in anthropology, where social structure frequently has been characterized in terms of relationships between smaller constituent units such as lineages and clans. Formal attempts to characterize households in this way have been rare, however, and almost completely descriptive. Nevertheless, household structure may provide a way of linking small-scale sociocultural processes to global structural properties of communities, in much the same way that family composition mediates between postmarital residence and demographic processes on the one hand and household composition on the other.

Such an approach to communitywide social structure poses serious methodological problems. One of the most difficult arises from the variety and complexity of large structures and the resulting difficulty in characterizing them in productive ways. The multiplicity of large structures contrasts sharply with household structures, whose variety and complexity are relatively narrowly limited, making it possible to characterize them economically. In fact, it has been possible to construct an inventory of discrete household structures which more or less effectively captures the full range of variation (for example, Hammel and Laslett 1974) and which has provided insights that have led to more interesting models exemplified in this volume. Although the full range of variation in properties of large structures is far too complex to yield to such straightforward enumeration, it is possible to approximate this kind of capability using recently developed social network methods. Whatever method we may use to characterize global structure, that method must be capable of representing a broad array of different types of domestic units and must illuminate the analytical relationships between household structure and the broader global structure.

My specific objective in this paper is to use results from recent social network research to explore the relationship between household structure and community structure. Although many of the issues I address have more general impact, my analysis will be concerned with Thai ethnographic materials, and I will conclude with a discussion of field data recently collected in a small village about 40 miles north of Bangkok.[1]

ETHNOGRAPHY OF THAI FAMILY AND HOUSEHOLD STRUCTURE

Thailand provides an ideal ethnographic case for investigating the relationship between household and community structure since more traditional approaches to Thai society have not yielded very satisfactory results. The difficulties seem to be far more extreme than those routinely faced in peasant communities. The Thai show little interest in kinship in the more standard ways; it is not unusual to find people who do not know the names of their grandparents, for instance, and who may not even know the names of their deceased parents or siblings. In much of the country communities do not provide good natural units, since settlements are often dispersed in the fields or stretch along rivers and canals. Buddhist temples (*wat*) sometimes provide some focus for social organization, but this too is variable. Some otherwise more or less natural communities have no *wat*, while others may have more than one; the abbot may be strong and influential or he may be ineffective. In short, the *wat*'s influence may range from very strong to negligible. In most places there are few community rituals or cooperative work projects (the government generally maintains irrigation facilities, for instance), and the administrative hamlets and subdistricts established by the government tend to correspond rather badly with whatever natural community boundaries do exist. There are no voluntary associations, ritual kinship, or formal social control mechanisms (for example, the blood feud)—in short, few of the well-known features of social organization found elsewhere in the world.

The upshot of these discouraging conditions is that little research has focused directly on Thai social structure. Perhaps the most influential contribution to the subject is John Embree's (1950) characterization of Thai society as "loosely structured," by which he meant that a great deal of variation in individual behavior is sanctioned. Although this essentially negative idea has recently fallen from favor, it has colored research in Thailand for 30 years, giving researchers a charter to attribute their failure to find regularities in social behavior to "loose structure." To this day Thailand remains a "problem case" in world ethnography.

One topic that has yielded results is that of family and household structure, which has captured the interest of many researchers (Keyes 1975; Piker n.d.; Mizuno 1971; S. H. Potter 1977; J. Potter 1976; Foster 1975, 1977, 1978*a*, *b*). There is general agreement that the household has an important place in Thai society, partly because rice production, the backbone of the Thai society, is primarily a domestic enterprise. Most labor is mobilized within the family/household unit except during transplanting and harvesting periods, and even then it is the domestic units that exchange and hire labor that cannot be provided from within. Domestic units are also consumption units, whose members often manage resources jointly. In many ceremonial activities households are important organizational units, and they play an important part in Thai informal "social security" networks.

In addition to a concern with Thai household and family structure as such, much of the literature on Thai domestic units strains toward the global structural perspective I wish to address here. The topic has been raised in a particularistic way, however, without considering the formal methodological or theoretical problems that must be solved to make the approach generally useful (see Mizuno 1971, however, for a partial exception). Before turning to my own analysis, I will put these specific methodological and theoretical issues in sharper focus by examining three ethnographic works that suggest ways that Thai domestic units combine to form larger structures.

Although there is much variation among Thai households, virtually all investigators agree on the essentials of the domestic development cycle, which constitutes a stem family system. Ideally, sons move to their wives' parents' houses and daughters remain in their own parents' house after marriage. Before a second daughter marries, the first must establish a separate household, nearby if that is possible (see Keyes 1976; Piker n.d.; Mizuno 1971; Foster 1975, 1978*a*,*b*). Various contingencies may of course arise—for instance, no daughters may be born to a couple, or an unmarried child may stay in the parents' household—but most produce straightforward transformations of the basic cycle. Although there is some terminological confusion, in all the discussions cited nuclear families often combine to form households consisting of coresidents in the same house.

With regard to building on the basic family cycle to construct larger structures, several common themes also emerge, but important differences occur, too. The most straightforward extension is described almost identically by Keyes (1976) and Mizuno (1971), who, however, use different terminology. In each case the unit is a kind of agricultural cooperative in which several families exchange labor and share tools and other resources. Such units grow out of the domestic development cycle and consist of the parents' (stem) family and the families of married daughters who have established independent households inside or outside the physical boundary of the parents' compound. At the death of the parents and distribution of the parents' land, the agricultural cooperative unit splits and the different households separate and form independent domestic units. The cooperative units therefore last but a single generation, unlike the stem family, which in some sense maintains continuity through several generations. This simple extension of the basic stem family development cycle in itself does not go far toward generating global structure and is easily accommodated in the general notion of domestic unit, creating a kind of "superhousehold."

Keyes (1976) carries this line of reasoning further, noting that the "superhouseholds" are the constituent units of the *wat* community and are also the units represented at "town meetings." Here we have a communitywide structure composed of domestic units. Moreover, Keyes says that the villagers themselves seem to see their village at least partly in these terms, suggesting that this formulation may be important in villagers' understanding of their social environment and that norms may be couched in terms of such a global structure.

Piker (n.d.), again beginning from the basic family development cycle, makes an extension that is similar to and in some ways more complex than Keyes's "domestic units." He defines units (which he calls "kindreds") that are composed of the households formed as a result of the removed residence pattern and the stem family development cycle (that is, a husband and wife with their married daughters' families, some of which live in separate households). He then goes on to describe patterns found in various kinds of aid exchanges between households within the kindreds, including "exchanges of resources and assistance (such as interest-free cash loans, loans of rice and work animals, assistance with farm work and other labor, and often exchange of cooked food at meal times if comembers reside in the same neighborhoods or neighboring compounds)" (Piker n.d.:102). That the kindreds arise from operation of the family development cycle is all the more interesting because Piker characterizes them more or less independently in terms of aid and other exchanges (for example, as clusters of households linked by exchange relationships). Moreover, Piker defines different kinds of kindreds on the basis of their internal structure; he classifies them as "hierarchical" and "sibling" kindreds, tying the exchange relationships between households directly to the development cycle.

In addition, Piker notes that an individual and presumably, by implication, an individual family may be a member of more than one kindred. This structure is similar to Keyes's "*wat* community" insofar as it incorporates an entire community in a single global structure. The point is rather similar to that made by Keyes, who explains that although people use kin networks for aid, the recruitment principle is previous coresidence in the same domestic unit. Both Keyes's principle and Piker's idea of global extension differ from the "*wat* community" idea or the "town meeting" idea by specifying a relation to tie households together to form larger units.

Mizuno (1971) suggests one final kind of extension of the basic domestic cycle. He says the Thai group of kin called *phi naung* is basically a bilateral kindred (using the term differently than Piker does) consisting of all the descendants of four grandparents and their siblings. The members of this set of individuals provide a resource for an ego (the person whose grandparents define the set) when ego needs "assistance at various stages in life cycle, cooperative works, exchange of labour, or visiting and traveling" (1971:99)—a list of relations similar to those associated with Piker's kindred. The notion of *yad phi naung* introduces the family again since this new set is likely "to include immediate family members of the bilateral kinsmen" (1971:99). Mizuno does not try to combine kindreds to build larger structures. It is often said that ego-centered bilateral units such as kindreds overlap and thus give rise to complicated structures. This is a gross understatement of the complexities of the matter, however, for to understand aggregate structures composed of several kindreds one would have to consider not just overlap but also the kinds and degree of overlap and other relationships between various emergent units (such as families) and individuals. The amount of information needed and the complexity of the processing would be simply overwhelming, not just for analysts but probably also for the actors themselves.

An important but rather obscure point in all of this is that where there is coresidence, the coresident units are often regarded as internally undifferentiated and used to construct larger structures. We see this most clearly in the combination of "households" to form Keyes's "domestic units," Mizuno's "multi-household compounds," and Piker's "kindreds." Beyond that we see this presumption of internal homogeneity in the use of these larger units to form global structures—for example, the *wat* community and the suggested overlap structure composed of Piker's kindreds. In the households themselves and in the large kindreds described by Mizuno, the Thai maintain the internal structure of the family in all of its detail, and this is recognized by the ethnographers. We find no suggestion that either families or kindreds be put together to form structures larger than households. For kindreds we've seen that to do so would give rise to impossibly complex structures. It is possible to maintain the internal structure of families that combine to form households only because the size and consequent complexity of the larger units are severely limited by coresidence (or a normative image of it). All of this suggests that we might see coresidence (or some ideal of it) as providing a natural way of translating relationally defined units such as households into something more manageable for constructing communitywide structure.

Although these observations are suggestive, we are still left with the question of how to synthesize these various ways of constructing global structure out of family or household units. We are faced with two types of problem. First, there are the methodological problems mentioned above, which can now be stated more concretely. The arguments in the ethnographic discussions of social structure are all carried out in a kinship idiom. Although this is illuminating as far as it goes, it is not adequate to accommodate all elements. Aid relations, coresidence, and other nonkin elements can be included in the formulation only nominally or in an ad hoc way. It is precisely the relationship between nonkin relations and kinship that we wish to investigate, but to do so requires that they be represented independently and in a form that allows comparison. In a similar vein, we lack a vocabulary to characterize the structure of emergent larger units (such as Piker's kindreds) and global structures (such as the *wat* community). We do not have so much as a language to discuss the analytical relationships between household and community structure. Second, we do not have at hand a theoretical position that will accommodate the diverse types of aggregate domestic structures and bring them into a single argument with some explanatory or at least interpretive power.

A NETWORK APPROACH TO EXTENDING THE DOMESTIC DOMAIN

How can we represent the various properties of families, households, larger social structures, and the relations between them in a way that allows us to investigate variation in global structure productively? One strategy is to regard all the various kinds of domestic units as potentially present in one degree or other in all villages. We can then investigate the ways the domestic units are linked by different kinds of relations, and we can examine their structural importance to the larger society. From a structural perspective at least three basic elements must be present in any analytical scheme that will accomplish those ends.

First, we need a general way of representing all of the various kinds of domestic units. We can do this by recognizing that all domestic units are composed of smaller units. Families and households are composed of individuals, for instance, but sets of families may be seen as comprising households, households as comprising larger domestic units, and so on. The most straightforward way to represent these units is as graphs—that is, as sets of points, some or all of which are connected by lines (Harary 1969; Foster and Seidman 1981, in press). The constituent parts are represented by the points and the relationships between the parts by lines. The internal structure of the units—the configuration of points and lines—may vary considerably and can be characterized in graph theoretic terms. One type of graph, which will be of interest later, is one in which every point is connected by a line to every other. Such units are internally undifferentiated and therefore have little structural interest, since all such units of the same size are identical. This being the case, little structural information is lost by reducing each such unit to a single point. This type of unit, called a "complete graph," provides a natural way of representing categories, for example, individuals who have the same occupation or who live in the same house.[2] Other kinds of units are more diverse internally and contain more "structural information," much of which would be lost by reducing them to points (Foster and Seidman, in press).

The second element necessary in the analytic scheme is the ability to represent relationships between units, such as relationships between families or households. Like the units themselves, relationships can be represented in graph form with lines representing the relationships. This kind of representation is useful, since it can accommodate any well-defined relation, and unlike the kinship idiom of most structural analysis in anthropology there is no difficulty in accommodating friendship, labor exchange, or other relations along with kinship. The generality of this kind of notation is also its weakness, however, since there are no inherent constraints on the kinds of patterns that can be produced or on the ways these patterns can be transformed or combined. The kinship mode of analysis is of interest precisely because the logic of human reproduction provides such constraints, thus limiting the kinds of patterns that can be produced. For instance, families have their characteristic structure partly because a man cannot be his own son and because men don't marry their brothers. The presence of these constraints in kinship gives rise to a natural, if primitive, computational facility for structural analysis. The utility of such constraints is in many ways analogous to "constraints" on certain arithmetic operations; the notion *is greater than* is useful because not all numbers are greater than, say, five. Identifying such natural constraints is necessary if the graph theoretic approach is to be useful beyond providing notation.

The third element necessary to the analytical scheme is the identification of useful, well-defined transformations of graphs. One simple kind of transformation of graphic structures suggested by the Thai material is what Foster and Seidman (in press; 1981) have called "reduction," in which structural units of a specified form (for example, maximal complete subgraphs)[3] are reduced to points, and some relation on the original set of points is used to induce a new graph on the set of new points. For example, suppose we have two graphs, the lines of one representing friendship relations between members of a village, and the lines of the second representing siblingship. We could identify cliques (maximal complete subgraphs) in this friendship graph. Each clique could be "reduced" to a point and a new graph made of these points, with a line linking any two cliques with members who are siblings, thus producing a graph of cliques linked by sibling ties. This seems to be exactly the sort of transformation Keyes suggests when he says that the *wat* community is comprised of domestic units: the domestic units could be represented as points, and this collection of points represents the *wat* community. What is lacking in Keyes's suggestion is any sense of the relationships between units, for presumably the "community" is more than a set of units but is a set of units connected by various relationships. Similarly, Keyes's "domestic units" can be represented as reduced graphs; the basic structural units that are reduced to points are households (sets of people living in the same house), and in this case he also gives us information on the kinds of relations that link the constituent units—relations of joint agricultural production.

These reductions are analytically productive because there is ethnographic justification for making them; the people themselves in a sense make the reduction and presumably act accordingly in some measurable degree. In contrast, neither Piker, Mizuno, nor Keyes gives us ethnographic justification for collapsing the families that constitute a household to undifferentiated points. Families are units in a kind of generative sense, but they do not function as undifferentiated units. In any case reduction of this kind would result in a loss of structural information which does not occur when reducing households defined (in analysis or in the natives' cultural constructions) as coresidence units. Despite Piker's interest in the internal structure of his kindreds, he states that individuals may be members of different kindreds and thereby suggests a reduced-graph approach to linking the kindreds. In this case information on the internal structure of the units is lost, but he seems to suggest that for at least some purposes the loss is unimportant.[4]

For our present purposes three general points emerge from this brief discussion of network methods. First, the graph theoretic representation allows us to represent any kind of unit and any kind of relationship between units. Second, the reduction process provides a way of translating relationships between individuals, households, or other units into analytically useful representations of larger social structures such as communities. The reduced graph then becomes the object of structural analysis. Third, the analytical usefulness of any particular reduction depends on the choice of units and of relations, which must be ethnographically and theoretically justified. We have seen that Thai ethnography provides a charter for some reductions but not others.

Regardless of how effective this method might be, variation in possible community structures is great. A structural fishing expedition is unlikely to succeed in the absence of theoretical ideas to guide the choice of structural units and relations and help interpret their relationship to global (that is, communitywide) structures. Several features of Thai society suggest that "collectivistic" (Ekeh 1974) exchange theory associated with the work of Levi-Strauss (1949), Sahlins (1965), and others would be particularly promising (Foster, in press). On the one hand, exchange theory is well suited for the kind of analysis proposed here, since it deals with discrete structures. On the other hand, many important Thai social relations, both between individuals and between domestic units, are explicitly couched in terms of exchange: labor exchange, aid, ceremonial exchanges.

There seem to me to be three relevant ideas in the structural exchange literature. One concerns the degree to which properties of a given global structure are sustained through time. In Levi-Strauss's (1949) theory the question concerns a contrast between matrilateral and patrilateral cross-cousin marriage. The general question for our purposes is whether different kinds of households and related sociocultural practices produce analogous continuity and discontinuity. Second is the question of whether characteristic structures are hierarchical or egalitarian. Closely related is the notion of structural centrality (Freeman 1977). The third concerns the degree to which equivalences in exchange are reckoned to achieve direct balance or to achieve indirect, perhaps long-term, and even rather abstract, conceptual balance. Joining all three of these ideas are theoretical linkages, which are beyond the scope of the present discussion. Although all of these ideas can be seriously questioned, they have sufficient intuitive validity to excite a great deal of interest from anthropologists of various theoretical persuasions and with various topical interests, and I have used them here to guide my examination of data from a small Thai village.

SOCIAL STRUCTURE OF THA SUNG

Tha Sung was once both a "natural" village unit and a government administrative unit. About 40 years ago, however, boundaries of administrative hamlets were adjusted and the village was consolidated with a larger, neighboring village called Ban Klang to form Hamlet no. 2 in subdistrict Ban Ngiw. Although the two villages now form a single administrative unit, there is little else to unite them socially. The people of Tha Sung are ethnically Thai while those of Ban Klang are Mon; those of Tha Sung go to a Thai *wat* called Wat Paa Ngiw while those of Ban Klang attend a Mon *wat* called Wat Song Phii Nong.[5] A sidewalk runs the entire length of Ban Klang from Wat Song Phii Nong to the border of Tha Sung, where it stops short. There is little social interaction between the two villages—few friendships, few marriages, and little participation in each other's ceremonies.

This extreme segregation is surprising, since the administrative hamlets do have significant political, economic, and health-care functions that give people common interests. Moreover, Tha Sung and Ban Klang do form a single continuous settlement. Although the children go to different primary schools (one at Wat Song Phii Nong and one at Wat Paa Ngiw), they go to the same secondary school, which is located adjacent to Tha Sung. None of this translates into significant interpersonal relationships between members of Tha Sung and Ban Klang. Tha Sung has retained its identity, suggesting the presence of a relatively strong, solidary social structure (cf. Kunstadter this volume).

Tha Sung village contains 15 houses and has a total population of 82. There are no unifying physical features such as sidewalks, and walking there sometimes is difficult. Occupationally the village is extremely diverse, with no less than 25 occupations (counting both husbands' and wives') among adults in the 15 houses; only three houses are engaged in rice farming. The modal category is "retired." In several families both the husband and wife were born and raised elsewhere. Wat Paa Ngiw is directly adjacent to, but not within, the village.

There are two serious departures from general Thai postmarital residence practices. First, the requirement that parents furnish land for their children is not generally applicable. Given that most families have independent incomes, there are economic advantages for several families to pool resources and live in the same house, and in some cases several married children do live with their parents. Second, the matrilocality rule is not carefully observed.

Given this ethnographic sketch of Tha Sung one would not expect to find Keyes's and Mizuno's multihousehold agricultural production units or, given the diversity of occupations, other kinds of multihousehold production units. Moreover, given the advantages for the formation of large households, the neolocal residence pattern that generates the Keyes and Mizuno units is attenuated. To define multifamily domestic units comparable to those described by Keyes and others, we will have to construct them of relations other than relations of production, and the domestic development cycle may play a secondary role. In short, to pursue this line of inquiry, we must carefully define some meaningful units and meaningful relations between them. These units will be *various kinds* of domestic units, and in keeping with the social exchange orientation outlined earlier, we will focus on two kinds of exchange relations.

Ten of the 15 households in Tha Sung consist of single nuclear families, while 5 are composed of 2 or more nuclear families.[6] All 5 multifamily units can be described completely by linking nuclear families together with descent ties. Exchange relations within the households show several structural regularities, one of which concerns aid relations. In our interviews the head of each nuclear family was asked to name persons from whom he or she would ask to borrow several thousand baht (1 baht = U.S. $0.05) in an emergency—for example, to pay medical expenses. Eight such aid choices were made within the households—at least one from each multifamily household—and each was directed to a member of an older generation. In every case where a member of the senior generation (either husband or wife) chose a person in Tha Sung, the choice was directed to the head of a multifamily unit. Clearly the internal structure of these units is hierarchical, at least as respects this aid relation.

Data on attendance at funerals shows a second, related feature. In three of the five multifamily units, people in the younger generation volunteered the information (no question of this sort was asked) that they relied on their parents to represent them at such affairs. In one household (O) no one went to any funerals. In the fifth (G) most responded either that they could not remember the names of the deceased whose funerals they attended or that they attended every funeral. Because both the husband and wife in the senior generation in this case were born in villages some distance away, it is conceivable that they attended few or no funerals within the village. Thus, though the data are far from conclusive, household units seem to be regarded by the villagers as functional units for attending funerals, but they are internally differentiated on the basis of kinship precisely to identify "representatives" at funerals.

Internal structure of the households is therefore clearly sociologically important—even in relations between units. It is equally clear that even in this tiny village the overall structure would become impossibly complex if we tried to define it while maintaining all the internal structure of the households and families. To so define them would be tantamount to "adding" households, families, and aid and funeral-attendance relations to a kinship chart for the entire village. Conceived in this way, the structure would be far too complex to be of analytical utility and would probably be too complex for the villagers themselves to understand as a coherent community structure.

We can achieve dramatic simplification if we adopt the reduction strategy discussed above. The first step is to redefine the domestic units to eliminate internal structure, thus giving us a charter to reduce them to points and form a reduced graph. Redefining the household as a coresidential unit is straightforward and seems justified both by the general Thai ethnography that I briefly described above and by my own data. We must also choose an appropriate relation for the reduced graph, which must be induced by some relation or relations plus this new set of points. This new graph or graphs will now become our representation of global structure.

An obvious prospect for this kind of reduction is the aid relation, which represents a kind of indirect reciprocity with solidarity (for example, see Sahlins 1965). Strong, connected substructures in the graph of this relation should represent aid units not unlike Piker's kindreds, though such units would be weaker because of the intermittent extension of aid compared with more regular exchanges in production activities.

Figure 4.1A shows the aid network for Tha Sung, where the circles represent coresident units. If we disregard the direction of the arrows, we see only one maximal complete subgraph larger than two points (L,M,N)

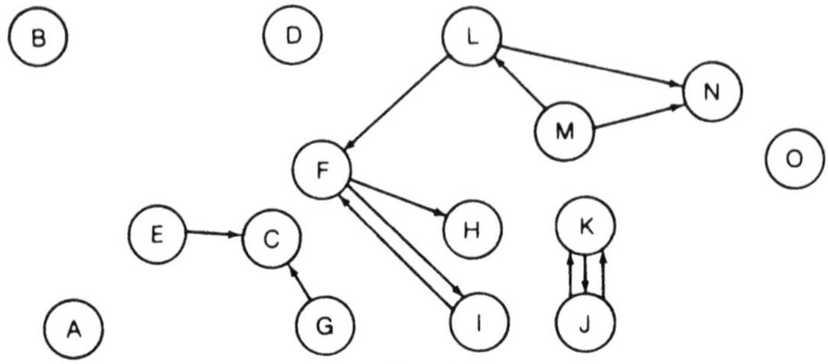

Fig. 4.1*a*

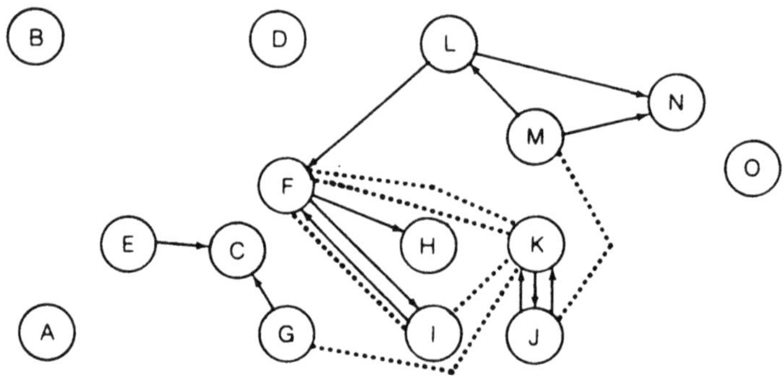

Fig. 4.1*b*

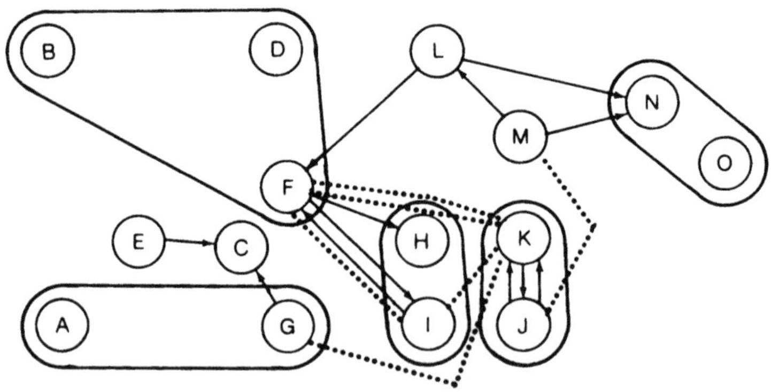

Fig. 4.1*c*

Figure 4.1A shows aid choices concerning persons from whom villagers could borrow money. The circles represent households—i.e., coresidence units. Figure 4.1B adds the relation on coattendance at the same funeral (represented by dotted lines). Figure 4.1C adds information on the kin groupings based on current or prior coresidence in the same family; each unit is encircled. The units containing E, I, and K are also related but by more distant kinship ties. B was not interviewed.

Fig. 4.1
Aid, Attendance at Funerals, and Kinship in Tha Sung

plus six consisting of two points—clearly not a very interesting structure. We might "weaken" the completeness criterion in a controlled way in an attempt to identify larger units. One way of doing so is to search for two-plexes (Seidman and Foster 1978*a*,*b*), which are cliquelike units in which each point is connected to all but one other point. There are five two-plexes greater than two points (EGC, FHI, IFL, LMN, HFL) and one clique of two points (KJ). While this does produce units similar in a way to Piker's kindreds, it is still less than satisfying, since the units are small and for the most part are linked very tenuously. We might construct a reduced graph of the two-plexes, but there is neither ethnographic nor theoretical charter to do so. It is worth noting, however, that F seems to have a central position in this graph and unit LMN is the "strongest" unit with more than two elements.

The aid relation used here is, of course, a strong one, and we would not necessarily expect villagers to request aid from anyone in the absence of a strong personal relationship. We might therefore make our structure more dense by superimposing a somewhat weaker relationship of indirect reciprocity. Figure 4.1B shows the aid relation with added ties for coattendance at the same funeral within the past year. This is an important indirect reciprocity tie and is explicitly seen as such by the villagers, for people contribute money and/or labor to the occasion. In addition, coattendance reflects shared social interest and relationships and brings people together in face-to-face interaction. Although the residents of Tha Sung attended over 25 funerals in the past year, the overlap in attendance is surprisingly meager. Nevertheless, it casts new light on our aid structure by bringing together all the different aid units. More important, however, are the seemingly close ties of the units containing FI and the group KJ, suggesting that they may occupy a central position in the village exchange structure and weakening the importance of LMN and EGC.

Given this more interesting structure and the obvious close ties between aid, friendship, and kinship, we might well return to the kin relations and try to generate a graph resembling this composite aid structure. One obvious tactic is to begin with an idea suggested by Keyes—that the reduced graph be induced by the relation "has lived in the same family." This strategy makes good ethnographic sense because many aid choices are made within households, and we might expect to find that ties continue to be active after household fission. This procedure yields the result shown in figure 4.1C.

Five different kin groups emerge, spanning 11 of the 15 households in the village and leaving 4 households isolated. Of the 12 aid choices among the household units,[7] only 2 appear within these kin units (K and J choose each other, and even that is a special case, since J contains the families of a former wife, married child, and married granddaughter of the head of house K). The implication seems clear that at least the kin unit based on previous coresidence is of little importance to the aid network in Tha Sung. It is interesting to note, though, that the groups containing F, K, and I are related by more distant kin ties, forming a larger kin group that contains nearly half the households in the village and 3 of the 5 multifamily households.

The most striking feature of figure 4.1C is that the households joined strongly by the funeral relation are senior households in the large kin group—in a sense heads of the constituent kin units. This points not only to the considerable coherence of that set of kinsmen but also emphasizes its social separation from the rest of the households in Tha Sung. The latter point is further underscored by the nature of the two funeral relationships not in this group. G and K jointly attended a funeral in Ban Klang, which takes on significance in the light of the fact that most of the aid choices from G go to Ban Klang and that the head of K was headman of the consolidated Ban Klang/Tha Sung village for 40 years. The tie between J and M is a lateral tie between younger people, and M is a member of no kin group in the village.

Given the village's internal kinship and exchange structure, it would be satisfying if we could circumscribe it with one or more still weaker indirect reciprocity relations. We can do so by adding attendance at major ceremonial events (the traditional New Year and the beginning and end of Buddhist Lent) and coattendance at the same *wat*, all of which are indirect reciprocity relations, like funerals, though weaker. At this level the village is indeed seen as a unit, though still a weakly integrated one, and the social isolation of a small number of households is emphasized (fig. 4.2).

The question remains whether we can interpret these results in terms of the exchange-theory ideas with which we began. This is a difficult enterprise, since we have only a single, rather unusual village, but some observations can be made. The question of whether the structure is hierarchical can be answered affirmatively insofar as there are at least three levels of incorporation into the exchange system. Inspection of figure 4.1C shows that the large kinship grouping is the core of the village society and all else is peripheral. At the same time, within the large group both the pattern in the relations and the nature of the ties indicates that the senior families of the three subgroups form an inner core whose periphery is the remaining set of families within the group. This struc-

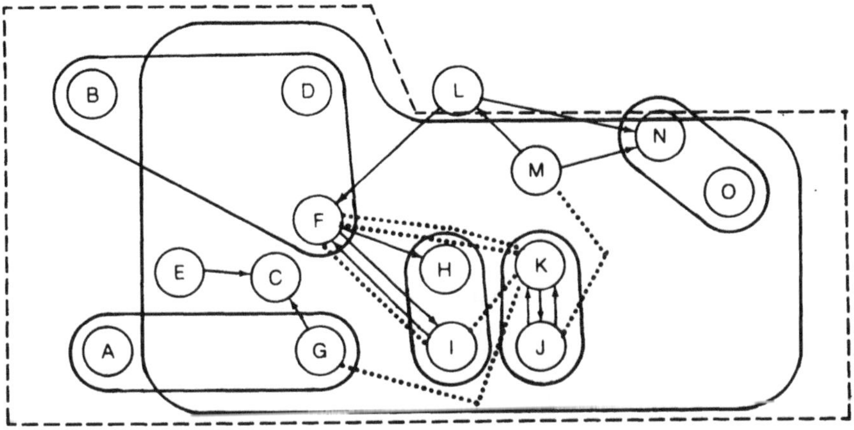

This figure is the same as figure 4.1C with three additions. The large kin group has been encircled. The line outlining the entire village except house L represents the relation "co-attendance at Wat Paa Ngiw"; the parallel line, which also excludes houses A and B, represents the relation "coattendance at major annual festivals" (traditional new year, beginning and end of Buddhist Lent). The position of house B is actually problematic, since the occupant was not interviewed.

Fig. 4.2
Exchange Structure of Tha Sung

tural hierarchy is informed by the fact that K is the former headman, I the subdistrict doctor, and F the owner of a substantial amount of land (40 *rai*) who plants yet an additional 20 *rai* (25 *rai* is a respectable holding).

Closely related to this informal notion of different levels of inclusion is the more formal notion of centrality in graphs, which illuminates several features of the network which are hard to see by informal inspection. One widely used concept of centrality is based on the intuitive idea of "betweenness" in a communication network. Points are central "to the degree that they stand *between* others and can therefore facilitate, impede or bias the transmission of messages" (Freeman 1977:36). A useful measure of betweenness-centrality has been proposed by Freeman (1977). By this measure K (the former headman) is by far the most central, with a centrality index of 25.5. F follows with an index of 17.5, and, perhaps surprisingly, G is next with a score of 16. G's high score results from E and C's dependence on him for their ties to the rest of the network. Other values are much lower than those of F, K, and G—7.5 for L, for instance, and 6.5 for J. I is particularly interesting. Although this household is strongly integrated into the structural core of the village by ties to both F and K, I has a betweenness-centrality of zero, since no two houses depend on I for their linkage.

Assessing the stability of the exchange structure through time is more complex. One approach might be to focus on the fact that stem families are in a sense corporate units with a life exceeding the lives of their individual members. One might expect to find lasting relationships between the units, much as among lineages in some unilineal societies. That does not seem to be the case. Although the exchange structure is firmly embedded in kinship relations in a general way, generating the inter-household structure from kin relations did not work. The lack of a determinate relationship between kin relations and exchange notwithstanding, the internal structure of the households changes during the domestic development cycle in such a way as to give the units different kinds of exchange relations with other units at different phases of the cycle. This is quite unlike the kinds of structures generated by lineages and similar units, which act as corporate units and also retain essential internal structural properties. We would not then expect to find any detailed, discrete structural properties of the reduced graphs which will remain constant if we make new observations in the future.

These inferences can be empirically observed by removing the most central households from the network. The heads of households F and K are both elderly men—aged 68 and 79, respectively—and their actual removal could occur in the near future. F lives with a married son and married daughter and their families, but neither child has any ties outside the house. K lives with his wife, all children having moved away. The effect of removing F (see fig. 4.3A) is to increase the centrality of K, G, and J. Removing K (fig. 4.3B) alters the structure dramatically: G is disconnected from the network and M becomes the most central household in the network. When both F and K are removed, the entire structure fragments into two small components and several isolated households. One can only conclude that the network is extremely fragile.

Finally, as I have noted repeatedly, these are indirect exchange relationships of the kind often said to foster solidarity. This is interesting because, for all the sparseness of the network, it is nonetheless true that the village of Tha Sung has retained its identity for a long period in the face of significant conditions for integration—even after incorporation into a consolidated administrative hamlet with Ban Klang. In view of the fragility of the network, this apparent solidarity has a questionable future.

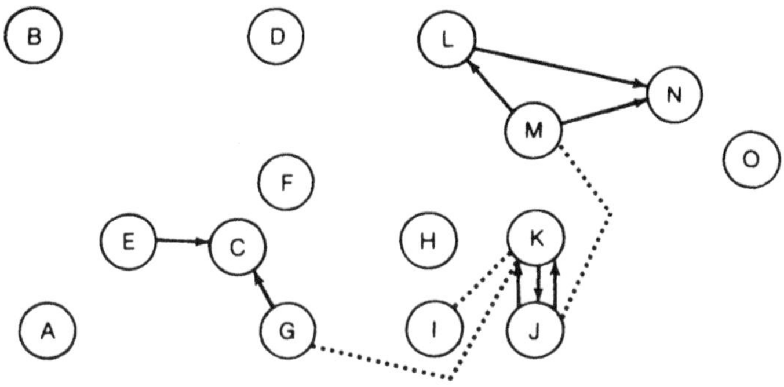

4.3A

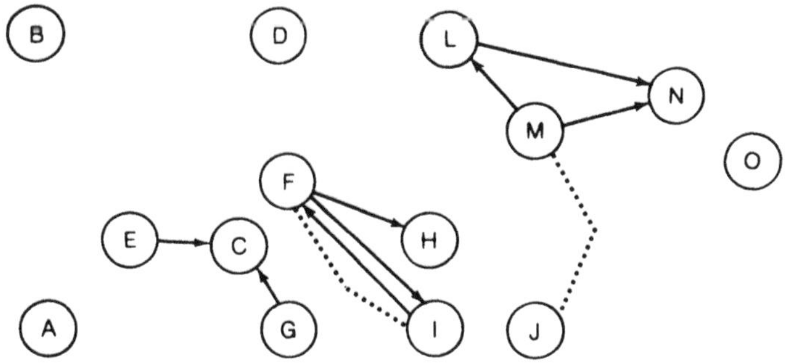

4.3B

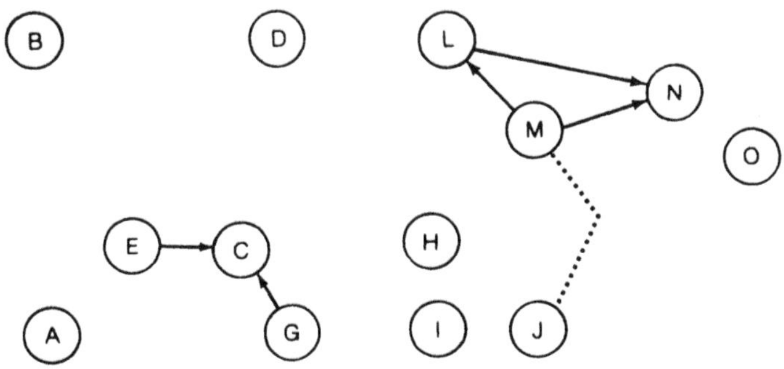

4.3C

Figure 4.3A shows the effects of removing house F from the network; the centrality of K, G, and J are increased. In figure 4.3B house K is removed, altering the structure more fundamentally. When both houses F and K are removed, the entire structure fragments (figure 4.3C).

Fig. 4.3
Effects of Removing Key Figures from the Exchange Network

CONCLUSION

My objective in this paper was to examine the ways in which domestic units combine to form larger social structures. This is an important and relatively neglected aspect of household and family structure. The topic raises difficult methodological and theoretical problems that I have addressed in terms of recent social network research. Analysis of Tha Sung data yields promising results, in view of the few and on the whole unsatisfying previous successes in the analysis of Thai village society. While the data analysis, theoretical formulation, and method all require a great deal of further development—I've scarcely begun to address the kinds of problems raised by Hammel's contribution to this volume—and while it would surely be an error to claim that all social organization can be accommodated by a scheme building on family and household structure, the issues addressed seem to have wide applicability in other Thai villages and outside Thailand. The mode of analysis adopted here is directly in the tradition of social structural analysis in anthropology. The significance of the results is largely that I am able to do in a Thai village a kind of structural analysis that has been so profitably done in other societies but which until now has yielded virtually no success in rural Thailand.

NOTES

1. The research on which this paper is based is still in progress under support from the National Science Foundation, Grant no. BNS-80 13507. The paper was written while fieldwork was still in progress, though data collection in Tha Sung was complete. Fieldwork began in early April and continued through most of August 1981. Some of the data were collected by general observation and extended interviews by myself, my Thai collaborator, Dr. Chavivun Prachuabmoh, and four research assistants. In addition, a set of more formal, censuslike interviews were conducted, which included a sociometric question on to whom one would turn to borrow money and other questions on cooperation and attendance at various ceremonies and other occasions. Our intent was to interview the head of every nuclear family in four villages with a long, censuslike schedule and to interview the spouse with a shorter instrument containing essentially the aid question and other items about ceremonial cooperation. In fact, some families in the village described here were not interviewed, either because someone was unwell (one person), uncooperative (one person), or unavailable when the interviewing was done (one family).

2. In this latter case the points would represent individuals who live in the house; the relation linking them would be defined as "coresidence in the same house." There would, of course, be other relationships—e.g., kinship—and the

household could be represented using these relations. In that case, the internal structure would likely be very different. The choice of relation depends on the investigator's analytical interests.

3. A maximal complete subgraph is a complete subgraph of a larger graph to which no other point can be added while still maintaining the property of "completeness." In figure 4.1A, for example, L,M,N, is a maximal complete subgraph since each point is directly tied to the other two and since that property would not be present should any other point be added. M,N is also a complete subgraph, but it is not maximal since L can be added and the resulting graph is still complete.

4. There are more complex kinds of reduction which make it possible to retain the internal structure of the units that have been reduced to points. More can be said about the relationships between the internal structure of the units and the properties of the graphs produced by the reduction process (Foster and Seidman 1981 and in press). These complexities are not pertinent to the analysis that follows except insofar as maintaining internal structure makes the resulting "total reduced graphs" extremely complex. If the constituent units are of any type other than complete subgraphs, the total reduced graphs may be highly variable in the sense that many nonisomorphic structures can be produced with the same units and same relationships by simply varying the way the internal structure is defined.

5. It should perhaps be noted that ethnic diversity of this kind is not unusual in Southeast Asia, and we should not make too much of its role in separating Ban Klang from Tha Sung. Since Leach's (1954) influential work in Highland Burma, it has been widely known that ethnicity does not set up barriers between social worlds in Southeast Asia but rather is an important organizing principle in much social organization (see Kunstadter's paper in this volume; also see Moerman 1965; Kirsch 1973; Kunstadter 1967; Golomb 1978; Keyes 1980; and Foster 1982 for other examples of the ethnic organization of society).

6. I use the term *nuclear family* here in a special way to include not only the sets of people (including father, mother, and children) but also any residual of such a set that has been diminished by death, by divorce, or by the children's growing up and leaving the family.

7. It should be noted that of 48 aid choices made by the heads of families and their spouses, more than half were made outside the village. This is, of course, extremely important, but I have not been able to take account of it in a systematic way here. For purposes of my analysis the distortions are minimal since the ties are extremely dispersed, and seldom if ever do members of two families choose the same person outside the village. Eight choices were made within the households, leaving only 12 among household units.

REFERENCES

Ekeh, Peter P.
1974 Social Exchange Theory: The Two Traditions. Cambridge: Harvard University Press.

Embree, John
1950 Thailand: A Loosely Structured Social System. American Anthropologist 52:181–93.
Foster, Brian L.
1975 Change and Continuity in Thai Family Structure. Journal of Anthropological Research 31:34–50.
1977 Social Organization of Four Mon and Thai Villages. New Haven, Conn.: HRAF Press, HRAFlex Books.
1978*a* Domestic Development Cycles as a Link between Population Processes and Other Social Processes. Journal of Anthropological Research 34:415–41.
1978*b* Socioeconomic Consequences of Stem Family Composition in a Thai Village. Ethnology 17:139–56.
1982 Commerce and Ethnic Differences. Papers in International Studies, Southeast Asia Series, no. 59. Athens: Ohio University.
In press An Exchange Network Approach to Thai Social Organization. To appear in a festschrift to Professor William Gedney. Ann Arbor: Michigan Papers on South and Southeast Asia.
Foster, Brian L., and Stephen B. Seidman
1978 SONET-I: Social Network Analysis and Modeling System. Vol. 1. User's Manual. Binghamton: State University of New York, Center for Social Analysis.
1981 Network Structure and Kinship Perspective. American Ethnologist 8:329–55.
1983 A Strategy for the Dissection and Analysis of Social Structures. Journal of Social and Biological Structure 6.
Freeman, Linton C.
1977 A Set of Measures of Centrality Based on Betweenness. Sociometry 40:35–41.
Golomb, Louis
1978 Brokers of Morality. Honolulu: University Press of Hawaii.
Hammel, E. A., and Peter Laslett
1974 Comparing Household Structure over Time and between Cultures. Comparative Studies in Society and History 16:73–109.
Harary, Frank
1969 Graph Theory. Reading, Mass.: Addison-Wesley.
Keyes, Charles
1975 Kin Groups in a Thai-Lao Community. *In* Change and Persistence in Thai Society, ed. G. W. Skinner and A. T. Kirsch, pp. 274–97. Ithaca: Cornell University Press.
Keyes, Charles, ed.
1980 Ethnic Adaptation and Identity: The Karen on the Thai Frontier with Burma. Philadelphia: ISHI Publications.
Kirsch, A. Thomas
1973 Feasting and Social Oscillation: Religion and Society in Upland South-

east Asia. Southeast Asia Program, Ithaca: Cornell University, Data Paper 92.

Kunstadter, Peter, ed.
1967 Southeast Asian Tribes, Minorities and Nations. 2 vols. Princeton: Princeton University Press.

Leach, E. R.
1954 Political Systems of Highland Burma. Cambridge: Harvard University Press.

Levi-Strauss, Claude
1949 Les Structures Élémentaires de la Parenté. Paris: Presses Universitaires de France.

Mizuno, Koichi
1971 The Social System of Don Daeng. Center for South East Asian Studies, Discussion Papers 12–22. Kyoto: Kyoto University.

Moerman, Michael
1965 Ethnic Identification in a Complex Civilization: Who Are the Lue? American Anthropologist 67:1215–30.

Piker, Stephen
n.d. A Peasant Community in Changing Thailand. Manuscript.

Potter, Jack
1976 Thai Peasant Social Structure. Chicago: University of Chicago Press.

Potter, Sulamith Heins
1977 Family Life in a Northern Thai Village. Berkeley, Los Angeles, London: University of California Press.

Sahlins, Marshall
1965 On the Sociology of Primitive Exchange. *In* The Relevance of Models for Social Anthropology, ed. M. Banton, pp. 139–236. London: Tavistock.

Seidman, Stephen B., and Brian L. Foster
1978*a* A Note on the Potential for Genuine Cross-fertilization between Anthropology and Mathematics. Social Networks 1:65–72.
1978*b* A Graph-theoretic Generalization of the Clique Concept. Journal of Mathematical Sociology 6:139–54.

PART II

Household Morphology and Activity

5

Sheep Ranchers and Sugar Growers: Property Transmission in the Basque Immigrant Family of the American West and Australia

William A. Douglass

The purpose of this paper is to probe a major lacuna in the literature on family form and function in historical perspective, namely, the nature of the immigrant family. Reference is to the persistence (or lack thereof) of donor societal familial structures and norms among migrants embedded in host societies characterized by differing cultural traditions. The potentialities and problems of the approach will be highlighted by means of comparative treatment of the intergenerational transmission of property within Basque immigrant families in the American West and Australia.

The European family in its many variations has received the greatest attention to date in terms of sheer scholarly output within the budding fields of family history and historical demography (see the majority of essays in Laslett and Wall 1972; Wrigley 1972; Goody, Thirsk, and Thompson 1976; and Wachter, Hammel, and Laslett 1978; for an exception see Krishnan 1976). Given the wealth, historical depth, relative comprehensiveness, and accessibility of European data sources, researchers have been able to make detailed reconstructions of various regions' family and household structures for remote periods in time. It is not surprising then that many of the methodological and theoretical advances within the field (as well as its controversies: see Laslett 1978) are generated from European case studies material and their comparison (see Heers 1974 and Flandrin 1979).

A recurring theme in much of the literature is the relationship between family structure and ethos on the one hand and ecological and economic factors on the other. Burns (1963) finds that the stem family occurs in many mountainous environments throughout Europe and is an adaptation to alpine conditions. Silverman (1968) contrasts the extended family pattern of central Italy with the nuclear familism of southern Italian society and accounts for the difference in terms of their distinctive land tenure arrangements that in turn are reflective of topography. Similarly, the impact of economic developments, such as industrialism, on "traditional" family systems has been documented extensively (see Goode 1963 and Levine 1977). Internal migration from rural to urban environments *within* a particular society is found to cause changes in family organization (Goode 1963; Smith 1972). There is then considerable evidence suggesting that family systems are attuned to their physical and social settings and are prone to modification when these contextual factors change.

Given this scarcely startling conclusion as well as the impressive available information on European family systems *and* the role of Europe as one of the world's major staging areas of emigration, there is a surprising paucity of literature on the European family in ultramar contexts, that is, the immigrant family.[1] I believe that this lack results both from simple neglect and from thorny conceptual concerns that are more easily finessed than addressed.

Most European-oriented family history specialists have concerned themselves with internal change within particular European family systems—their evolution or revolutions—while treating emigration as either irrelevant or epiphenomenal. Researchers viewing the family from the perspective of host societies (for European emigrants notably the United States, Canada, Australia/New Zealand, South Africa, and southern South America) have resorted either to *disjunction* or to *syncretism*. By disjunction I refer to the tendency to examine, for example, the American family sui generis, establishing the colonial family as its historical baseline and working largely without reference to its Old World antecedents (see Seward 1978). Syncretism refers to the technique of ignoring Old World regional variations by referring to entities such as the Spanish family (Kenny 1976) or the Italian family (Gans 1962), thereby disregarding the internal diversity in family organization on the Iberian and Italic peninsulas. At times syncretism is pushed to the extent of discerning *the* European family, which is then contrasted with its New World counterpart.[2] Understandably the approach has tempting heuristic applications if the purpose is to explain tendencies and trends within the American family. An archetypical, frozen European family form provides a good foil against which to highlight the dynamics of New World familism. Unfortunately, typological comparison avoids the question of the extent to which there is persistence of Old World family forms in the New World setting or their modifications.

In sum, I contend that detailed analysis of the immigrant family is critical both to the study of New World family systems and to a fuller understanding of the constraints and potentialities within European ones as they adapt to changing conditions. To illustrate the point I shall examine family structure within a sample of Basque sheep ranchers of the American West and sugar farmers of North Queensland, Australia.

THE OLD WORLD BASQUE FAMILY

The nineteenth-century sociologist Frederic Le Play (1895) cited rural Basques as a prime example of a stem family (*famille souche*) society. This observation has been confirmed repeatedly by subsequent observers (Unamuno 1902; Lhande 1908; Echegaray 1922; Caro Baroja 1944, 1958; Douglass 1969, 1971, 1972, 1975; Greenwood 1976). Among the Basques the stem family ethos not only pervades world view but is reinforced in customary law and ancient statutes (Vicario de la Peña 1901). To this day in matters of inheritance, particularly the critical right to transmit a patrimony intact to a single heir, the two Spanish Basque regions of Vizcaya and Navarra are exempted from the partible inheritance provision of the Spanish Civil Code. Just as tellingly, in parts of the Spanish Basque area where the code applies as well as throughout the French Basque country (where inheritance is dictated by the Napoleonic Code), the Basques have developed elaborate subterfuges designed to effect integral transmission of the patrimony (see Lhande 1908, 1910). Quitclaims and both real and simulated sales between siblings are common. Mortgaging the farmstead in order to compensate the disinherited with the proceeds is another tactic. The designated heir emigrates for as long as required to amass sufficient savings to satisfy the lien. He then returns to resume the status of male head of household.

The stem family system was highly attuned to the ecological realities of the Basque country. The mountainous topography meant that arable land was at a premium. Only a small portion of the average ten-hectare *baserria* (farmstead) was suitable for plow agriculture, the remainder being pasture and forest. The typical *baserria* was therefore barely capable of supporting a single stem family in agriculture: hence the explicit recognition that the units had to be preserved intact over time. It was unthinkable, indeed morally reprehensible, to sell individual parcels. Persons received their social identity from their house name rather than their surname.[3] Consequently, within rural Basque society social continuity was expressed in terms of immutable farmsteads on both the physical and social landscapes, most of which have persisted unchanged for several centuries.

Impartible transmission of farmsteads from generation to generation, the moral strictures requiring that farmsteads not be divided, and the stem family system of social organization were all mutually reinforcing. Additionally, there were mechanisms to accommodate vagaries in the development cycle of the domestic group. One common recourse for the understaffed[4] domestic group was the practice of adoption. A niece or nephew living in an overexpanded household was the prime candidate. Lacking such, an infant might be secured from an orphanage. In either event the adopted person was fully incorporated into the family and might even emerge as the selected heir.[5] A parallel practice was for the handicapped domestic group to contract the live-in services of an adolescent drawn from an overstaffed household. The servant received little more than room and board, and the arrangement often lasted for several years. At its conclusion he/she might be given a lump sum payment, a dowry, or passage to the New World.

Land banking was another tactic available to the understaffed domestic group. Particular fields could be let out on short-term lease arrangements to stronger neighboring households. This provided a modest income while ensuring that the fields did not revert to secondary growth through neglect.

Access to communal resources provided yet another mechanism permitting stem families to cope with vagaries in their developmental cycle.[6] Expanding domestic groups could bid for tracts of the communal pastures, thereby augmenting the household's pig, sheep, and cow carrying capacity. Stands of timber could be purchased for felling and then sold as lumber or processed into charcoal. Chestnuts were gathered and sold.

Finally, contraband and seasonal labor migration were ploys utilized by overstaffed households. Young women found employment as domestics in the nearby coastal resorts or as far away as Paris. Gangs of young men formed logging crews in the Landes region and the Alps.

Such were the options allowing expanded domestic groups to employ their excess labor productively until such time that out-marriage, permanent emigration, aging of the membership, or death more or less brought the household's labor potential back into line with its resource base.

Modern developments further underscore the extent to which the traditional Basque stem family system was highly attuned to its ecological and economic settings. Given the waning importance of peasant agriculture in the twentieth century and the topographical constraints on mechanization of agriculture in the region, the inheritance system has entered a crisis phase. Whereas the most prestigious status within rural Basque society[7] had been *etxekojaun* ("lord of the household") or *etxekoandrea* ("lady of the household"), that is, an owner of a *baserria*, potential heirs increasingly competed to avoid inheriting with its attendant obligations of continuing in agriculture while caring for elderly parents until their death. The situation was exacerbated by spiraling values of farmsteads when put to other than agricultural uses. A growing Basque paper pulp industry made it attractive to plant pines (Douglass 1975). The trees required little care, grew rapidly in the area's climate (maturing in 25–30 years), and promised long-term returns of windfall proportions. The land itself soared in value as real estate for tourist chalets (Greenwood 1976).

In light of the declining commitment to the peasant agricultural way of life and the trend toward long-term cash cropping and real estate sales, the disinherited siblings of the heir became less and less willing to waive claims against the patrimony. Understandably, this has resulted in considerable rancor and litigation. What is surprising, however, is the tenaciousness of the traditional system given the modern realities. To this day in many Basque villages the impartible inheritance system endures and deviations from it are severely criticized.

Rural Basques provide a classic example within the European literature of a system of stem family social organization. Recent developments have undermined much of the system's viability, but the stem family ethos persists as an integral part of rural Basque world view. Breakdown within the system is closely related to the declining commitment to agriculture as peasant holdings are converted into business enterprises.

Such is the context from which Basque emigrants were drawn. We may now examine Basque familism in two ultramar contexts, the American West and Australia, where I focus on sheep ranchers and sugar growers—households with landed patrimonies. For inclusion in the sample the family patrimony must have been established by an Old World-born Basque immigrant and have been (or failed to be) transmitted at least once to a New World-born heir or heirs. Such New World transmissions will then be examined against the backdrop of the preceding discussion of Old World Basque stem family ethos and system of social organization.[8]

BASQUE EMIGRATION HISTORY

The Basque country has long been one of Europe's major emigratory staging areas (Douglass and Bilbao 1975). On the one hand the stem family system of social organization generated many disinherited siblings who were prime candidates for emigration. On the other, the Basque country was politically divided between Spain and France, giving Basques access to both Spanish and French overseas colonies. Consequently, Basques played key roles as mercenaries, missionaries, mariners, and merchants in colonial enterprise.

With the demise of Spain's empire in the nineteenth century the formerly elitist emigration was converted into an exodus of peasants and manual laborers disposed to try their luck elsewhere. Latin America continued to be the favored destination of the Basque emigrants since most were bilingual in Spanish.[9] At the same time there was a willingness to emigrate to other areas in response to perceived opportunity.

In this respect Basques joined the Atlantic transfer of Europe's "huddled masses" in search of a better life. For the Basque emigrant, however, this was seldom a quest for permanent security on a modest but comfortable scale in a new country. Rather, the paramount concern was to find an opportunity whereby through hard work, personal privation, and risk-taking the emigré could amass sufficient capital to purchase a farm or launch a business back in the Basque country. Many emigrated, but few left with the intention of never returning (see Arnould, Segalen, this volume).[10] Most Basque emigrants do eventually return to Europe after a sojourn abroad that may be measured in decades.[11]

BASQUES IN THE AMERICAN WEST

The siren song of the California gold rush proved just as irresistible to Basques as to most other nationalities. The Basque contingent in the ranks of the pioneers was drawn from several sources. Some traveled directly from Europe, but the majority were reemigrants—men who had previously established themselves in Argentina, Chile, Peru, and Mexico. Quickly disillusioned in the mining camps, many Basques turned to other activities.

Many of the Basque immigrants drawn to the American West from southern South America were experienced herders under open range conditions, for the Basques had established themselves as sheepmen on the pampas by the 1830s (Douglass and Bilbao 1975). The vast underutilized expanses of Southern California presented the Basques an opportunity to repeat their earlier South American experience, and during the 1850s Basque livestockmen became well established in California. A few acquired ranch properties but most were itinerants, "tramps" to their detractors, who practiced sheep transhumance on the public domain. An outfit consisted of the herder/owner, a burro and pack outfit, and 1,000 or more ewes and their lambs. As the herd expanded the operator would send to Europe for a kinsman or fellow villager and employ him as a herder. The new man might take his wages in ewes, running them alongside those of his employer until he had sufficient numbers to establish his own itinerant sheep outfit and strike out in search of new rangeland.

By the turn of the century Basque sheepmen had spread throughout most livestock districts of the American West. Theirs was a lonely lot that almost precluded family life. The owner/herder spent the entire year living in a tent on the open range. A few of the men were married and left their wives back in Europe; others set up households in small towns in the sheep districts, visiting their families infrequently. The majority of itinerant sheepmen, however, remained bachelors throughout their sojourn in the United States, selling out at some point in order to return to Europe to establish a family.

By the beginning of the present century the itinerant Basque sheepman was a figure reviled in the American West. Settled livestockmen regarded public lands contiguous to their own holdings as an extension of their private patrimony, even though theoretically those lands were open to anyone on a first-come basis. For these ranchers the Basque itinerants were "foreign" interlopers who exploited American resources while lacking a permanent commitment to the region's future. As such they were berated in the press, harassed in the courts, and bullied on the range (Douglass and Bilbao 1975).

Ultimately the confrontation was resolved by land law legislation creating the national forest system in the timbered summer pasture high country and grazing districts in the desert wintering areas. The intent of the legislation was to regulate livestock access to the public lands. Its target was clear: henceforth aliens were to be excluded from the ranges while grazing allotments were to be awarded solely to landed Anglo livestockmen (Douglass and Bilbao 1975).

The era of the itinerant Basque sheepman was over. Many of the displaced returned to Europe disillusioned. Others became wage employees of settled outfits. At the same time some Basques responded by becoming American citizens and acquiring ranch properties. This latter group provides the corpus from which my sample of Basque ranching families was drawn.

BASQUES IN AUSTRALIA

The history of immigration in nineteenth-century Australia differs notably from that in the American West. The several Australian states, serving as penal colonies for part of the century and protected British possessions for all of it, received limited non-British immigration. To be sure, Australia experienced its own mining crazes that attracted persons from the four corners of the globe, but the thrust of official policy was to favor Britons, tolerate northern Europeans, discourage southern and eastern Europeans, and exclude nonwhites (Price 1963; Willard 1974; Yarwood 1968).

The issue of non-British immigration came to a head in the sugar districts of the state of Queensland. Sugar cultivation in Australia began in the 1860s (Livick 1954:2) and gradually encompassed a discontinuous 2,000-mile belt of the continent's eastern coastline. In the cooler districts of northern New South Wales and southern Queensland small-scale European farmers employing white laborers produced and harvested sugar that they sold to a central mill. In the tropical districts of central and northern Queensland, however, a plantation system emerged akin to that of the American South and the Caribbean.

Such enterprises operated on a grand scale, employing hundreds of laborers to cultivate thousands of tons of sugar for the plantation's own mill. While the plantations employed a variety of ethnic groups, including Chinese, Japanese, Singhalese, Malays, and Arabs, the backbone of the industry was the Kanaka, or Pacific Islander. Recruiters, "blackbirders" to their detractors, combed Melanesia for workers who were sometimes kidnapped but more frequently given contracts that amounted to little more than abject peonage (Palmer 1973; Wawn 1973).

The system was not without its critics. Some objected on humanitarian grounds while others feared for Australia's racial purity. By the late 1880s opponents included many of Queensland's leading politicians. The Pacific Islanders Act of 1885 dictated that Kanaka labor be eliminated over the next five years (Easterby 1932:10). The plantation owners were ultimately successful in obtaining a reprieve, but the portent of things to come was sufficient to effect a change.

Two developments were of major interest. First, the giant of the industry, the Colonial Sugar Refining Company, implemented the central mill system on its Queensland holdings. The company began to divest itself of land, facilitating credit to small farmers while limiting its operations to milling and refining. Second, the plantation owners initiated a search for alternate sources of labor. Many opted for Asians, but this was clearly a stop-gap measure of limited potential given widespread national opposition to nonwhite immigration. Consequently, some argued that a viable source of European immigrants had to be developed.

At the time this was a bold experiment, since it was commonly held that whites were incapable of hard physical labor under tropical conditions (Courtney 1975). Following climatological reasoning, however, some suggest that southern Europeans might be suited for the task, certainly more so than their northern counterparts. Consequently, in 1891 some Queensland growers recruited over 300 Italians for work in the fields, promising to sell small sugar properties to the new immigrants at some future date (Borrie 1954:9). Many of the Italians failed the test, opting for nonagricultural employment. But a core succeeded and established the bases for chain migration from southern Europe to northern Queensland.

Creation of the Australian Commonwealth in 1901 spelled the end of the Kanaka system. The new nation implemented the White Australia Policy of immigration that prohibited the introduction of nonwhites. Those Pacific Islanders present in Queensland were to be repatriated over a six-year period. As a result efforts to recruit southern Europeans for the canefields intensified during the first decade of the century. In 1907 the Colonial Sugar Refining Company brought a contingent of 200 Catalans from Spain while aiding established Italian farmers to recruit kinsmen and acquaintances in Italy.

The first Basques appeared in Queensland about this time. The early arrivals were not part of any official recruitment but rather were mariners who jumped ship in Sydney. Lured by rumors of opportunity in the sugar districts, they made their way northward where they secured employment as canecutters. The cane gangs consisted of eight or ten individuals who contracted their services to small farmers on a piece-work basis. The enterprising member of a good gang was in a position to earn far more than the going wages in other manual occupations.

This was an era of considerable expansion in the sugar industry. In the Johnstone, Herbert, and Burdekin districts, areas that by World War I had considerable populations of southern Europeans, marginal brushland could be purchased for nominal sums. Two or three canecutters might pool their savings, acquire a property, and clear it during the off-season. After bringing the land under cultivation one would remain there year-round to care for the crop while the others continued in canecutting. The combined earnings were used to acquire another property and the cycle repeated until each partner had a farm. Established as individual farmers, the men were then in a position to send to Europe for relatives or fellow villagers, establishing a pattern of chain migration.

In this fashion between 1900 and 1930, or when the Great Depression and World War II slowed the movement, many southern Europeans entered north Queensland. The Basque contingent in their ranks remained small, probably never surpassing more than 200 individuals,[12] but several Basques acquired sugar properties and established families in the sugar districts. This is the group that provided the Australian sample for my subsequent analysis of the Basque immigrant family.

PROPERTY TRANSMISSION IN THE IMMIGRANT BASQUE FAMILY

The following is an analysis of intergenerational transfer of landed patrimonies in 53 Basque-American and 26 Basque-Australian families. Criteria for inclusion are that the male founder must have been Old World-born, married, and the parent of offspring that reached the age of majority (and hence qualified as potential heir[s] of the property).[13]

The sample for the American West is drawn from areas of Basque settlement in southern Idaho, southeastern Oregon, and western and northern Nevada. The Australian cases are derived from the Herbert, Johnstone, and Burdekin river districts. While the total for Australia is low, it is significant because it represents the universe of Basque-owned sugar farms on the continent.

Table 5.1 details the intrafamilial pattern of ownership and working relationship in the 79 Basque-American and Basque-Australian immigrant families in which a landed patrimony either was (or could have been) transferred successfully between generations. In 21 households—

TABLE 5.1
PROPERTY OWNERSHIP BY FAMILY FORM

Family form	Pattern of property transmission	American West		Australia		Combined	
		Number	%	Number	%	Number	%
Nuclear	Patrimony not transferred between generations. Either rejected by potential heirs or never proferred	16	30	5	19	21	26
Stem	Parents continue in agriculture with one married son (or daughter)	21	40	12	46	33	42
Extended	Parents continue in agriculture with two or more married sons (or daughters)	16	30	9	35	25	32
	Totals	53	100	26	100	79	100

26 percent of the total—the family ownership of the patrimony remained nuclear. No intergenerational transfer was made to potential heirs either (1) at the discretion of the founding donor couple or (2) because of the unwillingness of the candidate[s] to inherit with the stipulation that they continue in agriculture. Rather, the properties were sold and inheritances resolved with the liquid assets. In 33 instances—42 percent of the total—a stem family transmission and postinheritance working arrangement were effected. In 25 cases—32 percent of the total—extension encompassed two or more married siblings remaining in the family enterprise with their parents, including 6 instances of three married brothers doing so.

The question of postmarital residence of heirs requires consideration. In only a few instances did the donor couple and heir(s) coreside in a single dwelling. Others opted for a compound living arrangement with each nuclear family inhabiting closely contiguous but separate dwellings. But in the majority of cases of extended families each nuclear unit resided at considerable distance from its counterparts.

The prevalence of dispersed postmarital residence arrangements is largely a product of historical developments in ranching and sugar farming. In both industries the trend throughout the twentieth century has been for aggrandizement of land holdings. The typical turn-of-the-century 160-acre homestead in the American West or 10-acre sugar farm in Australia is far too small to be a viable agricultural enterprise in the contemporary economic climate. Hence today's ranch or sugar farm usually encompasses two or more formerly independent properties, each with its own dwelling. The present proprietary extended family is therefore likely to have multiple dispersed dwellings at its disposal. In sum, my correlation of family form is with property transmission and working arrangements but not necessarily with coresidence.

DISCUSSION

Before discussing the preceding data regarding the Basque immigrant family in light of Old World Basque family organization I should note one caveat. In the immigrant contexts I am examining developments so recent as to preclude treating them as an *institutionalized* system. I have noted the Old World rural Basque penchant for the stem family living arrangement and transmission of landed property—a system reinforced by legal codification, mythology, world view, and moral stricture. There is no comparable discernible consensus among either Basque-Americans or Basque-Australians regarding the *proper* disposition of sheep ranches or sugar farms. Nevertheless, an analysis of patterns within the immigrant sample suggests some interesting parallels and contrasts with the Old World Basque system of family organization.

Consider two hypothetical contingencies deriving from the host society. The Anglo-Saxon legal tradition of both the United States and Australia lent itself to the preservation of the stem family arrangement, were Basque immigrants so inclined. In both host societies the donor couple is at liberty to select a single heir while disinheriting his/her siblings. Yet both American and Australian societies display a strong strain of nuclear familism. Consequently, if Basque immigrants were acculturating fully to the host society, one might have anticipated a high incidence of individual, independent property ownership by nuclear family units. Yet in fully 58 cases (or 77 percent of the sample), property transmission and working arrangements were made either along stem or further extended family lines.

Regarding the question of the persistence, or lack thereof, of the stem family arrangement there is a curious anomaly. In 33 cases—42 percent of the total—the patrimony was transferred in this fashion. Yet informants were moot on the point, even denying that it was done intentionally and expressing surprise at its considerable statistical incidence. To be sure, in 8 of the 33 cases the selected heir was an only child; however, this still leaves a considerable number in which in practice, if not by conscious predilection, Basque immigrant families effected single-heir inheritance with a continued postmarital working and in some cases coresidential living arrangement between heir and parents.

In most cases extension was patrilineal. In 4 of the 21 instances in which there was no intergenerational transfer of the patrimony, all of the potential donors' offspring were female. Informants were explicit in attributing the sale of the patrimony to this biological eventuality. In only 4 of the 33 stem family cases was the selected heir a daughter (in 2 of these households the daughter was an only child). In only 2 of the 25 cases of extended families was one of the heirs female.

This male bias within the system is consonant both with the Old World Basque reality and circumstances in the two host societies. All of the Australian sample and all of the Idaho and Oregon Basque-American families (N = 21) are from Vizcaya, where male primogeniture is the inheritance norm. The remaining Basque-American families derive from regions of the French Basque country where male inheritance is preferred if not prescribed.

At the same time both ranching and sugar farming are primarily male activities. The small-scale ranch or farm tends to be a family enterprise in which from an early age sons become accustomed to working with their fathers. Consequently, even among non-Basque American ranchers and Australian farmers there is a tendency in intergenerational transfer of the patrimony to follow male lines.

Probably the most fascinating finding is the incidence of patrilineally extended families in which two or more married sons share ownership and working arrangements on the patrimony with their donor parents. Again the issue may be considered from the standpoint of conditions both in the host societies and in the Old World system of family organization. There are several striking parallels in the historical development of the ranching and sugar farming complexes considered here. Both were economic activities that emerged under frontier conditions in harsh, sparsely settled environments. In sheep ranching and sugar farming a seasonal demand for herders and canecutters was met by a transient, largely unreliable labor force.[14] Within both industries there has been progressive pressure to "get bigger or get out." Consequently, the successful rancher or farmer was faced with increasing his holdings simply in order to survive in agriculture throughout his active adult years.

Considering that the Basque rancher or sugar farmer began as a herder or canecutter, he achieved ultimate success by dint of privation and self-sacrifice. Aggrandizement and consolidation of the property was as much an obsession as a calculated series of business decisions. Patrilineal extension of ownership provided a ready means for the founder, in his waning years, to avoid the painful dissolution of the fruits of a lifetime of struggle. Indeed, many heirs continuing in agriculture were aware that they were "humoring" their immigrant parents by remaining on the ranch or farm and were willing to speculate about selling out once the donor couple had fully retired or died.[15]

Patrilineal extension of ownership secured for the founding immigrant a reliable source of labor. All of the sheep ranches and sugar farms in this sample were owner-operated. Although the owner/operator's net worth was sometimes calculated in the millions of dollars, his life-style differed but little from that of his menial laborers. Incorporating adult sons into the enterprise reduced a man's dependence on the shifting population of seasonal laborers.

It is interesting to speculate on the implications of patrilineal extension in host society contexts against the backdrop of Old World Basque inheritance practices. I have noted that the Old World Basque stem family system of property transmission is finely attuned to the Pyrenean ecological constraints of a nonexpandable land base. In the frontier conditions of both the American West and Australia, however, Basque immigrants were not only able but were practically required to expand their holdings in order to survive and prosper. Patrilineal extension was not only possible in such circumstances but even an efficacious strategy for attaining the goal of consolidating a viable agricultural enterprise. Stated simply, the penchant for patrilineal extension among Basque immigrant families in the American West and Australia raises questions concerning the conservative commitment among Old World rural Basques to a stem family system of social organization. Even in Europe that system may be merely a compromise and potential way station within a system that would encourage further patrilineal extension were the ecological constraints not so formidable.

I note that such an interpretation is consonant with Hammel's analysis of changes within the Serbian *zadruga*. Hammel (1972) argued that the fully elaborated joint family was an adaptation to frontier conditions and an expandable resource base. By the nineteenth century, however, the region had been fully settled and there was a marked reduction in the size and complexity of the *zadruga*. Hammel (1972:368) notes, ". . . the reduction in mean size was underlain by a shift from the classic *zadruga* form of patrilocal and fraternal extension toward the stem family pattern in which only a single son usually remains on the land. It is important to note that the causal factors in this change involve no major shift in the basic ideology of kinship but only the response of behavioral patterns to demographic and ecological alterations." The Basques and Serbians may well represent variations of the same type of underlying kinship system.

CONCLUSION

At the outset I noted that the study of the immigrant family against the backdrop of its Old World origins is fraught with difficulties and hence neglected. I believe that the foregoing treatment illustrates many of the problems and possibilities inherent in this area of inquiry. Hotly contested issues within the family literature such as the Laslett-Berkner debate (Laslett 1978) regarding the significance and interpretation of the statistical incidences of family form within a particular society become greatly complicated by inclusion of data on emigrant diaspora. The emigrant family functions within host society economic, social, and legal environments that differ radically from those of their Old World homeland. It is possible to argue that many outcomes result from host society factors, Old World penchants, or possibly a combination of both. The present analysis shows that if the reference points are the founding immigrant and his first-generation offspring, the recency of events precludes speaking of an institutionalized immigrant family system characterized by its own explicit value system. Indeed, the informants themselves provide conflicting rationales for their behavior. The investigator cannot take comfort in the adage "But we've always done it this way!" so frequently elicited when interviewing in situ representatives of long-standing societies. Rather, the uprooted immigrant in expressing his lot is more likely to comment simultaneously on his alienation from his cultural heritage and his lack of integration within the host society.

It is myopic for the family specialist to examine immigrant families without reference to the preimmigration system of familism from which they derive or to ignore familism within an emigrant diaspora while studying family organization in a particular Old World society. In neither instance does a broadened perspective necessarily hold the key to understanding the system, but it may certainly provide the scholar with many important clues.

NOTES

1. For a notable exception see Cronin 1970.

2. This practice leads to simplistic and untenable generalities such as W. Lloyd Warner's (1962:18) statement, "The ancestral family system of all the Continental European groups who have migrated to America was patriarchal, the mother and children being subordinated to the authority and discipline of the father. . . . Because of the attachment to the land certain sons continued with the family even after marriage, extending the family unit through several generations to become a *grosse Familie*. . . ." Gans's classic study of the Leavittowners provides another example since we are told, regarding members of the white working class subculture, that "many are Catholics, and of Irish, Italian, and Southern or Eastern European peasant backgrounds. The vestiges of this origin are particularly strong in family life" (1967:25). Gans then describes their common family system and contrasts it with that of the predominantly Anglo lower middle and upper middle classes. The syncretic family form of European Catholic peasants then becomes a function both of Old World background and lower class status with no systematic treatment of either.

3. In any event the surname reflects the house name since most surnames were derived from existing house names when persons were required to assume surnames in the late Middle Ages. For example, Etxeberria, the most common Basque surname, means "Newhouse." If, however, Manetx Etxeberria comes to reside on the farmstead Bekosubi he is known locally as Bekosubi'ko Manetx or simply Bekosubi.

4. A unit might be unable to exploit its available farm resources because of untimely deaths, crippling accidents, chronic illnesses, or childless marital unions.

5. While single-heir inheritance characterizes rural Basque society as a whole, there is considerable regional variation in how the candidate is determined, ranging from male primogeniture in Vizcaya to parental discretion irrespective of sex or age order in Navarra (see Douglass 1971).

6. In clear recognition of this fact municipal councils strenuously resisted the nineteenth-century effort by central governments to disentail village commons by transferring the lands to private ownership (Gómez Chaparro 1967; Goyhenèche 1961:62).

7. Excepting that of priest or nun.

8. It should be noted that in every case the founding immigrants departed the Basque country between 40 and 70 years ago. This means that they left before developments detrimental to the stem family system gained their current ascendency; that is, they were socialized into the more traditional set of values and might have been expected to act in accordance with them in later life.

9. I refer primarily to Spanish Basques. But French Basques were also oriented to South America. Given their proximity to the Spanish frontier and involvement in movement of contraband across it, many French Basques know Spanish. In any event, French speakers found learning Spanish an easy task. It should also be noted that Spanish Basque emigrants far outnumber their French Basque counterparts. The population of the French Basque area is barely 200,000 persons, or about one-twelfth the total for the Basque country as a whole.

10. In the course of interviewing hundreds of Basque immigrants in Australia, the Philippines, the American West, and several countries of Latin America I have encountered only two men who claim to have left Europe without any thought of returning. But, of course, some changed their minds. Those who failed found it difficult to face the inflated expectations of their Old World kinsmen and fellow villagers. Some enjoyed such fabulous New World success that they were reluctant to relinquish it for a new start back in Europe. Most common, however, is the case of the man who tarries abroad for so long that his children become functional adult members of the host society. Reunion with the family of orientation by returning to Europe then risks separation with the family of procreation.

11. Migration is frequently more a process than an event. The transfer of persons of a particular domestic group from one social setting to another (or others) may transpire over a period of several years through the movements of its individual members. Migration may be a strategy for maintaining the domestic group intact, albeit in a new context (Darrock 1981), or it may signal dissolution of the donor domestic group. The process is also reversible, for the return of individuals and even entire domestic groups to their natal community is always a possibility (Bovenkerk 1974). Migration, then, is much less definitive than birth, marriage, or death as a social mechanism affecting recruitment or dissolution of domestic groups.

Migration poses significant problems for students of family form and function in past times. Most evidence is constituted by census enumerations and there is the obvious problem of determining the motives of enumerators. Censusing a population is a tedious business, usually undertaken only for some specific purpose such as taxation or tithing. In such cases the coresidential membership of a household becomes a convenient, readily discernible, and hence countable unit on the social landscape. Persons present at the time of the exercise are included (only once, one hopes); absent family members are rarely counted. The migration factor then weakens the case considerably for inferring family organization as perceived by the actors themselves solely from household enumerations. It is significant that Wachter, Hammel, and Laslett (1978) found it necessary to exclude migration in their seminal computer simulation of statistical frequencies of stem family households in a community characterized by a rigidly applied stem family ethos.

To illustrate from contemporary Basque contexts, migrants are drawn from the ranks of *both* married land owners (*etxekojaunak*) and their unmarried siblings. It is not unusual for the married migrant to spend between 10 and 20 years in the American West as a solitary sheepherder remitting his earnings to his household. Such an individual, though physically absent, is inevitably listed by the Old World census enumerator (sometimes, but not always, with a parenthetical notation like "in Idaho"). Conversely, the unmarried sibling who emigrates abroad is never included in subsequent village household censuses. Insofar as he remains single, however, he retains full jural membership in his natal household. News of his death abroad triggers the elaborate year-long cycle of funerary ritual and mourning complete with a block of wood serving as a surrogate coffin during a burial ceremony. There are extreme cases in which an emigrant uncle who has failed to communicate with his family for 40 years returns unannounced from abroad to resume residence in the household now headed by a nephew whom he has never met!

12. In the aftermath of the Second World War the industry experienced a severe labor shortage. Agents were dispatched to Europe to secure workers. More than a thousand Basques entered Australia under the plan. Because of the recency of their entry, their experiences are excluded from the present treatment.

13. Both in the American West and in Australia single Basque males often acquired a livestock or farming operation, either alone or in partnership with other bachelors, before eventually selling out to return permanently to Europe. Married couples commonly operated a ranch or farm while their children were young, then ultimately returned to the Basque country to live during their offspring's childhood. Similarly, the urban growth of cities like Boise, Idaho, and Reno, Nevada, absorbed some family-operated Basque outfits before intergenerational transmission became an issue. All of the above cases are excluded from consideration.

14. In both the American West and Australia Basques gained a group reputation for dependability and dedication to hard work. The profligacy of the nonimmigrant herders and canecutters produced the negative stereotype of the hard-drinking, violence-prone drifter which in contrast enhanced the fame of the Basques.

15. This tendency for lineal extension of family groupings as a strategy for retaining accrued agrarian holdings and wealth has been documented for the northeastern United States in the eighteenth century (Henretta 1978) and for western Canada in the nineteenth century (Gagan 1978).

REFERENCES

Borrie, W. D.
1954 Italians and Germans in Australia. Melbourne: F. W. Cheshire.

Bovenkerk, Frank
1974 The Sociology of Return Migration: A Bibliographic Essay. The Hague: Martinus Nijhoff.
Burns, Robert K.
1963 The Circum-Alpine Culture Area: A Preliminary View. Anthropological Quarterly 36:130–55.
Caro Baroja, J.
1944 La Vida Rural en Vera de Bidasoa. Madrid: Consejo Superior de Investigaciones Científicas.
1958 Los Vascos. Madrid: Ediciones Minotauro.
Courtney, P. P.
1975 The White Man in the Australian Tropics: A Review of Some Opinions and Prejudices of the Pre-war Years. *In* Lectures on North Queensland History; 2d ser., pp. 57–65. Townsville: James Cook University of North Queensland.
Cronin, Constance
1970 The Sting of Change: Sicilians in Sicily and Australia. Chicago: University of Chicago Press.
Darrock, A. Gordon
1981 Migrants in the Nineteenth Century: Fugitives or Families in Motion? Journal of Family History 6 (4):257–77.
Douglass, William A.
1969 Death in Murelaga: Funerary Ritual in a Spanish Basque Village. Seattle: University of Washington Press.
1971 Rural Exodus in Two Spanish Basque Villages: A Cultural Explanation. American Anthropologist 73 (5):1100–1114.
1972 The Basque Peasantry: Closed or Open? Nord Nytt 2:99–104.
1975 Echalar and Murelaga: Opportunity and Rural Depopulation in Two Spanish Basque Villages. London: C. Hurst and Co.
Douglass, William A., and Jon Bilbao
1975 Amerikanuak: Basques in the New World. Reno: University of Nevada Press.
Easterby, Harry T.
1932 The Queensland Sugar Industry: An Historical Review. Brisbane: Queensland Government Printer.
Echegaray, Bonifacio de
1922 La Vida Civil y Mercantil de los Vascos a Través de Sus Instituciones Jurídicas. Revista Internacional de Estudios Vascos 13:273–336.
Flandrin, Jean-Louis
1979 Families in Former Times: Kinship, Household, and Sexuality. Cambridge: Cambridge University Press.
Gagan, David
1978 Land, Population, and Social Change: The "Critical Years" in Rural Canada West. Canadian Historical Review. 59 (3):293–318.
Gans, H. J.
1962 The Urban Villagers: Group and Class in the Life of Italian-Americans.

New York: The Free Press.
1967 The Leavittowners: How People Live and Politic in Suburbia. New York: Pantheon Books.
Gómez Chaparro, Rafael
1967 La Desamortización Civil en Navarra. Pamplona: Institución Príncipe de Viana.
Goode, W. J.
1963 World Revolution and Family Patterns. New York: The Free Press.
Goody, J., J. Thirsk, and E. P. Thompson, eds.
1976 Family and Inheritance: Rural Society in Western Europe, 1200–1800. Cambridge: Cambridge University Press.
Goyheneche, Eugène
1961 Notre Terre Basque. Bayonne: Éditions Ikas.
Greenwood, Davydd
1976 Unrewarding Wealth: The Commercialization and Collapse of Agriculture in a Spanish Basque Town. Cambridge: Cambridge University Press.
Hammel, E. A.
1972 The *Zadruga* as Process. *In* Household and Family in Past Times, ed. P. Laslett and R. Wall. Cambridge: Cambridge University Press.
Heers, Jacques
1974 Le Clan Familial au Moyen Âge: Etude sur les Structures Politiques et Sociales des Milieux Urbains. Paris: Presses Universitaires de France.
Henretta, James A.
1978 Families and Farms: *Mentalité* in Pre-industrial America. The William and Mary Quarterly (3d ser.) 35 (1):3–32.
Kenny, M.
1976 Observations on Contemporary Spanish Families in Mexico: Immigrants and Refugees. *In* Mediterranean Family Structures, ed. J. G. Peristiany. Cambridge: Cambridge University Press.
Krishnan, P., ed.
1976 Family and Demography. Journal of Comparative Family Studies 7(2).
Laslett, P.
1978 The Stem-family Hypothesis and Its Privileged Position. *In* Statistical Studies of Historical Social Structure, ed. Kenneth W. Wachter, Eugene A. Hammel and Peter Laslett, pp. 89–111. New York: Academic Press.
Laslett, P., and R. Wall, eds.
1972 Household and Family in Past Times. Cambridge: Cambridge University Press.
Le Play, Frederic
1895 L'Organisation de la Famille selon le Vrai Modèle Signalé par l'Histoire de Toutes les Races et de Tous les Temps. Tours: A. Mame et fils.
Levine, David
1977 Family Formation in an Age of Nascent Capitalism. New York, San Francisco, London: Academic Press.

Lhande, Pierre
1908 Autour d'un Foyer Basque: Récits et Idées. Paris: Nouvelle Librairie Nationale.
1910 L'Émigration Basque. Paris: Nouvelle Librairie Nationale.
Livick, B. B.
1954 Origin and Development of the Central Mill and Small Farm System in Queensland. Manuscript. Colonial Sugar Refining Company Archives. Box N.I.O., folder 3.
Palmer, George
1973 Kidnapping in the South Seas. Blackburn (Vic.): Penguin Books.
Price, Charles A.
1963 Southern Europeans in Australia. Melbourne: Oxford University Press.
Seward, R. R.
1978 The American Family: A Demographic History. Beverly Hills and London: Sage Publications.
Silverman, S.
1968 Agricultural Organization, Social Structure and Values in Italy: Amoral Familism Reconsidered. American Anthropologist 70 (1):1–20.
Smith, Robert J.
1972 Small Families, Small Households and Residential Instability: Town and City in "Pre-Modern" Japan. *In* Household and Family in Past Time, ed. P. Laslett and R. Wall, pp. 429–472. Cambridge: Cambridge University Press.
Swierenga, Robert P.
1980 Dutch Immigrant Demography, 1820–1880. Journal of Family History 5 (4):390–405.
Unamuno, Miguel de
1902 Vizcaya. *In* Derecho Consuetudinario y Economía Popular en España, ed. Joaquín Costa, II, vol. 2, pp. 37–66. Barcelona: Manuel Soler.
Vicario de la Peña, Nicolás
1901 Derecho Consuetudinario de Vizcaya. Madrid: Imprenta del Asilo de Huérfanos del Sagrado Corazón de Jesús.
Wachter, K. W., E. A. Hammel, and P. Laslett, eds.
1978 Statistical Studies of Historical Social Structure. New York, San Francisco, London: Academic Press.
Warner, W. Lloyd
1962 American Life: Dream and Reality. Chicago: University of Chicago Press.
Wawn, William T.
1973 The South Sea Islanders and the Queensland Labour Trade. Canberra: Australian National University Press.
Willard, Myra
1974 History of the White Australia Policy to 1920. Melbourne: Melbourne University Press.

Wrigley, E. A., ed.
1972 Nineteenth-century Society: Essays in the Use of Quantitative Methods for the Study of Social Data. Cambridge: Cambridge University Press.

Yarwood, A. T.
1968 Attitudes to Non-European Immigration. Stanmore (New South Wales): Cassell Australia.

6

Marketing and Social Reproduction in Zinder, Niger Republic

Eric J. Arnould

Biological reproduction always takes place within a determinate structure of relations of production, distribution, and consumption and occurs simultaneously with economic activity; thus demographic processes "reflect the . . . mechanisms through which a society organizes the creation and reproduction of the relations of production" (Meillassoux 1975: 43–44). Hausa communities in Zinder province in the Niger Republic have adopted new, specialized production strategies in response to the development of local market opportunities. As a result of market development some communities may depend directly on products produced in the industrialized nations and marketed locally for some of their subsistence needs, and thus their biological reproduction is contingent on capitalist production. They may have to purchase necessary tools and other productive inputs made abroad in order to continue to produce. One might therefore expect such adaptations to a change in the economic climate to alter the demographic conditions necessary for the social reproduction of the household system in Zinder. Marriage and alliance relationships might also be affected by changes in the conditions of production (Godelier 1975).

In some precolonial societies of the Sahelian cereals zone social reproduction was linked to the production process through the juridicopolitical control elders exercised over junior members of society. Through exchange of bridewealth (produced by junior men) and spouses between households, the elders converted the material products of economic activity into kin and alliance relations that in turn, determined the morphology and tasks of domestic groups. Meillassoux (1975), from whom this interpretation is borrowed, has suggested that the reason production and reproduction are based on social relations within the household and the Sahelian village community today is that international capital has no reason to disrupt these structures. Labor and agricultural products from precapitalist African domestic production processes are cheaper for capitalist firms to buy than those produced through the capitalist mode of production. By perpetuating the village community capitalists economize on the long-term social security and welfare costs that must be paid to workers in the capitalist core, and when African goods and labor are not desired by capitalist consumers the communities can be left to their own devices, or so capital presumes. Hence, capital maintains precapitalist modes of production and reproduction as subordinate elements of more inclusive social formations articulated through exchange.

Meillassoux's hypothesis smacks of reification, but the data presented below confirm that household organization and social reproduction in Zinder retain precapitalist elements but display sensitivity to local and global production and exchange relations. The data were gathered as a response to three questions: First, what is the structure and organization of social reproduction in the three communities? Second, does marketing contribute to the articulation between local social reproduction and the world market economy? Third, in what ways do local communities actively shape and reinterpret exogenous economic pressures within and through local structures of reproduction?

Cross-sectional studies of other communities confronted by a dominating capitalist system provide specific hypotheses about changes in household morphology and task performance which inform my analysis of the three communities in Zinder. Among these hypotheses are decreasing household size with agricultural intensification (Netting 1965; Raynaut 1976); lessened span of intrahousehold cooperation as dryland farming becomes a less important component of the total farming strategy (Raynaut 1976; Hill 1972); intervillage variability in the adoption of extending or intensifying marriage strategies with the availability of land and labor (see Linares, this volume; Reyna 1972); increasing gender-based polarity within households and a trend toward duolocal residence with increasing economic contributions of women to the household fund (Arnould and Henderson 1982; Sanday 1974); elevated fertility as a form of labor recruitment (see Hackenberg, Murphy, and Selby, this volume) in a context of increasing duration and incidence of male labor migration (Amin et al. 1974); class specific patterns of household morphology emerging from common precapitalist antecedents (Löfgren 1974; Rapp n.d.); and strong links between variants in household form and the incidence of cash cropping (Raynaut 1976; see Wilk, this volume).

THE REGIONAL MARKETING SYSTEM

The province of Zinder in the Niger Republic is an area of 145,430 square kilometers in the heart of the central Sudan in the Sahelian region of West Africa. The provincial economy is based on mixed farming and crafts production, and although industry is weakly developed, the commercial sector manifests what Hackenberg, Murphy, and Selby (this volume) call "commercial involution," a state akin to Geertz's (1963) agricultural involution. Development activity is dependent on foreign aid (Arnould 1982:64ff, 71ff).

Exchange occurs through the activities of thousands of part-time producer/traders and full-time merchants in over 80 periodic weekly markets and through a set of interlocking government marketing boards that try to control the prices and supplies both of agricultural products and key imports like salt.

The market system has developed since colonial times. The French established a dendritic network of groundnut export markets that facilitated the emergence of local central-place mechanisms toward the end of the colonial period (Collins 1974). The modern system exhibits elements of a precolonial network market system (C. A. Smith 1976:39–41) insofar as certain markets are glutted with local manufactures and prices for some goods are poorly correlated between distant markets (Arnould 1982: 196ff), and the market system has encouraged only moderate development of a regionwide division of labor. Thus prices for pottery are poorly articulated between markets, and because of poor transport facilities and localized glut, pot traders from one of the study villages were forced to resort to itinerant trading to generate adequate demand for available supplies.

The economy also manifests elements of a dendritic mercantile system in that imports, particularly new inputs to production, are very expensive because of outmoded transport infrastructure and are poorly distributed outside of the central entrepots like Zinder town (C. A. Smith 1976: 33–35). At the same time state-controlled marketing boards keep producer prices for basic cereals artificially low, monopolize urban redistribution of cereals, and control collection of groundnuts for export through politically expedient but economically irrational channels (Arnould 1982: 70ff).

The economy also has elements of a redistributive system for garden produce. Produce is bulked at a large number of small markets, like the Gada market near one of my study communities, and is then immediately retailed or wholesaled in a much higher order central place without passing through intermediate centers.

There persists an archaic relay system by which livestock passes from north to south, changing hands in numerous intermediary markets like the Mirria market near one of the study communities.

Three markets were important in this study. Zinder market is a primate center (C. A. Smith 1976:32) where goods, capital, supply, demand, transport infrastructure, credit, and administrative functions are concentrated to the detriment of secondary centers. Historically the center of regional handicraft production (Arnould 1981), Zinder still provides a much reduced tanning community with a livelihood. The National Company for the Collection of Hides (SNCP), like other government marketing boards, maintains its headquarters here and through a network of contract merchants monopolizes the export of high quality hides, depriving the handicraft tanners of untanned export-grade hides and driving up prices for other untanned hides.

Mirria market is a secondary center that is almost as important as Zinder. It is important as a stop on the relay system and as a produce market. It is glutted with locally produced pottery. An outlet of the Nigerien Company for Food Products (OPVN) assures a relatively stable supply of food while proximity to Zinder ensures availability of large supplies of imported goods.

Gada market is primarily a retail market. Groundnut marketing, monopolized by the Nigerien Company for Groundnuts (SONARA), was extended to this bush market within the past 20 years. Grain sales at controlled prices were monopolized by the government within the past 5 years. Recently, with the paving of the road to Nigeria, Gada has become a produce bulking market, albeit on a small scale so far. As in most tertiary markets in Zinder, the choice and supply of nonlocal products in Gada is limited and uncertain, particularly during the season of cultivation.

THE STUDY COMMUNITIES

Maidoki

Maidoki is located about 50 kilometers south of Zinder town. It lies 5 kilometers east of the paved road to Nigeria, but no road links the village to Gada market, some 7 kilometers to the north on the main road. The village lies on slightly evolved lithosols formed on semistabilized sand dunes that are subject to severe wind erosion because of scanty vegetation. Between the dunes are heavy hydromorphic soils with a relatively high humus content located on the margins of small ponds and employed for dry season gardening. While fertile, these soils are difficult to manage because of the presence of dissolved potassium carbonate (natron) in the water. About 400–500 millimeters of rain are received from May to July annually.

The soil supports a bush vegetation of the grassy woodlands series. Trees with well-defined trunks like *Acacia albida, Hyphaene thebaica* (a palm), *Tamarindus indica* (the tamarind), and the wild custard apple (*Anona senegalensis*) coexist with short annual grasses and a perennial *andropogon* species.

Modern infrastructure is nonexistent in Maidoki. There is no cement well, school, veterinary service, nursery, or clinic nearby. The government-sponsored cooperative headquartered in Gada, however, began active intervention in village production habits in the late 1960s.

The villagers number 266 and are of Kanuri-Hausa extraction. They make three main uses of the natural environment. The remaining bush land is harvested for fruits, palm leaves, medicinal herbs, firewood, and potash. Bush and fallow lands are available for livestock pasture. During the short rainy season the dune soils are planted with millet, sorghum, cowpeas, and groundnuts. Small gardens are cultivated with capsicum peppers, onions, squash, sugar cane, cassava, rice, and tree crops.

Mean household farm size in Maidoki is 15 hectares, large by regional standards, while additional women's fields averaged 0.8 hectares. Most men possess fallow land and practice crop rotation. Dry season crops are planted in association.

The mean value of seed sown on 15 family farms was $13. Groundnuts are monocropped, and groundnut seed costing each household head an average of $15 is obtained on loan from the state. Each woman's seeding cost for cereals was about $3, while groundnut seed cost each of them about $4.

Mean yields of family farms were about 1,800 kilograms of grain, at a rate of about 190 kilograms per hectare, which is half of the country average. Women's fields yielded about 209 kilograms per hectare, primarily because of denser sowing. The average market value of produce from a family farm was $473, and about 16 percent of the harvest was marketed. The average value of groundnut production after repayment of loans was $70.

Between 1976 and 1980 food production was inadequate to meet household needs. A total deficit of about 6000 kilograms of grain was reported for 15 households for these years. Women's contributions to the household fund made up some of the deficit, but this was a violation of cultural norms of gender behavior. Women produced an average of 203 kilograms of grain a year, worth about $86, and groundnuts worth about $33 each year.

Men supplement their incomes with gardening, which nets on average about $22 per year, with income from commerce and craft production, which provides an average of $112 per year and with livestock sales worth on average $233 per year. Gardening is an increasingly important component of production strategies, although gardening is an old practice. Livestock has also been an important component of the domestic economy but is an increasingly important source of income. An average household owned 24 animals, 78 percent of which were small ruminants. The average value of a household's herd was $933. The average market value of a man's herd was about $733, that of a woman was about $235. Men own more large livestock. There were considerable variations in household income on the order of 3:1.

Kadafan Tulu

Kadafan Tulu is located just a few kilometers southeast of the Mirria market, to which it is connected by a well-traveled earthen track. It is situated on tropical ferruginous soils that have a tendency toward aeolian erosion and leaching. Even where leaching is not severe, these soils have limited agricultural value. The microenvironment of the village includes an extensive drainage basin. Seasonal runoff from distant hills creates an intermittent swamp around Kadafan Tulu which provides clay and supports bird populations but is also a breeding ground for malaria-carrying mosquitos and guinea worm. The natural flora is characterized by woodlands savannah vegetation, and the seasonal watercourses support considerable stands of trees.

All available land is employed in rainfed hoe cultivation of millet, sorghum, and cowpeas. There are no gardens and no fallow or bush land. Villagers own cattle and small ruminants, but most animals are entrusted to a village herdsman who pastures them along a watershed as far as 75 kilometers from the village. The most important use of local natural resources is the extraction of clays and the women's production of a utility pottery sold throughout the province.

Claiming autochthony, the village at present has a population of 356 persons, who, like those in Maidoki, live in four separate hamlets. There is a 45-year-old cement well, now inadequate for village needs. Ten children attend a primary school a few kilometers away. Government services, a clinic, secondary schools, and the palace of the traditional local emir are located in Mirria.

Mean household farm size in Kadafan Tulu was seven hectares, but only two women possessed personal farm plots. There is no fallow land, and only in-field rotation of associated crops is practiced. The mean value of seed sown on 15 farms was about $13, the same as in Maidoki, but the seeding rate per hectare was about double. Groundnuts are not sown because of poor performance and the greater utility of subsistence crops.

Mean yield was about 1,611 kilograms for each family farming unit (FFU), but such units were larger on average than in Maidoki because of land shortage. Yields per hectare were higher in Kadafan Tulu: 302 kilograms per hectare, mainly a result of better rainfall and soils and more intensive seeding and weeding practices.

The average value of farm production in Kadafan Tulu was about $607, but only an average of 8 percent of the harvest was marketed, half the figure for Maidoki. Over a two-year period 15 households in Kadafan Tulu suffered a net food deficit of 2,500 kilograms, but villagers employed a higher consumption standard than in Maidoki. Intrahousehold variation in total annual production was more marked in this village than in Maidoki, on the order of 4:1.

Instead of cultivating, almost all adult women produce pottery, using a combination of coiling and molding techniques. Thirteen different types of pots are produced, but water vessels predominate. Average annual production is about 34,000 vessels, worth about $19,000. Sixty percent of sales revenues, however, accrue to the male pot traders, who are the women's relatives and neighbors. Each of the 110 producers stands to earn an average of $69 per year from pot sales. But the nine principal potters each earned about $212, and eight groups of two to four cognatically related women (32 in all) accounted for 47 percent of the output. There was thus considerable stratification in output and income among women, which contributed to economic stratification.

Livestock is as important a store of value in Kadafan Tulu as in Maidoki. Men own large numbers of donkeys (for use in the pot trade) as well as small ruminants. The average man's herd was worth $400. Women owned small ruminants and cattle, but ownership of the latter was concentrated among nine major pot producers. The average woman's herd was worth $474. Eleven households owned an average of 17 beasts of which 79 percent were small ruminants. The average household's herd was worth about $909.

Angoal Majema

The tanners' quarter, unlike the other two communities, is located in an urban environment: a corner of the *zengou* (one-time caravan stop and Tuareg quarter) of Zinder town. Modern Zinder, a city of 60,000 persons, now surrounds the *zengou*, including the present tanners' quarter. The tannery now lies about 500 meters northwest of the old *zengou*, where it was moved by early French authorities.

The first tanners were brought to the walled city of Zinder from Bornu in the 1850s as slaves of Sultan Tanimum. Later, as freed men, some two hundred tanners labored in the household of a great precolonial merchant. Today, just 21 men labor independently to support their households.

One nearly exclusive system of production is practiced in Angoal Majema: tanning and trading of hides. Annual hide production of the 15 full-time tanners and their 6 most active dry season apprentices amounted to 16,500 hides. Goat and sheep hides and small goat skins used in rugs accounted for 40 percent of output; they are mainly destined for tourist consumption. Cowhides account for another 16 percent of output and are usually sold to be used as buckets by Tuareg or Fulani pastoralists. The value of cowhides exceeds the value of goat and sheep hides.

The tanners vigorously downplay individual specialization, emphasizing instead their common heritage. Nevertheless, individuals tailor output to match their physical strength, to meet long-term agreements with certain regular clients among the leatherworkers, and in line with personal proclivities.

The approximate net income from hide sales is about $14,000 annually. Mean income among full-time tanners was $868 but ranged from $469 to $1,386. Vigorous men specializing in cowhides and maintaining large households and employing many dry season apprentices earned higher incomes.

In addition to tanning men rent empty compounds inherited from deceased or migrant relatives, trade hides to the state marketing monopoly (SNCP), sell raw materials to other tanners, and market finished leather goods. In one case an individual acts as the *muzzein* at a local mosque. These occupations are an important arena for experimentation with new forms of entrepreneurship and are limited to this urban context.

Women have few sources of income because they are placed in Moslem seclusion after marriage. If there is an unmarried daughter or other girl coresident in her household, a woman may prepare food for sale to the tanners and other consumers, earning up to $100 per year. Some women earn up to $50 per year from the sales of decorative leather horse collars. Most women, however, are completely dependent on their husbands for consumer goods and pocket money.

UNITS OF REPRODUCTION

What then are the local units of reproduction that are the object of study? I make a distinction between the conjugal family unit, the family, and the household. The conjugal family unit (CFU), consisting of a married couple and their offspring, is sometimes called a simple elementary family. In general, the family may be thought of as the set of cultural expectations of what domestic groups and domestic relationships should be like, that is, a normative or ideational component of modes of reproduction (Rapp n.d.:78; Reyna 1976). The family refers to normative rules, those of recruitment and devolution, for example (see Carter, this volume). The household, on the other hand, is a dynamic empirical unit (albeit a culturally particular one; see Yanagisako, this volume) in which reproduction and other important tasks, commonly including production, transmission, pooling, and distribution, take place (see Wilk and Netting, this volume). In defending their ideals or norms of family and in acting on them, people adopt household strategies that provide the dynamism and variability so evident in most systems of social reproduction (see Kunstadter, this volume).

In some African societies application of these concepts is problematic (see Linares, this volume; Woodford-Berger 1981), but in Hausa society the three concepts have emic referents. The CFU corresponds to the Hausa *iyali*. *Family* is translated by a number of words, including *iyali, gida, dengi, iri,* and *waje,* depending on the context and inclusivity intended. This discussion largely sets aside the complex symbolic content of familial concepts in Hausa society. Finally, the concept *household* corresponds to the Hausa *gida*, or multiple CFU coresidential dwelling cluster, and to various meanings attached to the concept of the *gandu*, or family farming unit (FFU) (Hill 1972, 1977), which are discussed in detail below.

AN IDEAL OF HOUSEHOLD MORPHOLOGY AND ORGANIZATION

Greenberg (1947), M. G. Smith (1955), and Nicolas (1960) have provided descriptions of the Hausa *gida* (household) and *gandu* (multiple family farming unit) which have become the classical referents against which contemporary variations in Hausa domestic organization are compared (see, for example, Hill 1972 and Goddard 1973). Problems of reification aside, this description, with modifications contributed by my informants, does approximate the emic ideal in Maidoki and of elder men in Kadafan Tulu, although not the ideal of younger men in the potters' village. It does not correspond to the actual or remembered household organization of the tannery, which was already influenced by urban market forces in the precolonial period. Nor does this model adequately encompass the range of present-day household structures in any of the three communities. Nevertheless, as an ideal type, some of the elements of which are actualized in all three communities, this description of the household is a worthwhile point of departure for a discussion of household morphology and task organization.

Each Hausa farm village was built up around a core family group (*dengi*) composed of agnatic kinfolk. The fundamental unit of residence, production, distribution, transmission, and reproduction was the *gida*. At a mature stage of the domestic cycle the *gida* was a patrilocal multiple family household (Wheaton 1975:607) of at least two generations depth and comprising the conjugal family units (*iyali*) of the household head (*mai gida*) and his married sons and their children (Greenberg 1947). Some wealthier *gida* contained farm slaves.

The *gida* was essentially a family farming unit (FFU) distinguished from other FFU by usufructory rights of tenure to dune (*jigawa*) and marsh (*fadama*) lands (Raulin 1965), control of its own granary, and disposition of the labor power of its active members.

The household head (*mai gida*) partitioned the household land into *gandu* (collective) and *gamana* (individual) parcels. Men worked together on the *gandu* five days a week, and junior men in *gandu* and wives worked on their *gamana* one day a week. The *mai gida* held the fruits of *gandu* production in trust and was obliged to feed, clothe, and pay taxes and ceremonial expenses of his household from the *gandu* produce during the agricultural season (Greenberg 1947:195). With the help of the extended agnatic kin group the *mai gida* ensured that his sons and daughters would marry. Individuals and junior *iyali* fed themselves during the dry season from the fruits of the *gamana* and, in addition, used *gamana* produce to participate in ceremonial events and exchanges (baptisms, marriages, funerals). *Gandu* produce could never be sold; *gamana* produce could be, but the bulk of production took place on *gandu* plots.

On the death of the *mai gida* the inheriting sons did not immediately divide the land and slaves but continued to work together, the eldest brother assuming the role of *mai gida*. At this stage of the developmental cycle the *gida* became a *frérèche*. As the families of the brothers grew, they divided the patrimony. Usually junior brothers were compelled to clear new bush lands.

Small households in the traditional setting could overcome temporary or seasonal labor bottlenecks by calling young men in the village to participate in a labor party (*gayya*), a form of interhousehold labor exchange. *Gayya* were also called by young men to meet labor service obligations to their wives' parents (Nicolas (1960:412). *Gayya* were instrumental to the social reproduction of the community because they enabled smaller and poorer households to cope with accidents of demography or illness that threatened their viability.

Interlocking conditions have been cited as favoring extension of this sort of household system over a very large part of the Sahel: long fallow hoe cultivation, limited agricultural productivity, a complex agricultural calendar with seasonal labor bottlenecks, periodic localized crop failure, abundant land, a low level of development of transport and intraregional commerce, the weakness of supralocal political institutions, high fertility, and the necessity for local defense (Greenberg 1947; Nicolas 1960; Burch 1972; Hill 1972; Raynaut 1973; Faulkingham and Thorbahn 1975; Lovejoy and Baier 1975).

Problems of Description and Comparison

Description and comparison of contemporary household morphology in Zinder is complicated by the lack of definitive criteria for discretely bounding household units and by interhousehold variation in the organization of tasks both within and between the communities.

In European historical demography the criterion of coresidence for household membership (a morphological distinction) is commonly used (see Wilk and Netting, this volume; Douglass, this volume). If this criterion were naively applied in Zinder, then every CFU would be counted separately because every CFU occupies a walled compound including a dwelling for every wife. In addition, seasonal migration commonly results in temporary reshuffling of personnel between households. In Hausa-speaking areas, therefore, few have employed the coresidence criterion alone to define households.

Some (Norman 1967; Hill 1972, 1977) have used the basic unit of production—the family farming unit (FFU) or the *gandu*—as the basic household unit. Although farmers now equate *gandu* with FFU whether or not the *gandu* conforms to the multiple CFU ideal household described above, this definition of the household is adequate for most descriptive purposes. Application of this criterion of cooperation in production yields fairly consistent data on the mean size of family farming units not only for the communities I studied but also for other Hausa communities as well. The data in table 6.1, column 3, confirm this.

Defining the household as the FFU or production unit is not entirely satisfactory if other tasks are employed as criteria of household membership. As Goddard (1973) showed, there is considerable variability in the allocation of household tasks among members of CFU within FFU in different communities even though all farmed land in common (see below).

People in the communities I studied actually seem to employ a multivariate definition of the *gida*, or household. Members of a *gida* reside close together in clusters of compounds (see Wilk, this volume) and labor on

TABLE 6.1
COMPARATIVE MEASURES OF HOUSEHOLD SIZE

Location	Mean size of conjugal family unit (*iyali*)	Mean size of family production units	Mean number of CFU/*Gida*[f]	% of *Gida* with married sons
Maidoki	4.9 (N=42)	7.8 (N=28)	1.5	68
Kadafan Tulu	3.6 (N=77)	6.9 (N=39)	1.8	34
Angoal Majema	5.0 (N=22)	5.5 (N=21)	1.0	N/A
Central Niger[a]	4.6	7.6	1.7	
Tudu, Tahoua province[b]		19.0		
Maradi province[c]		5.7		
Katsina Nigeria[d]		5.09		24
Sokoto[e]				
Riverine			2.4	69
Accessible			2.2	58
Remote			2.0	36

SOURCES: [a]Pool and Piche 1971; [b]Faulkingham and Thorbahn 1975; [c]Raynaut 1976; [d]Hill 1972; [e]Goddard 1973.

[f]In this table *gida* are defined as equivalent to household production units, which are termed *gandu* in the rural areas.

gandu fields together. But *gamana* plots consume more labor time than was true in the past, and the distinction between *gandu* and *gamana* has grown fuzzy, so that any CFU may consider itself the proprietor of a *gandu* if other criteria of comembership in another household are not met. In addition, there is tremendous variation from the ideal in the degree to which junior householders participate in agricultural tasks such as field clearance, granary construction, and fencing gardens, which contributes to qualitative differences between *gandu* organization among *gida*. There is also considerable variation in pooling of dry season income.

Hausa also employ the criterion of reproduction (see Wilk and Netting, this volume) to distinguish households from one another, a fact not given sufficient attention in the literature. Members of a *gida* include those for whom marriage and tax payments are paid by the household head. All men who assume these tasks, as well as responsibility for feeding and clothing their dependents, are considered to be household heads, and those for whom they assume these tasks are said to be members of their households. Men do not, however, necessarily farm with the man who pays their taxes and marriage expenses. An old man who pays taxes for his dependents lists a different set of household members than a junior man from this unit who has contributed to his own and other householders' tax and marriage payments with earnings from migration or commerce. Be this as it may, only when a CFU ceases to contribute to the household fund from which subsistence, taxes, and ceremonial expenditures are drawn does it conclusively lose membership in its parent household. In summary, then, the multivariate definition of the household that is employed by my Hausa informants and the existence of variation in intrahousehold pooling and distribution resulting from changing patterns of marriage and migration leads to a confusing overlap in household boundaries and uncertainty when dividing households from one another.

MARRIAGE PATTERNS

Marriage alliances transform the material products of economic activity into new reproductive units through ceremonial exchanges. While native models for marriage and the behaviors associated with it determine the nature of resulting households, intercommunity variations in marriage patterns are indicators of divergent responses to changes in the climate of production and exchange effected by the articulation of capitalist and precapitalist modes of production in Zinder. Table 6.2 summarizes marriage data.

TABLE 6.2
MARRIAGE, ENDOGAMY, AND DIVORCE

Population structure	Maidoki	Kadafan Tulu	Angoal Majema
Marriages in sample	117	167	37
% Endogamous	17	41	27
% Exogamous	83	59	82
Marriages per man[a]	3.3	2.4	2.1
Wives per husband	1.3	1.06	1.07
Mean age at first marriage	17.5 (N=40)	20.1 (N=68)	25 (N=25)
Mean age at first marriage, men under 30	17.0	19.2	24.5
Mean age at first marriage, men over 30	17.1	21.3	26.5
Total marriages 1977-1980	13	17	6
Total divorces 1977-1980	3	6	3
% Polygynous men	28.8	17.0	10.0

[a]Marriages include all marriages past and present of men in the sample.

Marriage is viewed as the normal state of affairs for sexually mature people in Zinder. Polygyny is also valued, especially by urban dwellers in closer contact with the Islamic world. In the past polygyny was an indicator of wealth, of the individual's ability to mobilize the labor of a large number of persons. It was the presence of sons in *gandu* and farm slaves which enabled senior men to accumulate wives through their display of wealth.

Maidoki

Table 6.2 shows that 13 marriages and 3 divorces between 1977 and 1980 brought the number of married men in Maidoki to 52. There are just 1.3 wives per man, and only 29 percent of married men are polygynous. Rates of polygyny in other Hausa villages commonly reach 37 percent (Hill 1972; Raynaut 1973). Today polygyny is a good indicator of the control of money wealth rather than labor. The three wealthiest men in Maidoko each have three wives; two of these men earned their wealth in groundnut marketing while the third is the chief. Six other duogynists earned money in livestock trade or as Muslim clerics. The others are vigorous cultivators and marketers of garden produce and groundnuts. In short, polygyny today is related to success in marketing products in demand in Gada.

Men average 3.3 marriages in their lives. High rates of divorce and remarriage are probably related to economic insecurity. Although men claim that most divorces occur as a result of disobedience to the husband or jealousy between cowives, conflict between spouses is commonly caused by failure of the husband to provide an adequate level of support for a wife or wives (see Saunders 1978, 1979).

Though the rate of polygyny is low and divorce is common, the proportion of men of marriage age who actually do marry reaches nearly 100 percent in Maidoki. It is almost impossible for a man to survive as a solitary in the agricultural economy of the village in which autarchy is an ideal and the sexual division of labor is complementary.

Age at First Marriage in Maidoki. The age of first marriage of both men and women in Maidoki seems to be decreasing. The causes of the decrease in age and the now near universal marriage of eligible adults can be found in the market system. Lowered age at first marriage among older men was made possible by the inclusion of Maidoki in the groundnut collection network in the 1940s. Unlike cereals cultivation, groundnut cultivation was neither gender nor age specific, and because groundnuts were grown on individual farm plots (*gamana*), proceeds from sales were not preallocated for intrahousehold redistribution by the household head (Nicolas 1962). Individual groundnut sales made it possible for men to amass the goods necessary to marry off their sons earlier than before, and the income also allowed young men to pressure their fathers into allowing them to marry earlier.

Today men may arrange earlier marriages for their sons, knowing that their sons will eventually migrate in search of cash and hoping to ensure that more of the migrant's off-farm income makes its way back to the village than it would if the son were not married. The recent marriage of three men at age 16 may also indicate that senior men are responding to temporary market opportunities by financing early marriages. In other words fathers are arranging marriages for their sons whenever harvests permit the accumulation of a small surplus instead of waiting until their sons reach a more culturally appropriate age when harvests may be poor. It is also possible that in response to unfavorable producer prices farmers are marrying off their sons earlier in an attempt to shift some of the burden of household maintenance and social reproduction onto their sons' shoulders, since all married men should assume responsibility for their families' subsistence needs. Paradoxically, the result of these moves is to promote the earlier partition of *gandu* and the creation of smaller *gida*.

Kadafan Tulu

In the potters' village 17 marriages and 6 divorces during my 15 months of study brought the number of married men in the village to 75, as shown in table 6.2. Only 17 percent of men are polygynous, with 1.1 wives per married man. Married men average fewer marriages in their lives than in Maidoki, just 2.4. Here polygyny is quite strictly related to the control of money wealth since marriage costs are almost as high as in Zinder town and the bridewealth should contain expensive imports. Only three men keep three wives: one is the village chief; the others are elderly men who rent donkeys to the young pot traders.

Three polygynous men, one of them with three wives, are married to divorced or widowed village potters under an unusual marriage formula called *je ka da kore ka* ("go with your bow"). *Je ka da kore ka* marriage derives its name from the tensions inherent in the relationship between the husband and woman's grown male children, the latter of whom are jealous of the rights of sexual access which normally inhere in the marriage contract. In this arrangement the wives remain in their prenuptial residence close to their grown, married sons. Wives receive periodic visits from their husbands, but they do not perform the usual household tasks expected of a Hausa wife. Instead they manage their own and their sons' compounds as if they were household heads; the sons farm and trade pots produced by their mothers. Indirect evidence from pottery trader purchase patterns in the village indicates that senior men enter into this type of marriage contract primarily to enable their own sons to obtain pots produced in their wives' compounds. Women seem to enter into these marriages of convenience primarily to preserve their respectability, their income from potting allowing them financial independence. Such marriages thus result in the constitution of matrifocal and matrilocal households.

Age at First Marriage in Kadafan Tulu. Table 6.2 shows that the average age at first marriage in Kadafan Tulu was higher than in Maidoki, the agricultural village. Nor are all eligible men and women of Kadafan Tulu married. These facts seem to be related to the higher money costs of marriage and the greater proportion of household income and bridewealth that must be earned as cash. Marital conflict is endemic in this community, as it is not in Maidoki, primarily because of greater sexual polarity attendant on the elevated contribution of women's income to household funds and because of men's difficulties in setting themselves to work independently and successfully. As in Maidoki, first marriages are brittle and usually end in divorce.

Angoal Majema

The number of married men in the tanners' quarter increased over the two years of this study from twenty-four to twenty-five. Only 10 percent of married men are polygynous. Marriages are also more stable here than in the rural communities; tanners average only two marriages in their lives.

The existence of stable monogamous households is linked to various economic peculiarities of Zinder town, which are in turn linked to its position at the apex of the regional market system. Among these peculiarities are the extremely high cost of marriage and the lack of economic opportunities for secluded married women. Stability is also facilitated by the relative security of tanning as a means of livelihood, but polygyny is limited by the low level of income: most tanners cannot afford to support a second wife and her children.

The resistance of married women also discourages the formation of polygynous households. Because secluded urban wives do not work for cash incomes, cowives are forced to share whatever revenues the household head allocates to them. Unlike rural women, for whom a cowife lessens domestic chores, urban women oppose polygyny. Monogamy and marital stability are two factors contributing to the constitution of tanners' households as independent economic units.

Age at First Marriage in Angoal Majema. Late age at first marriage seems to be characteristic of the tannery, although women marry younger than do men. In the past senior tanners delayed the marriages of their sons and apprentices in order to reap full benefit from their labor. Today master tanners no longer assume the marriage expenses of their apprentices, although they do finance their sons' marriages. Marriages can be contracted earlier today because young men may freely enter the market with their own hides. They did not have this freedom in the days of the caravan trade. But the age of first marriage remains high because of the inflation of bridewealth costs under the influence of standards of consumption adopted by commercial and political elites.

Exogamy and Endogamy

Table 6.2 shows that the three communities vary with respect to rates of exogamy. This can be linked to patterns of participation in the marketing system.

Maidoki. Eighty-three percent of Maidoki marriages are exogamous. They are almost invariably patrilocal. Maidoki is linked to some two dozen neighboring communities by marriage alliances. Wealthy men sometimes seek alliances in market towns of a higher order than Gada to facilitate commercial activities, but most men seek alliances in agricultural villages. Affines are a potential source of seed, cuttings, and money loans, and in times of local crop failure affines in a distant village may be a source of food aid. In other words, men prefer to rely on their network of marriage alliances in order to obtain inputs to production as well as food in periods of crisis rather than on the market system, which has proved to be unreliable in this regard.

Most wives come from within a 15-kilometer radius—a day's walk. Women favor this arrangement for the same reasons as men; in addition, proximity allows them to participate in ceremonies linked to social reproduction in their natal villages. Their mothers may more easily attend them in childbirth as well.

Kadafan Tulu. Of the 187 marriages ever contracted by married men in the potters' village, 41 percent were endogamous, far more than in the agricultural village. Endogamy is linked to the high value of commercialized pottery. Men value alliances with skilled potters because of the stable and growing money revenue from pottery.

Women also prefer endogamous unions. Daughters who marry locally retain access to means of production located near the village, and both mothers and their daughters can look forward to intensive dry season cooperation in domestic tasks and pottery production when the absence of male migrants lightens their household tasks.

Marriages are sometimes contracted with close relatives, particularly parallel cousins, such as father's brother's daughter. Such marriages are termed *armen gida* (see Saunders 1978). They pose several advantages to the allied households: they significantly reduce marriage costs, keep scarce agricultural land within a single patriline, keep valuable female labor within the household, and strengthen ties of cooperation between brothers who cooperate in a single household. Although *armen gida* is practiced in both rural communities to strengthen bonds between agnatic kin, it is more popular in Kadafan Tulu where there are more financial advantages to it. Thus endogamy and *armen gida* tend to intensify the possibilities for intra- and interhousehold pooling and redistribution of agricultural and potting revenues while large women's revenues tend to destablize households.

Angoal Majema. Almost 82 percent of the marriages contracted by the tanners are with nontanning households, but only a quarter of marriages are contracted outside of Zinder town. Tanners favor alliances with Muslim clerics, but surprisingly few marriages are contracted between tanners and their most dependable customers, the leather workers. Exogamous marriages are usually contracted with distant kinfolk in rural communities. Such alliances usually facilitate a sporadic flow of millet and apprentices to the workshop in the dry season and entail the reciprocal hospitality of the senior tanners to apprentices and other travelers to Zinder town.

LABOR MIGRATION

Meillassoux (1975), Amin (1974), and Ouedraogo (1977) argue that seasonal labor migration is destructive to the reproduction of Sahelian household systems because it disrupts relations of production in which elders control the labor of junior household members and its fruits. Lovejoy and Baier (1975) and Faulkingham (1976) argue, on the contrary, that labor migration is a component of long-term strategies of social reproduction in the Sahel linked to periodic climatic crises. Meillassoux (1975) and Grier (1981) argue that *modern* migration of wage laborers enables capital to exploit labor at or below reproduction costs because capital relies on the village community to reproduce future workers. In so doing capital disrupts without replacing prior patterns of intergenerational cooperation and decreases the chances of long-term social reproduction.

In Zinder household morphology, task performance, and the structure of social reproduction are all affected by seasonal migration, which assumes different forms in each community because of their differing positions within the regional marketing system.

Maidoki and Kadafan Tulu

In 1978–79, 20 men from Maidoki and 44 men from Kadafan Tulu migrated during the dry season. Eighty percent of the men between ages

16 and 30 in Maidoki and between ages 16 and 45 in Kadafan Tulu have participated. Men from Maidoki migrate for three months or less while those from Kadafan Tulu commonly migrate for four or five months at a time.

Most men from Maidoki worked irregularly at commission sales jobs in Zinder town or in Nigeria. The average value of their remittances amounted to about 20 percent of the average value of *gandu* production and about 84 percent of the average value of a *gamana*'s yield in Maidoki. Clothing is distributed to the migrant's wife, children, and parents, and small amounts of money may also be distributed.

Men migrating from Kadafan Tulu found more regular employment than those from Maidoki as itinerant tea sellers, Muslim clerics, and bonnet embroiderers in Kano. Men are commonly employed by the same merchants each year, or the men reside with the same senior clerics. Three clerics from Kadafan Tulu were recently killed in religious rioting in Kano. It is uncertain what effect the expulsion of aliens from Nigeria in early 1983 will have on productive strategies in this village.

In 1978–79, migrants returned with cash and goods equal to half the value of women's annual pot production of $18,000. The average migrant's income is equal to 35 percent of the value of average *gandu* production. Migrant income thus represents a larger share of total household income in Kadafan Tulu than in Maidoki. But most migrants seem to redistribute their earnings through ceremonial exchanges, marriage payments, debt repayments, and purchases of prepared foods rather than turning their earnings over to the nominal head of their household, as senior men still believe they should. Migrating men frequently establish independent households rather than cope with interminable disputes over household pooling. Migration seems to be linked to the small number of CFUs per household in Kadafan Tulu (see table 6.1).

Angoal Majema

Two different migratory processes affect household morphology and task performance in the tanners' quarter. Urban educational and employment opportunities in Niamey, the capital, and the mining districts around Agadez and Arlit are inducing the tanners' natural offspring to seek individual solutions to the problem of meeting urban consumption standards. From the perspective of youth the paternalistic patron-apprentice norms that historically governed behavior in the tannery appear an anachronistic impediment to individual gain (see Verdon 1978). There is thus regular attrition of the tanners' sons out of the craft and out of the neighborhood as well.

A process of immigration occurs simultaneously with the process of emigration just described. Each year 7 to 12 young men from the bush come to the tannery to work during the dry season when demand for cowhides is at its peak. The tannery provides a setting in which these young men can earn the cash necessary to supplement cash crop revenues and subsistence stocks produced in the bush. In order to gain access to the means of production they must dedicate some of their labor power to tasks set for them by the master tanners. Nonetheless, experienced apprentices can earn between $50 and $100 in three to four months of work.

Occasionally one of the immigrating apprentices decides to settle in Angoal Majema permanently and establish a new household there. While this pattern is not without historical precedent, what is new and reflects the development of open market for hides in Zinder is that these immigrants now establish economically independent households within the quarter without accepting the control of senior tanners over the allocation of household resources and their labor.

HOUSEHOLD MORPHOLOGY

Table 6.3 identifies household types, mean size, and dependency ratios of the *gida* censused in the three communities. There are significant differences in the distribution of household types and in their sizes, but dependency ratios appear less variable.

Maidoki

In Maidoki 44 percent of the households are simple and 56 percent are complex. About one-quarter of the simple households consist of CFUs at the beginning of the domestic cycle, the parent household having been dispersed by the death of the senior household head. Another quarter consist of households at the end of the domestic cycle in which an elderly couple and grandchildren, whom they have adopted, live together. Adoption of grandchildren is traditional in Hausa society and one of the means by which the ratio of workers to consumers between households is regulated. The other half of the simple households in Maidoki consist of the CFUs of young men who have chosen to break away from a possible multiple family household arrangement. Some of these men's brothers, however, participate in multiple family households. Overall, less than 10 percent of the total number of possible multiple family households are not actually so organized in Maidoki.

TABLE 6.3
Household Type, Size, and Dependency Ratios

	Household types[a]																		
	Solitary			Elementary			*Frérèche*			Stem			Multiple[b]			Houseful			Total
Community	N	S	D[c]	N	S	D	N	S	D	N	S	D	N	S	D	N	S	D	N
Maidoki	1	1	1.0	11	4.5	2.2	2	15	1.5	0			13	9.5	1.9	0			27
%	3.7			40.6			7.4						49.1						100
Kadafan Tulu	2	1	1.0	11	3.4	1.7	6	7.3	1.2	4	3.8	1.5	13	9.4	1.6	2	10	1.5	39
%	5.2			28.2			15.3			12.8			33.3			5.2			100
Angoal Majema	1	1	1.0	16	5.0	3.8	0			1	6.0	2.0	3	9.6	3.3	0			21
%	4.7			76.1						4.7			19.2						99.7
Total	4			38			8			6			29			2			87
Percentage	4.5			43.2			9.1			1.8			23.1			2.3			100

[a]N = number
S = mean size
D = dependency ratio $\frac{\text{persons aged 0–15 and 65+ years}}{\text{persons aged 16–64}} \times 100$

[b]Refers to households with at least two agnatically related CFUs of two-generation depth.

[c]Wives are included as dependents only in Angoal Majema where Islamic seclusion limits their income- earning opportunities.

Kadafan Tulu

In Kadafan Tulu about 34 percent of households are simple and about 56 percent are of the multiple variety when cooperation in agriculture is the sole criterion of household membership. But Kadafan Tulu exhibits a greater diversity of household types than does Maidoki. Included are three matrifocal joint family households created through the *je ka da kore ka* marriage strategy discussed above and housefuls composed of the CFUs of unrelated men. *Frérèche* are also relatively more numerous than in Maidoki.

Angoal Majema

The tanners' quarter exhibits a drastically different range of household types, sizes, and dependency ratios from those of the two rural communities. Here elementary families predominate, though many consist of CFUs for which there is potential for the formation of *frérèche* or multiple family households. In fact only 19 percent of households are of the multiple family type, and housefuls that one would have expected to find, given the history of immigration to the tannery, do not exist. Average CFU size is greater than in the rural communities, and dependency ratios are much higher than in the rural households. High dependency ratios indicate the extent to which the burden of social reproduction falls on the shoulders of the household heads. The high ratio is an artifact of the lack of economic opportunities for secluded wives, which in turn is linked to Islamic ideology concerning gender roles and the division of labor which is most strongly observed in the major cities of Niger, like Zinder. The ability of household heads to sustain the large number of dependents in their households is made possible not only by revenues earned from tanning but by income from other commercial endeavors.

HOUSEHOLDS AND PRODUCTION UNITS

Table 6.1 presented data on the size and composition of family production units, and the size of the CFU corresponds to theoretical expectations of family size in a society like that of Niger (Burch 1972). While family size in Kadafan Tulu varies somewhat from the theoretical norm, this may be an artifact of the large size of the median age cohorts. Family sizes in these communities are also comparable to those reported for other Hausa villages.

Both rural communities in Zinder have more than a single CFU per farming unit on average, while in Angoal Majema, where farming has all but been abandoned, the tendency for the *gida* to be reduced to the single CFU is just about complete. This is an outgrowth of the commercial strategies of household heads in the tannery, just as multiple households are a part of the autosubsistence strategy of household heads in the most rural community, Maidoki.

Although mean FFU size is quite large in both Maidoki and Kadafan Tulu, there is a considerable range in size and quality of the work force fielded by each household. It should be borne in mind that 30 percent of the household heads in Maidoki and 34 percent of the household heads in Kadafan Tulu farm alone or with the help of their wives and small children only. These figures are similar to those reported for Katsina, Nigeria, where Hill (1972:17) found that 50 percent of household heads farmed alone. The low figure reported for Kadafan Tulu derives from the shortage of farm land that makes sharing farm work a necessity.

Task Performance

The figures reported in table 6.1 show few differences in the internal organization of production units in the rural communities, but the organization of both productive and reproductive functions does differ substantially.

Ideal or Complete Gandu. Older men in Maidoki and in Kadafan Tulu said they lived in households that corresponded in morphology and task performance to the ideal or complete *gida* described above. Complete *gida* are preserved morphologically in both villages today, but they are based on changing tasks and diversified resources and are associated with social stratification.

Nearly 70 percent of *gida* in Maidoki contain married sons. In riverine Sokoto a similar percentage (see table 6.1) was associated with a relatively low degree of off-farm income. Households in Maidoki are indeed reliant on on-farm activities for their income. Nevertheless, the ideal *gida* morphology and division of labor occurs only in a few households that not only cultivate many fields and large gardens, have high fertility overall, and dispose of enough labor to respond quickly to seasonal shifts in labor demand but also possess large livestock holdings derived from success in the groundnut trade. Neither the possession of abundant land nor labor alone is sufficient to ensure that the household conforms to traditional models. It is also necessary that land and labor be employed in producing commercially valuable goods and that the household have large reserves.

In Kadafan Tulu the number of married sons in *gandu* is relatively low, but the incidence of complete *gandu* is lower still. Barma, the village chief, is one of the few men to maintain a household conforming morphologically to the traditional norm, but he is unusual in other respects. The two married men in his *gandu* were matrilateral relatives whose bridewealth he provided and whose taxes he pays. Of the six fields they cultivate together, two were purchased and one is an interest-free loan. The household pools pot-trading revenues as well. The two young men trade the pots produced by two of Barma's wives as well as those produced by their own wives and by one of the young men's mothers. Barma lends the two men donkeys and in return receives a half share of the trading revenues. The other half is split between the traders and the producers. Barma also derives income from a share of village taxes and from village grain sales to the state marketing monopoly. A few other households, some *frérèches*, some matrifocal, correspond in broad outline to this pattern.

In both rural communities new commercial resources, livestock, and pottery allow some households to preserve the precolonial household ideal, yet few households can muster the necessary resources given the shortage of livestock in Maidoki and land in Kadafan Tulu. Two other kinds of household morphology and organization were found in the two villages which differed from the ideal pattern.

Land Gandu. The household organization of a number of FFUs in Maidoki corresponds to Goddard's (1973:214) description of the land *gandu*. In this case the land held in usufruct by the household may be subdivided among daughter households while the *mai gida* lives. Subordinate men contribute to marriage and tax payments from individual enterprise but retain a larger share for themselves. The participation of subordinate men in *gandu* activities (excepting cereal production) is limited by migration and other individual economic activities. Distribution and pooling is reduced at the level of the multiple family household, and individual CFU provide for more of their own needs than was true in the past.

Land *gandu* are also associated with a shift in inheritance patterns which tends to hasten division. Youngest brothers often remain at home while older siblings migrate. The former participate more fully in *gandu* activities and are more likely to inherit the paternal *gandu* under an informal system of ultimogeniture. Inheriting sons, however, must assume primary care for aging parents. If migrating sons were excluded from my count of men in *gandu* because of their lessened contribution to maintenance and reproduction, then land *gandu* might be said to resemble a stem family household system more closely than the ideal multiple family system. Land *gandu* describe the majority of FFUs in Maidoki which lack access to the commercial resources available to households that approximate the ideal pattern. Disinclination to obey the authority of the *mai gida* and his first wife (*uwar gida*) on the part of young men and their brides is also cited as a reason for lessened cooperation and early division of the *gandu* by the older folks in the village.

Cooperative Gandu. The most radical departure from the ideal *gandu* is to be found in Kadafan Tulu. Individual CFUs that share *gandu* fields pool labor and resources during the rainy season of cultivation, but for most of the year male labor migration and women's pottery production act as an effective curb to extensive cooperation. In other words, high individual incomes act to disrupt older patterns of cooperation and pooling. The land is not divided only because there is a serious shortage of land. Thus defining households as FFU in this village yields overestimates of effective household size.

Barely a third of *gandu* contain married sons. Nor are all members of a *gida* necessarily active even in cereal production, the mainstay of the Sahelian village community and essential to the preservation of the multiple household. As in Katsina (Hill 1972) and Maradi province of Niger (Raynaut 1976) individual commercial activities have reduced the scope of intra-CFU cooperation, pooling, production, and participation in reproductive activities.

While the degree of cooperation between agnates has declined, women play an increasingly important role in the constitution of households. For long periods of the year, while the men are away, women assure the survival of their households from pottery revenues. During the dry season some senior women maintain matrifocal compound clusters in which there is a high level of cooperation in domestic tasks and pottery production. Some women have gone so far as to pay the marriage expenses of their sons and daughters. Women also participate far more intensively in the network of ceremonial exchanges than men. While women's public role is no greater than in Maidoki or Angoal Majema, their financial contribution is greater than the men's in many households.

The increased role women play in assuring the persistence and reproduction of their households leads to antagonism between spouses. Conflicts between husband and wife over the disposition of the wife's labor, like parallel conflicts between brothers, fathers, and sons in *gandu*, contributes both to the high divorce rate and to declining cooperation among related households.

SUMMARY AND CONCLUSION

A number of questions and hypotheses enumerated at the beginning of this paper concerning the relationship between marketing and systems of social reproduction in Zinder can now be evaluated. Commercial opportunities and constraints, ideals and past experiences of domestic life combine to create new and varied patterns of household morphology and task performance. In Maidoki the old ideals are retained: the multiple CFU *gida* is the point of social reference for most people. The types of households censused seem to reflect various stages in the traditional developmental cycle. But the internal structure of the *gida* based on the authority of senior household heads has changed and intrahousehold cooperation lessened because of the effects of labor migration and new commercial strategies of cash cropping.

In Kadafan Tulu few people still cling to the old ideals but rather make creative use of elements of traditional household forms to establish new units of social reproduction, such as housefuls, matrifocal compound clusters, and households based on patrilateral parallel cousin marriage oriented toward pottery production and marketing. Many of the household types censused do not conform to stages in the traditional developmental cycle. There is a tendency toward duolocal postmarital residence, and gender-based polarity is increasing because women make a greater contribution to household reproduction than is sanctioned by traditional norms.

In Angoal Majema the old ideals associated with the patron-apprentice workshop/household have evolved into a more vague statement of communalism: "we are all of one family." Men still cooperate informally in the workshop and a few retain apprentices, but apprentices are no longer controlled as they were when the master tanners monopolized access to raw materials and to markets. Most households are elementary in form, and most are quite autonomous as regards maintenance and reproduction. In addition, the Islamic ideology tends to strengthen androcentric bias in the construction of gender identities (see Linares, this volume) and thus seems to be promoting greater gender inequality in this urban central place where women's economic contribution to the household is less than in the rural communities.

In all three communities memories of intrahousehold cooperation are at variance with the limited and variable arrangements observed. Instead, each community exhibits patterns of household organization which are sensitive to the differing, new commercial opportunities and constraints available. As was hypothesized, manipulation of commercial strategies seems to promote economic stratification in household morphology and task performance. Thus, those who have gained wealth by production of cereals, groundnuts, garden produce, and livestock in Maidoki are most likely to be polygynous and to live in multiple households (see Netting 1982). Successful cash cropping is related of necessity to larger household size, given the ideology of family and the low level of development of productive technique which prevails. Nongardeners, blacksmiths, and those who dispose of a small labor force are poorer and live in elementary households.

In Kadafan Tulu successful pot producers or traders are more likely than others to live in multiple family households. Although some may be matrilocal, others approximate the paternal *gandu* ideal. Nonpot traders and clerics are forced to migrate and tend to live in elementary family households or in multiple CFU *gida* that approximate the ideal only during the brief periods of dry season residence.

In Angoal Majema large household size correlates with control of a diversity of economic resources peculiar to urban Zinder, in addition to vigorous tanning and kin ties in distant villages. Small households rely for their income on tanning alone. Overall, maximum household size decreases as dry farm income becomes less important in the domestic economy and the economic value of children declines from the agricultural to the urban artisanal setting. Thus, changing economic circumstances contingent on the market allow fewer households to realize the cultural ideal appropriate to successful farmers and artisans in the past (see Hill 1972; Goddard 1973; Raynaut 1976).

Household morphology, marriage patterns, and migration seem to be closely related and are in turn sensitive to the demand for labor and local products. Continued emphasis on subsistence farming in Maidoki favors exogamous marriages, which tends to strengthen the *gandu* system of social reproduction, while specialization in pottery production favors endogamous unions in Kadafan Tulu. Endogamy and *armen gida* are favored by a mode of social reproduction based on the commercial success of individual households rather than successful subsistence farming at the level of the entire community.

In the tannery in Zinder elite consumption standards favor later marriages and more stable unions, while the limited degree of cooperation between households favors a strategy of alliance based on considerations of cost and prestige unique to each household. Consequently, social reproduction is closely tied to the economic prosperity of Zinder as a whole.

In all three communities migration is an important variable in the construction of households and their internal organization. In Maidoki migrants leave because of severe local cash shortage, which is a result of low producer prices for most agricultural products. Most migrants, however, leave in order to earn enough cash to return to the village and take up permanent residence there.

In Kadafan Tulu there is a longer tradition of migration and a greater spirit of economic individualism associated with the high level of pottery trading begun in the southern groundnut market places of the 1940s and evident more recently in other markets. Many clerics and commission traders, however, leave in order to protect their personal incomes, and they maintain a residence in Kadafan Tulu only to farm and to obtain a wife.

Migration at the levels it reaches in the two rural communities tends to be self-sustaining (Rey 1971) and leads to modifications in household form. Migration seems to be associated with the land *gandu* in Maidoki and the cooperative *gandu* in Kadafan Tulu because of the ruptures it creates in the organization of production and in the control and flow of resources within the household. While the absence of young men during the dry season relieves pressure on available food supplies, greater responsibility for household maintenance and reproduction falls on the shoulders of women, a phenomenon more advanced in other parts of Niger. The rapid redistribution of remittances into consumption goods through ceremonial exchanges diverts resources from productive investments beneficial to the reproduction of the traditional *gida* and strengthens economic individualism.

In Angoal Majema a simultaneous process of emigration and immigration has created a unique situation. The social reproduction of the tannery is a function of immigration of young men from the bush, which in turn is caused by low agricultural prices on local markets. But each tanning household is largely dependent for its maintenance on the productive activity of one man, which is a function of emigration and the democratization of the market place. This represents a drastic change in the organization of production and exchange from traditional models.

While decisions affecting household organization, age at marriage, endogamy, and migration, which in turn affect household morphology, have been sensitive to local labor needs and market opportunities, demographic rates are less subject to these rapid local adjustments. High fertility is a recruitment strategy pursued by households in rural areas while lower fertility characterizes households in the tannery. High fertility in Kadafan Tulu, however, is incompatible with the low local demand for labor. An ideology favoring high fertility is still shared by all the communities, although this seems to spring from an older premarket, subsistence orientation of agricultural communities. Dependency ratios are also markedly similar for all communities and household types and do not seem sensitive to differences in individual productivity as defined by the market value of locally produced products. But in the purely cash nexus of the tannery where decreased demand has reduced the overall size of the tanning community but high unit value makes individual output fairly valuable, dependency ratios are higher. In short, household morphology and structures of social reproduction are sensitive to changing market conditions that now mediate most productive activities. Structures of biological reproduction have been less sensitive to these changes in the past 50 years.

REFERENCES

Amin, S.
1974 Introduction. *In* Modern Migrations in West Africa, ed. S. Amin. International African Institute. London: Oxford University Press.
1975 Neo-colonialism in West Africa. New York: Monthly Review Press.
1976 Unequal Development: An Essay on the Social Formations of Peripheral Capitalism. New York: Monthly Review Press.

Arnould, E. J.
1981 Petty Craft Production and the Underdevelopment Process in Zinder, Republic of Niger. Dialectical Anthropology 6:61–70.
1982 Regional Market System Development and Changes in Relations of Production in Three Communities in Zinder Province, Niger Republic. Ph.D. Dissertation, University of Arizona.

Arnould, E. J., and H. K. Henderson
1982 Women in the Niger Republic. University of Arizona, Tucson: Consortium for International Development. Office of International Agriculture Programs, Women in Development Program, Working Paper no. 1.

Burch, T. K.
1972 Some Demographic Determinants of Average Household Size: An Analytical Approach. *In* Household and Family in Past Time, ed. P. Laslett and R. Wall, pp. 91–102. Cambridge: Cambridge University Press.

Collins, J. D.
1974 "Government and Groundnut Marketing in Rural Hausa Niger: The 1930s to the 1970s in Magaria." Ann Arbor: University Microfilms International.

Faulkingham, R. H.
1976 Fertility in Tulu. Manuscript.

Faulkingham, R. H., and P. F. Thorbahn
1975 Population Dynamics and Drought: A Village in Niger. Population Studies 29 (3):63–77.
Geertz, C.
1963 Agricultural Involution: The Process of Ecological Change in Indonesia. Berkeley and Los Angeles: University of California Press.
Goddard, A. D.
1973 Changing Family Structure among the Rural Hausa. Africa 43 (3): 207–18.
Godelier, M.
1975 Modes of Production, Kinship, and Demographic Structures. *In* Marxist Analyses in Social Anthropology, ed. M. Block, pp. 3–28. London: Malaby Press.
Greenberg, J.
1947 Islam and Clan Organization among the Hausa. Southwestern Journal of Anthropology 3 (3):193–211.
Grier, B.
1981 Underdevelopment, Modes of Production, and the State in Colonial Ghana. African Studies Review 24 (1):21–48.
Hill, P.
1972 Rural Hausa: A Village and Its Setting. Cambridge: Cambridge University Press.
1977 Population, Prosperity, and Poverty: Rural Kano, 1900 and 1970. London: Cambridge University Press.
Löfgren, O.
1974 Family and Household among Scandinavian Peasants: An Exploratory essay. Ethnologia Scandinavica 1974:17–52.
Lovejoy, P. E., and S. Baier
1975 The Desert-side Economy of the Central Sudan. The International Journal of Historical Studies 8 (4):551–80.
Meillassoux, C.
1975 Femmes, Greniers, et Capitaux. Paris: Maspero.
Netting, R. M.
1965 Household Organization and Intensive Agriculture: The Kofyar Case. Africa 35:422–29.
1982 Some Home Truths on Household Size and Wealth. Manuscript.
Nicolas, G.
1960 Une Village Haoussa de la Republique du Niger: Tassao Haoussa. Cahiers d'Outre-Mer 13:420–50.
1962 Aspects de la Vie Économique dans un Canton du Niger: Kantche. Cahiers de d'Institut de Science Économique Appliqué, series 5, no. 5, no. 131, pp. 105–88.
Norman, D. W.
1967 An Economic Study of Three Villages in Zaria Province. Samaru Miscellaneous Paper 19. Samaru, Zaria: Institute for Agricultural Research.

Ouedraogo, O. D.
1977 L'Émigration et la Dynamique de L'Activité Productive à Zogore (Haute Volta). Manuscript. Dakar: IDEP.
Pool, D. I., and V. L. Piche
1971 Enquete sur la Fécondité au Niger Central. Methodologique no. 2. Niamey, Niger: Centre Nigerien de Recherche en Sciences Humaines (CNRSH).
Rapp, R.
n.d. Peasants and Proletarians from the Household Out: An Analysis from the Intersection of Anthropology and Social History. Manuscript.
Raulin, H.
1965 Travail et Régimes Fonciers au Niger. Cahiers de l'Institut de Science Economique Appliqué, series 5, no. 9, pp. 119–140.
Raynaut, C.
1973 Structures Normatives et Relations Électives: Étude d'une Communanté Villageoise haoussa (Niger). Paris: Mouton.
1976 Transformation d'un Système de Production et Inégalité Économique: Le Cas d'un Village haoussa (Niger). Canadian Journal of African Studies 10 (2):279–306.
Rey, P. P.
1971 Colonialisme, Neo-colonialisme, et Transition au Capitalisme. Paris: Maspero.
Reyna, S. P.
1976 The Extending Strategy: Regulation of the Household Dependency Ratio. Journal of Anthropological Research 32 (2):182–198.
Sanday, P.
1974 Female Status in the Public Domain. *In* Women, Culture and Society, ed. M. Rosaldo and L. Lamphere, pp. 189–206. Stanford: Stanford University Press.
Saunders, M. P.
1978 Marriage and Divorce in a Muslim Hausa Town (Mirria, Niger Republic). Ann Arbor: University Microfilms International.
1979 Women's Divorce Strategies in Mirria County, Niger Republic: Cases from the "Tribunal de Premier Instance." Paper presented at the 22nd annual meeting of the African Studies Association, Philadelphia, Pennsylvania.
Smith, C. A., ed.
1976 Regional Economic Systems: Linking Geographical Models and Socioeconomic Problems. *In* Regional Analysis, vol. 1, pp. 3–65. New York: Academic Press.
Smith, M. G.
1955 The Economy of Hausa Communities in Zaria. Colonial Research Study no. 26. London: Her Majesty's Stationery Office.
Wheaton, R.
1975 Family and Kinship in Western Europe: The Problem of the Joint Family

Household. Journal of Interdisciplinary History 5 (4):601–28.

Verdon, M.

1978 African Apprentice Workshops: A Case of Ethnocentric Reductionism. American Anthropologist 6 (3):531–42.

Woodford-Berger, P.

1981 Women in Houses: The Organization of Residence and Work in Rural Ghana. Antropologiska Studier 30–31:2–35.

7

Nuclear Is Not Independent: Organization of the Household in the Pays Bigouden Sud in the Nineteenth and Twentieth Centuries

Martine Segalen

The size and structure of the household are sensitive to and dependent on several factors. Size and structure are correlated with the social and cultural environment; they are directly subject to demographic factors and inheritance practices and, as such, their study can be useful in understanding changes in the family which are linked to the industrial revolution, urbanization, and industrialization.

When data make it possible the household should be analyzed in reference to a larger context. Though we know kinship groups are not corporate in our complex societies, kinship nonetheless plays an important part in building network organization. We can observe the kinds of social interaction that run along the network lines and try to relate household structures and tasks to a larger familial organization.

Studying the household in reference to a larger kin network is particularly necessary when cross-cultural comparisons are made or when rapid changes occur, as is the case in the area of Brittany studied here. Yet this approach raises a methodological problem. Only anthropologists can use different criteria of household membership, since they can examine ongoing exchanges and interaction, whereas the historian dependent on census lists has to stick to the implicit criterion of coresidence.

In this paper[1] I shall analyze the household (1) as a coresiding domestic group and (2) as a task-oriented unit (following Wilk and Netting, this volume). To assess the effects of economic and social change on households, I shall also observe them in their kin-based network.

A COUNTRY IN UPHEAVAL

An area with a long tradition of agriculture, Saint-Jean Trolimon, and more generally the Pays Bigouden Sud (Hélias 1975) in the southern part of Finistère, is looking for a future. Long an area of small farming where land was held by bourgeois owners living in towns, the property was purchased by its tenants at the end of the nineteenth century and beginning of the twentieth century. As a result of partible inheritance practices, the farms were continuously divided, and by the 1950s they were much too small to allow the numerous children (this is an area of high demographic fertility) to stay on the estates as farmers. Consequently, few children remained on the farm, and most of them emigrated, leaving for Nantes or Paris to work in factories or frequently as highway patrolmen. These emigrés inherited a plot from their parents' estate and often built a house where they still return on holidays. I shall consider in the last section of this paper these "episodic" domestic groups.

Active farms at present have a small size: 17 are over 20 hectares, 50 around 10, and 30 under. Farmers are aging: most of them are 60 years old and over, two are under 50, and only one is 25. Only a few of them have managed the difficult conversion to modern agriculture, abandoning polyculture crops and turning to intensive hog or cattle raising.

When I started fieldwork in 1974, the village was experiencing a crisis, with a declining and aging population, an uncertain future regarding the structure of agriculture, and most of the farmers having no heir to take their land after them. In the area there is no large industry, but only small plants creating little new employment. Quimper and Audierne are mainly commercial and administrative cities. The only prosperous sector is that of fishing on the coast. Some revenues are derived in summer from low-income tourism.

Yet in 1979, 1980, and 1981 the situation has altered quickly by the coming of age of a new generation, sons or grandsons of farmers who have decided not to emigrate as the previous generation did but to try to find employment locally and live in the area where they were born and socialized. These young men's decisions have spurred the building sector, which in turn has created jobs. Popping up around the countryside are individual tile-roofed, rough-cast houses with stone-framed

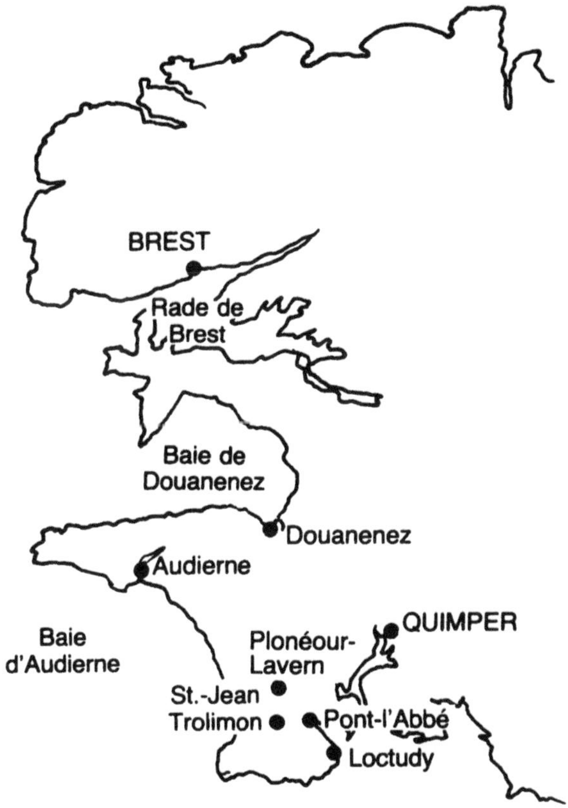

Brittany and the Pays Bigouden

Scale: 1/100,000

doors and windows; these so-called traditional *maisons bretonnes* have nothing in common with the thatched-roof farmsteads always hidden behind trees and located in the recessed parts of the estates. On the contrary, the new houses are spread in anarchic disorder all over the countryside, to be seen and admired from far away.

Until the 1921 census 90 percent of the population of St.-Jean lived in scattered hamlets—*ker*—consisting of clusters of two to ten farmsteads; the village was nothing more than a crossroads with the church surrounded by the graveyard, the school, the *mairie*, a few cafés, and some small farms. Since then, the number of inhabitants living in the countryside has decreased and the small town is growing as young people build their houses along the main roads and especially in the two housing estates, one private, one promoted by the commune.

Most young men find employment in the building sector: they are carpenters, plasterers, plumbers, and heating specialists, working either as independent *tacherons* or employed by local firms. Women are employed in Pont-l'Abbé, Audierne, or Quimper as workers in the canning industry and employees in the various administrative offices or businesses. The present social structure of the population is thus intermediate between country and town, between agriculture and crafts or industry. In the past there was always an important interaction between country and local towns, with cultural and economic influences flowing in both directions. These interactions are now so strong and frequent that the boundaries between country and town are blurred. We must then scrutinize relations between family change and socioeconomic changes, the latter being so sudden that they were relatively unpredictable less than ten years ago. What changes do we observe in household structural organization and in the kinship network? How do these alterations correlate with the general changes that have taken place within the last 60 years?

CHANGES IN HOUSEHOLD STRUCTURES

I examine two types of households here: the farmer's household, where residence, family, and work are usually integrated, and the households of craftsmen and employees, where residence and work are dissociated. In the first case the domestic group shares a house attached to a farmstead that is a working tool; the house in the second category is only a place of residence.

The Laslett typology reveals the changes that have taken place between 1921 and 1981 (table 7.1).

The number of solitaries has increased spectacularly, the number of simple family households remains relatively stable, the number of extended family households has decreased, and the number of multiple households has slightly decreased.

We must be very careful when comparing the categories of fixed typologies (Segalen 1977:227) because their connotation changes when important social and economic changes occur. We cannot infer from the stability of a category of household the stability of the household's internal organization; nor can we infer from a change in categories a change in the household organization. Besides, categories take on a different meaning according to the system of values. With these difficulties in mind, what can we conclude from table 7.1?

The increase of solitaries is the result of a complex interplay between demographics, social policy, and norms. Lower mortality and longer life

TABLE 7.1
HOUSEHOLD STRUCTURE CHANGES FROM 1921 TO 1981

	1921	1975			1981[a]
		Total population	Agriculturally employed	Retired and nonagriculturally employed	
Solitaries	6.9	24.5	9.0	34.7	29.05
No family	1.4	3.6	3.3	3.8	—
Simple family	67.3	63.8	79.8	53.3	67.2
Extended family	18.6	4.5	5.6	3.8	3.7 (extended and multiple family combined)
Multiple family	5.8	3.6	3.8	4.4	
Total number of households	230	232			296

[a]The 1981 figures are not taken from a census list but have been communicated by the Secretary of the Mairie, whom I thank here.

expectancy account for the increase in the number of old, widowed people. The welfare state provides for them, whereas in former times they were dependent on their children. Nowadays, retired agriculturalists can live on old-age pensions. In addition, the norm is now that adult generations live independently. Emigration has often left older people alone, with kinship ties loosened by physical and cultural distance. Even when children live nearby, they prefer to see the old mother or father staying alone, visiting frequently in the parent's house. Thus, the increase in the number of aged solitaries accounts for the development of old-age clubs, where once a week the old people of the village gather to chat over a cup of coffee, play cards, or knit. The decrease in extended family households is the reverse side of the increase in the solitary category. Old people who were formerly kept at home are now independently housed.

Beyond these changes the most remarkable feature concerning household structure over the last 60 years is its stability. Percentages in simple family and multiple family households are almost identical. What can we conclude from this data? The nuclear domestic group appears to be the cultural norm while the multiple family household is a sign of family crisis or marginality. Living in a separate house right after marriage is practically a condition to marriage, and often a young couple will postpone their wedding until they can settle immediately on an independent basis. Thus, kin-tied couples sharing the same house appear as the poorest ones, integrated with difficulty into modern society. Generally, we find in these cases an old couple still farming a small estate and a daughter or son with spouse sharing the same old, uncomfortable house. The son or son-in-law goes out to earn a salary in a factory while the young woman helps the old people work the land and take care of the cattle. These two categories—nuclear and complex—refer then to drastically different situations if we oppose them to similar ones 60 or 100 years ago.

In the nineteenth century simple and multiple configurations of the domestic group alternated along the family life cycle, and the succession of various phases appeared as "normal." Assuredly, the model was oriented toward independent nuclear households, but sharing the roof of the parents was culturally accepted until the early twentieth century.

The alternation of phases of simple, multiple, and extended family households appears then both temporary and structural. A young couple would start in their parents' farmstead, then leave it and settle independently one, two, or five years later as the size of their family grew. When their children in turn got married they too would spend a temporary period on their parents' estate until they found a free farm. Generally, the youngest son or daughter and his or her spouse would take over the farm from the aging parents or on their death. Coresidence appears to have been structural for parents once their children got married while it was temporary for the young couple at the beginning of their own family cycle.

Not all households, however, experienced this sequence of nuclear, multiple, and extended phases. There is a marked hierarchy among peasants, and only richer households could afford to be extended or multiple, accommodating young couples and their children or older parents. The structural alternation of phases is the sign of a relatively well-to-do farmstead. Each estate would feed a relatively fixed number of people, or it could be said that the size of the farm needed a fixed amount of human work. When children grew up and got married, they would replace servants that were only needed as long as children were too young to work effectively. This is why, when we observe a household along its life cycle, the number of people—household head and wife, children, relatives, servants—remained fairly constant when technical means of production remained unchanged. In contrast, the poorer households, those of very small tenants or day laborers, could not afford to feed a large number of people. Among this group existed a majority of nuclear domestic groups. The older parents rarely coresided with their married children, and even the older children could not remain with their parents. When they reached eight or ten years of age, they were placed as servants in the larger farmsteads of the area. The stability of a nuclear household in the nineteenth century was generally a sign of great poverty.

This comparison shows us how cautious we must be when manipulating the categories of a typology that covers different meanings and situations under the same headings. But a further question arises as we consider household organization. Can we infer that the younger, most active section of the population living as nuclear domestic groups are totally separated from the other related domestic groups? If it is true that "the household social unit responds more flexibly and sensitively to changes in the socio-economic environment than do larger aggregations such as kin groups and settlements" (Netting 1981), it is yet impossible to examine household organization as if the house where a domestic group resides were separate from others. Only in connection with the wider kin networks linking individuals and households can changes taking place in household organization be significantly described.

A few decades ago Talcott Parsons supposed that family changes, under the effect of industrialization, cohered with the nuclearization of the household and the severance of extended kinship ties. Historians have since demonstrated that households were nuclear in a large section of Europe before industrialization started (Laslett 1972). Anthropologists like Jack Goody (1972) have also emphasized that family changes took place not so much inside domestic groups but within kinship networks linking the various domestic groups.

Another common assertion concerning the present-day family is that the interaction is more or less limited to the married children and both sets of parents, as if the rest of the kinship network had only a insignificant, symbolic importance. The material concerning the Pays Bigouden Sud shows on the contrary that domestic group organization is strongly connected to kinship networks, revealing a seeming paradox: nuclear households are nowadays highly dependent on kin for the organization of their tasks, probably more dependent than they were in former times of extended or multiple households. I put forth this hypothesis after long observation of contemporary life in this region. This hypothesis could not be derived from the examination of census lists, which give kinship ties inside each domestic group but not between them. Before presenting the contemporary situation, I shall briefly discuss the importance of kinship ties in this peasant society under the traditional way of life that prevailed until the early twentieth century.

DOMESTIC GROUPS AND KINSHIP NETWORKS IN THE NINETEENTH CENTURY

I am not concerned here with the structure of the kinship network but with the amount and type of services, help, and goods that were exchanged between domestic groups or between individuals within the domestic group. In the latter category we can mention the mother-daughter bond, which was very strong even if the two were physically separated, and involved cooperation in child care, cooking, healing, and similar activities. The bond between siblings might be reinforced as they became godparents of their nephews and nieces. The services exchanged between domestic groups could include material help between kin-linked domestic groups on such occasions as ploughing, harvesting, and threshing, which required a lot of manual labor. Yet when children settled independently, they did not necessarily work with their parents. Young people often found farms relatively far from their parents' properties, and if we consider the state of the roads in that period, they often could not set up a work team. Work cooperation was thus often based on neighbor networks. The organization of work also associated richer and poorer domestic groups; the small holder would come and help the larger farmer during the ploughing period and the latter would lend his horse and plough implements to the former to till his small plot of land. It appears then that the work force was formed inside the household but at times required pooling between households, either kinfolk or neighbors, according to the stages of the annual labor cycle.

Distribution processes were also correlated with household size and structure and depended on the amount of resources to be pooled or exchanged inside the household or between households. A farm produced agricultural products and animals. Grain and calves are the product of a yearly cycle; poultry, eggs, dairy products, and garden vegetables also come out of the hen house and garden. These products could be used directly, transformed into money, or fed into another product category. Grain, for instance, could be kept in the house for food preparation, fed to the calves, or sold on the market, which implies an additional step, for between production and distribution decisions had to be made regarding the pooling/distribution strategies of the household (see fig. 7.1).

Inside the house, generally managed by the head woman, food was distributed according to a social hierarchy. The male household head received the largest servings and the best pieces, followed by older children, male servants according to an internal hierarchy, women, fe-

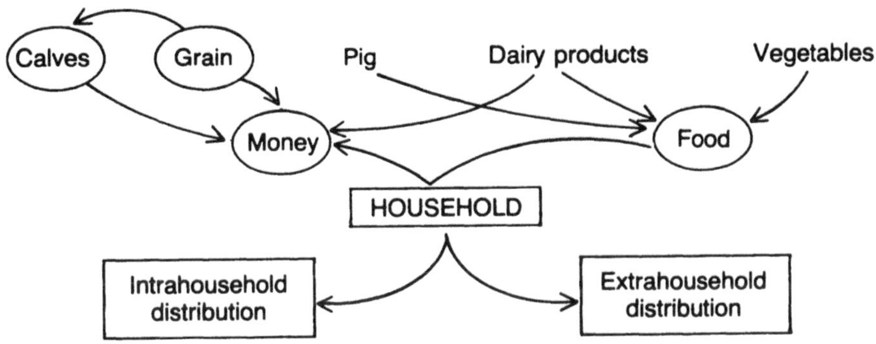

Fig. 7.1
Intra- and extrahousehold distribution within the farmyard

male servants, and younger children. Money was given to servants as a salary and to young married couples waiting to settle on an independent farm. Adult unmarried children did not receive any salary. A balance was struck between the number of servants, coresiding married children, and unmarried adult children. At some periods in the yearly cycle, when work forces were pooled during harvesting, for example, households reserved products generally sold for money to be distributed among other households when needed for collective cooking and eating. Products were also distributed at family gatherings, baptisms, and marriages whose rituals were accompanied by enormous quantities of food or at annual family *pardons*—religious feasts. Aside from agricultural products, some money was otherwise produced and used by the household, but it had to be set aside as a separate category related to the inheritance cycle. Money entered and left the household according to the stage of the family life cycle: shares were received from brothers and sisters or given to them; dowry installments were received from parents or given to children after marriage. There was a constant process of income and expenditure, linking related households of parents, children, brothers and sisters, grandparents, nephews, and nieces.

Intrahousehold and extrahousehold pooling clearly appears to have been linked to surpluses obtained from farming; only large farms could keep a large number of people inside the household and also engage in more extrahousehold transactions, staging more important marriage feasts, which yielded more prestige and important symbolic rewards. The smaller day laborer's household achieved the balance between resources and items distributed on a lower level. Among resources were a small cereal harvest and some daily wages coming in on an irregular basis (there were no long-term work contracts). Supporting resources were thus low and fragile and all mouths could hardly be fed, which put a strain on children to leave the farm as soon as possible. We find no extended households. Not only was there little extrahousehold distribution but in fact the whole economy was vulnerable. Around 1850 and at the turn of the century hordes of families turned to begging on the roads and worked their way down to the coast where they found employment as fishermen or workers in the canning industry.

Households were also connected to larger social networks from which they received various types of services. Along these networks flowed information concerning the whole area (since settlement was scattered) about farms that had become available and about young girls and boys who might make good matches. The wide kinship and alliance networks offered a pool of spouses, as the habit was to marry not so much inside a line (consanguineous marriages) but between lines who had already married two of their children. Of course, as anthropologists have so often demonstrated, belonging to this or that kindred gives the individual material, social, cultural, and political privileges (for instance the titles *maire* and *conseiller municipal* remained in the richest lines and passed on regularly from generation to generation) and more generally set every individual's place and rank within the society.

In the nineteenth century in the Pays Bigouden Sud the norm was clear. Households should be nuclear but tightly bound by kin and neighbor relationships. Coresidence was always a temporary solution to the problem of a limited number of farms available to young couples in a time of population increase. Children were socialized to leave the family farm; all but the two younger children knew they would have to settle on their own, and certainly not very close to their parents' farm. Nuclear family households and mobility inside the area were two characteristics of the local social structure. Having an independent household was certainly a value; thus, around 1900, when a farmer managed to buy a large farm, he would divide it into two parts (giving money to the unlanded heirs) and set up two different houses for a brother and a sister to live separately with their spouses. This norm, however, could only be achieved by a section of the population, given the economic and demographic situation. Nevertheless, the concept of the nuclear household was strongly embedded in wider social networks whose presence was indispensable, whether for pooling, distribution of help, work, or information. In a different manner this holds true today.

PRESENT-DAY DOMESTIC GROUPS AND KINSHIP NETWORKS AMONG FARMERS

The peasant household is today as it has been in the past a family, work, production, and consumption unit, but its structure and organization have been profoundly disturbed by the social, agricultural, and more general economic changes affecting the area. A radical restructuring of agriculture is under way. Because most farms are too small for the requirements of modern agriculture large sums of money are necessary to modernize them. What happens most often is that when a farmer retires, his land is bought by a contractor if it is good enough to be worked, and the farm buildings cease to be used. The production unit disappears, and the houses are sometimes rented to tourists. When individual farmers carry on their family enterprise, they often shift to intensive pig or cattle breeding, but very few are in this category. Now in the *ker* where one could once count two to ten farms, there remains but one farmer, which makes traditional neighborly cooperation difficult. The households are always nuclear; if the children do not migrate, most of them leave agriculture for another activity and settle, sometimes close to their parents, sometimes in the nearby area (I will examine these domestic groups in the next section).

Young couples who take over the estate left by an old farmer must enlarge it and must cooperate with their own parents. Independence of the nuclear peasant domestic group implies interdependence in work, unlike the system prevailing in the nineteenth century. Farmers driving their tractors and other huge mechanical equipment are a common sight on the road during the months of July and August. Usually you are seeing a father driving to his son's farm, or the reverse. If cooperation between near kin is not possible, the farmer draws on a widely dispersed group of similar, commercial agriculturalists. Thus nuclear domestic groups are organized on an interdependent basis for the temporary times of heavy work.

Daily tasks rest with the farmer and his wife, but self-sufficiency seems frail and threatened. If a farmer is physically handicapped, he finds it difficult to hire help, based as it now is on a precarious professional network. In former times when peasants were numerous, if a labor problem arose a servant or a worker could be hired or a parent or neighbor would come to help. We also observe here, in contrast to other areas of France, that farmers' wives put in a lot of work on the farm, mainly because they are deprived of the help of servants, unlike their forebears. Household organization, though internal to the domestic group, appears directly dependent on external factors both connected with the kinship network and social and economic conditions. Nuclear households, though in conformity with the norm of independence, are a heavy liability in the organization of daily routines and production work of farmers.

DOMESTIC GROUPS AND KINSHIP NETWORKS TODAY: NONFARMERS

Farm children who decided to quit agriculture often left the area altogether in the 1950s. This was a period of large internal migrations in France, when industry developed quickly and towns grew into cities with large suburbs. Leaving agriculture and the area was part of the individual's search for "modern" culture, a new way of life, and a higher standard of living. Thirty years later city lights seem less attractive. Most young people now endeavor to remain where they were born and find employment locally. Those who have received only a basic education often find jobs in the building sector. Once married, these young people settle independently in their own houses, but the organization of the domestic group is strongly dependent on the parents' household and more generally on the kinship network. Examples abound warning us against equating nuclear households and an independent way of life.

Most young couples, children or grandchildren of farmers, inherit a piece of land on which to build a house. Living independently is the norm, and while the young couple's house is being erected they prefer to rent a small apartment or cram into a room, even though they could have been accommodated by their parents. Building the house—the nutshell of the domestic group—is a kin-based operation. Because it is possible to assemble a team of relatives who have complementary technical skills, most of the work is done without the intrusion of a commercial firm.

This operation is accomplished on an exchange-of-services basis during weekends and holidays. Only the building materials are bought. Let us take the example of Pierrot and Gilbert B., two brothers; one is a plumber, one is employed by the most important building contractor of the area. Their father is a retired mason, a job that sons of the poorest farms would often take in the 1920s. Their mother, Léonie, inherited a small plot of land right in the center of the town. When Pierrot and Gilbert married two years ago, each received a share of the land, which was divided into three parts, the third portion being kept for Marie-Claire, the youngest, and still single, sister. In August 1979, during his month of vacation, Gilbert dug the foundations of his house, laid the concrete stone of the cellar, and raised the plaster walls. All this work was done with the help of a team composed of his father, father-in-law, brother, brother-in-law, uncle, and cousin. Besides having personal relationships with local entrepreneurs through his work, Gilbert was able to borrow the crane free of charge and his brother-in-law transported the building materials in a truck lent by his employer. Day after day, weekend after weekend, the team of kin built the house; it was necessary to pay only for the wooden frames and the roof, tasks for which no technical skills were represented among the men working together. All other operations were performed on an exchange basis. Gilbert helped his brother build his house a few months later and will give a hand, when the time comes, to his cousin and brother-in-law. These free services were made possible because of the particular skills commonly found in the area and among the occupations of the relatives; building houses creates mutual dependency between households and is one among the many services, goods, and types of information exchanged along kinship networks.

Once the house is built, the young couple moves into a nuclear family household. Yet this domestic group is extremely dependent on the parents' household. In the farming system the household was an integrated unit of residence, work, production, and consumption. Now these functions of the domestic group have been split.

The house is the place of meals, leisure, private time; work takes place elsewhere in the area. The young man may work as a craftsman on various sites, the young woman may be employed in one of the various small mills or offices of the nearby towns. The woman's work is generally indispensable because her salary helps pay off the loan contracted on the house. Because of the young woman's absence, the parents provide help in daily activities. This is possible because the house of the young couple is built relatively close to the parents' home. Contrary to the example of Pierrot and Gilbert, who have built near their mother, I have observed a strong tendency for daughters to build near their mother's house. The help coming from the parents' house increases when a baby is born. A grandmother may keep the baby at her house all day long, sometimes all week long. In addition, she may take over a lot of the cooking for the young couple. Pierrot and Anne-Marie, for example, have a son whom Anne-Marie brings to her mother-in-law every morning with the baby food prepared in a thermos bottle, the mother thus retaining control of the baby's feeding.

Sometimes the ties between the household of the young couple and that of the parents is much stronger, and integration seems to increase as the life cycle unrolls and children grow up. Consider the case of Fernand Le B., a plasterer, son of a farmer, and Annick T., his wife, employed as an accountant in one of the canning factories of the area. Their home is built 200 meters from that of Annick's mother, Jeanne, a farmer's widow who shares her house with a sister, Marie, a spinster and retired social worker. Annick goes away to work all day and her two children are totally in the charge of her mother. Jeanne belongs to a car pool to drive the children to school and she keeps them at night during the week. Moreover, when Fernand has the occasion to come home for lunch, he eats at his mother-in-law's house. The entire group—parents, children, grandmother, and aunt—eat the evening meal during the week at Jeanne's house.

Thus Fernand and Annick's house is virtually an empty shell, only used on Sundays when the washing machine is put to work or on a few social occasions. Moreover, the socialization of the children is principally assumed by the older generation. This contrasts with the general assertion that modern children are brought up in isolated households with poor interaction between generations. In the Pays Bigouden Sud at least, we can observe the active role of the grandmother, who as a native Breton speaker may speak poor French and convey to grandchildren a limited French vocabulary. Here then continuity between generations is ensured by choice, and there is no conflict about the accepted model of socialization.

A number of social exchanges take place around food. We have seen that Jeanne and her sister Marie, who carry on a limited amount of farming and keep a single hog each year, feed their household and that of Jeanne's children mostly from their domestic production. The hog is killed and cut up at home and distributed between the two households: home freezers are now a staple of domestic equipment. In all households whatever gardening parents carry on is done mostly to give produce to children, relatives, and friends whose menus benefit from the abundant fruits and vegetables. The traditional feminine focus on the hen house continues everywhere and is always a means of integration between households. This is evident in the household of Mathilde, married to Marcel, who works as a mechanic in a gardening appliances retail business. Her house is separated from that of her mother, Marguerite, by a garden and a small patch of land where she grows grain for the poultry. The grain is harvested by a contractor and stored in the garage; each week Mathilde gives her mother the necessary amount to feed the chickens and the rabbits. Once a week, Marguerite, who supervises the hen house, kills a hen and plucks it for Mathilde to cook for the Sunday lunch that Marguerite will share at Mathilde's house. The domestic organization of both houses, one nuclear, one composed of a "solitary," is based on a dense exchange mainly through food, which integrates both households to the point that they are one. The mother-daughter bond is permanently activated for general help, for the socialization of children, and for the exchange of food, which carries a symbolic dimension.

Gardening, traditionally a woman's activity, tends to become a man's activity for nonfarmers. Two hours of daily intensive work in these gardens produces enormous amounts of food surpluses that compel extrahousehold distribution, lest the vegetables and fruits be wasted. This sharing calls into question the common assertion that households are nonproductive and function only as consumption units. Such surpluses in the Pays Bigouden Sud are exchanged on a continuous, casual basis, unlike nineteenth-century practice, and are not linked to exclusive family gatherings (marriage meals, for instance, now take place at restaurants). When we compare farmers' households to nonfarmers', a striking difference is evident. Farmers have a smaller surplus of food since they don't have as much time to tend their gardens as nonfarmers and all that is produced is given to children but not to neighbors or relatives. Thus the amount of exchange and the possibility of interconnectedness between households is much greater among nonfarmers' households than among farmers'.

While parents are still active in farming, children carry out many agricultural tasks for them, even though the children are often full-time craftsmen. I have noted that old farmers who have not renovated their traditional techniques have difficulty finding help. But if their children live only a few hundred yards away, although sometimes even farther, the parents receive the needed help. Children give a hand during periods of heavy work, drive the tractor, plow, saw, and help bring in the hay or harvest in summer. When houses are close, integration in daily work is stronger. For instance, Marie-Louise L., married to a tractor salesman, takes out her mother's cows every day, milks them, and gives a hand to her mother who lives in the farm just behind the house. Marie-Louise's children eat and sleep at their grandmother's house. From the main road you see only the brand-new house, standing proudly, pretending to be the sign of a "modern," independent way of life. Once you have met Marie-Louise and her husband, you realize that most family and work transactions take place in the old farm, hardly visible from the road. The new house is only a facade.

The integration of two households sometimes restores a productive function to the young couple's unit. Henry M. is the director of the local branch of the Credit Mutuel (farmers' bank); his wife, Bernadette, is listed as a housewife with no activity. Yet she speaks of her *petite boutique*, referring to her chicken and rabbit raising activity. In this case again her house is a few hundred yards from that of her parents, aging farmers.

They provide her with the grain to feed the chickens, which she sells to a small circle of patrons, friends, and relatives. She could easily lengthen the list but wants to keep the business small.

In this transitional situation from agriculture to a more diversified economy, households have forgotten neither their peasant origins nor the cultural norms linked to them. Parents' and children's domestic groups are strongly integrated, even though each unit appears to be a nuclear family, and this integration increases with the nearness of the houses. Proximity of houses is at once a consequence and a cause of this tight relationship. A constant reciprocal flow of services, contacts, and psychological help takes place, resulting in deeply intertwined household organizations, despite their formal and material separation. In some extreme cases we observe that the children's house appears as an empty shell where very few familial or social activities take place, most of them occurring at the parents' house. Should these links be severed, household organization would be greatly disturbed. Household integration between adjacent generations probably attenuates as the life cycle rolls on and parents get older, providing fewer resources and having to be supported in their turn. But at present, given the age structure of the population, the major part of intrahousehold productive activity is still carried on by the older parents.

The integration of households of parents and children separated by greater distances is still tight for those couples who have remained in the region but not in the village. Early in the morning young women drive their babies to their mothers' houses to be kept during the day or to attend school in the village where grandparents reside. For those young people who live in town and come only on weekends, the household integration of both domestic groups is nevertheless strong. The young couple may have settled in a small apartment in a low-rent housing development and both work in town, Monday through Friday, having little contact with neighbors. Friday arrives and the young couple with the children rush to one of the grandparents' houses. Most of the social life takes place on weekends, with family celebrations, visits, and similar activities. When the young couple goes back to town on Sunday evening, the car's trunk is loaded with fresh fruits, vegetables, and poultry from the parent's garden and hen house. So even during the week in town, purchases at the supermarket are limited. Should a difficulty arise with a child, such as a mild illness, he or she is driven to the grandparent's house to be cared for. Grandparents also keep the children during the holidays.

Living in town seems to be dictated only by economics. There is little sentimental attachment to the apartment where the conjugal family unit resides. If home is a place where one has a sense of belonging, it is at the parents' house or at the dream house of the future. The town apartment could be compared to a temporary campsite, an extension of the original household where the conjugal family unit migrates under the constraint of making a living. It is forsaken as soon as a location closer to home becomes possible.

The parent-child bond is preeminent but by no means the only significant kinship tie. I must briefly mention that other types of relationships are active and have multiple consequences for household organization. Nuclear households are certainly not isolated from their kin. We have seen these bonds activated during the building of houses, but they can also be observed at work in daily life. Because of high local mobility, kinship networks spread over the whole area, and people often have relatives living as sailors on the coast. A number of exchanges go on although not as developed as with parents, and they figure significantly in the food budgets or at least in food quality. Sailors come in for a visit on Sunday, bringing in buckets of Dublin bay prawns, and when the visit is paid back, apples or fresh vegetables from the garden are brought along. Aside from these active food exchanges, a lot of information related to the state of the local labor market follows the lines of the kinship networks. An individual's first job is frequently provided by a relative.

Kinship beyond the nuclear family in our society is often said to be limited to an informal network rather useless save for its symbolic functions. Parallel assertions refer to the loss of functions of the nuclear household. Hammel took up this theme in conference discussions. In this study I have observed that neither proposition accounts for Breton rural household organization, which, though formally nuclear, is dependent on parent-child ties and on cooperation with other affines and kin. Considered as a whole, this network is hardly merely symbolic; the household, embedded in its kinship network, retains a number of important functions. It is clear that if we had to measure 1981 household structure not in terms of coresidence but in terms of food and service exchanges, the figure of the multiple or extended households shown in table 7.1 would have to be multiplied by that of nuclear households. A look at the interaction between households of those siblings who have built secondary residences provides other evidence of the relationship between household and kinship networks.

SECONDARY RESIDENCES ARE NOT DEAD HOUSES

When farmers realize that none of their children will take over the working farm, they often decide to divide the property into as many lots as they have children. Those children who have migrated generally build for themselves a large house where they plan to retire and where they go for the holidays. Generally, secondary houses have a negative connotation locally. Villagers resent the settlement of outsiders and assert that their presence brings little to the local economy and disturbs the collective life. But in this case the secondary residents are not foreigners but children of the village who are easily integrated when they come back. Villagers discover that the migrant has not amassed a fortune or necessarily made the best choice in going away. There is no open hostility between those who have remained and those who, having left, come back regularly to their house. Neither is the house an empty shell totally cut off from the relatives' houses. An important interaction goes on through the gardens. For example, there is the Kerfilin farm (see figs. 7.2 and 7.3) of Yves D. and Marie-Louise T., who bought their farm in 1910 and divided it between two of their children around 1930. Their son Yves married Marie-Louise Le B. and until Yves retired he worked the farm with the help of his daughter, Yvonne, who is married to a secretary at the *mairie*. Yves's son Jean left in the 1950s to be a highway patrolman and live in Nantes. From his farm Yves gave a land allotment to his daughter, who built a house close to the farm, and to his son an eighteenth-century freestone cattle shed, turned into a secondary residence. Marie-Louise D. married Corentin G. (now deceased) with whom she had five children; one of them, Lisette, died; Marie Thérèse, the last daughter, has built a house near her parents-in-law in Pont-l'Abbé with her husband, who is a carpenter. The son Corentin, a bachelor of 50 years, works the farm and shares his mother's house. Jean G. is a plumber in Quimper and Raymond a highway patrolman in Paris. Both sons have received a patch of land and built houses there. Close to the old farm, there are now four new houses, one occupied all year round, the others episodically by siblings and cousins. Between these units is woven a strong network of services on which the various household organizations are more or less dependent. In summer, for instance, brothers, cousins, and their children help Corentin with the heavy work. Despite the absence of salaried servants, help is never a problem. Jean, who lives in Quimper, comes to help his brother regularly during winter work. These city dwellers have not forgotten the farm work. Corentin, who lives permanently on the farm, tills his brother's and cousin's gardens, which are ready for sowing or harvest when the relatives arrive from Quimper, Nantes, or Paris. If vegetables ripen after they have left, Yvonne or Corentin will harvest them. Though there are occasional clashes, the children appreciate the relative benefits of both urban and country ways of life.

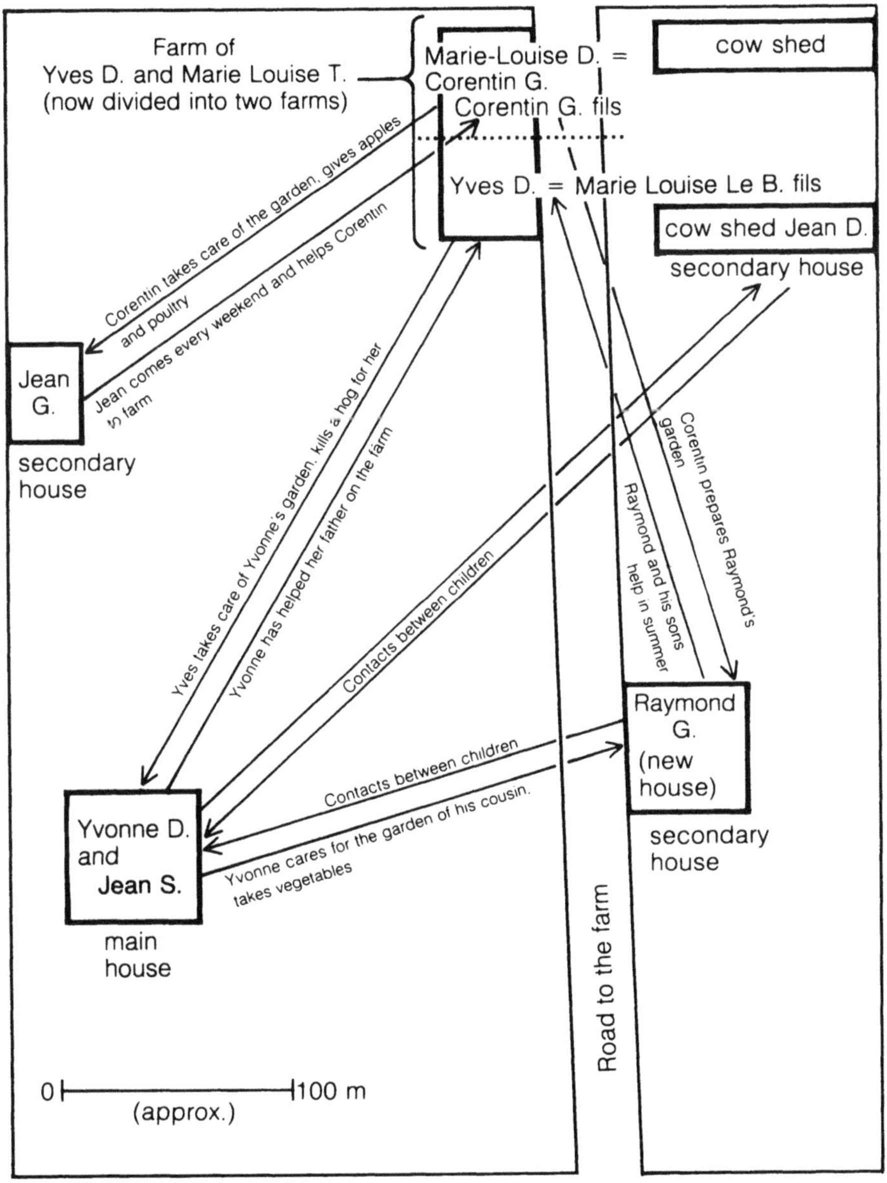

Fig. 7.2
Help and Exchanges between Kin-tied Households at Kerfilin

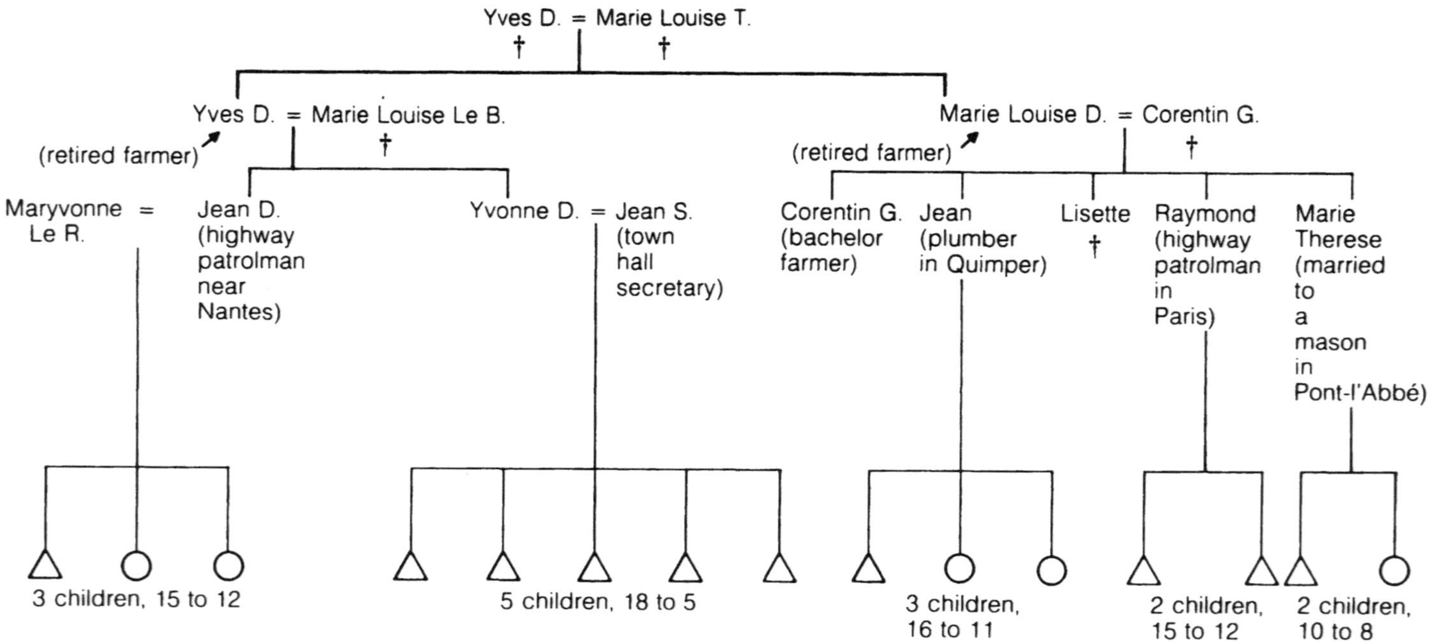

Fig. 7.3
Kerfilin Family Genealogy

These examples are certainly not particular to Brittany. Douglass points to similar links between Basque households and migrants to the New World and refers to the "constant feedback of returnees" (Douglass 1975:124–25).

WHERE NUCLEAR IS SYNONYMOUS WITH INDEPENDENT

A few households do not participate in these tight-knit kin networks. Some local residents are true strangers who have come from other areas of France. In a rural housing development a few couples and their children live a secluded life. Their household structure is nuclear, their organization is independent, and strongly so, since kin are distant and neighbors are felt to be too close. Outside their work they have little interaction with other people. Their neighbors, who are participating in the system I have described, preserve their social distance yet are inquisitive about the newcomers' personal lives. Under the proclaimed norm of independence, which is never attained in this kind of environment because real privacy is almost impossible, neighbors will neither interfere with the newcomers nor do anything to integrate them into the network. Stranger households are both isolated and spied on.

We can observe the consequences of this isolation on the newcomer household organization. In local households participating in the network, salaries are supplemented by free help, food, and exchanged services of all kinds. The newcomer couple has only its own earnings to rely on. Should a crisis occur, help is obtained with difficulty, and neighbors blame the crisis on the couple itself. The only way for a newcomer to have access to local society is to enter one of its associations, which is easier for men; hunting or football clubs accept newcomers and will provide some social interaction. For the women, it is more difficult, especially if they do not work; they will have to turn to the nearest city for social activity. We can perhaps credit the important increase in the number of clubs and associations in France, which is a recent phenomenon, to the lack of integration of newcomers in existing networks.

PEASANTS INTO CRAFTSMEN, EMPLOYEES, AND INDUSTRIAL WORKERS

Considering the changes that have occurred over the last 50 years we see a society moving from an agricultural base to a modern type of economy. Using the household as a variable to observe change in the village, one can say that a shift from a multiple or extended family household (for richer farmers) to a nuclear one seems the most striking characteristic. If the household organization behind that structural change has also been altered, it nonetheless displays a strong continuity in patterns of pooling and cooperation. Considering the lack of geographical mobility in the nineteenth century these patterns may now even be stronger than they were in former times. Even when close, parent and child households were not then integrated to the same degree as they are now. When children, after a period of coresidence, finally settled independently, they did not cooperate as they do now. There was no common cooking and less regular help from grandmothers because these women still had to take care of their own younger children. When children replaced their parents and took over the property or the lease on retirement of old parents, their help was important but could be replaced by paid labor.

The strong integration observed now between households is partly linked to the new demographic situation in which younger married and older generations have a potential of 25 years of cooperation ahead of them. The new household cooperation is linked as well to a reversal in attitudes about mobility. Because of overcrowding, elder children of farmers were brought up with the obsession of leaving the house. Mobility inside the area was prescribed by the social system in which we find the combination mobility/temporary coresidence/independent household unit. Today the combination is rather stability/independent residence/strong household cooperative network and close attachment to household of origin.

To summarize the characteristics of family change, it can be stated that in farmer households, family, work, residence, and production are all integrated. Parents inhabiting the house make up the main work team, even if it has to be enlarged occasionally. Most of the production is consumed at home. Today wage work is separated from the household, which is mainly residential; work often takes place away from home and outside the village. Inheritance practices do not tie married children together since they can attain independence with a salary. This evolution has been frequently described in explanations of the transformation of complex households into nuclear ones. Yet previous frameworks of analysis have been much too schematic to account for the situation described here in the Pays Bigouden Sud. A house itself implies work; building it is a family affair. Once it is built, it is ceaselessly transformed. The organization of tasks around food show that continuous exchange patterns create a strong bond between households.

If during the nineteenth century the difference between households was mainly of degree and not of kind, nowadays two different models emerge, revealing an increase in social differences between farmers and nonfarmers. This difference can be measured by the degree of exchange that goes on between households. Farmers feel solitary and cut off from the community, which they tend to resent, whereas nonfarmers are the most active through the household networks. This situation has consequences on the political level; since 1974 there have been no farmers on the Conseil Municipal, though 50 percent of all household heads are still employed in farming.

This cleavage between the two groups must not hide the important change taking place. Though some of these peasant households always had kin connections with the nearby town, household networks today link urban and rural environments. In the model of social change presented here there is no sharp break between country and urban life but a continuity, which flows in both directions. These networks help individuals and domestic groups adapt to social, economic, and cultural change. Domestic groups both acknowledge and implement a traditional stock of norms and values geared to work and perpetuated by kinship links. At the same time the groups absorb and accept modern urban standards of independent nuclear family residence as embodied in French national culture and the mass media. The structure of the domestic group, supposedly the sign of modernity, has an organization linking it to the past, thus attenuating the shock of turning peasants into Frenchmen (Weber 1976). This is not to say that the modern family structure is only a sign of continuity with the past. It is also linked to the new constraints of spatially separate jobs and improved economic status.

One final question remains unanswered. Why do people behave as though they wanted to live independently, building costly, separate houses, while maintaining intense interfamily cooperation?

We have a residential model that extols independence. All young couples abide by that norm in building their own houses. Only marginal people, the poor or those considered within the group as "backward," do not or cannot conform. Yet the practice of domestic organization seems to violate the model and the norm as young couples and their parents and relatives interact actively. The contradiction, however, is only an apparent one, and the behavior becomes coherent if we consider that this organization is the result of choice, not imposition. The choice is to deliberately carry on familial and social values. (The alternative—to migrate and set up a true independent domestic group—exists for those who do not choose to perpetuate these traditional values.) The formal nuclear structure of the modern domestic group in the Pays Bigouden Sud is the sign of recognition of modern values; the possibility of independence is preserved. The tight interaction between households is the sign of a desire for continuity. Households help integrate tradition into modernity.

NOTES

1. Contrary to my previous approach (Segalen 1977), I will not deal with family life cycles here. I shall oppose two "snapshots" of the organization of the household: that of today against that I will refer to as "traditional," the latter pertaining mainly to the nineteenth century. As a point of reference, I have chosen the year 1921, when population was at its maximum and the system had reached its apex before it collapsed.

This research has been supported by funds granted by the Centre National de la Recherche Scientifique, within the Action Thématique Programmée (ATP) of l'Observation Continue du Changement Social et Culturel (OCS).

REFERENCES

Douglass, William A.
1975 Echalar and Murelaga: Opportunity and Rural Exodus in Two Spanish Basque Villages. Guildford and London: Billing and Sons.
Goody, Jack
1972 The Evolution of the Family. *In* Household and Family in Past Time, ed. Peter Laslett and Richard Wall, pp. 103–24. Cambridge: Cambridge University Press.
Hélias, Pierre
1975 Le Cheval d'Orgueil. Paris: Plon.
Laslett, Peter
1972 Introduction. *In* Household and Family in Past Time, ed. Peter Laslett and Richard Wall. Cambridge: Cambridge University Press.
Netting, Robert McC.
1981 Balancing on an Alp. Cambridge: Cambridge University Press.
Segalen, Martine
1977 The Family Life Cycle over Five Generations in a French Village. Journal of Family History 2 (3):223–36.
Weber, Eugen
1976 Peasants into Frenchmen. Stanford: Stanford University press.

8

The Urban Household in Dependent Development

Robert Hackenberg, Arthur D. Murphy, and Henry A. Selby

This essay[1] on social reproduction delineates how the poor majority of households in two secondary cities—one in Mexico (Oaxaca City) and one in the Philippines (Davao City)—seek to survive, maintain themselves, and sometimes prosper under the contemporary conditions of dependent development. Like other writers in this volume we take the household as the unit of decision making and, collaterally, the locus of negotiation of the interests of its members. We define the household as those who regard themselves as living together such that their memberships are elicited by the census query "Who lives in the house?" We have been mindful of Yanagisako's admonition (this volume) that it is dangerous to impute strategies to people whose goals we have not bothered to understand. Our response is to point to five years of work on the topic of goals and strategies of urban householders in Oaxaca which has been reported elsewhere (Murphy 1973; Murphy and Stepick 1978; Stepick 1974; Stepick and Murphy 1977) and so need not be rehearsed here, except to say that our imputations in both Oaxaca and Davao City in no way run counter to that previous work.[2]

Our paper differs from many in this volume because it examines the conflicts of interest between three parties: the state, the household, and the individual. The relationships between these three are complex and vary greatly over time according to the changes that take place in the definition of the state's interests in the household, the age structure and composition of the household, and the economic and political conditions that structure the relationship. We explore only one configuration of the triad. We observe and analyze the behavior of the household as it attempts to blunt the attempts of the state to interfere in its internal affairs (see also Löfgren, this volume). The state needs a skilled and disciplined work force to man its industries in the formal economy of modern, capitalist firms and enterprises. These needs are met through recruitment of members from the households of the poor majority. Recruitment is effected through wage and benefit incentives, which are exceptionally attractive compared to rewards to be found in the small scale, informal economy of family firms and self-employed workers where the poor are mostly employed.

The state often wins. The forces of national and international capitalism are difficult to resist. When the state wins, those members of the household with the most attractive credentials leave their relatives and coresident kinfolk behind and form new households in the same city, or they migrate, effectively severing ties to their households and families of orientation. The result is plain to see in all but a handful of underdeveloped countries: the coexistence of individual mobility, economic development, and increases in aggregate measures of economic performance side by side with mass poverty. The households of the poor which lose their members also lose their battle for economic betterment. They sink into that familiar destitution that plagues the poor majority in developing countries.

Sometimes the household wins and through the combined efforts of three generations of kinfolk or grown children living together and working for the common good they are able to rise from destitution to a tolerable level of poverty and to achieve the beginnings of a decent life for all the members. Usually such families succeed by arranging jobs for their members in the informal economy. Usually they achieve economic success through economies of scale in consumption and the increase in earning power that comes from shared budgets and pooled earnings. The strategies of the successful households defeat the goals of national economic planners because they ignore the opportunities of the formal sector, provide little disciplined labor for industry, and organize their activities in the interstices left by inadequate and distorted formal economic development.

Since economic and social success depends on the deployment of a large number of workers, successful households tend to reproduce at a high rate or have significantly larger memberships than unsuccessful households, thereby defeating the aims of the state in the imposition of a policy of restricted fertility. In addition, they defeat the aims of the state by implicitly refusing to bow to the demands of credentialism, by failing to make those investments in their members' human capital, through education, that make them attractive to the state and its enterprises. But by denying the state the appropriation of their members, these households maintain their membership and their cohesiveness and are able to work together to enlarge the consumption pool and maintain themselves in a nearly satisfactory way.

We study the results of this struggle between state and household at one point, roughly, in two quite different intermediate cities of the third world. This is an essay on the dynamics of the household in confronting the state in dependent development.

DEPENDENT DEVELOPMENT

Dependency theory is more an argument than a theory, but if we may cavil at the standard theory we would say that it is less interested in the reactions and strivings of the exploited than it is in delineating the historical, sociological, cultural, and economic forces that coadjust to exploit them. Dependency theorists in Latin America at least view urban household formation as affected by massive migrations to the city brought about by capitalist penetration of the rural hinterlands, rationalization of agricultural production, and reduction in the need for peon labor, all of which act to create a rural proletariat that responds to unemployment or loss of land by moving to the city. The scale is immense. Since populations gather where resources accumulate, it is not surprising to see tremendous urban growth under these conditions of urban capitalism. The city and, in particular, the primate city becomes the most dynamic economic center of the country and attracts both capital and labor as a result. The urban household in this formulation emerges as fairly helpless. It breeds ("and the poor get children"), and it sweats and suffers and experiences the poverty, suffering, and travail that is the lot of most human beings. The urban household is not supine perhaps, but it is at the mercy of gigantic forces it can neither channel nor comprehend; it is adrift in a political economy to which it must always adapt.

It is in this last step of this formulation that we take leave of dependency theory, for we are interested in the ways that the household fights and opposes the interests of the state. As anthropologists, we are able to view these struggles at close range and therefore have greater empathy and understanding than a census analyst or econometrician might.

We are not alone in attempting to revise dependency theory as it bears on the household (see Arnould, this volume). Roberts (1973, 1974) studied the Peruvian situation with a careful eye on the ethnography of the household and the small firm and found surprising vitality in the form of a rejuvenated labor-intensive, small scale development taking the place of large factories that were removed to the capital city. And in a vein similar to that of this paper, Arizpe (n.d.) sketched the responses of the rural households in Mexico to agricultural development that had left them increasingly poorer over the years. The strategies employed by the townfolk in two *municipios* where Arizpe studied differ little from those of the urbanites of Davao City (Philippines) and Oaxaca (Mexico).

The household, then, is a vital institution made up of members who are well versed in its interests and perforce compelled to battle the most powerful forces in its environment: the blandishments and enticements of the state in the form of opportunities generated by development and the desires of some of its members to better themselves economically at the expense of the other members.

THE CITIES

The Mexican city of Oaxaca is very different from Davao City in the Philippines, and not just because of the cultural contrasts between the two countries. The Philippines is a much poorer country than Mexico, even though its per capita income growth rate over the past two decades has been only fractionally less than Mexico's: 2.6 percent compared to 2.7 percent.[3] The per capita income of the Philippines at U.S. $600 is 37 percent as much as Mexico's, although this is at least partially offset as an index of well-being by the greater degree of inequality in the distribution of income in Mexico. In other ways the countries are similar. In both we find that the service sector is the important contributor to the distribution of gross domestic product. Both have high population growth rates: in the decade from 1960 to 1970, Mexico showed 3.2 percent while the Philippines showed 3.0 percent. In the next decade, from 1970 to 1980, Mexico showed 2.9 percent while the Philippines were slightly lower at 2.6 percent. Both have high total fertility rates (5.0 for Mexico and 4.8 for the Philippines), and both have experienced dramatic declines in the crude death rate over the past decade: 36 percent for Mexico and 47 percent for the Philippines.

The most important economic differences between the two cities lie in their relationship to their national economy. Oaxaca, at the time the data were collected (1977), was a poor, backward, unindustrialized city, untouched by petroleum development. Davao City, in contrast, was a thriving, bustling center on the economic frontier.

The two cities exhibit similar rates in the distribution of household types and attributes, which is surprising in the light of their cultural, historical, and geographical dissimilarity. We find the same kind of strategies successfully operating in both, leading us to suspect that the results reported in this paper are part of a more general pattern.

The rest of this essay is divided into five sections examining the general economic situation; the demographic conditions; the activities, structure, and composition of the household in the light of these constraints; the economic opportunities for the majority poor in both cities as well as possible strategies for upward mobility; and a regression model for Oaxaca that tests some of the components of the household strategies laid out in the sections on household composition and economic opportunities.

ECONOMIC CLASSES

In order to compare the household and individual attributes of people in differing economic circumstances in the two cities, we have partitioned the cities into three economic groups: the marginals, the poor, and the middle and upper income groups (or "middles" for short). As is often the case with comparative research, the partitions are less than perfectly satisfactory. Hackenberg, in his original study (1976), divided his population into three groups according to their income and the style of life enjoyed in their neighborhood. He called these three groups "poor," "middle," and "upper" and noted that the percentages of the population that fell into the three categories were 38 percent, 34 percent, and 28 percent, respectively. Rather than attempt to establish ethnographic parallels between the two cities' populations or corresponding monetary cut points for the three classes, we took roughly the same proportions for the groups in Oaxaca. The marginals' monthly household incomes range from zero to U.S. $44.25 (in 1972 dollar values) for Davao City and from zero to U.S. $50.60 for Oaxaca, giving households in both cities slightly above the minimum salary, which is calculated for a single individual and is inadequate at that (see table 8.1 for data summary). The poor group's household incomes range from U.S. $44.25 to U.S. $51 for Davao City and from U.S. $50.60 to U.S. $99 per month for Oaxaca. We changed the names for the economic groups so that they would better describe economic conditions and so that it would be difficult to interpret them as social classes (they are not).

The Income Situation

Hackenberg (1976:17) has noted, "In his address to the World Bank Group in Nairobi on September 24, 1973, Robert McNamara described absolute poverty: 'a condition of life so degraded by disease, illiteracy,

TABLE 8.1
ECONOMIC CLASSES IN DAVAO CITY AND OAXACA

Economic class	Upper bound		No. households		% Population	
	Davao[a]	Oaxaca	Davao	Oaxaca	Davao	Oaxaca
Marginal	$44.25	$50.60	380	559	38	36
Poor	$51.00	$99.00	325	420	34	34
Middle	—	—	284	430	28	30
Total			999	1409	100	100

[a]Cut points were defined so that the same percentage of households (roughly) would appear in each class in both cities: 38 percent of the population would be in the marginal class, 34 percent in the poor class, and 28 percent in the middle class. All money figures are expressed in 1972 U.S. dollars.

malnutrition, and squalor as to deny its victims basic human necessities. Absolute poverty is the life of some 800 million individuals who must survive on incomes estimated at 30 cents a day.' " The median income of P343 received by a six-person household in Davao City is equal to U.S. 28 cents per person a day, while the median monthly income of MN $2,518 in Oaxaca for a household average of 5.3 members is equal to $15.60 per person, or U.S. 52 cents per day.[4] By the McNamara standard, 50 percent of the people of Davao are living in absolute poverty, compared to 18 percent in Oaxaca.

Income Distribution

The distribution of incomes in both cities is highly skewed (see table 8.2), more so in Oaxaca than in Davao City. This is in line with Kuznets's (1965) finding that the initial stages of economic development are accompanied by an increase in income inequalities.

We can calculate the level of poverty in the two cities in two ways: by estimating the proportion of people in absolute poverty or by comparing household income level with the nationally defined minimum salary. Ahluwalia, Carter, and Chenery (1979) have calculated that 33 percent of the population of the Philippines and 14 percent of the population of Mexico live in absolute poverty.[5] The minimum salary standard gives a slightly different picture since it is defined for the region and not the country as a whole. The minimum salary is the official government minimum standard of income required by the individual wage earner for subsistence. It usually underestimates the real cost of living and is generally regarded as a less than adequate minimum standard. But still one

TABLE 8.2
HOUSEHOLD INCOME IN DAVAO CITY AND OAXACA

Income range	Davao City (%)	Oaxaca (%)
Below 1 minimum salary	15	25
Below 2 minimum salaries	55	68
Below 3 minimum salaries	75	83
Below 4 minimum salaries	84	89

can compare the proportions of households in each city to see the degree to which they attain the minimum salary standard. The minimum salary standard per month for Davao City is $37.50 and for Oaxaca $61. By this criterion the people of Oaxaca are worse off than those in Davao City, emphasizing their relatively extreme poverty as a result of their living in a backward economic zone in a newly industrialized country.

Individual incomes are distributed in a similar fashion—clearly unequally in both cities but more unequally in Oaxaca than in Davao City. In Davao City the median individual income of the poor group is 8 percent more than that of the marginal group, while the comparable figure for Oaxaca is 54 percent. Similarly, the median individual income of the middle in Davao City is 34 percent more than that of the poor group; the comparable figure for Oaxaca is 76 percent. The figures in the two cities are closer when one considers median household (and not individual income—even though the interclass differences are greater. The median household income of the poor is 14 percent more than that of the marginals in Davao City, while in Oaxaca the figure is 93 percent. At the next economic level, in Davao City the median household income of the top group is 93 percent greater than that of the poor, while in Oaxaca the figure is 102 percent. These figures, along with the absolute values for mean and median income for both individuals and households, are given in table 8.3.

Recognition of the skewed distribution of income in both countries is important since it shows that aggregate measures misstate the level of well-being of the majority of the citizens. Despite the higher median income of Mexico compared to the Philippines, the distribution of incomes is so skewed in Oaxaca that an even greater proportion of households fall in the lower intervals of the distribution, as in table 8.3. The data on income show clearly that the term "majority poor" applies equally to the citizens of Davao City and Oaxaca.

TABLE 8.3
INCOMES OF INDIVIDUALS AND HOUSEHOLDS, DAVAO CITY AND OAXACA

	Monthly individual income[a]		Monthly household income	
Economic class	Davao City	Oaxaca City	Davao City	Oaxaca City
Marginals				
Median	32.85	50.49	44.85	51.32
Mean	36.65	155.80	50.25	51.03
Number of cases	549	682	380	559
Poor				
Median	35.40	77.52	51.30	98.91
Mean	45.45	286.76	73.65	94.29
Number of cases	509	546	335	420
Middle class				
Median	47.40	136.38	83.70	200.00
Mean	65.40	369.71	121.80	598.80
Number of cases	497	679	284	430
Total population				
Median	36.45	65.21	51.45	84.21
Mean	48.15	263.50	78.45	230.37
Number of cases	1555	1907	999	1409

[a]All income figures are monthly, expressed in 1972 U.S. dollars converted at the 1972 rate of exchange.

Jobs and Employers

Table 8.4 gives a summary of the kinds of jobs held by people in Davao City and Oaxaca. Despite the transparent differences in the economies of the two cities and despite the dynamism of Davao City compared to the stagnation of Oaxaca, the structure of the two economies, from the perspective of employment, is amazingly similar. To no one's surprise very small numbers of the urbanites engage full-time in agricultural pursuits. The distribution of employment over the seven major categories in both cities is quite similar. Tertiary sector employment predominates, with half of the working population engaged in either sales or services, and only one-fifth in manufacturing and construction.

In both urban employment pictures the majority of workers engage in essentially "nonproductive" pursuits: no goods are being produced by four-fifths of the population. The economy revolves around distribution of goods and the provision of services, as one would expect in areas where the informal rather than the formal economy provides the majority of jobs.

TABLE 8.4
Occupational Groups by Economic Class

Occupational group	Economic Class															
	Marginals				Poor				Middle				Total			
	Davao		Oaxaca		Davao		Oaxaca		Davao		Oaxaca		Davao		Oaxaca	
	N	%	N	%	N	%	N	%	N	%	N	%	N	%	N	%
Agriculture	32	2.1	43	2.1	17	1.1	35	1.7	13	0.8	37	1.8	62	4.0	91	4.5
Sales	95	6.2	217	10.8	150	9.8	188	9.3	128	8.2	257	12.8	371	24.2	662	32.9
Service	112	7.3	189	9.4	123	8.0	105	5.2	79	5.1	71	3.5	314	20.4	373	18.5
Manufacturing/ construction	153	10.0	167	8.3	97	6.3	146	7.3	47	3.1	96	4.8	297	19.3	409	20.3
Clerical/ management	46	3.0	82	4.1	51	3.3	112	5.6	99	6.4	266	13.2	196	12.8	460	22.9
Transportation/ communication/shipping	78	6.1	—	—	46	3.0	—	—	31	2.0	—	—	155	10.1	—	—
Professional	20	1.3	3	0.1	25	1.6	2	0.1	95	6.3	12	0.5	140	9.2	17	0.1

Hackenberg (1976:32), studying the employment profile from Davao City, commented in a way that fits Oaxaca well too: "The association of [better] income with sales and service jobs, and of [marginal] income with the industrial sector, reveals that the preindustrial forms of employment contain greater promise of upward mobility. Jobs associated with industry have sharply reduced frequencies among the middle and upper class."

Production jobs are not necessarily skilled jobs. In fact, in typical Oaxacan light industries as many as half the industrial jobs are unskilled. Hackenberg (1976:32–33) found that the match between skills and employment in Davao City economy was extremely poor: "Only one quarter of the skilled workers are engaged in industrial employment, twice that number fell within the clerical and office manager category. Production jobs . . . appear to be the unskilled sector of the economy."

So the employment profiles of the two cities are remarkably similar, as are the changes in employment profile across economic classes. The informal economy clearly dominates the employment picture, and the cities can be characterized as involving more and more people handling proportionately smaller and smaller amounts of output in a system of "commercial involution" well designed to maintain a large population at or near the poverty level while providing jobs for all.[6]

Employment and Unemployment

Employment rates of the heads of households, the principal wage earners, are high in both cities. Since both countries lack a social security net, there is no way that a household can survive without paid employment. So, while underemployment remains high, unemployment is unthinkable: household heads almost always have jobs, even if they are not the most attractive nor remunerative. Table 8.5 shows how high employment rates are (ranging from a low of 90 percent to a high of 99 percent) and how little they vary across the economic groups.

Spouse and child employment varies a good deal. In both cities it is the key to the maintenance of an above-marginal economic status—more so in the Philippines, where women have a longer tradition of labor force participation, than in Mexico, where women are comparatively underrepresented even though the rate at which they are increasing in the work force is high. Similarly, the Philippine city shows relatively higher rates of employment of children and more distantly related household members.

The Philippine household is larger (see table 8.5) and relies on numbers for success. On this count it does very well. A quick observation of the obvious differences between different economic groups is that attain-

TABLE 8.5

EMPLOYMENT OF HOUSEHOLD MEMBERS BY ECONOMIC CLASS, FREQUENCIES PER 100 HOUSEHOLDS

Economic class	Male household head employed		Spouse employed		Children employed		Others employed		Total[a] employed	
	Davao	Oaxaca	Davao	Oaxaca	Davao	Oaxaca	Davao	Oaxaca	Davao	Oaxaca
Marginals	89.9	97.0	14.7	12.7	23.2	8.6	15.8	6.0	145.0	124.0
Poor	94.9	99.0	23.9	15.0	20.3	10.9	11.6	12.0	152.0	140.0
Middles	95.1	99.0	30.6	22.0	27.8	14.1	22.5	20.0	175.0	172.0

[a]The additional members reported in this column who do not appear in the row are household members who are present and working, close enough relatives as to avoid the appellation "other," which is reserved for distant relatives or nonrelatives. A working uncle or nephew or brother would appear in this column but not in the other column since (in Oaxaca) he is not an "other." He is an "other" in Davao City, however, and such are the delights of doing comparative quantitive work in two different areas, at two different times, with two different kinds of assumptions.

ment and maintenance of advanced economic status depends almost entirely on the ability of the household to deploy more members into the work force. The changes in work force participation by rising economic status are monotonic.

The Informal Economy

The majority of workers in the marginal and poor categories work in the informal economy (see Hart 1973 and Sethuraman 1976 for general discussion). By this term we mean small-scale enterprises employing ten or fewer workers (largely family-owned-and-operated enterprises) with little access to capital or credit which operate on the principle of autoexploitation. Typically these firms are engaged in the tertiary, or service, sector of the economy, and the workers that are employed are unskilled (in the formal schooling sense) and earn low wages (rarely more than minimum wage). Additionally, since these enterprises lack formal status, employers do not provide fringe benefits, pensions, unemployment benefits, or any form of company credit to the employees (although, as Ekstein 1975 shows, personal loans from the owners of such enterprises are sometimes made to employees to tie them more closely to the enterprise). Typical informal enterprises include auto repair shops, small scale manufacturing of items like shoes or paper bags, and very small scale shops—*tienditas* in Latin America (as studied by Peattie 1975) or sari-sari shops in the Philippines. These last are characteristically informal in their structure, dealing with the distribution of goods on a very small scale, offering credit in very low amounts, operating on exceedingly small profit margins (when profit is made at all), and functioning more as a labor sink than a profit maximizing operation. These enterprises outnumber formal sector enterprises, especially in secondary cities, such as those studied in this paper, by an estimated two orders of magnitude. Hackenberg, for example, noted that there was one sari-sari shop in Davao City for each 11.5 inhabitants. But they do absorb labor.

The informal economy provides jobs for the majority poor in secondary cities, and its structure impinges on and constrains the strategies adopted by them.

The informal economy of Oaxaca is well characterized by this description. Five important characteristics of the Oaxacan people and households have been outlined by M. H. Kim (1982).

1. Most of the people who work in the informal economy are poor. Two-thirds of the household heads in the marginal category work in the informal sector, and 89 percent of the workers in the informal

sector earn no more than the minimum wage (compared to 69 percent of the formal sector workers).

2. The educational levels of people who work in the informal sector are low. They average three years of schooling, while the formal sector workers average 7.5 years of schooling.
3. The majority (54 percent) of the jobs held in the informal sector are short term, lasting less than one year, compared to 2.3 percent of the formal sector jobs.
4. Mobility is limited. Although 70 percent of the workers under 25 years of age are employed in the informal sector, there is no tendency for workers who have lived longer in the city to be any better represented in the formal sector than the younger workers.
5. The wage structure of the informal sector is low and homogeneous, as seen in tables 8.1 and 8.3. We have already discussed the wages of the informal sector workers and the distribution of income.

To reiterate: almost 90 percent of the workers in the informal sector earn no more than the minimum wage, which wage is widely recognized as insufficient, at least by 50 percent, for the maintenance of a well-nourished, minimally housed household. And a glance at the income distribution for Mexico shows that the first six deciles of the distribution earn 16 percent of the income (compared to the top decile's 49 percent), yielding a Gini coefficient of .54. This suggests a homogeneity of incomes among the majority (Carnoy 1979:80–82).

This homogeneity has important implications for households that depend on the informal sector for work, as do the majority in both cities. If all jobs pay more or less the same inadequate wage, then there is no advantage from self-improvement through on-the-job training or further education. The only way to secure a higher payoff for one's labors is by moving to a city where there are better wages. And since wages are tied to the minimum salary and the minimum salary supposedly reflects the costs of living in different cities, the only dramatic improvement that can be secured is through international migration. Since the costs of this strategy are high, most households cannot use it, and for all intents and purposes they are stuck where they are socially, physically, and economically. This set of economic constraints has important implications for household structures.

Household Strategies

Our description of the situation of the majority poor in these two secondary cities allows a better understanding of household response.

We can divide this response into four strategies:

1. Maintain membership intact and work as a collective to pool earnings and achieve economies of scale in consumption.
2. Enlarge the household's work force as much as possible.
3. Control the degree of dependency. There are two methods: either one can control fertility or one can increase the number of workers in the household. In Davao City both strategies are used, whereas in Oaxaca households eschew fertility control and increase workers only.
4. Try out different household forms. In Oaxaca, for example, we find greater variability in household arrangements—larger numbers of matrifocal and female-headed families and slightly larger numbers of male-only households as well. We view this variety as evidence for the manipulation of household structure and composition in an effort to achieve the same efficiencies that arise from dependency control.

In short, by looking at the characteristics of households in the different economic classes in both cities, we can see evidence for the struggles of the household to make use of what opportunities are realistically afforded to the majority by the state and by the international economy. We can compare the households that have been relatively successful in this struggle with those that have not and examine the degree to which the successful ones differ from the less successful in the implementation of the four strategies.

DEMOGRAPHIC CONDITIONS

Birthrate

We find differences in fertility (see table 8.6) between Davao City and Oaxaca across economic groups. In both cities the poor and the marginals display very high crude birthrates (between 34 per thousand and 50 per thousand). Oaxaca has uniformly higher birthrates than Davao City and shows little change across economic groupings. Davao's fertility falls with rises in class.

The birthrates are high in both cities, with only the middle group in Davao City approaching the crude birthrate of industrialized countries at 15.[7]

Dependency

The control of dependency in the household is more important than fertility. We compare this across economic groups in both Davao City and Oaxaca in table 8.7, which gives the median age by city and economic group. We note immediately that the marginals in both cities are younger than the other groups, in Oaxaca quite dramatically so (14.8 years for the marginals, as compared with 16.1 overall). The maturity of the household (as measured by the mean age of the head of household) increases with higher economic standing in Oaxaca,[8] suggesting that a portion of the cause of destitution lies in the age of the household head and the household's place in the domestic cycle.

TABLE 8.6
CRUDE BIRTHRATES BY ECONOMIC CLASS, DAVAO CITY AND OAXACA

	Crude birthrate	
Economic class	Davao City	Oaxaca
Marginals	41	47
Poor	34	50
Middle	20	42
Total	32	46

TABLE 8.7
MEDIAN AGE AND DEPENDENCY MEASURES BY ECONOMIC GROUP FOR BOTH CITIES

	Median age		Ratio of dependents (age 0-14) to members in most productive age range (15-34)		Number of workers	
Economic group	Davao	Oaxaca	Davao	Oaxaca	Davao	Oaxaca
Marginal group	16.9	14.8	1.38	1.26	1.45	1.25
Poor group	17.9	17.6	1.13	1.38	1.52	1.40
Middle group	19.9	17.8	0.76	1.19	1.75	1.72

Not only are the marginal households somewhat younger than the other economic groups but their dependency ratios are also higher. If we compare the proportions of the population in the economically most productive range, we note that there is a strong tendency for dependency ratios to decline with higher economic standing.

The data conceal a most interesting pair of related processes that bear mention. In Davao City households do better if they control the structure of dependency by importing income-earning adults into the household. In Oaxaca the number of incomes also increases with economic standing, but the number of "imported" adults does not increase as quickly as does the number of children. As the data in table 8.8 indicate, Oaxaca households increase their numbers and efficiency by reproduction while Davao City households bring new members in from outside the nuclear family.

HOUSEHOLD FORMATION

It is interesting to see the impact of the conditions of urban economic life on the efficacy of residence rules, for the effects of the rule are quite different in Oaxaca and Davao City. Since fertility is uncontrolled in Oaxaca and since dependency therefore has to be controlled through the manipulation of adult membership, Oaxacan households must have flexibility in making their household arrangements. The citizens of Davao City can and do use fertility control to achieve reduced dependency ratios.

TABLE 8.8
HOUSEHOLD MEMBERSHIP BY ECONOMIC CLASS

Economic groups	Male household head & spouse		Number of household members (Mean)		Number of children		"Extra" adults in household	
	Davao (%)	Oaxaca (%)	Davao	Oaxaca	Davao	Oaxaca	Davao	Oaxaca
Marginal class	90	73	6.08	4.74	3.47	2.60	.69	.14
Poor class	92	85	5.89	5.30	3.29	2.90	.74	.40
Middle class	87	81	6.25	5.74	2.85	3.20	1.54	.54
Total	90	76	6.06	5.26	3.20	2.80	.86	.40

The jural rule of postnuptial residence in both Davao City and Oaxaca is that a household be headed by a monogamous male. In Oaxaca, however, we find that there is a much lower percentage of households following the rule. As table 8.8 indicates, only 73 percent of the Oaxacan households are headed by married males. In 22 percent of the households there is no married couple whatsoever. This kind of flexibility, sketched long ago by Hammel (1961), discussed in Buchler and Selby (1968), and described with passion and depth by Oscar Lewis (1961, 1968) is necessary in those cases where there are no controls on fertility and where efficient wage-earning collectives must be formed in violation of the jural rules of household formation.

In Davao City the jural rule is followed probably to the extent that is demographically possible: the percentages do not stray far from 90 percent male headedness.

THE HOUSEHOLD STRATEGY

The elements of the survival strategy for the marginal and poor people of both cities are now fairly clear. It can be summarized under four points.

1. There can be only slight expectation that the economic fortunes of the household will improve with age, as we can tell from cross-sectional data on the median ages of the household heads in the economic groups in the two cities. So economic survival with possibilities for advancement has to come from the conscious organizational efforts of the households.
2. Big households are better than small households, as far as positioning the household for advancement is concerned. The data for Davao City do not show the advantages of size too well, but the Oaxacan data are unequivocal: household sizes rise with economic class.[9]
3. Most important of all are the number of incomes. The Davao City data show this dramatically, but the Oaxacan data are comparable. To survive, more than one income is needed. A single income guarantees not genteel poverty but true hardship, with all its attributes: nearly constant illness in the house, unceasing crying by the babies, hungry stomachs, feelings of weakness, even hypochondriasis and low energy levels. Incomes are not necessarily best "recruited" from among the nuclear family members. Distantly related family members and unrelated people can be incorporated into the household and contribute to it.

4. The final element of the common strategy is the control of dependency. Obviously there are two ways of decreasing the ratio: (1) a household may decrease the number of unproductive workers by restricting fertility, by giving up children for adoption or by denying household membership to the elderly; or (2) a household may increase the number of productive workers by putting children to work earlier, importing adult members into the household, or keeping older people at work longer.

The control of dependency is crucial to the economic success of the household in both Davao City and Oaxaca. In Davao City both ways of decreasing dependency are used; in Oaxaca fertility is unrestricted and efficiencies are achieved by increasing the number of workers. Table 8.7 provides the appropriate figures.

These are the major outlines of the strategies that seem to be dictated for poor and marginal households in these two cities of the third world. Because the countries are so different and the role played by the cities within each country so different as well we are led to think that the solution being converged on in both cases could be fairly general.

But before we conclude we would like to test our descriptive model of the responses to social and economic conditions by observing how these variables interact in the three groups and by estimating the strength of the relationships. We do so in the last section of this paper, which presents a simultaneous equations model of the most important variables that have been discussed so far. Since only the data for Oaxaca are available in disaggregated form, we are only able to test the model there.

A TEST OF THE EFFICACY OF THE HOUSEHOLD STRATEGY

This test shows that the major outlines of our theory about household organization are correct. The more successful households within the marginal and poor categories are those that deploy more workers into the work force, and the number of workers is best given by the size of the household. Furthermore, household size is not determined so much by the presence of an extended family (undoubtedly true in Davao City) but by the maturity of the household and the ability of the household to control its expenses and reduce the proportion of its income spent on food. Finally, we show that the quality of the household head's job plays an important role only in the higher income groups, where investments in education make sense. For the marginals the informal economy provides the only opportunities for advancement.

The Structural Model

Equations 1 through 4 present the structural model showing how household income is affected by the kinds of jobs held by household members and by household composition, organization, and management. The variables are defined in table 8.9. Equation 1 accounts for household income, while equations 2 through 4 examine its determinants. Equation 2 models the determinants of the number of workers in the household and equation 3 the determinants of household size. Equation 4 examines the determinants of job classification or the quality of the job held by the household head.

$$(1)\ \log(Y)_{HH} = a_{11}NW + a_{12}J_n + a_{13}J_1$$

$$(2)\ NW = a_{21}HS + a_{22}EXT + a_{23}Y_1$$

$$(3)\ HS = a_{31}AGE + a_{32}BM + a_{33}EXT$$

$$(4)\ J_1 = a_{41}ED_1 + a_{42}AGE_1 + a_{43}SEX_{HH}$$

The system was solved simultaneously as a structural equations model on the SPSS G3SLS subprogram. It accounts for 34 percent of the variance; 53 percent of the coefficients surpass the 1.64 level, which is conventionally taken as the .05 significance level for "true" *t*s. The R^2 is average for cross-sectional research dealing with anthropological or sociological data. The system is run for all three economic groups and coefficients are compared within groups to see which variables are significantly different from zero and among groups to assess the relative importance of each variable in determining the value of the dependent variable for each economic grouping.

Equation 1: Household Income

The log of household income was predicted by three variables: the number of workers in the household, the quality of the job held by the head of household (on a seven-point scale running from casual laborer to independent professional), and the quality of the jobs held by secondary workers in the household (on the same scale).

Examining table 8.10, we can see that the number of workers is the most important variable to all economic groups. It is also the *only* important variable to the marginal group, as we suggested it would be earlier in the discussion when we noted the homogeneity of jobs and wages in the

TABLE 8.9
DEFINITION OF VARIABLES IN THE MODEL

Endogenous variables		
Y_{HH}	=	Total household income
NW	=	Number of workers in the household
J_n	=	Quality of the jobs of the other household members on a four-point scale (summed for up to four secondary workers)
J_1	=	Quality of the job of the principal wage earner on a seven-point scale from 1 (farm laborer) to 7 (entrepreneur or professional)
HS	=	Number of members in the household (household size)
EXT	=	Extended family organization (dummy variable)
BH	=	Budget management efficiency: a nine-point scale that measures the ability of household members to keep down the proportion of household income spent on food, given the number of children
ED_{HH}	=	Educational attainment of the household as a whole—all members
Exogenous variables		
Y_1	=	Income of the household head, in minimum salaries
AGE_1	=	Age of the household head
EA_1	=	Educational attainment of the household head
SEX	=	Sex of the household head (positive indicates male)

formal sector where marginals are employed. Since the dependent variable is expressed in logarithmic units, the regression coefficients can be taken as elasticities, and it is impressive to see the percentage increase in income that is predicted from the addition of one extra worker: 164 percent for the marginal group and 173 percent for the poor and middle group.

The importance of the quality of the employment of secondary workers in the household and the household head varies significantly among the economic groups. The *t* values show that job quality matters not at all to the marginal group. They are not better off if they have better quality jobs, just as we suggested in the discussion on the informal sector and the need for households to put members into any employment rather than queue up for high quality jobs.

Indeed for secondary workers this indiscriminate strategy works in all economic groupings. It matters not what kind of job the second and third worker may have, provided a job is held. The number of secondary workers holding white collar jobs is very small indeed, approximately

TABLE 8.10

DETERMINANTS OF HOUSEHOLD INCOME FOR THREE ECONOMIC GROUPS

Marginals (N = 363)						
Log (household income)	= 2.08	(number of workers)	- 2.84	(quality of job of secondary workers)	+ .18	(quality of job of household head)
t	=	(3.41)		(-1.15)		(0.56)
Poor (N = 298)						
Log (household income)	= 2.40	(number of workers)	- 1.43	(quality of job of secondary workers)	+ .08	(quality of job of household head)
t	=	(8.65)		(-2.49)		(2.46)
Middle (N = 312)						
Log (household income)	= 2.97	(number of workers)	- 1.92	(quality of job of secondary workers)	+ .17	(quality of job of household head)
t	=	(5.53)		(-3.39)		(2.74)

2 percent of the marginals, 4 percent of the poor, and 11 percent of the middles.

But for the head of the household job quality does matter if the household is a member of the poor or middle group. Members' economic status is improved when they land formal sector or government jobs. They are the households in the top 60 percent of the income distribution, some of whom stand to profit by development as it is being implemented in Mexico. And, as we shall see shortly, theirs are the kinds of jobs that are affected by formal education and the possession of credentials. But, for the marginal group, the impact of high quality jobs on household income is nil.

Equation 2: The Number of Workers

The number of workers in the household is decisive in determining its welfare, as the first equation showed. But what determines the number of workers in the household differs for the different economic groups. For the marginals, as the *t* scores indicate, both household size and the presence of an extended family are important in increasing the number of workers. But the extended family is not important for the poor group, where only household size is significant in increasing the numbers of workers in the household.

But the importance of the extended family in providing workers in marginal households is somewhat ironic in that the frequency of extended households is only 18 percent, compared to 21 percent for the poor people and 25 percent for the middles. The crucial role of extended families in building the household, combined with the rarity of their appearance, underscores the extreme difficulty under which the marginal households operate.

The last variable in the equation is defined as preset in value, or exogenous.[10] We theorized that households where the head had a higher income would attract more "imports," distant relatives, and, indeed, grown and/or married children to the household. As Herlihy (this volume) has argued, people collect where the resources are, the world over. And, as we have underscored in the earlier parts of the paper, households that are better off have larger numbers of workers. The inclusion of the household head's income in this equation shows the direction of causality in the wealth/size correlation, since higher household heads' incomes do not produce larger numbers of workers. The relationship between the household head's income and the number of workers (see table 8.11) in the household is insignificant for all three economic groups.

It seems that larger household memberships generate higher numbers of workers, which in turn generates higher income levels for the households, rather than higher income households attracting larger numbers of people to share in higher standards of living. What is occurring in the Mexican urban household is not sharing of poverty but rather increased levels of material well-being being generated by increased efficiencies in the organization of the domestic work force.

TABLE 8.11
DETERMINANTS OF NUMBER OF WORKERS IN THREE ECONOMIC GROUPS

Marginals (N = 363)						
Number of workers	= 0.20	(household size)	+ 1.45	(extended family)	- .001	(income of head of household)
t	=	(11.06)		(2.34)		(-0.64)
Poor (N = 298)						
Number of workers	= 0.27	(household size)	- 0.99	(extended family)	- .001	(income of head of household)
t	=	(6.36)		(-0.76)		(-0.46)
Middle (N = 312)						
Number of workers	= 0.73	(household size)	- 13.83	(extended family)	+ .030	(income of head of household)
t	=	(0.82)		(-0.52)		(0.42)

Equation 3: Household Size

Household size was not surprisingly the one important variable in determining the number of workers for both the marginals and the poor. In the third equation we tested the determinants of household size, hypothesizing that there would be three predictors: the effectiveness of household budget management (and in particular the way in which food expenses were controlled so as to generate funds for the purchase of consumer goods), extended family organization, and household maturity (as measured by the age of the household head). The results were clear for the marginal and poor groups, and consistently equivocal for the middle group (see table 8.12). Budget management and household maturity are important determinants of household size, but extended family organization is not (though, as we noted, it contributes to increasing the number of workers among the marginals).

Efficient budget management is an index constructed to reflect the degree to which households fall above or below the median in the proportion of household income they spend on food, given the number of children in the household. Households that spent below the median proportion of their income on food do well on the index, and vice versa. This is, in a sense, a cruel but realistic measure.

The majority of the urban population, the marginal and poor groups, have little opportunity to generate savings. Only the more successful members of the groups can afford to buy consumer goods, which are used not only for the purposes for which they were designed but also to store

TABLE 8.12

DETERMINANTS OF HOUSEHOLD SIZE FOR THREE ECONOMIC GROUPS

Marginals (N = 363)						
Household size	= 1.07	(efficiency of budget management)	−0.50	(extended family)	+0.07	(age of head of household)
t	=	(7.80)		(−0.20)		(4.66)
Poor (N = 298)						
Household size	= 0.92	(efficiency of budget management)	−3.09	(extended family)	+0.0008	(age of head of household)
t	=	(5.04)		(−0.62)		(3.86)
Middles (N = 312)						
Household size	= 0.08	(efficiency of budget management)	+21.41	(extended family)	+0.03	(age of head of household)
t	=	(0.09)		(0.72)		(0.52)

value, as savings accounts, during periods of high inflation. Such goods are a form of security against economic catastrophes like severe illness (see Higgins 1974 for ethnographic documentation). The only way the urban poor can possibly save money is by ruthless economies in the area of greatest expenditure—the food budget. After all, between 50 and 60 percent of their total household income is spent on food. Households that do save by this method are able to attract new members. And only large households can pool consumption expenses so as to reduce the proportion of the household income spent on food.

This relationship goes two ways. Inspection of the regression coefficients associating increased efficiency with household size shows what we would expect: the largest effect is found with the marginal group, the next largest with the poor group, and there is no significant effect at all for the most successful 30 percent in the population—the middles.

We thought that maturity of the household would be significantly associated with household size, and this again is true for the marginal and poor groups—the poor majority. Thus, we have to retract to some degree the rather pessimistic view we held earlier about the irrelevance of time in healing the wounds of extreme poverty. As household heads age, their households do get larger, and larger households are associated with larger numbers of workers and thereby with increased household income. But the relationship is indirect at best and for that reason attenuated, and in no way does it provide the household with a rationale for waiting in the hope that things inevitably are going to get better. They will improve, but *only* if the household can make full and effective use of the household formation strategies that we have delineated. Time is a benefit in principle, but only a contingent benefit.

Equation 4: The Quality of Employment

The quality of the job held by the household head (see table 8.13) is important in generating higher income for the poor and middle groups but not for the marginals, as was stated in the first equation. The *range* of jobs held by each income group is quite different, however. For example, only 30 percent of the marginals have jobs as good as clerical posts in the private or public sector, compared to 51 percent of the poor group and 64 percent of the middle group. But even with the marginal group credentialism is so strong that the educational attainment of the head of household is significant in determining who gets good jobs. The importance of education is high for the poor group (as can be seen from the regression coefficients), but it diminishes for the middle group, where 64 percent of the householders hold these jobs.

TABLE 8.13
DETERMINANTS OF JOB QUALITY FOR THREE ECONOMIC GROUPS

Marginals (N = 363)					
Quality of job of household head	= 0.73	(educational attainment) +0.14	(age of head of household)	-0.81	(sex of head of household)
t	=	(3.23)	(3.67)		(-0.83)
Poor (N = 298)					
Quality of job of household head	= 0.74	(educational attainment) -0.005	(age of head of household)	+2.17	(sex of head of household)
t	=	(2.94)	(-0.14)		(2.54)
Middles (N = 312)					
Quality of job of household head	= 0.54	(educational attainment) +0.04	(age of head of household)	+1.09	(sex of head of household)
t	=	(4.30)	(1.23)		(1.40)

We had expected that age would be negatively associated with the holding of better employment, based on the increasing levels of education in Mexico. This does not seem to be the case. Age is only a factor for the marginal group, where low-paying salaried jobs in municipal or state government are held by men (mainly) who have been around long enough to acquire them through personal contacts and years of service.

We had also felt that we would tend to see employment discrimination against women in the data, reflected by female household heads holding less desirable jobs than males. This is only true for the poor group; in the marginal and the middle groups there is no significant relationship between the sex of the head of household and the desirability of the job held.

Interpretation of the Equations

What does the model tell us?

1. The key to raising household income in each economic category is the increase in number of workers.
2. The key to survival for the marginals is the insertion of workers in the informal economy. And since wages in the informal economy are low and nearly invariant, one job will do just about as well as any other.

3. While the poor and middle groups may do well to invest in education for the head of the household, as things stand now such investments are wasted on secondary workers, as they are on the primary workers in the marginal group. There are no returns to these investments.
4. The key to deploying larger numbers of workers is household organization. A large household is necessary and for the marginal and poor groups the large household is attainable if members are exceptionally prudent in budget management. Large households make prudent budget management easier, to be sure, because households can take advantage of economies of scale in consumption, but we feel that frugal budget management and restrictions of the diet are necessary to provide that minimal amount of spending money that can produce progress in daily life.
5. Household organization involves the organization and even manipulation of kinfolk as well, especially sons and daughters-in-law. Extended families are infrequent among the marginal groups but very important in creating the conditions for additional workers in the household.

What the model shows then is that the argument that was developed in the earlier half of this paper, based on data for both Davao City and Oaxaca, is testable and is true when the test is carried out on the Oaxaca data.

We shall conclude with two related sets of thoughts that contrast our analysis with contemporary government policy.

The Mexican government feels that fertility must be restricted rapidly if Mexico is to continue to progress. Our data show that this is not true. Given the current set of economic and political arrangements, including the contemporary distribution of income and wealth in Mexico, the marginal and poor groups have but one recourse: to withdraw into themselves and organize themselves into large, closely related collectives that work together in order to survive. Children and their begetting are important facets of this strategy. Though the government says that "the small family lives better," the data from Mexico and from the Philippines show quite clearly that the large household lives better, for good and sufficient reason.

A second concluding point: The government encourages households to make sacrifices in order to educate their children. Our data show that among the poorer groups in the city this sacrifice is unnecessary. To the degree that households in the marginal and poor groups embrace the "informal economy" strategy, education is largely wasted. While the government adopts policies that generate niggardly amounts of formal sector employment and expansion of the informal economy expands in proportion to the formal economy, sacrifices for education make little sense.

There is another way of viewing education, as government planners well know. Education is a road out of the *colonia popular* into the lower middle class world for the selected few who take it. But when the educated members of households depart, they leave behind the ruins of the only strategy that could possibly have assisted their families out of the poverty they are themselves escaping (with luck and perseverance). The households they leave remain poor, effectively robbed both of the investment made on the fortunate member's behalf and of the only means of salvation.

The answer to this terrible dilemma is as obvious as it is difficult and unlikely: a complete change of the political and economic arrangements on the national and international level so that the majority of the people here and in other countries of the third world are not robbed of the means to health, a decent life, and hope for their children. As things now stand, we cannot expect less than a continuing hostile dialogue between the households of the majority and the apparatus of the state, resulting in distorted and unbalanced development on the one hand and unwelcome intrusions into the household's field of operations on the other.

NOTES

1. We would like to acknowledge the invaluable support of INDECO-Mexico, the Institute of Latin American Studies at the University of Texas at Austin, and the Dean Rusk Center for International Law at the University of Georgia. We would like particularly to thank Lic. Luis N. Rubalcava Rosas, Arq. Jose Ma Gutierrez, and Lic. Ignacio Ruiz Love in Mexico and Bill Glade and Al Saulniers in the United States. Eric Chetwynd of USAID put the Murphy-Selby pair in touch with Hackenberg and facilitated a kind invitation on the latter's part to a conference at the East-West Center, where the topic (The Intermediate City in Asia) was instantly, if not officially, broadened to The Intermediate City in the Pacific Basin on the arrival of the Mexicanists, Murphy and Selby, one of whom was from Canada.

2. Full accounts of the survey procedures can be found in Hackenberg (1976) for Davao City and Murphy (1979) for Oaxaca. In each case a two-stage sampling procedure was followed to permit random sampling within enumeration districts (in the case of Davao) and neighborhood types (in the case of Oaxaca). The final sample contained 2.5 percent of the Davao City households and 5 percent of the Oaxacan households. The total number of households sampled amounted to 1,005

for Davao City and 1,547 for Oaxaca. Statements relating to the whole city and to the enumeration districts or neighborhood types are representative of those populations.

3. The figures in this section are taken from the *World Development Report, 1981*, published by the World Bank.

4. The Philippine peso figures are calculated at 1972 values of U.S. 15 cents to the peso. The Mexican figure is somewhat more complicated since it involves changes in exchange rates between 1972 (our base year) and the year the data was collected (1977). The Banco de Mexico publication *Indicadores Economicos* for March 1981 takes 1978 as base year (= 100) and calculates the consumer price deflator as 100 in 1978, 85.1 in 1977, and 35.7 in 1972. In 1972 the exchange rate was 12.5 pesos to the dollar; in 1977 it was 22.7. In order to calculate the U.S. dollar equivalent, multiply the 1977 peso figure by .044 to obtain the 1977 peso equivalent, then multiply by .76 to correct for inflation from 1972 to 1977 and the change in the rate of exchange that took place with devaluation in 1976.

5. Bergsman (1979, table 2) has noted that the income shares of the bottom 40 percent of the income distribution are 14.3 percent for the Philippines and 7 percent for Mexico.

6. "Commercial involution" is adapted from Geertz's "agricultural involution," which describes the case where more and more labor inputs produce ever diminishing marginal returns—but much employment.

7. See the World Bank's *World Development Report, 1981*, table 18. The figure 15 is a weighted average for 1979.

8. The median ages for the household heads in the city of Oaxaca are: all = 37.6; marginals = 36.3; poor = 37.8; middles = 39.5.

9. During the Conference on the Household at which this paper was given, R. M. Netting and Rick Wilk presented, in tabular form, a collation of data bearing on the "large household hypothesis." They presented 23 historical and ethnological examples that showed a clear correlation between household size and economic standing.

10. Exogenous variables are those determined to be outside the system. They enter the system with preset values. In this model we are taking the income of the head of the household as preset because we are interested in determining the direction of causation in the wealth/size hypothesis.

REFERENCES

Ahluwalia, Montek S., Nicholas Carter, and Hollis B. Chenery
1979 Growth and Poverty in Developing Countries. World Bank Working Paper 309 (May).

Arizpe, Lourdes
n.d. Relay Migration and the Survival of the Peasant Household. Manuscript.

Bergsman, Joel
1979 Growth and Equity in Semi-industrialized Countries. World Bank Staff Working Paper 351 (August).

Buchler, Ira R., and H. A. Selby
1968 Kinship and Social Organization. New York: Macmillan.

Carnoy, Martin
1979 Can Educational Policy Equalize Income Distribution in Latin America? Westmead (Hants), England: Saxon House for the International Labor Organization.

Ekstein, Susan
1975 The Political Economy of Lower Class Areas in Mexico City: Societal Constraints on Local Business Prospects. *In* Latin American Urban Research, ed. Wayne Cornelius and Felicity Trueblood, vol. 5. Beverly Hills, Calif.: Sage.

Frank, A. G.
1970 Urban Poverty in Latin America. *In* Masses in Latin America, ed. I. L. Horowitz. New York: Oxford.

Hackenberg, R.
1976 The Poverty Explosion: Population Growth and Income in Davao City, 1972. Philippine Planning Journal (April).

Hammel, E. A.
1961 The Family Cycle in a Coastal Peruvian Slum and Village. American Anthropologist 63:989–1005.

Hart, K.
1973 Informal Income Opportunities and Urban Employment in Ghana. The Journal of Modern African Studies 2 (1):61–89.

Higgins, Michael
1974 Somos Gente Humilde: The Ethnography of a Poor Urban Colonia. Ann Arbor, Mich.: University Microfilms International.

Kim, M. H.
1982 Informal Economy in an Intermediate City in Mexico. M.A. thesis, University of Georgia.

Kuznets, Simon
1965 Economic Growth and Structure. New York: Norton.

Lewis, Oscar
1961 Children of Sanchez. New York: Random House.
1968 A Study of Slum Culture: Backgrounds for La Vida. New York: Random House.

McGee, T. G.
1980 Labor Markets, Urban Systems, and the Urbanization Process in Southeast Asia. Paper delivered at Workshop on Secondary Cities, Honolulu, Hawaii, July 16–28, 1980.

Murphy, Arthur D.
1973 A Quantitative Model of Goals and Values in Coquito Sector, San Juan, Oaxaca, Oaxaca. M.A. thesis, University of Chicago.
1979 Urbanization, Development, and Household Adaptive Strategies in Oaxaca, a Secondary City of Mexico. Ph.D. Dissertation, Temple University.

Murphy, Arthur D., and Alex Stepick
1978 Economic and Social Integration among Urban Peasants. Human Organization (Winter).
Murphy, Arthur D., and Henry A. Selby
1979 Tipologia de Vivienda: Un Estudio Socioeconomico de la Ciudad de Oaxaca. INDECO-Mexico. CIDIV (October–November), pp. 42–81.
Peattie, Lisa
1975 Tertiarization and Urban Poverty in Latin America. *In* Latin American Urban Research, ed. Wayne Cornelius and Felicity Trueblood, vol. 5. Beverly Hills, Calif.: Sage.
Roberts, Bryan
1973 Cities of Peasants. Beverly Hills, Calif.: Sage
1974 Center and Periphery in the Development Process. *In* Latin American Urban Research, ed. Wayne Cornelius and Felicity Trueblood, vol. 5. Beverly Hills, Calif.: Sage.
Selby, Henry A., and Arthur D. Murphy
1982 The Role of the Mexican Household in Making Decisions about Migration to the United States. Occasional Paper no. 4, Series on Social Change in Latin America. Philadelphia, Pennsylvania: Institute for the Study of Human Issues.
Sethuraman, S. V.
1976 The Urban Informal Sector: Concept, Measurement and Policy. International Labor Review 114:69–82.
Stepick, Alex
1974 The Rationality of the Urban Poor. Ann Arbor, Mich.: University Microfilms International.
Stepick, Alex, and Arthur D. Murphy
1977 A Comparison of the Economic Status of Two Urban Colonias in Oaxaca, Oaxaca, Mexico. Paper presented at the annual meetings of the American Anthropological Association, Houston, Texas.
World Bank
1982 World Development Report, 1981.

9

Households in Process: Agricultural Change and Domestic Transformation among the Kekchi Maya of Belize

Richard R. Wilk

The principal objective of this paper is to describe the process of transformation of household groups among the Kekchi Maya under economic stimulus. The emphasis on process distinguishes this discussion from others that attempt to demonstrate the ways in which household groups adapt to changing circumstances. This difference in mode of explanation is crucial in avoiding the abuses of functionalism which ecological anthropologists have so frequently (and often justly) been accused of (Yanagisako 1979; Orlove 1980).

As the editors mention in the introduction to this volume, one of the most useful ways of determining the causes of household transformation is comparison of household organization over time or between places. Such comparisons cannot by themselves demonstrate causality—they only set the stage for explanation. For example, to show that swidden-farming Kofyar have large households while intensive-farming Kofyar have small households (Netting 1965, 1969) only demonstrates covariation and does not explain why this difference exists. What we lack are arguments explaining the link between farming practices and domestic groups in a causal manner instead of merely proposing a plausible explanation after the fact.

My research among the Kekchi in Belize (Wilk 1981*a*, 1981*b*) began as an attempt to replicate Netting's study of changing agriculture and domestic organization among the Kofyar, but I made a more explicit attempt to trace causal relationships. The data collected among the Kekchi seemed to contradict the Kofyar case. I found that households became larger and more complex as agriculture became more intensive, rather than vice versa. Yet the contrast between the two cases provides the key to more general and more specific properties of domestic groups. Instead of talking about intensive versus extensive agriculture (or Goody's [1976] comparable hoe versus plow contrast) we can now define more specific attributes of agricultural systems which affect domestic groups. Agricultural production can then be related to general models of the processes by which production of all kinds is organized within household groups on a cross-cultural basis.

A second objective of this paper is to point out the effect of household classifications and typology on the way we perceive and measure household change. The transformations I will describe in Kekchi domestic groups are realized in the changing nature of kinship ties, in the exchanges between individuals, and in the relations between conjugal families. The size and composition of the group of people living together under a single roof does not change very much (see Löfgren, this volume). Furthermore, what changes there are in size and composition of domestic groups are not consciously perceived by the Kekchi themselves as anything but expectable qualitative variations in kinship behavior and exchange relationships.

This example calls long-standing definitions of the household into question and emphasizes the usefulness of the kind of multistranded approach to defining the household advocated by Hammel (1980 and this volume) and Wilk and Netting (this volume). My analysis also points out the interplay of exchange, ideology, and reciprocity in counterpoint to the strength of tradition, which acts to maintain structural form despite drastic organizational change. Other contributors to this volume make similar points, though in other cases traditional forms seem to exert a greater constraint on pragmatic action (for example, those cases discussed by Wolf, Carter, Douglass, and Plakans). Elsewhere I have speculated about some of the historical and economic reasons for the fluidity and adaptability of Kekchi domestic groups (Wilk 1981*a*).

THE ETHNOGRAPHIC SETTING

The Kekchi are a Mayan-speaking people who were confined to the broken upland region of Alta Verapaz in Guatemala from prehistoric times to the nineteenth century. Protected by Dominican missionaries from the time of the conquest (see Saint-Lu 1968), their homeland was

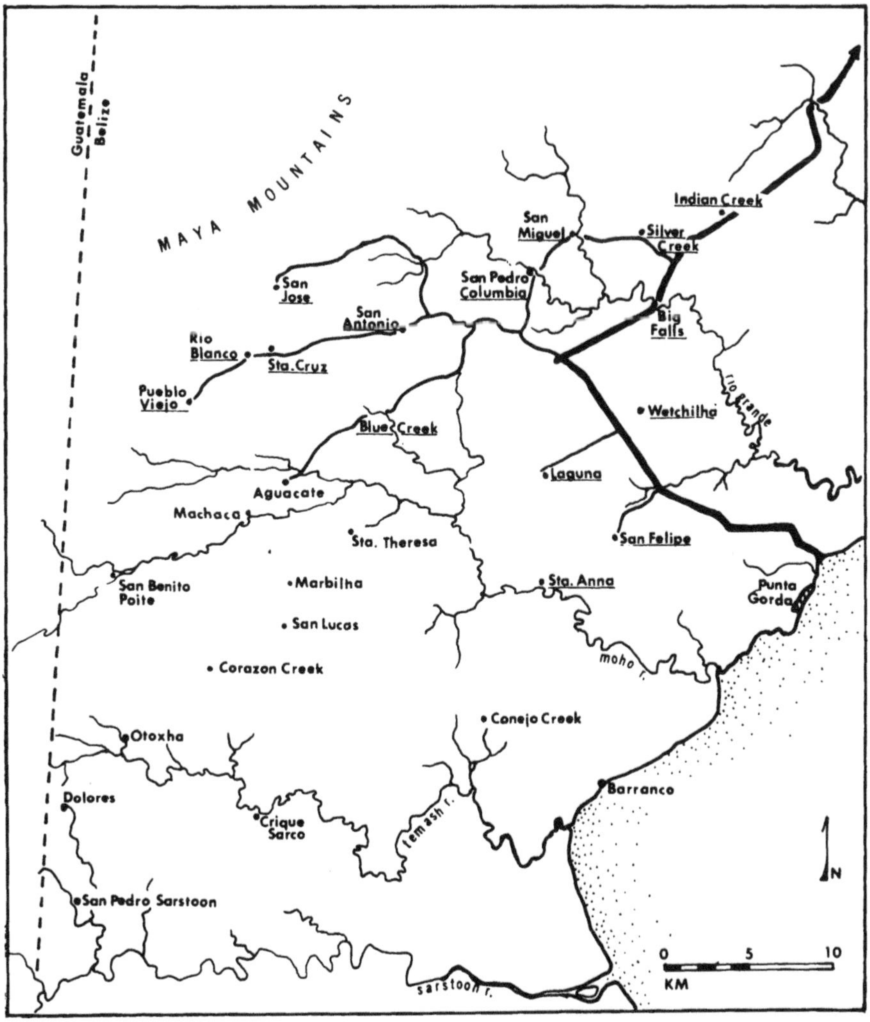

Southern Belize

Northern zone villages are underlined, southern zone settlements are not. Punta Gorda is the District Town. Thick line is main highway connecting with the capital in the north; thin lines are feeder roads.

literally invaded in the late nineteenth century by ladino, English, and especially German entrepreneurs who began a coffee industry using forced native labor on expropriated native lands. Continuing inroads into the land and labor needed for subsistence and strengthened oppression have led many Kekchi to flee into adjacent lowland areas to the north in Peten (Adams 1965), to the south in the Izabal region (Carter 1969), and eastward to the Toledo district of Belize.

The first Kekchi to arrive in Belize were brought there around 1890 as laborers on a German-owned plantation in the far southwestern corner of the country. At about the same time Mopan Maya from eastern Peten also began to migrate into Belize, where they occupied the largest single area of good swidden lands in the northern uplands of the Toledo district. As more Kekchi entered the district, they spread along the southern rivers, creating small, dispersed hamlets of up to 200 inhabitants. The northern part of the district, where all of the Mopan are concentrated, has always had more contact with the world economy than the more isolated southern forests have. By 1914 the large Mopan settlement of San Antonio was connected to the district capital of Punta Gorda, which lies on the coast (and is inhabited mainly by Black Caribs and East Indians). In the mid-1960s both San Antonio and Punta Gorda were tied into the national road network and began to develop closer economic and political ties with the rest of the country to the north.

This historical pattern of development resulted in great differences between the northern and southern parts of the Toledo district which are partially mirrored in cultural and social differences between Kekchi and Mopan (whose languages are mutually unintelligible). In the northern zone population densities are higher and the economy is highly oriented toward participation in the national economy. Major cash crops are rice and beans (the staples of the urban Creole population), and large areas are being cleared by foreigners for cattle ranching. The southern zone economy is still based on swidden agricultural production of subsistence crops, though considerable numbers of pigs are raised for cash sale (Wilk 1981*b*).

Considerable movement takes place between the two zones. Beginning in the 1950s many Kekchi left southern villages and moved to establish new villages along the expanding northern road network, where they could market cash crops. This influx of population, in concert with the growth of the cattle industry, has fueled increasing competition for land with access to the northern roads. The movement north continues, however, fed by accelerating migration across the border from Guatemala, where Kekchi have borne the brunt of political and economic oppression during the present insurgence. The southern zone villages are growing slowly today, adding population from Guatemala and losing some to the northern zone. The population of these villages at present ranges from 36 to 240 inhabitants; the villages' subsistence economy is intact.

My research took advantage of the north-south gradient of change in the district to contrast a subsistence economy with one based largely on cash production. The majority of the research was conducted in Aguacate village, which is situated on the border between north and south and where cash crop production was introduced in 1972. Additional material was gathered in one village in the southern zone (Santa Theresa) and one village on the road network in the northern part of the district (Indian Creek).[1]

LAND RESOURCES AND DOMESTIC ORGANIZATION

Many studies of variation in household organization have focused on settled land-holding peasant societies. This has led to an elaboration of models that view households as property-holding institutions, organized and affected by rules of transmission and inheritance (see Goody 1969, 1972, 1976; Berkner 1972; Netting 1981). At the same time anthropologists generally recognize that households also play an important role in the organization of production and the distribution of what is produced. The analytical problem posed by these overlapping spheres of activity is a serious one (see Wilk and Netting, this volume). How do we separate the structural elements of the household which respond to production and distribution from those tied to the group's role in property holding and transmission?

The Kekchi in the far southern part of the Toledo district in Belize provide an opportunity to solve this analytical problem because they do not own the land they work and are unable to transmit property rights between generations. Since 1914 the territory occupied by the Kekchi has been divided into Indian reserves by legislative acts of the colonial government, and this policy continues under the new independent government. In the reserves established around major villages land is legally held by the government and can be cultivated by any Indian who lives in that village on payment of a nominal yearly fee. Practical administration of the land in a village is left in the hands of the village *alcalde*, who is chosen annually by the village members. He works with an informal council of village elders or with the more formal elected village councils that have been established recently in a few communities at the instigation of the government (see Howard 1977 and McCaffrey 1967).

TABLE 9.1
MEASURES OF MAN/LAND RATIOS IN THREE STUDY VILLAGES

	Santa Theresa	Aguacate	Indian Creek
ha. of levee soils suitable for matahambre[a]	275.00	163.00	0.0
ha. of good to fair milpa soils[b]	3,050.00	2,981.00	3,293.75
ha. of poor milpa soils	1,256.25	175.00	943.75
ha. of unusable soils	465.25	2,025.00	331.25
ha. of usable soil per household[c]	218.20	110.63	70.60
ha. of good to fair milpa soil per household	145.30	99.36	54.90
ha. of good to fair milpa soil per person[d]	30.20	19.11	10.10

[a]All soil areas were calculated from soil maps published in Romney (1959) using a modified version of site catchment analysis. Five km. radius circles were drawn around each village center and the areas of soils within the circle were calculated. The five km. limit corresponds closely to the actual distance which Kekchi farmers will go to farm. The circle was modified for Santa Theresa and Aguacate to exclude soil areas which are claimed and used by other villages and so are not available to farmers. In Indian Creek the excluded area has been purchased by cattle ranchers and the catchment was expanded outside the five km. circle to include a pocket of fertile land that is used by Indian Creek farmers because it can be reached quickly by a logging road.

[b]The soil classifications are a combination of the descriptions and chemical analysis published by Romney (1959) and my own interview data. Poor milpa soils are only used under special conditions, if they are very close to a road for instance. All of the area figures should be reduced in practice by about 30 percent because many areas with good soil are actually unusable because of rough topography.

[c]This figure includes the first three soil categories.

[d]The population of Indian Creek is an estimate based on sample data, school rolls and informant's statements.

Informal tenure arrangements of varying kinds are found within villages, enforced only by the consent of the village members, since no legal tenure is possible. In most southern zone villages the population density is so low that suitable swidden lands are still widely available. As long as the fallow cycle of most fields is longer than 10 years, no degrees of ownership or rights to reuse are recognized or desired. As the catchment analysis in table 9.1 demonstrates, population is much higher in relation to land resources in the northern zone villages than in the south, and this does affect land-use practices and rights. When population pressure on land increases, fallow cycles are shortened and different areas of land acquire different values for agriculture, depending on how far they are from the village and how long they have lain fallow. Consequently, where better land becomes hard to find, we see a system in which continuing usufruct rights are recognized, the rule being that the man who first clears a plot from high forest retains the right to use the field again after it has been fallowed.

Few villages have yet reached the degree of land shortage at which access to swidden land is a serious consideration in the formation of domestic groups. But in a number of villages another more scarce kind of land has become an important element of domestic strategy. Here I refer to the seasonally inundated levees of the major rivers, which are capable of supporting annual cropping of maize and other subsistence crops during the dry season. The greater long-term productivity of these soils and their ability to produce during the season when swidden agriculture in the surrounding hills is not possible gives the levee areas a high value.

In some of the southern villages, of which Santa Theresa is an example, there is enough levee land in relation to population to avert competition. In these villages use rights to a levee plot have no continuity—they lapse if the field is abandoned for more than a year. In other villages where population is greater in proportion to the area of levee land available (Aguacate is an example), rights to levee plots do have continuity and resemble outright ownership. The plot can be loaned, given as a gift, or inherited but cannot be sold. The effects of land scarcities of various kinds on strategies of domestic group formation will be considered below after I devote some space to defining the domestic unit and describing its variability.

HOUSEHOLD VARIABILITY

One problem with existing definitions of the household for the Kekchi case is the use of coresidence as a defining criterion for the unit. Gonzalez (1969), Bohannan (1963), and Laslett (1972) all argue that members of the household must live under a single roof to be considered a discrete unit. As Hammel (1980) and Wilk and Netting (this volume) point out, coresidence is only one of a number of activities that household groups perform. In some cases it makes sense to look at other activities when defining the household group in a particular setting. Anthropologists working in Latin America and the Caribbean have encountered this problem often, for in these areas it is common to find groups that eat together, work together, share child rearing and other obviously domestic activities but live in separate houses. Anthropologists should not be forced to abandon the term *household* for describing or discussing these units or to resort to tortuous terms like *nonresidential extended family* (Nutini 1968).

I have chosen to designate Kekchi households on the basis of the activities of production and distribution (see Wilk and Netting, this volume, for definitions) rather than coresidence. The group that actually inhabits a single house I will call the *dwelling unit,* which does in some cases form a household by itself. These single dwelling unit households are called *independent households* while a household composed of more than one dwelling unit is a *household cluster.*

Members of an independent household form a tight cooperative group that shares meals on a daily basis. All household members share in child-care duties, in tending the household livestock, and in maintenance of the dwelling itself. All males in the household who are over 14 years old (school is mandatory until this age) cooperate daily in the household's agricultural fields under the command of the male household head. Whatever is produced by any household member, through agriculture, wage labor, hunting, fishing, or gathering, is brought back to the household to be shared.

The only exception to this apportionment rule occurs with rice fields and the money derived from the sale of rice (this crop is not usually eaten by the Kekchi, although they grow it in large quantities).[2] Young men who live with their fathers are permitted to cultivate rice and keep a part of the cash derived from its sale. In practice this division of the household rice fields is more ideal than real, since most of the time the rice fields are adjacent and are worked cooperatively by all men in the household.

Though meals are rarely formal occasions, all household members eat the same food from the same pot. All female members of the independent household share in processing and cooking food for meals, but the exact allocation of specific duties tends to vary with the number and age of the female household members.

In household clusters arrangements for production and consumption are considerably more complex and varied than those I have just sketched in independent households. One way to deal with the variation in household clusters is to scale them along an axis between extremes I label *tight* (many overlapping activity groups and spheres) and *loose* (greater separation of activities).

In a tight household cluster all adult males of the component dwelling units coordinate their daily agricultural labor and often work together. Yet each male dwelling unit head has his own cornfield and his own granary in the cornfield. The cornfields of all cluster members are usually adjacent, and members freely borrow corn from one another. Rice fields, if present, are owned by the individual dwelling unit heads, though again there is close cooperation in all productive tasks and the fields are usually adjacent. All of the household cluster's rice will be harvested and marketed in a single operation. Pigs may be owned communally by the entire cluster if it is a tight one, with the cash from their sale divided equally between dwelling unit heads. Chickens and ducks, on the contrary, are individually owned and fed by each married woman in the cluster.

Labor exchanges between the males of a tight household cluster are transacted through an explicit rule of generalized reciprocity. This means that a careful reckoning of who owes whom how many days of labor is not kept (such reckoning is kept by males who live in separate households). Among comembers of a household cluster it is considered uncouth to expect or discuss reciprocity, while outside the household there are explicitly stated norms of labor exchange, and borrowed days of labor are usually returned within a few weeks.

In a tight household cluster continual sharing of food takes place. When a domestic animal is slaughtered or a wild animal killed, the meat is distributed among the component dwelling units or, if the quantity is limited, one woman will cook a large meal in which all cluster members partake. Gathered wild foods and harvested vegetables are shared in similar ways, and the household cluster may plant and tend a single garden plot for vegetables, root crops, and fruit trees.[3] Many other tasks related to the maintenance of the household site—keeping weeds down, care of pigpen and chicken coop, or cleaning trails—are also shared by members in a tight cluster.

Each dwelling unit within the household cluster has its own hearth and kitchen area, but in a tight cluster more than half of the meals each week are eaten by all the cluster members together in one kitchen. As well as sharing in many tasks of food processing and preparation, the adult female members of a household cluster tend to be involved in constant complex exchanges of child-care duties. Most of the day is spent visiting back and forth between dwellings. Nevertheless, each individual female dwelling unit head is responsible for maintaining her own house, and minor craft production (pottery and weaving) is still done individually.

In a loose household cluster the cooperative ties that bind individuals in different dwellings are fewer and weaker. The corn fields of the dwelling heads may not be adjacent, and there is less frequent labor exchange in all productive tasks. If corn is exchanged between dwellings a count may be kept and there will be an explicit expectation of reciprocity within a reasonable period of time. Pigs are penned, fed, and sold separately. There is still a great deal of sharing of food, but fewer meals are taken by the entire group together, perhaps as few as five meals per month. Garden crops and fruit trees are no longer planted in one location, and there is less coordination and planning of the year's production by the cluster head. Female tasks also seem to be performed together less often, with less sharing of the burden of child care on a daily basis.

So far I have defined three different kinds of social group on the basis of (1) the frequency of exchange of food and other resources by members, (2) the frequency with which the members associate together in work groups, (3) the quantity of crops, property, and goods held in common, and (4) the degree to which the activities of the group are planned and directed by the head of the unit. From this functional perspective we can see the independent household as a single, undifferentiated group in which all of the above quantities are constant and the household cluster as a group in which there is internal differentiation in these measures, the component dwelling unit at one level and the entire cluster at another level. In a tight household cluster the individual dwelling unit is less distinguishable, less "decomposable" (Simon 1962), from the cluster itself. The dwelling unit economy is melded into that of the larger unit. The loose household cluster is much more a complex differentiated unit, with the dwelling unit economy embedded in but distinguishable from the household cluster. This nesting of units offers a degree of adaptability and flexibility that the tight cluster lacks, but as we shall see below it also makes the management and maintenance of interpersonal relationships within the unit more complex and difficult.

The differences between the units discussed here are not emicly recognized by the Kekchi. There is no word for "household cluster." But there are ideological boundary markers and material symbols that directly reflect the nature of economic interaction between dwelling units. One such marker is the rule of reciprocity, which I have mentioned above. The difference between a pair of independent households and a pair of dwelling units within a household cluster is marked by the distinction between explicit rules of balanced reciprocity between the former and generalized reciprocity between the latter. This is especially evident in male labor exchange: if men keep count of the work days they trade, they are not members of the same household cluster.

The physical placement of dwellings is another overt symbolic expression of the relationship between inhabitants. Tight household clusters tend to be spatially tight, the houses almost touching and oriented to face onto a common *plazuela*. Loose household clusters are spatially more dispersed, less formally planned, and the separate dwellings may not even be visible to one another. The spacing of dwellings is also used as an expressive symbol, a means of communicating about the nature of ties between households and even of changing those ties. One older man in

Aguacate expressed dissatisfaction with his sons by moving and rebuilding his house over 100 meters away from their cluster, on top of a hill looking down on them. When his relationship with his sons improved (the argument was over the father's autocratic control of the scheduling of the sons' labor), he once again moved his house down the hill to fill in the empty side of their plaza.[4]

So far in this discussion I have avoided any mention of the morphology of the households I have described. Before going on to consider how households change and realign the multistranded economic relations between their members, I will make a short foray into a more conventional description of the kinship relations and structural configurations around which the economic interrelationships are woven.

HOUSEHOLD MORPHOLOGY

Independent households are usually composed of a nuclear family group, normally a married couple and their children. A widowed parent is sometimes taken into the household, though never in the role of household head. The high rate of divorce and death leads to a large number of fragmented nuclear families; many children end up living with a step-parent. In case of divorce children usually go with the mother, though sometimes a woman's new husband will not tolerate children by a previous marriage and the children must be sent to live with other relatives. These children sometimes wander from household to household for many years until they reach the age when they are economically valuable (about 12 or 13).

Two special circumstances can lead to more than one nuclear family living within a single independent household. The first is the custom of postmarital residence, in which a couple lives with one of their parents for one or two years after marriage. Postmarital residence is normally patrilocal, though the couple may choose some other arrangement if the husband has only a step-father or if his parents have a dwelling crowded with many other children. Postmarital coresidence normally ends when the couple's first child is born. Three-generational households are not common.

Multiple nuclear families also live under a single roof if they are recent immigrants to a village and do not have the labor resources necessary to build more than a single house at first. In a newly settled village I recorded four nuclear families living in a single dwelling, though most members planned to move out as soon as the first year's crops were in and there would be time to build new houses.

The developmental trajectory of a household cluster is much more complex than that of the independent household, though it can best be seen as the composite of several concurrent nuclear family cycles. Household clusters are usually formed when a married couple that has been living in patrilocal postmarital residence moves out after having a child. They build a new house adjacent to that of the husband's parents, usually forming a tight bond of reciprocity with them. There is, however, no cultural rule that prescribes a patrilocal household cluster after a son's marriage, and in many villages a significant portion of postmarital residence is uxorilocal or neolocal.

The choices of different residence locations after marriage create a number of recognizable, simple structural types of household clusters. This is somewhat complicated by the decisions of couples that later have a chance to join established clusters. Taking together all of the nine villages I visited, I found seven different kinds of household clusters:

1. Patrilocal household clusters: Nuclear family plus family (families) of married son(s)
2. Uxorilocal household clusters: Nuclear family plus family (families) of married daughter(s)
3. Uxoripatrilocal household clusters: Nuclear family plus families of married son(s) and married daughter(s)
4. Fraternal clusters: Families of two brothers or two half-brothers
5. Sororal clusters: Families of two sisters or half-sisters
6. Extended sororal clusters: Families of two sisters and one of their husband's step-parents
7. Unrelated clusters: Two or more families connected by distant or fictive kinship ties

This list by no means exhausts the possibilities, many more of which are reputedly present in villages that I did not visit. These categories are again not emic ones, but they do seem to bear some relation to the activity-based division of household clusters into loose and tight. Patrilocal and uxorilocal household clusters tend to be tight, with a preponderance of tight clusters being patrilocal. In Aguacate village, for instance, the only tight household clusters were patrilocal ones. Loose clusters, on the contrary, span all morphological types. This corresponds with the Kekchi ideal of a special emotional tie, a bond that permits and condones unbalanced reciprocity, between father and son and between mother and daughter. This bond is not felt between siblings, compadres, or other kin.

The household cluster is clearly flexible in composition, allowing a freedom of choice of membership far beyond the restrictive bounds of the developmental cycle of an individual domestic group. Though it is feasible to plot all of the possible transition probabilities and paths for change from one form to another over time, such a lengthy task would not answer the basic question of why these arrangements are chosen by different people at different stages of the life cycle. I will take two approaches to explaining this variability, the first distributional and the second based on a detailed study of the economics of productive labor.

HOUSEHOLD DISTRIBUTION

Striking differences exist between the three study villages in the number and frequency of the different morphological household types defined above, though there is little difference in the size or composition of individual dwelling units. Because of the nature of these differences, a census study that used the house as the unit of counting and measurement would find little difference from place to place. The researcher should keep this example in mind when examining census records—my own attempts to trace Kekchi households over time using census records were frustrated by this same confusion over units of analysis (see Arnould's essay, this volume for a similar boundary-definition problem).

Table 9.2 lists the absolute and relative frequencies of independent and

TABLE 9.2
FREQUENCIES OF DIFFERENT HOUSEHOLD TYPES IN STUDY VILLAGES

	Santa Theresa	Aguacate	Indian Creek
Total population[a]	101	159	54[b]
Dwelling units[b]	21	30	10
Mean size, dwelling units	4.8	5.3	5.4
Independent households	17	10	1
Mean size, independent households	5.0	5.7	8.0
Household clusters	2	8	5
Mean dwellings per cluster	2.0	2.5	2.2
Mean cluster size	8.0	11.9	[c]

[a]Total population of Indian Creek is really about 320. The listed figure is for the village sample of ten households.

[b]Dwelling units are individual houses, whether clustered or not.

[c]Only one cluster in the village was entirely censused, so I have no meaningful figures for this settlement.

clustered households in the three study villages. Note that the census of Indian Creek village is only a small random sample of the village population. It is clear from this figure that dwelling size does not vary greatly from village to village. Rather, the differences between villages are found mainly in the higher proportion of independent households in Santa Theresa, a higher frequency of household clusters in Aguacate and Indian Creek, and the larger number of persons in the Aguacate household clusters.

A further difference between the villages is revealed in table 9.3. Here the households are broken down by cluster types, using the typology developed above. The differences between Aguacate and Indian Creek are striking. The frequency of patrilocal household clusters in Aguacate is far higher than in the other settlements. It should not surprise us, given the low frequency of patrilocal household clusters in Indian Creek, to find that most of the clusters there fall toward the loose end of the relational spectrum while those in Aguacate tend to be tight. Though we would expect the patri- and matrilocal clusters in Santa Theresa to be tight on the basis of their kin structure, they are quite loose and the interactions between members are more similar to what we find in Indian Creek. Explaining these differences requires some detailing of the patterns of labor mobilization within households.

AGRICULTURE, LAND, AND LABOR

Table 9.4 brings together the data on variability in household form in the three study villages and information on land availability and the frequency of cash cropping. There is an obvious and strong correlation between lower availability of land, higher frequency of cash cropping, and a low frequency of independent households. A larger sample of villages would have allowed a statistical treatment of this covariation, which might tell us something about the relative strength of association

TABLE 9.3
CASH CROPPING, LAND AVAILABILITY, AND HOUSEHOLD FORM IN THE THREE STUDY VILLAGES

	Santa Theresa	Aguacate	Indian Creek
Percentage independent households	81.0	33.3	10.0
Ha. good and fair soil per person	145.2	99.4	54.9
Percent dwelling units growing rice	0.0	36.7	70.0

TABLE 9.4
FREQUENCIES OF CLUSTER TYPES IN THREE STUDY VILLAGES

Cluster type	Santa Theresa	Aguacate	Indian Creek
Patrilocal	1	7	1
Matrilocal	1	0	0
Patri-matrilocal	0	1	1
Fraternal and unrelated	0	0	3
Total	2	8	5

between variables. Instead, the detailed data on productive systems collected in Aguacate village permits me to trace the often subtle causal linkages between land, production strategies, and household organization in a way that statistical analysis cannot.

To begin I must elaborate on the discussion of labor scheduling in Wilk and Netting (this volume). Some agricultural tasks can be performed as a sequence of operations by a single individual, in a mode I will call *linear scheduling*. Other kinds of tasks, however, require a number of workers to coordinate their labor at the same time in what I refer to as *simultaneous scheduling*. Furthermore, simultaneous scheduling occurs in two types: that in which all workers do the same job at the same time (*simple simultaneity*) and that in which there is a division of labor and workers do different tasks at the same time (*complex simultaneity*). These distinctions are loosely based on those made by Terray (1972).

Many tasks can possibly be accomplished by any of the three kinds of scheduling; a Kekchi man can build a pigpen by himself, or he can call together a work group and do the job with them in a simple or complex division of labor. But in reality every kind of job is defined by a set of time limits, contingencies, and scales that make one kind of scheduling more efficient than another. In other words, some ways of finishing a job are better than others. In fact, the nature of the job itself has a direct effect on the size, structure, and composition of the group that will complete it. And a change in the number or nature of jobs to be done will have an effect on the composition of work groups.

Of course, people will not always choose the most efficient kind of scheduling to accomplish a particular task. The societal division of labor by sex, as Linares (this volume) points out, places a real limit on the possibilities of choice. Although the sexual division of labor is itself changeable, such division seems to lie at the core of so many other aspects of culture (gender constructs, for instance) that it tends to remain stable.

Norms of reciprocity in labor exchange, like those discussed above among Kekchi household cluster members, also place limitations on the possibilities of task organization, and their application can result in the performance of tasks in seemingly inefficient ways.

The general cultural ethos relating to work also limits an actor's options in choosing the most efficient way to finish a job. Among the Kekchi an often invoked norm is that communal labor is better than solitary work. All work, it is said, is more pleasant and goes faster when done by a group. I cannot deny that work is often a social activity during which important activities—learning of skills, exchange of information, and verbal play—take place. At the same time people are not slaves to norms, and the fast and efficient completion of a job is the goal of a great deal of pragmatic thought in every culture. When the Kekchi find that a labor group would be an inefficient means of accomplishing a task, they readily forgo the pleasures of the group and work alone. Like many other peoples, the Kekchi seem capable of invoking a norm daily and violating its precepts hourly.

The extent of Kekchi pragmatism is demonstrated by their willingness to change the size and composition of labor groups when such a change is more efficient. To show the causes of these changes more precisely and to detail their social consequences, I will develop the contrast between villages where land is plentiful (as in Santa Theresa) and villages where land has become a more limited resource.[5]

Villages with plentiful land practice subsistence agriculture on a highly communal basis. A single large wet season cornfield is cleared, burned, and planted by a labor group consisting of all of the adult males in the community. The same large group builds corn storage sheds in each household's portion of the field and then harvests and stacks the crop in each. By working together to build a pig-proof fence, the group can choose a field site very close to the village.[6] If any man desires to enlarge his field or interplant a quantity of other crops among the corn, he does this on his own or with the help of members of his household. The yearly schedule of labor inputs to agriculture is relatively level, with three major peaks when corn fields are cleared, planted, and harvested (see fig. 9.1).

A low man/land ratio means that well-fallowed high forest land is close to the village site and average corn yields are high (2.83 kilograms per man-hour of labor) and quite reliable. Because of the high yields, the village rarely plants a dry season river-levee corn crop (called *matahambre*). There is also little need to interplant root crops or other plants as a dietary supplement. Aside from agricultural tasks done by the village work group, all other work in agriculture is performed by individuals in a linear manner or with household labor. Women perform much more

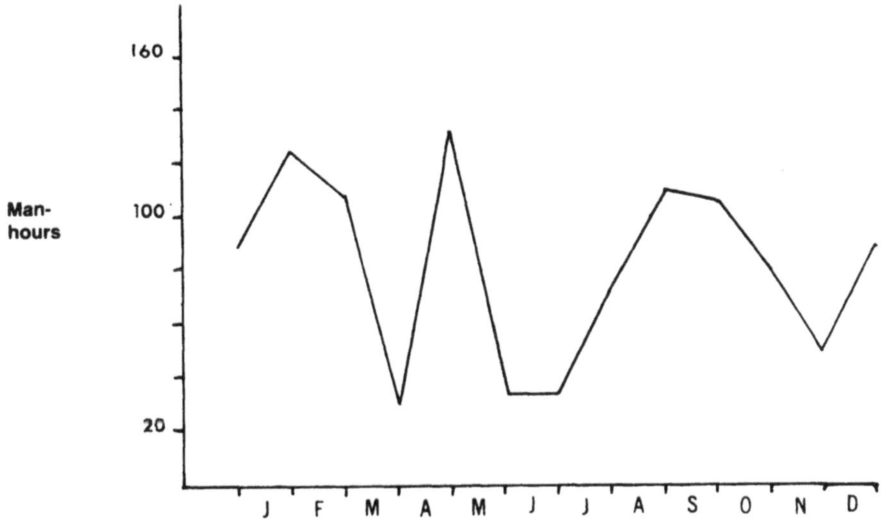

Fig. 9.1
Annual Labor Inputs to Wet Season Corn Production

The line represents an average farmer's monthly labor inputs in wet season swidden agriculture. The peaks occur during clearing (January–March), planting (April–May) and the harvesting-storage seasons (August–November). These bottlenecks are met through labor exchange; the farmer works alone during the rest of the year. This is typically the entire annual productive cycle in southern zone villages, with only hunting, fishing, and planting a few minor crops to complicate the schedule.

agricultural labor than in villages that have less land, visiting fields to work with their husbands up to seven times a month. The pooling of labor in the large village exchange-labor group tends to minimize the disparities in production between those households with large labor forces (those with more adult male children) and those with a single male.

Thus, when land is plentiful, usually in small or relatively recently settled villages, most yearly agricultural production can be effectively carried out by the community labor group or by the individual household. There is no agricultural task that requires the formation of intermediate-sized labor groups with any frequency. The independent household consisting of the conjugal (nuclear) family unit is therefore a viable productive group.

This is the situation in present-day Santa Theresa. A newly married couple there almost always chooses neolocal residence in an independent household because they have little incentive to stay with either set of parents to form a household cluster. They perceive the ties of reciprocity and obligation within the household cluster as burdensome: if the male were living in his father's household cluster he would end up giving his father more days of labor than he would receive. This occurs because during the time that a boy is growing up in his father's household, his labor belongs to his father and he is at his father's beck and call. This pattern of unbalanced reciprocity tends to continue after the son marries and is culturally formulated in the normative ideal that "sons owe respect to their fathers." Unless the son feels that he stands to gain something in return for this unbalanced labor exchange, he will have little incentive to live with or even near his father and will choose the independence of neolocal residence. Similarly, if the couple resides near or in the wife's parents household cluster, the wife will end up carrying a burdensome share of her mother's child-care, cooking, and cleaning duties.

The decision to set up a separate independent household after marriage is not without social problems. A man's father tends to feel that he has a right to his son's labor and may continue to make demands even if the son's new house is located across the village. The young couple, for their part, expect their parents to give them some pigs and chickens as a start for their livestock enterprise. There is a lot of personal variation in the ways these issues and obligations are settled, but enough rancor is often generated to drive the younger married couple out of the village. They may move to another village to establish their independent household, or they may join another, looser household cluster where the reciprocity between members will be more balanced.

This is one of the many points where household formation processes articulate with regional patterns of mobility and settlement. Although there is no rule of exogamy among the Kekchi, villages are so small and interrelated that incest prohibitions usually force people to seek spouses outside their natal village. A postmarital residence choice is thus also a choice between villages, not just a choice between which set of relatives to live with and what possible economic relationships to establish with them. *Regional* variation in the abundance of land and the availability of access to markets and transportation therefore affects residence choices, sometimes as much as the considerations of production mentioned above. At marriage a household may leave the village for another that has more land or is closer to the road, even if there is no quarrel with a parent.

The independent household/community work group system I have described undergoes change when man/land ratios increase. Basically, pressure on land resources requires changes in agricultural techniques and the scheduling and timing of agricultural labor. This in turn leads to changes in labor group composition and to changes in the balances of power and exchange between kin. The outcome of residence decisions therefore tends to be quite different, and a different form of household group results.

One immediate effect of greater population in relation to land is that farmers must go farther and farther from the village to find well-fallowed land. Because travel time to and from the field and transportation of corn back to the village constitute a major part of the yearly labor devoted to agriculture, increased distance to fields reduces effective yield per man-hour. As a result, when well-fallowed land becomes distant enough—about 45 minutes one-way travel time—some farmers find that they can get equal yields by using shorter-fallowed land closer to the village. When "high bush" is more than 45 minutes away, "low bush" closer to the village actually yields more per man-hour, although because of increased animal predation and marginal fertility, those low-bush yields are more variable.

A variety of strategies therefore becomes possible among village farmers during the wet season. Those who want to maximize yield (usually younger men with few dependents) clear fields in closer low forest while men who want to minimize risk with a more reliable harvest (often older men with many dependents) grow their corn in distant high forest.

The operation of the village communal labor group is disrupted when households pursue diverse strategies; high and low bush are cleared at different times by different techniques. The fine scheduling that keeps labor exchanges in a large work group balanced tends to break down when members each have different requirements. High forest requires complex simultaneity during clearing, because it takes teams of four men to safely cut large buttressed forest trees. Secondary forest, in contrast, can be cleared in a linear manner by groups of any size.

The general decline in total yield per man-hour and the reduced reliability of the harvest, which both follow from higher man/land ratios, require many farmers to cultivate a dry season *matahambre* corn crop to make up their shortfall. *Matahambre* fields are cleared in November and harvested beginning in February, a schedule that conflicts with the beginning and end of the main wet season swidden field. These timing conflicts exacerbate the scheduling problems of the village labor group. Communal harvesting seems to break down first, as individual labor needs tend to vary most widely at this time of year. The farmer finds himself unable to call on a corporate village labor group when it is needed, and individually organized exchange labor groups become harder and harder to actualize because each farmer's labor needs and scheduling are out of step with the others' requirements.

At the same time the increasing complexity of the agricultural cycle leaves the farmer with less flexibility in his own labor allocation. More and more he finds that several tasks have to be done at the same time (complex simultaneity) and that many of the tasks must be carefully scheduled within strict time limits. *Matahambre*, for instance, must be planted within seven days after the field is cleared and prepared, otherwise new growth will have a head start on the young corn and laborious weeding will be required. Figure 9.2 depicts the increasing complexity and the many scheduling overlaps in the Aguacate annual agricultural cycle.

The decline of the village labor group imperils the autonomy of the independent household. Household labor and the village work group can no longer fill all the year's labor scheduling needs.[7] There are many times when the farmer needs small, flexible groups of workers which are larger than just the male membership of his house.

Some independent households meet these needs by forming smaller, task-specific labor-exchange groups with other households. A man who wants to plant his *matahambre* field will go from house to house until he finds four or five other men who are making *matahambre* and who are willing to come and help him for a day. He will have to negotiate to pay back a day's labor to each of these men, hoping that this won't disrupt the

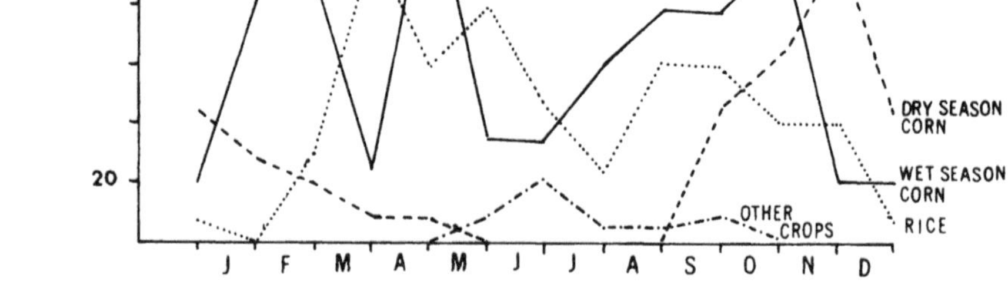

Fig. 9.2
Annual Labor Inputs in a Northern Zone Village

The lines indicate monthly labor expenditures for four different productive systems that operate simultaneously in most northern zone villages. These are approximations of averages for groups of farmers—individual farmers may use a different schedule, yet the problems of coordination and overlap remain. "Other crops" are those interplanted in the wet season corn field or the rice field.

scheduling of the next set of tasks he has set for himself. The complications involved in such scheduling are often formidable, since the date of each day of exchanged labor has to be negotiated separately.

The household cluster provides an alternative and more flexible solution to these problems by constituting a group of adult males who can call on one another frequently and coordinate their efforts to deal with scheduling conflicts and labor bottlenecks. When diverse tasks must be done at the same time, the cluster can divide its labor for greater effectiveness. One man can spend two or three days camping at his cornfield, protecting it from wild animals, knowing that other members of his cluster will haul in corn from their fields in order to provision his household. The larger labor unit can harvest *matahambre* and begin to clear the next year's swidden field at the same time.

Pooling of the household's production also provides benefits to all its members. Often one member will clear a field in high forest while another will use low forest, thus combining low-risk and high-yield strategies. More constant supply of fruits, vegetables, and meat is ensured as well as greater reliability in the corn supply—temporary shortages can be made up from another cluster member's granary.

These advantages change the balance in postmarital residence decision making. Married couples now find more benefits to staying in a parental household cluster; they can see that as they begin to have children they are going to have more and more dependents but no new labor resources until the children are older. If they join a cluster, their parents will help to support and care for those children. The disadvantages of unbalanced labor reciprocity are counterbalanced by sharing produce and by the enhanced security the group offers.

Most clusters formed in this way are patrilocal ones because the core is a group of men who have acted as a cooperative labor group over many years (as the sons grew up). These clusters tend to be tight because of the dense network of labor exchange and pooling of resources binding the two units together. The tightness is enhanced by parental tendencies to maintain control over many of their children's resources, such as pigs and minor crops.

Villages like Aguacate which are composed of many tight household clusters tend to have a dispersed settlement pattern. Clusters mark their autonomy by establishing themselves at a distance from other houses. Clusters also tend to have greater locational permanence than independent households. The economic advantages of the household cluster seems to be an incentive for remaining in a village, and permanent improvements to the house site may be made (leveling, ditching, planting ornamentals and fruit trees). The solidarity of the household cluster also provides a unified front in village politics, and all recent *alcaldes* in Aguacate have been the heads of household clusters.

EFFECTS OF CASH CROP PRODUCTION

When cash crops such as rice are added to a situation of growing land shortage, many of the processes of household aggregation outlined above are strengthened. Rice and beans, the major cash crops, conflict with the subsistence corn production system in their labor requirement schedules. Households find that rice and bean production demands that even more cropping operations be performed at the same time. Pooling and coordinating labor within the household cluster becomes an attractive solution as scheduling problems increase in complexity. Cash crops are grown using the same methods as corn, and the cash crops compete for land with subsistence crops. Effective land shortage increases, and even with increasing dependence on levee lands, some households find it increasingly difficult to meet subsistence needs as well as produce for market. Heads of independent households are among the first in a village to have to seek wage labor (outside the community) during slack times of the year.

Household clusters garner further advantages in cash crop production because they can accumulate and concentrate more capital for investment in herbicides and fertilizer and because they are more capable of taking risks when new opportunities open up (as has happened with apiculture recently). Greater capital also enables commercial expansion. A common arrangement has a father lending his son money to establish a small shop in the cluster; the son tends to do less work in the cornfield but receives a steady supply of corn from his father in exchange for goods from the shop. In some villages the members of a cluster may cooperate in purchasing a truck and setting up a pig wholesaling operation. Comparisons can be found in other parts of the world where the large household has been an effective unit for taking advantage of new commercial opportunities (see Hunt 1965; Singer 1968).

Why are so many of the household clusters in Indian Creek—the progressive, roadside, cash-cropping village—nonpatrilocal and loose? The explanation is partially that the village is quite new and composed of unrelated households assembled from many different villages. But there also seems to be a more fundamental cause, one related to a change in the balance of power in household clusters that follows from greater population pressure on land and a larger degree of participation in cash crop farming. Older men with many dependents know that it is to their advantage to get a recently married couple (with few dependents) to form a cluster with them. Young couples are aware that they have a certain bargaining power and that they have a choice of people with whom they can affiliate. A loose household cluster often results because the junior units in a patrilocal or matrilocal cluster can now assert their independence more successfully. Other households, often the most "progressive" ones that depend on purchased foodstuffs to some degree, prefer to form loose clusters with more distantly related households because these units offer the advantages of sharing and coordinating labor in production without the common pooling of cash and food for consumption. Such loose clusters allow the individual dwelling unit to pursue cash production and accumulate goods without requiring that the proceeds be shared evenly among members of the unit.

CONCLUSION

This short presentation does not do justice to the complexity of the household system among the Kekchi or to the multitude of ways in which the household is tied to economic, political, and ideological elements of Kekchi culture. Yet even this brief discussion sheds some light on several more general aspects of household organization and the dynamics of change.

First, it is clear that household change cannot be adequately described, much less explained, solely through the use of static typologies. The actions that *define* the household are as changeable as the units themselves, and any classification that fails to take this into account confuses the most obtrusive object of study—the household group—with the more important *subject* of study—the dynamic and adaptive abilities of that group (see discussion in Medick 1976). We must look at what households do, in both the ideological and material realms. This in turn requires us to view households as decision-making bodies (see, for example, Carter and Merrill 1979) and as adaptable "survival vehicles" (Adams 1981).

But households are not individuals, and what they do is the product of negotiation, exchange, and individual decisions. I have therefore tried to focus on the internal processes of balance and exchange which affect the life course of conjugal units and their choices for aggregation or separation. This problem has been touched on in the work of those who apply decision-making theory to residence decisions (and discussed explicitly by Barth 1967), but otherwise few anthropologists have been interested in the flow of exchange within households. Carter's household history approach (this volume) shows promise as a means of objectively assessing the causes and consequences of economic balancing in these contexts.

Second, this paper argues that household clusters increase in frequency because population pressure and cash cropping require a set of activities that household clusters are better suited to perform than independent households. This example relates to other discussions of the economic roles of large households. Both Befu (1968) and Sahlins (1957) have discussed the advantages of a large household group for pooling consumption and providing simultaneous labor in production. Pasternack, Ember, and Ember's "incompatibility theory" (1976) makes a more general point about the need for large groups to cope with conflicting labor needs. My analysis generaly supports these hypotheses, but at the same time none of these schemes pays adequate attention to alternatives or to balances of costs and benefits within the household. It is not the diversity of Kekchi production alone which places a premium on a large group, it is also the growing simultaneity of the tasks that have to be done. Large households are not the only possible solutions to this kind of problem—under certain circumstances the Kekchi communal labor group makes a large household labor group unnecessary.

A more general question I have not approached is why the Kekchi respond so quickly and readily to changing environmental circumstances with new domestic arrangements. Other groups discussed in this volume seem to show considerable ideological resistance to realignment of their households for a number of reasons (see, for example, Kunstadter, or Linares). We must work toward explanations that specify why economic adaptation takes place in some cases and why it doesn't in others. In the Kekchi case the key seems to be that economic adaptation has not required breakage of any preexisting norms or rules of household or kinship behavior. The most definite Kekchi rule of household formation demands that three generations shall not coreside in the same house. As a result married couples move out of the parental house after the birth of their first child. Household clustering allows conformation with the letter of the rule. Couples still move out and build their own house after their first child is born—but now they build their house adjacent to a parental house and maintain an economic unity.

Old rules of kinship are also reinterpreted and readapted to the new household form. The subordination of adult males to their fathers, a fact of life in household clusters which is unknown in the independent household system, is accomplished by an extension of the rules of children's behavior toward parents. Fathers and sons in household clusters justify their nontraditional relationship by reference to the very traditional rule that sons should always obey their fathers. This rule is applied, in an independent household system, only to sons who have not yet married. The household cluster is justified by a stretching of accepted modes of behavior to fit new situations.

In closing I would like to return briefly to the implicit theoretical underpinnings of this paper, namely, the concept of the household as an activity group offered in Wilk and Netting (this volume). There we mention that cultural change can be conceptualized as a shift in the size and level of the groups that perform various activities. This concept provides another way of looking at changes in Kekchi households. We could say that the village at present is losing its role as a productive group, the household is taking on new responsibilities for distribution and management, and the individual conjugal family is perhaps temporarily losing its independence in reproduction. While the household is certainly not the only level at which this kind of change can be studied, it seems to hold the most promise for explaining culture change in a dynamic, actor-oriented way.

NOTES

1. The research on which this paper is based was supported by the University of Arizona Graduate Program Development Fund, a grant-in-aid from the Wenner-Gren Foundation for Anthropological Research, and a Dissertation Improvement Grant from the National Science Foundation (BNS 7814205). I would like to thank my coeditors and the conference participants for constructive criticism of this paper and for generally expanding my awareness of household organization. I must thank as a (large) group all of the people who have read and offered comments on the many drafts of this paper.

2. This applies only to villages in the northern zone, where rice is a common cash crop. The practice of individual management of rice yields seems to have developed because young unmarried males first introduced rice farming as a source of cash into new villages and areas that had previously practiced only subsistence farming.

3. Over 50 domestic plants are grown in addition to corn and rice. The most important are manioc, sweet potato, plantain, and beans.

4. All groups of dwellings which are close together are not necessarily household clusters. Sometimes limitations in the number of available house sites leads to dense concentrations of houses which are not clusters as defined here. Households must, however, be located within about 30 meters of one another if they are to be a household cluster.

5. In this more general discussion I draw on the work of other anthropologists who have worked in the Kekchi, particularly Howard (1974, 1977) and McCaffrey (1967). Erasmus (1956) and Guillet (1980) also give important discussions of labor group formation and change.

6. Any field within about 1.5 kilometers of a village must be fenced to keep out pigs. Single farmers find it easier to go beyond "pig range" than to fence a small field, but if a large group clears adjoining fields they can protect the larger area with less work per person. This increases the efficiency of production by minimizing the amount of time wasted traveling back and forth to the field to work or to carry the crop home.

7. Some very few households which have two or three working-age male children—obviously a short-lived stage of the household cycle—do seem to manage quite well on their own. Not coincidentally, households at this stage are usually the ones that try to pioneer new areas and establish villages of their own.

REFERENCES

Adams, Richard N.
1965 Migraciones Internas en Guatemala: Expansion Agraria de los Indigenas Kekchies Hacia El Peten. Guatemala: Centro Editorial "Jose Pineda Ibarra."
1981 The Dynamics of Societal Diversity: Notes from Nicaragua for a Sociology of Survival. American Ethnologist 8 (1):1–2.

Barth, F.
1967 On the Study of Social Change. American Anthropologist 69:661–69.

Befu, Harumi
1968 Ecology, Residence, and Authority: The Corporate Household in Central Japan. Ethnology 7:25–42.

Berkner, Lutz K.
1972 Rural Family Organization in Europe: A Problem in Comparative History. Peasant Studies Newsletter 1:145–54.

Bohannan, Paul
1963 Social Anthropology. New York: Holt, Rinehart and Winston.

Carter, Anthony, and William Merrill
1979 Household Institutions and Population Dynamics. Washington, D.C.: Agency for International Development.

Carter, William E.
1969 New Lands and Old Traditions: Kekchi Cultivators in the Guatemalan Lowlands. Gainesville: University of Florida Press.

Erasmus, Charles
1956 The Occurrence and Disappearance of Reciprocal Farm Labor in Latin America. Southwestern Journal of Anthropology 12:444–69.

Gonzalez, Nancie S.
1969 Black Carib Household Structure. American Ethnological Society, monograph 48.

Goode, William J.
1963 World Revolution and Family Patterns. New York: John Wiley.

Goody, Jack
1969 Inheritance, Property, and Marriage in Africa and Eurasia. Sociology 3: 55–76.
1972 The Evolution of the Family. *In* Household and Family in Past Time, ed. Peter Laslett and Richard Wall, pp. 103–24. Cambridge: Cambridge University Press.
1976 Production and Reproduction. Cambridge Studies in Social Anthropology, no. 17. Cambridge: Cambridge University Press.

Guillet, David
1980 Reciprocal Labor and Peripheral Capitalism in the Central Andes. Ethnology 19 (2):151–69.

Hammel, E. A.
1980 Household Structure in Fourteenth-century Macedonia. Journal of Family History 5:242–73.

Howard, Michael
1974 Agricultural Labor among the Indians of the Toledo District. National Studies (Belize) 2:1–13.
1977 Political Change in a Mayan Village in Southern Belize. Katunob Occasional Publications in Mesoamerican Anthropology, no. 10. Museum of Anthropology, University of Northern Colorado, Greeley.

Hunt, Robert
1965 The Developmental Cycle of the Family Business in Rural Mexico. *In* Essays in Economic Anthropology, ed. June Helm, pp. 54–80. American Ethnological Society. Seattle: University of Washington press.

Laslett, Peter
1972 Introduction: The History of the Family. *In* Household and Family in Past Time, ed. Peter Laslett and Richard Wall, pp. 1–89. Cambridge: Cambridge University Press.

McCaffrey, Colin
1967 Potentialities for Community Development in a Kekchi Indian Village in British Honduras. Ph.D. Dissertation, University of California, Berkeley.

Medick, H.
1976 The Proto-industrial Family Economy: The Structural Function of the Household during the Transition from Peasant Society to Industrial Capitalism. Social History 3:291–315.

Netting, Robert M.
1965 Household Organization and Intensive Agriculture: The Kofyar Case. Africa 35:422–29.
1969 Ecosystems in Process: A Comparative Study of Change in Two West African Societies. National Museum of Canada Bulletin, no. 230. Ottawa.
1981 Balancing on an Alp. Cambridge: Cambridge University Press.

Nutini, Hugo
1968 San Bernadino Contla: Marriage and Family Structure in a Tlaxcalan Municipio. Pittsburgh: University of Pittsburgh Press.
Orlove, Benjamin
1980 Ecological Anthropology. Annual Review of Anthropology 9:235–75.
Pasternack, Burton, C. Ember, and M. Ember
1976 On the Conditions Favoring Extended Family Households. Journal of Anthropological Research 35 (2):109–24.
Romney, D., ed.
1959 Land in British Honduras. Colonial Research Publications, no. 24. London: Her Majesty's Stationery Office.
Sahlins, Marshall
1957 Land Use and the Extended Family in Moala, Fiji. American Anthropologist 59:449–62.
Saint-Lu, André
1968 La Verapaz: Espirit Evangelique et Colonisation. Paris.
Simon, Herbert
1962 The Architecture of Complexity. Proceedings of the American Philosophical Society 106 (6).
Singer, Milton
1968 The Indian Joint Family in Modern Industry. *In* Structure and Change in Indian Society, ed. M. Singer and B. Cohen. Viking Fund Publication, no. 47. Chicago.
Terray, Emmanuel
1972 Marxism and "Primitive" Societies. Monthly Review Press. New York.
Wilk, Richard R.
1981*a* Agriculture, Ecology, and Domestic Organization among the Kekchi Maya of Belize. Ph.D. Dissertation, University of Arizona.
1981*b* Pigs Are a Part of the System: A Lesson in Agricultural Development. Belizean Studies 9:122–29.
Yanagisako, Sylvia
1979 Family and Household: The Analysis of Domestic Groups. Annual Review of Anthropology 8:161–205.

10

Serf Emancipation and the Changing Structure of Rural Domestic Groups in the Russian Baltic Provinces: Linden Estate, 1797–1858

Andrejs Plakans

Because few communities in premodern Europe took household censuses regularly enough to create data in a continuous series, researchers dealing with household change in the long term ordinarily have had to use the regional or even the national level in their analyses, with different communities providing evidence for different time periods (Laslett and Wall 1972).[1] Two other correctives for the same problem are cross-sectional analysis controlled for age and microsimulation (Berkner 1972; Wachter, Hammel, and Laslett 1978). While the conceptual problems created by these approaches do not exist in an actual census series, such a series creates other difficulties and raises other questions, especially when confronted with an hypothesis formulated in general terms. Consider, for example, one of the hypotheses the organizers of the Seven Springs Conference asked participants to consider, namely, that "household organization responds sensitively to changes in the environment while preserving certain formal similarities over long periods of time" (Netting and Wilk 1980:1). This proposition seems straightforward, but when it is tested against such empirical data as the succession of Russian tax censuses, which I will examine below, the next steps are not all self-evident. What are "households" in this concrete historical population, and what do we examine in them to detect a "response"? How inclusively do we define the historical "environment" that emits the "changes" to which households respond, and what do we measure in order to say whether a response has been "sensitive"? What characteristics of the household comprise its "formal" features, and for how many generations do we need data to be able to say that we have dealt with the responses over "a long period of time"? Finally, how close to each other do the elements of a time series have to be in order for us to claim that we have examined household change in the same population rather than in two essentially different populations that happen to have lived in the same area? There are few settled conventions regarding these matters in the existing corpus of historical investigations of the household, particularly with respect to areas in which community studies of the traditional type have never cleared the ground for more specialized inquiries. Premodern eastern Europe is one such area, and an investigation of its household history must therefore involve, as a preface to a description of structural changes, some account of the socioeconomic environment within which households existed.

SECOND SERFDOM IN EASTERN EUROPE

The classifications "free people" and "hereditary serfs" in premodern population enumerations of eastern Europe are a stark reminder that in these areas of the continent structural analysis cannot take for granted that what shows up in the sources was the result of implementation of time-sanctioned rules of coresidence. Free people—landed nobles, renters, clergy, estate officials, and estate artisans—had relatively free choice in residential matters, but they were always a small minority (3–4 percent) of the population of a given landed estate. Serfs, by contrast—the hereditarily servile people (*Erbuntertänige*) or those whose "bodies" were "owned" (*Leibeigene*), to use the German designations from the documents of some of these areas—were always a vast majority. Their living arrangements came into being as the result of an as yet inadequately understood process involving customary rules and the bending of such rules as well as the regulations created by landowners in their role as the local government. Sometimes these regulations influenced structures directly through the people involved, as in the case of pronatalist landowners who sought to depress ages at first marriage by fining fathers whose children had not married by a certain age. Sometimes the influence was indirect, as in the case of restrictions on the use of lumber as a building material. Sometimes, presumably, there were no regulations at all, or what regulations existed were circumvented. In all such historical populations generalizations about typicality have to recognize that the composition of households could be altered suddenly by a landowner's decision to relocate entire families to other estates or to bring new ones in, to block the customary passage of headships from father to son, and even to divide complex family groups. These decisions could be made without any reference to peasant custom or preference, though they were probably never so frequent as to keep an estate's population in constant turmoil.

These managerial proclivities on the part of eastern European landowners made serfdom in the early modern period of European history sufficiently different from its medieval counterpart for historians to speak of it as a "second serfdom" (Blum 1957). Attitudes toward land were now different than they had been: landed property had come to be perceived as a means to profit rather than as a basis for self-sufficiency, and managed agricultural activity aimed at increasingly distant markets. These changes were part of the agrarian history of the Russian Baltic provinces as well, where in the course of the fourteenth and fifteenth centuries a series of crusades sanctioned by the papacy had resulted in the creation of a new, German-speaking landowning order and the start of the enserfment of the native Latvian- and Estonian-speaking populations. In the course of the sixteenth and seventeenth centuries these serf estates became tied to an eastern and western grain market, and the Baltic landowners, by the end of the eighteenth century had developed considerable expertise in fitting their activities to market requirements (Dunsdorfs 1973:440–502; Schwabe 1928:255–83).

The creation of a permanent rural labor force through enserfment had been an unremitting process, which was slowed somewhat in the seventeenth century when the Baltic area came under Swedish rule and the Vasa dynasty, for reasons of imperial control, sought to check the autonomy of the Baltic landowners. But when the third partition of Poland in 1795 brought the last of the Baltic provinces (Kurland) into the Russian Empire, there were few peasants left who could move about freely and who had ownership rights to the land they worked or the premises on which they lived. The Baltic estates in the last decades of the eighteenth century could not rival in size or in the number of their resident peasants those of the great Russian landed families, but their owners were as firmly in control as their Russian counterparts. After their incorporation into the empire, all three Baltic provinces (Estland, Livland, and Kurland) became subject to the imperial head tax and to the military recruitment laws and therefore had to be enumerated in the so-called "revisions of souls," which had been started in Russia proper under Peter the Great (Kabuzan

1971; Vahtre 1973; Brambe 1982:13–23). The resulting census-type population listings are the principal sources for detailed information about the domestic domain of the Baltic peasantry from the end of the eighteenth century to the end of the revision series in 1858.

During the seventeenth and eighteenth centuries the enserfment process in the Baltic provinces changed the personal status of thousands of peasants, but it did not alter the physical appearance of the countryside. On some 2,000 large and small estates scattered farmsteads lay isolated from one another by expanses of field, pasture, forest, and marshland. At times several farmsteads formed a cluster, but both the Swedish land surveys (cadastres) of the seventeenth century and the subsequent Russian revisions demonstrate that in this area the historian deals not with nucleated villages but with discrete compounds of farm buildings in which the residents had far more daily interaction with one another than they did with the other peasants of the estate.

The pattern of dispersed farmsteads became the basis of the estate's economy, which can best be understood as a mixture of constraint and autonomy, freedom and control. There was movement of people between farmsteads but relatively little across estate boundaries. The estate owner required from each farmstead a labor force of a certain size to work the demesne, but he seems not to have been particularly interested in the structure of the group from which this labor force was drawn. The passage of farmstead headships between generations could follow custom as long as this did not bring into the headship a person who was likely to be a poor manager of the farmstead. The creation of new farmsteads was not entirely impossible, especially when new land was cleared, but the costs of creating a new set of buildings (normally at least five structures) would be balanced by the estate owner against the lesser costs of increasing the number of inhabitants in the existing farmsteads. Marriages did not entail the creation of new farmsteads, but the place of residence of newly married couples was not prescribed. Judging by the records, some peasants practiced *Hälftnerschaft*, which involved two separate peasant families coresiding in a single farmstead and dividing the labor responsibilities and the yield. But these arrangements remained informal and did not mean, from the owner's point of view, any permanent division of the farmstead and its land. In a certain sense the farmsteads, their buildings, and their land were the persisting features of these estates. The estates could be sold and bequeathed, and the human population on them could grow and diminish and circulate in and out of the farmsteads without much disturbing the number of farmsteads or the living space available in each of them (Kundzins 1974). The central position of the farmstead in the rural areas of the Baltic provinces remained essentially unchanged during the two centuries of peace that followed the Great Northern War (1700–1721) and lasted almost without interruption until World War I.

The youngest generation enumerated in the first analyzable fiscal census (or revision) in Kurland (1797) therefore should be considered the most recent link in a chain of generations which had had considerable experience in adjusting to the constraints created by the settlement pattern and by serfdom. These features of the Baltic countryside had had ample time by 1797 to become what Fernand Braudel has called "structures of long duration," that is, factors of social life which "live on for so long that they become stable elements for an indefinite number of generations: they encumber history, they impede and thus control its flow" (Braudel 1972:18). The dominant residential patterns in the 1797 revision reflect how this "control" had been worked out. But the *entire* revision series is useful for another purpose: it provides information not only about the last decade of serfdom but also about the period *after* serfdom was formally abolished in 1817. In that year the imperial government and the Baltic *Ritterschaften* (corporations of the nobility) introduced a new peasant law (*Bauerverordnung*) that simultaneously initiated a 15-year-long process transforming the Baltic serfs into free subjects of the tsar, created a degree of peasant self-government, and began to modify restrictions on freedom of movement. When the youngest serfs listed in the 1797 revision began to take up adult responsibilities and to make decisions about the composition of the farmsteads whose headships they had inherited, the factors they took into account were radically different. At least in principle the revisions carried out after emancipation reflected the results of household decisions made in a changed environment.

Unfortunately, the revisions were carried out according to an imperial schedule and not by reference to events of importance to the regional history of the Baltic area. The first revision in 1797 in Kurland was in reality a giant listing of the entire provincial population, estate by estate, farmstead by farmstead, individual by individual. In principle, the revisions were to be carried out every fifteenth year, but in practice the intercensal periods varied considerably. The next revision in Kurland was made in 1811, but in line with the *ukaz* (ukase, edict) that called for it, only males were counted. This method having proved unsatisfactory, full counts were resumed in 1826, and this practice was followed in the subsequent revisions in 1833, 1850, and 1858. Thereafter no province-wide enumeration of any kind was carried out until 1881, when the Baltic German authorities decided to take a provincial census using modern techniques of counting. Only the aggregate results of this have been published (Ergebnisse der baltischen Volkszahlung . . . 1884). The 1881 census was followed in 1897 by the first modern census for the empire as a whole. The timing of the revisions proper therefore gives us intercensal periods, starting in 1797, of 14, 5, 10, 7, 7, and 8 years, respectively. This short history of population surveys in the Baltic, however, disguises incompleteness of the records for most localities at the estate level of analysis. In some estates the 1833 revision was not carried out at all, and a very few estate archives (*Güterarchiven*) managed to preserve the entire series.

Continuity from one revision in the series to the next was considerable. Each farmstead had a unique number and name and appeared in the same place in each of the successive revision books. The estate scribes used each revision document as the basis for the subsequent one, as illustrated in figure 10.1. The figure shows the column headings for the 1797 and the 1811 revisions. The 1797 revision was the first full count of the Kurland population, and in its columns 1 to 4 contained the names and ages of all free (*Freygeborene*) and enserfed (*Erbuntertänige*) people in each estate, by gender, as well as the names and ages of those who had fled from the estate (*Entlaufene*). Fourteen years later, in 1811, the names and ages in the 1797 revision were repeated in the first two columns (5 and 6), creating a kind of a baseline population for that year. Column 7 in 1811 contained annotations about each individual of the 1797 population: whether he had died, if he had moved and where, and so forth. In addition column 7 also indicated those who had been born between 1797 and 1811. Column 8 in 1811 then repeated the ages of all the people who were alive and living in the estate in 1811, and this information was in turn repeated, as another baseline, in the first columns of the next revision in 1816. In these ways each revision document in the series was linked to earlier and subsequent ones and contained, among other things, valuable information about the movement of individuals between census years. In many cases it is possible to track individual peasants from their first appearance in the record to their disappearance and to know why they disappeared. Though in the Baltic area the revisions were carried out in German, with column headings written in German, this general format was approximately the same as was used in Russia proper, as the work on revision documents from serf estates in the interior of Russia attests (Czap 1978, 1982).

Even these records contain problems, of course. When, for example, an individual appears in two successive censuses as living in one farmstead in the first and in another in the second, we do not know whether the latter residence represents the only move he made in the intercensal period or the last in a series of moves. There is also the problem of underregistration, though this, as best as can be established, does not in

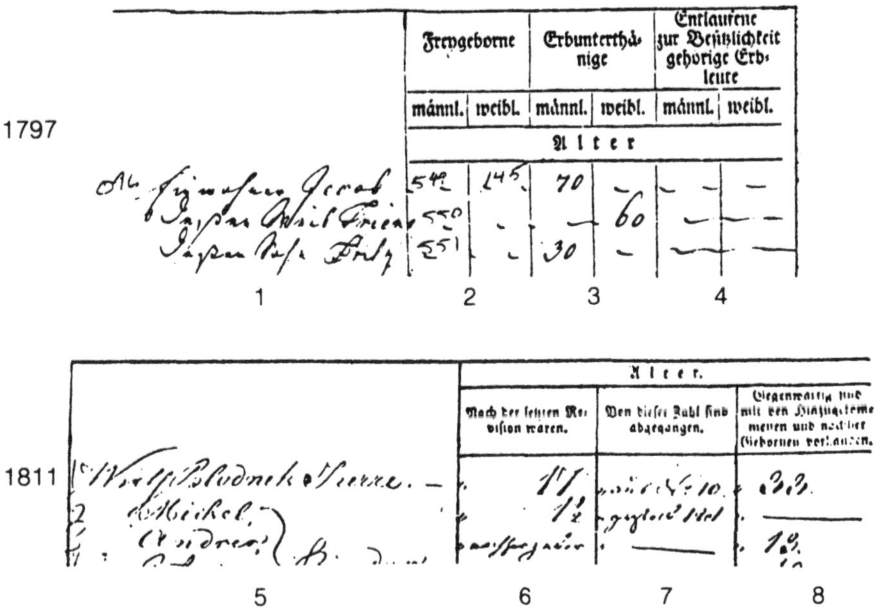

Fig. 10.1
1797 and 1811 revisions

most cases lead to serious statistical error (Palli 1980). Inevitably, the one estate we have chosen to examine has to serve as a trial case. There were something like 2,000 serf estates in the Baltic provinces at the beginning of the nineteenth century and some 650 in Kurland. At the individual estate level one should therefore expect a variety of outcomes as each entered and went through the emancipation period. Given the current archival policies of the Soviet Union, where the original revisions documents are located, drawing a sample from the entire revision is impossible. Whether the changes in the one estate we will look at were representative or not must therefore remain an unanswered question.

LINDEN ESTATE AND EMANCIPATION: OVERALL CHANGES, 1797–1858

The estate Linden was a large, privately owned estate in the south-eastern section of Kurland, close to the Lithuanian border.[2] The property made its first appearance in the inheritance records of the Baltic in the sixteenth century, and by the middle of the nineteenth century it had been part of the landed patrimony of the von Plettenberg and von Mengden families for several hundred years (Kurläudischer Güterchroniken 1895:112–36). In 1844 the last representative of the Plettenbergs sold the estate to the von Hahns, another noble lineage, for the sum of 150,000 rubles. In 1797 the nearly 2,000 people in Linden (see table 10.1) gave it a substantially larger population than the average for Baltic landed estates, which was approximately 600 serfs (Plakans 1976:361; forthcoming). In 1797 Linden's revision listed altogether 111 farmsteads (*Gesinde*), with a mean size of about 17 people per farmstead. Linden also had 12 other residential units (such as taverns, estate farms, and a mill), which housed mostly free people, and a farm set apart for the Lutheran clergyman (*Pastoratshof*), which had 4 serf farmsteads that have been included in the total number of 111.

I will not take up in detail the structure of the farmsteads at this point except to note that in 1797 the Linden farmsteads resembled other Kurland farmsteads both in average size (in persons) and in being polynucleated coresidential groups. The residents of each farmstead *normally* included two or more conjugal family units (CFUs: husband, wife, children), the most important of which was the CFU of the head (*Wirth*). Also, frequently coresiding with the head's CFU were CFUs of males kin-linked to the head as well as CFUs of farmhands (*Knechte*) and various other people (such as *Beywohner* or *Bettler*).

Earlier analyses of other estates from the 1797 Kurland revision have suggested the existence among these serfs of two different kinds of

TABLE 10.1
LINDEN: GENERAL CHARACTERISTICS, 1797–1858

	Revisions			Census
	1797	1826	1858	1881
Total population	1982	2407	2326	2310
Sex ratio	95	91	85	86
Percentage of population in farmsteads	96.5	97.5	82.5	59.1
Number of farmsteads listed in revision or census	111	115[a]	115[a]	101[b]
Average size (persons per farmstead)	17.2	20.5	18.3	15.4
Range	6-27	7-28	2-39	N/A

[a]In 1826 one farmstead was listed as vacant; in 1858 ten were listed as vacant (see text).

[b]This figure in the 1881 census includes 12 so-called *Knechts-establissement*, which correspond to the 1858 farmsteads that housed farmhands but had no heads (see text).

familial experience, stated in structural terms. Not all heads of farmsteads headed multiple family groups (two or more kin-linked CFUs), but the individuals who headed such groups were almost exclusively farmstead heads. Not all simple family configurations (only one CFU) were headed by farmhands and lodgers, but when peasants in these categories had families in coresidence they almost never included relatives beyond wives and children (Plakans 1975). Acquisition of a headship at an early age meant a degree of residential permanence and a good chance that in due course the individual's CFU would develop into a multiple family group. Membership in the other status categories used in the revision connoted impermanence and the separation of the family of birth from the family of marriage.

It is an open question whether we should conceptualize these two kinds of familial experiences in terms of "landed" and "landless" peasants. During the period of serfdom no peasant had ownership rights to the land he worked, and in this sense all Baltic peasants were landless. Yet it is also clear from the revision documents that landowners allowed usufruct rights to be passed from one generation of peasants to the next, so that acquisition of a headship *could* be the start of permanent occupancy of a farmstead. But this did not mean a long-term monopoly. Looking at the origins of heads in the revisions after 1797 makes it clear that *Knechte* (farmhands) could become heads and heads could "descend" into the lower rank for a variety of reasons. Classification in one or another of these groups in one revision year is not an infallible indicator of an individual's status in the next revision.

The final decades of the eighteenth century saw a great deal of criticism of the prevailing socioeconomic arrangements in the Baltic countryside. Serfdom was attacked as inhuman, there were calls for its abolition, and restrictions were placed on the use of corporal punishment of serfs. Serfdom was finally abolished by a series of edicts in 1816 in Estland, 1817 in Kurland, and 1819 in Livland, about 40 years before emancipation took place in the rest of the Russian Empire.[3] These measures granted serfs "freedom of the person"; henceforth Baltic peasants were to be entitled to all of the rights of the peasant order (*Bauernstand*).

The emancipation process was a drawn-out affair, lasting until 1832. On each Kurland estate the peasantry was divided into three groups: farmstead heads and their families, farmhands and their families, and peasants working on the manor farm (Schwabe 1928:341–47). Each of these was divided further into 8 groups and, depending on local circumstances, "freedom" arrived for each of these 24 subpopulations at different times over the period of the next 15 years. This guarded procedure was said to be necessary to avoid the unrest that many thought would follow emancipation. To control the situation even more, each freed group was limited initially in its movement to the parish in which it was living; then, several years later, these persons could seek their fortunes outside the parish but only within the district in which the parish was located. Finally, in 1832, all peasants were given the right to move freely throughout the entire province of Kurland, but the right to cross its boundaries without special permission did not come until 1863, after the last of the revisions. Between 1832 and 1863 out-migration from rural areas to cities and towns was governed by a complex formula designed to prevent the countryside from being depopulated.

Unrestricted movement within the province was certainly one of the most important new factors in the lives of the Kurland peasants, and this liberty is crucial for an understanding of the subsequent history of the rural domestic group. But at least as significant was the fact that personal freedom was not accompanied by an expansion of the right to own land. Indeed, in this matter there could not even be appeal to customary use rights. As compensation for what they claimed to be the loss of their stable labor force, landowners were granted absolute rights to all landed property. Henceforth the relationship between a farmstead head and a landowner was to be spelled out in a written contract, in principle freely negotiated by both parties. These contracts called for the payment of rent in the form of money and labor, but agrarian historians agree that the postemancipation landowners preferred labor rents to any other kind. As late as 1861, when labor rents were about to be abolished, 55 percent of the farmsteads in the adjoining province of Livland were still being held entirely on the basis of labor rents, 19 percent on the basis of a mixture of labor and money, and only 23 percent on the basis of money rents alone (Svabe 1958:275). During the period from 1832 to 1858, most farmstead heads were still required by their rental agreements to have in their farmsteads a labor force sufficiently large to meet the farmstead's own labor needs and to supply laborers to the estate owner. Now, however, the matter was no longer regulated by custom or subject to unilateral changes imposed by the landowner.

The emancipation edicts also absolved estate owners of any responsibility for the general welfare of the peasants residing on their properties. The obligation to render assistance and to solve local disputes was transferred by the emancipation edicts to rudimentary organs of self-government created at the county (*pagasts*) level: the board of elders, the county court, the county orphanage, the county poorhouse, and the county granary. The revision documents of Linden reflect these changes. In the earlier revisions legal responsibility for the correctness of the data was assumed by the estate owner (whose signature closed each revision book), but after 1817 the principal signatories were the members of the board of elders, most of them farmstead heads in Linden. The board of elders also took care of payments of the head tax and determined who was to be sent to serve in the army. It also issued the internal passports, requests for which became more frequent as restriction on geographical mobility relaxed.

As we can see in table 10.1 these momentous changes in the status of the Linden peasants and in the role they played in local-level government were not accompanied by equally dramatic changes in the statistics pertaining to the size of the farmsteads (cf. Wilk, Löfgren, this volume). But if we look more carefully at the "weight" of the population in farmsteads in the total population, it is possible to say that the position of this traditional residential group was eroding. The number of farmsteads increased but slightly between 1797 and 1826, apparently to help accommodate the population increase in the estate during that period. But after 1826 the numbers diminished. Though in 1858 all of the farmsteads listed in 1797 were still in the record by name and number, altogether ten of them were noted as being vacant, which probably meant that their land had been added to the manor farm which was being worked directly for the benefit of the landowner. Moreover, of the farmsteads listed in 1858, 13 did not have heads (*Wirth*) but contained only farmhands (*Knechte*), with one of these designated as a "chief farmhand" (*Grossknecht*). A number of farmsteads had therefore been transformed into a kind of barracks housing the wage laborers employed by the landowner. (These units were designated in the 1881 census as *Knechts-Establissements*, though in 1858 they are still referred to with the traditional name of *Gesinde*.) By 1858 farmsteads proper were still the majority of the residential groups, but their number had declined. Only 82 percent of the total peasant population was living in these proper farmsteads in 1858, which was a drop from the 96–97 percent of the earlier period. A glance at the post-1858 decades suggests that this decline was in fact a trend. In the Baltic census of 1881 the proportion of all Kurland peasants living in farmsteads was 58 percent, in contrast to 88 percent for the whole province in 1797 (Ergebnisse . . . , 1884; Keyserling 1805). The proportions for Linden in these two years were 96.5 percent and 59.1 percent. Whatever else the emancipation had accomplished, it made the farmstead more vulnerable. At the termination of a contractual agreement, the landowner could simply add a farmstead's land to his own consolidated farm, and he could transform the farmstead into a new kind of coresidential group, unprecedented in the history of the estate.

GEOGRAPHICAL MOBILITY

The lines containing figures for total population and sex ratio in table 10.1 suggest that the period of emancipation (1817–32) was a turning point of another kind for the peasants of Linden. After continuing growth during the last decades of serfdom, the total population of the estate appears to have stabilized at a higher level after 1826. By contrast, the sex ratio seems to have fallen to a lower level after that date. While the 1858 sex ratio could be questioned because that revision was not a modern census, the sex ratio based on the 1881 count, which was a formal census, corroborates the decline. These figures imply that the Linden males were responding to the relaxation of restrictions against movement and bring us to the question of how best to utilize the revision data for a more careful look at the subject of mobility.

The enserfment of the Baltic peasant population in the sixteenth and seventeenth centuries had as one consequence the reduction of the rate of geographical mobility. We have no way of proving this statement, because the only systematic surveys—the land cadastres—in these earlier centuries dealt with economic matters and contain only fragmentary figures about local populations. There are no surviving successive household listings that would permit the kind of population turnover studies carried out for villages in seventeenth-century England and elsewhere (Laslett 1977). The statement about Baltic geographical mobility in the prenineteenth-century period thus has to remain a hypothesis. Yet, as hypotheses go, this one does not seem unreasonable. To claim that enserfment "immobilized" the peasant population—to use a word frequently associated with premodern eastern Europe—would be to say too much. It is quite true, however, that unless movement out of a serf estate took the form of flight, each individual instance, after enserfment, was the result of negotiations between individual peasants and the owners of estates. If the landowner wished to move peasants with or without their families, the question was of course resolved unilaterally. But serfs themselves had no such liberties. There appears to have been continual skirmishing in eighteenth-century Kurland between the ducal house of Biron (the nominal ruler of the province) and individual members of Kurlandic nobility. The ducal house wanted to bring about maximal freedom of movement, at least for peasant women who wanted to marry across estate boundaries, while the nobles wanted to restrict all such rights. None of these questions was ever resolved in any decisive way, and the serfs of Kurland entered the nineteenth century relatively restricted.

Such general information and data from a small pilot study lead us to believe that population turnover in Kurland serf estates before emancipation was probably not as high as in the English villages examined by Peter Laslett in his well-known Clayworth and Cogenhoe study. If in Clayworth one can speak of a turnover rate of about 60 percent in the 12-year period between 1676 and 1688, in the small Kurland estate of Autzenbach that rate stood at about 37 percent in the 14-year period from 1797 to 1811 (Laslett 1977:65; Plakans 1978). That is, 60 percent of the Clayworth population and 37 percent of the Autzenbach population differed from the earlier listing. Yet the gross turnover statistic does not tell the whole story for the serf estate. The greater persistence of the Autzenbach population in general was not accompanied by fixity at the level of the coresidential group (farmstead). Of the Autzenbach serfs who were listed in both the 1797 and 1811 revisions about three-quarters (72.9 percent) had moved from one farmstead to another within the estate. This pattern of low out-migration but considerable internal movement was also characteristic of Linden in the latter part of the eighteenth century, as shown in the first column of table 10.2. Since table 10.2 is based on different data from the Autzenbach study's, however, I will spell out in some detail how the figures in this table should be understood.

TABLE 10.2
MOVEMENT OF MALES IN LINDEN, 1797–1858

	1797-1811	1816-1826	1850-1858
Percentage of males recorded in intercensal period as moving within, into, or out of Linden			
1. Moved within Linden	86.4%	85.8%	68.7%
2. Moved from Linden to another estate	.2	.2	11.3
3. Moved from Linden out of Kurland	0	0	7.1
4. Recruited into army service	8.9	6.5	7.1
5. Fled from Linden	4.3	3.0	N/A
6. Moved into Linden from outside	0	3.4	5.6
	99.8%	99.9%	99.8%
Total number of males	392	487	672
Number of males moving annually (N/years in intercensal period)	26.1	44.2	73.8
Contribution to change in male population by movement	-52	-30	-133
Annual contribution to change in male population by movement	-3.4	-2.7	-16.6

Table 10.2 does not analyze turnover but surveys the movement of Linden males in three intercensal periods. Each revision began with a baseline population (a list of the people present in the last revision year), spelled out in the next column what had happened to each member of this population in the intercensal period, and listed the population of the current revision year. The "comment" column therefore contained information not only on what had happened to the earlier population but also on what the origins were of the people who had not been in the estate when the earlier revision was taken. The total in table 10.2 thus represents the total number of males who were "in motion" in the intercensal period: moving from one farmstead to another in Linden, leaving Linden, or moving into Linden from the outside. I have used a "males only" approach because the 1811 revision listed only males. Without this revision we would not have comparative statistics for the preemancipation period, because the 1797 and 1816 revisions (both of which contained males and females) were separated by the 1811 count and thus were not directly linked. The use of females in a mobility inquiry would be problematic in any case, for the movement of married women would have to be inferred from comments about their husbands.

Table 10.2 makes clear that in all of the intercensal periods—before, during, and after emancipation—most of the male movement that took place involved movement *within* Linden, not only in terms of percentages but of absolute numbers. Since the total population of the estate increased substantially between 1797 and 1826 (see table 10.1), we would expect a rise in the absolute numbers of movers in the earlier period. But the numbers of movers continued to increase even after emancipation, when the total population of the estate stabilized. Items 2 to 6 in table 10.2 suggest that the male peasantry was responding to the decreased restrictions on mobility. The proportion of men moving out of Linden to enter the imperial army remained proportionately about the same in all the intercensal periods. The number of peasants who fled, of course, ceased to be a relevant category by the last intercensal period. But the other aspects of movement suggest major changes. Whereas in the first two intercensal periods movement out of Linden to other estates in Kurland and out of Kurland represents a tiny proportion of total movement, by the last period these two categories have come to encompass nearly one-fifth (18.4 percent) of all movement. Correspondingly, movement into Linden from the outside had also become far more pronounced. If we recalculate some of the figures in table 10.2 and take into consideration only those statistics implying unforced movement (items 1, 2, 3, 6), then it appears that the number of men who were involved in moving for the purpose of improving their economic lot had risen from the first to the last intercensal period by 84.3 percent. Yet we must not forget that movement as such was not new; it was departure to and arrival from the outside that marks the establishment of a new pattern in the postemancipation period.

The calculations at the bottom of table 10.2 suggest that Linden was not an estate in which the male population was ever satisfied to stay put. Annual movement of all kinds was high even before emancipation, and by the last intercensal period it had almost tripled. Moreover, each period of documented movement ended with a loss of males, reflecting a chronic condition throughout the half-century under observation. Here, then, we have the beginnings of an explanation for the low sex ratio shown in figure 10.1. We cannot infer from table 10.2 the reasons for male movement, but at least one figure in the table—that for movement out of Kurland—suggests that this movement had concrete goals. During the last intercensal period movement *within* Kurland had become relatively easy, but departure from the province was still in principle extraordinarily difficult unless the individual presented proof of future employment at the point of arrival. Some 74 men in Linden apparently could demonstrate that they had been promised a job elsewhere and therefore secured permission to leave. If such figures were to show up frequently in other estates, then the 1860s law permitting out-migration from the province was to some extent an admission that such migration was already a major phenomenon.

HEADSHIP, WORK, AND MARRIAGE

Though the migration evidence demonstrates that the Linden peasantry responded to the relaxation of restrictions, we should keep in mind that in the last intercensal period Linden had some 2,300 people. In this light the 74 or so persons (about 3 percent) who moved annually in these years does not seem overimpressive. Perhaps it is best to think of the mobility pattern in the years between 1832 and 1858 as transitional, for this period shared with the preemancipation years the high incidence of internal movement yet also contained the new element of out-migration. Out-migration did not become more pronounced until the last restrictions on movement were gone and urban areas had been forced to drop their barriers to in-migrants. There were other changes of this transitional sort taking place in Linden, which are perhaps best seen not as entirely new patterns but as a mixture of the old and the new. Because of space limitations we cannot discuss all of these in detail, but in table 10.3 I have summarized the statistics of some of the more important changes. They deal with the people who in the postemancipation years occupied the positions of heads (*Wirthe*) and farmhands (*Knechte*) and with the ages at which people married.

Enserfment had been carried out to provide an estate owner with a permanent labor force. The most effective way to transfer part of the labor a farmstead population had at its disposal to the landowner's direct use was to encumber each farmstead with an obligation to send a certain number of workers (some with a horse team) to the manor farm every week. The entire group was then assigned daily or weekly tasks by the bailiff. Given the settlement pattern in the Baltic area, these labor dues were attached to each farmstead rather than to some larger grouping such as a village. The system was complicated, but it did have the virtue of allowing the farmstead head to know from one year to the next (providing the obligation was not changed on short notice) how many able-bodied (*arbeitsfähige*) persons he needed in the farmstead. It was the head who recruited the labor force, and this gave him an important position in the

TABLE 10.3
CHANGES IN SELECTED FEATURES OF LINDEN POPULATION, 1797–1858

	1797	1826	1858
Farmstead heads	111	114	92
1. Mean age of heads	45.0 years	41.5 years	40.8 years
2. Percentage of married heads	98.2	96.4	94.7
Heads and farmhands			
1. Ratio of heads to farmhands in adult male population	1:1.7	1:3.0	1:3.4
2. Percentage of all adult males classified as relatives of head *and* farmhands	0	13.6%	2.7%
Single individuals (as percentage of population in age group)			
Males			
20–24	66 (78.2%)	130 (59.2%)	95 (69.4%)
45–49	19 (10.5%)	39 (2.5%)	37 (2.7%)
Females			
20–24	67 (47.7%)	88 (50.0%)	109 (60.5%)
45–49	3 (0)	17 (0)	79 (11.3%)

estate's economy. He was something of an "officer," being responsible not only for the labor needs of the farmstead itself but also for those of the estate farm.

In view of the importance of this "office" in the preemancipation period, landowners had always retained veto rights over the candidate and as a result had seen to it that the head was always a mature man, that is, one who was married. As table 10.3 shows, there were few unmarried heads, and this characteristic of the headship persisted after emancipation when landowners no longer had much say in the matter. Farmsteads maintained their high average size and their dual labor obligation. Evidently, the allocation and supervision of tasks among men and women in the farmstead required the presence of a head's wife. The documents hint in later years that her status was more important than it had been previously: in the later revisions she is referred to increasingly as *Wirthin* rather than simply as *Weib* (wife) of the head. Yet the mean age of heads decreased after emancipation, which may mean that headships were becoming less partriarchal and more meritocratic. Though it would be misleading to posit absolute differences between the skills required to run a farmstead successfully in the pre- and postemancipation periods, the transformation of agricultural practice in the Baltic area in the nineteenth century suggests that younger heads might have been able to handle the job better (Strods 1972; Svarane 1971). Certainly by the middle decades of the century (our last intercensal period), "scientific" farming had become a prime concern of Baltic German landowners, who had also sought to involve "their" peasants in this movement.

If the men who occupied the position of *Wirth* in the postemancipation period were generally younger, those who occupied the position of farmhand (*Knecht*) were more numerous. As table 10.3 shows, the ratio of heads to farmhands in Linden doubled over the 60-year period under observation. In the past this statistic has always produced long and generally fruitless debates among Baltic historians about the "sharpening of rural class conflict," but in recent years the problem has come to be seen as more complex because of a more realistic view of social structure. Analysis of local structures in Linden, for example, requires that we account for the relatives of heads, for individuals were described in the revision as working as farmhands for a relative, a type that table 10.3 suggests was becoming more numerous. A more general formulation of the question would ask about the precise structural position of all farmhands who had relatives as heads somewhere in the estate, probably a substantial part of the farmhand population even in mid-century when out-migration had not yet reached very high levels. One Soviet Baltic historian concludes that

> in the 20s, 30s, and 40s of the nineteenth century farmhands and heads cannot be seen as separate classes but rather as long-term social groupings within the peasant class. Part of the farmhand population had been farmhands for several generations, but another part continued to be drawn from younger members of the heads' families. Brothers and sisters of heads frequently remained as farmhands in the farmsteads of their relatives or in other farmsteads. (Svarane 1971:196)

So even in postemancipation decades, just as in the years of serfdom, siblings who did not gain access to a headship probably migrated out. Though the loosening of migration restrictions produced a response, it did not produce a total turnover in the landless population, with all farmhands being in some sense outsiders. The classification of peasants, on an estate-wide basis, as *either* farmhands *or* relatives of heads would lead to a simplified view of the social structure of the population.

Another kind of change was at work in Linden, a change, however, that can better be studied in populations larger than the one we have at our disposal. Still, we may take the statistics regarding marriage ages in Linden in table 10.3 to be a local-level example of what historical demographers have noticed about the Baltic area in general, namely, that the timing of marriage here was closer to the western European than to the Russian model (Coale, Anderson, and Härm 1979:148–55). Males and females in the Baltic tended to marry somewhat later than in the eastern parts of the empire, and more of them remained unmarried throughout their whole lives. Table 10.3 reflects this, though imperfectly; but what is most interesting about the long-term trend in this small sample is the noticeable convergence of the age at marriage of both sexes. The proportions of single males in the ages groups 20–24 and 45–49 described a downward trend, while those for females an upward one. Were these trends to continue then in the second half of the nineteenth century, marriage in Linden would certainly have come close to being "companionate," that is, there would have been a relatively small age difference between husband and wife (Laslett 1977:13). It is impossible to say why this trend existed in Linden, or why by 1858, before any noticeable industrialization had occurred in the Baltic provinces, the proportions of unmarried women in Linden in the two crucial age groups were already close to comparable figures for such countries as Austria, France, and Italy in 1900 (Hajnal 1965:102–3). All we can do at this time is take notice of these characteristics of marriage and leave for the future a more searching analysis of the reasons behind them.

THE STRUCTURE AND COMPOSITION OF FARMSTEADS

Some of the changing features of Linden described in the foregoing sections could have affected the structure and composition of farmsteads directly by altering the numbers and kinds of CFUs in the population. Increased out-migration could have produced a fall in the number of CFUs at risk and thus a simplification of structure; a slightly higher marriage age (if that was the consequence of a noted convergence of marriage ages for men and women) would have had the same result. The decrease in the total number of farmsteads by 1858 could have produced a higher proportion of people in each farmstead who were related to the head. Increased proportions of kin of the head might not have been the result, however, if the higher number of persons who were moving about *within* the estate included more brothers and sisters of heads than ever before. In order to be able to make some of these connections we have to establish what was the composition and structure of the Linden farmsteads. The next three tables are devoted to that task.

The most widely used conventions for household analysis are not entirely satisfactory for looking at the Baltic farmsteads because of the high proportion of farmhands and other types of nonheads in the estate in both the pre- and postemancipation periods (Hammel and Laslett 1974). I have commented on these difficulties elsewhere with respect to the 1797 revision, and the same problems continue in the other revisions (Plakans 1975). Simply stated, because farmsteads continue to be large, we have to be on guard against assigning them to structural categories by reference to a minority of the inhabitants, that is, the heads. Yet it will not do to assume that the farmsteads were "housefuls" composed of several "households," for there is nothing in the data that would support belief in such internal divisions, at least in the period we are studying. A way out of this dilemma is to use two separate ways of classifying these groups: one that uses the socioeconomic identity of the constituent CFUs and another that makes use of the ties among the members of the head's familial group.

Table 10.4, in which the first kind of classification is used, depicts the changing nature of polynucleation. The farmsteads in which the only CFU was that of the head were a small minority throughout the period, and those in which the only CFUs were those of the head and of the head's relatives (such as married brothers) diminished in importance over the years. The most telling changes in the long term were connected with the married relatives of the head. They were numerous enough in 1797 to make the most complex compositional category the dominant one (even if barely), but their numbers in 1826 had grown so large that six out of every

TABLE 10.4
COMPOSITION OF FARMSTEADS BY REFERENCE TO CORESIDING CFUs

Type	1797 %	1826 %	1858 %
CFU of head only	3.6	5.2	2.1
CFUs of head and of coresident relatives only	19.8	7.0	4.2
CFUs of head and of farmhands only	37.8	27.2	76.8
CFUs of head, coresident relatives and farmhands	38.7	60.5	16.8
Total CFUs	111	114	92

ten farmsteads had at least three kinds of CFUs: the head's, the head relatives', and the farmhands'. But this situation did not continue. After emancipation fewer relatives of the head evidently married and fewer stayed with him after their marriage, and this must have enlarged the number of migrants reported in table 10.2. By the end of the period the principal type of farmstead was one in which the head and his family of marriage relied on a labor force composed almost entirely of unrelated married farmhands. Yet not all farmsteads were polarized in this fashion. In about one-eighth the labor force still contained married relatives of the head. The trend, more than likely, was in the direction of the bipolar type because in 1858 emigration from Kurland was still restricted.

Table 10.4 is based on an ad hoc classification scheme that ignores unmarried people; it is really tailored to fit only the Linden data base. Table 10.5, however, employs categories not generally in use for historical sources, though in using them we have to ignore all residents of farmsteads not related to the head. This scheme has the advantage of allowing comparisons, even though such comparisons will be between family *households* elsewhere and the *dominant familial group* in the farmsteads. We can observe in table 10.5 that Linden had a high proportion of complex heads' family groups throughout the entire period we are observing. Even in 1858 complexity (multiple plus extended families) was still characteristic of the dominant families in about half (47.8 percent) of the farmsteads, a drop, to be sure, from the much higher levels present earlier (77.4 percent in 1797; 69.1 percent in 1826) but still considerably higher than in the West even in centuries before the nineteenth.

TABLE 10.5
STRUCTURE OF FAMILIAL GROUP OF FARMSTEAD HEADS, 1797–1858

	1797		1826		1858	
Type[a]	N	%	N	%	N	%
Simple family						
Married couple alone	0		1		8	
Married couple with children	25	22.5	34	30.4	40	52.1
Widower with children	0		0		0	
Extended family						
Extended upward	5		4		14	
Extended downward	2	18.0	0	10.4	0	23.9
Extended laterally	6		6		4	
Combinations a-c	7		2		4	
Multiple family						
Secondary units up	11		10		4	
Secondary units down	23		29		6	
Units all on one level	18	59.4	9	59.1	6	23.9
Frérèches	3		8		4	
Other	11		11		2	
Number of farmsteads classified	111	99.9	114	99.9	92	99.9

[a]Categories adapted from Laslett and Wall 1972:85 and Hammel and Laslett 1974:72–109

It is also clear that there was a marked trend in heads' family structure over the 60-year period. Structural simplicity increased in both of the census years after 1797. By the end of the period simple structure characterized the plurality of cases, a reversal of the 1797 situation when multiple families (containing more than one conjugal family unit) had been in the plurality. Extended forms (containing one full CFU and one or more unmarried relatives) were a strong subtheme in all three years and became somewhat more important by the end of the period than they had been at the beginning. The continued existence of extended forms, however, is less remarkable than the changes that had taken place in the relative proportions of the simple and multiple families. Evidently fewer married sons remained with their fathers, fewer married brothers continued to live together after the old head died, and fewer married kinfolk were willing to be recruited into a labor force of a kinsman when this individual took over a vacated farmstead. The relatives who did not stay with the heads left the estate or sought positions in other farmsteads, where they entered the revision documents as "farmhand" and not as "kin of head." These data show that as opportunities for migration increased, the significance of the multiple form as a characteristic of heads' families diminished.

There is another vantage point from which we can examine the changing structure of the dominant groups: we can look at the specific individuals who composed these groups rather than at their overall structure. This method brings out both the changes and the continuities somewhat better. Table 10.6 examines the kinship relation (to the head) of all persons coresident with the head, excluding the head's spouses and children, and places each person into an exclusive kinship category. Again, by comparison with figures available for western European communities in earlier centuries the Linden figures appear to be high throughout the period. But the entire set of persons classified as coresident kin was decreasing in size.

TABLE 10.6
CORESIDENT KIN OF HEAD, 1797–1858
(excluding spouses and offspring)

Type[a]	1797 %		1826 %		1858 %	
Parents	7.7	31.2	8.9	25.8	17.7	42.7
Siblings	23.5		16.9		25.0	
Spouses of offspring	7.7	16.9	13.5	29.1	7.2	16.8
Grandchildren	9.2		15.6		9.6	
Spouses of siblings	7.7	25.2	7.0	21.5	6.4	23.2
Nephews	9.5		9.9		7.2	
Nieces	8.0		4.6		9.6	
Affines	20.1		16.8		8.6	
Others	6.2		6.7		8.6	
	99.6		99.9		99.9	
Coresident kin as proportion of population in farmsteads	17.5		14.6		7.4	
Percentage of farmsteads with coresident kin of head	79.4		70.4		55.4	

[a]Categories adapted from Laslett and Wall 1972:81

By 1858 the proportion of coresident kin in the entire farmstead population was less than half of what it had been at the outset, the sharpest reduction coming in the decades after the emancipation process had been completed. In addition, the number of farmsteads with coresident kin had diminished, particularly so after the end of emancipation. Yet it was also true that the major types of kin represented in the coresident kin population in 1797 were still represented in the 1858 population, though not to the same degree. The proportion of members of the head's family of birth had increased, largely because of the increase in coresident parents of the head. The proportion of kin in the conjugal families of the heads' offspring had remained nearly the same by 1858, as had the proportion of kin in the conjugal families of the heads' siblings. The only major category that showed a steady decline was that of affines—relatives of the head through marriage—but even that category registered what could be termed a strong presence (nearly 9 percent of all coresident kin in 1858). In light of this information it is possible to conclude that even though the new order witnessed many changes in the nature of the farmstead, the heads' groups that entered the complex structural categories in 1858 did so for about the same reasons as at the beginning of the period.

These several approaches to farmstead composition and to the structure of heads' familial groups illustrate again that during the decades covered by the revisions no radical alterations in the compositional and structural forms of rural residence occurred. The personal status of peasants had indeed changed, in a manner of speaking, overnight, but this had not resulted in so great a transformation of living arrangements as to make the farmsteads unrecognizable. Indeed, by 1858, a generation after the emancipation process had been concluded, the analyst of the revisions still finds himself in generally familiar territory: farmstead names had not changed nor had the socioeconomic terminology used by the enumerators to classify people. The farmstead with its characteristic subpopulations of heads, relatives of heads, and nonrelated farmhands of various kinds was still the dominant form of rural coresidence. The most significant new factor in the situation—the "change in the environment" to which the farmstead populations "responded"—was the increased opportunity and perhaps incentive for movement; and these acted so as to increase the numbers of people who moved within Linden as well as of those who moved in and out of the estate. In the postemancipation decades movement of all kinds was becoming a significant demographic characteristic and migration had initiated processes of change whose ultimate effects cannot now be documented.

THE FARMSTEAD IN THE LONG TERM

Like many other historical sources, the Baltic revisions began too late to allow for empirically grounded statements about the origin of the patterns in the last decades of serfdom and ended too early to tell us about further changes in the second half of the nineteenth century, when additional reforms continued to affect the Baltic countryside. The various tables I have presented contain a suggestion that the numbers for 1797 and 1826 may be the tail end of a longer trend: the total population rose between these two years and started to decline afterwards (table 10.1); the variety of CFUs in farmsteads increased until 1826 but decreased afterward (table 10.4); the number of farmsteads headed by multiple families of heads held steady during the earlier period but dropped sharply subsequently (table 10.5). Without equally precise nominal data for the pre-1797 period we cannot know whether the statistics for 1797 and 1826 represent some final phase of development of an enserfed population or even perhaps a drop from some higher levels. At the other end of the series we have only the numbers from the census of 1881 (table 10.1), several of which (mean size, sex ratio) suggest that the 1858 figures may have been the start of some sort of new equilibrium. But in 1881 we cannot tell very much about the familial composition of the farmsteads or about the structure of the heads' groups and whether these two important measures had undergone changes in the period between 1858 and 1881.

After 1858 the socioeconomic environment continued to change; in fact, the revisions stopped just on the threshold of one extremely significant event. In the early 1860s the Baltic landed nobility began to sell to the peasants the land they worked and occupied, thereby creating for the first time since the Middle Ages the possibility of peasant landownership unencumbered by labor dues or labor rents. These transactions began in 1863 and in the first year 359 farmsteads in Kurland were purchased by their peasant occupants. By 1868 a total of 1,321 farmsteads had been sold to peasants, and by 1885 a total of 8,974, or about 40 percent of all the farmsteads in Kurland, had become peasant property in the full sense (Svabe 1958:314–15). Peasant proprietorship continued to expand until World War I.

This important development was accompanied by one other, which increased the outflow of the population from the Kurland countryside. Starting in the early 1860s a series of imperial decrees relaxed existing restrictions against migration across provincial boundaries and into urban areas. Though the urban population of the Baltic provinces increased by 193 percent from 1863 to 1897, the rural population increased by only 11 percent (Svabe 1958:544). It is frustrating in the extreme not to know, and not to have any possibility of knowing, what effects these two major developments had on farmsteads in terms of the components we have been discussing. The question I raised in the beginning—what is a sufficient period of time to document real change in household form?—therefore has no other answer in the Baltic area, as in so many other areas of the European past, except that which is supplied by the dating of the sources. During all the centuries farmsteads have existed it is only possible to make a detailed, time-based, study of changes in their makeup in the 60 years surveyed here.

That unfortunately is not the only problem. Ironically, the very care with which the Baltic enumerators organized the data by naming each farmstead and carefully separating it from the rest and by stating that people moved to and from farmsteads and not to and from subunits of farmsteads makes it difficult to use the conventional understanding of *household* in any analysis. If on the one hand we define the farmstead as a household, we run into the problems of classification referred to earlier. If on the other hand we look for some way of breaking the farmstead population into smaller analyzable units, the multiple criteria by which this is usually done appear inadequate. The use of kinship to draw the lines will not produce groups that lived and ate separately; the groupings of persons according to the work they did will not produce groups that were also procreative or kinship units; and the use of socioeconomic labels such as *Wirth* or *Knecht* to create coequal groupings will downplay the important fact of unequal authority and will also create the problems of how to classify unlabeled relatives of the head and how to treat unmarried farmhands who were labeled as relatives. These difficulties raise the general question of whether all listings from the European past can be fitted into a comparative framework. It is certainly possible to believe that in some corners of the European continent, such as the Baltic, a combination of historical forces created coresidential groupings that functioned tolerably well but in most respects were unlike those in more central regions.

Moreover the useful definition of *household* adopted for Linden will possibly not be relevant elsewhere in the Baltic. My scepticism in this matter derives from a survey of farmsteads carried out by the Statistical Committee of the Livland nobility in the adjoining province in 1884 (Materialien . . . , 1885:233, 237). The Livland statisticians wanted to find out, among other things, about the living and eating arrangements among Livland peasants. In the survey they asked two questions to which we would have liked to have the answers for our period as well.

The questions were: Did heads of farmsteads and farmhands have separate living spaces (*Wohnungen*) in the farmstead? and Did heads and farmhands, as a rule (*in den Regel*), eat together or separately? We can consider the answers from two adjacent districts in Livland, where farmsteads were as typical a form of rural settlement as in Kurland. In Wenden district the 5,151 farmsteads that responded (90.6 percent of those surveyed) said that in 18.3 percent of the cases heads and farmhands lived separately and in 12.3 percent of the cases ate separately. If we were to use these facts to define the *households* in Wenden, the only alternative would be to view the entire farmstead as a single unit. In the adjoining district of Wolmar, however, the 2,945 farmsteads responding (92.2 percent of the total) observed that in 70.4 percent of the cases heads and farmhands had separate living quarters and that in 64.4 percent of the cases the two groups ate separately. A definition of *household* here would be tempted to use the idea of a farmstead as a "houseful" containing several households. Judging by other socioeconomic criteria these two adjacent rural districts did not differ, but in one of them the lines between groupings in farmsteads were much more sharply drawn than in the other. We know nothing more about these farmsteads, except that the problem of definition and comparability would be as great there 60 years after emancipation as it is in the revisions we have surveyed.

At the outset of this analysis I suggested that a series of household censuses solves some problems but creates others. The Linden series has proved to be a good example of how elusive unambiguous conclusions can be, even when the characteristics of a baseline population are well known and repeated enumerations of this population take place according to the same format. Even if in Linden we do not know how long the 1797 structures had been in existence, the 1797 revision gives us a good starting point. The hypothesis that "household organization responds sensitively to changes in the environment while preserving certain formal features over long periods of time" appears eminently testable by reference to the subsequent elements of the revision series; and the emancipation of serfs, which from the sociolegal viewpoint was the preeminent fact of Baltic rural life in the first half of the nineteenth century, certainly seems like the type of "environmental change" to which household organization could be expected to respond "sensitively." Yet when all is said and done it is a fair question whether the connections we had hoped to establish firmly have indeed been made and whether the serial evidence we have at our disposal in this particular case is sufficient to confirm or negate the hypothesis. In a larger perspective the problem at hand is a variation of the difficulties historians have been encountering when seeking to verify behavioral propositions by reference to historical evidence (Berkhofer 1969:46–74).

In a very general sense we can take the hypothesis as having been verified. There was a change in the "environment" in which the Linden farmsteads existed, and in the context of the new conditions that this change—emancipation—brought into being we have been able to detect "responses": an increase in the number of farmsteads in which the resident CFUs were only those of the head and of the farmhands unrelated to the head; a decrease in the number of farmsteads in which the head was surrounded by a complex group of kinfolk; an erosion of the farmstead's position as the typical coresidential group in Linden; an apparent decline in the age at first marriage of males and a rise in that of females; and an increase in the number of males who moved about in the intercensal periods. At the same time the baseline (1797) organization of the farmsteads was not transformed dramatically since by 1858 the last revision presents us with a picture that is still familiar. But to have identified these features of this 60-year period does not mean that we have been able to exit the realm of associations and enter the realm of causality, in the sense of being entirely satisfied that the Linden case study provides a thorough exploration of the impact of serf emancipation on household organization, even in only the Baltic setting.

There is first the problem that the revision series is a series of single-year censuses and not continuous data about each of the farmsteads that emancipation affected. In order to make a tight connection between the behavioral consequences of emancipation and household structure we would need to be able to examine the structural history of each farmstead individually in order to establish whether the changes we seek to attribute to emancipation could not be explained in some other fashion as well. Now household data of this sort are not known to exist in historical Europe, and they certainly do not exist in the Baltic area. Consequently, it is difficult to know whether the new patterns identified might not be more readily explainable by reference to, for example, the developmental cycles of the constituent families of farmsteads rather than to the general condition of personal freedom introduced by emancipation.

Second, the series I have analyzed cannot give us an ultimate explanation of what we seek because, by force of circumstances, it pertains to the internal history of a single estate. Stated in its simplest terms, the problem is the lack of comparative information for the Baltic area. Social historians of the Latvian-speaking area of the Baltic have not explored the "domestic domain" of the pretwentieth-century peasantry and therefore we do not know the extent to which the Linden outcome is generalizable. Several fragments of information introduce a sobering note. In the estate of Pinkenhof, which with its 126 farmsteads is comparable in size to Linden, the revision series suggests a different pattern of household development during the postemancipation period. If in Linden we can document a decrease of the farmsteads headed by heads' family groups with complex structure, in Pinkenhof groups with this structure showed an increase: 38.8 percent of the farmsteads are complex in 1816 and 49.5 percent in 1850. In Pinkenhof, moreover, the actual outcome is the reverse of what one would expect, for Pinkenhof was a patrimonial estate of the major city of Riga, lay on its outskirts, and thus was within the magnetic field of the labor market of that city. If anything, the relaxation of restrictions against migration in Pinkenhof should have shown a decline of complex farmsteads, that is, the Linden pattern. Instead, Linden—an estate located in the fertile and purely rural area of Kurland—reveals the patterns we would have expected for an estate located close to a major nonagricultural labor center.

Even more disturbing are the results of recent research on the structure of serf households in the interior of Russia. The results of research carried out by Peter Czap of Amherst College (Czap 1982) for the estate of Mishino in Riazan province are instructive because they are also based on a series of revisions (though a somewhat longer series than Linden's) but deal with decades *all* of which fall in the preemancipation period of Russian history (before 1861). This series therefore records structural change entirely within the period of serfdom. Czap finds that as far as household complexity is concerned there are long-term patterns even under serfdom: an uninterrupted rise in the proportion of complex households from 1782 to 1822, then an uninterrupted fall in this proportion from 1822 to 1850, and signs of an upturn from 1850 to 1858 (Czap 1982:12). Such trends in a serf estate that never experienced emancipation during the time covered by the series place a very large question mark after the connections I have sought to make in Linden. They raise the possibility that in Linden some kind of long-term pattern of decline of complexity might still have taken place even if emancipation were removed from this equation. It is these fragmentary but nonetheless suggestive trends in household data from other serf estates that force me to end on a tentative note. Nonetheless, the Linden data have permitted us to identify the elements that a thoroughly convincing explanation of the impact of emancipation would have to consider in the rest of the Baltic area, in Russia after 1861, and in the many other parts of central and eastern Europe where time-based collections of household evidence have to be reviewed from the perspective of sociolegal changes.

NOTES

1. I gratefully acknowledge the assistance of National Science Foundation Grant BNS–7926704 (Anthropology Program) in parts of the analysis contained in this chapter and the support of the International Research and Exchanges Board in providing for travel to Riga in the Latvian Soviet Socialist Republic to obtain the primary sources.

2. Originals of the Linden revisions are to be found in the Central National Historical Archive (*Centrālais Valsts Vēstures Arhīvs*) in Riga, Latvian SSR, USSR, fond 630, op. 1, d. 411 I.

3. For a general but thorough survey of serf emancipations throughout Europe see Blum 1978.

REFERENCES

Primary Sources

1884 Ergebnisse der baltischen Volkszählung vom 29. December 1881. Teil III. Ergebnisse der kurländischen Volkszählung [Results of the Baltic Census of 29 December 1881: Part III. Results of the Kurland Census]. Mitau: Steffenhagen.

1895 Kurländische Güterchroniken [Histories of Kurland Estates]. Neue Folge, Band 1. Mitau: Steffenhagen.

1885 Materialien zur Kenntnis der livländischen Agrarverhaltnisse [Materials for the Study of Agrarian Relations in Livland. Riga.

Secondary Sources

Berkhofer, Robert F., Jr.

1969 A Behavioral Approach to Historical Analysis. New York: Free Press.

Berkner, Lutz K.

1972 The Stem Family and the Developmental Cycle of a Peasant Household: An Eighteenth-century Austrian Example. American Historical Review 77:398–418.

Blum, Jerome

1957 The Rise of Serfdom in Eastern Europe. American Historical Review 62:807–836.

1978 The End of the Old Order in Rural Europe. Princeton: Princeton University Press.

Brambe, R.

1982 Rīgas iedzīvotāji Feodalisma perioda beigās [The Inhabitants of Riga at the End of the Feudal Period]. Riga: Zinatne.

Braudel, Fernand
1972 History and the Social Sciences. *In* Economy and Society in Early Modern Europe, ed. Peter Burke. New York: Harper and Row.
Coale, Ansley, Barbara Anderson, and Erna Härm
1979 Human Fertility in Russia since the Nineteenth Century. Princeton: Princeton University Press.
Czap, Peter
1978 Marriage and the Peasant Joint Family in the Era of Serfdom. *In* The Family In Imperial Russia, ed. David Ransel. Urbana: University of Illinois Press.
1982 The Perennial Multiple Family Household, Mishino, Russia, 1782–1858. Journal of Family History 7:5–26.
Dunsdorfs, Edgars
1973 Latvijas vēsture 1710–1800 [The History of Latvia 1710–1800]. Stockholm: Daugava.
Hajnal, John
1965 European Marriage Patterns in Perspective. *In* Population in History, ed. D. V. Glass and D.E.C. Eversley. Chicago: Aldine.
Hammel, Eugene, and Peter Laslett
1974 Comparing Household Structure over Time and between Cultures. Comparative Studies in Society and History 16:73–109.
Kabuzan, V. M.
1975 Izmeneniia v razmeshchenii naseleniia Rossii v XVIII–pervoi polovine XIX v., po materialam revizii [Change and Distribution of the Population of Russia in the Eighteenth and the first half of the Nineteenth Century, According to Revision Materials]. Moscow: Nauka.
Keyserling, P. E. von
1805 Beschreibung der Provinz Kurland [Description of the Province of Kurland]. Mitau.
Kundzins, Pauls
1974 Latvju sēta [The Latvian Farmstead]. Stockholm: Daugava.
Laslett, Peter
1977 Family Life and Illicit Love in Earlier Generations. Cambridge: Cambridge University Press.
Laslett, Peter, and Richard Wall, eds.
1972 Household and Family in Past Time. Cambridge: Cambridge University Press.
Netting, Robert McC., and Richard R. Wilk
1980 Prospectus for Conference on Households: Changing Form and Function. Typescript.
Palli, Heldur
1980 Estesvennoe dvizhenie selskogo naseleniia estonii 1650–1799 [Natural Increase of the Rural Population of Estonia 1650–1799]. Tallinn: Eesti raamat.

Plakans, Andrejs
1975 Seigneurial Authority and Peasant Family Life: The Baltic Area in the Eighteenth Century. Journal of Disciplinary History 4:629–54.
1976 Familial Structure in the Russian Baltic Provinces: The Nineteenth Century. *In* Sozial geschichte der Familie in der Neuzeit Europas, ed. Werner Conze. Stuttgart: Klett.
1978 Population Turnover in a Serf Estate: Autzenbach 1797–1811. Paper given at the Conference on Marriage and the Family in Historical Perspective, Brigham Young University.
Forthcoming The Familial Contexts of Early Childhood in Baltic Serf Society. *In* Family Forms in Historic Europe, ed. Richard Wall and Peter Laslett, Cambridge: Cambridge University Press.

Schwabe, A.
1928 Grundriss der Agrargeschichte Lettlands [Basic Agrarian History of Latvia]. Riga: Bernhard Lamey.

Strods, Heinrihs
1972 Lauksaimniecība Latvijā pārejas periodā no feodālisma uz kapitālismu [Agriculture in Latvia in the Period of Transition from Feudalism to Capitalism]. Riga: Zinatne.

Svabe, Arveds
1958 Latvijas vesture 1800–1914 [History of Latvia 1800–1914]. Stockholm: Daugava.

Svarane, M.
1971 Saimnieks un kalps Kurzemē un Vidzemē XIX gs. vidū [Farmer and Farmhand in Kurland and Livland in the Middle of the Nineteenth Century]. Riga: Zinatne.

Vahtre, Sulev
1973 Eestimaa talurahvas hingeloenduste andmeil 1728–1858 [The Peasant Population of Estonia According to the Results of the Soil Revisions 1782–1858]. Tallinn.

Wachter, Kenneth W., Eugene A. Hammel, and Peter Laslett
1978 Statistical Studies of Historical Social Structure. New York: Academic Press.

PART III

Households as Persisting Cultural Forms

11

Family Life and the Life Cycle in Rural China

Arthur P. Wolf

In the Western world marriage creates new families by robbing old families of their children. In China marriage gives old families a future by exchanging daughters for daughters-in-law. If a family has no sons or is in desperate need of labor, a daughter may remain in her parent's home where she is joined by her husband, and in this case the husband may agree to assign one or more of his children to his wife's father's descent line. More commonly and ideally, the wife joins her husband's family and bears children all of whom are assigned to his descent line.

Since families that are expanded by marriage must eventually divide, the history of a Chinese family is one of regular expansion and contraction. Small units grow into large units as sons marry and produce children, and these large units are then reduced to small ones again by division and the death of the senior generation. How large a family becomes depends on how many sons it raises, how early the sons marry, how many children they produce, and how long the group endures before it is divided. Some families reach their maximum with a membership of only 4 or 5 people; others expand into great households with as many as 40 or 50 members. The cycle varies from case to case, but all families experience more or less regular fluctuation in size and complexity.

Having investigated elsewhere the stages through which Chinese families normally pass, my purpose here is to examine the relationship between the family cycle and the life cycle. Are these two temporal processes correlated? In other words, does the type of family experienced by children, adolescents, young adults, and the aged vary systematically, each phase in the life cycle carrying the individual forward to another phase in the family cycle? The question is important because behavior that is commonly attributed to a phase in one of these cycles may, if the cycles are coordinated, be better attributed to a parallel phase in the other cycle. On the one hand, problems associated with stages in the life cycle may be rooted in tensions generated by a type of family; on the other, tensions seen as characteristic of a type of family may reflect problems people encounter at certain stages of the life cycle.

The data reported in this paper were drawn from household registers compiled in nine districts (*li*) in northern Taiwan during the years 1906–45. Since these communities have been described in detail elsewhere, it will suffice for present purposes to say that in 1905 all but a handful of their inhabitants were farmers, and most of these tenant farmers (Wolf and Chieh-shan Huang 1980: chap. 3). The few exceptions were craftsmen, boatmen, camphor workers, tea pickers, and border guards whose task it was to defend against raids by head-hunting aborigines. By 1945 a few men had left agriculture to work in coal mines or a large winery built with Japanese capital, but the majority remained farmers tilling someone else's fields. In sum, my subjects were Chinese peasants whose hard life was somewhat ameliorated but not transformed by the Japanese colonial presence.

The Taiwan household registers have also been described elsewhere and need not detain us here (Wolf and Chieh-shan Huang 1980: chap. 2). The reader who is not familiar with these magnificent records need only know that in taking the family as the basic unit of the registration system, the Japanese did not impose their conception of the institution on their Chinese subjects. After experimenting with a system that took the physical house as the basic unit, the Japanese settled on the *chia* (family) as the most appropriate unit and wisely left it up to the natives to define the term. All that they required of people was that they register as members of one and only one *chia*. Thus we may be confident that the family preserved in these records is a product of Chinese custom and not an arbitrary creation.

The Taiwan household registers provide us with family histories that are not only accurate but unusually detailed. It is up to us, however, to decide what is significant in these histories. Age provides a convenient and meaningful way of dividing the life cycle into segments. But what criteria should we employ to define the phases of the family cycle? Large Chinese families seldom pass a year without witnessing a birth, a death, a marriage, or an adoption. Which of these many changes should we take as marking a transition to a new stage in the developmental cycle?

My solution to this problem views the Chinese family as composed of building blocks I call *nuclear units*. To qualify as a nuclear unit a group must contain either a conjugal link or a filial link. I accept as nuclear units married couples with or without children, widows or widowers with a child or children, and never-married or divorced persons with a child or children. I call a nuclear unit that stands alone as an independent household an *elementary family*. A household that does not qualify as a nuclear unit is termed a *subelementary family* if it has two or more members and a *solitaire* if it has only one member. In my nomenclature an elementary family becomes an *augmented elementary family* with the addition of persons who do not themselves constitute a nuclear unit, while the addition of a second nuclear unit in a lower generation creates a *stem family*. Though some authorities believe Chinese farm families rarely achieved forms more complex than that of the stem family, this was definitely not true of rural Taiwan (see, for example, Levy 1965). Many families raised two or more sons all of whom married and remained members of their natal household. So long as one or the other of the parents remain in the household, I call families of this type *grand families*. More often than not grand families were divided into simpler units before both parents died, but there were many exceptions. These exceptions I term *frérèches*. "Grand" says that a family contains a minimum of three nuclear units two of which are in the same generation and descended from the third; *frérèche* says that a family contains two or more nuclear units that do not have a common ancestor present in the household.

Since the family types created by this scheme have a long history, I should say that they were not adopted because they came recommended by convention. I chose them because the distinctions drawn reflect my view of what matters most in the evolution of a Chinese family. In the usual case an elementary family becomes a stem family with the marriage of the eldest son; a stem family expands to a grand family when a second son marries; and a grand family is reduced to a *frérèche* with the death of the senior generation. Each change disrupts existing relationships and moves the family one stage closer to dissolution. The first introduces in the role of daughter-in-law a woman whose only hope of personal autonomy is division of her husband's natal family; the second makes division a tangible possibility by providing the younger brother with the means of establishing an independent household; and the third removes the only people who can hold divisive tendencies in check.

Though the question of how these stages in the family cycle relate to the life cycle appears simple, it is not easily answered. By linking the Japanese household registers with those maintained by the present government we could trace the experience of most people born in 1905 from birth to death, but there is no point in doing so if one is interested in how the Chinese family cycle related to the life cycle. The changes of the past 40 years have been so overwhelming that the conditions obtaining when these people were born were already relics of the past by the time they died. There would be no way of discovering whether the trends associated with age were a function of age or the result of changes in the family system. Thus we have no alternative but to pick a point in time and treat the experience of the younger people as representative of that of the older people at earlier ages. There are obvious dangers in pasting up lives in this fashion, but these difficulties are no greater than those involved in trying to disentangle intrinsic and extrinsic change.

For reasons that will become apparent as we proceed, I have chosen January 1, 1946, as my point of analysis. Since by this time the changes initiated by the Japanese had affected all but the most isolated communities, the conditions in our nine districts cannot be taken as representative of traditional China. During the 50 years of Japanese occupation infant mortality had declined, literacy had risen, cities had grown enormously, and many people had left agriculture for other forms of employment. But despite all this, the family retained its traditional form. The data reported in table 11.1 reveal a gradual rise in family size and complexity, but there is no evidence of a fundamental change in the family. The changes are demographic, not structural, quantitative, not qualitative. I am confident that if my analysis could be repeated for 1906 the results would not differ markedly from those obtained for 1946.

Before turning to the evidence from the household registers, we need to consider what we can expect to find. Imagine a population in which all women married virilocally at age 20, bore two sons and two daughters in rapid succession, and then died on their sixty-fifth birthday. Imagine further that men married at age 25 and remained members of their natal household until both parents died. If the men in this population also died at age 65, the life cycle and the family cycle would show close coordination. Since brothers would be about the same age and would marry at about the same time, most children would be born into grand families, and they would all grow up as members of grand families. By the time they reached early adolescence, however, their grandparents would die, the family would be divided, and they would spend late adolescence in simple elementary families. The older son's marriage would then establish a stem family, and this would be quickly replaced by a grand family created by the younger son's marriage, the result being that young

TABLE 11.1
DISTRIBUTION OF FAMILIES AND POPULATION BY FAMILY TYPE AT FIVE-YEAR INTERVALS, 1906–1946

		Percentage of families by family type					
Year	Number of families	Solitaire	Subelementary	Elementary	Augmented elementary	Stem	Grand
1906	1,491	2.4	1.0	36.3	7.9	31.5	20.9
1911	1,608	4.3	1.5	35.1	6.4	29.7	22.9
1916	1,826	5.3	2.3	36.5	4.8	31.9	19.3
1921	1,944	5.6	2.1	35.0	4.3	32.7	20.4
1926	2,056	5.0	2.1	31.4	3.5	33.6	24.4
1931	2,203	4.8	1.0	29.7	3.4	34.7	26.5
1936	2,372	5.0	1.6	28.6	3.5	33.6	27.7
1941	2,554	4.1	1.9	28.5	3.2	34.2	28.2
1946	2,873	3.5	2.0	32.8	4.0	31.6	26.2

		Percentage of population by family type					
Year	Number of people	Solitaire	Subelementary	Elementary	Augmented elementary	Stem	Grand
1906	9,133	0.4	0.5	23.7	6.4	31.4	37.6
1911	10,577	0.7	0.6	23.1	5.1	28.4	42.3
1916	11,486	0.8	0.9	24.8	4.0	32.6	37.0
1921	12,651	0.9	0.8	22.7	3.4	32.8	39.5
1926	14,231	0.7	0.8	20.2	2.7	31.7	44.0
1931	16,072	0.7	0.3	18.0	2.4	31.4	47.2
1936	18,139	0.7	0.5	17.4	2.6	30.0	48.8
1941	20,326	0.5	0.6	17.4	2.3	29.9	49.4
1946	22,173	0.5	0.7	21.3	3.0	29.0	45.7

adulthood would see these men return to the family form of their childhood. One turn of the cycle being completed, the process would be repeated. Middle age would find our subjects living again in elementary families spawned by division of their parental household, and old age would see them presiding over grand families created by the marriages of their sons.

Such close coordination of the life cycle and the family cycle can only occur if two conditions hold. First, the family cycle must be regular and follow a nearly uniform course. If some families never achieve a form more complex than that of the stem family and only achieve that briefly, while others grow so large and complex that division produces stem and grand families, there can be no more than a loose relationship between the two cycles. Many people will never experience life in a complex family, while many others may know nothing else. Second, the great majority of all children must be born during the same phase of the family cycle. If children are born during all the phases of the cycle, those born at the same time will experience a coordination of the two cycles but the population as a whole will not. Those born early in the cycle will grow up as members of grand families, while those born late in the cycle will not experience life in a grand family until they marry.

Evidence to be reported elsewhere indicates that the cycles followed by the families living in our nine villages were surprisingly uniform. Most families moved from elementary to stem, stem to grand, and then back to elementary and stem again by way of division. But there were many exceptions. Tracing families over the 40 years covered by the Japanese registers, I found some that never rose above elementary and others that never fell below grand. Moreover, we know that births were not confined to one phase of the family cycle. Not only did women bear children from their late teens through their early forties but, because they did, brothers were commonly separated by many years in age. Thus even when births were concentrated in the early years of marriage, they were not necessarily concentrated in one phase of the cycle, young women joining the family as it developed. In the extreme case the youngest of several brothers might marry just as the eldest's wife reached the end of her reproductive career.

Consequently, we can expect only a weak relationship between the life cycle and the family cycle if we treat our nine villages as an aggregate. But weak though it is, there is a definite relationship between the two cycles. Table 11.2 reports the proportion of all males living in each of six family types at ages 1 through 75. We see (most clearly in the graphs displayed in fig. 11.1) that as men approach age at marriage, the proportion living in elementary families declines, falling to a low of 11.9 percent at ages 25–29. After that the figure climbs steadily to a peak of 32.8 percent at ages 45–49 and then falls precipitously. The decline in adolescence in the proportion of men in elementary families is accompanied by a modest rise in the proportion in stem families and a sharp rise in the proportion belonging to grand families. Stem families decline from a high of 33.3 percent at ages 20–24 to a low of 20.4 percent at ages 40–45 and then rise to a peak of 40.7 percent at ages 60–65. Grand families remain close to 40 percent among men aged 25–40, decline to a low of 21.7 percent among those aged 45–55, and then rise to a zenith of 53.1 percent among the elderly.

What we see in these figures is a muted expression of the domestic cycle followed by most families in our nine districts. As men pass from

TABLE 11.2
MALES BY AGE AND FAMILY TYPE
ALL MEN LIVING IN NINE DISTRICTS JANUARY 1, 1946

		Percentage of men by family type					
Age	Number of men	Solitaire	Subelementary	Elementary	Stem	Grand	Frérèches
0–1	195			19.0	30.3	36.9	13.9
1–2	227			20.3	29.1	37.0	13.7
2–3	218			25.7	22.0	36.7	15.6
3–4	250			25.2	23.2	32.8	18.8
4–5	208			28.4	23.1	35.1	13.5
0–4	1,098			23.8	25.4	35.6	15.2
5–6	210		0.5	27.1	25.2	33.8	13.3
6–7	202		0.5	25.3	19.8	35.6	18.8
7–8	208			30.8	24.5	30.8	13.9
8–9	203		0.5	37.0	17.7	25.1	19.7
9–10	173		1.2	26.0	24.9	28.3	19.6
5–9	996		0.5	29.3	22.4	30.8	17.0
10–11	174		1.2	28.7	25.3	32.2	12.6
11–12	189		1.1	30.2	25.4	24.9	18.5
12–13	152		2.0	23.0	21.7	34.2	19.1
13–14	183		2.7	26.2	28.4	24.6	18.0
14–15	188		1.6	25.5	31.4	25.0	16.5
10–14	886		1.7	26.9	26.6	27.9	16.9
15–16	167		1.2	24.0	31.1	19.8	24.0
16–17	166		1.8	30.1	31.3	19.3	17.5
17–18	149		2.0	26.2	30.2	24.8	16.8
18–19	132		1.5	30.3	28.8	22.0	17.4
19–20	133		0.8	28.6	32.3	23.3	15.0
15–19	747		1.5	27.7	30.8	21.7	18.3
20–21	120		0.8	29.2	26.7	29.2	14.2
21–22	132	0.8	3.8	24.2	30.3	29.6	11.4
22–23	115	0.9	0.9	19.1	33.9	28.7	16.5
23–24	115	0.9		14.8	36.5	29.6	18.3
24–25	112	1.8	0.9	14.3	40.2	30.4	12.5
20–24	594	0.8	1.4	20.5	33.3	29.5	14.5
25–26	118	1.7	0.9	11.9	32.2	35.6	17.8
26–27	88			8.0	31.8	40.0	20.5
27–28	104			17.3	32.7	33.7	16.4
28–29	99	2.0		10.1	33.3	40.4	14.1
29–30	78			11.5	30.8	37.2	20.5
25–29	487	1.0	0.2	11.9	32.2	37.2	17.7

TABLE 11.2 (Continued)

		Percentage of men by family type					
Age	Number of men	Solitaire	Subelementary	Elementary	Stem	Grand	Frérèches
30–31	84	1.2		23.8	22.6	35.7	16.7
31–32	88	2.3	1.1	27.3	27.3	31.8	10.2
32–33	83	2.4	1.2	14.5	27.7	37.4	16.9
33–34	85	2.4	1.2	23.5	23.5	30.6	18.8
34–35	97	1.0		23.7	21.7	43.3	10.3
30–34	437	1.8	0.7	22.7	24.4	35.9	14.4
35–36	66		1.5	21.2	18.2	45.4	13.6
36–37	88		1.1	21.6	22.7	33.0	21.6
37–38	100	1.0		26.0	25.0	33.0	15.0
38–39	74			28.4	20.3	39.2	12.2
39–40	72	1.4	1.4	26.4	20.8	29.2	20.8
35–39	400	0.5	0.8	24.8	21.8	35.5	16.8
40–41	87			27.6	21.8	33.3	17.2
41–42	69			31.9	20.3	31.9	15.9
42–43	94		1.1	37.2	19.2	25.5	17.0
43–44	66		1.5	30.3	24.2	25.8	18.2
44–45	71	4.2		35.2	16.9	21.1	22.5
40–44	387	0.8	0.5	32.6	20.4	27.7	18.1
45–46	73		1.4	43.8	23.3	16.4	15.1
46–47	58	3.5		29.3	31.0	22.4	13.8
47–48	78	2.6	1.3	33.3	24.4	24.4	14.1
48–49	55			27.3	21.8	21.8	29.1
49–50	35	5.7		22.9	37.1	25.7	8.6
45–49	299	2.0	0.7	32.8	26.4	21.7	16.4
50–51	36			25.0	33.3	16.7	25.0
51–52	42			26.2	31.0	23.8	19.1
52–53	42			23.8	28.6	31.0	16.7
53–54	54			24.1	33.3	18.5	24.1
54–55	38		2.6	21.1	42.1	18.4	15.8
50–54	212		0.5	24.1	33.5	21.7	20.3
55–56	35			25.7	34.3	22.9	17.1
56–57	31			22.6	38.7	19.4	19.4
57–58	32			18.8	34.4	34.4	12.5
58–59	40			10.0	42.5	30.0	17.5
59–60	31			6.5	41.9	32.3	19.4
55–59	169			16.6	38.5	27.8	17.2

TABLE 11.2 (Continued)

		Percentage of men by family type					
Age	Number of men	Solitaire	Subelementary	Elementary	Stem	Grand	Frérèches
60–61	42	2.4		16.7	47.6	23.8	9.5
61–62	28	3.6		17.9	42.9	25.0	10.7
62–63	37	5.4		5.4	24.3	37.8	27.0
63–64	33			12.1	36.4	33.3	18.2
64–65	32	3.1		3.1	53.1	31.3	9.4
60–64	172	2.9		11.1	40.7	30.2	15.1
65–69	117	1.7		6.8	39.3	41.0	11.1
70–74	56	1.8	1.8	8.9	32.1	41.1	14.3
75+	32			3.1	37.5	53.1	6.3

childhood to adolescence, they marry and so do their brothers, expanding elementary families into stem families and stem families into grand families. The result is a sharp decline in the proportion of men in elementary families and a sharp rise in the proportion in grand families. The proportion belonging to stem families also rises but less dramatically because the transformation of elementary to stem is largely offset by the simultaneous transformation of stem to grand. At age 25 these trends are reversed. Since most of the men in the cohort have already married, the flow of new stem families into the population is reduced to a trickle. This, combined with the continuing transformation of stem to grand, precipitates a sharp decline in the proportion of men living in stem families. Surprisingly, this is accompanied not by a rise in the proportion of men in grand families but by a dramatic increase in the proportion living in elementary families. The reason is that by this time the families of men born late in the developmental cycle have begun to divide. The dissolution of these complex households floods the system with elementary households and simultaneously offsets the emergence of new grand families.

With very few exceptions, brothers will all have married by the time any one of them reaches age 40. Consequently, this is the point at which dissolution of old grand families overcomes the emergence of new ones and the proportion of men living in grand families enters a decline. The proportion in elementary families continues upward as the older grand families split into their constituent parts, but the downward trend in the

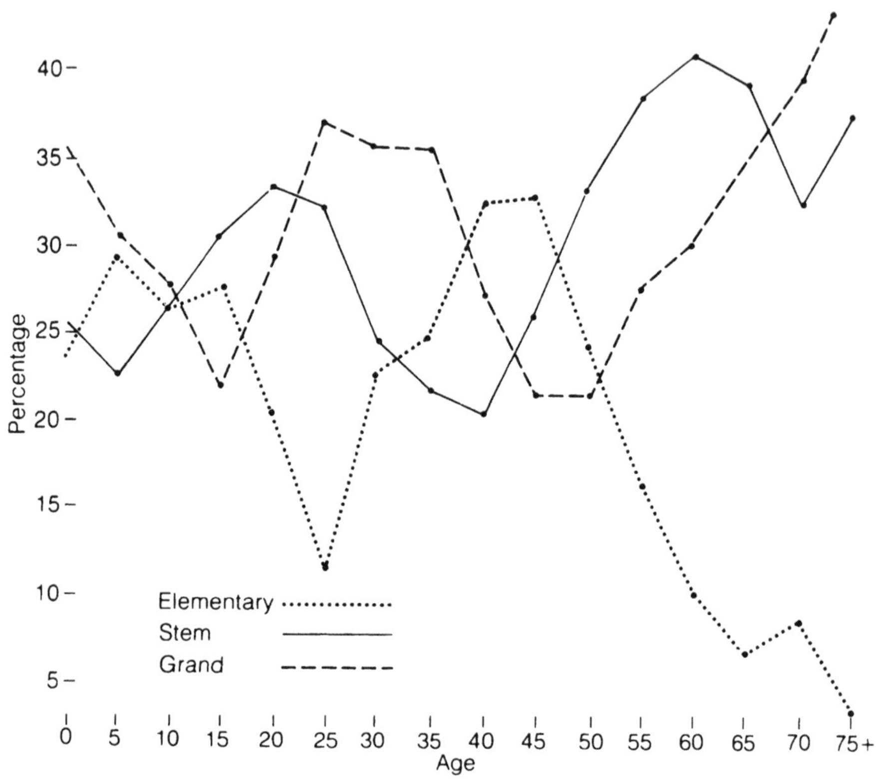

Fig. 11.1
Proportion of Males in Elementary, Stem, and Grand Families

proportion of men in stem families is reversed. Men whose brothers have all married include many whose sons are ready to marry. Thus the proportion of men living in stem families begins to rise at about the same time as the proportion belonging to grand families begins to decline.

Despite a rise in the rate at which elementary families are converted to stem families, the proportion of men living in elementary families continues to rise until age 50, the flood of elementary families produced by the dissolution of mature grand families overwhelming the loss resulting from conversion of elementary to stem. By the time most men reach age 50, however, they have already divided their natal household with their brothers, and this, together with a rising rate of marriage among their sons, sets the whole process into reverse. Elementary families are converted to more complex forms faster than they emerge from family division, and the proportion of men living in simple families plunges, while the proportion living in stem and grand families shoots upward. The result is that by the time men reach age 65 almost all are living in complex families.

I turn now from men to women. Table 11.3 (summarized visually in fig. 11.2) shows that as women pass from childhood to adulthood and thence to old age, they experience much the same sequence of family types as men. The only significant differences are in the timing of the transitions—women reach certain critical points in their careers a few years earlier than men—and in the form of family life experienced in old age—most women pass the last years of their lives in stem families while most men pass their last years in grand families.

The first difference, that in timing, reflects the fact that women marry before men. Since marriage transforms elementary to stem and stem to grand, women pass the critical transitions a few years earlier than men. The second difference is more interesting because the explanation is not so obvious. Why do we find most old women in stem families and most old men in grand families? Part of the answer follows from the fact that like their sisters in many societies, Chinese women tend to outlive their husbands. As a result, they are more likely to survive to see their sons marry and divide their natal household, the old mother forming a stem household with one or the other of her male offspring. But biology does not provide a complete answer. Women's social inferiority is at least as important as their biological superiority. Though many Chinese women establish a matriarchy on sentiments nourished in childhood, they cannot control their adult sons as effectively as their husbands can, simply because formal authority and rights in property are vested in men. Consequently, women are more likely to pass their last years as members of stem families, not only because they tend to outlast their husbands but also because having survived them, they are unable to prevent division of the household.

Having seen that the life cycle and the family cycle are correlated for both men and women, we now try to refine our view of the relationship. I have argued that the fit between the two cycles varies with the degree to which births are concentrated in time. One implication of this hypothesis is that people who are born at different times experience different family careers. Since women do in fact bear children over a 30-year period, it follows that the family careers experienced by their offspring may differ, depending on whether the children are born early or late in the mother's reproductive career. Is this in fact the case? And if it is, how great is the difference? Is it so small that it can safely be ignored for most purposes? Or is it of such magnitude that students of the Chinese family risk disaster if they fail to heed its presence?

TABLE 11.3
FEMALES BY AGE AND FAMILY TYPE
ALL WOMEN LIVING IN NINE DISTRICTS JANUARY 1, 1946

Age	Number of women	Percentage of women by family type: Solitaire	Subelementary	Elementary	Stem	Grand	Frérèches
0-1	150			26.6	20.6	33.3	19.3
1-2	212			20.8	25.0	36.3	17.9
2-3	211			21.3	26.0	38.8	13.7
3-4	192			21.8	23.9	40.1	14.0
4-5	188		0.5	28.1	25.5	28.7	17.0
0-4	953		0.1	23.5	24.5	35.7	16.3
5-6	233			27.8	26.6	30.9	14.5
6-7	191		0.5	25.1	25.1	27.7	21.4
7-8	191		0.5	25.6	25.6	30.8	17.2
8-9	197		0.5	29.4	22.3	27.9	19.7
9-10	189		0.5	31.7	19.0	31.2	17.4
5-9	1,001		0.4	28.0	23.9	29.8	18.0
10-11	199			31.6	25.1	24.6	18.5
11-12	187		0.5	31.0	20.8	28.8	18.7
12-13	173		0.5	22.5	24.8	33.5	18.4
13-14	165	0.6	1.2	29.6	24.8	24.8	18.7
14-15	170		1.1	35.2	18.8	28.8	15.8
10-14	894	0.1	0.7	30.1	22.9	28.1	18.1
15-16	162		1.2	22.8	28.3	33.3	14.1
16-17	150		0.6	23.3	24.6	30.0	21.3
17-18	171		0.5	32.1	26.9	28.6	11.6
18-19	138		2.1	28.2	26.0	22.4	21.0
19-20	167		1.1	16.1	31.1	37.7	13.7
15-19	788		1.1	24.5	27.5	30.7	16.1
20-21	128	0.7	1.5	14.8	31.2	37.5	14.0
21-22	154			15.5	38.3	27.9	18.1
22-23	121		0.8	11.5	36.3	38.0	13.2
23-24	121		1.6	13.2	27.2	43.8	14.0
24-25	125		0.8	14.4	29.6	37.6	17.6
20-24	649	0.2	0.9	14.0	32.8	36.5	15.6
25-26	93	1.0		19.3	31.1	26.8	21.5
26-27	82		2.4	25.6	17.0	37.8	17.0
27-28	100			18.0	33.0	31.0	18.0
28-29	85		1.1	25.8	20.0	35.2	17.6
29-30	87	2.2		21.8	20.6	42.5	12.6
25-29	447	0.7	0.7	21.9	24.8	34.5	17.5

TABLE 11.3 (Continued)

Age	Number of women	Solitaire	Subelementary	Elementary	Stem	Grand	Frérèches
		Percentage of women by family type					
30–31	74			17.5	18.9	48.6	14.8
31–32	113	1.7	0.8	29.2	15.9	35.3	16.8
32–33	87	1.1		25.2	21.8	32.1	19.5
33–34	90			21.1	22.2	42.2	14.4
34–35	82			37.8	15.8	26.8	19.5
30–34	446	0.7	0.2	26.5	18.8	36.8	17.0
35–36	74			29.7	18.9	35.1	16.2
36–37	88	1.1	1.1	26.1	19.3	35.2	17.0
37–38	76	1.3		22.3	25.0	30.2	21.0
38–39	72			37.5	23.6	23.6	15.2
39–40	82			26.8	20.7	36.5	15.8
35–39	392	0.5	0.3	28.3	21.4	32.4	17.1
40–41	67	1.4		31.3	23.8	20.8	22.3
41–42	69		1.4	42.0	14.4	18.8	23.1
42–43	76			31.5	27.6	26.3	14.4
43–44	60	1.6		25.0	31.6	25.0	16.6
44–45	65	1.5		41.5	26.1	18.4	12.3
40–44	337	0.9	0.3	34.4	24.6	22.0	17.8
45–46	59			33.8	40.6	16.9	8.4
46–47	53			26.4	32.0	18.8	22.6
47–48	59	1.6		35.5	28.8	22.0	11.8
48–49	62	1.6		22.6	33.9	24.2	17.7
49–50	37	2.7		13.5	43.2	8.1	32.4
45–49	270	1.1		27.4	35.2	18.9	17.4
50–51	28			17.9	32.1	32.1	17.9
51–52	49			24.5	42.9	14.3	18.4
52–53	47		2.1	8.5	40.4	31.9	17.0
53–54	35			2.9	48.6	25.7	22.9
54–55	36			8.3	47.2	27.8	16.7
50–54	195		0.5	12.8	42.6	25.6	18.5
55–56	32			3.1	50.0	31.3	15.6
56–57	32			18.8	34.4	34.4	12.5
57–58	32			12.5	40.6	46.9	
58–59	34			8.8	47.1	26.5	17.7
59–60	36			13.9	47.2	33.3	5.6
55–59	166			11.5	44.0	34.3	10.2

TABLE 11.3 (Continued)

Age	Number of women	Percentage of women by family type					
		Solitaire	Subelementary	Elementary	Stem	Grand	Frérèches
60–61	50		2.0	2.0	42.0	34.0	20.0
61–62	40	5.0		12.5	52.5	22.5	7.5
62–63	45			4.4	42.2	35.6	17.8
63–64	30				53.3	33.3	13.3
64–65	27			7.4	48.2	40.7	3.7
60–64	192	1.0	0.5	5.2	46.9	32.8	13.5
65–69	120		1.7	10.0	40.0	40.8	7.5
70–74	81		2.5	4.9	48.2	38.3	6.2
75+	80	2.5	3.8	2.5	47.5	38.8	5.0

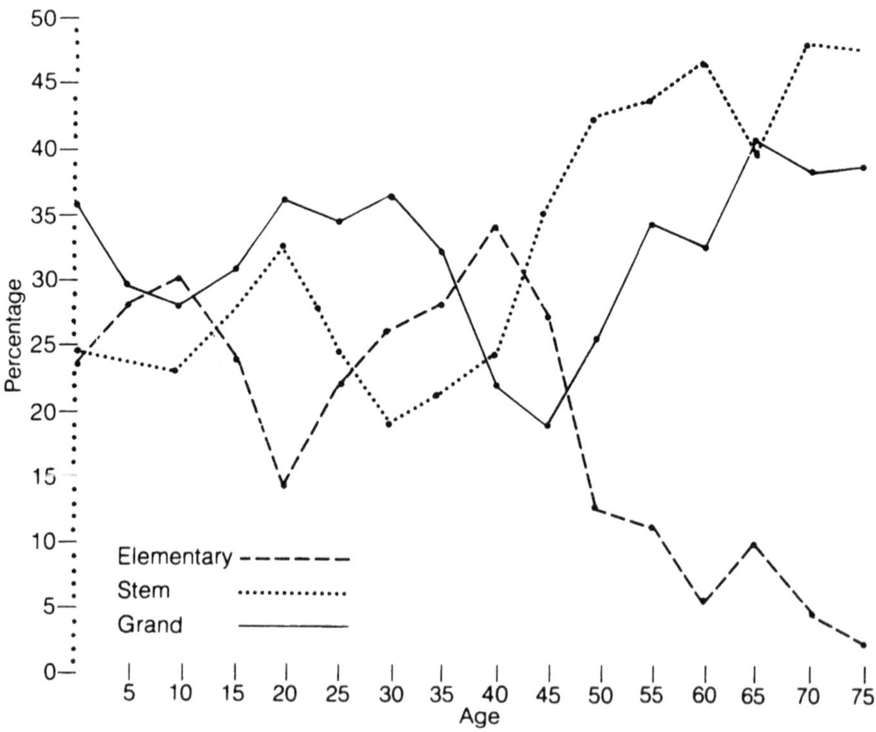

Fig. 11.2
Proportion of Females in Elementary, Stem, and Grand Families

In fact, the family careers of men born early exhibit a trajectory that differs markedly from those of men born late (see table 11.4). The magnitude of the difference is evident in figure 11.3. The data displayed there contrast the careers of early-borns and late-borns by comparing the proportion living in elementary families at ages 0–65. During the early years of life the paths taken by early-borns and late-borns are inversely related. Where the proportion of early-borns in elementary families begins at 11.6 percent at ages 0–4 and rises sharply to 31.4 percent at ages 15–19, the proportion of late-borns in elementary families starts at 42.0 percent at ages 0–4 and falls abruptly to 14.0 percent at ages 15–19. After age 20 the figures for early-borns decline to the low level found among late-borns, but the convergence at ages 25–29 is short-lived. Immediately thereafter the figures for late-borns begin a steep ascent, rising to 30.8 percent at ages 30–34, 41.8 percent at ages 40–44, and finally 44.8 percent at ages 50–54. Meanwhile, the figures for early-borns also rise but only after a five-year delay and to only one-half the height. In fact, the experience of men born early and late in their mothers' reproductive careers does not converge until after age 55 when both groups are found in complex rather than elementary families.

The differences displayed in figure 11.3 are, of course, a result of the fact that the female life cycle and the family cycle are related. Boys born early in life are born into complex families because their mothers' marriages have created complex families; those born late in life are born into elementary families because by then the families created by their mothers' marriages have been divided. The only difference to be explained is the greater proportion of late-born men living in elementary families during the middle years of their life. Ultimately, the reason for this difference is that Chinese women bear children from age 15 through age 50. Because the active reproductive period extends over so many years, a family's eldest son is often many years older than the youngest son. Thus when division occurs one son may be 45 with a married son of his own, while another is 25 and only recently married. The former passes quickly from a grand family formed by him and his brothers to one founded by him and his sons. The latter leaves the complex family headed by his father just as he enters the middle years of life and does not see another emerge until 20 years later when his sons marry.

Because many of the women living in our nine districts were born elsewhere, I do not know their mother's age at birth and cannot duplicate table 11.4 for women. This lacuna must eventually be filled, but I doubt if it will change the conclusions suggested by the present analysis. Tables 11.2 and 11.3 argue that when we allow for the effects of such obvious differences as age at marriage the family careers of men and women follow similar routes.

TABLE 11.4
MALES BY AGE, FAMILY TYPE, AND MOTHER'S AGE AT BIRTH
ALL MEN LIVING IN NINE DISTRICTS JANUARY 1, 1946

		Mother aged 15-19 Percentage of men by family type					
Age	Number of men	Solitaire	Subelementary	Elementary	Stem	Grand	Frérèches
0-4	132			9.1	35.6	40.9	14.3
5-9	104			19.2	28.9	37.5	14.4
10-14	115		1.7	23.5	16.5	38.3	20.0
15-19	112		0.9	30.4	30.4	21.4	17.0
20-24	89		1.1	25.8	36.0	22.5	14.6
25-29	59	1.7		15.3	45.8	28.8	8.5
30-34	50	6.0		10.0	32.0	42.0	10.0
35-39	48	2.1		18.8	27.1	39.6	12.5
40-44	56			21.4	33.9	25.0	19.6
45-49	37			24.3	29.7	40.5	5.5
50-54	34			17.7	35.3	26.5	20.6
55-59	17			17.7	23.5	23.5	35.3
60-64	23			4.4	39.1	34.8	30.4
65+	16			25.0	31.3	25.0	18.7

		Mother aged 20-24 Percentage of men by family type					
Age	Number of men	Solitaire	Subelementary	Elementary	Stem	Grand	Frérèches
0-4	272			12.9	33.5	40.4	13.2
5-9	233		1.3	24.9	23.6	36.9	13.3
10-14	207		0.5	28.5	15.9	39.1	15.9
15-19	219		1.8	32.0	24.2	23.7	18.3
20-24	169		1.8	28.4	34.3	23.7	11.8
25-29	121	1.7	0.8	11.6	33.1	27.2	25.6
30-34	84			13.1	28.6	40.5	17.9
35-39	104			22.1	22.1	41.4	14.4
40-44	86	1.2		30.2	20.9	34.9	12.8
45-49	90	1.1		27.8	26.7	25.6	18.9
50-54	42			19.1	33.3	28.6	19.1
55-59	33			9.1	45.5	27.3	18.2
60-64	27	7.4		18.5	37.0	18.5	18.5
65+	25				40.0	52.0	8.0

TABLE 11.4 (Continued)

Mother aged 25-29
Percentage of men by family type

Age	Number of men	Solitaire	Subelementary	Elementary	Stem	Grand	Frérèches
0-4	239			23.0	19.3	45.2	12.5
5-9	252		0.4	27.4	17.9	32.9	21.4
10-14	229		2.3	31.9	24.9	24.5	16.6
15-19	160		1.2	34.3	29.6	16.6	18.3
20-24	130			18.5	34.6	24.6	22.3
25-29	85			9.4	34.1	42.4	14.1
30-34	115	0.9	0.9	22.6	21.7	39.1	14.8
35-39	86			22.1	25.6	41.9	10.5
40-44	94	2.1		26.6	19.2	37.2	14.9
45-49	54			37.1	25.9	22.2	14.8
50-54	42			14.2	38.1	26.2	21.4
55-59	18			44.4	38.9	11.1	5.6
60-64	15	6.7			53.3	20.0	20.0
65+	25				44.0	48.0	8.0

Mother aged 30-34
Percentage of men by family type

Age	Number of men	Solitaire	Subelementary	Elementary	Stem	Grand	Frérèches
0-4	215			30.2	19.5	29.8	20.5
5-9	201			34.8	22.4	26.4	16.4
10-14	165		2.4	26.1	37.0	21.8	12.7
15-19	120		1.7	20.0	40.0	17.5	20.8
20-24	78		5.1	15.4	35.9	35.9	7.7
25-29	106	0.9		8.4	24.5	51.9	14.2
30-34	85	2.4	2.4	31.8	20.0	32.9	10.6
35-39	63	1.6	4.8	27.0	11.1	33.3	22.2
40-44	55		1.8	49.1	16.4	16.4	16.4
45-49	40		5.0	32.5	27.5	10.0	25.0
50-54	15			20.0	46.7	20.0	13.3
55-59	25			12.0	40.0	32.0	16.0
60-64	14			28.6	42.9	28.6	
65+		6.7			33.3	40.0	20.0

TABLE 11.4 (Continued)

Mother aged 35–39
Percentage of men by family type

Age	Number of men	Solitaire	Subelementary	Elementary	Stem	Grand	Frérèches
0–4	133			42.1	15.8	25.6	16.5
5–9	125			45.6	24.0	20.0	10.4
10–14	98		3.1	24.5	36.7	14.3	21.4
15–19	69		1.5	17.4	43.5	20.3	17.4
20–24	62	3.2		14.5	24.2	45.2	12.9
25–29	61			16.4	29.5	41.0	13.1
30–34	42	4.8		35.7	21.4	28.6	9.5
35–39	39			38.5	18.0	23.1	20.5
40–44	42		2.4	40.5	14.3	9.5	33.3
45–49	27	7.4		40.7	33.3	11.1	7.4
50–54	19			47.4	15.8	26.3	10.5
55–59	6			16.7	50.0	16.7	16.7
60–64	13			15.4	38.5	30.8	15.4
65+	6				50.0	33.3	16.7

Mother aged 40+
Percentage of men by family type

Age	Number of men	Solitaire	Subelementary	Elementary	Stem	Grand	Frérèches
0–4	74			41.9	29.7	17.6	10.8
5–9	45		2.2	17.8	26.7	22.2	31.1
10–14	44			6.8	54.6	22.7	15.9
15–19	38			7.9	28.9	50.0	13.2
20–24	38	5.3		10.5	26.3	42.1	15.8
25–29	22			4.6	18.2	40.9	36.4
30–34	23			21.7	13.0	30.4	34.8
35–39	15			20.0	13.3	40.0	26.7
40–44	13			46.2	7.7	15.4	30.8
45–49	7		14.3	42.9	14.3		28.6
50–54	10			40.0	30.0	10.0	20.0
55–59	6				33.3	16.7	50.0
60–64	6				66.7	16.7	16.7
65+	4			25.0	50.0	25.0	

The more important task for the future is to discover the extent to which the relationship between the family cycle and the life cycle varies with social status. Though I think Maurice Freedman (1966:44–45) and Marion Levy (1965:9–10) exaggerate the difference between the rich and poor versions of the Chinese family, there is certainly a difference. What we see in the data presented in this paper is a compound product of the

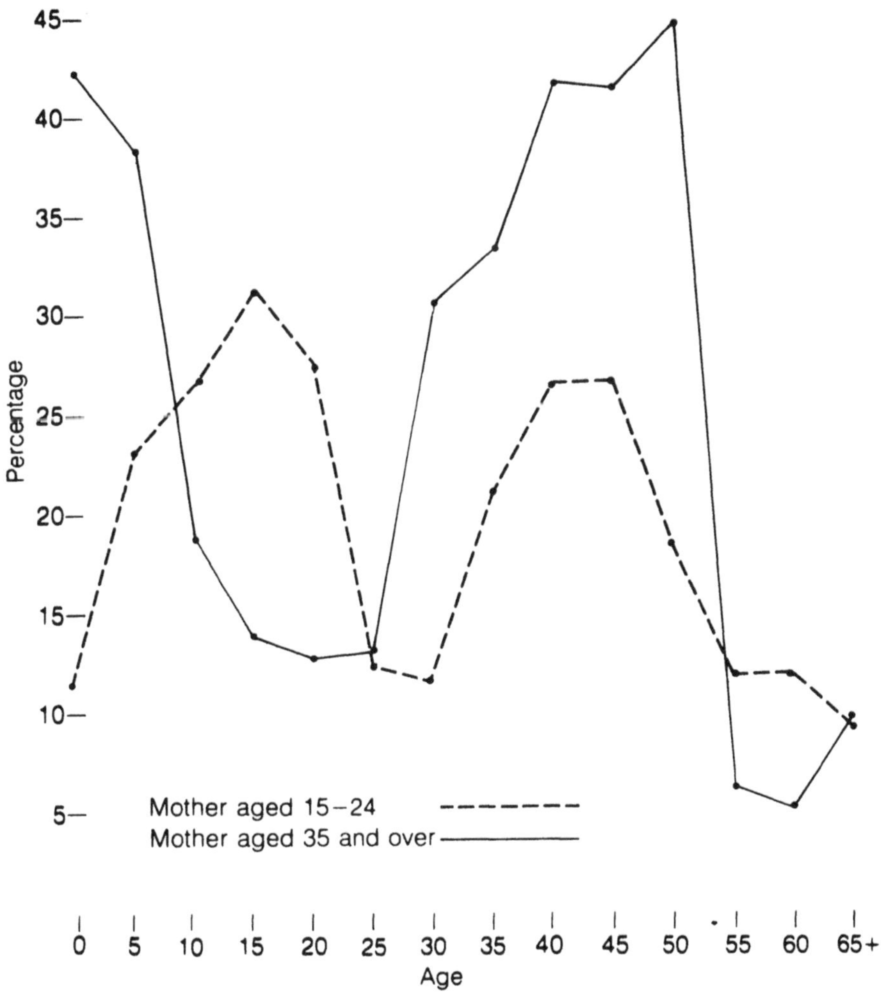

Fig. 11.3
Proportion of Men in Elementary Families by Mother's Age at Birth

family cycles followed by farm laborers, tenant farmers, rich peasants, and a few petty landlords. My guess is that when these strata are analyzed separately the results will reveal differences and thus strengthen the relationships reported here.

What are the implications of these findings? Does it matter that the life cycle and the family cycle are correlated? What follows from our discovery that the correlation varies with the individual's point of entry? Would it be worth the effort to determine whether the relationship between the two cycles varies with social status? The frank answer to these questions is that we do not know. Psychologists have never asked whether the various forms of the Chinese family leave distinctive marks on the individual. But let us assume that they do. Let us imagine that a person's experience of different forms of the family has enduring consequences that vary with his age at the time of exposure. If these consequences include the ability to deal effectively with subordinates, it could be that some Chinese families divide earlier than others because their heads were born in different phases of the cycle. And since the family careers of children at the top of a sibling set are necessarily different from that of those at the bottom, behavior commonly attributed to sibling position may be better attributed to family organization. There is even the possibility that by concentrating births in one phase of the life cycle, the birth control programs promulgated throughout China may inadvertently reduce individual variation. I make no claims for any of these hypotheses. My only purpose is to suggest why the relationship between the family cycle and the life cycle is worth further attention.

REFERENCES

Freedman, Maurice
1966 Chinese Lineage and Society. London: The Athlone Press.
Levy, Marion J., Jr.
1965 Aspects of the Analysis of Family Structure. *In* Aspects of the Analysis of Family Structure, ed. Ansley J. Coale et al. Princeton: Princeton University Press.
Wolf, Arthur P., and Chieh-shan Huang
1980 Marriage and Adoption in China, 1845–1945. Stanford, Calif.: Stanford University Press.

12

Cultural Ideals, Socioeconomic Change, and Household Composition: Karen, Lua', Hmong, and Thai in Northwestern Thailand

Peter Kunstadter

The wisest thing I heard on my return from the 1981 Wenner-Gren conference on household form and function was a remark I overheard on Fifth Avenue: "If you can't learn from the past, and you can't predict the future, you better stick to the details." With this rationale I resort to crude empiricism in attempting to answer several kinds of questions about household composition.[1]

1. Are there consistent patterns of distribution of household types within given ethnic groups suggesting a regular adherence to cultural ideals of household composition? Does the distribution of household types vary systematically between ethnic groups with different cultural ideals?
2. Is there an association between the basic economic type of a community and the distribution of household types within that community?
3. Are there regular changes in distribution of household types associated with basic socioeconomic changes and with patterns of demographic change?

I believe it is necessary to look at statistical distribution of household types as well as cultural ideals because it is impossible for all households to conform to the ideals (assuming they want to do so) because of stochastic demographic processes and because it is by no means certain that all households attempt to conform to the cultural ideals.

My excuses for dealing with something as prosaic as household composition are two. First, despite the existence of a few ethnographic anomalies, most people in most societies at most times live in households, membership in which is usually based on kin relationships of marriage and descent, which are simultaneously a combination of dwelling unit, a unit of economic cooperation (at least in distribution and consumption), and the unit within which most reproduction and early childhood socialization takes place. Thus the kin-based household seems to be an important social unit in all (or almost all) societies, with widely proliferating implications for many important aspects of behavior, including reproductive and other demographic behavior.

Second, various arguments have been made concerning the relationship between population processes and the forms and functions of the household—for example, the Coale-Levy argument that most people in any society live in nonextended family households (1965) and that this must be so because of the exigencies of birth and death rates. Thus they would argue for at least the statistical primacy of the nuclear family household. There is also the somewhat dubious conventional wisdom that as modernization and urbanization proceed, there is a tendency toward nuclearization of the household, with many implications for population distribution on the fine-grained scale and more tenuous implications for birth and death rates. Perhaps, conversely, there is the less frequently stated argument that household composition is the subject of very deep-seated cultural norms that persist despite changes in other aspects of society (for example, the persistence of the patrilineal-patrilocal extended family household of the Chinese throughout millennia of Chinese history despite radical changes in Chinese socioeconomic and political conditions, as discussed in Wolf's contribution to this volume).

This paper considers community differences and changes in household composition over the past decade in a mixed ethnic population in northwestern Thailand. The study area as a whole includes highland Lua' villages, highland Karen villages, a highland mixed Karen and Hmong village, lowland rural Karen villages, mixed ethnic suburbs surrounding a market town, and the market town itself containing northern Thai, central Thai, Shan, Indian, Chinese, Pa-O, and other ethnic groups. Data were collected in community surveys in the late 1960s and in the same communities in 1980 and 1981. This paper, based on a portion of the study, deals with data from a highland Lua' village, highland and lowland rural Skaw Karen communities, the highland mixed Hmong and Karen community, and lowland suburbs with large Skaw Karen and Lua' populations. The data presented here are from hand tabulations and should be considered preliminary.

STUDY DESIGN: CROSS-SECTIONAL AND LONGITUDINAL COMPARISONS

The available data allow us to make cross-sectional and longitudinal comparisons at the community level rather than considering in detail the history of changes in individual households. Cross-sectional analyses will compare distribution of types of household composition between different ethnic groups and between different kinds of communities of the same ethnic group to investigate two kinds of questions. First, are there systematic differences in the distribution of household composition between different ethnic groups living under approximately the same demographic and economic conditions? If so, this supports the not very surprising conclusion that cultural differences are important determinants of household composition. Second, are there systematic differences between different communities of the same ethnic group living under different demographic and economic conditions? If so, this supports the conclusion that demographic and economic differences are related to household composition within a single cultural tradition. Longitudinal comparisons within and between ethnic groups, where trends of demographic and economic change are known, will allow us to determine whether the cultural differences in household composition persist or tend to converge in some standard pattern under the pressure of these changes.

METHODS

Quantitative data in this paper are based on a socioeconomic and demographic survey conducted in the late 1960s covering 30 communities in Mae Sariang and Mae La Noi districts of northwestern Thailand and a similar survey in April 1981 covering the same communities plus a few additional ones. Every household in each of the surveyed communities was censused. Based on responses to a question on relationship of household members to household head, diagrams summarized the composition of each household. Household headship was usually assigned by respondents to the eldest married (or ever-married) male. Current research on household functions suggests that the *head* defined in this way is not necessarily the economic decision maker in the household. Each household was classified according to its composition, ethnic group, and location (table 12.1).

Where possible, we reinterviewed to clarify incomplete or ambiguous responses to as to specify relationship. In Thai the term *lan*, for example, may refer to grandchild, niece, nephew, or distant relative belonging to a younger generation. We attempted to learn about de jure (legally registered) and de facto membership (actually living in or considered to be a permanent member of the household by household members) and to learn the reasons for discrepancies in household composition based on these two definitions. People who were considered to be temporarily away at school or at work were included in our definition of household membership; people who had moved out permanently were excluded, even if their legal registration had not been changed.

My description of ideals of household composition in the various ethnic groups is based on long familiarity gained through extensive fieldwork in the area (for Lua' and Karen see Kunstadter 1966, 1972, 1978, 1980; for Hmong see Geddes 1976). Typology of the communities is based on the environment (highland versus lowland) and predominant economic activities carried out within the community. Highland communities are those located above 500 meters. Their traditional economies are based on subsistence rice swiddening on communally held land. Lowland rural communities, below about 400 meters, generally have a mixed cash and subsistence crop economy based on individually held irrigated fields. The urban community is centered around the market and district administrative offices and is occupied primarily by merchants, civil servants, and other wage earners. Suburbs, on the geographical margins of the market town, were originally agriculturally based communities but are increasingly the site of resettlement of newcomers, including civil servants and other wage workers as well as migrants from highland villages. The boundaries between suburban and urban communities have become increasingly blurred in the past ten years.

Frequencies of household types were tabulated for each community in this study. It is evident from a casual examination of the tabulations that not all households of a given ethnic group conform to that group's ideal pattern. This results in part from stochastic demographic processes (such as death or the sex of offspring) beyond the control of family members as well as violation of the ideals (such as failure to marry or to bear children) which constrain the availability of people to live in a given type of

TABLE 12.1

HOUSEHOLD COMPOSITION, ETHNIC GROUP, AND LOCALITY

	Highland				Lowland			
	Lua'		Karen		Rural Karen		Suburb Karen	
Household composition	1967	1980	1968	1981	1969	1981	1969–70	1981
Single person								
Male: sep/div								
widowed	1		2	2		1		1
nev. married								
Fem.: sep/div					1			1
widowed	3	1	8	3	5	5		
nev. married								
Institution, nonkin (HH/people)								
Single generational								
Married couple	3	1	4	3	4	6	3	1
Siblings			1					
Sib. + unrelated								
Nuclear (two gener.)								
Hu + Wi + Child.	16	29	61	95	35	32	35	43
Nucl. + Hu Ch.	4	2	4	1				
Nucl. + Wi Ch.	2						2	3
Nucl. + Ch. both			1					1
Nucl. + othr. rel.			4			1	2	3
Nucl. + nonrel.								1
Incomplete nuclear								
Male head: sep/div							1	
widowed			2		1			
unknown				2				
nev. married	1							

TABLE 12.1 (Continued)

	Highland				Lowland			
	Lua'		Karen		Rural Karen		Suburb Karen	
Household composition	1967	1980	1968	1981	1969	1981	1969–70	1981
Fem. head: sep/div							2	3
widowed	3	3	3		3		1	5
unknown				3		4		2
nev. married								
Inc. Nuc. + other		1						1
Other two-generational (pre-three generation)								
Patri.: 1 cur. mar.				1				
2 current marriages	2						1	
Matri.: 1 cur. mar.	1		1	2	1			
2 current marriages		1	2	10	2	1		
Three-generational								
Patri.: 0 cur. mar.								2
1 current marriage	10	11				1	1	1
2 current mar.	1			1				1
Matri.: 0 cur. mar.	1		3	1	1	1	5	2
1 current marriage	1	3	8	5	2	2	3	8
2 current marriages	1	1	10	13		2	2	
Other: 0 cur. mar.								
1 current marriage								2
2 current marriage								
Four-generational								
1 current marriage								1
2 current marriages		1						

household. Moreover, there are alternatives to living in a kin-based household (for instance, living in a Buddhist temple, living in jail) and alternatives to the "normal" household form associated with socioeconomic and demographic changes (such as the high rates of widowhood associated with epidemic mortality or noncoresidence of spouses associated with work opportunities away from the home community). Analysis of these distributions in relation to the cultural ideals and the factors affecting actual composition of households is the subject of this paper.

FACTORS AFFECTING HOUSEHOLD COMPOSITION

Households are coresidential social and economic units, usually based on kinship or fictive kinship ties. As such they are subject to change as a result of alterations in the basic economic system, constraints on housing, or redefinitions of kinship obligations. A typology of household composition may be developed on the basis of a limited number of characteristics or variables. For purposes of this paper and the tabulations on which the analyses are based I have considered the following variables: number of persons in the household; relationship of household members (institutional or nonkin versus those based on ties of marriage or descent); number of generations; number of current marriages; postmarital residence (patrilocal, matrilocal, bilocal).

Composition of any household and the distribution of household compositions in a community result from the working through time of the various forces that determine who joins and who leaves the household and the circumstances under which household fission or fusion may take place. Because some of these forces act repetitively and in sequence (as in sequences of birth and death, marriage and dissolution of marriage), families that make up households may be viewed as undergoing life cycles (see also Wolf, this volume). Because the human species reproduces by single births over a period of years, the pattern of repetition of events will never be exactly in phase in all households in a community. Thus a community will *always* exhibit a range of household types, representing not change but rather the distribution of households (or families within households) at different points on the cycle. Some systems (for example, that of the Lua', described below) imply the minimization of such cycling as it applies to households, emphasizing household continuity through transmission of obligations to ancestral spirits, identification of the house structure with those spirits, rules of postmarital residence, and the associated presence of multiple generations and several marriages within a single household. Other systems emphasize discontinuity of households through the absence of any systematic sentimental association of house and ancestral spirits, postmarital neolocality, or rules of household fission.

The basic variables determining household composition and the distribution of types of households within a community are, first, cultural rules that restrict or enjoin, more or less strictly, who joins and who leaves the household and, second, demographic conditions that establish the probability with which individuals can be expected to join or depart the household by birth or death. Both of these basic types of variables are subject to change in response to conditions external to the household.

The most easily examined type of change is demographic. Changes in both death and birth rates have been noted in the study area. In recent history death rates have fallen rapidly in the study populations. If we assume certain common cultural features of the area (such as extremely rare infanticide, fairly high desire to marry and bear children), the potential consequences for household composition from decline in the death rate, in the absence of fertility control, include the following:

1. Higher survival rate of children, and larger children sets per household.
2. Fewer married couples without surviving children.
3. More couples with completed families having surviving children of both sexes.
4. More couples surviving intact to the completion of their own reproduction.
5. More parents and more couples surviving to the age of grandparenthood.
6. Higher youth dependency.
7. Higher old age dependency.
8. Higher probability that household-level demographic characteristics will permit the realization of ideals of marriage (because the ideal marital partners prescribed by kinship rules are more likely to exist).
9. Higher probability that household-level demographic characteristics will permit the realization of ideals concerning multigenerational family households (because of the increased probability of survival of grandparents).
10. Higher probability of the possibility of conflicts between siblings over inheritance (because of the higher probability that siblings of the same sex will survive to the age of marriage and reproduction).
11. Fewer widows and orphans.

12. More children who survive to the age of marriage who have surviving married siblings (this implies that at the same time it is demographically possible to achieve an extended, multiple-generation household there will be at least the potential for the creation of more nuclear family households).

Fertility control may have the following consequences for birthrate and thus for household composition:

1. Decline in the number of children born per couple.
2. More limited range of completed family size.
3. Some degree of control over the sex composition of the set of children in accord with ideals of household composition by stopping reproduction when the ideal has been achieved (for example, one child of each sex or at least one son).
4. Consequences for achievement of ideal household composition depend on the extent to which total number and sex distribution of offspring are limited.

Migration, the third variable in the demographic equation along with changes in birth and death rates, may have varied consequences for household composition, depending on who moves (age, sex, birth order) and the relationship of movement to household of orientation and procreation and depending on whether movement is by individuals or by household groups.

Socioeconomic changes have many possible effects on household composition. Modernization, for example, may allow many normal family functions to be substituted by infrastructural services or market purchases (for instance, piped water and electricity may be substituted for carried water and gathered fuel or food may be bought and housing may be rented instead of being produced by family members). Compared with a subsistence economy, a market economy makes it much easier for individuals to live outside a normal family household. Likewise, wage labor may be substituted for labor exchange based on ties of kinship, so some of the functions of large extended family households as units of production may be lost. For these reasons urbanization and modernization are generally thought to result in individualization or at least nuclearization of household structure. Socioeconomic changes in the study area have proceeded rapidly along the lines of modernization, commercialization and, to a certain extent, urbanization. Thus we may look for evidence of the consequences of both demographic and socioeconomic changes on household composition.

THE STUDY AREA IN THE 1960s

Until the mid-1960s the portion of northern Thailand discussed here was relatively isolated, although it had long been crossed by a caravan route connecting the valley of the Ping (the major river of northern Thailand) with the Salween drainage and the market towns of eastern Burma. Traditionally these highlands were occupied by dispersed, permanently settled villages of Lua' and Karen subsistence rice swiddeners. The rural lowlands were occupied by villages of northern Thai, Shan, and Karen wet rice farmers. The district town served as an administrative center and as a market for the surrounding region.

A dry season road was completed connecting the town with the Ping valley in the late 1950s, and an all-weather road was completed in 1965. Commercial and administrative expansion followed almost immediately, along with a variety of development projects, beginning with road construction and a large irrigation project in the valley. In the early 1960s the unpaved streets of the town were lined with wooden houses. Electricity was available for a few hours in the evening from an erratic generator; an ice plant had opened mostly to provide ice for cold drinks. Consumer goods were limited in variety and high in price. The market, open only early in the morning, was irregularly supplied with fresh meat and local seasonal fruits and vegetables. Administrative services were minimal.

By 1970 the town streets were being paved and lighted and work had begun on a district hospital. There was occasional taxi service every day linking the town with Chiang Mai, Thailand's second city. A telegraph line was completed to supplement the radio telephone. Consumer goods from throughout the world began to be stocked in stores, and the town was opened to tourism. Rural areas were still relatively isolated, though by 1970 many of the lowland villages could be reached by motorcycle in the dry season. Transportation in and out of the highlands was still by foot.

Death rates apparently started to fall in the lowlands after World War II. Major communicable diseases (smallpox, malaria) were controlled and food supplies and medical care improved. Fertility control was apparently already being exercised in town by traditional means when modern family planning was introduced in the early 1960s. By 1970 family planning was spreading to some rural lowland villages but was still very rare in the highlands. Death rates remained relatively high in the highlands, primarily from infectious diseases, but continued to fall in the lowlands, especially in town.

The basic economy of the region was agricultural, with little emphasis on cash crops. Some seasonal agricultural wage work was available in the lowlands and some of the construction projects provided jobs, but most of the wage work was done by lowlanders, some of whom moved into the area for this purpose. There was little or no wage work available in the highland villages, where the traditional subsistence economy persisted, based on subsistence swiddening plus some irrigated rice farming. Some highlanders came to the lowlands in the dry season to seek wage work as a supplement to their income. Lightweight market goods (such as plastic sheeting, a few canned goods, matches, flashlights) were added to highland material culture and replaced traditional items, but there was no mechanization or chemicalization of highland agriculture. Even in the lowlands traditional methods of growing traditional crops persisted.

Government schools, limited to the four primary grades, opened in the highlands. Christian and Buddhist missionaries were active among the animistic highlanders and their lowland ethnic cousins. Despite these changes, the life of highlanders was lived much as it had been before, and even in the lowlands, outside of town, people were not very deeply involved in the market economy.

CHANGE IN THE 1970s

The 1970s were years of rapid change, especially around the town. By 1981 transportation had impoved markedly throughout the area. There are several daily buses, including air-conditioned service, connecting the new bus station in town with the province capital to the north and with Chiang Mai. Dry season roads now reach many rural communities, including many of highland villages. Commerce and administrative services have expanded, especially in town. Dependable electric power is available day and night in town and suburbs. Town streets are now lighted and water is piped to all houses in town and to many in the suburbs. Several new markets have opened. The main market is now open all day and receives daily supplies of meat, fish, and produce from all over Thailand. Local shops are well stocked with the latest models of radios, refrigerators, motorcycles, and pickup trucks. There are two cinemas and an air-conditioned hotel and a commercial bank. The old wooden houses and shops are being torn down to make way for multistory concrete buildings. The new district hospital has opened to replace the old second-class health station, and new secondary schools have been built in the suburbs.

Death rates have continued to fall, as have birthrates in town. In the highlands, where use of birth control is relatively recent and still not completely accepted, fertility remains high and the population has grown rapidly. Resources are now perceptibly scarce in the highlands, as the amount of swidden land available per capita declined in the past decade by as much as 50 percent in some villages. Migration to the lowlands offsets some of the highland population growth and conversion of more areas to irrigated farming compensates for some of the rest. The limits of expansion of highland irrigated farming are being rapidly approached because of scarcity of water and suitable land.

Land in highland villages, formerly a communally held and community managed resource, is rapidly being converted to individual ownership. Wage-labor opportunities are expanding in rural areas, including the highlands, in association with development projects, which helps supply the increasing demand for cash to buy manufactured goods. Even heavy items (galvanized metal for roofing, diesel-powered rice mills) are now being introduced into the highland villages, and traditional crafts (which once occupied much of the time of women) are disappearing as people turn to purchased items. Schools are now open to the sixth grade in many highland villages, and primary education has become accessible to most children (although not all parents choose to send their children to school). Many of the highlanders have been converted to Christianity, and this, along with scarcity of resources and changing agricultural practices, is weakening the authority of traditional animistic village leaders. By the end of the 1970s space for building houses, formerly freely available, was dwindling, as were locally gathered building materials and the supply of domestic water.

In the lowlands the distinction between the urban area, the suburbs, and even some of the nearby rural communities (including the lowland rural Karen community tabulated here) is becoming blurred. Family planning has been accepted on a large scale by most ethnic groups in the lowlands (except for Moslem Indians and some of the newcomers from the highlands), death rates remain relatively low, despite a resurgence of malaria, but population growth appears to have been high because of immigration. Immigrants continue to come from the highlands, but people from other lowland areas of Thailand now contribute much more to the rapid population growth around the town than do highlanders. Housing shortages and the increase in land values in town became acute, and townspeople began to move to the "suburbs" where they could afford land or buy houses. As communities became less homogeneous, more Hmong and Karen and Lua' participated in ethnically mixed marriages.

I now turn to the ideals of household composition held by various ethnic groups in the study area and compare them with the actual distribution of types of household composition.

KAREN HOUSEHOLD COMPOSITION

The ideal Karen household consists of a married couple, their unmarried children, their youngest married daughter and her husband and children. An older married daughter moves to a new house (and a new household) when her younger sister marries. When a parent appears to have reached the age when death may occur, he or she will move into a separate small house (to avoid spirit contamination of the main house when he or she dies), but the move into this new structure does not establish a new household economic unit, for the elderly person continues to eat with his or her child's family. Married sons generally move to the village and house of their bride, but occasionally they are reluctant to establish coresidence and will often bring their wife back to live in their own village (though not in their parents' household), especially if the son's parents have farmland to which he has access. The household is the unit of agricultural production, and household labor is regularly supplemented by exchange labor from relatives and neighbors.

Tabulation of household composition from several different kinds of Karen communities in 1968 (table 12.2, column C) reveals an overall similarity in the frequency distribution of various types of households: in the highland communities a total of 65.8 percent of the households were composed of various kinds of nuclear families: 53.5 percent simple nuclear (Hu+Wi+Ch), 7.9 percent amalgamated nuclear (including children from other marriages of the parents), 4.4 percent incomplete (one parent) nuclear. All of the extended family households (totaling 21.1 percent) were extended along matrilineal lines. Tabulation of household types in a lowland rural Karen village surveyed in 1969 (table 12.2, column E) showed a similar pattern: 63.6 percent simple nuclear, 7.3 percent incomplete nuclear, total 70.9 percent nuclear; all of the extended family households, totaling 10.9 percent were extended along matrilineal lines. Composition of Karen households in a suburb surveyed in 1969 and 1970 (table 12.2, column E) followed almost the same pattern: 59.3 percent simple nuclear, 6.8 percent amalgamated nuclear, 8.5 percent incomplete nuclear, total nuclear 72.9 percent. Extended family households comprised 22 percent of the total, and 84.6 percent of these were matrilineally extended. In other words, extended family households did exist, along lines consistent with the Karen ideals.

TABLE 12.2
PERCENTAGE DISTRIBUTION OF MAJOR TYPES OF HOUSEHOLDS

	Highland				Lowland			
	Lua'		Karen		Rural Karen		Suburban Karen	
Household type	1967 A	1980 B	1968 C	1981 D	1969 E	1981 F	1969–70 G	1981 H
Single person	8.0	1.8	8.8	3.5	10.9	10.5		2.5
Single generational	6.0	3.6	4.4	2.1	7.3	10.5	5.1	1.2
Nuclear:								
Simple	32.0	52.7	53.5	66.9	63.6	56.1	59.3	53.1
Amalgamated	12.0	3.6	7.9	0.7		1.8	6.8	9.9
Incomplete	8.0	7.3	4.4	3.5	7.3	8.8	8.5	12.3
Total Nuclear	52.0	63.6	65.8	71.1	70.9	66.7	72.9	75.3
2-generation:								
Patri.	4.0			0.7			1.7	
Matri.	2.0	1.8	2.6	8.4	5.5	1.8	1.7	
Total 2-generation	6.0	1.8	2.6	9.2	5.5	1.8	3.4	

3-generation:								
Patri.	22.0	20.0		0.7		1.8	1.7	4.9
Matri.	6.0	7.3	18.4	13.4	5.5	8.8	16.9	12.3
Other								2.5
Total 3-generation	28.0	27.3	18.4	14.1	5.5	10.5	18.6	19.8
4-generation:								
Patri.		1.8						
Matri.								1.2
Total 4-generation		1.8						1.2
Total ext.:								
Patri.	26.8	21.8		1.4		1.8	3.4	4.9
Matri.	8.0	9.1	21.1	21.8	10.9	10.5	18.6	13.6
Other								2.5
Total extended	34.0	30.9	21.1	23.2	10.9	12.3	22.0	21.0
Households	50	55	114	142	55	57	59	81

[a]Inconsistencies in totals of cells as a result of rounding.

LUA' HOUSEHOLD COMPOSITION

The ideal Lua' household consists of a married couple, their unmarried children, their youngest married son and his wife and children. Older siblings are supposed to marry before their younger siblings. An older married son should preferably move to a new house and establish a new household before or shortly after his younger brother marries. Rules of patrilocal postmarital residence may be violated (and in fact frequently are) when the household has no sons. In this case, especially if the household has property, such as an irrigated field, a son-in-law may move in and will become incorporated into the household as a full member (which includes obligations to the patrilineal spirits of the household and other kin-defined duties). As in Karen highland villages, the household is the unit of agricultural production, and there is an elaborate system of kin-based labor exchanges.

Household composition in one Lua' village surveyed in 1968 (table 12.2, column A) revealed a total of 52 percent nuclear family households: 32 percent simple nuclear, 12 percent amalgamated nuclear, and 8 percent incomplete (one parent) nuclear. Extended family households comprised 34 percent of the total, and most of these (76.5 percent) were patrilineally extended.

CROSS-SECTIONAL COMPARISONS: KAREN VERSUS LUA'

The highland Karen and Lua' communities (see table 12.2, columns A and C) were very similar ecologically, economically, and demographically. All communities had an economy based on a mixture of subsistence swiddening and irrigated rice farming, supplemented with a small amount of wage labor. All had relatively young age distributions, representing the result of high birthrates and fairly high death rates. Assuming the data presented here are representative of Karen and Lua' communities in general, the comparison of data from Karen and Lua' highland villages shows a majority of the households are nuclear or incomplete nuclear, but the proportion of nuclear family households is much higher among Karen communities. Preference for lineality is indicated in the extended family households, as shown by the predominance of matrilineal extended family households in Karen communities and the contrasting prevalence of patrilineal extended family households in the Lua' community. These results suggest that the actual distribution of household types reflects cultural ideals.

HMONG HOUSEHOLD COMPOSITION

Unlike Karen and Lua' highlanders, who have traditionally been subsistence rice swiddeners living in settled communities, Hmong have a mixed subsistence (rice and maize) plus cash crop (opium) economy and live in villages that often split apart and move. Hmong household heads attempt to maximize the size of their households by extending them patrilineally through clan-exogamous marriage of their sons and through polygynous marriages. The ideal Hmong household consists of a man and his wife or wives, their unmarried children, their married sons and those sons' wives and children, and married grandsons and their wives and children. Unlike the Karen and Lua', Hmong household heads attempt to maintain the extended multigenerational family household with as many married sons as possible. Such households usually break up after the father (head of household) dies. Women who marry into the household are completely incorporated into the husband's clan, along with their children, after the high brideprice (now equivalent to several thousand U.S. dollars) has been completely paid. If a husband dies before the brideprice is paid, the widow and her children return to her father's (or brother's) household, for until the brideprice is paid the children remain members of their mother's clan.

The household is the unit of agricultural production, and in general household products are pooled and redistributed by the household head. This is one way he can accumulate the necessary funds for brideprice and thus enlarge the household size and labor force. This retention of control of household money by the household head is one of the chief reasons for household fission, particularly when brothers cannot agree on division of the household produce (Lee 1981).

Hmong households (table 12.3) in the one mixed Hmong-Karen community in our study population show the effectiveness of Hmong household heads in shaping their households to conform to their ideals. There were only 23.6 percent nuclear family households (17.7 percent simple nuclear, 5.9 percent incomplete nuclear). Extended family households comprised 76.5 percent of the total, and all of these were patrilineally extended; 29.4 percent of all households had four current marriages intact.

CROSS-SECTIONAL COMPARISON: HMONG VERSUS KAREN

The one mixed Hmong-Karen community (see table 12.3) has an economy based on subsistence swiddening of rice and cultivation of opium as

TABLE 12.3
SUMMARY OF PERCENTAGE DISTRIBUTION OF TYPES OF HOUSEHOLDS IN A MIXED HMONG AND KAREN VILLAGE, 1981

Household types	Hmong	Karen
Nongenerational		
Single person		
Multiple person, nonkin-based		
Single generation		
Married couple or siblings		
Two-generation, not extended		
One current marriage (simple nuclear, amalgamated nuclear)	17.7	50.0
Incomplete nuclear	5.9	16.7
Two-generation, extended	11.8	8.3
Three-generation, extended	64.7	10.0
Four-generation, extended		
Total nuclear + incomplete nuclear	23.6	66.7
Total extended	76.5	33.3
Number of households	17	12

a cash crop. Although it seems reasonable to assume that Hmong household heads attempt to maximize the size of their households in order to increase their labor supply for growing opium (thus increasing their disposable cash income), it is interesting to note that Karen households in this community (also growing rice plus opium) conform to the pattern already outlined for other Karen communities. Two-thirds of the households were nuclear (50 percent simple nuclear, 16.7 percent incomplete nuclear) while one-third were matrilineally extended. Thus, within the same agroecosystem ethnic ideals of household composition seem to predominate as the determinant of frequency distribution of household types rather than the apparent demands for labor in order to maximize household income.

A possible explanation for the difference between Karen and Hmong distributions of household types under the same agroeconomic setting is related to settlement and migration patterns and their implications for use of household labor. Karen highland villages tend to be permanent settlements; intervillage migration of individuals associated with marriage is common, but movements of entire households (in search of land) are much less common, and any moves tend to be over relatively short distances. Labor exchange between kin-related households is possible and common, even after migration. The Hmong population in Thailand has been expanding rapidly, and Hmong villages on the leading edge of expansion have often been temporary aggregations of households around a small land resource that may be quickly consumed in their form of swiddening. Fellow clan members may call on one another for support (usually on ritual occasions), but there is little exchange of labor between households. A much higher proportion of Hmong labor than Karen comes from within the large extended family household or is hired for payment in cash or kind. Karen household organization, combined with their pattern of limited migration, seems flexible enough to adapt to the labor requirements of cash cropping as well as to subsistence farming.

The strength of cultural ideals in determining frequency distribution of household types is also suggested in comparisons of Karen household composition in different community types over time.

CROSS-SECTIONAL COMPARISONS: KAREN VERSUS KAREN 1968–70

Karen communities surveyed in 1968–70 (see table 12.2, columns C, E, G) represented a range from fairly isolated highland villages to households in a mixed ethnic suburb on the edge of the district town. As already indicated, there seemed to be an overall pattern of similarity in the distribution of household types, emphasizing nuclear family households, with almost all of the extended family households being matrilineal. More detailed comparisons of the data from the three community types (highland, lowland rural, suburban) in the 1968–70 surveys indicates that:

1. Single person households were relatively common in the highlands (8.8 percent, all widowed) and in the rural lowland communities (10.9 percent, mostly widowed), compared with none in the suburb.
2. The highest proportion of single generational family households was found in the rural lowlands (7.3 percent), followed by the suburb (5.1 percent) and the highland villages (4.4 percent).
3. The total proportion of nuclear family households was slightly higher in the suburb (72.9 percent) and the rural lowland community (70.9 percent) than in the highland villages (65.8 percent).
4. Extended family households are more common in the suburb (22 percent) and the highlands (21.1 percent) than in the rural lowland community (12.3 percent).

5. The highest proportion of three-generational extended family households (18.6 percent) was found in the highlands; the lowest proportion of this type was in the rural lowland community.

The observed differences do not fall into a neat pattern along a folk-urban or other single dimensional continuum such as might be predicted on the basis of agricultural versus nonagricultural occupations. The high proportion of single person households is not the result of alternatives to family-based activities but rather the result of high mortality that leaves many widows and widowers. Extended family households do not vanish with the approach to urban living conditions—they are just as frequent in the suburb as in the more traditional, subsistence agricultural highland villages. As of the late 1960s Karen cultural patterns seemed to predominate over local socioeconomic conditions in determining the distribution of types of household composition.

CROSS-SECTIONAL COMPARISONS: KAREN VERSUS KAREN, 1981

When we examine the distribution of household types in the same communities surveyed in 1981 (table 12.2, columns D, F, H) we find that:

1. Single person households now occur in the suburb (2.5 percent) but less often than in both the highlands (3.5 percent) or in the rural lowland communities (10.5 percent), where these households consist entirely of widowed persons.
2. Single generational family households are also much more common in the rural lowland community (total 10.5 percent) than in the highlands (2.1 percent) or the suburb (1.2 percent).
3. The total proportion of nuclear family households is highest in the suburb (75.3 percent), intermediate in the highlands (71.1 percent), and lower in the rural lowland community (66.7 percent).
4. Extended family households (including two or more generations) are most common in the highlands (total 23.2 percent), intermediate but common in the suburb (21 percent), and least often found in the rural lowland community (12.3 percent).
5. The highest proportion of three- and four-generational extended family households is in the suburb (21 percent), followed by the highlands (14.1 percent) and the rural lowland community (10.5 percent).

Again, the observed distributions do not appear to follow a neat pattern. Differences between the communities are similar to those observed a decade earlier. Karen cultural patterns of household composition have persisted despite the recent socioeconomic changes.

LONGITUDINAL COMPARISONS: LUA' 1967 VERSUS 1980

The differences in distribution of household types between 1967 and 1980 in the highland Lua' village may be summarized as follows (see table 12.2, columns A, B):

1. Single person households have declined from a total of 8 percent in 1967 to 1.8 percent in 1980, associated with a lower frequency of widows in the population.
2. Single generational households have declined from 6 percent to 3.6 percent of the total as a result of the decline in number of childless couples (childless couples may be either newlyweds, married with no surviving children, married with only children who have moved out, or infertile).
3. The total proportion of nuclear family households has risen from 52 percent to 63.6 percent. This increase results entirely from the larger number of simple nuclear families in 1980, which in turn appears to be the result of a high rate of new household formation by children of the post-Second World War baby boom who were still unmarried when surveyed in the late 1960s.
4. The total proportion of extended family households has declined from 34 percent to 30.9 percent, probably as a result of the increased formation of new nuclear family households, referred to above.
5. Three- and four-generational extended family households form a slightly higher total proportion in 1980 (29.1 percent) than in 1967 (28 percent) and now comprise 94.1 percent of all extended family households, compared with 82.4 percent in 1967.
6. The proportion of matrilocal-based households appears to be slightly higher in 1980 (9.1 percent) than in 1967 (8 percent), perhaps because two Karen men have married into the village in that period.

The overall impression is that traditional Lua' household composition patterns have persisted. The changes observed seem to have resulted more from a decline in the death rates of both children and adults than from the systematic consequences of socioeconomic change in this highland village.

LONGITUDINAL COMPARISONS: KAREN 1968–70 VERSUS 1981

I will treat the comparisons of each community type separately and then consider the overall pattern of change during this period.

Highland Communities (Table 12.2, columns C, D)

1. The total proportion of single person households has declined from 8.8 percent in 1968 to 3.5 percent in 1981, because of a decline in widowed persons.
2. Single generational households have declined from 4.4 percent to 2.1 percent.
3. The total proportion of nuclear family households has increased from 65.8 percent to 71.1 percent, associated with a decline in the proportion of incomplete and amalgamated nuclear family households and an increase in the proportion of simple nuclear family households in 1981.
4. The total proportion of extended family households has increased from 21.1 percent in 1968 to 23.2 percent in 1981.
5. Three-generational extended family households are now a lower proportion of all extended family households (60.6 percent in 1981 versus 87.5 percent in 1968).
6. There is now a small number of patrilineal extended families (1.4 percent), whereas there were none in the highlands in 1968.

As with the Lua' highland village, these changes seem to be a result of a declining death rate and population increase. Lua' apparently accommodated to land shortages some time ago by allowing matrilocal marriages in a nominally patrilineal patrilocal system. Apparently the corresponding change (allowing patrilocal households in a nominally matrilocal system) is just now taking place among these highland Karen communities as land resources become perceptibly scarce.

Lowland Rural Community (Table 12.2, columns E, F)

1. The total proportion of single person households has remained about the same in 1981 (10.5 percent), compared with 1969 (10.9 percent).

2. The proportion of single generational households has increased slightly from 7.3 percent in 1969 to 10.5 percent in 1981.
3. The total proportion of nuclear family households has declined from 70.9 percent in 1969 to 66.7 percent in 1981.
4. The total proportion of extended family households has increased slightly from 10.9 percent in 1969 to 12.3 percent in 1981.
5. Three-generational extended family households are now a higher proportion of all extended family households (85.7 percent in 1981 versus 50 percent in 1969).
6. There is now one patrilocal household (1.8 percent), contrasted with none in 1969.
7. This community now contains two non-Karen households and five households in which one of the heads is non-Karen (10.9 percent of all households in this community), contrasted with none reported in 1969. (Note: percentages reported in this summary are based on Karen households only.)

There seems to have been no consistent pattern of change of household composition in this community over the past decade. The traditional Karen pattern of household composition seems to have remained, despite the community's becoming almost a suburb of the rapidly expanding town.

Karen in a Suburb (Table 12.2, columns G, H)

1. The number of single person households has increased from none in 1969–70 to two in 1981 (2.4 percent).
2. The proportion of single generational households (married couples without children in the household) has declined from 5.1 percent to 1.2 percent.
3. The total proportion of nuclear family households has increased from 72.9 to 75.3 percent while an increase in amalgamated nuclear family households and of incomplete nuclear families (mostly headed by women) has compensated for a decrease in the proportion of simple nuclear family households.
4. The total proportion of extended family households has declined slightly from 22 percent in 1969–70 to 21 percent in 1981.
5. Three- and four-generational extended families now comprise all of the extended family households, compared with 84.6 percent of this type of household in 1968–69.
6. The proportion of patrilocal households has increased slightly, from two households (3.4 percent) in 1969–70 to four households (4.9 percent) in 1981.

7. There is considerably more intermarriage of Karen and non-Karen in this community now. (Note: percentages reported in this summary are based on Karen-headed households only.)

Again there seems no strong or consistent pattern of change in pattern of household composition over the past decade, even in this community that has been exposed to rapid socioeconomic change.

LONGITUDINAL COMPARISONS: NORTHERN THAI IN A SUBURB, 1969–70 VERSUS 1981

Data from another rapidly growing ethnically mixed suburb (table 12.4) show that the ethnic composition has shifted from a predominance of Lua' in 1969–70 to a plurality of northern Thai and mixed Thai households in 1981. Migration of lowlanders from other parts of Thailand

TABLE 12.4
CHANGE IN ETHNICITY OF HOUSEHOLDS IN ONE SUBURBAN COMMUNITY, 1969–1981

Ethnicity of households	Proportion of community 1969–70 (%)	Proportion of community 1981 (%)	Change in % of community	Population increase 1969–70 to 1981 (%)
Northern Thai	23.2	36.0	+12.8	264
Central Thai	0.5	2.9	+2.4	1200
Shan	0.5	0.5	0.0	100
Northeastern Thai	0.0	0.2	+0.2	–
Mixed Thai	11.6	16.4	+4.8	232
Lua'	55.3	34.4	–20.9	46
Mixed, Lua' head	2.1	2.5	+0.4	175
Skaw Karen	2.6	2.0	–0.6	80
Po Karen	0.0	2.0	+2.0	–
Mixed, Karen head	0.5	1.6	+1.1	600
Other, other mixed	3.7	1.6	–2.1	0
Number of households	190	445		134

has clearly played a major role in the growth of this suburb in the past decade. Interethnic marriage, especially mixed marriage in which the household head is Thai, is apparently increasing at a rate higher than the overall growth in number of households.

Changes in distribution of types of household composition among northern Thai households in this suburb between 1969–70 and 1981 (table 12.5) are as follows:

1. The total proportion of single person households has increased from none in 1969–70 to 6.9 percent of all households in 1981 (most of these are females).
2. The proportion of nonkin-based households has risen from 2.3 percent (all of which were composed of males) to 18.7 percent (including one all-female household).
3. The proportion of single generation households has declined from a total of 4.5 percent to 2.5 percent; in contrast to 1969–70 there were no childless couples as independent households in 1981.

TABLE 12.5
SUMMARY OF PERCENTAGE DISTRIBUTION OF TYPES OF HOUSEHOLDS IN A MIXED ETHNIC SUBURB

	N. Thai		Mixed, Thai head	
Household type	1969–70	1981	1969–70	1981
Nongenerational				
Single person		6.9	N/A	N/A
Multiple person, nonkin-based	2.3	18.7		17.8
Single generation				
Married couple, siblings	4.5	2.5		6.8
Two-generation, not extended				
One current marriage (simple nuclear, amalgamated nuclear)	36.6	42.6	81.8	57.6
Incomplete nuclear	11.4	3.8	N/A	N/A
Two-generation, extended	2.3	2.4		2.7
Three-generation, extended	36.3	10.7	18.1	15.1
Four-generation, extended	4.6			
Total nuclear + incomplete nuclear	48.0	46.4	81.8	57.6
Total extended	43.2	12.1	18.1	17.8
Number of households	44	160	22	73

4. The total proportion of nuclear households declined from 50 percent to 42.6 percent, and most of the decline results from the absence of incomplete nuclear households in 1981.
5. The total proportion of extended family households has declined radically from 43.2 percent in 1969–70 to 13.1 percent in 1981, in contrast to what has been found in other communities.
6. The matrilineal bias in extended family households is clearly evident (74 percent of the extended households were matrilineally extended in 1969–70, 72 percent in 1981).

These results suggest the changing character of the northern Thai population in what has now become in part a "bedroom suburb" of wage workers. In the past decade a substantial number of unmarried people, and probably young married couples without children, have moved into what had been a more stable, largely agricultural community characterized by a large proportion of extended family households. What seems to be happening is not "nuclearization of the family household" but individualization associated with migration. Because most of the northern Thai migration has been recent it is too soon to tell if these migrants will settle permanently and if they will eventually create extended family households of their own.

Lua' in the Suburb, 1969–70 versus 1981 (Table 12.6)

1. The total proportion of single person households among Lua' in this community has declined from 9.6 percent to 5.3 percent, with widowed females still constituting the bulk of such households.
2. There were no nonkin-based Lua' households in 1969–70 or in 1981.
3. Single generation households have declined from a total of 5.8 percent to 4.7 percent.
4. The total proportion of nuclear family households has declined from 64.1 percent in 1969–70 to 59.7 percent in 1981; this decline results entirely from a lower proportion of incomplete nuclear family households in 1981.
5. The total proportion of extended family households has increased from 21.2 percent in 1969–70 to 30.9 percent in 1981, associated with a marked increase in matrilineally extended family households that now exceed the number of the traditionally favored patrilineally extended ones.

TABLE 12.6
SUMMARY OF PERCENTAGE DISTRIBUTION OF TYPES OF HOUSEHOLDS IN A LUA' HIGHLAND VILLAGE AND IN A MIXED ETHNIC SUBURB, LATE 1960S AND 1981

	Highland[a]		Suburb[b]	
Household type	1967	1980	1969–70	1981
Nongenerational				
Single person Multiple person, nonkin-based	8.0	1.8	9.6	5.3
Single generation				
Married couple, siblings	6.0	3.6	5.8	4.7
Two-generation, not extended				
One current marriage (simple nuclear, amalgamated nuclear)	44.0	56.3	48.8	51.1
Two-generation, extended	6.0	1.8	1.0	3.9
Three-generation, extended	28.0	27.3	20.2	
Four-generation, extended		1.8		
Total nuclear + incomplete nuclear	52.0	63.6	64.1	59.0
Total extended	34.0	30.9	21.2	27.0
Number of households	50	55	105	153

[a]Note: This is the same Lua' highland village tabulated in table 12.1.
[b]Note: These households live in the same Mixed Ethnic suburb tabulated in table 12.5.

There is no evidence of individualization or nuclearization among these Lua' households. The observed changes seem to be the result of the combination of several factors. The pattern of migration from the highlands appears to be changing from one emphasizing incomplete family units (for example, widows and orphans) unable to make a living in the highlands because of traditional patterns of division of labor to one in which complete family households move because of land shortages or other widespread conditions (such as insurgency) in the highlands. Once in the lowlands the norm of the extended family household is maintained (or renewed), but the traditional patrilineality may be abandoned because it is no longer relevant for ritual or for access to swidden land and because of ethnic intermarriage. The classification of ethnicity used here is based on ethnicity of household head and spouse (if any), which obscures the fact that in many of the matrilineally extended Lua' family households a northern Thai immigrant male has married into the family.

Mixed Ethnic Households with Thai Head, 1969–70 versus 1981 (Table 12.5)

1. There are (by definition) no single person households.
2. The proportion of nonkin-based households (consisting largely of employees of a lumber company) has increased from 0 percent to 17.8 percent.
3. The proportion of single generation childless married couples, including both newlyweds and couples all of whose children have died or moved out, has increased from 0 percent to 6.8 percent.
4. The total proportion of nuclear family households has declined from 81.8 percent to 57.6 percent, because of a decline in simple nuclear family households (Hu+Wi+Ch), from 68.2 percent to 45.2 percent of all nuclear family households.
5. Extended family households that constituted 18.1 percent in 1969–70 made up 17.8 percent of all households in 1981.

Frequency distribution of the mixed ethnic households is distorted by the large proportion of nonkin-based households. If these are excluded from the tabulation, the proportion of extended family households actually increased over the past decade. The nonkin-based households consist of individuals (such as government workers sharing government housing, lumber company employees rooming together) living together because of the nature of their jobs and living apart from their normal family-based households. Most of these people are male, and many are married. This is an important new phenomenon associated with economic development, but it is still too soon to know the long-term consequences. The complement of these men is women who report themselves to be married but whose husbands are absent from the household. Such women are found in several of the communities not yet tabulated, where in general they appear to be members of extended family households.

The distribution of household composition types in this suburban community clearly cannot be understood apart from the recent patterns of immigration into the community. Although it might appear from the overall figures that "individualization" is occurring, this has happened only among northern Thai and mixed ethnic households and may be associated with recent migration rather than with modernization in the form of a shift from agriculture to wage work.

CONCLUSION

Clear differences in frequency distributions of types of household composition between Lua' and Karen highland villages are consistent with the cultural ideals of the two groups and have persisted over the past decade despite a series of similar changes and pressures to which these villages have been exposed. Cultural differences between Hmong and Karen household composition are also very clear within the same village, despite the similar economic bases of the Hmong and Karen households. Socioeconomic changes over the past decade appear to have had a relatively minor impact on Karen or Lua' household composition in communities representing a range of socioeconomic conditions. There seems to be a slight tendency for unilinear systems to accept modification of their rules to accommodate to economic conditions and thus become at least slightly ambilineal (or ambilocal).

The data presented here do not support the idea that early stages of modernization or increasing participation in the wage labor market leads to nuclearization of the household. In fact, the extended family households are as alive and well in the most urbanized of the Karen and Lua' communities as in the most traditional. For the most part, changes in household composition (such as decline in single person households and decline in the proportion of amalgamated nuclear family households) in both the Lua' highland and suburban communities and in the Karen highland, lowland rural, and suburban communities seem more likely to have been a result of demographic changes (especially decline in the death rate) than a consequence of socioeconomic changes (such as increase in nonagricultural occupations or increase in commercialization of all relationships). Despite the socioeconomic changes, extended family households seem to be persisting in both Lua' and Karen communities, even in those communities that are quite urbanized and in which the majority of the adults are wage workers, not subsistence farmers.

Analysis of distribution of household types within the mixed Karen and Hmong highland village and in mixed ethnic suburban communities indicates the importance of disaggregating data on household composition by ethnicity: significant differences would have been obscured had this not been done. Northern Thai and other Thai groups in suburban communities show more changes (or differences) in household structure than do Lua' and Karen. A substantial proportion of married people live apart from their spouse as a result of job transfers (nonlocalized marriages), and there is much greater variability in household composition than is shown among either Lua' or the Karen in communities analyzed so far. The differences may be associated with the traditional flexibility of Thai family structure (see Foster, this volume) as well as with modernization, but in part they are clearly associated with more recent immigration of the Thai groups into these communities. Wage-working Karen and Lua' in these communities have jobs near their homes.

One difficulty in basing a study of change in household form and function on frequency distributions of household forms is that a similar form may be produced by different means and may encompass different functions while similar functions may be accomplished by different household forms. For example, single person households may be young, unmarried individuals, divorcees without children, or widows; a married couple without coresident children may be newlyweds, parents all of whose children have died or moved out, or an infertile couple; pooling of labor may be confined to the household, or may involve an interhousehold exchange system; a multigenerational extended family household may be a cooperating economic unit or may represent two or more largely independent subunits living together because of a housing shortage; and physically distinct entities may be an economically cooperating unit (see Segalen, this volume).

I have tried to sort out some of these possibilities by looking at age and marital status of household members, but a complete understanding of changing form and function requires more data on details of function (such as pooling and division of resources within the household) and on the individual histories (see Carter, this volume) of household formation, growth, and fission (for example, how was the decision made regarding postmarital residence or the establishment of an independent household).

Longitudinal data presented in this paper suggest that the dynamics of household form and function are complex and involve many variables in addition to the predominant form of local economy. In some circumstances ideals of household composition may persist as powerful forces in determining the frequency distribution of household types irrespective of major changes in the predominant demographic or economic conditions external to the household. Local historical circumstances that influence household form temporarily (local epidemics resulting in numerous incomplete households or patterns of individual and household migration) may be overcome within a single generation, and extended family households may reassert themselves after more normal conditions of mortality and residential stability have returned.

NOTES

1. This paper is based on data collected with support from the National Science Foundation (current grants BNS 7914093 and BNS 8040684). Fieldwork was conducted under the sponsorship of the National Research Council of Thailand.

REFERENCES

Coale, Ansley J., et al.
1965 Aspects of the Analysis of Family Structure. Princeton: Princeton University Press.

Geddes, William Robert
1976 Migrants of the Mountains: The Cultural Ecology of the Blue Miao (Hmong Njua) of Thailand. Oxford: Clarendon Press.

Kunstadter, Peter
1966 Residential and Social Organization of the Lawa of Northern Thailand. Southwestern Journal of Anthropology 22 (1):61–84.
1972 Demography, Ecology, Social Structure, and Settlement Patterns. *In* The Structure of Human Populations, ed. G. A. Harrison and A. J. Boyce, pp. 313–51. Oxford: Clarendon Press.
1978 Subsistence Agricultural Economies of Lua' and Karen Hill Farmers, Mae Sariang District, Northwestern Thailand. *In* Farmers in the Forest, ed. P. Kunstadter, E. C. Chapman, and S. Sabhasri, pp. 74–133. Honolulu: University Press of Hawaii.
1979 Ethnic Group, Category, and Identity: Karen in Northern Thailand. *In* Ethnic Adaptation and Identity: The Karen on the Thai Frontier with Burma, ed. C. F. Keyes, pp. 119–63. Philadelphia: Institute for the Study of Human Issues.
1980

Lee, Gary
1981 Ph.D Dissertation. University of Sydney, N.S.W., Australia.

13

Explicating Residence: A Cultural Analysis of Changing Households among Japanese-Americans

Sylvia Junko Yanagisako

The point of this paper is that households must be explicated as well as enumerated. I mean by this that we cannot understand the changing composition of households or the changing activities of household members without treating households as units of cultural meaning—and as particular ones at that. I do not mean that households (or, rather, the variety of social forms glossed by that term) cannot be compared across cultures, but before we attempt such comparisons we must recognize these units for what they are. Such recognition, I hope to show here, requires a cultural analysis of the system of symbols and meanings by which people construe these units and the configuration of activities, emotions, and dilemmas they attach to them. Because households—like all social facts—are shaped by symbolic processes, a symbolic analysis must be undertaken not merely as a colorful embellishment to a functionalist theory of changing household form and function but as a central component in analysis of that change.

The changes in urban Japanese-American households described in this paper have commonly called forth a functionalist explanation in which domestic groups "adapt" by adjusting form and function to exogenous (usually economic or ecological) factors. In rushing hastily to a functional analysis of households, however, we risk replicating what we have come to recognize as the limitations of treating the family as a functional unit (Yanagisako 1979). Having conceded that the family is more usefully conceived as a cultural construct—that is, as a dense configuration of meanings with normative implications—rather than as a discrete social entity linked invariably with a distinctive function or set of functions, the temptation is to console ourselves by salvaging a functionalist theory of the household. Accordingly, we expect in any society to be able to identify households that are empirically isolable, social units performing empirically observable functions. Yet systematic investigations such as have been undertaken by several authors in this volume (Laslett, Linares, Segalen) demonstrate that households are no different from families with regard to their discreteness and functions; neither their boundaries nor their functions are unequivocably apparent.

A functionalist entrenchment around the household has at the minimum three unfortunate consequences. First, as Wilk and Netting (this volume) note, it impedes recognition of the significant variations in the productive, distributive, and reproductive activities of coresidential units in any given population. Second, as Segalen's research (this volume) on a Breton farming community demonstrates, it may lead us to attribute an illusory "independence" to coresidential groups when in fact activities and functions crosscut them. Finally, it can trick us into reifying households in such a way that we come to misconstrue them as social actors endowed with human consciousness. As a result, we have households that not only have goals but that fashion strategies, adapt to the vicissitudes of a transforming modern world, and even think of themselves as households. The ambiguous epistemological status of the household betrayed by our less than rigorous language reveals the extent to which we have slipped dangerously into anthropomorphizing what is more productively construed as a cultural construct. In the following analysis of changing Japanese-American households, I argue that the imputation of a unified household strategy, rooted as it is in the assumption that those who live together share a collective motive and will, obscures the social process through which individuals negotiate the relations that give form to households despite different and sometimes conflicting goals, strategies, and notions about what it means to "live together."

I do not deny that there are empirically observable sets of people living together in any society who participate in empirically observable activities, but rather I claim that labeling such sets of people *households* does not describe accurately the activities they share or the structure of their relations (Yanagisako 1979; Sanjek 1982). Neither do native terms that we roughly translate as household describe the social organization of these units. For like *family* and *household* such terms refer to cultural maps that serve as normative guides for social action and its interpretation rather than as analytic models.

Once we recognize the household as a cultural construct that enables the natives to make common sense of the diverse range of activities in which overlapping groups of people engage, we must ask how that recognition can help us to make analytical sense of that complexity. The explication of a cultural construct—no matter how rich and elegant—is not an anthropological end in itself but an integral step toward the understanding of patterns of social action. Furthermore, despite the concession by those such as Hammel (this volume), whose efforts have been directed toward discovering the "noncultural" determinants of household form, that "an unambiguous and strictly followed cultural rule" has a greater effect on the proportion of household types than do differences in demographic rates, most of us concede that such rules are rare. The same can be said of cultural constructs, which are frequently ambiguous, rarely generate clear-cut directives for action, and are inaccurate predictors of the actions of individuals or groups.

Yet the normative ambiguity of cultural constructs should not prompt us to pursue a research strategy aimed at discovering the ways people discard cultural maps in order to contend with the "objective" conditions of their lives through means of a practical consciousness. For such a strategy unproductively dichotomizes meaning and action. Instead, that normative ambiguity should lead us to recognize that the meanings people attach to living together in households are often more complex, dynamic, and inconsistent than we have tended to think and that not all the members of a society or, for that matter, a single household necessarily share the same meanings. Making analytic sense of this insight into the symbolic character of the household hence requires that we unpack the household as a cultural construct just as we have done in the case of the family (Collier et al. 1982; Löfgren, this volume; Rapp 1978; Schneider 1980) to explicate the symbols and meanings of which it is constituted. In other words, we must subject cultural constructs and sentiments about households to as much scrutiny as we have the observable forms of households.

CHANGING HOUSEHOLDS: A JAPANESE-AMERICAN CASE

Japanese-Americans in Seattle, Washington, like other Japanese-Americans in West Coast urban communities, offer a case of kinship change which is a somewhat unique variation of the much discussed separation of production from the household. The Seattle Japanese-

American community originated in the 1890s with the immigration of young and for the most part unmarried men from farming families or small-town entrepreneurial families in the southern prefectures of Japan. During the initial "frontier period" (1890–1910) of the community these men worked primarily as wage laborers.

Between 1910 and 1920, as a consequence of the Gentlemen's Agreement (1908) between the United States and Japan, the number of first-generation males actually decreased because of curtailed immigration and the return of many immigrants to Japan. The arrival of wives and brides, however, more than compensated for the decrease in the male population, and a period of marriage and family building began, accompanied by a growth in the community's economic, religious, and social institutions. The economic boom accompanying the United States' entry into World War I brought about an expansion of Japanese businesses and services catering to white workers and Japanese farmers in the surrounding rural areas. But the expansion of the community was short-lived. The growing anti-Japanese sentiment that had already led to the passage of discriminatory laws in California brought about similar restrictions in Washington. In 1921 the state of Washington passed an Anti-Alien Land Law denying foreign-born Japanese the right to lease or own land. A year later, in *Takao Ozawa* v. *United States*, the U.S. Supreme Court upheld the ineligibility of Japanese immigrants for citizenship through naturalization. Two years later the Immigration Act of 1924 cut off further immigration from Japan and further crippled the community's economy. After 1924 the growth of the Seattle Japanese population was entirely a result of births of the second generation.[1]

Just prior to the outbreak of World War II the Japanese in the Seattle community were mostly self-employed in small businesses, whereas in 1932 Miyamoto (1939:71) classified 74 percent of the Japanese in Seattle under "trades" or "domestic and personal services." The Japanese small businesses were restricted to a narrow range of service-oriented enterprises, including hotels, groceries, grocery stands, produce houses, restaurants, greenhouses, gardening services, barber shops, laundries, and peddling routes. A comparatively small percentage (19 percent) of Japanese remained in wage-earning, working-class occupations.

The events that followed the outbreak of World War II destroyed the entrepreneurial character of the community. The imprisonment of the entire Japanese population on the West Coast of the United States—immigrant Japanese citizens and second-generation U.S. citizens alike—resulted in the forced sale or abandonment of businesses and the liquidation of assets. From extensive studies of "relocation camps"[2] and follow-up studies of the resettlement[3] that began with the closing of the camps in

1945, we know of the disruption of family relations, the decline in the first generation's political and parental control, and the economic and social hardships Japanese-Americans faced in attempting to rebuild their communities. We know too that the majority of the Japanese-Americans who returned to Seattle after the war did not resurrect their businesses but instead moved into wage and salaried employment (Miyamoto and O'Brien 1947).

By the end of the war the majority of first-generation men were over 55 years old; the majority of first-generation women were in their late forties and early fifties. Many couples who had small family businesses before the war were forced back into the unskilled, low-paying jobs in which they had begun their occupational histories. Less than a third of the men in my first-generation marriage sample (N=24 couples) who had been self-employed entrepreneurs at the outbreak of the war were in the same line of business in 1946. The others were either unemployed or had taken wage-earning jobs as janitors, kitchen helpers, or handymen. The women who had worked in family businesses before the war experienced the same shift to wage work. Again, less than a third of the women in my marriage sample who had been self-employed were occupied in the same business in 1946. Almost as many were unemployed or housewives. But the largest number (almost half) were found in wage work. Women who had worked with husbands to operate hotels, grocery stores, and laundries became domestic servants, chambermaids, seamstresses in garment factories, and cannery workers.

After the war the children of the first generation, who by the 1960s had surpassed whites in median school years completed, moved into predominantly white-collar managerial and professional occupations. Second-generation Japanese-American men in Seattle today exhibit higher percentages of college graduates, white-collar employment, and professional occupations than white men in Seattle. Less than 29 percent of Japanese-American men are self-employed businessmen.

The political history that shaped the character of Japanese immigration to the United States had an effect on the age structure of the Japanese-American population which persists to the present. It created relatively discrete, nonoverlapping generations (Thomas 1950). The concentration of the marriages of the first generation during the period from 1907 to 1924 in turn concentrated the births of the second generation and created a distinct bimodality in the age structure of the pre-World War II population. Second-generation marriages were similarly concentrated and so produced a third generation, the vast majority of whom were under 30 in 1970. Japanese-Americans are consequently one of those rare populations in which historical events have rendered kinship-defined generations simultaneously temporally defined birth cohorts. The discreteness of the three generations continues to be recognized by Japanese-Americans and is reflected in their usage of distinct terms (Issei, Nisei, and Sansei) for each generation.

Households in Japan

The first generation (Issei) of Japanese-Americans came from the villages and small towns of a rapidly industrializing Japan in which the household was the primary kinship unit. From Issei accounts of the rules and practices of household succession, inheritance, and postmarital residence in their communities, it appears that these immigrants' households of orientation were stages in the developmental cycle of stem family households. The perpetuation of the household was ideally achieved through primogenitural succession and inheritance. The eldest son of the head of the household succeeded to the headship, managed the household's productive enterprise, inherited the bulk of its property, and worshipped its ancestors. If the eldest son died, was deemed incompetent, or chose to leave the household in favor of some other pursuit, a younger son would replace him. Where there were no sons, the head would adopt a son or son-in-law (*yōshi*) who acquired the head's surname and the same jural status as a biological successor.

The system of primogeniture generated two distinct kinds of marriages and households: those that involved a successor and those that did not. The marriage of a successor entailed the movement of a woman (or a man if it was a *yōshi* marriage) from one household to another and the simultaneous transfer of rights over her procreative and productive capacities. The bride in a successor marriage moved into a household consisting of her husband, his parents, and his unmarried siblings. The siblings of the successor would subsequently marry and leave the household, and as the parents grew older the successor and his bride would succeed to the offices of househead and house mistress. In a nonsuccessor marriage the bride and groom established their own conjugal family household. If such a nonsuccessor household were endowed with sufficient landholdings or other resources to ensure its economic viability in the community, it might eventually evolve into a stem family household on the marriage of its successor. Nonsuccessor sons who lacked such endowments were forced to marry uxorilocally as *yōshi* or to emigrate to other rural areas where land might be obtained or to towns and cities where they sought employment or engaged in trade. If their fortunes allowed it, these migrating sons would eventually marry and establish new households that were economically and jurally independent from their natal households.

Forty percent of the Issei in my marriage sample grew up in stem family households in Japan. In all these cases the Issei's fathers were the successors to the household, whether through birth or adoption. The other 60 percent of the Issei were raised in conjugal family households or incomplete conjugal family households if the father was deceased or had emigrated to the United States.

Households in Seattle before World War II

Although approximately half the Japanese men who immigrated to the United States were successor sons, the great majority of Issei couples lived in conjugal family households before the war. Only 4 of the 24 couples in my Issei marriage sample lived with either spouse's parents in Seattle. The reason for this low incidence of stem family households is simple: the households to which the Issei expected to succeed were located in Japan. So were the parents with whom the couple expected eventually to reside.

In spite of the vast geographical distance separating Issei couples from these households in Japan, at the time they married almost all Issei successors planned to return to take their place as the next household head. Indeed, their reasons for emigrating were inextricably linked with their goal of succession. Issei successors worked overseas to amass savings that would allow them to expand the household's property or business enterprise. Without these savings their parental households had insufficient resources to sustain another generation. In some cases the remittances sent by the Issei were necessary to support parents and younger siblings in Japan. Hence, return was not economically feasible until sufficient wealth had been accumulated for the expansion of landholdings, the capitalization of a business venture, or a comfortable retirement.

For a great many Issei successors—as well as for the nonsuccessors who also had hopes of accumulating savings that would allow them to resettle in their natal communities—that return never came. Yet before World War II successors and nonsuccessors alike attempted to keep open their options for return to their natal communities. Not only did they send remittances, and sometimes children, to buttress their claims to households in Japan but they exhibited the signs of a generation committed to reproducing stem families that could be transplanted in Japan.

Among the actions that spoke of the Issei commitment to the stem family was their differential treatment of eldest sons and junior sons, including the privileges they afforded the eldest son and the authority he was granted over his sisters and younger brothers. Yet more convincing evidence lies in Issei plans for their children's future occupations. All children were expected to contribute to the household, whether through work in the family business and home or through the wages they earned. But eldest sons were more often groomed to take over the family business. In some cases only the eldest son worked in the family business while other sons and daughters were encouraged to find work elsewhere. In other cases all children worked in the family business, but only eldest sons were taught about its finances and management. Issei who had hopes of expanding family businesses or of diversifying into new enterprises sometimes went beyond mere on-the-job training and sent first sons to receive formal training in business, accounting, and related fields.

The Issei arrangements of their children's marriages before World War II also evince parental expectations of their future relationship with eldest sons and wives. The brides the Issei desired most for their eldest sons had the personal attributes of a *yome* (young bride) who could be incorporated into their household. Kibei women (Nisei raised in Japan) were particularly popular with Issei parents who wanted a dutiful, "Japanese" bride uncontaminated by "American" ideas. Given their plans to return to their home communities in Japan, the Issei were at the same time interested in arranging marriages that created or reinforced kinship (*shinrui*) ties with households in these localities. Not all prewar Nisei marriages were arranged by the Issei. But even when the Nisei had initiated the marriage or chosen the spouse, their parents soon became active participants in the marriage arrangements. Here again the actions of the Issei—including the payment of wedding costs for eldest sons (which ran counter to the American norm of the bride's parents' responsibility for wedding costs)—suggest a parental strategy for establishing future claims on the couple. Prewar marriages of eldest sons therefore ranged from those whose arrangements seemed to proclaim unequivocally that this was a successor marriage intended to perpetuate the household to those whose arrangements left ambiguous the common or divergent expectations of parents and children.

Households in Seattle after World War II

The coincidence of the incarceration and its aftermath with the period in which most Nisei were marrying exacerbated the ambiguities in their relationships with their parents and raised new questions during a critical phase in the development of filial relationships. The instability of filial relations during and after the war is starkly displayed in the residential histories of Nisei married couples. Figure 13.1 maps the changes from 1940 to 1970 in the percentage of Nisei couples in my marriage sample (N=48) living in stem family households.

In 1940 half of the eight Nisei couples in my sample who had already married were living in stem family households. The lower incidence (30 percent) of such households during the war was undoubtedly affected by the housing policies of the War Relocation Authority, which assigned each newly married couple a separate room in the camp barracks. By 1946, immediately after the closing of the camps, the percentage of Nisei couples living with parents had risen to a peak of 65 percent. This unusually high rate of stem family households was stimulated by the severe housing shortage and high rates of unemployment in the initial resettlement years. The decline in stem family households to just under 20 percent of married couples by 1950 coincided with a period of increasing occupational mobility and job security. When money and housing were less scarce, the proportion of Nisei living with parents decreased. This decline was not caused by the death of the Issei but to the movement of either the Issei or Nisei to a separate residence. After 1960 the percent-

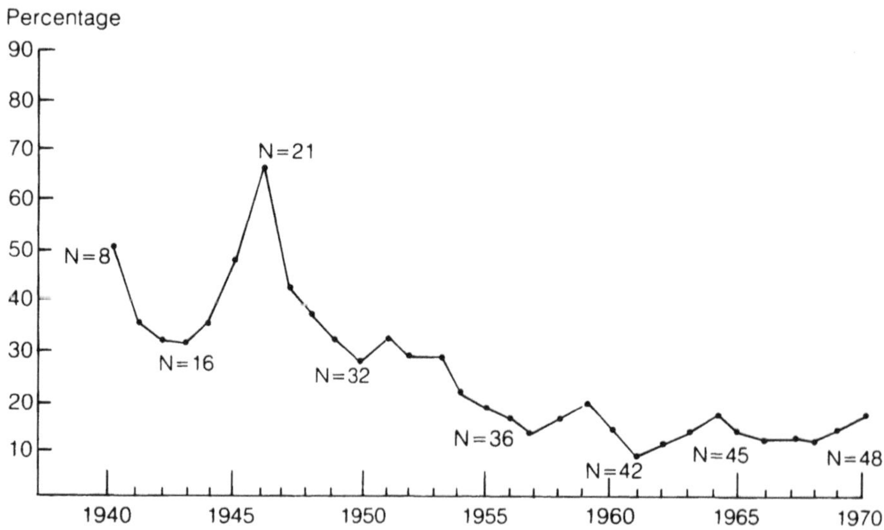

Fig. 13.1
Percentage of Nisei Married Couples Living in Stem Family Households, 1940–70

age of Nisei couples living with parents stabilized at a low level between 10 and 18 percent.

When we examine the postmarital residence patterns of different birth-order Nisei sons, the Issei prewar expectations appear at first glance to have been somewhat more fulfilled than indicated above. Table 13.1 shows that two-thirds of Nisei first sons and their wives lived virilocally for some period of time during the first ten years of marriage. Later birth-order sons and their wives, in contrast, did so in less than a third of my cases. The mean number of years of virilocal residence, moreover, was greater for first sons than for other sons.

But while first sons and their wives were more likely to reside virilocally for some period of time, not all of them did. More important, most of them did not live virilocally exclusively during the first ten years of marriage. Indeed, there were considerable shifts in the composition of households in which Nisei couples lived, whether the husband was a first or junior son. These shifts are apparent in table 13.2, which displays the combinations of residence types experienced by Nisei couples during their first ten years of marriage.

Slightly more than a fifth (22 percent) of first sons lived virilocally for their entire first ten years of marriage. A similar percentage (28 percent) lived neolocally for those years. But more frequent (44 percent) among first sons was some *combination* of two or more residence types. Junior sons exhibit a similar frequency (48 percent) of some combination of two or more residence types. They differ from first sons in that they were just as likely to live uxorilocally and neolocally as they were to live virilocally

TABLE 13.1
Frequency of Virilocal Residence of Nisei Couples by Husband's Birth Order During First Ten Years of Marriage

	First sons		Junior sons		
	N	%	N	%	All sons
Virilocal residence for at least one year	12	67	8	28	20
No virilocal residence	6	33	21	72	27
Total	18	100	29	100	47

Mean number of years of virilocal residence:
First sons: 6.8 years
Junior sons: 4.2 years

TABLE 13.2
COMBINED TYPES OF POSTMARITAL RESIDENCE OF NISEI COUPLES BY HUSBAND'S BIRTH ORDER DURING FIRST TEN YEARS OF MARRIAGE

	First sons		Junior sons	
	N	%	N	%
Virilocal only	4	22	0	0
Uxorilocal only	1	6	2	7
Neolocal only	5	28	13	45
Two or more residence types	(8)	(44)	(14)	(48)
Virilocal and neolocal	5	28	6	21
Uxorilocal and neolocal	0	0	6	21
Virilocal, uxorilocal, and neolocal	3	16	2	7
Total	18	100	29	100

and neolocally, while first sons and their wives tended toward a combination of virilocal and neolocal residence. Among *both* first sons and junior sons, however, almost half changed residence type at least once during the first ten years of marriage.

Changing Households and Changing Filial Relations

By 1960 both the genealogical and social relationships in stem family households in the community had altered. Couples who had just married, if they were not residing neolocally, were more likely to be living with the elderly parent or parents of the wife.[4] When we contrast the postwar decline in occupational and economic position of the Issei with concurrent social mobility of the Nisei, it is obvious that the relations of dependency that existed in prewar stem family households no longer characterized those of the 1960s. Nisei couples living in stem family households were not the junior, subordinate members of the husband's parents' household but more often the dominant couple in a household they were willing to allow the wife's parents to join. In between these two periods Nisei couples had passed through a period of shifting, short-term coresidence with either or both sets of parents.

Residence patterns alone do not tell us about the social organization of residence units or about their ties with other units. Indeed, the most notable feature of households after the war is that they were accompanied by a wide range of economic and social arrangements. Although some Nisei couples lived and worked with the husbands' parents in a family enterprise, most Issei and Nisei members of stem family households worked in separate wage-earning and salaried jobs. And while they shared in the cost and preparation of meals, they did not always pool their earnings and savings in a common fund. Instead, in many households each couple paid for a portion of the household's operating expenses while keeping the rest of their earnings in separate bank accounts. At the time of residential separation each couple left with its own conjugal fund intact.

Just as residential units were not necessarily productive units, so productive units were not necessarily residential units. Some Nisei couples worked with the husband's parents in a family business but resided neolocally. In these cases the husband's father usually controlled the finances of this residentially dispersed productive unit, allocating a portion of the earnings to his son. Eventually the son gained control of the business and its earnings. By the time his parents retired completely from working, the son and his father would have negotiated an agreement as to the parents' continuing share in the business earnings. What had been a single family unit of production (albeit residentially separate) eventually evolved into a corporation structured by specific (if not legally binding) contractual agreements.

Finally, after the war Nisei couples had a range of residential and economic ties with the wife's parents. Some lived for long periods of time with them, a few permanently. Again, the financial arrangements in these stem family households varied. Although the members rarely worked together in a common business enterprise or pooled their earnings in a common fund, they sometimes jointly purchased the home in which they lived. In other cases the Issei couple or widowed parent were guests in a home owned and maintained by the daughter and her husband.

ADAPTATION AND STRATEGIES IN SEARCH OF MOTIVES

It should be apparent by now why these changes in Japanese-American households seem to invite a functional explanation of the kind in which domestic groups adjust form and function in response to exogenous factors, among which economic factors are primary. The decline in the frequency and duration of stem family households, the transitional period of unstable residence, and the shift toward uxorilocal residence in later stem family households might be cast as a "functional adaptation" to the postwar occupational character of the community. Were we to employ a model in which households fashion adaptive strategies, the shift from stem family household to conjugal family households might be explained as a response to the shift from family business to individual wage, which obviated pooling the labor of so large a group. The rise in the rate of uxorilocal residence might be seen as replacing the pooling of father's and son's labors with that of mother's and daughter's labors, specialized in nurturant and reproductive functions, as productive work is removed from the household.

The attribution of strategies to households, however, assumes a consensus among household members as to their shared goals, which are often implicitly posited to consist of little more than bare survival or social mobility. While I have no quarrel with the claim that people everywhere, including the poor in the dependent cities of the third world, act strategically on their own behalf rather than passively accepting their economic and residential fates (see Hackenberg, Murphy, and Selby, this volume), I do object to the transference of consciousness and volition from humans to households. Such a transference rests on the claim that all members of a household share the same goals and strategies or, if they do not, that some (most often women and children) are so powerless as to have their actions determined by the goals and strategies of others (most often adult men). Hence the seemingly benign metaphor of household as human agent too readily camouflages the different and sometimes divergent goals of its members, which are disclosed by analyses that attend to age and gender hierarchies within domestic groups. Research on women's domestic strategies (Collier 1974; Lamphere 1974; Wolf 1972) in societies where women are denied legitimate authority over households forces us to recognize that an individual's refusal to passively accept his or her economic and residential fate brings strategy and struggle inside households as well as between households and external institutional structures.

Were we to reject a consensus model of households, we might adopt a conflict model in which individuals in different structural positions pursue divergent strategies of self-interest. In this less solidary tale of change the Issei attempts to reproduce the stem family might be read not as adaptation to an occupational niche of small business but as an effort to control their children's labor and thereby enhance their economic security. The postwar decline in stem family households then might be attributed to the increasing ability of Nisei to throw off the yoke of parental control because of their increased access to jobs and income outside the community.

If the consensus model of household strategy must be faulted for naively conferring a Durkheimian single-mindedness to social collectivities, the conflict model of household struggle runs the risk of too readily assuming that what drives human action is a universal self-interest or a pan-cultural will to power rather than culturally constructed goals and motives. Hence, even leaving aside the issue of whether stem family households are better suited to fulfilling the needs—productive or otherwise—of petty capitalists than those of wage earners, there is the problem of imputing strategies to people whose goals we have not yet bothered to understand. Put another way, we have read meaning into residence without pausing to investigate the meanings held by the actors themselves.

In the following section I pursue just such an investigation of meaning as the initial step toward an analysis of the changing household forms described in the previous section.

KAZOKU, SUCCESSION, AND THE PERPETUATION OF SOCIAL IDENTITY

A useful strategy in a cultural analysis is to first identify the core constructs that people use to organize complex systems of relationships. *Household* is not a core construct for the Issei; nor, as we shall see, is it for the Nisei. *Kazoku* is such a construct for the Issei.

When Issei enumerate the membership of the *kazoku* in which they lived in Japan, they appear to describe households; yet the *kazoku* in which the majority of them claim membership today are residentially dispersed families. In their childhood *kazoku* Issei include all individuals who resided under one roof at the period in question. For almost all Issei this included only kin with whom they were connected by blood, marriage, or adoption. If the individual was raised in a stem family household he or she included as members of the childhood *kazoku* (in addition to parents and siblings) the father's parents and any of his siblings residing in the household. If the individual was raised in a conjugal family household he or she included only parents and siblings. Issei who had nonkin servants or farm workers living in their homes also included them as members of the *kazoku*.

When asked to list the current members of their *kazoku*, Issei respond in a couple of ways. Most list their spouse (if surviving), any surviving children and their spouses, and grandchildren. A few also include their grandchildren's spouses. Coresidence is not a requirement and, indeed, is irrelevant to the way most Issei define their contemporary *kazoku*. A couple of women, however, used residence criteria in defining the membership of their present *kazoku*. Both of these Issei were widows living with a married daughter and her spouse and children. Each widow included in her *kazoku* only the daughter, her husband, and their children. Unlike Issei living apart from their children, they excluded all their other children and grandchildren.

There are some obvious differences between the units the Issei identify as their past *kazoku* and those they identify as their present ones. First, the genealogical composition of these two sets of *kazoku* is different. The *kazoku* of the Issei's childhood and early adulthood never included married siblings; indeed, the Issei insist that married siblings are by definition members of two different *kazoku*. In contrast, except for the two widows living with married daughters, the Issei list all their children (married and unmarried) and their spouses and children as members of their present *kazoku*. In doing so they greatly expand the lateral genealogical range of *kazoku* membership. This change in *kazoku* composition, however, does not indicate a change in the Issei conception of *kazoku* but rather reflects a change in their position from members of a junior generation to members of a senior generation. Just because the genealogical referent of *kazoku* is contingent on ego's position in a family developmental cycle does not mean that the other referents of *kazoku* have changed. In addition, however, except for the *kazoku* of the two widows living with married daughters, no present Issei *kazoku* is characterized by the common residence, common hearth (shared meal preparation), common budget, or common productive enterprise of their childhood *kazoku*.

Despite these differences in the genealogical composition and functions performed by the Issei's childhood *kazoku* and their present ones, the core meaning of *kazoku* has remained unchanged. That meaning lies neither in genealogical or residence criteria nor in any specific set of functional characteristics. Rather, *kazoku* refers to those on whom one can, or at least should be able to, depend for enduring, unconditional loyalty and support. In the Issei's eyes the people on whom one can legitimately make such claims today in America are one's children and their spouses and perhaps one's grandchildren.

Given this meaning of *kazoku*, it is not surprising that only those Issei who live with a married child employ residence as a criterion in defining their present *kazoku*. Those Issei who do not—and they comprise the majority of their generation today—are understandably reluctant to employ a criterion that would exclude all their children from the domain of primary claims.

If one can make such claims on the children with whom one does not reside, it would seem to follow that the Issei have no financial stake in living in stem family households. The Nisei, moreover, uniformly assert that adult children should assume financial responsibility for needy parents, and their actions generally bear this out. Yet the Issei's actions after the war demonstrate that many of them attempted to form stem family households even though it was clear that their children had other desires.

The key to understanding the Issei's postwar attempts to form stem family households lies in a further examination of their notion of succession. When we return to a consideration of prewar attempts to maintain claims of succession to households in Japan, it is obvious that here too Issei were not motivated only by economic goals. Issei successors, after all, were not in line to inherit substantial property holdings or even enterprises capable of generating enough income to support themselves and their spouses, children, and parents. Indeed, most Issei successors had emigrated because the household's property was insufficient to support its next generation. I do not know the size of the Issei's parental household property and wealth. But when placed in the context of the economic history of Japan at the turn of the century, the Issei's recollections of their parents' occupations provide sufficient evidence of their economic circumstances. That not only the Issei but in many cases their fathers and brothers emigrated to work in America suggests that they were members of the growing class of Japanese who had insufficient landholdings to subsist as full-time farmers. Even those Issei whose parents and brothers never emigrated grew up in households that were supported in part by petty trade, home craft production, or wage labor.[5] In short, Issei successors to "farm" households were hardly intent on maintaining their claims to that status because it entitled them to inherit the means of production. In some cases, where their parents were tenant farmers, succession did not even entail the inheritance of the small plot of land on which the family home sat.

Instead, what lay behind the Issei's attempts to buttress their claims of succession to households in Japan was their desire to maintain their claim to a place and thereby a social identity in their natal community. Of course a nonsuccessor could return to his natal community and establish a household there. Indeed, that was the goal of many of the nonsuccessor Issei. But the possibility of returning to set up a new household did not have the symbolic security of the return to an established household with a recognized place and social history in the community.

After the war the vast majority of Issei no longer held such a claim to a viable place in a community in Japan. And hence their desire was to have an unambiguous successor who would perpetuate their social identity in the Japanese-American community and by so doing establish for them a continuing place in the community and, by extension, in the United States. That the Issei would rely on their children for the establishment of such a claim to a place in American society is understandable, particularly in light of their marginal status in a country that denied them citizenship for so many years.

FAMILY, SIBLING EQUALITY, AND THE TRANSMISSION OF LOVE

Although the Issei uniformly translate *kazoku* as "family," the Nisei construe the latter term as a core construct endowed with a rather different system of meanings. *Family* for the Nisei denotes neither a single, genealogically defined group of people nor one whose composition changes in predictable ways over the individual's life cycle. The membership of a person's *family* varies from one context to another, even at a particular stage of the life cycle. Which one of several sets of kin is the relevant *family* in which a Nisei includes himself depends on the occasion, activity, or normative expectation he has in mind. If defined by genealogical criteria, therefore, *family* shares the polysemic character of many kin categories explicated by anthropologists—including the Nuer lineage (Evans-Pritchard 1940).

In the context of discussions about coresidence, however, *family* refers to a married couple and their unmarried children. The conjugal pair is the proper core of the coresidential family and the "love" and "unity" manifested in this relationship is what, for the Nisei, shapes the other relationships in the family. There is absolute unanimity among the Nisei that it is far better for a married couple to live apart from their parents. Living with parents after marriage is a "burden" not only because there are bound to be disagreements over the management of the household and the rearing of children but because it stifles the spontaneous interaction between husband and wife. Nisei who have lived in three-generation households after marriage portray them as tolerable but unsatisfactory arrangements that intrude on personal "privacy" and "independence." "Two families," they say, "cannot live together happily under one roof."

The Nisei do concede that some circumstances necessitate coresidence with parents. If financial resources are inadequate to support parents in a separate household, if parents require physical care, or if the parents simply cannot manage living alone, then they must be taken into the child's home. Few Nisei are willing to send their elderly parents to a nursing home if they can provide them with adequate care at home. If a Nisei sibling set has an unmarried member, he or she is considered the best candidate for coresidence with parents. Such a residential unit, the Nisei reason, can be a comfortable arrangement as it does not interfere with a conjugal relationship. If all children are married, the Nisei say it is better for the parents to live with daughters rather than sons. The closer emotional bond between mother and daughter makes it easier for them to get along on a daily basis. Having been brought up in her mother's household, a daughter already understands her temperament, housekeeping style, and kitchen practices. And as women "stay at home more" and "run the household," the relationship between the two women is considered more critical than the relationship between the two men.

The burden of coresidence with parents should be shared equally by all married daughters. Accordingly, Issei are often sent to live with one daughter for a year or two and then transferred to a second daughter's household. The Nisei recognize that this practice has serious drawbacks—especially in the case of senile or disabled Issei—as it often seems to exacerbate their physical and mental decline. Consequently, one daughter often ends up bearing the primary burden of coresidence—an inequity that may generate resentment among sisters.

The Nisei's normative statements about coresidence, along with their normative statements about other claims and obligations of family members, in particular those between themselves and their Issei parents, reveal that they have unraveled and redistributed among members of the sibling group the bundle of rights and duties that their parents at least initially attached to the successor son (Yanagisako 1975). Underlying these norms for the distribution of filial rights and duties are several key constructs.

First, the division of components of the successor role and their assignment to sons or daughters employs gender constructs shared by Issei and Nisei. The Nisei, for example, assign sons the financial responsibility for aging parents because it requires going "outside" the family to "work," hence entering into what is construed as the male domain. Likewise, the assignment of coresidence responsibility to daughters is in accordance with women's symbolic placement "inside" the home.

Second, what the Nisei say about filial relationships and indeed all family relationships evinces a conception of the family as a unit that should be bound by "love" rather than just by "duty." To the Nisei a strong family is unified by love and its expression rather than merely by rules and obligations. It is for this reason that Nisei say they try to openly demonstrate their affection for their children, as difficult as it is to overcome their "Japanese" inhibitions.

Third, and closely linked with the above construct of the family, is a belief in sibling equality. When the Nisei assert that sisters should share equally the burden of taking needy parents into their homes just as brothers should contribute an equal or "fair" share to the support of their parents, they are speaking of a general commitment to the absence of differentiation, hierarchy, or any form of inequality among siblings. Aside from gender differences, Nisei siblings are inherently equal human beings, and any attempt to undermine this equality leads to dissension and the destruction of the family.

The combination of the belief in sibling equality with the construct of the family as a unit bound by love means that parental love must be distributed equally among all children regardless of birth order or gender. Not only parental affection and attention but any commodity that passes from parents to children must be equally distributed. The Nisei accordingly are adamant about the equal division of inheritance. A parent who wills all his or her wealth, however paltry, to one child is a parent who did not love all children equally. And those Nisei who received smaller shares or no shares of parental wealth feel unloved and rejected by their parents. The brother who appropriates more than his equal share of parental property symbolically hoards his parents' love and denies it to his siblings.

HOUSEHOLDS AS NEGOTIATED FORMS

The Nisei assignment of coresidence responsibilities to daughters is part of the normative distribution of the claims and obligations that they contend the Issei and "Japanese tradition" had unfairly concentrated in the successor son. At the same time coresidence of parents and married children is to be avoided if possible because it brings parents into a (coresidential) family in which they do not belong and where they can only interfere with the proper fulfillment of the conjugal relationship. The placement of parents in the home of *one* of their children, moreover, subverts the equal flow of "love" from parents to all members of the sibling group, and vice versa. Hence, by impeding the flow of conjugal love and creating an inequity in the flow of filial love, the residence of parents in the home of a married child threatens the very stuff of which the Nisei family is constituted.

The Issei's resistance to the Nisei division of filial responsibilities and claims among siblings is likewise rooted in a coherent system of meanings. In the Issei system of meanings coresidence with a married child signifies that one has an unambiguous successor who will perpetuate one's social identity and thereby transmit the very stuff of which filial relationships are constituted. The Issei aversion to residential arrangements that deny them such an unequivocal successor can be traced to their own household histories rather than merely to a trans-Pacific "Japanese tradition."

For many of the Issei the demise of their parental household in Japan was preceded by the kind of division of the successor role among siblings that their children now prefer. The household histories of the Issei reveal that most successors who left Japan to fulfill their financial duties, leaving their siblings to fulfill other components of their roles, eventually had no household to return to and hence no place in their natal community. Even those who had not seen the end of their own natal household in Japan had seen households disappear from communities through the emigration of its children. For the Issei those households generated not only offspring without filial pasts in new communities but parents without filial futures and therefore without a continuing place in the community. Division—whether of duties, rights, or inheritance—symbolizes for the Issei a social demise they have already had to bear in one community and one country.

Given the different meanings that Issei and Nisei attach to coresidence of parents and married children, the postwar decline in the frequency and duration of stem family households, the transitional period of unstable residence, and the shift toward uxorilocal residence in later stem family households can hardly be characterized as the outcome of a unified household strategy. If the members of these households acted strategically, they did so in pursuit of goals that were far from uniform and, in the case of the two generations, often in conflict. The changing form and function of Japanese-American households were the outcome of a dynamic negotiation between two generations who read different meaning into residence and accordingly fashioned different residential strategies.

The explication of residence and the meanings people attribute to particular household forms as well as particular configurations of household functions need not confuse the "epistemological status of household" (Hammel, this volume) by confounding an analytic category with a folk category. Neither should it impede cross-cultural comparison. Instead, our household strategy should begin with an explication of folk constructs which displays the culturally specific and quite possibly divergent meanings and motives behind residential strategies. Having done so, we can go beyond the crude comparison of distributions of household types across regions and nations. Rather than pursuing generalizations about the disembodied ratios of household forms, we may then pursue generalizations about the social processes through which people with culturally constructed goals and strategies act to create those ratios.

NOTES

1. In 1920, 76 percent of the 7,874 Japanese in Seattle were immigrants from Japan and only 24 percent were U.S. born. By 1930 the proportion of immigrants in the population of 8,448 had declined to 53 percent and the proportion of U.S. born had risen to 47 percent (U.S. Bureau of the Census 1930: 2:1231, table 27).

2. See, for example, Bloom 1943, Daniels 1971, Spicer et al. 1969, Thomas and Nishimoto 1946.

3. See Broom and Riemer 1949, Broom and Kitsuse 1956, Thomas 1952, Thomas and Nishimoto 1946, Miyamoto and O'Brien 1947.

4. For a more detailed comparison of postmarital residence patterns of four Nisei marriage cohorts see Yanagisako (in press).

5. The Issei, moreover, came from those prefectures in Japan that had been most penetrated by the rapidly expanding monetary economy. These areas were also characterized by high rates of tenancy in the late nineteenth and early twentieth centuries (Smith 1959; Fukutake 1967). Thus, even where the Issei's parents were engaged in farming, it is unlikely that they owned most of the land they farmed. In 1910 tenants who owned less than one-tenth of the land they cultivated made up 27.8 percent of farm households in Japan; part-tenants who owned between 10 and 90 percent of the land they cultivated comprised 40 percent of the farm households (Fukutake 1967:10). The vast majority of Issei whose parents were "farmers" undoubtedly were members of these two categories rather than the category of owner-farmers who owned more than 90 percent of the land they cultivated.

REFERENCES

Bloom, Leonard
1943 Familial Adjustments of Japanese-Americans to Relocation: First Phase. American Sociological Review 8:551–60.

Broom, Leonard, and John I. Kitsuse
1956 The Managed Casualty: The Japanese-American Family in World War II. Berkeley and Los Angeles: University of California Press.

Broom, Leonard, and Ruth Riemer
1949 Removal and Return: The Socio-economic Effects of the War on Japanese Americans. Berkeley: University of California Press.

Collier, Jane F.
1974 Women in Politics. *In* Women, Culture and Society, ed. M. Z. Rosaldo and L. Lamphere, pp. 89–96. Stanford: Stanford University Press.

Collier, Jane, Michelle Z. Rosaldo, and Sylvia Yanagisako
1982 Is There a Family? New Anthropological Views. *In* Rethinking the Family: Some Feminist Questions, ed. Barrie Thorne, pp. 25–39. New York: Longman, Inc.

Daniels, Roger
1971 Concentration Camps USA: Japanese-Americans and World War II. New York: Holt, Rinehart and Winston, Inc.
Evans-Pritchard, E. E.
1940 The Nuer: A Description of the Modes of Livelihood and Political Institutions of a Nilotic People. New York: Oxford University Press.
Fukutake, Tadashi
1967 Japanese Rural Society. Translated by R. P. Dore. Ithaca, New York: Cornell University Press.
Lamphere, Louise
1974 Strategies, Cooperation, and Conflict among Women in Domestic Groups. *In* Women, Culture, and Society, ed. Michelle Z. Rosaldo and Louise Lamphere, pp. 97–112. Stanford: Stanford University Press.
Laslett, Peter
1981 Family and Household as Work Group and Kin Group: Areas of Traditional Europe Compared. Paper presented at the Prato Meeting, April 1981.
Miyamoto, Frank Shotaro
1939 Social Solidarity among the Japanese in Seattle. Seattle: University of Washington Press.
Miyamoto, S. F., and R. W. O'Brien
1947 A Survey of Some Changes in the Seattle Japanese Community since Evacuation. Research Studies of the State College of Washington 15: 147–154. Pullman, Washington.
Rapp, Rayna
1978 Family and Class in Contemporary America: Notes toward an Understanding of Ideology. Science and Society (Summer), pp. 278–300.
Sanjek, Roger
1982 The Organization of Households in Adabraka: Toward a Wider Comparative Perspective. Comparative Studies in Society and History 24 (1):57–103.
Schneider, David M.
1980 American Kinship: A Cultural Account. 2d ed. Chicago: The University of Chicago Press.
Smith, Thomas F.
1959 The Agrarian Origins of Modern Japan. Stanford: Stanford University Press.
Spicer, Edward H., et al.
1969 Impounded People: Japanese-Americans in the Relocation Centers. Tucson: University of Arizona Press.
Thomas, Dorothy Swaine
1950 Some Social Aspects of Japanese-American Demography. Proceedings of the American Philosophical Society 94:459–80.
1952 The Salvage: Japanese-American Evacuation and Resettlement. Berkeley and Los Angeles: University of California Press.

Thomas, Dorothy Swaine, and Richard S. Nishimoto
1946 The Spoilage: Japanese-American Evacuation and Resettlement. Berkeley: University of California Press.
U.S. Bureau of the Census
1930 Population Composition and Characteristics. Vol. 3, part 2: Census of Population. Washington, D.C.: Bureau of the Census.
Wolf, Margery
1972 Women and the Family in Rural Taiwan. Stanford: Stanford University Press.
Yanagisako, Sylvia J.
1975 Two Processes of Change in Japanese-American Kinship. Journal of Anthropological Research, 31:196–224.
1979 Family and Household. The Analysis of Domestic Groups. *In* Annual Review of Anthropology, ed. B. J. Siegel, A. R. Beals, and S. A. Tyler, pp. 161–205. Palo Alto, Calif.: Annual Reviews, Inc.
In press Transforming the Past: A Cultural History of Japanese American Kinship. Stanford: Stanford University Press.

14

The Family as a Knot of Individual Interests

Peter Laslett

In the year 1604 there was an outbreak of plague in the cathedral city of Salisbury in England, and the civic authorities found themselves having to support 411 out of some 2,000 households that comprised the population. So many of the breadwinning members of these households fell sick that they could not keep their domestic groups going unaided, and in the event about half of those citizens died. No doubt the support of the city was a supplement to the means of subsistence these households could still provide for themselves. No doubt also sources other than that of the city were called on to help out: communal assistance, as from the church and charitable institutions; the kin of those in the households affected; their neighbors and friends. But without the final resort of Salisbury as a political entity, all these persons might have perished, and a fifth of the domestic groups that made up its society would have ceased to exist.[1]

Every citizen of Salisbury can therefore be said to have had a vital interest in the existence and continuation of that city as well as the existence and continuation of the domestic group to which he or she belonged. Even in this preindustrial society the security of the individual could not wholly be assured by the household in which he or she lived, secured insofar as this could ever be done in that era. Threats to the security of the individual, threats that it was of the first importance to avoid, will be classed here as demographic and economic. In Salisbury during the plague a particular demographic vicissitude became so severe as to exceed the power and resources of some domestic groups and demonstrated their insufficiency to protect the interests of individual members.

In other cities, towns, and villages, or even regions, economic vicissitudes such as failure of the harvest or collapse of a market could not be adequately met by familial organization either. But on the whole most demographic and economic eventualities could be withstood by people living familially in traditional Western European nonindustrial society. This must have been the case for the other four-fifths of Salisbury families in 1604. The interests of people in being born, bearing children, marrying, or resisting death for as long as possible—in dying well when that inevitability arrived—indeed in arranging for every *rite de passage*—all were intertwined in the conjunction of individual interests at play in the familial group. These interests constitute my subject here. I shall even tend to talk as if the family group could actually consist in such a knot of individual interests.

Neither the family group nor any other social institution can be apprehended more than partially in terms of the individuals who compose it or in terms of their interests. To these always must be added the social structure in which the family group is placed, together with the social pressures at play, the economic and productive imperatives, the social norms, traditions, expectations, regulations, secular and religious, which limit and to some degree fashion the behavior of individuals and the groups to which they belong. Taken together, these social factors are sometimes said to determine the familial group, its composition, its comportment. To go as far as this, however, is to make the error opposite to that of supposing that the family group consists entirely of individuals and their interests and that its policy and activities are directed exclusively by them.

My object here is to make a brief and preliminary attempt to establish how far external social elements set boundaries to the interests and activities of individuals within the familial group and how far social elements accord with such interests and actions. The subject therefore is the reciprocal interplay at work in a particular historical situation. This will be for the most part the situation of the familial group in preindustrial Western Europe, especially in England. But I shall make comparative reference to other past familial systems spread across the surface of Europe in historic times as well as occasionally to those that anthropologists examine in the contemporary world. The issue of how far the family group has itself a collective interest, even a collective life, over and above the interests of its constituent members will finally have to concern us as well. As so often happens in discussions of the family, we can only proceed by drawing further distinctions and implications.

The classification of interests into demographic and economic, for example, is not entirely satisfactory. All economic losses or gains—in earning power, earning opportunities, possession or control of productive resources—may have demographic consequences, encouraging or discouraging births or marriages, raising or lowering mortality. The theorists of protoindustrialization, for example, have proposed a particular application of this principle, which could be of considerable importance. The argument is that productive arrangements and conditions as well as composition of the family group in protoindustrial households largely determine age at marriage and number of children. Though the generality of this proposition is in doubt, researchers from the time of Malthus have recognized that levels of subsistence have a controlling influence over births, marriages, and deaths. The whole story of population development and industrialization in England has recently been reformulated in these terms.[2]

Similarly, demographic events can often be economic events. The death of a breadwinner is in itself an economic disaster, and the much greater vulnerability of family groups to such disasters is one of the features distinguishing preindustrial from industrial and backward from advanced societies. A fortunate marriage was also more likely to mean an economic uplift. Even the birth of a potential earner was an economic advantage in the long run, if nearly always an added liability in the short. Moreover, the category morbidity—liability to illness short of death—has to be added to the more usual demographic categories in order to grasp the type of vicissitude it was in the individual's interest to provide against. The half of the population of the Salisbury families we have referred to who survived the plague of 1604 must have been nursed back to health by their domestic groups, aided by the city perhaps, but never dependent on it. A better way of classifying the vicissitudes we have to consider might be as the individual's *life chances*, divided into predominantly demographic and predominantly economic.

The word *family* in my title is neither self-contained nor self-explanatory, which is why I have otherwise preferred the expression *domestic group, coresident domestic group,* or more usually *household*. For one thing this group in the preindustrial West and in many other social structures was not confined in its membership to kin and affines, immediate or distant. Other persons could and did belong to it, and they were not usually related to its members by kinship, only quite rarely in England. These persons were, first, servants, who made up more than an eighth of all household membership in preindustrial England, and, second, such resident relatives as there were, along with those who have been entitled *inmates* (the traditional English term), that is, boarders, lodgers, and visitors. The life chances of these individuals were bound up with the persistence of the domestic group in which they found themselves, even though they did not belong to the kin-related part of the family.[3] The employers of English servants tended them when they were sick—indeed they were required to do so by law. It is unfortunately true that when plague was about, a servant was likely to be in danger from the domestic group in which he lived, since plague was communicable. But there can be no doubt that in the terrible situation in Salisbury in 1604 servants and inmates alike had a powerful interest in the domestic group of their membership since they could expect support and care from this source above all others.

The word *family* is also ambiguous, since it refers to the extended kin relations of a particular individual, or kinship as a network in itself, as well as a coresident domestic group. My subject is this group, and it might seem rather odd to think of kin in terms of individual interest. In Salisbury in 1604 we can be certain that at least some, perhaps most, of these family groups were assisted in their predicament by nonresident kin, in the city or outside it, because of what we know of the normative role of kinship in traditional Western society. It was particularly in such emergencies that kin connection could be invoked, as well as in other critical passages in the life course such as birth, marriage, death, migration, the getting of jobs, or the "placing" of sons or daughters. The most tangible form of such help in Salisbury was no doubt the offer by relatives of a home for the duration of the plague to all who could afford, or could be spared, to leave the site of infection. This was the usual way of ensuring that the individual did not catch the disease. Those relatives within reach certainly offered personal services in the way of helping with cooking, with the supply of food, even with money.

In this way members of a household did have a tangible interest in its kin connections. The more there were of these connections, the better for each family member, since this spread insurance against risk, both demographic and economic. The more influential the kin the better, for the personal careers of many successful persons in the past can be shown to have been assisted by the use that individual was able to make of well-placed kin connections. But we must remember that obligations of this kind were reciprocal and that a large circle of badly placed kin peculiarly subject to ill health or poverty could be a liability. What is more, for lesser favors like borrowing money or giving a testimony in court, in every matter not marked by familial emphasis, friends and neighbors were as important as kin, sometimes more important, at least in traditional English society. In the village of Terling in Essex at about the time of the plague in Salisbury "neighbours and personal friends selected from them seem to have played the supporting role that in other societies might have been played by the wider kin group" (Wrightson and Levine 1979:102; see also Macfarlane 1970 and R. M. Smith 1979).[4] The standing of a family group in a community then did affect the interests of its members, and we can imagine that in Salisbury in 1604 there was much neighborly assistance to those families with the plague. There were after all large numbers of households there that managed to do without city support although they were also affected by the epidemic.

The interest of members of a household in its wider kin-group connections apparently did not extend to more than partial and temporary assistance. The permanent upkeep of an individual or of another family group in face of demographic or economic disablement does not seem to have been a feature of kinship in traditional English society, and neighborly assistance was only extended this far in the special case of beggars. There could have been a norm requiring prosperous people to give support to widowed, orphaned, or crippled relatives for long periods of time, but we have found little to indicate that in this particular society, and perhaps in western or northwestern Europe generally, this convention of individual and familial behavior was ever of much import. Even in Italy, where kinship solidarity is supposed to have been greater than in England, the unfortunate in the cities looked to the civic authorities and charitable foundations for continuing support, perhaps in greater numbers than in England, and over the whole period from the fifteenth to the nineteenth century.[5] In any case the extent and effectiveness of the kin network was itself subject to demographic chance and vicissitude. A person or a family might have many relatives or few; there might be more at some times than at others, all because of births, marriages, and deaths. It is for reasons of this kind that it is possible to say that in matters of permanent dependency, in the societies I am studying, the only finally reliable source was the collectivity.

NEOLOCALITY AND FAMILIAL SELF-INTEREST

A look at the relationship of nonresiding relatives with a family group and with its constituent interests abruptly changes our perspective. Martine Segalen describes in her contribution to this volume how in Brittany of the 1980s family groups are sometimes virtually maintained by relatives living close by, though by relatives of one type only, by the parents of the head or his wife. Even here the word *maintenance* means more in the way of personal service than financial support, although money is occasionally contributed. Providing essential help with the upkeep of the household and with child rearing so that the younger couple can work away from their home all day, often in the city, is the crucial contribution. Without this help, the new house, not infrequently actually built by the younger husband with the assistance of his father or father-in-law, cannot be afforded or the family maintained at present levels of living. The interest of these younger married couples in their relationship with their parents outside their household is quite apparent. If "standard of living" is to be reckoned as a constituent of life chances, which would be appropriate in our affluent generation, then their life chances are dependent on their links with their families of origin, links that are external, not internal, to their own households. This is a contemporary example, and there can be no doubt that such behavior is widespread in the industrial world of the 1980s. It is entirely wrong, as we shall see, to think of such an attitude on the part of parents as an historical novelty. Nevertheless, it is interesting to notice the extent to which the relationship depends on demographic good fortune.

Not everyone has his parents, or even one parent, alive in the early years of his marriage, even in our long-lived generation. It has been reckoned in fact that at age 35 on average a married couple will have three and a quarter out of their four parents alive in contemporary France. In eighteenth-century France the average was much less, only just over one of the four parents would still have been living at about the time when such assistance could be offered to a married couple at this stage in household formation (Le Bras 1982: table 1).[6] Moreover, it is not certain how many of these surviving parents would have had the resources 200 or 300 years ago to behave in the way Segalen describes, though certainly those capable would have been only a fraction of those with such resources now. Here we have an issue of some significance in comparing the family of the present with the family of the past. We have to decide the case on the basis of a hypothetical situation. How many parents of the eighteenth century would have done what parents of the late twentieth century do had they had the opportunity and the means?

Two other features of such a situation command our attention. One is that the interest of the older couples in the sense of their own life chances is not involved to any great extent in maintaining such a relationship; that is not what persuades them to behave in this way. Some elements of reciprocal interest could certainly be at issue, since the parents of any married couple can expect something in the way of support from their married children in any case. The more they help their married children, the more they may get from them when they need it, which is an illustration of the intricate and often unexpected way in which individual interest interacts with social expectation. For there is and has been, always and everywhere, a social norm requiring grown children to take responsibility for elderly parents. But the balance of advantage may be rather complicated. In the Breton case the senior couple may actually be assisting their grown children in leaving the family house, where they might perhaps have gone on living with their parents. In this sense such behavior reduces the cohesion of the parental family group as a residential unit at the same time as it affirms the strength of familial or kinship bonding.

This leads us to the second circumstance of note. The actions we are discussing bring into being, spatially if not socially, a new independent family household, in no way a continuation of that of the older parents, although itself often situated not far away on the family plot itself. Both generations collaborate in the practice of neolocal residence—a household comes into being at the marriage of the head, lasts as long as his lifetime and that of his spouse (or of his final spouse), and then disappears. A constituted household cannot be divided so as to form new households and it cannot be inherited or survive a change of generations; in fact it cannot survive for any longer than one family cycle. Household headship cannot be transferred from father to son or between any two persons, except perhaps from a dying spouse to a surviving spouse. Neolocalism in such an uncompromising form must be regarded as a polar case that can be contrasted with the logical opposite case in which new households are never formed at marriage but always by division. Here the headship can pass from father to son or from any nominated individual to any other, and the household normally survives more than one family cycle; it may in fact be perennial (see Czap 1983; Czap 1982, on serfs in imperial Russia).

Neither polar model has probably ever existed in a pure form anywhere, but taken together these models can be used as the extremes of a spectrum along which conventions of household formation can be ranged. In table 14.1 the degree of approximation to pure neolocalism is used to distinguish four sets of tendencies apparent in the social structures of traditional Europe. The English household is taken as the type case for the western, entirely neolocal pole and the Russian serf household as that for the contrasting eastern pole. You will see that it is possible to place the famous stem family, an intermediate form between the western and eastern poles, by the use of the table. In the stem family, which is here presumed to be one of the characteristics of the middle European area, though not widespread even there, one child, the designated heir, inherits the headship and takes over a household at the retirement or death of his predecessor. Marriage is thus distinct from household formation. In fact, the heir is usually portrayed as a son

TABLE 14.1

SETS OF TENDENCIES IN DOMESTIC ORGANIZATION IN TRADITIONAL EUROPE

	Sets 1 and 2 Northern and western		Sets 3 and 4 Southern and eastern	
	1	2	3	4
Overall criterion	West	West/central or middle	Mediterranean	East
Occasion and method of group formation				
a 1 Formed at marriage of household head	Always	Usually	Seldom	Never
a 2 Formed by fission or fusion of existent household(s)	Never	Sometimes	Frequently	Always
a 3 Marriage important to household formation	Always	Usually	(Seldom)[a]	Never
a 4 Takeover of existent household by new head	Occasionally	Frequent	Frequent	Usual
Procreational and demographic criteria				
b 1 Age at marriage, female	High	High	Low	Low
b 2 Age at marriage, male	High	High	High	Low
b 3 Proportions marrying	Low	Low	High	High
b 4 Age gap between spouses at first marriage	Narrow	Narrow	Wide	Narrow
b 5 Proportion of wives older than husbands	High	Very high	Low	High
b 6 Proportion of widows remarrying	High	Very high	Very low	Very low
Criteria of kin composition of groups				
c 1 Proportion of resident kin	Very low	Low	High	High
c 2 Proportion of multigenerational households	Low	Low	High	Very high
c 3 Proportion of households headed by never-married women	High	High	(Low)[a]	High
c 4 Proportion of solitaries	Very high	High	Low	Absent
c 5 Proportion of no-family households	High	High	Low	Absent
c 6 Proportion of simple-family households	High	High	Low	Low

c 7 Proportion of extended-family households	Quite high	High	Low	Low
c 8 Proportion of multiple-family households	Very low	Low	High	Very high
c 9 Proportion of complex-family households (c7 + c8)	Very low	Low	High	Very high
c 10 Proportion of frérèches	Absent	Low	High	Very high
c 11 Proportion of stem-family households	Very low	High	Low	Low
c 12 Proportion of joint-family households	Absent	Low	Very high	Very high
Criteria of organization of work and welfare				
d 1 Addition to household of kin as workers	Rare	Common	Very common	Universal
d 2 Added working kin called servants	Rare	Common	?	Irrelevant
d 3 Addition to household of life-cycle servants	Very common	Very common	Not uncommon	Irrelevant
d 4 Married servants	Uncommon	Common	?	Irrelevant
d 5 Attachment to household of inmates as workers	Very rare	Common	?	Occasional
d 6 Mean number of adults per household	Low	High	Very high	Maximal
d 7 Mean number of households of ⩽ 3 persons	Very high	High	Very low	Very low
d 8 Mean number of persons of working age (15–65) per household	Low	Medium	Very high	Very high
d 9 Household head described as laborer, journeyman, out-servant, cottager	Often	Sometimes	Never	Never
d 10 Household head described as pauper	Often	Sometimes	?	?
d 11 Attachment of secondary household to houseful	Absent	Common	Absent	Absent

[a]Exceptions to the suggested classification are known to exist.

SOURCE: R. Wall, J. Robin, and P. Laslett 1983; table 17.5. The reader is referred to that volume for the meaning of entries in the table and the character of the regions. The notion of such a spectrum originated in October 1981 at the discussions that form the basis of the present volume.

already married, residing with his wife and child in a household headed by his father, and not in a household brought into being by his wife and himself.[7]

My concern here is with the interests of members of the family, primarily the coresident family but also the extended family, in maintaining such a familial form. But the table, as will be seen, is not simply concerned with the kinship structure of households. Their productive lineaments are also shown as varying between sets of European tendencies in a way that displays some correlation with neolocalism. Before we approach the household as a work group, however, I will make some general observations on household formation, household survival over more than one family cycle, the interest of individual household members, and the social norms at play in familial systems. Something must also be said about the rules that maintained such systems in being.

NOUMENAL NORMS

Let us begin by agreeing that the patterns of behavior we are considering can scarcely have arisen from the rational comportment and calculated decisions of all the members of all the populations in question.[8] The unlikelihood of such an explanation can be illustrated from the behavior of the population of the contemporary United States, which has a claim to be the best instructed population of its size that has ever existed and so perhaps the most likely to adopt rational criteria for decisions on marriage and residence after marriage. This illustration may seem at first sight to take us away from the family as a knot of individual interests, but we will not stray far.

Americans today divorce with unparalleled frequency and procreate fewer and fewer children. Yet it is as certain as analytic demography can make it that each and every one of us will live a large part of her or his remaining life as an elderly person. It is equally certain that during the final years he or she will be dependent for contact with the rest of society and for psychological support on one of his or her own offspring, usually a daughter. Yet Americans persist in behaving in such a way as to lower the probability of engendering such a daughter at all. They also live their sexual and procreative lives so as to ensure that when they reach the later stages of their lives such a daughter, if she should have made an appearance, will be less disposed than ever before to undertake the responsibilities so valuable to the aged individual. This is because Americans now tend to undergo a whole history of visiting unions, consensual unions, marriages, divorces, and remarriages which must make filial relationships diffuse and uncertain, very different from that solidary interconnection of aging parent with biological offspring which has been characteristic of the Western monogamous familial system.

The American example does not portray rational, calculated behavior, and it evidently goes on in ignorance of the implications for the life chances of the individual. We have to conclude therefore that such wisdom as does influence such decisions and behavior is for the most part collective wisdom. It may owe something, perhaps a good deal, to custom, tradition, even to religious belief. Parsing the content of religious revelation, myth, or symbolism in such a way as to explicate rules for collective social survival has been a favorite pastime of anthropologists. But it is evident that normative regulations are inefficient, for norms are not always obeyed. Indeed, one of the functions of norms in a society is that they should be disobeyed, for it is in disobeying them that the opportunity arises for affirming social and cultural values and for assigning praise or blame. These are all essentials of the social process.

I have asserted that the neolocal rules describing the western family place responsibility for procreation fairly and squarely on the individual or couple who do the procreating. It is they who have to find the resources to establish a household, to live independently for as long as economic or demographic vicissitude makes this possible, and to maintain and train to independence any offspring they engender. Very little of this responsibility can be shifted to the immediately or to the more distant kin, as we have seen. Yet these rules of household composition are not ethical norms in Western society. Defiance of them does not bring with it the sanctions of public shame prompted by religious or clerical condemnation or sententious declarations by spokesmen for the community about a rent in the social fabric.

If the rules of household composition are contrasted with rules of procreational behavior as these have been established in Western culture and its Christian code, the contrast is conspicuous. Having children outside marriage was, and to most respectable English or American persons still is, morally unacceptable behavior, subject to diatribes from the pulpit, the magistrate's bench, and the political rostrum. "Living in sin," homosexuality, and engendering children outside marriage do appear to what Americans call the "moral majority" as evidence of social decline and to the social scientist as symptoms of anomie. Yet there is good reason to believe that the normative rules forbidding such behavior are not, and have never been, obeyed as consistently as the rules of household composition (see Laslett, Oosterveen, and Smith 1980: chap. 1).

In the London proletarian community of Bethnal Green, for example—an area notorious all over Victorian England for the wickedness of its ways and perpetually cited as an example of social decay—the English nuclear family model appears with monotonous regularity in the households recorded by the census authorities in 1851, 1861, and 1871.[9] I have accordingly decided to name regulations of the kind that govern familial formation *noumenal normative rules*, noumenal as opposed to phenomenal and normative because they refer to decisions that are perceived as matters of choice, even if they do not usually raise ethical issues in themselves. Such rules seem to exist, or to have existed, without public sanctions and without internal conscientious sanctions either. They are like nothing as much as the natural laws of Thomas Hobbes: rules of prudence, rules that everyone agrees are secure, advantageous, and desirable. They can be regarded as socially encoded programmatic rules, on the computer analogy, and they have the outstanding characteristic of being permanent parts of the social structure.

To identify certain regulations as noumenal normative rules, and to include rules of household composition among them, may be as far as we shall get in explaining why it is possible to descry the range of variation in domestic group composition across the continent of Europe which is set out in table 14.1. Such an identification tells us nothing, of course, about how such rules arose and why they differed from area to area, although geography, climate, and economic organization must have been important. Nor does it attempt to explain why some regulations are of this character while others—those to do with sexual behavior perhaps or those that might have to do with providing for old age—are not. Possibly some or most of the social regulations we encounter are of this kind; rules of postmarital residence seem to be noumenal norms to a considerable extent. The degree of fuss made about a social rule—its phenomenology so to speak, the extent to which it is subject to legislation, formal or informal, politically based or custom based—is most decidedly not to be taken as a reliable indication of how far it is likely to be programmatic. The implication may be indeed that the less a regulation is discussed, protested, made the subject of symbolism or demonstrations, such as the famous charivari with which sexual or marital misdemeanor was sometimes greeted, the more likely it is to be spontaneously, silently, persistently obeyed.

Such would certainly be the case with the neolocal rule in English institutional and imaginative life. I have been hard put to find a single reference to the undesirability of living after marriage with parents or with a spouse's parents in the whole body of English literary output. Yet here was a behavioral rule that seems to have been almost universally obeyed, from the earliest period, in the thirteenth century, for which we have analyzable evidence, until the present day, in all social classes, in all English regions, in the countryside as well as in the towns.[10]

PERPETUATION, SUCCESSION, AND SELF-INTEREST

Once established as regulations of social life, the forms characteristic of the various European regions could be and were made use of to serve the interests of members of domestic groups, sometimes serving the interests of some at the expense of others. As I have already hinted, this is always so in a relationship between individual interest and social regulation. A theological tag could be adapted to express that relationship: society proposes, the individual disposes.

It is also true that situations might arise in which the life chances of household members might be better secured by modifying the regulations: a grandmother or even a grandparental couple might be allowed to take up residence in a household previously formed on neolocal principles because this arrangement maximizes overall household income, the level of child nurture, and the support of the grandparents as they age. It could perhaps be claimed that the stem family principle existed, in part at least, because of the interest of all household members in the continuity and permanence of a domestic group endowed with the resources that should serve in an emergency to help even nonresident relatives. The perennial multiple household could perhaps be supposed to perform these services to an even greater extent.

But these benefits might be attained at palpable cost to the individual, harming his or her life chances by reducing the freedom to provide for the future by founding a new domestic group. There are probably other ways in which these regulations might conflict with freedom of choice.[11] What is more, the domestic group even under the "Eastern" regime is not exempt from the consequences of extreme economic and demographic circumstances.

This is not the occasion to dwell on the relevant evidence, but the history of serf peasant households and of the self-perpetuating stem family households of Japan shows that some flourished, some were impoverished, some grew in size, some shrank and even disappeared. The Russian *mir*, or village community, and the landlord himself are perpetually found intervening in the affairs of individual households to keep them viable, which was one of the reasons for the redistribution of village land. The extent to which the life interests of the individual were better secured by differing degrees of departure from the neolocal principle is an interesting topic in its own right, about which little is yet known. In the last resort individual life chances clearly depend on the interplay between family and collectivity under all forms of social structure, never on family and kinship alone.

I have tended to talk of the life chances of the individual in terms of permanency, as if the length of a lifetime were always more important than its quality. This is to generalize from extraordinarily unfavorable conditions, such as those in Salisbury in 1604, or from an extraordinarily hostile environment, such as that facing some contemporary tribal societies. The limitations of such analysis have to be fully recognized, for such extreme conditions are generally regarded by anthropologists as exceptions (see Turnbull 1973).[12] Nevertheless it could be claimed that the values of expressiveness and personal achievement are ordinarily provided outside the family group, certainly in agricultural and industrial societies. Among hunter-gatherer peoples, for instance, hunting itself, undertaken to acquire food for household support, and military organization and activity provide such opportunities.

Qualitative values, insofar as they have to be public, then have little relevance to our subject. Military activity, on the contrary, has another and quite distinct connection with it, because such activity is justified for security reasons. Here it is the security of the collectivity that is in question, and the collectivity in a sense also represents the life chances of individuals, of every single individual in a given population. The collectivity, if successfully protected in this way, will ordinarily outlast all members of its population and all the other institutions they bring into being, including their familial groups. From the point of view of the interest of the individual, supporting the state, if such exists, certainly makes sense. The family is insufficient.

The life chances of an individual household member may depend to a varying extent on the permanency of the family group. But these life chances do not require the continuation of the domestic group into an indefinite future, as is the case with the state. The life chances are fostered simply by a high probability that the domestic unity will last long enough to provide security as long as the individual member stands in need of it. Under neolocal rules this means effectively until death for the household head and his spouse (say, 25 or 30 years after household formation in traditional Europe); the remaining time of departure from the household for infants and children is perhaps 10 or 12 years on average. For servants in England the next hiring fair set a limit—this was on average no longer than six months.[13] At the Eastern pole of family organization a whole lifetime might be at issue for nearly all members. No individual's life chances in any family group demand greater intervals of time, so the manner in which such relative permanence is secured is of little importance from the individual point of view. It follows that particular provisions for ensuring the continuance of the domestic group after a change of headship—that is, patrilocal residence rules—must be largely social in character. They represent a society-level variable at play on familial organization.

The possibility of conflict between such social rules and the interest of individuals should not escape us. Even given the intervals I have specified for security purposes, the termination of a family group in accordance with neolocalism might well affect the life chances of individual members, to some extent, especially those of young children. We shall have to return to the question of conflict of interest as well as to the question of continued life of the household group over time, but a warning is necessary concerning the unqualified and definite language I have used. The problems of how to define the domestic group as continuing over more than one cycle, and of how to define the family cycle itself are exceedingly complex and have not to my knowledge been solved.[14]

We may return with these considerations in mind to the motives of the middle-aged or elderly Bretons and their antecedents. Where familial rules were not neolocal, of course, such behavior could not arise. Parents did not help their married children establish households; children did not in fact establish their own households at all. But in preindustrial neolocal England it was a recognized practice of mothers and fathers to do their best to "set up" each of their children with the required skill in earning, and even with the capital, to marry. The resources this transferred downward between the generations were often considerable. The evidence for such transmission goes against the theory that modernization or industrialization causes a reversal of wealth flows between generations, that is, the passage of wealth from children to parents before the demographic transition but from parents to children thereafter.[15] Though I have claimed, with the required qualification, that if the interests of Segalen's senior couples in providing for old age are not involved in what they do, it is possible that an interest of a different kind could be at play. An identification with the subsequent careers of their offspring is a well-known feature of the attitude of parents, and the success of these children in establishing themselves familially in the changed world in which they will go on living could well be part of such an attitude.

When the familial model is not a neolocal one and where headship is transferred so as to secure a degree of permanence in the domestic group over time, succession is much less rigidly conventionalized than might be expected, even though as we have seen it is legitimated by social regulation. Inheritance is not strictly followed. It is not necessarily a son who is selected to succeed but the fittest person for the responsibility. This was true of the large scale *mezzadria* (sharecroppers) household of central Italy as it was for the Russian serfs. In Austrian peasant households in which stem succession was important, a bastard or even a servant might finally attain to the headship of a household, and the succession of the widow of the last head was commonplace (see Czap 1982; Poni 1978 on the *mezzadria*; Mitterauer 1983).

We may say in fact that it was no part of the interest of household members exactly how succession to headship was brought about. Members would indeed follow their common as well as their individual interest in modifying those rules whenever their life chances required it. A serf owner, or landlord, might do so too, or at least attempt it, but in such cases their own life chances were much less involved. We can pursue the discussion no further here, but we are at a crux in the relationship between socially originated succession of household formation rules, economic imperatives, and the life chances of individuals.

THE FAMILY DYNAMIC AND THE WIDER COLLECTIVITY

I now turn to the economic and productive functions together with the class position of the household, emphasizing the collective interest of the domestic group. There can be no doubt that the accepted portrayal of the preindustrial household as a work group strongly suggests that it had a collective interest, even a collective life. The peasant family group working on its own plot of land with no employees from outside and no work done by any member for another employer must have had a high level of integration for working purposes and accordingly an interest shared by every member. As depicted by Chayanov, the great Russian observer of peasant living in its final phase in his country, everything was subordinated to the membership of the working family. The size of the farm was fitted to their numbers rather than their numbers to the size of the farm. Collaboration in production must have extended and consolidated that common interest in shelter and subsistence which we have already dwelt on and must have given structure to those interests shared by most members. We might also point to the interest of the younger members in the socialization functions of the household, of the older ones in such entertainment and relaxation as it might provide.

Such a picture of integrated interest, attitudes, and policy is equally representative of the craftsman's family household, producing its wares for sale and buying supplies with the income thus obtained. Even the *mezzadria* sharing its output with the landowner, or the serf household whose members were owned by the estate and its boss, or the exploited domestic units under the putting-out system (where the capitalist owned the material, the product, and even the productive instruments), all must have had the same characteristics. There is evidence that in England during the nineteenth century the protoindustrial households of nailers in the Midlands may have been disciplined by the productive process, and by the nailer himself, to a greater extent than in wholly preindustrial times, as marginal returns decreased and the competition of the factories threatened extinction. Family households in nonindustrial societies, combining productive and reproductive functions, seem to constitute an outstanding example of a group with a community of interests comprising the individual interests of its members, exhibiting perhaps a general will of a psychological and moral character which might delight the heart of Jean-Jacques Rousseau. It is certainly at the center of that all-inclusive, personality-fusing, social-psychological construct given the name *Gemeinschaft* by Ferdinand Tönnies.

It is understandable that historians and sociologists of the family should talk of a family dynamic deriving from this unanimity of interests. These scholars postulate an interest of the domestic group as a whole that overrides that of each of the group's members, an interest that enables the domestic group to react in a strategic way to the imperatives imposed by class, productive conditions and fluctuations, political, economic, demographic, and epidemic developments. For Tamara Hareven, for example, family strategies condition not only individual choices but social choices as well. Bodnar insists in his instructive study of the formation of the American working class that precisely because domestic group interests opposed the interests of individuals, tensions have arisen between family and individual members, though in general family interest has tended to prevail.[16]

To recognize the presence of friction, indeed to admit that conflict must always have been part of the authoritarian familial group, requires us to assume that such unity as a family group possessed was the outcome of bargaining and compromise, instrumental as well as affective relationships. This is an important truth. But collective family strategy might have existed nonetheless. When dealing with an emergency situation such as that of the plague in Salisbury, we are tempted to think of individual families as taking action, having a policy as unities of this kind. It is important also to bear in mind that all face-to-face societies, even if they are best regarded as knots of interests rather than as crystalline, unbreakable wholes, do modulate the behavior and outlook of individual members as well as their conceptions of their own interests (cf. Laslett 1956).

Apart from the well-known dangers and difficulties of regarding groups as having a life independent of their members and a communal will of their own, closer examination of familial life in the past requires me to reject the dominance of family over individual interests. Attention has already been drawn to the fact that membership of the familial group in preindustrial Europe was not a constant over decades, years, or even months and that various classes of household members lived in the household for varying periods, some of them for very short periods indeed.[17] Such variability in residence seems unlikely to give rise to a communal interest or a general will. These are concepts more appropriate to the collectivity, if appropriate at all, because membership of the collectivity is for life, for everyone except emigrants. Even the perennial multiple family household is scarcely of this character.

Such facts as are known about the extent to which households were work groups also raises difficulties for the general interest or general will of that microsociety. An appreciable proportion of households in traditional Europe turn out not to have been work groups at all, and rather less of the production in the era before the factory actually went on within the individual household than has been assumed: rather more by collaboration between households, certainly in collaboration with employed outsiders, and some of it wholly apart from familial organization.[18] It seems probable that the extent to which households were work groups varied from area to area on the European continent in accordance with ecology and technical development and that this also showed some correlation with degrees of neolocalism. There are also interesting indications that in historic Europe work groups were perceived as familial when they were not so and that familial groups were perceived as independent productive units when in reality many of their earning members worked away from the household all day. Even in medieval cities such as Coventry in the fifteenth and early sixteenth century it was possible for the earning head of a household to spend as much time away from his family group as the industrial or office worker of our own society. This was a common, not an exceptional, experience.[19]

CONGRUENCE AND CONFLICT IN THE INTERESTS OF HOUSEHOLD MEMBERS

To make a clear and satisfactory analysis of the relationship between household production and membership in a wider collectivity it would be necessary to examine in detail the interest, the roles, and above all the power of every class of member of households of every type and in every region or economy. This is a task far beyond my present purpose, but one or two statements can be made all the same. Infants and children clearly have the greatest interest in the family household since their life chances depend almost wholly on its existence and persistence, on their being accepted and retained as members. But children also have the least power to affect the household's decisions and none whatever to carry them out. The servant or inmate with no expectation of inheritance, no recognized share in the pool of resources beyond his or her keep and his or her exiguous wages, and only temporary membership had the least interest and little more power than children.

The head of the family, perhaps especially the head of the neolocal household of the West, must be accorded the next largest individual interest (after that of children) and the greatest effective power. Male dominance was an established fact, and to the masculine governor were reserved all the satisfactions of marital life. No other member, except his wife, was officially permitted sexual expression, and everyone was to some degree under his discipline. It is tempting to think of the household of an English, a Dutch, or a northern French landholder, farmer, or craftsman as being an extension of his personality; insofar as it had a collective interest, will or strategy, it was his.

Although the patriarchal theorists of traditional Western Europe took this absolutist view,[20] it scarcely fits the facts of any European area. For one thing, about one-fifth of all households in England between the sixteenth and the nineteenth century were not headed by masculine patriarchs at all but by women. The official head of neither the Italian *mezzadria* (the *reggitore*) nor the Russian serf household was in such a monarchical position, and in the western and northwestern regions the ability of the official patriarch to will for the household as a whole was in practice severely limited. Such a domestic monarchy would have to rely for its effectiveness on the extent to which the head had exclusive control of the resources of the household, and the fewer these resources the less such control might mean.

In the view of the only contemporary who ever made such a reckoning, Gregory King, over half the "families" of England in 1688 were poor and dependent. Moreover, it was of the essence of the seventeenth-century household community that all monies, and especially those derived from earnings, were pooled. Studies of the disposition of this pool show that it was generally not the man of the house who managed earnings but his wife, the *reggitrice* in the Italian *mezzadria*. At the lowest social levels the miscellaneous earnings of wives and children might be as much as a half or more of total income, and we know that some laboring fathers had to mind the children some evenings so that the wife could go on with the cottage handicraft that helped to keep the family above water. The more modest the resources, it would appear, the more likely was it that the wife would manage such money as there was to be managed.

We may imagine that conflicts of interest between the head and other wage-earning household members might be more acute when a family was poor than when it was comfortable. All this follows from the fact that only a minority of households were unified work groups, creating their own resources within themselves, and a majority lived on a family fund coming from miscellaneous inputs from activities outside the household. Among the laboring classes of eighteenth-century Britain, then, or among the textile households of northern cities of eighteenth-century France, or among the émigré households in New England a century later, familial authority might well be lax, conflict of interest quite pronounced, and the only structural principle other than that of the reproductive unit within the domestic group (if such were present) would have been the family fund from which family needs were met.[21] Such a unity could scarcely be thought of as having a general interest, and the term *family strategy* seems as inappropriate here as it does if attached to the will of a patriarch.

It is in relation to these domestic groups, and of those farther below them still, the proletarian households, that the notion of a common family interest or strategy seems most often to be applied. When we reach the truly possessionless households, however, those for which economic or demographic vicissitude has been too extreme, we find ourselves faced with the collectivity once more. In England, anyway, a considerable part (or all) of the miscellaneous income of such family groups came from the Poor Law funds. What is more, it can be shown that the Poor Law authorities pursued a consistent policy of keeping these dependent households in being rather than disbanding them and putting their members in institutions or combining one family group with another. This brings us back to Salisbury in 1604 and the actions of the civic authorities in maintaining households. It draws our attention once again to the inadvisability of looking on families, households, or familial systems as ever likely to be wholly self-sufficient or independent in respect to the collectivity that surrounds them, except perhaps in social structures organized entirely differently from those of preindustrial Europe and from the others discussed in the present volume. We may have here, in the variable role of the collectivity in ensuring the welfare of the membership, a criterion for comparing one social structure with another whose importance has been hitherto unsuspected.

We cannot overlook the much more familiar observation that the collectivity in its turn—and especially that manifestation of it which acts for the whole population and all its interests, the state—cannot be regarded as independent of the family in which it has a perennial, ineluctable interest. Reproduction and the nurturing and primary socialization of children has never been undertaken by collective instruments, except under extraordinary circumstances when the collectivity has established orphanages or, as in southern Europe in late medieval and early modern times, hospitals for foundlings, in each case with conspicuous lack of success. In spite of the claims of the utopians from Plato until our own generation, it still seems to be true that the collectivity cannot do for itself what families and family groups have always done for human populations—maintain the population in existence over time.

The usual definition of the differences between industrial and nonindustrial societies is one that makes the claim that production was dependent on the family before the coming of industry made it a wholly collective matter. We have seen that this assertion cannot be wholly supported. In nonindustrial societies production does have its site ordinarily in the household and does have household members as its work force, but not always, and perhaps never necessarily. This is certainly not the case in the sense that a productive association has always had to be coterminous with a reproductive association in societies we are disposed to call nonindustrial.

Once the distinction between productive and reproductive functions is accepted, the discussion may branch out in many directions. All require a great deal more information than we yet possess and much more analysis and reflection than has yet been undertaken, certainly in the present brief essay. The shift of emphasis implied by my title "The Family as a Knot of Individual Interests" has strategic importance to the study of social structure generally. When we think of a family group reacting to an economic or demographic vicissitude or making decisions and adopting policies to safeguard and enhance the life chances of its members, we must certainly think of this group as possessing something in the way of collective life. There is the inertia that all continuing associations display, however small they are and impermanent their membership. There is the reluctance of all parties to insist on their individual interest to the point of open friction and their unwillingness to risk a breakdown. There is the powerful influence of attitudes handed down from previous members of the group and even inherited from earlier generations, especially where neolocalism is not the familial rule. There are also pressures from the collectivity, as we have seen, promoting familial solidarity and continuity. But in my view none of these can transcend the character of the family group as a knot of individual interests, even if this concept makes it difficult to grasp how household decisions are arrived at and a strategy pursued. To think otherwise is to misunderstand our subject. We may have to reckon with the existence of rules of familial behavior which lack all public manifestation, but we are not required to believe in the real personality of familial groups.

NOTES

1. I have taken this example of Salisbury in 1604 from Paul Slack (1979:58) with its references. Other instances could certainly be found.

2. See E. A. Wrigley and R. S. Schofield (1981), chapters 8–10 and appendix 10. For the shortcomings of the protoindustrialization theory in these respects, see R. A. Houston and Keith Snell, "Proto-industrialization: Theory and Reality," forthcoming.

3. The model of the domestic group followed here is that elaborated at Cambridge, in which, however, inmates share not the *household* but the *houseful* (those residing in a distinct set of premises with the others). Contemporaries in preindustrial England would usually call all these unities by the same name—*family*—as well as the lineage and extended kin; see P. Laslett and R. Wall, eds. (1972), chapter 1. There are other models that draw a less rigid distinction between the family group on the one hand (i.e., usually the spouse and/or the children of the household head with coresident relatives) and servants or inmates on the other hand. In one such model lodgers and boarders are regarded as being members of the household as much as servants or even kin. The society for which the best case can be made for this model is probably nineteenth-century North America; see below and, e.g., Modell and Hareven (1973) and M. B. Katz (1976).

4. It may be significant that in earlier English usage a person's "friends" included his kin and affines, or those of them with whom an individual was in contact.

5. See S. J. Woolf and J. Goodman, "Household and Family in Early Nineteenth-century Italy," an unpublished paper at the Cambridge Group, 1982. In Florence around 1810, a quarter of the population (in Rome a third) applied to such sources for relief, which must imply, as the authors state, that the support of the extended kin was not forthcoming or was insufficient. Paupers from the surrounding countryside came into these cities for the purpose. That permanent sustenance from relatives was occasionally offered in England nevertheless is evident from that remarkable record of the interrelationships in the seventeenth-century English village of Myddle (see Richard Gough 1981:191). On page 192 a case of maintenance by neighbors alone is cited. In general, however, such occurrences seem to have been noted because they were exceptional, and they were exceptional even for quite close relatives.

6. It can be added that the number of brothers and sisters a person in his thirties would have on average is fewer now than it was in the past (under two as against three or a little over in the cases simulated by Le Bras), so that there is not so much potential competition between grown children for parental assistance.

More detailed figures of this kind, giving complete distributions of extant relatives for a range of demographic schedules, are in preparation at the Cambridge Group.

7. In Mitterauer's opinion only families that exhibit this structure at some stage in the family cycle are true stem families; if the heir comes in from outside at his father's retirement and takes over the headship, allowing the older man with his wife and any remaining children to stay on, that is not a true stem family, as Berkner and others have supposed. But there are many forms of the stem family principle, producing a widespread and in my view rather tedious debate on whether it was ever widespread in Europe; see Laslett (1978).

8. The discussion of noumenal normative rules in the next few paragraphs was introduced verbally into the exchanges of the October 1981 conference that gave rise to the present volume. The discussion on norms was based on a contribution I prepared for a symposium, How Humans Adapt, which took place in November 1981. My contribution, entitled "Demographic History in Relation to Human Adaptation," has been published in Ortner 1983.

9. Research of Martin Clarke at the Cambridge Group. The theory of anomie is now in retreat among social scientists.

10. There were interesting and important variations in other respects in the composition of the English households from place to place and time to time, as in the numbers and types of relatives per household, lodgers per household, servants per household, headship rates, and so on. See R. Wall (1982: chap. 16).

11. A conversation in April 1982 with an old lady who had spent her girlhood in a *mezzadria*, a large-scale multiple household that she said contained 24 people who had been engaged in sharecropping in the region of Bologna in Italy, seemed to confirm these observations. She talked at length about the pleasure of companionship and mutual entertainment at that period of her life but insisted that it had a fatal disadvantage. Everyone lacked liberty. She later married a smallholder and they founded a nuclear family of their own, in which they were living as a couple in the empty-nest stage of the family life cycle.

12. Turnbull's conclusions do not seem to be generally accepted by those qualified to judge.

13. On annual hiring fairs in England and on the disposition of servants to change households every year or two, see Kussmaul (1981). No comparable study of servants in Europe as a whole has yet been attempted, but see chapter 1, and Hajnal's contribution to Wall, Robin, and Laslett (1983).

14. See Laslett (1983*b*) on neolocalism and its structural significance for its references to work in progress or in contemplation. I insist there that it is the family that undergoes *cycles*, not the individual (who has a *life course*), not the household (which has a *history*) and not the domestic group as a whole, to which events occur in a noncyclical manner. Vagueness and confusion about these distinctions is widespread, and many seem to have wrongly assumed that these problems have already been satisfactorily settled.

15. See the work of J. C. Caldwell as summarized and criticized in R. M. Smith (1981). Repetitive examples of "setting up" each child successively can be conveniently found in Gough (1981). It can be regarded as implied in neolocal

principles, though by no means all of the resources necessary for establishing new households came from the parents of the spouses-to-be. They themselves accumulated all they could for the purpose and in this way retained resources that might otherwise have gone upward to the older generation.

16. Compare Hareven (1974), Bodnar (1980), and Gribaudi (1982). For the authoritative portrayal of domestic group relations in the past as instrumental, see Anderson (1971).

17. See Mitterauer and Sieder (1982, chap. 3). For them it is the family of industrial society which shows long-term stability in membership rather than that of the *ancien régime*, which, apart from the high rate of turnover of its members, had varying membership in relation to productive organization and requirements. The fleeting character of this membership has been confirmed wherever historical data make it possible to follow the household's course over time—in Belgium, in Italy, even in the Baltic States as well as in England or Austria.

18. See Wilk's contribution to this volume for a contemporary Caribbean example of interhousehold collaboration to form work groups, a circumstance that persuades Wilk to give up the household as a useful unity for social analysis, apparently for all purposes as well as for production.

19. See Laslett (1983*b*), the chapter having the title "Family and Household as Work Group and Kin Group: Areas of Traditional Europe Compared." Compare the position of male breadwinners absent in the city in contemporary Africa, whose own familial groups are necessarily weakened in cohesiveness but who do not join, and dilute, other familial groups for working purposes.

20. The most extreme declaration is found in the *Patriarcha* of Sir Robert Filmer (written in the 1680s) (ed. P. Laslett, 1948). See also G. Schochet, *Patriarchalism in Political Thinking* (1975). Filmer and his followers believed that despotism was the only natural form of government because the state was interchangeable with the family (the household), and the head of the household was by nature a despot over his domestic subjects.

21. For household economies of this type, often female headed, see, e.g., Louise Tilly (1979). For the partnership between man and wife in traditional households, see Laslett (1983*c*, chap. 4), and especially Martine Segalen (1983).

22. See Laslett (1979). Investigation of Poor Law policy in nineteenth-century England shows that the principles set out above were not always respected at that time.

REFERENCES

Anderson, Michael
1971 Family Structure in Nineteenth-century Lancashire. Cambridge: Cambridge University Press.

Bodnar, J.
1980 Immigration, Kinship, and the Rise of Working Class Realism in Industrial America. Journal of Social History 14:45–66.

Czap, Peter
1983 A Large Family: The Peasant's Greatest Wealth. Serf Households in Mishino, Russia, 1814–1858. *In* Family Forms in Historic Europe, ed. R. Wall, J. Robin, and P. Laslett. Cambridge: Cambridge University Press.
1982 The Perennial Multiple Family Household. Journal of Family History 7:5–26.

Filmer, Robert
1948 Patriarcha (orig. 1680). Edited by P. Laslett. Oxford: Blackwell.

Gough, Richard
1981 The History of Myddle (orig. 1701). Edited by David G. Hey. Harmondsworth: Penguin.

Gribaudi, Maurizio
1982 Stratégies Migratoires et Mobilité Relative entre Village et Ville. Population 37e année 6:1159–83.

Hareven, Tamara
1974 The Family Process: The Historical Study of the Family Cycle. Journal of Social History 7:322–29.

Houston, R. A., and Keith Snell
Forthcoming. Proto-industrialisation: Theory and Reality. The Historical Journal.

Katz, M. B.
1976 The People of Hamilton, Canada West: Family and Class in a Mid-nineteenth-century City. Cambridge: Harvard University Press.

Kussmaul, Ann
1981 Servants in Husbandry in Early Modern England. Cambridge: Cambridge University Press.

Laslett, Peter
1956 The Face to Face Society. *In* Philosophy, Politics, and Society, series 1, ed. P. Laslett. Oxford: Blackwell.
1978 The Stem Family and Its Privileged Position. *In* Statistical Studies of Historical Social Structure, ed. K. W. Wachter, E. A. Hammel, and P. Laslett. New York: Academic Press.
1979*a* The Family and the Collectivity. Sociology and Social Research 63: 432–42.
1979*b* Family Life and Illicit Love in Earlier Generations. Cambridge: Cambridge University Press.
1983*a* Demographic History in Relation to Human Adaptation. *In* How Humans Adapt. Ed. Donald J. Ortner. Washington, D.C.: Smithsonian Institution.
1983*b* Family and Household as Work Group and Kin Group. *In* Family Forms in Historic Europe, ed. R. Wall, J. Robin, and P. Laslett. Cambridge: Cambridge University Press.
1983*c* The World We Have Lost Further Explored (Being the 3rd Edition of The World We Have Lost). London: Methuen.

Laslett, Peter, K. Oosterveen, and R. Smith, eds.
1980 Bastardy and Its Comparative History. Cambridge: Harvard University Press.
Laslett, Peter, and R. Wall, eds.
1972 Household and Family in Past Time. Cambridge: Cambridge University Press.
Le Bras, Hervé
1982 Evolutions des licns de famille au cours de l'existence. *In* Les Ages de la Vie. L'Institut National d'Etudes Demographiques.
Macfarlane, A.
1970 The Family Life of Ralph Josselin. Cambridge: Cambridge University Press.
Mitterauer, Michael, and Reinhard Sieder
1982 The European Family: Patriarchalism to Partnership from the Middle Ages to the Present. Oxford: Blackwell.
Modell, John, and Tamara Hareven
1973 Urbanisation and the Malleable Household. Journal of Marriage and the Family 35:467–79.
Poni, Carlo
1978 Family and "Podere" in Emilia Romagna. Journal of Italian History 1:201–34.
Schochet, Gordon J.
1975 Patriarchalism in Political Thought. Oxford: Blackwell.
Segalen, Martine
1983 Love and Power in the Peasant Family. Oxford: Blackwell.
Slack, Paul
1979 Mortality Crises and Epidemic Disease in England, 1485–1610. *In* Health, Medicine, and Mortality in the Sixteenth Century, ed. Charles Webster. Cambridge: Cambridge University Press.
Smith, R. M.
1979 Kin and Neighbours in a Thirteenth-Century Suffolk Community. Journal of Family History 4:219–56.
1981 Fertility, Economy, and Household Formation in England over Three Centuries. Population and Development Review 7:595–622.
Sieder, R., and M. Mitterauer
1983 The Reconstruction of the Family Life Course. *In* Family Forms in Historic Europe, ed. R. Wall, J. Robin, and P. Laslett. Cambridge: Cambridge University Press.
Tilly, Louise, and Joan W. Scott
1978 Women, Work, and Family. New York: Holt, Rinehart and Winston.
Turnbull, Colin
1973 The Mountain People. London: Cape.
Wall, Richard
1982 The Household, Demographic and Economic Change in England, 1680–1970. *In* Family Forms in Historic Europe, ed. R. Wall, J. Robin, and P. Laslett, chap. 16. Cambridge: Cambridge University Press.

Woolf, S. J., and J. Goodman
1982 Household and Family in Early Nineteenth-century Italy. Cambridge Group. Manuscript.
Wrightson, K., and D. Levine
1979 Poverty and Piety in an English Village: Terling, 1525–1700. New York: Academic Press.
Wrigley, E. A., and R. S. Schofield
1981 The Population History of England, 1541–1871. London: Edward Arnold.

PART IV

Synthetic Models of Household Change

15

Households in the Early Middle Ages: Symmetry and Sainthood

David Herlihy

The history of the early medieval household has for several years attracted the close attention of scholars, but we are still far from a satisfactory appreciation of its experiences, of the forces that molded it and the shapes it assumed, across this long span of human history.[1] And of all periods of the Middle Ages, the years of transition from the ancient to the medieval worlds, from approximately the fifth through the eighth centuries, are at once pivotal and perplexing. The age witnesses the meeting and blending of different social and cultural systems—Roman and barbarian, Christian and heathen. What kinds of households can be observed in the early Middle Ages?

In this paper I shall examine two topics central to the study of early medieval households. The first is the emergence of the household as a standard, commensurable unit in social surveys. When, and under what conditions, did governments ("chiefs," in this context, might be the better word) first utilize a count of hearths as a measure of a community's size and productive capacities? The second topic is the character and structure of families and households among early medieval elites—the stratum of society our scanty sources best illuminate.

HOUSEHOLDS AS COMMENSURABLE UNITS

Social analysts have developed many useful definitions and typologies of households, applicable to many societies at many times (Laslett 1972).

They have not, however, to my knowledge, satisfactorily addressed this closely related issue: the historical use of households as standard units in surveys and assessments. The adoption of this tactic implies that households had come to possess a certain commensurability across society. Put another way, society itself, in terms of its households, was acquiring a certain symmetry; no matter in what direction the surveyor looked, toward urban or rural areas, toward rich or poor, the households he discerned bore more resemblances than differences. The use of hearth lists in the distribution of taxes further implies that households were assuming roughly comparable roles in the production of wealth.

When do communities first show predominantly commensurable households? To this question I can offer only a partial answer, for two reasons. Limited competence requires that I restrict these observations to historic societies directly linked to the Western tradition. And our sources allow us to judge not truly the structure of societies, only the techniques adopted by surveyors in estimating their size and resources. Still, even this indirect evidence has manifest interest. Could there have been a radical divergence between the eye of the surveyor and the society he was seeking to measure?

The ancient Mediterranean world maintained a long tradition of censuses and surveys. Perhaps the most famous of them are the nine censuses recorded in the Bible.[2] Thus, according to the Book of Numbers, God directed Moses and Aaron to "take the sum of all the congregation of the children of Israel by their families and houses, and the names of everyone, as many as are of the male sex, from twenty years old and upwards, of all the men of Israel fit for war. . . ."[3] The males were to be grouped and counted according to families and kin, but they, and not the family or hearth, remained the target of the survey. So the hearth was not a basic unit in any tax survey described in the Bible.

According to the Greek historian Herodotus, Amasis, king of Egypt, every year recorded the occupations of his subjects, but here adult males, and not households, were the object of his inquest.[4] The Greeks themselves were the first to develop a theory of household organization. This was "economics," the science of ruling households, and was closely related to "politics," the science of governing cities.[5] Greek theorists, like the Romans after them, equated the household either with the persons (wife, children, slaves) subject to its head, or, still more commonly, with its possessions. "The household," wrote Xenophon, "looked to us to be the totality of possessions."[6] The management of property thus became a central concern of "economics," but the household envisioned in Greek theory was clearly big and rich and could not have been typical of society as a whole.

The Romans were the great census takers in the ancient Mediterranean world. Every five years special officers, the censors, were required to register citizens liable to bear arms or pay taxes and prepare an inventory of their possessions. We have fragmentary results of their efforts dating from 225 B.C., and the practice was continued into the imperial period, apparently until the reign of Vespasian (A.D. 69–79) (Kubitschek 1899; Brunt 1971:15–25). As the empire grew, the government imposed similar censuses and assessments on the provinces. But neither in counting its subjects nor in assessing their wealth did the Romans make use of household units. In the period of the late Empire (fourth and fifth centuries) the Roman government developed an elaborate, and for historians still opaque, method of tax assessment, known as the *capitatio–iugatio.*[7] *Capitatio* involved a count of heads, presumably able-bodied workers; *iugatio* was an estimate of land area and its productivity; and, in ways that are less than clear, animals too were factored into the assessment. The methods were so intricate as to cause wonder: why did not the Roman assessors simply count by households and assign an assessment to each? We can only speculate: perhaps Roman agriculture still remained mixed, with many single family farms alongside great estates worked by gangs of slaves. These latter productive units could not be readily assessed by a count of households.

It can be further argued that the ancients lacked a clear concept of the hearth or household, as a moral entity, comparable and commensurable across society. If for the Greeks the household or family was usually equivalent to its possessions, to the Romans it seems commonly to have included only members, but not all the members: the wife or wives, children and slaves, but not the chief. The jurist Ulpian (second century A.D.) thus writes: ". . . in strict law we define the family as the many persons, who by nature or law are set under the authority of an individual, such as the *paterfamilias.* . . ."[8] Isidore of Seville, a writer of encyclopedic interests who died in 636, avers that *familia* derives from *femur* "loin" and means in the strict sense "offspring."[9] The Romans, to be sure, had words for hearth (*focus*) and for household gods (*lares, penates*). *Focus* meant the physical hearth or, in late Latin, the fire within it (cf. Italian, *fuoco*). It also was used to symbolize the collectivity of households, as in the rallying cry *pro aris et focis,* "for altars and hearths." But *focus* seems rarely to have been used as a metaphor for households, and it never represents a coresidential domestic unit common to all social levels.[10]

Only in one area of Roman institutions and life do households appear as equivalent units in a social array: the foundation of new settlements or colonies. Since the early Republic the Roman government had rewarded veteran soldiers with grants of land. Grouped into colonies, the veterans worked their farms primarily with the aid of their families; they could have owned few or no slaves.[11] These farms were units of production as well as residence, and this made them particularly suitable for surveys.

The appearance and use of commensurable household units thus seem intimately related to the extension of family-based, or peasant, agriculture over the soil of the empire. Perhaps this close association with peasant agriculture also explains why the ancient censors utilized hearths so rarely in their work. The unit could not be easily used to assess large, slave-run estates (or big ranches in the pastoral regions). Then, too, ancient societies showed enormous variations in the range of wealth, from patricians owning thousands of slaves to the slaves themselves, pitiful chattel, most of whom were herded into barracks. Household units, with their implication of a rough equality across society, could not measure the size, wealth, and productivity of such socially cleaved communities. Phrased in different fashion, the households of the ancient world seem to have been for the most part incommensurable, and the household system, of which they were a part, asymmetrical.

The full appearance of commensurable domestic units set within a symmetrical household system had to await, it would appear, the demise of ancient slavery and its replacement in most areas of the former Roman Empire by peasant agriculture. The Venerable Bede (d. 735), in his *Ecclesiastical History of the English People*, gives perhaps the most dramatic example of the new usage. He routinely estimates the size both of small estates and of entire regions of England in terms of *familiae*, or families (he doubtlessly was thinking "hides," farms large enough to occupy the labors of a single household). In doing so, he claims to be following "the customs of the English." But on the Continent too, from about 700 or even somewhat earlier, our sources make allusion to counts of households. From the late eighth and ninth centuries, the family farm, called variously *mansus, focus, familia, casata, casa massaricia* (in Italy), *hufe* (in Germany), *hide* (in England), becomes the basic unit of manorial and fiscal assessment.[12] It is interesting to note that in these medieval hearth lists the manor house is assimilated for purposes of assessment to the family farm. It is commonly called *mansus indominicatus*, "lordly farm." Ancient commentators on the household gave exclusive attention to the large and rich domestic units; they made no pretense that these were standard in society. Medieval surveyors, however, made the humble peasant hearth and farm the units by which the entire community should be measured.

Although the emergence of the family farm is a dominant theme of early medieval social history, still we know little about the domestic arrangements of the humble in pre-Carolingian times. We are better, though never well, informed about elite families and households during these darkest centuries of the Middle Ages.

ELITE FAMILIES AND HOUSEHOLDS

To enter the homes of the elite is necessarily to review, even if briefly, the character of our surviving sources. In broadest terms the sources of medieval social history fall into three principal categories. The first and perhaps the most revealing are so-called "documents of practice"—administrative records, chartularies or collections of charters, surveys, and similar documents (see Herlihy 1975). Better than any other kind of social document, these records tell us what every historian fundamentally wants to know—what really happened. For some places and periods of the Middle Ages these documents of practice are marvelously abundant. But they are not abundant for the epoch that interests us here. Records of this type survive in fairly continuous series only from about A.D. 750. To penetrate back into older times is to do so without the help of our surest documentary guides.

The second type of record I shall call normative and didactic—laws, commandments, and exhortations to obey the laws and commandments. Here we find much aid in our search for families. The great collections of Roman law redacted in late antiquity—the Theodosian Code of the fifth century and the Justinian Corpus Iuris Civilis of the sixth—have preserved numerous imperial enactments concerning marriage, many of them dating from the fourth century.[13] The barbarian codes of Western Europe, written roughly between 500 and 800, and the later but still primitive brehon law of Ireland similarly yield many references to marital arrangements, inheritance, and the like.[14] But biases are also present. The laws reflect the desires of kings and emperors, not truly the behavior of people. And the laws, even the barbarian codes, are already heavily colored by the memories of Rome and the teachings of the Christian Church.

Since the foundation of the church, Christian writers commented profusely on marriage and family life and the moral problems connected with them. And yet these didactic writings do not serve the purposes of social history as well as their prolixity might promise. They largely concentrate on those aspects of the conjugal and parental tie which primarily concerned Christian ethics: impediments to marriage arising out of consanguinity, affinity, age or intent; the purposes and practice of sex; divorce and concubinage; the reciprocal obligations binding husbands, wives, and children. The model of medieval marriage, emerging from the legal and didactic literature, is thus very narrow. Moreover, long retaining a near monopoly on literacy, these didactic authors inevitably leave the impression that the ecclesiastical model of marriage was a realistic one, that it accurately describes the behavior of medieval people. The most recent research on the medieval family now calls this assumption into question—for Merovingian Frankland (Wemple 1981; McNamara and Wemple 1977), for early Ireland (Power 1977), for twelfth-century France (Duby 1978), for twelfth- and thirteenth-century Iceland (Jochens 1980).

But what was common behavior within the communities of the early Middle Ages? The principal hope for enlightenment would seem to be a third category of sources: narrative. The early Middle Ages boasts several informative chroniclers: Gregory of Tours in Frankland, the Venerable Bede in England, to name only the most famous.[15] But for social history they are rivaled in value by another type of narrative account that is even more abundant: the lives of saints.

Saints who purportedly lived in the early Middle Ages are numerous. Let us bound the period with exact dates: 476, the year traditionally used to mark the end of the Western Empire, and 751, when the coronation of Pepin, according to long convention, introduces the Carolingian age. The standard bibliography of saints' lives—the two volumes and supplement of the *Bibliotheca Hagiographica Latina*—lists by name 3,276 saints who lived before 1500.[16] Better than a quarter of them—866 by my count—purportedly flourished between 476 and 751. Early medieval saints nearly equal in number the 925 holy men and women, almost all of them martyrs, who earned their crowns during the age of persecutions. The early Middle Ages are in fact more crowded with saints than any other period of medieval history.[17]

As a distinct literary genre saints' lives have this characteristic—this advantage—from the point of view of the social historian: the lawgiver and didactic writer look forward, with a view to correcting future behavior. The early hagiographer frequently, even usually, looks backward into a world still unregenerated by Christian faith. The saint often contends with the heathen past and, in contending, illuminates.

To be sure, early hagiography presents formidable difficulties of interpretation. Commonplaces abound: stereotypical persons, acts, situations. Few lives of the early Middle Ages were written by authors who had a personal knowledge of their holy subjects. Many modern scholars, over many generations, have wrestled with these delicate questions of *Quellenforschungen*. In the now common opinion the early lives are rarely to be trusted in exact detail, in their depictions of real events. But they offer authentic insight into cult and culture. Do they not illuminate social behavior as well, specifically the behavior sanctioned by the fading pagan order?

One set of purportedly early lives requires special heed and handling. These are the lives of Irish saints. The principal setting of these lives is of course Ireland, but the saints in their famous peregrinations wandered widely, and allusions to Britain, to Gaul, and even to Italy are frequent.[18] The named saints of Ireland for the period roughly before 800 are many, nearly a hundred in number (see Plummer 1925:171 ff.). This small land, set on the margins of the world, earned the title it is given in one of the lives, the *insula sanctorum*.[19]

The tradition by which these many lives have reached us is obscure. They are principally preserved in three great manuscripts, all of them apparently written in the fourteenth century. Internal evidence—references, for example, to the Norman conquest of England—indicate that they were probably composed in the late eleventh and twelfth centuries.[20] But all of them pretend to recount the lives of saints who flourished in early Christian Ireland, soon after the time of St. Patrick, in the sixth and seventh centuries. These lives thus hover like a mist over some 800 years of Irish and European history, without firm moorings. But they possess certain striking qualities. The rhetorical bombast that obscures many continental lives is here restrained. They are rich in homely allusions—to the tending of flocks and herds, to the making of cheese and butter, to the daily activities of peasants, shepherds, artisans, bards. Most important for our purposes, they populate the landscape with living families and households and describe domestic arrangements in vivid detail. But can the picture of social life they offer be trusted?

Many scholars have commented on the aura of archaism which permeates these lives.[21] The Irish saints, for example, often ride about in chariots driven by an *auriga*, or charioteer. One of the three great hagiographical collections, the Codex Salmanticensis, formerly the property of the Irish College of Salamanca in Spain, is especially noteworthy for its archaic flavor. In the fourteenth century copyists and editors tried to rid all three collections of incidents and allusions thought to be unedifying, but the censors of the Salamanca Codex proved especially inept. *Felix culpa!* The codex, for example, contains a rare reference in medieval hagiography to delousing. The young saint Molua is depicted picking lice from the hair of an aged friend.[22] The service must have been frequently performed in medieval society, but it is not the usual stuff of pious legend. The codex also treats in startling fashion a not uncommon hagiographical topic: the plight of the pregnant nun.

Nuns, rendered pregnant usually through illicit love affairs, appear fairly often in saints' lives. The story of the nun of Watton, related by the twelfth-century Cistercian abbot Aelred of Rievaulx and recently reexamined by Giles Constable (1970), is a well-known version of the incident. In the tale, in order to save the convent from scandal, the Virgin Mary herself secretly delivers the nun's baby and spirits it away, presumably to a safe haven. None of these incidents that I have so far read manifests any hostility toward the fetus or baby, however tainted its origins. Indeed, in the early thirteenth-century life of the abbess St. Erendruda of Salzburg the saint and her helpers make strenuous efforts to aid the child. One of Erendruda's nuns becomes pregnant. As the time of her delivery draws near, desperate and fearing punishment, she calls on the devil for help. "Oh devil," she pleads, "assist me in this my gravest difficulty, and I shall give you the baby I shall bear, body and soul, into eternal damnation."[23] But the abbess's brother, a saintly priest, learns of her design, rescues the baby from the clutches of the devil, and, in the words of the Life, "had him at once baptized and given to a nurse to be reared, until he be instructed in the Catholic faith. . . ."[24]

Much in contrast to this benign treatment of the illegitimate child, the Life of the Irish saint Kieran, in the version preserved in the Salamanca Codex, betrays a harsh spirit of vengeance. A petty king (*regulus*) named Dimma abducts a "noble and beautiful girl" from a convent founded by Kieran's mother and takes the girl to wife. The enraged saint seeks him out and through his miraculous powers forces him to relinquish the girl. The story continues: "When the man of God returned with the girl to the monastery, the girl confessed that she had conceived in the womb. Then the man of God, led by zeal for justice, not wishing that the seed of vipers should quicken, making the sign of the cross on the womb, caused it to empty."[25]

The text is unambiguous: the saint miraculously aborts the fetus.[26] Both the Irish penitentials and the brehon laws, themselves archaic sources, forbid induced abortions, even of illegitimate fetuses (see Power 1977:33, 65). The saints' lives, in sum, seem to hearken back to an even more ancient epoch.

Early hagiography, insular and continental, thus carries us to a strange, occasionally savage world, still largely influenced by traditional heathen customs, still only slightly touched by a crude Christianity. I shall here pretend that the lives reveal what they purport to show: social life in barbarian Western Europe at the origins of the Middle Ages. This much at least may be safely affirmed: The social system that emerges from these lives does possess, as I hope to illustrate, a certain inner logic and coherence. The images of families the lives contain are worth examining, even if we do not know where exactly those images belong in space and time.

The questions I shall apply to these documents are the following: What kinds of marriages are evident within them? What were the roles of household members, of women and children in particular, whose experiences often provide the most revealing insights into household organization?

All of the marriages we encounter in the lives seem monogamous. But legal monogamy did not, as we shall shortly see, preclude the formation of other forms of sexual liaison. The legal wife is the *domus domina*, the mistress of the household, as she is called in the Life of St. Brigid of Ireland.[27] She also performs certain other critical services for the household and family. When the four half-brothers of Brigid try to force her into marriage, they advance two reasons. Through her vow of virginity, they complain, "she avoids that for which God made her, and in her obstinacy so lives, and is determined to live, so as not to want to make her father a grandfather and her brothers uncles."[28] She thus causes them "great shame and expense." Here, I believe, is an important insight. Brigid is the half-sister of these males, and indeed her mother is a slave. But their own mother—Brigid's stepmother—has been cursed with sterility and cannot produce another sister. Brigid offers her half-brothers their one possible link through a sister to the coming generation. They seem to be themselves unmarried, and no one of them is bothered by the celibacy of the others. Yet they insist that Brigid marry. This highlights the capital importance of the avunculate relationship in early medieval kinship systems. I shall return to this topic presently.

In urging her to marry, Brigid's brothers further argue that her husband, who will surely be noble, will be for them all, for brothers and for father, a champion and friend (*propugnator et amicus*).[29] The wife was thus critically important in defining the relations of her family of origin to other powerful persons and clans in the vicinity.

In keeping with the important services she rendered, the legal wife seems also to have controlled important wealth and to have wielded considerable influence, even power, over decisions made within the household. In both Ireland and on the Continent, the lives make clear that the groom, or his family, conveyed property to the bride, which she personally controlled.[30] This reverse dowry, probably best called bridewealth, included even land. In the Life of St. Mochteus, for example, a widow bestows on the holy man a field she received as part of her dower, an *agrum dotalem*.[31] Apparently some women accumulated wealth through gifts from their husbands, and even from other males, over the entire course of their marriage. In the Life of St. Fursa, a nobleman of Gaul reminds his wife of the "riches I have given you."[32] In the Life of St. Aed, a king bestows a gold and silver brooch (*spina*) on a woman who is clearly not his wife.[33] Wealthy women often appear in the tales. St. Fursa, when passing through Arras in Gaul, seeks hospitality from a lady named Ermenfleda, who owns "many possessions and moneys."[34] After the saint's death, his merits cure of illness another rich lady, who also holds "many riches and possessions."[35]

Women had the right to divorce their husbands and depart their households, taking their wealth with them. This gave them substantial power over their husband's behavior. The stepmother of St. Brigid threatens to leave her husband Dubthach if he does not sell his slave concubine, Brigid's mother, then pregnant with the saint.[36] Her threat carries real force, as she bends her reluctant husband to her will and later gains his acquiescence in her persecution of the young saint. So also, in Gaul, the lady Leutisinda berates her husband and threatens to abandon their marriage, if he continued to bestow their properties on St. Fursa.[37]

The legal wife in these elite households is rich and powerful, but her presence does not stop her husband from forming other sexual liaisons. The Life of St. Brigid offers a particularly lively picture of sexual relations inside and outside of legal marriage.[38] Dubthach, Brigid's father, is clearly a rich man, possessing large flocks and herds and extending the hospitality of his table to numerous guests. Perhaps he is also a Christian; at least he welcomes bishops to his table, with exultation and a smiling face, in the language of the Life. Besides his legal wife, he cohabits with a slave girl (*concubina*). When the story of Brigid's life begins, Dubthach has rendered both women, wife and concubine, pregnant. The Life utters not a hint of reproach against Dubthach for this violation of Christian marriage. On the contrary, the anonymous author rather reproaches the legal wife for forcing her husband through threats of divorce to get rid of his concubine. The wife is depicted as stupid and mad; she lacks matronly modesty and fails to show proper respect for her husband; she has an evil mind and she behaves like a raging beast.[39] She draws all this abuse because she objects to the presence of a concubine in her household. Dubthach is exonerated from all guilt, even for driving his pregnant concubine from his house. "My wife prevents me," he explains, "from being liberal and humane toward my concubine."[40]

The lives consistently show a tolerant attitude toward sexual relations outside of legal marriage. They describe, for example, again without a suggestion of reproach, the illegitimate births of several other saints. The noble father of St. Ailbe secretly sleeps with a slave girl, the concubine of King Cronan of Artaige.[41] The girl becomes pregnant, and the father, fearing the wrath of the king for impregnating one of his women, takes to flight. King Cronan assumes that the father of the baby was, like the mother, a slave, and in his fury orders that the child be exposed. Servants leave the baby in the wilderness, where a she-wolf finds him and suckles him along with her cubs. In spite of these inauspicious origins, the boy grows up to become a renowned bishop and, according to his Life, a second Patrick. Another example is King Echach and his three beautiful daughters. One of them falls in love with a noble warrior in her father's service, apparently seduces him, and bears a son by him without benefit of legal matrimony. She delivers the baby in secret, and the father spirits him away to his own country. The child, called Tigernach, also grows up to become a holy bishop and a famous saint.[42] And the father of St. Barr was born of an incestuous union of father and daughter, was exposed at birth, and was also suckled by a wolf.[43]

Although legal marriage was monogamous, these Irish aristocrats, like the Merovingian kings on the Continent, seem sometimes to have cohabited with two or more free women simultaneously. Dimma, the petty king who according to the Life of St. Kieran abducted the girl from the convent, makes her his wife, according to the text. But he seems already to have been married; at least, he has had two children by another woman, one of whom at the time of this incident was still being nursed.[44] Unions of this sort, made without benefit of contract, dower, and dowry, are often called in the scholarly literature by their German title, *Friedelehe* (from *fidila*, "beloved"). They were common among the Merovingian elites, and the Irish also seem to have possessed an analogous institution (see Wemple 1981:12–14).

Can these admittedly scattered references to early medieval families be interpreted in terms of a single, coherent system of marriage? According to the lives the maintenance of several sexual liaisons is unmistakably the prerogative of the wealthy and the powerful. The rich man, such as Dubthach, can afford to purchase a slave girl for a concubine and support her in his household. A petty king such as Dimma has the power to abduct the girl that he desires, and only a wonder-worker can retrieve her. The rescue of abducted girls gives frequent employment to these early saints, even as it gains much attention in the barbarian laws. St. Aed brings back several girls from the possession of kings who had abducted them.[45] On the Continent St. Rusticula of Arles was carried off by an impatient suitor when she was only five years old.[46]

Those males who possessed wealth and power used it to acquire women too. In anthropological terminology the common name for such a system is *resource polygyny*.[47] Even in societies where polygyny is legal, only the richest and most powerful males will usually command the resources needed for the support of several sexual partners. This anthropological model is suggestive, but it does not fit exactly the marriages and households portrayed in the hagiographic literature for two reasons.

First, while sexual liaisons were often multiple, legal marriage remained monogamous. And second, women were gathered into the households of the powerful not exclusively for sexual purposes.

Thus even the households of the early Irish bishops, who were celebrated for their chastity, seem to have accumulated women. The collections, for example, contain a curious passage on "the three orders of the saints of Ireland."[48] The first and indeed the holiest of the orders flourished from the days of St. Patrick and survived over four dynasties. Some 480 bishops, founders of churches, comprised it. "They did not," reads the passage, "spurn the administration of women and their company."

Our documents of practice, surviving from the middle eighth century, offer further evidence of this tendency for women to congregate in the households of the powerful. A partial survey from the monastery of Farfa in central Italy, redacted between 789 and 822, describes 299 dependent families plus the slaves attached to a manor house at Forcone.[49] The sex ratio for the entire population shows a dearth of women. Men outnumber them by a ratio of 122 to 100. But among the servants in the manor house women outnumber men by 73 to 23 in absolute count. Even this monastic estate enlisted proportionately large numbers of women into the immediate service of its lords.

The aggregation of women in a monastic manor house should again remind us that the attraction of women to rich and powerful males was not exclusively sexual. Women, according to the lives, performed numerous services for the family, all of them important, some of them essential. St. Brigid, when she labored under her stepmother's cruel dominance, was a jack-of-all-trades—or a jill-of-all-chores. According to her Life she milked the cows, tended the sheep and pigs, and helped in the harvest; she cooked, baked, made cheese and butter, and brewed beer; she waited at table, wove cloth, and nursed the sick.[50]

The Life of the German St. Liutbirg is even more explicit concerning what it expressly calls "the various skills which suit women" and the *muliebria opera,* "feminine labors."[51] A lady of the high nobility named Gisla encounters the young Liutbirg in a convent, observes her skill and virtue, and adopts her into her household. Liutbirg soon assumes a major role in the direction of household affairs, first for Lady Gisla, then for her son Bernard. Her biographer relates: "So completely did she assume the management of affairs, that the governance of the household rested almost entirely with her."[52] She wove cloth and ran a dye works. Dyeing seems to have been an exclusively feminine preserve, in Ireland and on the Continent.[53] Among the skills considered appropriate for women, at least for nuns, was reading. Young nuns learned to read the psalter as well as perform manual arts as part of their standard training.[54] Even some lay women mastered letters. The education of one tenth-century queen is described as "holy readings and work with the hands"[55].

Women thus tended to gather in the households of rich and powerful males, both for reasons of their sexual attraction and for reasons of service. A modified form of resource polygyny seems to have been a common model of aristocratic marriages and households in the early Middle Ages in Ireland and on the Continent as well. The model allows us to draw certain inferences concerning the social life of the epoch. We can now judge whether such inferences find support in the period's meager documentation.

One implication is this: resource polygyny tended to raise the incidence of sexual promiscuity within the community on the part of women as well as men. The rich man cohabiting with several women seeks to guard them from other men, but the task is difficult for two reasons. If some men claim many women, then other males will have none—on the assumption that the sexes are numerically balanced. They seek to overcome their deprivation through the purchase of a concubine, if they have the money; through abduction, if they have the power; or through seduction, if they have the charm. Moreover, the wife, like Dubthach's own, may resent sharing her husband's attentions and seek satisfaction, or even retribution, by cultivating her own extramarital affairs. And the disgruntled wife will have no trouble finding willing paramours.

Indeed, the women who appear in the lives are not passive sexual objects, moved about without acquiescence or resistance among powerful males. Women sometimes initiate these sexual liaisons. They repeatedly tempt the saints, although this may be only a hagiographical topos. The beautiful daughter of King Echach, mother of St. Tigernach, apparently seduces the saint's father. According to the Life of St. Kieran, a queen named Ethnea, wife of Engus, comes with her husband to a feast sponsored by another king named Concraidus.[56] She falls in love with her host and tries to seduce him. She is unable to consummate the adultery, but her failure does not indicate any lack of desire and effort on her part. One day St. Columba asks a young monk whether his mother is a religious woman. The surprised young monk replies that his mother is certainly of good morals and reputation.[57] The saint then instructs him to inquire from her about a certain grave sin—unnamed, but surely sexual. The abashed mother admits her guilt. In the same Life a layman expresses the fear that his wife, out of love for some younger man, may murder him.[58] Still another layman complains that his wife refuses to sleep with him, and only the saint's admonitions and power succeed in persuading her to fulfill her conjugal duties.[59] On the Continent the wife of St. Gangulf takes a lover and both successfully plot the saint's murder.[60] These are not passive women.

Even limited sexual promiscuity has the result of obscuring lines of descent through males. The issue of uncertain paternity emerges in the lives and is a frequent occasion for miraculous enlightenment. When a woman commits adultery, bears a child, but refuses to identify the father, St. Ailbe summons all the men of her village, as if all were equally suspect.[61] The baby at the saint's request names his father. In one of St. Brigid's miracles the saint in comparable fashion queries a three-year-old child and has him refute the allegations of his lying mother, who claims that a bishop is the father.[62] Both these women bore their children outside of legal wedlock, and but for miracles the paternity of the babies would have remained uncertain.

This situation is likely to impart to the male strong emotional ties with matrilineal relatives, even under the prevailing bilineal kin and inheritance systems. He has strong reason too for maintaining the rights of matrilineal relatives to shares in his inheritance. The children of his sister are certainly members of his clan and representatives of his stock—his *genus* and *semen* in the terminology of the Irish lives. And he has a better chance that his grandchildren through a daughter are his blood relatives than the grandchildren through a son. Both the continental and insular lives make frequent mention of the avunculate tie and other forms of matrilineal relationships. Duke Ludwin, who died ca. 713, "embraced with love" his maternal uncle St. Basinus, bishop of Trier, follows his counsel, gives up wife and rank to enter the religious life, and succeeds his uncle as bishop.[63] In Ireland, the maternal uncle of St. Alban, the bishop Ybar, is present at Alban's birth and blesses both mother and baby.[64] At age 12 the nephew joins his uncle and remains with him "many years." Their close spiritual fellowship is founded on the avunculate relationship. The nephew of St. Braccan, the son again of a sister, is a thief. He accidentally kills his uncle, and the crime is represented in the Life as especially heinous.[65] Three Irish saints—Cronan, Mobai, and Machonna—are parallel cousins (their respective mothers are sisters). Their spiritual relationship replicates the kinship tie running through women.[66] In the life of St. Ruadanus a man named Odo Guori flees for protection against an angered king to the bishop Senachus; the two are cousins, sons of sisters.[67] St. Fregius, uncle of St. Berach, takes the latter as a baby from his sister and nutures him, suckling him on his right ear.[68] Nephews often follow their maternal uncles into high office.

The surety and strength of matrilineal relationships buttressed the claim of daughters and their offspring to a share of the paternal inheritance. The various legal traditions of the early Middle Ages defined that share in various ways, but none of them excluded daughters from inheriting. All the traditions admitted them to the inheritance of movables; in regard to land, even in the worst cases, such as the famous Salic Law, women were postponed in relation to their brothers, not excluded. And they appear frequently in charters as holders of land.[69]

This modified form of resource polygyny also seems to have affected practices of child rearing. The presence of several mothers and several sets of offspring in the households of the powerful inevitably invited jealousy and dispute. Dubthach's legal wife, herself pregnant, is incensed when she hears the bishop prophesy that the offspring of her husband's concubine is destined to be mistress over her own sons and indeed over all Ireland.[70] Later she subjects the young Brigid to cruel persecutions. The wife of the king of Laigin, "like a faithless stepmother," tries to kill her husband's son, "for she feared that he would prevail over her own offspring."[71] Perhaps for their own protection young children were frequently, even usually, sent to be reared in different, often distant households. The foster mother is called in the lives the *nutrix*, as she assumed the duty of nursing the young child. The foster father is the *nutritor*. The bonds linking foster child and parents were often close. "Nature arranges," says the Life of St. Brigid, "that to those to whom they provide the milk of their flesh, nurses also offer the affection of their minds."[72] In the Life of St. Fintanus, a monk named Sinkellus tries to convert to the ways of righteousness both his natural father and his *nutritor*.[73] He brings the two men to St. Fintanus. The saint utters the gloomy prediction that the natural father will be numbered among the goats at the Last Judgment and adds, rather anticlimactically, that kings will also confiscate his property. But the foster father will be saved. Does this suggest that the services of the foster father were more meritorious than those of the natural parent?

I cannot review here the subsequent history of aristocratic marriages in the Middle Ages, except to make this single point. In the view of almost every historian, aristocratic marriages and households begin a transformation in Europe from the late eleventh and twelfth centuries (Duby 1970:12, bibliography). The new elite houses organize themselves along the line of male descent and become a kind of grouping of agnates. Aristocratic families then assume a family name, which is frequently associated with their place of origin, their ancestral castle or estate. They also adopt a coat of arms. Both family names and family arms proclaim the solidarity of the agnate lineage over time. Women no longer serve as the nodules through whom pass the surest kinship ties. They also lose their claim to a full share with their brothers in the family patrimony. Their fathers and brothers arrange for their marriages and provide the dowries that the changing terms of marriage now require. Barring unusual circumstances, the dowry marks the limit of the material support women receive from their families of origin. The status of women changes, even deteriorates, but there were compensations. The resource polygyny of the early Middle Ages, the effort of powerful males to acquire numerous women, created intense competition for their presence and their services. Women were subject to frequent abductions and to high levels of violence that disrupted their lives and perhaps even reduced their numbers in early medieval society.[74] Under the new marriage arrangements, women enjoy greater personal security, and they seem to be more evenly distributed across society.[75] And the married woman, unlike Dubthach's wife, now becomes the undisputed *domus domina*, the sole sovereign of her household.

The new lay model of aristocratic marriage often clashed with the church's teachings (a point emphasized in Duby 1978). Great laymen found the church's prohibition of marriage within prohibited degrees much too restrictive. Eager to arrange the marriages of their children, they also resisted the church's insistence that both bride and groom freely consent to their union. But this point must be emphasized: Prerequisite to the emergence of the new lay model was the success, always limited but nonetheless substantial, of the church's long campaign against extramarital sexual relations. As long as the elites of Europe, both men and women, cultivated multiple sexual liaisons, so the lines of agnate descent would remain obscure. So, too, any effort to define the elite family in terms of male solidarities would be frustrated. The increased authority of the church, arising from the eleventh-century reform and the new clarity and force of its teachings, were preconditions for this transformation of aristocratic marriages and of household structures in the central Middle Ages.

This rapid trip back to the exotic world of early medieval Ireland and of Europe has conjured up before us stimulating but elusive images. The risk remains that these shadowy portraits of saints and sinners might mislead us. Still, early hagiography invites us to view a world otherwise not easily visited. We must accept that invitation—and take that risk—if ever we are to trace the evolution of the medieval household across the full course of its history.

NOTES

1. For bibliographies of recent work on the history of the family, see Soliday 1980 and Erickson and Casey 1978.

2. For a review of biblical censuses and their much discussed meaning, see Westphal 1935.

3. Numbers 1:2–3.

4. Herodotus 1966, 2. 177. "It was Amasis who made the law that every Egyptian should yearly declare his means of livelihood to the ruler of his province. . . . Solon the Athenian got this law from Egypt and established it among his people; may they ever keep it: for it is a perfect law."

5. Aristotle 1946, pp. 1–38, in the first book of the *Politics*, discusses various meanings of *household* and concludes (p. 9): "We may make the assumption that property is part of the household and the art of acquiring property is part of household management" (i. 4).

6. Xenophon 1970, vi, 4 (p. 26).

7. Goffart 1974 and 1980 provides a recent discussion, with ample bibliography, of this long controverted topic.

8. Ulpian 1926. Dig. 50.16.195: ". . . iure proprio familiam dicimus plures personas, quae sunt sub unius potestate aut natura aut iure subiectae, ut puta patremfamilias. . . ."

9. Isidore of Seville 1911, Etym. 9.4.4: "Nam familia est liberi ex liberis legibus suscepti, a femore."

10. See the uses of the word cited in TLL 1900 (6.987).

11. See, for example, Livy 1957, 32.29.4: ". . . trecenae familiae in singulas colonias iubebantur mitti. . ." in regard to five colonies founded in Italy and 37.34.10 in regard to Spain, "sex milia familiarum conscribant, quae in eas colonias dividerentur. . . ." Both examples date from the third century B.C.

12. See, for example, Bede 1971, 3.24; Laws of Alamans and Bavarians 1979: cap. 21 (22). For a full discussion of the emergence of the family farm as an assessment unit, see Herlihy 1960.

13. Theodosian Code 1955. Corpus Iuris Civilis 1928–29. There is an English translation in 17 volumes, Corpus Iuris Civilis 1932.

14. See the recent translation of two of these barbarian codes, Laws of the Alamans and Bavarians 1979, with bibliography citing other editions and translations, pp. 16–24.

15. Portmann 1956 offers a survey of the depiction of women in early medieval sources, especially chronicles and saints' lives.

16. BHL 1909–1913.

17. The average number of saints per year is 2.32 under the Christian Roman Empire (313–476); 3.15 in Barbarian Europe (476–750); 1.15 in Carolingian Europe (751–850); 0.90 in the period 851–1000; 1.57 in 1001–1150; 1.65 in 1151–1347; and only 0.57 in the late Middle Ages (1348–1500).

18. St. Fursa, for example, "peregrina litora petens," journeyed "per Britanniam in Saxoniam," and eventually died in Gaul. See Codex Salmanticensis 1966:49.

19. Vita s. Abbani, Codex Salmanticensis 1966:256. "In occidentali plaga orbis est insula quedam . . . insula sanctorum nomine appropriate dicebatur."

20. Vita s. Brigidae, Codex Salmanticensis 1966:1: "Sed postquam Anglia dominos cepit habere Normannos. . . ."

21. See the comments of W. W. Heist on the "conservatism" of the Salamanca Codex, Codex Salmanticensis 1966:xi, and the remarks of Kenney 1927:1:294. Plummer, in his introduction to the Vitae sanctorum (1910:1:129–88), points out numerous survivals of "heathen folk-lore and mythology" in the lives of Celtic saints generally. Irish vernacular literature is similarly archaic. Chadwick (1970: 255) calls it "the oldest vernacular literature north of the Alps," although, like the Latin lives, it was not reduced to writing until comparatively late.

22. Vita prior s. Lugidi seu Moluae, Codex Salmanticensis 1966:132. "Alio die, quidam vir senex, de filiis Coilboth, caput suum in sinum pueri Lugidi reclinavit, ut puer a capite senis vermes colligeret."

23. De s. Erendruda virg. abbatissa Salisburgi in Bavaria, ASS, 5 Iunii, p. 583. "O diabole, fer mihi auxilium in hac maxima tribulatione, et dabo tibi hunc foetum quem producam, cum corpore et anima in damnationem sempiternam."

24. Ibid. " . . . fecitque puerum statim baptizari et tradi nutrici ad alendum, quousque in fide Catholica instrui posset. . . ."

25. Vita s. Ciarani saigirensis, Codex Salmanticensis 1966:348. "Tunc vir Dei, zelo iustitie ductus, viperium semen animari nolens, impresso ventri eius signo crucis, fecit illud exinaniri." In the expurgated version of the Life, the fetus simply vanishes. Vitae sanctorum 1910:1:221, "partus in utero evanuit."

26. Other allusions to the annihilation of fetuses, though not to abortions, are the following: Vita s. Aidi killariensis, Codex Salmanticensis 1966:172: "Intuens autem sanctus Aidus virginem que sibi ministrabat, vidit quod uterus illius, partum gestans, intumescebat. . . . Sanctus autem Aidus benedixit uterum eius, et statim infans in utero eius evanuit quasi non esset." Vita s. Cainnechi, Codex Salmanticensis 1966: 197: "Quedam virgo in vicino sibi loco habitans occulte fornicavit, et uterus eius partu intumuit. Que a sancto Kannecho postulavit ut uterum suum, quasi aliquo dolore tumescentem, benediceret. Cumque ille benedixisset eam, statim infans in utero eius non apparens evanuit."

27. Vita s. Brigidae, Codex Salmanticensis 1966:2, "sola domus domina."

28. Codex Salmanticensis 1966:15. "Illud refugit ad quod eam Deus fecit, et mente pertinaci sic vivit, et sic vivere disponit, ut nec avum patrem suum, nec avunculos esse velit fratres suos. Institutis Dei vanitatem suam anteponit . . . ad nostrum tam dedecus quam dispendium. . . ."

29. Codex Salmanticensis 1966:15. "Queramus aliquem nobilium, et certe repertu facilis erit, qui sit ei maritus et nostro patri gener, nobis autem omnibus propugnator et amicus."

30. The Merovingian St. Gangulf of Varennes, in repudiating his unfaithful wife, tells her that she may keep the *dos* he had given her for her support: "Illud denique, quod tibi in dotem sponsalicio iure dedi, ut vivere possis, habeto" (Vita Gangulfi martyris varennensis, p. 485).

31. Vita s. Mochtei, Codex Salmanticensis 1966:397. "Brigita vero se suumque dotalem viro Dei tradidit agrum. . . ."

32. Miracula S. Fursei, Codex Salmanticensis 1966:54.

33. Codex Salmanticensis 1966:177.

34. Miracula s. Fursei, Codex Salmanticensis 1966:51, "femina nomine Ermenefleda, que videbatur habere multas possessiones et pecunias."

35. Ibid., p. 55. "Erat quedam femina multas habens divicias et possessiones, sed valida infirmitate detinebatur cum suis hominibus . . ."

36. Vita s. Brigidae, Codex Salmanticensis 1966:1. ". . . verbis in virum amaris invehitur, de venditione puelle pertinaciter agit, unum iurans futurum ex duobus, aut puelle vendicionem aut suam ab eo separationem."

37. Miracula s. Fursei, Codex Salmanticensis 1966:54. "Fac me extraneam de tuo coniugio, si sic perseveras ut cepisti."

38. Codex Salmanticensis 1966:1–37.

39. Codex Salmanticensis 1966:2. "Hiis illa auditis, de stulta protinus efficitur insana, et verecundiam nesciens matronalem, neque maritalem magni faciens reverentiam, inhonestis sermonibus malignam mentem interpretatur . . . Cum que more furentis belue fremeret. . . ."

40. Ibid. "Impedimento, ait, michi est uxor mea, ne me liberalem et humanum mea reperiat concubina; quia si ista non venditur, illa amittetur."

41. Vita s. Albei episcopi, Codex Salmanticensis, 1966, p. 119.

42. Vita s. Tigernachi episcopi, Codex Salmanticensis 1966:107. "Predictus igitur rex Echacus cum tres filias pulcerrimas in palacio suo nutritas haberet, una ex eis, Derfraych, quendam virum nobilem de militibus patris sui, Lagnensem genere, nomine Corbreum, adamavit."

43. Vitae sanctorum 1910, 1:65.

44. Vita s. Ciarani saigirensis, Codex Salmanticensis, 1966, p. 348. "In una vero domorum dilectus filius regis erat dormiens derelictus. Hunc et alium suum filium. . . ."

45. Codex Salmanticensis 1966:177–78.

46. Vita Rusticulae sive Marciae abbatissae arelatensis, p. 341.

47. On the diffusion of various types of marriage arrangements, including polygyny, see Murdock 1967. On the relationship between uncertain paternity and an emphasis on kinship ties through women, see Kurland 1979, and Greene 1970.

48. For its appearance in the Salamanca Codex, see Codex Salmanticensis 1966:81–83.

49. De familiis Sanctae Mariae, Farfa, 1895, 5:254–73.

50. Vita s. Brigidae, Codex Salmanticensis 1966:10. ". . . nunc coci, nunc pistoris, modo subulci, non nuncquam opinionis, aliquando messoris, sepe textricis officium, et alia atque alia hiis viliora, tam domi quam foris . . . laudabiliter consummabat."

51. Vita Liutbirgae, p. 13: "ut diversarum artium, quae mulieribus conveniunt operibus." Ibid. p. 26: "multorum muliebrium operum artifex erat."

52. Ibid., p. 16: "ut rerum suarum fuerat custos atque fidelis dispensatrix."

53. Ibid., p. 13: "propter diversorum tincturam colorum." In Ireland too dyeing appears to have been an exclusively feminine enterprise. See Plummer's comment in the introduction to Vitae sanctorum 1910:ci.

54. See the typical passage in the Vita s. Dagaei, Codex Salmanticensis 1966: 392. "Quas [tres filias] literarum scientiam edocens, monasterium ad opus earum fundavit. . . ."

55. Vita Mathildis Reginae, p. 285: "sacras lectiones et manuum operationes."

56. Vita s. Ciarani saigirensis, Codex Salmanticensis 1966:350. "Considerans vero regina Ethnea egregiam illius Concraidi pulcritudinem, spiculo inordinati amoris vulneratur atque vulneris medelam apud Concradum esse fatetur."

57. De s. Columba abbate Hiensi. Vita prolixior auctore S. Adamnano abbate, ASS, 2 Junii, p. 204.

58. Ibid., p. 211.

59. Ibid., p. 224.

60. Vita Gangulfi 1920, p. 369.

61. Vita s. Albei, Vitae sanctorum 1910, 1:55. "Quadam die quedam mulier que oculte peperit per adulterium . . . Et ait: Ducantur ad me omnes viri qui habitant in una villa cum ea. . . ."

62. Codex Salmanticensis 1966:31. "Quomodo sanctum episcopum a falso crimine et mulierem a tumore liberavit."

63. De s. Leodwino seu Lutwino archiepiscopo trevirensi, ASS, 8 Sept., p. 172. "Amplectabatur amoris privilegio avunculum suum, sanctum videlicet Basinum. . . ."

64. Vita s. Abbani, Codex Salmanticensis 1966:256. "Sanctus ergo Albanus de claro genere Lageniensium ortus est. . . . mater vero, dicta est Mella, soror Ybar episcopi fuit."

65. Ibid., p. 269. "Hic latro extitit filius sororis sancti Braccani, abbatis monasterii Cluain Immurchuir."

66. Vita s. Cronani, Codex Salmanticensis 1966:275. "Qui itineris comitem . . . virum pudicum et sanctum, Mobai nomine, consobrinum suum, duxit: horum enim duorum et sancti Mochonna matres, tres erant sorores."

67. Ibid., p. 610.

68. Vita sancti Berarchi abbatis de Cluain Coripthe, Vitae sanctorum 1910, 1:76. " . . . solitus erat, ut matris mamillam, sancti Fregii auriculam sugere destram."

69. For a recent critical review of the texts dealing with Germanic kinship structure and inheritance customs, see Murray 1982.

70. Codex Salmanticensis 1966:2.

71. Vita s. Berarchi, Vitae sanctorum 1910, 1:78. " . . . uxor regis Lagenie . . . cogitauit arte maligna ut perfida nouerca interimere. Timuit enim quod proli sue preualeret. . . ."

72. Codex Salmanticensis 1966:9. "Ita enim a natura comparatum est nutricibus, ut quibus prebent lac carnis, prestent etiam semper affectum mentis."

73. Codex Salmanticensis 1966:34.

74. Our surveys of manorial populations in the ninth century characteristically show a shortage of women, most noticeable in the poorest social categories. This has suggested to some scholars that female infanticide was widely practiced. See Coleman 1974.

75. Under the conditions of marriage which come to prevail in the central and late Middle Ages, women must compete for husbands and wealthy women tend to marry downward, resulting in high sex ratios favoring men in the richest classes. This is much in contrast with the tendencies in early medieval society for women to gather in the households of the wealthy. See Herlihy and Klapisch-Zuber 1978:326–46.

REFERENCES

Primary Sources

Aristotle
1946 The Politics of Aristotle. Translated with an introduction, notes, and appendices by Ernest Barker. Oxford: Clarendon Press.

ASS
1643– Acta sanctorum quotquot toto orbe coluntur. Antwerp: Society of Bollandists.

Bede
1971 Baedae Opera historica. Translated by J. E. King. Loeb Classical Library. Cambridge: Harvard University Press.

Codex Salmanticensis
1966 Vitae sanctorum Hiberniae ex codice olim salmanticensi nunc bruselensi. Edited by W. W. Heist. Subsidia Hagiographica 28. Brussels: Society of Bollandists.

Corpus Iuris Civilis
1928–29 Corpus Iuris Civilis. Edited by P. Krueger, T. Mommsen, R. Schoell, and G. Kroll. Berlin: apud Weidmannos.

Corpus Iuris Civilis
1932 Corpus Iuris Civilis. Translated by S. P. Scott. Cincinnati: Privately published.

Herodotus
1966 Herodotus. With an English translation by A. D. Godley. Cambridge: Harvard University Press.

Isidore of Seville
1911 Isidori Hispalensis episcopi etymologiarum sive originum libri XX. Edited by W. M. Lindsay. Oxford: Clarendon Press.

Laws of Alamans and Bavarians
1979 Laws of Alamans and Bavarians. Translated by Theodore John Rivers. Philadelphia: University of Pennsylvania Press.

Livy
1967 Livy in Fourteen Volumes. With an English translation by B. O. Foster. Cambridge: Harvard University Press.

MGH
1826– Monumenta Germaniae Historica. Leipzig and Hanover: apud Weidmannos.

Regesto di Farfa
1895 Il Regesto di Farfa comilato da Gregorio di Catino. Edited by Ugo Balzani and I. Giorgi. Rome: Società Romana di Storia Patria.

Theodosian Code
1955 The Theodosian Code and Novels and the Sirmondian Constitutions: A Translation with Commentary, Glossary and Bibliography. Edited by C. Pharr in collaboration with T. S. Davidson and M. B. Pharr. Princeton: Princeton University Press.

Ulpian
1926 Die Epitome Ulpiani des Codex vaticanus reginae 1128. Edited by Fritz Schulz. Bonn: A. Marcus and E. Weber.

Vita Gangulfi
1920 Vita Gangulfi martyris varennensis. *In* MGH, Scriptores Rerum Merovingicarum, ed. B. Krusch and W. Levison. Hanover and Leipzig: apud Weidmannos.

Vita Liutbirgae
1939 Vita Liutbirgae virginis. Das Leben der Liutbirg. *In* MGH, Deutsches Mittelalter, vol. 3, ed. O. Menzel. Leipzig: K. W. Hiersemann.

Vita Mathildis
1841 Vita Mathildis Reginae. *In* MGH, Scriptores Rerum Germanicarum, vol. 4. Hanover: apud Weidmannos.

Vita Rusticulae
1895 Vita Rusticulae sive Marciae abbatissae arelatensis. *In* Passiones vitaeque sanctorum aevi merovingici, ed. B. Krusch. *In* MGH, Scriptores Rerum Merovingicarum, vol. 3. Hanover: apud Weidmannos.

Vitae sanctorum
1910 Vitae sanctorum Hiberniae. Edited by C. Plummer. Oxford: Clarendon Press.

Xenophon
1970 Xenophon's Socratic Discourse: An Interpretation of the *Oeconomicus*. By Leo Strauss with a new, literal translation by Carnes Lord. Ithaca and London: Cornell University Press.

Secondary Sources

BHL
1898–1913 Bibliotheca Hagiographica Latina antiquae et mediae aetatis, ed. Socii Bollandiani. 2 vols. Subsidia Hagiographica 6. Supplementi. Subsidia Hagiographica 12. Brussels: Society of Bollandists.

Brunt, P. A.
1971 Italian Manpower, 225 B.C.–A.D. 14. Oxford: Clarendon Press.

Chadwick, Nora
1970 The Celts. London: Penguin Books.

Coleman, Emily R.
1974 L'Infanticide dans le Haut Moyen Âge. Annales—Économies—Sociétés–Civilisations 29:315–35.

Constable, Giles
1970 Aelred of Rievaulx and the Nun of Watton: An Episode in the Early History of the Gilbertine Order. *In* Medieval Women (Dedicated and Presented to Professor Rosalind M. T. Hill), ed. Derek Baker. Oxford: Blackwell.

Duby, Georges
1978 Medieval Marriage: Two Models from Twelfth-century France. Baltimore and London: Johns Hopkins University Press.

Erickson, Carolly, and Kathleen Casey
1978 Women in the Middle Ages: A Working Bibliography. Medieval Studies 37:340–59.
Goffart, Walter
1974 "Caput" and Colonate: Towards a History of Late Roman Taxation. Toronto: University of Toronto Press.
1980 Barbarians and Romans, A.D. 418–584: The Techniques of Accommodation. Princeton: Princeton University Press.
Greene, P. J.
1970 Promiscuity, Paternity, and Culture. American Ethnologist 5:151–58.
Herlihy, David
1960 The Carolingian *Mansus*. Economic History Review 13:79–89.
1975 Quantification and the Middle Ages. *In* The Dimensions of the Past: Materials, Problems and Opportunities in History, ed. Val R. Lorwin and Jacob M. Price. New Haven and London: Yale University Press.
Herlihy, David, and Christiane Klapisch-Zuber
1978 Les Toscans et Leurs Familles: Une Étude du Catasto Florentin de 1427. Paris: École des Hautes Études en Sciences Sociales.
Jochens, Jenny M.
1980 The Church and Sexuality in Medieval Iceland. Journal of Medieval History 6:377–92.
Kenney, James F.
1927 Sources for the Early History of Ireland 1: Ecclesiastical. New York: Columbia University Press.
Kubitschek, W.
1899 Census. *In* Paulys Real-encyclopädie der classischen Altertumswissenschaft, ed. G. Wissowa, vol. 3, pp. 1914–24.
Laslett, Peter
1972 Introduction. *In* Household and Family in Past Time, ed. P. Laslett and R. Wall. Cambridge: Cambridge University Press.
Kurland, J. A.
1979 Paternity, Mother's Brother, and Human Sociality. *In* Evolutionary Biology and Human Social Behavior, ed. N. Chagnon and W. Irons. North Scituate, Mass.: Duxbury Press.
McNamara, Joanne, and Suzanne Wemple
1977 Marriage and Divorce in the Frankish Kingdom. *In* Women in Medieval Society, ed. Susan Mosher Stuard. Philadelphia: University of Pennsylvania Press.
Murdock, G. P.
1967 The Ethnographic Atlas. Pittsburgh: University of Pittsburgh Press.
Murray, Alexander Callander
1982 Studies in Germanic Kinship Structure and Society in Antiquity and the Early Middle Ages. Ph.D. Dissertation, University of Toronto.
Plummer, C.
1925 Miscellanea Hagiographica Hibernica . . . accedit Catalogus Hagiographicus Hiberniae. Subsidia Hagiographica 18. Brussels: Society of Bollandists.

Portmann, Marie-Louise
1958 Die Darstelling der Frau in der Geschichtsschreibung des früheren Mittelalters. Basel: Helbing and Lichtenhahn.

Power, Patrick C.
1976 Sex and Marriage in Early Ireland. Dublin and Cork: Mercier Press.

Soliday, G. L.
1980 History of Family and Kinship: A Select Bibliography. New York: Kraus Publications.

TLL
1900– Thesaurus linguae latinae editus auctoritate et consilio academiarum quinque Germanicarum. Leipzig: Teubner.

Wemple, Suzanne Fonay
1981 Women in Frankish Society: Marriage and the Cloister, 500–900. Philadelphia: University of Pennsylvania Press.

Westphal, Alexandre
1935 Recensement. *In* Dictionnaire encyclopédique de la Bible, vol. 2, pp. 531–32. Valence-sur-Rhone: Imprimeries réunies.

16

Households among the Diola of Senegal: Should Norms Enter by the Front or the Back Door?

Olga F. Linares

Households have been variously defined in the literature as coresident domestic groups (Hammel and Laslett 1974), as places where individuals reside (Reyna 1976), as agglomerations of "kin and non-kin ordered by norms specific to sex and marital status" (Smith 1979:286), and as processes rather than facts (Hammel 1972). Other scholars (for example, Berkner 1975; Goody 1972; Wheaton 1975; Yanagisako 1979) have avoided definitions and typologies, emphasizing instead the polysemic nature of the word *household*, which may connote a physical space, the individuals residing it, and the kinship ties binding coresident domestic units. As a handy but imprecise word for an institution characterized by flexibility, indeterminacy, and multiple functions, households are what households do. This trend away from rigid categories and definitions is a healthy one.

Nonetheless, if we want to analyze household changes in time and space, we must begin with common understandings, if not a common definition. The point of this paper[1] is to show that differences in households are only partially understood with reference to functional criteria and, furthermore, that the criteria used to compare households at different points in time or space may of necessity be overlapping or noncongruent. Thus, fathers and married sons may at one time or place have to be classified as forming one extended household because they live under the same roof and eat together. Yet at another time or place they would be put into the extended category because they regularly cultivate together, even though they live and eat in separate houses. Both attempts at classification would be correct if the household concept itself had shifted in social meaning; that is, if *household* no longer implied coresidence but rather coproduction. Even then, it might be possible to compare households along some sort of continuum from simple to complex. But we would have to consider not only what, and how many, functions (residence, production, transmission, and so on) are (or are not) shared by more than one conjugal family unit (CFU) but also how common tasks are perceived and organized. Qualitative changes in the meaning of interpersonal obligations may be as important in distinguishing among household types as more easily measured changes in size and form.

In the pages that follow I have considered the shift away from a reliance on fairly autonomous CFUs among "animist" Diola groups south of the Casamance river in southern Senegal toward larger, more complex units in "Mandingized" (and Islamized) Diola groups north of the river. The change toward more encompassing and differentiated units among the Diola is by no means unique. It is by now common knowledge that Goode's (1963) proposed evolution of large households in the direction of a single, nuclear modern pattern does not always work and is often reversed (Laslett 1965; Laslett and Wall 1972; Netting 1965, 1979; Wilk, this volume). What seems important to emphasize in this case is that in the process of "Mandingization" not only the form and function of Diola households changed but also their conceptualization. Households became what households were newly conceived to be. By treating the concept *household* as itself shifting and changing we may avoid the need to draw sharp lines around particular household variants.

Moreover, it may be necessary to conceive of changes in household functions and meaning as being embedded in more comprehensive cultural phenomena (see Barth 1966). For that reason differences in the size and form of Diola domestic units do not seem to correlate exclusively with changing labor needs in agriculture. Nor do they appear to be immediate responses to shifts in family norms or values narrowly conceived. Rather, among the Diola, these differences seem to result from more general shifts in the ideology that informs group behavior and in the norms and values that underlie proper social relations. The knotty question of how family norms and values are to be measured, whether they are antecedent to behavior or are the result of action-oriented changes, will not, however, be addressed in this paper. In situations of actual "contact" between asymmetrically conceived social units, such as between state-organized and acephalous peoples or between localized, particularistic religions and universalistic ideologies, the adoption of new cultural "norms" is seldom motivated by an explicit strategy. Following Bordieu (1977:27), I am using the word *norm* "in the sense of a *scheme* (or principle), immanent in practice, which should be called implicit rather than unconscious, simply to indicate that it exists in a practical state in agent's practice and not in their consciousness, or rather, their discourse."

This paper compares households in three groups of Diola peoples on both sides of the Casamance River. The first section, a discussion of regional ecologies, outlines the history behind the spread and subsequent "Mandingization" of the Diola. Next follows a description of how individuals fit into larger units on the basis of kinship and coresidence. The following sections will be detailed accounts of household activities involving transmission and production, storage and consumption, reproduction and socialization. The final section will be a plea for the restoration of a cultural dimension to explanations of household change, even at the risk of introducing some "vague polarities" (Goody 1972). In turning around the question from *how* households change to *why* they change, the appeal to norms and values seems unavoidable, indeed necessary.

The reader should be advised at this point that I have emphasized sociocultural divergences between the three villages rather than organizational similarities. Contrast in ideology and behavior between Sambujat, Jipalom, and Fatiya may appear to be too neat, too clearly drawn. This is not coincidental. The three villages were chosen for prolonged study precisely because they were located in each of three Diola zones whose cultural uniqueness had been previously noted by scholars (see Thomas 1957/58; Pelissier 1966). Moreover, I had already spent a year in Jipalom before deciding in 1966 to study Sambujat, an "animist" village near the Casamance River Delta reputed for its conservatism. My work in Fatiya began still later, in 1970, thanks to my assistant, who came from that village and kept insisting while we studied Jipalom that things were done "quite differently" back home. Still, I did not perceive the extent to which household organization diverged in the three villages until I went back to the field in 1981, outfitted with a preliminary copy of Wilk and Netting (this volume). I hope the following discussion serves to confirm the usefulness of their approach.

DIFFERENCES IN REGIONAL HISTORY AND ECOLOGY

The Diola, who occupy the southwest corner of Senegal as far east as the Soungrougrou River, are an aggregate nation of approximately 300,000 wet rice agriculturalists. Located in what is known as Basse Casamance, an area between the Gambia and Guinea Bissau, they border on the Manding peoples who occupy the Middle Casamance. Few historical accounts trace Diola history in any great detail, but most sources seem to agree that the Kasa region south of the Casamance River was one of the earliest Diola areas to be settled (Lauer 1969; Linares 1981). For that reason the closest linguistic relatives to the Diola, Manjaku, and Balanta are found in Guinea Bissau (Sapir 1971). Strictly speaking, the Diola are not part of Senegambia. Instead, they form the northernmost extension of the region in the Upper Guinea coast known as the "Rivers of the South," a swampy lowland coast occupied by predominantly rice-growing peoples (Rodney 1970:16).

The recent history of the Diola is marked by population movements and upheavals in large measure caused by the expansion and contraction of Manding (Malinke, Mandinko) peoples. Sometime before the fifteenth century, splinter groups of Manding started moving west from Mali, following the Gambia river. Their incursion, as well as the Europeans'

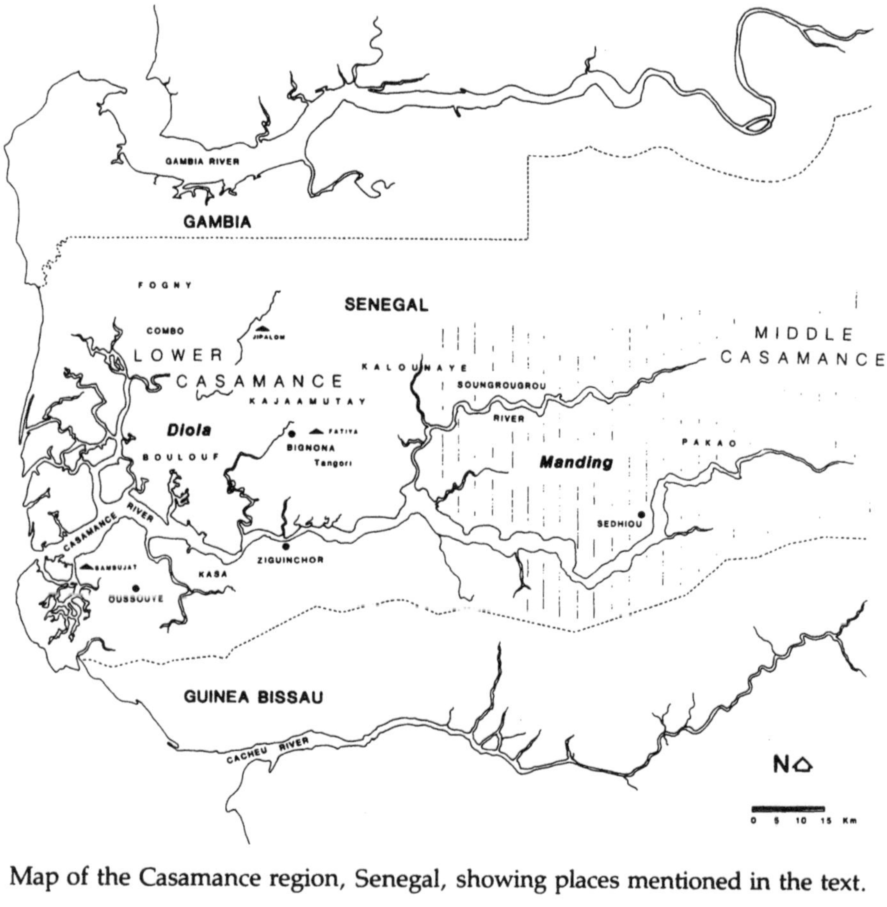

Map of the Casamance region, Senegal, showing places mentioned in the text.

escalation of slavery, and the Islamic *jihads* (or holy wars), kept the Casamance in political turmoil (Mark 1976). At or slightly before this time a branch of Diola-speaking Fogny (or Kujamutay), one of the two most important Diola dialects (the other is Kasa), began their spectacular expansion into territory formerly occupied by the Bainouk (or Banyun), a totally foreign trading group who had spread into the lower Casamance from eastern Senegal. "Diola and Mandinka territorial expansion occurred virtually at the same time and place. Population pressures on both groups forced them towards the relatively sparsely-populated Bainouk territories along both sides of the Soungrougrou" (Leary 1971:235). The Diola seem thus to have moved from areas of high population density around the Casamance River delta to lightly populated inland areas, following disruptions brought about by the Manding with their slave raids and maraboutic wars. According to Leary (1971) the Manding jihads against the Diola retarded the latter's conversion to Islam. When Islam began to make progress among the Diola at the turn of the century it was through peaceful means, through example and conversion.

Even today the Fogny-speaking Diola continue to spread and live among Manding peoples east and north of the Casamance River, all the way into the Gambia. Migration into the Boulouf, Combo, and Fogny areas obeys more pull than push factors, such as availability of land, the proximity of sources of illicit trade, and a long-standing labor market in the Gambia connected with seasonal groundnut farming (Swindell 1980). As a result of these movements the Diola are now divided into at least three major cultural zones (Mark 1976). In the Kasa area south of the Casamance River and west of the city of Ziguinchor, many Diola, other than those who have converted to Catholicism, have retained their traditional "animistic" religion. Directly north of the river, in the Fogny-speaking zone encircling the city of Bignona, most Diola have become Moslems. Finally, to the east and north of Bignona, Islamized Diola have been absorbed by the Manding, to the extent of abandoning Diola language and culture in the extreme northeast region of Basse Casamance known as Kalounaye.

The Diola villages I will be discussing in the three cultural areas outlined above were settled at different times. Sambujat is a "traditional" village practicing the *awasena* religion (from *kawasen*, to libate at a shrine). It is located in the Kasa area, near the Casamance delta, in a high-rainfall area within the department of Oussouye. Archaeological investigations suggest there was a Diola (?) village in this same spot as early as A.D. 200 (Linares 1971). Jipalom, my second village, is intermediate between the other two in geographic location and historical depth. Situated in the upper reaches of the Baila *marigot* (or tidal river channel), in the area

Fogny-speaking Diola call Kajamutay, Jipalom was settled probably in the nineteenth century by migrant farmers from the crowded area of Sindian to the north. Here, in the Kajamutay, conversion to Islam has occurred within the last 50 years. The third village, Fatiya, is in the drier Tangori zone east of Bignona, where Manding influences begin to be strongly felt. Although Tangori was a settled village by the 1850s, Fatiya is a recent pioneer Islamized village in the process of vigorous demographic growth. Official Senegalese village censuses by the Service de la Statistique listed the Fatiya population as 142 in 1958, 182 in 1964, and 233 in 1972. The total population and the size of villages are roughly comparable in the three areas (table 16.1).

Contrasts in rainfall, the size of *marigots*, tidal influences, types of soils, and other environmental differences in subregions in the Basse Casamance have been discussed in great detail elsewhere (see Dresch 1949, Pelissier 1966; Linares 1970, 1981) and need not be repeated here. In actual practice, the agricultural system of major Diola groups in the Kasa, western Fogny, and Mandingized eastern Fogny (beginning at Tangori) exhibit marked differences in land tenure, sexual division of labor, and consumption and distribution of agricultural produce. In Sambujat rice is grown intensively as a monoculture in tidal swamp paddies that are diked, desalinated, and irrigated. As elsewhere in the Kasa the sexual division of labor is cooperative: husband and wife, men and women, participate equally in rice-field work, even though each sex performs different tasks. The inhabitants of Jipalom started growing peanuts for cash, in addition to rice, perhaps as long as 50 years ago. The sexes

TABLE 16.1
A COMPARISON OF THE TOTAL POPULATION AND SIZE OF VILLAGES IN THE THREE STUDY AREAS[a]

Regions[b]	No. of villages	Total population	[Mean size of villages]
Loudia Ouloff	42	16,499	[393]
Kajaamutay	32	15,551	[486]
Tangory	87	30,308	[348]

SOURCE: Service de la Statistique 1972

[a]Using the G-test (see Sokal and Rohlf 1969), p. < 1 with two degrees of freedom. Differences are not significant.

[b]Loudia Ouloff and Tanghory are listed as *arrondissements* in the 1972 Senegalese village census and kept as such here. For the Kajaamutay area, where Jipalom is located, I have retained the preindependence *canton* designation, to wit, "Canton des Kadiamoutayes Sud" (Service de la Statistique, January 1958). With minor modifications I have used the 1972 census figures for the same villages because the old *canton* division is much closer to the Kujamaat culture area recognized by the Jipalom people than is the much more encompassing Sindian *arrondissement* used in the 1972 census.

complement each other by working together on both the rice and peanut fields. This is not true of Fatiya, or for that matter of any Mandingized Diola, among whom the sexual division of labor is complete. Women do all the rice and men all the cash-producing cultivation of groundnuts, even though the Fatiya Diola also grow millet, sorghum, and house orchard crops for domestic consumption and for sale. In table 16.2 I have summarized salient contrasts in the social organization of production in my three study villages. Aspects of this chart will be discussed in more detail later in this paper.

"CORPORATIONS" AT THE VILLAGE LEVEL

Among all Diola the most important residential unit beyond the conjugal unit and the household (described below) is the courtyard group (*fank* in Fogny, *hank* in Kasa; pl. *unk*). *Fank* or *hank* is a polysemic word meaning an open area or courtyard as a physical space, the group of individuals residing around this space, and the sibling corporation made up of classificatory brothers and sisters vaguely related in the male line. Whether the *fank/hank* unit is composed of one or more patronyms, it is strictly exogamous. It is also an important reference point for tracing both agnatic and matrilateral connections. An individual will give his/her *fank/hank* affiliation when asked where he was born or when asked where he "touches," that is, where he is a sister's son or matrilateral relative.

In Sambujat the 57 male household heads alive in 1981 were divided into nine *unk* varying considerably in size, the largest comprising 12 agnates, the smallest only 2. The men occupying a single *hank* form several subgroups that are linked predominantly by agnatic ties. Generally speaking, most subgroups of Sambujat agnates living in close proximity can demonstrate patrilineal links to a common forefather. All *hank* members usually own a palm grove together and tap the palms for wine without having to secure one another's permission. Two or more *hank* "brothers" may also own a cow in common, bought with the proceeds from the sale of palm wine, and share its progeny. The most important aspect of the *hank*, however, is not necessarily jointly held kin property but the *hank*'s function as a ritual corporation symbolized by the *hufila* shrine located at the entrance to the courtyard. *Hufila* is one of the most important Diola shrines (*bakiin*), and like all such shrines it is conceived as a "societe or table," a place where one eats communally. An "animist" Diola does not keep a chicken, pig, or goat for himself or his household; he takes it to a shrine to sacrifice it and share it with people. In this

TABLE 16.2

SOCIAL ORGANIZATION OF PRODUCTION AND LAND TENURE IN THE THREE VILLAGES

Villages	Agricultural system	Sexual division of labor in agriculture	Rights to land
Sambujat	Permanently cultivated tidal and rain-water swamp paddies. Deep fields recovered from the mangrove by diking, desalinating, ridging, and furrowing. Control of tidal waters in and out of fields by means of sluices. A rice monoculture. No peanuts, millets, or sorghum. Distribution of rainwater between paddies and drainage of excess water. Yields of up to 3,000 kg/ha. Households sell excess rice. No cash crops; no house-orchards. Extensive palm groves.	Cooperative: Men do all the preparation of the paddy fields using the fulcrum shovel. They build up the big dike and maintain the sluices. Occasionally men transplant and harvest. Women transplant, weed, and do most of the harvesting. Men tie up rice bundles. Adult men and youngsters are involved in the palm wine trade.	Residual rights vested in the *eluhol* and *unk*. Rights of use and disposition rest with household unit. Men can borrow extra land from uterine kin, but this is infrequent. Females members of agnatic groups cannot borrow or inherit fields. At the time of marriage, a girl's *hank* "brothers" cultivate a large field which she harvests. This is her "dowry."
Jipalom	Permanent swamp paddies; rain impounded in fields that are bunded and ridged. Some tidal paddies. Some drainage of rainwater. Yields 4,000 kg (?) per ha. Households not completely self-sufficient in rice. Rice grown for subsistence only. Shifting bush-fallow cultivation of groundnuts as cash crop. Tidal paddies have not been cultivated for the last decade because of drought.	Complementary: Men ridge and furrow the paddy fields using the fulcrum shovel (*kajando*). Men clear and ridge groundnut fields. They pull up, dry, and bag plants. Women transplant, weed, and harvest rice. They help weed millet fields. Women punch-hole groundnut seed, weed, and "beat" the plants. Men keep cash revenues from groundnuts. Women "own" the rice granaries. Men have smaller granaries.	Residual rights to land are vested in the patrifilial descent group. Rights of use and disposition rest with male heads of households. Sons are given some land before marriage; this land is theirs and their sons inherit it. A son gets land worked by his mother at time of her death. Agnatic women can be lent land but cannot inherit it. Men get usufruct rights by manipulating uterine ties. Peanut fields borrowed elsewhere.

Fatiya	Permanent rain-fed paddies. No tidal fields. No water control. No ridging and furrowing. Rice grown for subsistence. Yields of 2,300 kg per ha. Household must buy some of the rice it consumes. Shifting bush-fallow cultivation of groundnuts for cash and millet/sorghum subsistence. House orchard-garden crops for sale and subsistence.	Separate: All work in paddies is done by women; they prepare fields with a long-handled hoe. Women own the granaries and feed the family. All work in groundnut fields and house-orchards done by men. They work with the short hoe. They sell the crops and with proceeds clothe the family and pay the taxes. Plow has been introduced in the last decade. Eight "teams" in the village in 1981.	All land is "owned" by few patri-lineages tracing descent to village founders. Sons of these "families" inherit parcels at time of marriage. Agnatic women can be lent paddies, and if they marry a resident "stranger" their sons inherit the land. Resident "strangers" borrow rice paddies from village "owners." Groundnut fields are often owned outright. Paddies are lent to wife (or wives) of the "strangers."

particular case *hufila* is thought of as a father with children, each of whom lives with one of the *hank* agnates. *Hufila* is concerned with the welfare of resident agnates, with their marriage and future production of children. As such, it embraces under its protective mantle the in-married wives. The shrine or spirit also repels evil and can be asked for "things." Two elders of Sambujat are in charge of its propitiation, but if *hufila* "traps" a person by making him ill, the elders must libate at the shrine located in the *hank* of the particular individual concerned. As with many other shrines, the post of propitiator for *hufila* is inherited in a zig-zag fashion, ideally from father to brother's son, to father's son. The elders of the village, however, have a lot to say about who actually succeeds to the post.

Members of the same *hank* bury one another's dead, marry off their daughters and sisters with a proper dowry (consisting of enough rice for several years' consumption), and bewitch one another. It is the coresiding agnates who suspect one another of witchcraft if one of them produces much rice or has many children. The Sambujat chief, a purely secular figure in charge of matters dealing with the Senegalese administration, is always elected from among members of one *hank*, whereas the role of main priest (*aii*) always rotates among three *unk*. Finally, a new *hank* is formed when one or more of the male agnates fission off and establishes a new courtyard. This always involves setting up a new branch of the *hufila* shrine. Although in no way can the *hank* be called a "household," the *hank* is nonetheless a tight coresidential unit with many functions and a strong symbolic identity.

The same is not true of the other two sociospatial categories recognized by Sambujat inhabitants. The first (*eluhol*) is a shallow patrigroup composed of agnates who share the same patronym, who live near one another most of the time, and who can sometimes trace common descent. Slightly less encompassing is the patrilineal extended family (*buayu*) consisting of a man and his married sons or of two or more married brothers. Both of these descent groups are perceived as being potentially devisive by detracting from the cooperation that ideally binds *hank* members together. For that reason these categories are denied or at least deemphasized. Very rarely do they come up in daily conversations, and to my knowledge they are seldom referred to in songs, stories, or other forms of oral tradition. Their function is restricted to such matters as who may cultivate together. In short, in Sambujat the only large residential group that is conceptually emphasized is the *hank* or congregation of male agnates, plus their wives, living around a single courtyard.

The *fank* or courtyard unit is also important in Jipalom, where it is similarly symbolized by a shrine called "rope" (*kaneak*) having to do with wealth in children, women, and cattle. The elder in each *fank* is in charge of its propitiation. In the modern context "rope" is probably the most vital of all Diola shrines (Sapir, personal communication). A *fank* unit is usually referred to by the elder's name, such as "Malam's group" or "Abdoulaye's group." Although the predominant ideology of relationship between *fank* members is still agnatic—"brothers" living together around a common *fank*—several individuals are interconnected instead by matrilateral or affinal ties. Thus, two household heads sharing a common *fank* may turn out to be uterine kin because the father's mother of one individual (rather than the father's father) was born there. Sons of several female agnates who returned to live in Jipalom were also connected to the rest of the agnates via their mothers, not their fathers. In addition, an individual may be living with his mother's husband's son or he may be residing with vaguely related matrilateral kin who have lent him land.

The next most important Jipalom sociospatial category is referred to by another polysemic term, *eluup*, meaning a house as a physical structure as well as a loose patrilineal descent group whose elders claim to be related because their "forefathers were brothers." Following Schloss (1979 and in press) I will refer to this unit as a "house," with the understanding that it is not strictly speaking the equivalent of a lineage because its members cannot trace exact descent through known genealogical links; they also live in separate dwellings that are only in the same general vicinity. Nonetheless, in Jipalom the "house" is strongly corporate. It is an exogamous unit; its members also hold residual rights to land in common and often cultivate together. In the conception of Jipalom residents the "house" often plays a more important role than the smaller courtyard unit (or *fank*). Many songs that crop up at the time of circumcision, the most important village-wide ceremony, are concerned with the fate of a sad initiate whose "house" has been finished by illness and who is alone in the world. Even though the "houses" display great variation in size, both in space and through time, the 17 "houses" recorded in Jipalom in 1965 were still in existence in 1981, no "house" having disappeared or new one founded.

The Jipalom ward (*kalol*) is difficult to separate conceptually from the "house," except that it is larger and therefore more diffuse. There are five wards in Jipalom, one of them comprising three subwards in the process of fissioning. Located at some distance from one another, members of a ward often cultivate together, do not marry if they share the same patronym, and initiate their boys jointly in the same sacred forest. To summarize, in Jipalom a new social unit—the "house" (*eluup*)—has grown in importance and occupied the social space between the more restricted courtyard group (the *fank*) and the larger, somewhat more diffuse ward unit. The "house" of Jipalom is more or less equivalent in size and social significance to the *hank* of Sambujat. Conversely, the *fank* of Jipalom is smaller and less important than its linguistic cognate, the *hank* of Sambujat. When I did my most intensive fieldwork, the Jipalom *fank* averaged 2.57 agnates, compared to 7.56 agnates per *hank* in Sambujat.

Fatiya, which has roughly the same population as Sambujat (about 300 persons), is also divided into two wards of roughly equal size. But these two wards are at a considerable distance from each other, like the Jipalom wards. The ward where I did my most intensive work included three named courtyard groups (also called *fank/unk*); the other ward had four. Named courtyard groups include only those persons who claim descent from the original founding families. The rest of the male agnates, immigrants but not strangers (Shack 1979), belong to nameless *unk* and in the same manner as Jipalom are usually referred to in daily conversation by the dominant patronym, such as "the Jeju," "the Baji," or "the Sane." In 1981 the two largest of 17 existing *unk* with more than 6 married agnates each comprised members of the founding lineages. Most noticeable among these was the chief's *fank*, which in 1981 consisted of 16 adult men and women plus numerous children, actually all living in one enormous dwelling, thus forming one large coresidential household. Among non-founders, however, overall *fank* membership averaged only 2.8 agnates per *fank* in Fatiya in 1981, a number similar to that of Jipalom (2.7) but smaller than the average for Sambujat (6.2). Some Fatiya *unk* belonging to "strangers" are constituted of one adult male only, and several others include more than one patronym. The people of Fatiya no longer propitiate traditional spirits since they embraced Islam and became practicing Moslems; instead they pray together daily at one of several small mosques in the village and instruct their children in Koranic studies. With the exception of the founders, the Fatiya *unk* are smaller and more loosely structured than those of Sambujat. A distinction thus emerges between descendants of village founders and more recent immigrants. All male descendants of the original founders comprise one clearly defined group of three interrelated patrilineages living in three closely spaced *unk*. The remaining immigrants are grouped into many separate patrigroups. In addition, note that in several *unk*, households heads are absolute strangers to one another, having migrated to Fatiya from entirely different villages. Finally, the four resident Manding families of craftsmen are regarded as outsiders, but only from a kinship point of view; the men do not work the land but instead provide services. Thus, in the number of foreign-born men versus local agnates, Fatiya departs radically from the other two villages.

TRANSMISSION OF LAND AND AGRICULTURAL PRODUCTION

Any discussion of the Diola household must emphasize the importance of conjugal family units in Diola society. Regardless of location, all Diola share certain concepts and norms concerning proper spatial relations in the life cycle. A basic cultural principle dictates that some sort of separation of generations must take place at marriage. What happens after a son marries is crucial to the residential structure of the household. In all three villages a son and his new wife are expected to be independent. In Sambujat if a son has *sembe* (strength) he will build a separate house for himself and his wife as soon as he can. It is said that he and his wife should be able to receive their own visitors, be they strangers or his wife's kin, without "feeling shame." A new couple may be forced to continue living in separate quarters within his parents' home for two or three years until able to build their own home, but the couple forms a new CFU and a new elementary household (*butong*). The first house the man builds is usually made of local materials: compacted mud, earth floors, and a thatch roof. Rarely is a young man able to accumulate enough money from seasonal palm wine tapping to add such features as a covered porch or a corrugated zinc roof. Frequently, a young man constructs a house for his elderly parents, or for his widowed mother, before constructing his own house. Still, the period when generations coreside is very short in Sambujat, seldom more than four years. Incidentally, not a single instance of a married son coresiding with a father was recorded in 1981. This may be a result of the increasing frequency with which young couples are staying away in towns such as Ziguinchor and Dakar. Several instances in which young couples move from their parental residence to live in the same courtyard with a more distant relative while waiting to build their own place have nonetheless been recorded. The emphasis on privacy and separateness while living in close proximity is illustrated by the openness with which an elder may explain, in the presence of a friendly neighbor, that he is going to build a fence between them "so he can go in and out unnoticed."

The same general emphasis on residential autonomy was observed in Jipalom, but the period of parental coresidence, or residence with an older brother, while amassing the resources with which to build a new house seems to be longer in Jipalom than in Sambujat. (Unfortunately, I do not have "hard" data on this subject, but I can note that several of the young Jipalom married couples I knew in 1964 were still living under the same roof with their parents in 1970 but had constructed their own separate homes by 1977). At any one point (1981, for example), however, the number of conjugal family units living independently (in simple households) was as high in Jipalom as in Sambujat.

A radically different pattern emerges from a comparison of postmarital residence in Sambujat and Fatiya. A marrying son in Fatiya does not always move out of his parental home. Instead, he often occupies separate quarters within his father's house, which may be enlarged to accommodate him or his newly married brother(s). In table 16.3 I have summarized the types of households living under the same roof in the three villages in 1981. Solitary households comprise a widower or divorced man, elementary households have only one CFU, multiple households include a married father with a married son, and grand households have a married father, at least two married sons, and often the son of a deceased brother. We can, using the G significance test (see Sokal and Rohlf 1969), determine that Fatiya's residential pattern is quite different from that of the two other villages. In addition, if we break down the three-way comparison into dyadic comparisons, the only difference that is not statistically significant is that between Jipalom and Fatiya. To recapitulate, residential decisions made during the first stage in the developmental cycle of the household logically result in somewhat different household arrangements in our three villages. The ideal in Sambujat, and to some extent in Jipalom, is for a new pair to move out as soon as possible, whereas the Fatiya Diola prefer to enlarge the parental home to accommodate successive generations.

TABLE 16.3
A COMPARISON OF TYPES OF HOUSEHOLDS LIVING UNDER THE SAME ROOF[b]

	Solitary	Elementary	Multiple	Fraternal[c]	Grand[c]
Sambujat	7	37	0	0	0
Jipalom[a]	2	11	1	0	0
Fatiya	2	18	5	3	4

[a]One ward of Jipalom only.

[b]Using the G-test (see Sokal and Rohlf 1969), with eight degrees of freedom, $p < .005$. Differences are significant.

[c]Although Hammel and Laslett (1974) cluster fraternal and grand households together with multiple, I think that keeping them distinct is important in the Diola situation. Interpersonal relations are quite different in Diola households made up of two brothers (fraternal) than in households composed of a married son and his father (multiple). Where, as in grand households, there are several married "brothers" living with a household head who may be the real father to one son and a FB to another and where brothers do not usually share the same mother, the dynamics of mutual behavior may be very complex indeed.

Marriage also brings into existence a conjugal family estate. It is at this point that the transmission of landed property takes place. This process follows slightly different rules in the three villages. In Sambujat a father gives a marrying son a number of fields, and the latter immediately redistributes some fields to his wife for her use, keeping less than half under his control. As the father grows old, he keeps fewer and fewer fields. Every time a son marries, the father and his other already married sons assess the land anew, deciding what fields to give the newly formed pair. The low level of segmentation at which land is held means that a man has complete disposition over the fields he receives from his father at marriage and can lend them, pledge them, and pass them on to his own marrying sons at will. Meanwhile, the bride has harvested a large field that her own agnatic brothers have cultivated for her. The rice she brings as a dowry may feed herself and her husband for several years until the produce from their fields accumulates in their respective granaries.

In Jipalom, in contrast, a young man is given fields by his father, or father surrogate, several years before he marries; the bride does not bring with her a stock of rice. Thus, the son is expected to begin accumulating paddy in the space provided by his mother in her granary in anticipation of the time when he becomes independent by acquiring a wife. A third variant of land inheritance is illustrated by Fatiya, where land devolves from father to son only within the shallow patrilineages of the village founders. More recent immigrants get assigned rice fields by the members of the founding families in accordance with their needs. One strategy for getting more land is to keep on adding wives. Fields are "given" in the form of a loan; they revert to their owners when the borrower dies or divorces. Thus, marriage everywhere brings into existence a new unit of production and consumption—the conjugal family—with its associated rice fields and reciprocal labor obligations. Yet the transmission and "ownership" of land is by no means exactly the same in the three villages.

A few words now on the relationship between coresidence and forms of labor cooperation within the household unit. In table 16.4 I have classified conjugal units in the three villages using the same categories in table 16.3 (solitary, elementary, multiple, fraternal, and grand) but employing as the criterion of classification coproduction rather than coresidence. Thus I have grouped together those CFUs that year after year work together in one another's fields. Statistical comparisons indicate that the only significant difference is between Sambujat and Fatiya. Yet this difference may be an artifact of the classification. For example, if the "fraternal" and "grand" coproducing units were broken down into their constituent "multiple" households following the Hammel and Laslett (1974) terminology, the Fatiya-Sambujat difference would disappear

TABLE 16.4
COMPARISONS OF TYPES OF COPRODUCING HOUSEHOLDS THAT CULTIVATE TOGETHER IN THE THREE VILLAGES
(even though members may not live in the same house)[a]

Villages	Solitary	Elementary	Multiple	Fraternal[b]	Grand
Sambujat	7	27	8	3	1
Jipalom	1	8	1	2	0
Fatiya	0	19	1	2	4

[a]G-test scores (see Sokal and Rohlf 1969); S and J = 2.47 (not significant); S and F = 16.03 (significant); J and F = 7.99 (not significant).

[b]One of these fraternal households is of the *batiae* variety: two men who are classificatory brothers but come from different villages and have different patronyms.

(each would have 17 "multiple" units). Doing the same for the coresident units in table 16.3 would, however, only increase the differences. So it seems that differences in coresidential units between the three villages are not clearly reflected in household labor group organization. Whether married brothers and their parents live together or apart, the same number continue to cultivate together. From the Diola point of view this is as crucial, if not *more* crucial, than residing under the same roof.

Still, numbers by themselves may be deceiving in that they mask qualitatively important differences in productive relations. In Sambujat, for example, a son continues to cultivate with his father in a reciprocally egalitarian relationship. A father and his wife (who may or may not be the son's actual mother) will work side by side with a married son and his wife, in both the father's fields and in those he has transferred to his son. The son may rationalize his work as helping his aging father, but the father is not entitled to eschew his own obligations to his son. When harvest time comes around, however, each conjugal unit will take the produce of its fields to its own granaries in its own house. Food preparation and consumption is also separate (see following section). Now, in Jipalom, to quote from Sapir (1970:1330), "A father will never work his son's fields," though he will, if able, continue to work his own fields to a ripe old age. In other words, in Jipalom labor obligations are asymmetrical, from son to father, but not the reverse. This asymmetry is more pervasive and complete in Fatiya, where an able-bodied though elderly father often stops cultivating altogether and hires workers, occasionally also his sons, to do the farming of his peanut and millet fields. This is described as *anifan panajokulo* ("the old man will rest") and was as typical in the old days before the plow had been introduced as it is today, when there are eight teams of bulls and plows in the village. Incidentally, the plow is usually managed by the younger sons on behalf of the entire extended family. Needless to say, a father never cultivates his son's fields and, as I said, seldom cultivates his own fields if he is considered an elder. A slightly different pattern emerges for women. Cowives, mothers-in-law, and daughters-in-law are supposed, by Fatiya standards, to cultivate together in one another's fields. If one asks a Fatiya woman, "Do you cultivate with your cowife, or mother-in-law?" more often than not she will start on a long speech explaining, "Yes, and we also have one granary, one cooking place, and one serving bowl in common." The reality, however, is quite different. I censused many work groups in the fields in Fatiya in 1981 and only about 50 percent involved cowives working together. Slightly fewer cases were registered of a daughter-in-law working with a mother-in-law. In short, there is less than a 50 percent chance that the ideal of cooperation within the female coresident group is achieved in actuality. This then is an example of actual behavior overriding norms. Most Diola informants would also argue that no one is ever under an obligation to work for a village chief, a wealthy man, or a high-ranking elder. In fact, however, the matrilateral kin and strangers residing in Jipalom often cultivated for their "hosts": either for the classificatory mother's brother, in whose houses they resided, or for the Islamic cleric and his brother, in whose *fank* the strangers lived. The same was also true of the wealthy elder of the compound. Once a year his fields were cultivated by all the village men and women working together. In contrast, cultivating for the chief or the main "priest" would be unthinkable in Sambujat. But the Fatiya village chief, a descendant of one of the founding families, no longer cultivates his fields himself. His sons as well as recent immigrants do this for him on an informal and voluntary basis without receiving compensation. And every year all of the men of the village cultivate for a famous marabout (religious leader) who resides in a nearby town. Although it is generally true that such cooperation is largely voluntary and organized along age and sex lines, not hierarchy, the fact remains that in the more Islamized villages important persons may make subtle claims on outsiders, including their wives, for labor.

Numerous examples can be found in the literature of what is called the "extending strategy," or the expansion of household membership to include distant kin, friends, or servants, in order to meet labor bottlenecks at certain crucial junctions in the agricultural cycle (Sahlins 1957; Pasternak, Ember, and Ember 1976; Reyna 1976). As Yanagisako (1979) indicates, however, extrahousehold production may be organized along different lines in different cultures. Among the Diola extrahousehold labor is required at several points in the agricultural cycle, especially during field preparation, transplanting, and harvesting. Yet in no sense does this extra labor require a household "extending" strategy beyond the joint production of brothers or of fathers and sons. Extrahousehold labor is organized mainly along *hank/fank* lines. In order to document this point, let me for a moment elaborate on the organization of labor in these three villages.

In Sambujat the sexual division of labor in agriculture is essentially cooperative; both sexes work in the rice fields, though they tend to perform different tasks. Men use the fulcrum-shovel (*kajando*) to build up the bunds, keep up the dikes and sluices, ridge and furrow the nurseries, broadcast the seed upon them, ridge and furrow the fields into which their wives will transplant, and tie up the harvested rice into bundles. Women carry fertilizer to the fields, do the transplanting, and do most of the harvesting. It is not uncommon, however, to see Sambujat men transplant or harvest (though the reverse seldom occurs, namely, women cultivating with the *kajando*). All the resident men in one *hank*, including children above the age of 12 and elders who may be 50 years or older, may cultivate together for one another in what they view as a mutual aid society. Although *hank* agnates may work for only a pig or palm wine, the group often gets paid in cash. If they work for a *hank* member they earn less than if they work for an individual of another Sambujat *hank* or of another neighboring village. In either case, the money earned is saved for an important end-of-year religious ritual. Beyond the *hank*, larger work associations are comprised of two or more *unk* that cultivate together. Supra-*hank* cooperative units are usually restricted to one of the two main wards into which Sambujat is divided. Thus, for example, compounds A and B within the Tangen ward form a group called "Sapoti." It is said that not too long ago work groups involving several *unk* and sometimes even the entire village were common. Regardless of the size of these task groups, however, they recruit members from several generations. The only exception to this rule occurs in the modern context. Groups of young, unmarried men of the same age have formed what they call "clubs" whose members are not necessarily recruited by *hank*. The money they earn is saved to buy a phonograph or eventually to construct a youth's house.

Among Sambujat women extrahousehold labor is also recruited by *hank*, not on the basis of where a woman was born but on the basis of where she has married (all the in-married women of *unk* A form one group). These groups include women of all generations. Again, any woman from within the group or any woman from a neighboring village can engage the group, but outsiders pay more than the 2,500 francs CFA (about eight dollars) that a member contributes. The money paid to such a group is also pooled. It goes to pay for the big ceremony at the beginning of the rains, when palm wine and a pig are sacrificed to the shrine that represents the collectivity of in-married women of a particular *hank*. Finally, the Sambujat unmarried girls have also formed a club, which also works for pay. Sometimes they prefer to work for someone outside the village because they earn more. So the traditional cooperative unit in Sambujat is the collectivity of coresidential male agnates, or of coresident women, of different ages, living in one or more compounds and working together as a group. They work for one another or for an "outsider" and pool or share what they earn. More often than not, the "outsider" for whom they work is related to a member of the laboring group (Linares, n.d.). This happens, for example, when the men's *hank* works for a member's matrilateral relatives or affines or when the women's group labors for an out-married agnatic "sister." But in no way do these arrangements contradict the assertion that household composition in Sambujat is not altered to accommodate additional labor requirements.

In Jipalom large groups also work together in the rice fields and are constituted as follows. All the men of a *hank* or ward may work at the same time, but the elders usually work apart, in different parcels. All the in-married women from a ward or from a compound may also work together, but without recognizing age distinctions. In addition, the out-married female agnates, some of whom may be married within the village or within a small circle of intermarrying villages, occasionally come together to cultivate for one of their agnatic "brothers." Hence, a social distinction not present in Sambujat between task groups made up of locally born female agnates and task groups made up of women born elsewhere is recognized in Jipalom. Both groups work for a set fee. The money the in-married women make is usually put aside to pay for a ceremony involving the entire ward. Similarly, the money the female agnates make is used for ritual purposes; it is usually set aside for the girls' circumcision ceremony, which takes place every three or four years.

Fatiya illustrates yet a third variation in the organization of suprahousehold agricultural labor, for cooperative male work groups are in the process of disappearing with the recent introduction of the plow. Instead of laboring for one another individually or in groups, men now lend or rent one another their oxen and plows for preparation of the millet and peanut fields, which are exclusively male crops. Women, in contrast, continue to rely on cooperative work groups to prepare their rice fields. These groups sometimes attain very large numbers (32 or more women). Within each of the two large wards female work groups are divided by age classes. In the ward where I lived the younger married women's group numbered 24 while the older ladies' group numbered 14. It is said that in the old days the groups worked for each member several times and for a minimal fee. Nowadays, they work for each of the members only once and in strict rotation. The member for whom they are working pays the sum of 2,500 francs CFA for a whole day's work. A third work group, that of the unmarried girls, works for anyone who will pay them. There were 13 girls in the ward where I did my most intensive work, and together they were paid 500 CFA francs if they worked for one of the local women and 700 CFA if they worked for someone outside the ward. Hence, they get considerably less money as a group than do women of the two ascending generations.

The solution in all three villages to the need for extra labor at crucial times of the year is thus not accomplished through a household extending strategy. Instead, task groups organized on the basis of *hank*, "house," and ward labor for a member or for his kin. Except for the young unmarried boys and the young girls, the work groups in Sambujat comprise members of widely divergent generations. In Jipalom, on the contrary, the elder men and the younger men form distinct groups that may work at the same time but in different parts of a field or in different fields altogether. Women are recruited either on the basis of the compound or ward they married into or on the basis of the compound or ward they were born into and subsequently married out of. The younger folks also form a separate work group, as elsewhere in the Diola area. Finally, in Fatiya, men no longer work together in cooperative groups but instead lend one another or rent from one another teams of oxen, plows, and carts with which they prepare and harvest their peanut and millet fields. Fatiya women, however, continue to cultivate together, but in strict age-classes, the first comprising the younger married women, the second the elderly ladies. This growing separation of generations is reflected in many other organizational features of the Fatiya household.

OTHER HOUSEHOLD FUNCTIONS: STORAGE AND CONSUMPTION

Figures 16.1–3 portray house structures and compound arrangements within a *fank* or *hank* unit in each of the three villages under discussion. Particular attention should be paid to the distribution of granaries and to the location of kitchens or hearths where meals are cooked.

In Sambujat the conjugal family unit eats together—mother, father, and children all from the same bowl, except when the wife is menstruating, at which time she must eat apart. After a son marries, his wife is expected to cook for him in her own kitchen, either at their temporary living quarters or in their new house. It is not uncommon, however, for a young couple, if they are visiting his parents, to be invited to share a special meal with them. On this occasion the generations will also eat from the same bowl. In no instance is the young woman expected to cook for her mother-in-law or father-in-law; nor is she expected to feed her husband's widowed mother or father. Solitaries, who are numerous in Sambujat (there is a shortage of women), are expected to cook for themselves, unless they are senile or otherwise disabled.

I have already indicated that at harvest time each of the Sambujat households, that of the son or that of the father, takes the paddy harvested from his or her parcels to his or her own granary. From figure 16.1 we can see that the Sambujat wife and husband usually have separate granaries or separate places in the same granary located in a room inside the house. The granary is a secret place and is never shown to strangers, not even to other members of the *hank*. Granaries have no windows and may be connected to the wife's or husband's bedroom or to an anterior storage room, through private doors. Up to ten or more tons of rice may be stored in one granary, where wood is burned periodically to drive away insects. A woman's granary nourishes the family and also furnishes the rice given to visitors. The man's rice is for the "needs of the family." He sells it and buys clothing for his wife and children, or he uses it to feed work groups that are preparing their fields.

In figure 16.2 we can see that in Jipalom each cowife usually has her own granary, above the place where she cooks. These kitchen-granary combinations often constitute a separate, small structure in back of the main house or, less commonly, are placed on a part of the covered veranda found to the rear of the house. A Jipalom household head has his own granary also, but it is rarely a separate structure; more often it is a small place in the attic of his own house. As an informant put it, a man must have a place for his rice because his wife always takes the key to her granary with her wherever she goes. The rice stored in the man's granary does not feed the family; it is used to cook for important visitors and strangers. If a husband runs out of rice he would never try to take rice from his wife's granary without her permission.

Unmarried boys in Jipalom regularly eat with their fathers (their mothers eat apart with their daughters) until they marry, at which time a set of rules enforcing social separation in cooking and eating comes into play. Known under the collective name of *kujaama* (Sapir 1970), these rules take their name from a special shrine that "traps" the older, not the younger generation with severe stomach upsets. A married son can eat in the same room as his father or his father's brothers but not from the same bowl—nor may he use the same spoon unless he has performed a special

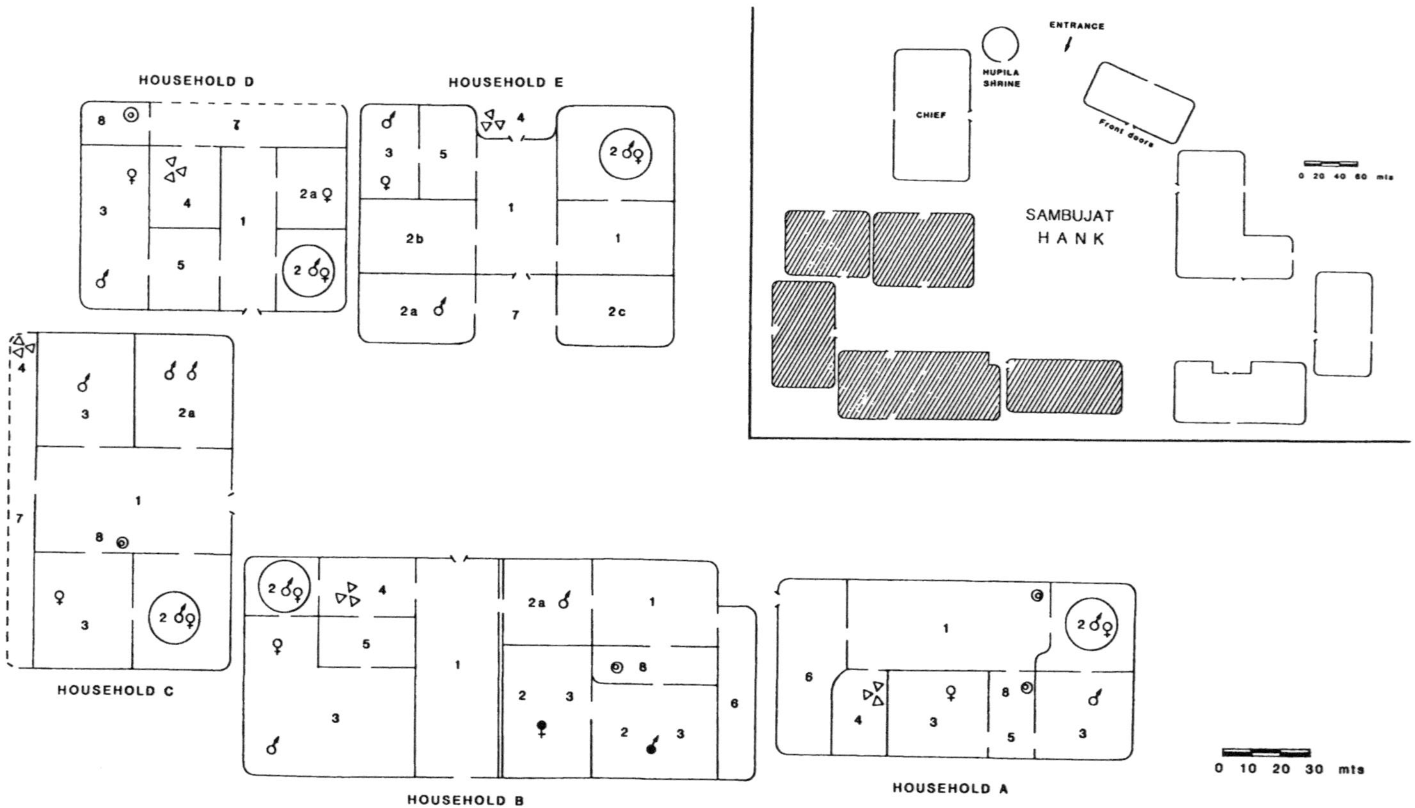

Fig. 16.1
Sambujat

Figure 16.1

A *hank* (compound) of Sambujat; stippled area represents households shown in detail. Key to rooms within each household:

1. *hulak*. Common hall/vestibule, also used for eating.
2. *emorum*. Bedroom: (2♂♀) conjugal family unit; 2a♂ unmarried sons and brothers; 2a♀ unmarried daughters and sisters; 2b guests; 2c others and/or empty.
3. *hubanten*. Granary: 3♂ husband's granary and/or place within a common granary; 3♀ wife's granary and/or place within a common granary.
4. *kañum* or *husil*. Kitchen/hearth, also indicated by .
5. *eñaten*. Storage place for baskets, etc., and/or anteroom to granary.
6. *hutuñ*. Pounding place for wife, or chicken coop, etc.
7. *eperoñ*. Verandah.
8. *báákin* (*hupila*). Household shrine. Also shown as .

Note: Household heads of A and C are full brothers. Household B was once two households separated by a wall; door was opened after old parents (♂ and ♀) died. They slept in their respective granaries. Household head of D and his wife are the parents of household head E.

"neutralizing" ritual. Similarly, a young wife should not cook for her mother-in-law or eat from the same bowl. The mother-in-law, however, can cook for her son and his wife in an emergency because they are "her children." Hence, older folks in the parental generation can cook for the younger generation, but not the reverse. This interdiction amounts to an explicit recognition of the dangers of encroachment by the older generation on the privacy and resources of younger household members.

In Fatiya cowives who get along moderately well often store rice in the same granary and cultivate the same parcels together. If they are not "in agreement," however, they will cultivate and store their rice separately. Cowives do not always thrive together. Thus, rather than cultivating with a cowife, a woman can choose to cultivate with the wife of her husband's brother or the wife of a son. She will then store her rice with the sister-in-law or daughter-in-law in the same granary. This arrangement may also pose difficulties, for younger women often complain of having to work with slower, elderly ladies. Whether wives and daughters-in-law cook in the same or in different hearths depends on the particular arrangement made by the household. Generally speaking, in Fatiya older women do not cook, whereas the younger women cook regularly for themselves and their husbands, contributing a small bowl of rice or millet to their husband's parents if these are elderly. The latter, as well as the cowives whose turn to cook is not up, contribute rice to those who are doing the

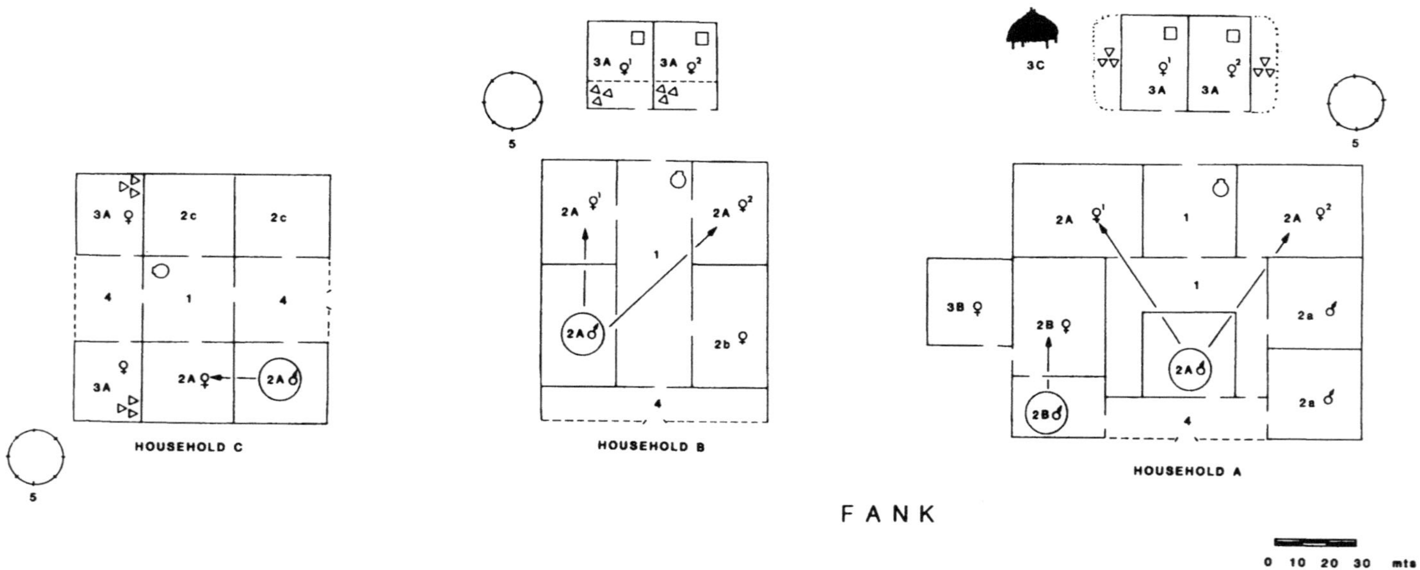

Fig. 16.2
Jipalom

Figure 16-2

Households within a Jipalom *fank* (compound). Key to the rooms within each household:

1. *jebir*. Vestibule/living room; ◯ water jug.
2. *kajíím*. Bedroom: (2A♂) household head, 2A♀^{1} his first wife; 2A♀^{2} his second wife; 2B♂ married son, 2B♀ his wife; 2a♂ unmarried son; 2b♀ widowed Z or FZ; 2c empty, and/or used for storage, and/or used for unmarried daughters, and/or sisters when they come home from the city during the agricultural season.
3. *buntuñ/fusil*. Granary/kitchen also shown by ▽▽▽: 3A♀^{1} first wife, 3A♀^{2} second wife; 3B♀ wife of married son; 3c granary for all the in-married women in the ward, who use the rice for socioceremonial occasions.
4. *kañon*. Covered porch/verandah.
5. *fuñoaf*. Bathing place. Used by everyone.
6. *eñaten*. Storage place for baskets, etc., and/or anteroom to granary.

Note: All three household heads are classificatory brothers of the *batiae* variety.

cooking. In addition, men regularly take their bowls to eat with an older brother or to eat at their father's house. Because of *kujaama*, the old man of the *fank* often eats alone in a separate room. Women also eat completely separately from the men, sometimes in different parts of the same house, and they usually share their bowl of rice if they are from the same generation or eat from separate bowls if they are not. These domestic practices are in marked contrast with those of Sambujat, where all women cook and sometimes men do too, and where parents and unmarried children of both sexes regularly eat together from the same bowl. A Fatiya married son or his wife are not prohibited from sharing the same bowl with his parents, though the occasion seldom arises.

MARRIAGE AND REPRODUCTION

Differences in the frequency with which plural marriages occur in our three villages are also striking. Marriage in Sambujat is predominantly monogamous; none of the men I knew in 1965, 1977, or 1981 had more than one wife simultaneously. Monogamy also prevails in Jipalom, but a substantial number of men (27 percent) had two wives. Finally, in Fatiya, monogamy and duogyny occur in almost the same frequency, with a nonnegligible proportion of all marriages (10 percent) involving three wives; a few additional cases involve marriage with four or more simulta-

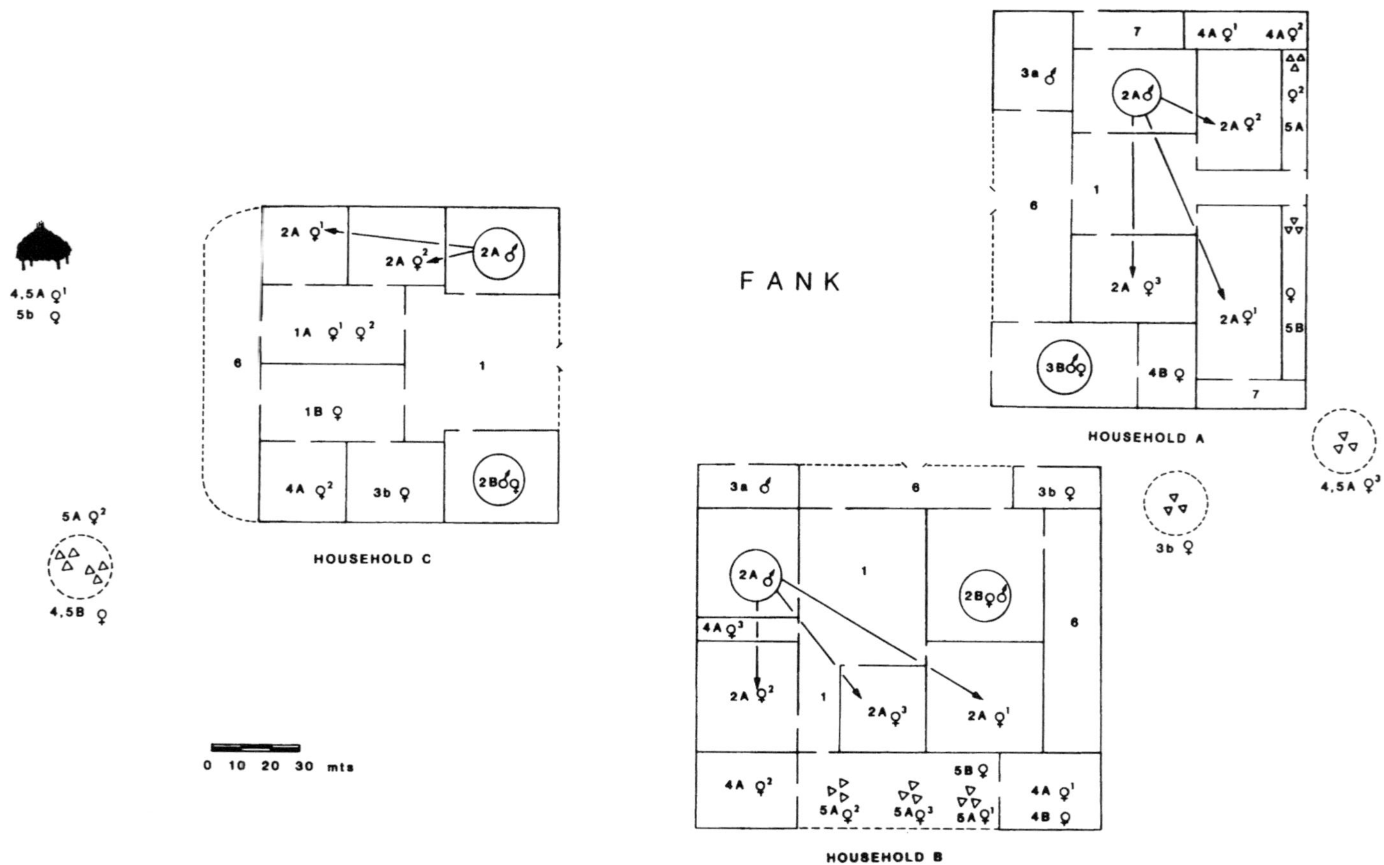

Fig. 16.3
Fatiya

Figure 16.3

Households of a Fatiya *fank* belonging to a founding family. Key to the rooms within each household:

1. *esalei*. Living room/vestibule.
2. *kalimbis*. Main and/or interior bedrooms for household head and/or middle-age son, (2A♂) household head, 2A♀ 1 first wife, 2A♀ 2 second wife, 2A♀ 3 third wife; (2B♂)♀ married son and his wife.
3. *epantrei*. Secondary and/or exterior bedroom: (3B♂ ♀) young married son and his wife; 3a unmarried sons; 3b widowed sister.
4. *bunturi*. Granary: 4A♀ 1 etc. for wives of household head; 4B♀ for wife of married son.
5. *fusil*. Kitchen/hearth: 5A♀ 1 etc., for wives of household head; 5B♀ for wife of married son.
6. *eperori*. Porch.
7. *epukus*. Closet/storage area.

Note: Household heads of A and B are full brothers. Household heads of A, B and C share the same father. Household head of C is the eldest brother.

neous wives. Statistical comparisons using the G-test (table 16.5) shows that the incidence of plural marriages is significantly different in the three villages.

Not only does the incidence of plural unions vary between villages but also the form that virilocal marriage takes. In Sambujat marriage is highly endogamous: 42 percent of all marriages in 1965 took place inside the village walls and another 48 percent with a village two kilometers away. The remaining 10 percent of the wives came from localities within an eight-kilometer radius. Although Sambujat agnates do not marry women from their mother's natal *hank*, they marry freely women from their mother's father's or mother's mother's *hank*. In fact, 15 percent of all marriages recorded in 1977 were of this type. An additional 16 percent of all marriages were between persons sharing the same patronym; in other words, patronymic exogamy is not enforced in Sambujat. Furthermore, a significant number of brothers within the same *hank* are married to sisters. Contrary to a strategy of out-marriage, whereby alliances are extended outside the local group, village in-marriage tends to reinforce existing ties by doubling up agnatic with affinal bonds, in short, by creating multiple cognatic bonds. In Sambujat close marriage seems to go hand in hand with a history of village isolation, of defense against slave raiding, and of resistance to outside forces, including Islam and Catholicism.

TABLE 16.5
A Comparison of Plural Marriages in the Three Villages in 1977[a]

	Number of simultaneous wives					
	0	1	2	3	4	G-test score
Sambujat	4	65	0	0	0	S and J = 36.62
Jipalom	4	80	32	3	0	S and F = 55.89
Fatiya	2	22	20	5	1	J and F = 11.39

[a]Using the G-test (see Sokal and Rohlf 1969), the critical value is 9.49. All differences are significant.

The Jipalom marriage statistics are somewhat different. Rather than in-marriage, we find a closed circle of intermarrying villages. Six villages, including Jipalom itself, accounted for about 80 percent of all in-married women. At a maximum distance of 12 kilometers apart, these villages are considered to be well within walking distance. They are also on the same side of the *marigot* in an ecological zone that includes swampland fields. Within the circle of intermarrying villages, exogamous unions are encouraged. Marrying too closely is discouraged, so that in Jipalom one should not marry within one's compound, where one was born, or within one's own ward, unless it be to a stranger living there. Marriage with uterine kin is also discouraged, and this includes marriage with a member of the FM's and MM's *fank* or courtyard group. (As noted, marriage with distant uterine kin is common in Sambujat.) The rule excluding uterine kin from marriage amounts to a mandatory recognition of the uniqueness and special nature of this relationship. Thus Jipalom wives and sisters circulate at marriage among a restricted number of villages but in a nondirectional, nonprescriptive way. Women marry out, and this is true even when they marry into another ward of Jipalom. But marriage takes place within walking distance so that female agnates retain important economic and mediatory roles within their agnatic environments.

Turning now to Fatiya, we see yet another variant of Diola marriage dynamics. The 82 wives married to the 50 Diola agnates of Fatiya in 1977 come from 24 different villages. Only 7 percent of the wives come from Fatiya itself. Some of the villages contributing wives are more than 25 kilometers away, clearly beyond walking distance. The strategies employed in securing wives in Fatiya are also more formal, or at least more "preferential," than in the other two villages.

Marriage rules clearly are simple in Sambujat, and only slightly more complicated in Jipalom. In Fatiya, however, the ideal marriage is formalized by an ideology of direct exchange between individual patrifilial groups located in numerous villages. The trend is in the direction of patrilateral cross-cousin marriage but without the development of an elaborate exchange mechanism. Twenty-five out of 60 marriages I recorded in 1977 (or 42 percent) fall in this preferential category, loosely defined. The rule that a man gets a wife where his father sent a sister (hence FZD [father's sister's daughter's marriage,] or an extension thereof) is observed, especially by men of status. By marrying a real or classificatory FZD, a man is marrying a woman who has uterine ties in his own compound and can therefore adjust easily to her new married environment. It is important to note that these arrangements are frequently in the hands of the FZ, who is terminologically distinguished by the same term used for HuM (husband's mother). It is the FZ who takes her own daughter or one of her husband's brother's daughters and gives back a woman to her own agnatic group. Thus, in contradistinction to a system of so-called generalized exchange, the Fatiya system of restricted exchange creates a sense of obligation on the part of small patrifilial groups to provide daughters and sisters where they took wives. Formal rules that dictate that a man can take a wife where one of his agnates in the past gave a sister, what in Sambujat amounts to a by-product of village endogamy, in Fatiya has become a preferential norm assuring a future supply of wives.

In keeping with other aspects of behavior, such as the complementary roles in agriculture and the importance of women in many ritual contexts, it is not surprising that in Sambujat conjugal relations are often easy, friendly, and above all founded on sexual equality. Husbands and wives frequently chat together. They consult each other and discuss matters of importance, arriving at common decisions about the children, family expenses, and other matters. As the sketch in figure 16.1 indicates, most couples also share the same bedroom (though each individual has a separate bed), except when very old, at which time one of the partners may sleep apart, usually in a corner of the granary. When a woman is menstruating, however, she must move out of the bedroom and sleep in the middle "hall."

Without exception in Jipalom if a man has more than one wife, each of the wives must have a separate bedroom (figure 16.2); the husband may or may not have a bedroom of his own, but he and his wives maintain separate beds. In Fatiya a man always has a separate bedroom and each of his wives also sleeps apart, as in Jipalom. In both villages a husband must also keep a very strict schedule of sleeping with each wife and making sure that whatever gifts are given to one are also given to the other(s). As I have indicated, cowives are not always in accord.

Although such matters are difficult to document, my general impression is that conjugal relations are qualitatively the same in all three villages (close and warm, or distant and hostile, as the case may be). Yet the "face" married partners present to the world—their social persona—varies in subtle but predictable ways. In Jipalom husbands and wives are generally friendly toward each other, but we begin to see formally constituted unisexual groups emerge: the in-married women, the women agnates, men who are in residence by virtue of matrilateral connections, agnates, and so forth. This does not mean, however, that women are more "solidary" or men more "cooperative" here than in Sambujat. It just means that their interactions are more formally organized. This is as true of group behavior as it is of individual behavior. Even such female Fatiya practices as curtsying in greeting one's husband or his brothers, praying separately from men at the mosque, or undergoing circumcision before marriage could be interpreted at some level as "mere formalities." On another level, however, these practices suggest that women's subordination and their emotional distance from their husbands increases as we go from Sambujat to Fatiya.

MANDING INFLUENCES AND ISLAM

As early as the sixteenth century Manding traders and Islamic religious teachers coming from the Fouta Djalon in Guinea and from the state of Gabou in which is now Guinea Bisau had settled sporadically in the Casamance (Leary 1971). In fact, the Portuguese chronicler Valentim Fernandes in 1507 described a powerful ruler (a *mansa* in the Manding language) who held sway over a portion of the Casamance River and owed allegiance to the sovereign of Mali. In the following centuries Manding traders continued to travel in the Lower Casamance, where they often served as middlemen for European slave dealers. At that time the Diola were both victims and profiteers in the slave trade. Following political and religious upheavals in the Fouta Djalon during the eighteenth century, more groups of Manding migrated into Middle Casamance where they established autonomous villages and what have been called protostates. Although ruled by a hierarchical system of hereditary chiefs and councils of elders and notables, the Manding protostates were only loosely federated. With the final migration of Manding from the Gambia and Fouta Djalon in 1890 began the Islamic *jihads*, or religious wars, against the pagans. Eventually these wars of conversion, directed against the Bainouk and the Diola, together with internal Manding revolts, led to the devastation of the northern Casamance provinces of Fogny and Combo. Manding religious aggression was finally ended by French "pacification" at the beginning of the twentieth century. This event "opened new roads to the Mandinka for proselytization and conversion of peoples they had been unable to conquer militarily" (Leary 1971:243).

To this day Diola attitudes toward the Manding are ambiguous. The Manding are identified with bringing trade to the area and with introducing the spiritual benefits of Islam to the Diola north of the river. That Islam represents to many Diola converts a superior moral code and provides an avenue for participation in a wider religious and economic community is made amply clear by recent studies (Mark 1976). Yet the memory of Manding warfare and slave raiding in the Fogny province still lives on. As late as the 1870s Diola slaves were sold to work in the peanut fields owned by Manding landlords in the Gambia. More recently, the French colonial powers assigned Manding rulers to the post of village chief in some Fogny Diola villages (Monteil 1980:79). But even though the Manding are identified with oppression in the past, their values have nonetheless permeated one Diola subculture in subtle ways. Recall that several Manding families actually reside in Fatiya. And because the Manding are somehow seen as more learned, pious, and worldly and as better politicians and merchants, they have been able to exert undue influence on their more egalitarian Diola hosts and guests. Some aspects of Manding social organization (described below) have transformed Fogny Diola society.

Space does not permit a review of the extensive literature on the Manding, who stretch "in the arc of some eight hundred miles, extending from the mouth of the Gambia in the northwest to the interior of the Ivory Coast in the southeast" (Dalby 1971:3). Despite a great deal of linguistic and cultural variation, there is some unity to Manding culture: "a strong sense of cultural identity and pride among the Manding themselves has been instrumental in maintaining this unity across unnatural colonial and post-colonial boundaries" (Dalby 1971:1). In general (and unavoidably superficial) terms Manding society is broadly characterized by patrilineal descent, with the original patrilineage being considered the "owner" of the land. Among the Gambian Mandingo (Weil 1971:251) a "patron patrilineage is called *jatiyo* ('host') and the client patrilineage is a *lungtango* ('stranger')." It also seems to be true of most Manding groups that strangers occupy a special position. Villages are pleased to receive strangers, for they add to the size and prosperity of the community, but only insofar as the original settlers retain some measure of control over the visitors (Hopkins 1971:109). A Manding stranger can become absorbed into another community through marriage to a local woman. Schaffer (1976; Schaffer and Cooper 1980) has made a study of Pakao, an ancient Manding outpost of the Malian empire located in what is now the Middle Casamance, a region bordering on Diola territory. To quote from his work (1980:45): "Mandinko think of lineages in terms of territory. Each lineage is led or 'commanded' by the eldest male. A minimal lineage is referred to as a 'household' and contains the houses of a man and his immediate family." Thus Schaffer equates a household among the Manding with a minimal lineage, emphasizing its corporate character. The same is true of a subhamlet, which he describes as a minor lineage, and the hamlet (*kabilo*), which he correlates with a major lineage. "Hamlets exchange women in marriage, and the various marital alliances and dissociations tend to correspond with the political alignment during crisis" (Schaffer 1976:311).

Hamlets in Pakao are divided into men and women's quarters, and this division is reflected in different agricultural tasks, the men growing peanuts and millets and the women cultivating rice. Further expressions of thoroughgoing sex polarity in Pakao society are found in separate organizations, formal leadership, circumcision, and labor arrangements as well as in particular male and female witchcraft secrets. Sex distinctions are not the only distinctions made. Villages in Pakao as well as among most Manding groups are also divided into age grades and age sets, artisan, noble and slave castes, chiefs and commoners, founders of the village and strangers, imams and marabouts. Thus, despite the notion of Islamic equality, there is much inequality in Manding society. This should not surprise us, given their history of empire formation and their role as conquerors and proselytizers (Quinn 1972). In fact, the well-known expansion of the Manding peoples may, according to Wright (1977:92), have involved "less the massive movement of people as typically portrayed and more the expansion of Mandinka ethnicity among previously non-Mandinka peoples."

The process of Mandingization could be separated from the introduction of Islam as a new religion (Trimingham 1959; Lewis 1980) and the introduction of peanuts as a cash crop. Mark (1976) has made an extensive study of socioeconomic change and Islamic conversion among the Diola Fogny of Boulouf, the region to the west of Jipalom and the Kajaamutay, *away* from the profoundly Mandingized areas east of Bignona and toward the Kalounaye. Here, in the Boulouf, between 1890 and World War II the introduction of cash crops and increased commercial transactions went hand in hand with the adoption of Islam. "Islam thus offered an identity and an ideology which facilitated the expansion of commercial and social relations with the outside world" (Mark 1976: abstract). Nonetheless, as Mark concludes (1976:185): "The Diola of Boulouf are a non-centralized, kinship-oriented society of sedentary subsistence farmers who, over a fifty-five year period, integrated themselves into the money economy, while also becoming predominantly Muslim." By itself Islam has not, in the Boulouf any more than in Jipalom, led in the direction of marked sex-role differentiation, unequal access to the means of production (namely, land), or political hierarchies. Because Mark equates the "traditional," pre-Islamic courtyard unit (what he calls a *fankafu*) with an extended family compound, he affirms that Islam, cash cropping, and migration contributed to the gradual dissolution of the extended family and eroded patriarchal authority among the Moslem converts of the Boulouf (1976:194). This is the opposite conclusion to the one I arrived at for the Mandingized Diola of Fatiya.

CONCLUSION

All Diola regardless of location place a great deal of emphasis on the independence and autonomy of the conjugal family unit. Nevertheless, this emphasis is translated into very different domestic structures in the three villages I have discussed. The CFUs of Sambujat are largely autonomous except for parents and their married sons, or two married brothers who may cultivate together. All other matters having to do with coresidence, consumption, storage, distribution, reproduction, and socialization take place within monogamous family units. Fatiya presents the opposite extreme with its complex households living under the same roof and sharing many activities. There is every indication that the incidence of complex households in Fatiya embodies the kinds of domestic relations this society particularly values (cf. Wheaton 1975). Thus, the large household of the much-respected Fatiya chief is often cited locally as a good example of a powerful and successful household that was able to retain its married sons living, laboring, and sharing domestic functions with their father and his wives. But, still, why should Fatiya people value complex households and Sambujat people, or to a much lesser degree Jipalom people, value small conjugal units? Are there extraneous reasons why complex households should be more functional, better adapted to the particular ecological or economic conditions present in Fatiya but absent from Sambujat? I hope to have shown convincingly that the family extending strategy does not present itself as *the* solution to meet labor needs in agriculture among the Diola. Extra hands to work in the rice fields are usually recruited from outside, not from inside the household.

In Fatiya the introduction of the plow has also rendered male cooperation obsolete. Adding extra wives does not seem to obey purely economic needs either; the more wives present, the more rice fields that an immigrant may receive, but also the more mouths he eventually has to feed.

Household changes among the Diola seem to be embedded in and accompanied by cultural changes of a more general and fundamental nature. Let me summarize some of the processes discussed in this paper as having been involved in the transformation from a Sambujat-like situation to one like that of Fatiya. Residential units above the household level have either proliferated (for example, the *eluup* or "house" of Jipalom), have become more loosely integrated (the *hank* of Sambujat versus the *fank* in Jipalom and Fatiya), or have become more differentiated (the immigrant groups versus the founding families of Fatiya). Descent ideologies have become more explicit (for instance, the Fatiya lineages). Strict transmission of property from father to son has been further complicated by rules that permit the pledging and borrowing of land from matrilateral relatives (in Jipalom) or the assigning of land by the founders of the village (in Fatiya). Reciprocal labor obligations between parents and their children (in Sambujat) have been reinterpreted to involve unilateral obligations from children to parents (in Jipalom) and from immigrants to village founders and important people like marabouts (in Fatiya). Household as well as suprahousehold work has become more differentiated along age and sex lines. The sexes and generations do not only work apart in Fatiya, in contradistinction to Sambujat and to some extent Jipalom, but they work on crops that have different economic functions and meanings. This increase in the sex polarity and in the recognition of generational differences is also reflected in the manner in which crops are stored, cooked, and consumed in the three villages. Finally, marriage takes very different forms in the three areas, from close in-marriage, monogamy, and status equality in Sambujat to polygyny (especially among the village founders), formalized and restricted exchange of women, and increased emotional distance between spouses in Fatiya.

Now clearly, at some abstract level, the processes of change outlined above have taken a similar course, toward increased role differentiation, complexity, asymmetry, and hierarchy. And the reason for this, I have suggested, has more to do with the adoption of Manding values—or what the Diola perceive as being Manding values—than with Islamization, cash cropping, or trade per se. That most Islamized Diola are themselves aware of how different Manding practices are from their own is clear from everyday comments by Jipalom residents: "I have never eaten millet, that is Manding" (said a proud elder); "We don't marry our cousins, but the Manding do" (commented a thoughtful man); "They cultivate Manding style" (sneered a contemptuous woman); "Elderly men do not farm and elderly women do not cook" (said a disapproving elder); "The Manding have ruined our women" (complained a young man referring to a girl's circumcision). Cultural distances between "animist" Diola of the Kasa and "Mandingized" Diola are even greater.

A word of caution may be appropriate here. I do not mean to imply that Mandingized Diola of Fatiya and northeast Lower Casamance have wholeheartedly embraced Manding ways. In Fatiya there are no age grades or age sets, no castes or village council, and no imam. Absorption of Manding cultùral features by the Diola has been highly selective as well as creative. For example, among most Manding a system of preferential matrilateral cross-cousin marriage exists, accounting for a substantial number of the marriages that take place in Pakao (Schaffer 1976: chap. 8). Elsewhere, the Manding of central and eastern Gambia also allow and in some instances actually prefer patrilateral cross-cousin marriage (Weil, personal communication). Although the Fatiya inhabitants have also taken up cross-cousin marriage, they have done so only in the Islamic patrilateral form (with the FZD).

Doubtless the introduction of cash crops may have "reinforced" Fatiya's burgeoning sex polarity and increased social differentiation. But the shifts in household structure and relations of production that we see in the Diola north and south of the Casamance River were probably the result of profound shifts in "family ideals or norms" (Berkner 1975:724) set in motion by contact between an essentially egalitarian people like the Diola and their more hierarchically organized Manding neighbors. Yet in trying to explain why the Fatiya inhabitants may have adopted Manding ways, I have made many assumptions. In fact, I have alluded indirectly to such problematical motivations as the quest for prestige, status enhancement, and "impression management" (see Barth 1966:3). How these matters are expressed in actual behavior is by no means easy to determine. The kinds of interactions that take place between Diola household members are largely qualitative, and as such they are difficult to classify and quantify. This in itself is no sufficient excuse to ignore them. Nor is there much to be learned "by separating actual behavior from the values upon which it is based" (Berkner 1975:735). Still, the thorny problem remains of how to avoid setting up as norms what has been obviously derived from observed practices. There may not be any way out of this dilemma. Perhaps, when all is said and done, new values come in, not through front and back doors but, like Diola witches, through windows and cracks.

NOTES

1. My fieldwork among the Diola was financed as follows: 1965–66, post-doctoral National Science Fellowship; 1970 (summer) Wenner-Gren Foundation; 1976–77, Smithsonian Institution Research Award; 1980–81 Smithsonian Institution, Fluid Research grant, and Wenner-Gren Foundation grant. The Smithsonian Tropical Research Institute (STRI), where I work, paid for my trip back and forth from Senegal so I could attend the Household Conference while in the midst of fieldwork. Special thanks to Maria Luz Jimenez for the preparation of the text and drawings and to Donald M. Windsor for the help with the computer. The following persons have read drafts of this paper and made helpful comments: Martin Moynihan, Robert M. Netting, J. David Sapir, Peter M. Weil, and Richard R. Wilk.

REFERENCES

Barth, Frederik
1966 Models of Social Organization. Royal Anthropological Institute of Great Britain and Ireland, Occasional Paper no. 23.

Berkner, Lutz K.
1975 The Use and Misuse of Census Data for the Historical Analysis of Family Structure. The Journal of Interdisciplinary History 4:721–38.

Bordieu, Pierre
1977 Outline of a Theory of Practice. Cambridge: Cambridge University Press.

Dalby, David
1971 Distribution and Nomenclature of the Manding People and Their Language. *In* Papers on the Manding, ed. C. T. Hodge, pp. 1–13. African Series, vol. 3. Bloomington: Indiana University Publications.

Dresch, Jean
1949 La Riziculture en Afrique Occidentale Annales de Géographie 58:295–312.

Goode, W. J.
1963 World Revolution and Family Patterns. New York: John Wiley.

Goody, Jack
1972 The Evolution of the Family. *In* Household and Family in Past Time, ed. P. Laslett and R. Wall, pp. 103–24. Cambridge: Cambridge University Press.

Hammel, E. A.
1972 The *Zadruga* as Process. *In* Household and Family in Past Time, ed. P. Laslett and R. Wall, pp. 335–73. Cambridge: Cambridge University Press.

Hammel, E. A., and P. Laslett
1974 Comparing Household Structure over Time and between Cultures. Comparative Studies in Society and History 16 (1):73–109.

Hodge, Carleton T., ed.
1971 Papers on the Manding. African Series, vol. 3. Bloomington: Indiana University Publications.
Hopkins, Nicholas S.
1971 Mandinka Social Organization. *In* Papers on the Manding, ed C. T. Hodge, pp. 99–128. African Series, vol. 3. Bloomington: Indiana University Publications.
Laslett, P.
1965 The World We Have Lost. New York: Scribner's.
Laslett, P., and R. Wall, eds.
1972 Household and Family in Past Time. Cambridge: Cambridge University Press.
Lauer, Joseph J.
1969 Rice in the History of the Lower Gambia-Geba Area. M.A. thesis, University of Wisconsin.
Leary, Frances A.
1971 The Role of the Mandinka in the Islamization of the Casamance, 1850–1911. *In* Papers on the Manding, ed. C. T. Hodge, pp. 227–48. African Series, vol. 3. Bloomington: Indiana University.
Lewis, I. M., ed.
1980 Islam in Tropical Africa, 2d ed. International African Institute and Hutchinson University Library for Africa. Essex: Anchor Press.
Linares, Olga F.
1970 Agriculture and Diola Society. *In* African Food Production Systems, ed. P.F.M. McLoughlin, pp. 194–227. Baltimore: John Hopkins Press.
1971 Shell Middens of Lower Casamance and Problems of Diola Protohistory. West African Journal of Archaeology 1:23–54.
1981 From Tidal Swamp to Inland Valley: On the Social Organization of Wet Rice Cultivation among the Diola of Senegal. Africa 51 (2):557–95.
In press Social, Spatial, and Temporal Relations: Diola Villages in Archaeological Perspective. Paper prepared for Burg Wartenstein Symposium no. 86, Prehistoric Settlement Patterns Studies: Retrospect and Prospect. University of New Mexico Press.
n.d. Technology, Ritual, and the Labor Process: Wet-rice Agriculture among the Diola of Senegal. Manuscript.
Mark, Peter A.
1976 Economic and Religious Change among the Diola of Boulouf (Casamance), 1890–1940: Trade, Cash Cropping, and Islam in Southwest Senegal. Ph.D. Dissertation, Yale University.
Monteil, Vincent
1980 L'Islam Noir: Une Religion à la Conquete de l'Afrique. Paris: Editions du Seuil.
Netting, Robert M.
1965 Household Organization and Intensive Agriculture: The Kofyar Case. Africa 25 (4):422–29.

1979 Household Dynamics in a Nineteenth-Century Swiss Village. Journal of Family History (Spring), pp. 39–58.

Pasternak, Burton, C. R. Ember, and M. Ember
1976 On the Conditions Favoring Extended Family Households. Journal of Anthropological Research 32 (2):109–23.

Pelissier, Paul
1966 Les Paysans du Senegal: Les Civilisations Agraires du Cayor à la Casamance. Saint-Yrieix: Imprimerie Fabregue.

Quinn, Charlotte A.
1972 Mandingo Kingdoms of the Senegambia. Evanston, Ill.: Northwestern University Press.

Reyna, S. P.
1976 The Extending Strategy: Regulation of Household Dependency Ratio. Journal of Anthropological Research 32:182–98.

Rodney, Walter
1970 A History of the Upper Guinea Coast, 1545–1800. New York and London: Monthly Review Press.

Sahlins, Marshall D.
1957 Land Use and Extended Family in Moala, Fiji. American Anthropologist 59 (3):449–62.

Sapir, J. David
1970 Kujaama: Symbolic Separation among the Diola-Fogny. American Anthropologist 72 (6):1330–48.
1971 West Atlantic: An Inventory of the Languages, Their Noun Class Systems, and Consonant Alternation. *In* Current Trends in Linguistics, ed. T. A. Sebeok, chap. 7, pp. 45–112. The Hague/Paris: Mouton.

Schaffer, David M.
1976 Pakao: A Study of Social Process among the Mandingo People of the Senegambia. Ph.D. Dissertation, Department of Anthropology and Geography, Oxford University.

Schaffer, David M., and C. Cooper
1980 Mandinko: The Ethnography of a West African Holy Land. Case Studies in Cultural Anthropology. New York: Holt, Rinehart and Winston.

Schloss, Marc R.
1979 The Hatchet's Blood: Spirits and Society among the Ehing of Senegal. Ph.D. Dissertation, University of Virginia.
In Press The Hatchet's Blood: Ehing Ritual of Separation.

Service de la Statistique
1958, 1965, 1972
Repertoire des Villages. Dakar: Ministere du Plan et du Development.

Shack, William A.
1979 Introduction. *In* Strangers in African Societies, ed. W. A. Shack and E. P. Skinner, pp. 1–17. Berkeley, Los Angeles, London: University of California Press.

Smith, Daniel Scott
1979 Life Courses, Norms, and the Family System of Older Americans in 1900. Journal of Family History (Fall), pp. 285–98.

Sokal, Robert R., and James Rohlf
1969 Biometry: The Principles and Practice of Statistics in Biological Research. San Francisco: W. H. Freeman.

Swindell, Ken
1980 Serawoollies, Tillibunkas, and Strange Farmers: The Development of Migrant Groundnut Farming along the Gambian River. Journal of African History 21 (1):93–104.

Thomas, L. V.
1957/1958
Les Diola. Memoire de l'Institut Francais d'Afrique Noire 55. Dakar.

Trimingham, J. Spencer
1959 Islam in West Africa. Oxford: Clarendon Press.

Weil, Peter M.
1971 Political Structure and Process among the Gambia Mandinka: The Village Parapolitical System. *In* Papers on the Mandinka, ed. C. T. Hodge, pp. 249–72. African Series, vol. 3. Bloomington: Indiana University Press.

Wheaton, Robert
1975 Family and Kinship in Western Europe: The Problem of the Joint Family Household. Journal of Interdisciplinary History 4:601–28.

Wright, Donald R.
1977 The Early History of Niumi: Settlement and Foundation of a Mandinka State on the Gambia River. Papers in International Studies, Africa Series no. 32. Ohio University: Center for International Studies.

Yanagisako, Sylvia
1979 Family and Household: The Analysis of Domestic Groups. Annual Review of Anthropology 8:161–205.

17

Family and Household: Images and Realities: Cultural Change in Swedish Society

Orvar Löfgren

The words *family, household* and *home* are three powerful notions in western culture which have also been used as conceptual tools in cross-cultural studies of domestic organization. While several generations of anthropologists have been arguing over the meaning of the term *family*, the difficulties in using the concept *household* have been given less attention (see Wilk and Netting, this volume).

In Western societies the three words have been used in many, often overlapping ways, not only to describe socioeconomic or genealogical categories and units of residence but also as images, metaphors, and symbols. This means that there are problems of cultural translation involved even in studies of domestic groups within our own society: *family, household,* and *home* stand for different things in different settings and epochs.

This paper explores some of these variations in Swedish society during the last three centuries. I focus on the considerable gap between normative ideas about how households ought to look or function and the actual patterns of household organization. The first part of this paper analyzes changes in domestic organization in Swedish peasant society in terms of household ideals and adaptive strategies in household formation and management. The second part deals with domestic life in Victorian middle-class settings and the ways in which this influential class tried to establish its notions of home, household, and family as normal and natural in relation to the domestic life of peasants and workers. Finally, I discuss some aspects of the Victorian heritage in twentieth-century household organization.[1]

DEMOGRAPHIC SOURCES AND SOCIAL REALITY

The problem of sources plagues all historical reconstructions of family and household. Not that there are too few of them; rather, they supply some types of information in abundance but remain silent about other aspects of everyday life.

Let me illustrate this problem with some examples from Swedish peasant society. Thanks to a long tradition of zealous bureaucrats Sweden has very good population records from the eighteenth century onward, which has made it possible to carry out quantitative studies of demographic change over long time spans. Especially during the last decade there has been a rapid expansion in studies of historical demography by Swedish historians and social scientists.

These excellent historical records, however, pose some problems. First of all, they reflect more of the culture and cognitive map of the administrators than that of the populace. Second, the information was collected for certain limited purposes, such as taxation and population census. This may seem trivial but it is important. We must always be aware of the problem of cultural translation in handling sources, in this case the translation of peasant culture and social life into administrative categories created by parish priests, judges, and tax collectors.

What I am advocating is not the classical type of source criticism. Such a treatment too often becomes the historian's monologue vis-à-vis the chosen source in which the scholar rarely questions his or her own cultural assumptions. Rather, we need to develop a type of cultural analysis in which a dialogue between the three concerned parties emerges: the peasants, their administrator, and the researcher. In such an analysis the problem of cultural translation is brought into the spotlight and the historical sources or records can be seen as cultural statements or texts open to several interpretations. We may, for example, learn about systems of social classification and folk taxonomies just by analyzing the order or hierarchy in documents such as a household list, a will, or an inventory. Who is included, who is excluded, who is at the top or at the bottom?

A traditional source-oriented approach may be especially dangerous in historical studies of household organization, both when judging the role of the household in everyday life and when assessing its resource base. In the first case we must always remember that classical population records are very household-oriented and thus tend to give the household a far more prominent position in the social landscape than it often had, at least in Swedish peasant society.

The organization of our abundant demographic information into two favorite administrative units—households and territorial districts (village or parish, for example)—has led to an exaggerated view of the social importance of these units in preindustrial society. Different types of sources underline the importance of other, less formalized social and economic units that were not given the status of administrative units. In order to appraise more realistically the kind of social and economic activities that were organized on a household basis we have to try to reconstruct the social web through which the individual households were integrated with other social units in the peasant community. A certain type of household may be viable only because a sophisticated and flexible system of economic cooperation between households exists whereby manpower and other economic assets are circulated between the units (see Segalen, this volume).

A typical eighteenth-century Swedish farm household was indeed part of a highly complex social organization that tied the domestic unit to a number of other social units both inside and outside the village community. These economic relations included systems of reciprocity in which neighbors pooled their labor for certain tasks during the farm year or cooperated in solving practical problems (concerning, for example, a funeral or a wedding feast). Another common type of cooperation took the form of shared ownership. Several households combined their resources to maintain a common smithy, a water mill, or a bull or shared a common natural resource, such as a meadow or a fishing ground (for the discussion of a similar pattern among Alpine peasants, see Netting 1976).

Perhaps it would be a good idea to start a contextual study of household organization by ignoring the household units and focusing on other types of social and economic units in the community which have often left so few traces in the traditional historical records. Such an approach may help us to get a less household-centered picture of social and economic life.

An ongoing research project at the Institute of European Ethnology in Copenhagen has attempted to develop this type of broad analysis placing the individual household in its local setting. A collection of detailed peasant diaries from the eighteenth and nineteenth centuries has been used to map the daily social and economic contacts between members of the farm household and the outside world. This material is then linked to analysis of more conventional sources like censuses, tax lists, and inventories. Such a painstaking analysis produces a much subtler picture of household organization, and we are able to get a richer and more detailed picture of the complex relations between households and between individuals of different household units (cf. Stoklund 1981).

Another problem in judging the viability of different household adaptions concerns the *resource base* of the individual household. In the traditional historical records we often find a heavy agrarian bias. Government authorities and local administrators viewed land, especially arable land, as the most tangible asset in the peasant economy. It was easy to measure and assess, easy to tax and control. We thus get abundant information on land ownership and land inheritance while the sources are silent on the less tangible assets of the peasant household.

In Swedish peasant society we can talk of a "hidden economy" made up of local resources and economic activities that were seldom registered or taxed but nevertheless formed an important base for the household economy. In many regions and among certain sectors of the population the carrying capacity of the household unit was more dependent on these assets than on land ownership. The reconstruction of such hidden economies is a difficult but necessary task in studies not only of the resource base of individual households but also of inheritance patterns, the division of labor, and other adaptive strategies.

ADAPTIVE STRATEGIES AND HOUSEHOLD ORGANIZATION

I have encountered these same problems in studying changes in household economy and family patterns in a Swedish coastal village between 1800 and 1970 (Löfgren 1977). Fishing was of great importance in the local economy, but the historical records from the nineteenth century spoke of this activity rarely. The occupational title *fisherman* does not occur in the records until the 1920s, illustrating the agrarian focus of the records. Before that time fishermen were registered as crofters, agricultural laborers, cottagers, or lodgers. From the administrative point of view, the important fact was that these fisherfolk were landless, not that they made their living from fishing.

In 1800 the coastal village of Bua had a population of approximately 300 villagers. The socioeconomic structure was relatively homogeneous, dominated by landowning peasants with only a few landless households. The element of ecological differentiation and economic specialization was small indeed. Farming was balanced between grain production and cattle raising for subsistence and was complemented by seasonal fishing. But during the first half of the nineteenth century the economic situation changed rapidly. Between 1800 and 1860 the local population doubled, mainly because of a drastically reduced mortality rate and an increase in fertility.

As in other Swedish agrarian regions this population increase was associated with a process of proletarization. While the number of landowning peasants remained relatively constant during these 60 years, the proletarian class trebled in size. This transformation of the social structure was connected with changes in the farming economy, which became increasingly oriented to market exchange and cash crop production.

How did the growing stratum of landless peasants survive in this local setting? They were forced into a pattern of subsistence on the periphery of the agrarian community of landowning peasants. The way they established new household units and built up their household economy became different from the farmers'. Their hidden economy, consisting of a complex utilization of many marginal resources, left few traces in the official records. Landless peasants became jacks-of-all-trades, combining small-scale fishing with wage labor on local farms, and created households based on a fishing, gathering, and gardening economy. A comparison of household strategies among landowning and landless peasants in the nineteenth century illustrates structural differences that can be observed in many other peasant settings of this period (see Löfgren 1978).

Among landless cottagers the household often functioned as a base of operations from which the household members left to perform different tasks, such as day labor and various gathering activities. Landless men in Bua went out fishing, worked as day laborers, and sometimes migrated to more distant regions. Children were sent away to work as farmhands at an early age in order not "to eat their parents out" and sometimes managed to send some earnings home. Women took in washing, tended their gardens, produced textiles for sale, and worked as day laborers on nearby farms. This type of *centrifugal* household organization was typical of many landless households and created a more flexible division of labor in the household than among the farmers. Although the household was often dispersed during long periods, it still functioned as an economic unit in which household members pooled their resources. Among landowning peasants the farm was more a focus or center of economic activities into which additional labor was recruited. Here the children had to "wait out their parents" in order to establish their own domestic units, and this created different types of social bonds between parent and child than in landless households. We can talk then of *centripetal* household organization among landowning peasants.

Such a comparison could be carried further. What differences did these two structural types of household organization generate in the relations between the members of the household, in sex and age roles, in authority patterns, and in conceptions of *home*? What kind of conflicts were most common?

This polarity, of course, represents a grand simplification. Among Swedish peasants we find a great range in household organization. The economic adaptation among different groups of landless peasants may illustrate this.

Children of agricultural laborers of the plains were a burden and were sent away to do wage labor as early as possible. But in regions where the landless could develop various types of cottage industries, children became an economic asset. A study of landless and smallholding peasants in a woodland region of Sweden illustrates this difference (Boqvist 1978). Here child labor was important for the various types of wood crafts that formed the foundation of the domestic economy.

In the same way, large households were an important asset among landless peasants who specialized in fishing. This was the case in late nineteenth-century Bua (Löfgren 1979), where fishing was primarily carried out by teams of three or four men. In the formation of fishing units we find a distinct pattern closely tied to the developmental cycle of the household. Before forming a household of his own a landless peasant often worked as a farmhand for some years, securing enough cash to build or rent a cottage on the outskirts of the village. After marriage it was not uncommon for the men to work in the U.S. for a couple of years and then return to their families with a small amount of capital that could be invested in a piece of land or some fishing equipment. As the sons grew up, they formed a family crew together with their father, though this had not always been the case.

Household crews became increasingly common as investments in fishing grew through the introduction of new types of equipment and bigger, motor-powered boats around the turn of the century. The growing capitalization of fishing made control and maintenance of capital a central issue, and family-based crews proved themselves to be the most convenient form of ownership. A fisherman who formed a team with his teenage sons secured an advantageous pooling of resources, all profits going straight into the household chest.

Rapid capital accumulation and investment was possible in this type of production unit. When sons established households of their own they continued to fish with their father and brothers, but when their own sons grew up they withdrew their share in the family enterprise and formed a new unit. The result of this economic strategy was a system of agnatic fishing clans and often a pattern of patrilocal clusters of houses (daughters never inherited any fishing capital).

This pattern could be interpreted at first sight in terms of a normative kinship system that was very different from that of the neighborhood farmers or the nonfishing cottagers. A processual analysis shows, however, that this recruitment pattern was a late phenomenon and was mainly a result of the modernization of fishing. It is better viewed as a flexible, economic adaptation in which certain stages of the developmental cycle of the household permit relatively rapid accumulation of fishing capital, which then can be distributed gradually to new households, in turn starting a new process of accumulation.

In my study of Bua I was early struck by the great variation and fluctuation that could be found in different households in the same community, between farmers and fishermen, between landowners and landless, between artisans and day laborers. There was no such thing as a clear local pattern of household organization. I also realized that to explain these variations I had to develop a historical and processual approach to household adaptations. Such a perspective could also help in understanding how different adaptative strategies had consequences for social relations within and without the individual household: in children's expectations of financial assistance from their parents, in the importance placed on kinship and family links, in the division of labor between men and women, children and elders.

FAMILY AND HOUSEHOLD IN A CHANGING PEASANT SOCIETY

Before the last decade few longitudinal studies of peasant kinship and household organization had been carried out in Scandinavia, but a number of mythical assumptions about the historical development of kinship and family patterns prevailed. The most important of these can be labeled the "devolutionary premise," or the tendency to see a gradual disintegration or deterioration in the importance of kinship links and the domestic unit over time. The starting point was the so-called "clan society" of the early Middle Ages where kinship links formed the basis of social organization in a number of contexts and where the kin group, rather than the family or the household, was the basic unit of society. After this stage came the era of the "extended family system," which gradually disintegrated with the advent of industrial society.

This evolutionary model has been taken to pieces by many scholars, but one of the first onslaughts was made by the Swedish ethnologist Borje

Hanssen in a number of empirical studies beginning in the early 1950s. It is primarily during recent years, however, that Hanssen's criticisms have influenced the debate on peasant household organization in Scandinavia (see Löfgren 1981:190ff).

In brief, Hanssen's argument, which is based mainly on local studies of southern Sweden and Denmark from 1600 to the present, is a provocative attempt to turn the classical evolutionary scheme upside down. The farther we move back in peasant history the fewer traces we find of a kinship-based and family-centered social structure. In the feudal villages of the seventeenth century, which are Hanssen's point of departure, the notion of a family in modern terms did not exist; nor were kinship links very important in the social and economic life of the village. The household was the primary unit and it was made up of both kin and nonkin (Hanssen 1979/1980; see also Plakans, this volume).

This was a society in which feudal and state control of the peasant economy was harsh and where sickness and death were a constant threat. Material conditions gave little scope for long-term planning. Possibilities for capital accumulation were slight and ownership and inheritance not very important factors in the life of the individual. Class differences were small. A farmer could easily end up as an impoverished cottager, and most farm children started their careers as servants on other farms. Both social and geographical mobility were marked.

According to Hanssen the eighteenth and nineteenth centuries saw the gradual emergence of a kinship ideology and a notion of the family unit that started to become more important than the concept household or neighborhood. This ideology is most marked among propertied farmers, who experienced times of growing prosperity with the gradual expansion of agrarian capitalism and the decline in feudal and state control of production. The new situation of economic growth also resulted in growing social stratification in the villages. In this process some households were more successful in adjusting to the new economic opportunities than others.

Ownership and control of property became more important as conditions of accumulation and investment improved. Farms became economic assets in ways that they never had been in the seventeenth century, and inheritance strategies became an important element in the management of family resources. Hanssen described the new kinship and family ideology that he saw manifested in many ways in the villages he studied. At its culmination toward the end of the nineteenth century, the prosperous farming class had opened a considerable social and cultural gap between themselves and the expanding class of agrarian proletarians: servants, farm laborers, and cottagers.

To what extent can Hanssen's findings be generalized? I find some of his basic assumptions convincing. First, there is his warning against taking kinship relations for granted in "traditional peasant society" and against confusing biological and cultural definitions of kin. Second, I find his emphasis on the links between family ideology and control of the distribution of household resources important. My main criticism is that Hanssen introduced an evolutionary premise instead of the traditional devolutionary idea, a notion of the gradual emergence of a kinship- and family-oriented social organization among Scandinavian peasants, based on *one* type of peasant adaptation. His research was also part of an ongoing polemic that led to problematic comparisons between family life among peasants and family life in contemporary society. Like many other students of the family, Hanssen tended to formulate his questions in a slightly dangerous way. We should not ask "Did the family unit and kinship links play a more or less important role in earlier times compared with today?" Rather, we should view the domestic unit or kinship as a cultural phenomenon that can be given varied emotional, social, and economic values in different settings.

The need to measure our own standards and values against those of earlier periods is a telling sign of contemporary uncertainty in attitudes toward the family. Behind many studies of the history of the family lurks an implicit comparison: was the family healthier, kinship links stronger, love of children less or greater, the role of elderly people easier, compared with today? Research often becomes part of the heated debate on the problems of modern family life or part of the search to find standards for a "natural" or "healthy" family. Clearly, we should reflect more about our own attitudes toward the family before embarking on a comparative study. In any case, it is important that we formulate research problems in a neutral form, such as "What types of primary groups fulfilled the functions of production, reproduction, or capital management in this society?" or "What is the content of the social relations labeled *kinship* or the unit called a *family* in this particular cultural setting?"

Hanssen's pioneer work has inspired many later students of Scandinavian household organization. The Danish ethnologist Palle Christianssen and the Swedish social historian David Gaunt have convincingly developed some of Hanssen's ideas and illustrated how the importance of kinship links and the household unit tends to vary in different ecotypes, periods, and social strata (Christianssen 1978; Gaunt 1977*a*, forthcoming). Thanks to their work and some other recent studies we know that variations in kinship ideologies as well as household structure and organization were considerable in Scandinavian peasant society and that changes over time cannot be compressed into any simple unilinear scheme of development.

CHANGING PERCEPTIONS OF THE HOUSEHOLD

One of Hanssen's central ideas was that the growing importance of the family unit in nineteenth-century peasant society illustrated the change from a household-oriented organization to a family-centered organization of primary groups. As we have seen in the example of Bua, the economic gap between landowners and landless grew in the village communities as part of the growing socioeconomic differentiation in Swedish peasant society. While more and more landless or smallholding peasants had to build up new patterns of household economy, the new class of prosperous farmers faced problems of capital management. They had to develop more elaborate marriage and inheritance strategies in order to maintain their economic position. As small-scale entrepreneurs in an increasingly market-oriented economy, they also reorganized economic interactions within the household unit.

The increased socioeconomic differentiation between the groups resulted not only in different material experiences in everyday life but also in a need for the farmers to increase the cultural distance from "the others." This process, described by Hanssen, included a new concept of the family and an interest in drawing sharper boundaries between the farm family and the rest of the household.

A fruitful field in which to study this cultural and social change is the altered positions of servants. In the earlier, more egalitarian social structure of peasant society the role of servant was usually linked to a certain stage in the life cycle. Most peasant children spent some period in their youth as servants in other households. It can be argued that the circulation of youths between village farms served as a way of balancing the unequal labor power of individual households resulting from variations in the size of the production unit and, more important, from changes in the developmental cycle of the household. Large households with many teenage children could supply smaller households with servants (see Löfgren 1974:25).

Another aspect of this change in status has been discussed by David Gaunt (1977*b*), who points to evidence that farmers thought they could exploit the work of hired servants more effectively than the labor of their own children.

Because of growing social stratification servants came to be recruited mainly from the class of landless peasants. The emerging class of more prosperous farmers became increasingly eager to dissociate themselves from the rest of the village and this wish influenced the internal relations of the farm household as well. Step by step, new social boundaries were created in everyday life. At first, these boundaries were most apparent in increased paternal control of children's marriage plans. Let me quote the reminiscences of a peasant woman from the nineteenth century:

> Master and mistress, children and servants, they all sat at the same table and ate off the same plate. They did the same jobs, and the daughters of the farmer shared the bed with the maids, just like the sons with the male hands. But if the question of marriage between servant and "free" arose, then the boundary appeared so sharp and so high that it couldn't be crossed, at least among more prosperous families.

The next steps included setting new boundaries within the household, separating servants from family members. Gradually the two groups ceased to share the same eating bowl at dinner and in some instances started eating at separate tables, later even in separate rooms. It was no longer considered proper for farm children to share sleeping quarters with the servants, who were moved to special quarters in the farm complex.

Farm work was also reorganized. Among the prosperous farmers the wife withdrew from hard manual labor, which was left to the servant girls. The master and the mistress of the farm no longer worked side by side with the servants in the fields but functioned more like supervisors.

The new boundaries were also manifested in village feasting and leisure. The children of farmers no longer socialized with the servants or the children of the cottagers. The social life of the village became much more segregated.

Such changes in everyday arrangements enable us to construct a timetable for the emergence of a new conception of the farm *family* and also to analyze how this process varied in time, space, and social dimensions in nineteenth-century society. "The time has long since passed when the servant was regarded as a member of the family," remarked one observer from southern Sweden in the 1890s. The important point here is that although the farm household may have had the same *composition* and *size* in 1800 and 1890, its internal structure had changed radically from a relatively well-integrated unit to a distinct family unit and a distinct group of servants. These two groups no longer mixed freely or shared the same tasks and were no longer united by the same emotional bonds of common identity.

These class boundaries drawn between family and servants on many farms caused new problems. Complaints about lazy or unruly servants increased as the old patriarchal structure withered away. The conflicting interests of the two groups became more obvious, and we find an interesting tendency among landowners to try to turn back the clock. Not that anyone tried to change the economic conditions that had produced this cultural change; rather, some tried to reintroduce the old patriarchal pattern that had been firmly founded in the so-called Lutheran unity of religious and secular authority in seventeenth-, eighteenth-, and early nineteenth-century Scandinavian society. As the father of his people, the king was God's representative and sat at the top of the patriarchal structure, which descended through clergymen and local representatives of state to the basic unit of society, the individual household. The master of the house represented the last link in this chain of authority. He was responsible for the moral conduct of all the members of the household.

Laments about the bad relations between master and servant were linked with a longing for the "good old days" when loyality and solidarity united all members of the household "living as one big family." Arguments for reintroducing some cultural manifestations of this old unity were bruited among the farmers. In Denmark some of them tried to revitalize the old peasant institution of servants and family members spending the evening together, working and talking, as an ideological expression of the *Gemeinschaft*, that no longer had any economic basis.

The nostalgia for a golden past in which society was based on big households and extended families, united in harmony under patriarchal guidance, is evident in many public arenas toward the end of the nineteenth century, when the old social order was disintegrating. It is important to remember that the evolutionary theory of the family and the myth of the "grand family" system has its roots in this social atmosphere. The conception of the "traditional house" became a powerful tool, an attempt to create an utopia, to return to a mythical past devoid of class conflicts and disobedience.

This dream is echoed in Ferdinand Tönnies's classical discussion of "Gemeinschaft und Gesellschaft," as three English scholars have pointed out:

> The house constitutes the realm and, as it were, the body of kinship. Here people live together under one protecting roof. Here they share their possessions and their pleasures: they feed from the same supply, they sit

> at the same table. The dead are venerated here as invisible spirits, as if they were still powerful and held a protecting hand over their family. Thus, common fear and common honor ensure peaceful living and cooperation with greater certainty. (Quoted by Davidoff, L'Esperance, and Newby, 1979:137)

The strong ideological and utopian connotations the concept *household* had in the contemporary debate is to be remembered. Another good example can be found in the influential writings of the German scholar Wilhelm Riehl, who in his studies of the family advocated a return to a social system based on "*Das ganze Haus*," the patriarchal household (see the discussion in Weber-Kellermann 1969).

The concept *household* was an important *root metaphor* (Ortner 1973) in eighteenth- and nineteenth-century society just as the concept *home* has become a powerful cultural image during the last century.

THE VIRTUES OF FAMILY LIFE AMONG THE VICTORIANS

The new ideas about home and family got their most distinct expression among the Victorian bourgeoisie. In this rising class the family no longer functioned as a production unit, and the cleavage of the household into family and servants had occurred much earlier than among farmers. If we want to find some of the roots of our modern conception of the family we need to take a closer look at the culture-building of this new and powerful nineteenth-century elite. One way of mapping this new ideology of the family is to look at the ways in which the Victorians described the domestic life of their social opposites, the "primitive" peasants or the "uncivilized" workers.

In Sweden we have a lot of evidence on Victorian reactions to the life of the "less advanced" peasants. Urban travelers in the nineteenth-century Swedish countryside were often shocked by peasant attitudes toward marriage, family life, and sex roles. The visitors' complaints were many: children were not given a proper upbringing; women behaved without modesty; love of home was lacking; and the virtues of privacy and propriety were not respected. Such comments may tell us more about the family ideology of the urban middle class than about peasant culture, but they also speak of a widening cultural gap in nineteenth-century Swedish society. One country doctor brings out this sense of difference especially vividly in his recollections of journeys in remote peasant areas around the turn of the century:

> For them [the peasants] there is no dividing line between public and private, all is public. Locks are never used in the isolated villages—night or day—and you never knock when entering a house.
>
> One light summer night I came to a farm where they used to take visitors in. The main door of the farm entrance was open as well as the door of the main building, but not a person was in sight. I had to walk through the whole house until I found the family sleeping soundly in the innermost room. The mistress of the house woke up, and I told her who I was and asked for a bed for the night. Well, that was no problem! She just got up and made me a bed.
>
> We normal middle-class people don't want to have strangers coming into the room where we are having a meal. The real old-fashioned peasants never worry about that. . . .
>
> We don't like to dress in the presence of strangers. That never bothers the peasants I am talking about here. And they just can't understand that type of feeling in others.

When visitors to peasant homes complained of the lack of privacy and the intolerable extent of communal living—the whole household (including guests) sleeping, dressing, eating, and working in the same room—it is clear that this complaint must be seen against the background of a rising cult of intimacy and privacy among the new middle class.

In the culture-building of the new middle class we can observe how a new class constructs its own moral and cultural charter. This cultural program opposed both the traditional and "immoral" aristocracy and the grey mass of ordinary people. The Victorian world view was characterized by an obsessive need for boundaries, for taboos and rituals of avoidance, and for hierarchy. New types of dividing lines separated public and private life, work and leisure, male and female, and class and class. The result was a new cultural framework for society, a totally novel organization of productive as well as social relationships.

This reorganization of everyday life and cognitive frames gave the concepts of home, household, and family new cultural meanings. For the Victorians these concepts became key symbols "which were good to think with": they were used as metaphors in a number of situations. They symbolized the "good and proper life." To understand how differently the Victorians viewed these concepts we have to see them as part of a more basic cultural structure: that of the polarity between public and private, production and nonproduction. A tentative representation of this cognitive structure would look something like this.

Private sphere	*Public sphere*
Home	Outside world
Family	Nonfamily
Leisure	Work
Personal and intimate relations	Impersonal and anonymous relations
Closeness	Distance
Love and legitimate sexuality	Illegitimate sexuality
Morality and purity	Immorality
Sentiment and irrationality	Rationality and effectiveness
Wholeness and harmony	Fragmentation and disharmony
The natural and unaffected life	The artificial and unnatural life

The sphere of home and family life thus becomes a sphere of reproduction where different moral and economic rules apply than in the harsh, outside world of production. The home comes to stand for emotional qualities, for love, protection, nurture, warmth, and cosiness, values that cannot (or must not) be measured in terms of money. It is striking that such a list of qualities in private and public spheres of Victorian life also provides a new model for female and male behavior. If we started to make the same type of list based on gender differences we would find that qualities attributed to the woman are also associated with the sheltered and warm home life. While her middle-class husband should be rational, effective, calculating, and career-oriented, she should be warm and loving, passive rather than active, a provider not of material but rather of emotional sustenance.

This is of course a simplified description of the dialectics between the two spheres of production and reproduction, between male/female gender constructs, but it may serve as a basis for further discussion.

How were these new ideas about family life related to everyday life? To what extent did they influence the organization of the Victorian household? Although in Sweden we have few systematic studies of variations in household size and composition in different classes and social strata for this period, it is possible to see some of the more important differences. The largest households are found in the small but influential upper class, not only because these households include servants of several kinds but also because they represent a more kinship-oriented life-style than in the Victorian middle class. The complex structure of these aristocratic households often evaded the census takers, but it is pictured in other sources (diaries, autobiographies, and letters, for example). Here we find a well-developed system of visiting through which young cousins, aunts, and other relatives stay for shorter or longer periods in the homes of their kinsmen.

Middle-class Domestic Life

Middle-class homes rarely had the space and resources for such visiting as took place in aristocratic homes, so it is in this bourgeois setting that we find the new ideals of the nuclear family anchored in everyday reality. We can exemplify this relation between world view and domestic life by looking at the material framework of family life, the Victorian middle-class home. (For a more detailed empirical analysis, see Löfgren 1979: 74–130.)

Building a home, for the Victorians, was not only a practical project—it was a *moral* one. In middle-class settings a man was supposed to marry only if he could finance an adequate home and support a wife, children, and at least one servant. If he was to be the provider, his wife was to be the guardian of the home and of the virtues of homeliness. She was responsible for making their house a *good* home.

Why did the Victorians choose to invest so much time, energy, and money in homemaking? Apart from their possession of far better material conditions for this project than earlier generations, it is important to understand that for the rising bourgeoisie the home was both a showcase to the outside world and a refuge from it. The family home became the stage on which the family demonstrated its wealth and social standing. In this period of unstable class boundaries the communication of status and social ambitions was of special importance, which increased the representational function of the home in middle-class settings.

At the same time the significance of the home as a private sphere and haven increased. The same economic class that administered the new capitalist industrial production system also created a compensatory world of intimacy, a refuge of coziness and warmth. The Victorian home became an antipole to the growing anonymity, rationality, and efficiency of the outside world. In this dialectical process the sweetness of home increased as the outside world became more complex and problematic.

Even the physical plan of the Victorian house in Sweden bears witness to this dual function of the home as stage and shelter. A number of spatial boundaries were drawn with the help of entrances, passages, doors, and sequences of rooms to separate public from private, servants from family, children from parents, and to sort out visitors of varying standing. An analysis of Victorian childhood reminiscences shows how much children learned about social relationships from the actual physical arrangements in the home, which became part of a silent and unconscious socialization process. It was as if the walls spoke to the children.

But these childhood memoirs must also be used carefully. Again we are faced with the problem of separating ideals and realities. It is evident that the unity of the small family group was given strong symbolic expressions through family rituals. For many Victorians the evenings when the family was gathered around the paraffin lamp are strong and emotionally loaded childhood memories, manifestations of intimacy and togetherness. These are times one *wants* to remember, although the truth was that contact with parents was often both restricted and formal.

For many children of this time the parents' bedroom was a forbidden territory. "Behind the dining room was a world I never entered, but where I guessed my parents had their rooms," recollects one Victorian. And he also remembered his father, the judge, visiting the nursery only once during his whole childhood. The same father later told his son that he considered the family the only real foundation of a civilized society, but as his son pointed out: "Home meant more of an intensive feeling of togetherness than of actual interaction." Another Victorian described how he as a young child shared rooms with the servants above his parents' apartment and had only the shadiest ideas about what went on downstairs.

This pattern of household organization was most common in the upper stratum of the middle class, where we often find the household divided into two units: the children, who spent most of their time with the servants, and the adults, who moved in their own sets. Separate nurseries were not common until the beginning of this century. Prior to this time the young children slept with the maid.

This arrangement produced its own problems. Middle-class family life was based on the availability of cheap female domestic help. Girls were recruited from peasant or working-class settings, and their position in the household was an uneasy one. Middle-class ideology stressed that they should be seen as members of the family, in the sense that they stood under the moral guardianship of the housewife. But they had to know their proper station: that of servant. They were both inside the family and safely outside it. Middle-class housewives often saw the inclusion of young servant girls in the household as a form of apprenticeship and moral guidance. The girls would get the opportunity to obtain good domestic manners and learn to manage a household. The girls themselves often had a more realistic picture of their position: they were poorly paid wage earners, not temporarily adopted members of the household.

Ambivalence toward servant girls increased because the young women spent so much time with the young children, leading to a clash of cultures. In the backstage area of the Victorian home, other values and ideas were being communicated. A proper middle-class upbringing thus stressed the necessity of the children to dissociate themselves from the culture the servants brought into the household. A child might turn to the maid for company, consolation, and bodily contact, but at the same time the parents told the child not to imitate the way she talked or acted: that was simply bad or inferior manners. Any analysis of the organization of the Victorian middle-class household must tackle this structural conflict, which Victorians often tried to suppress or ignore by defining servants as nonpersons in many situations. Children who grew up in these settings soon learned to differentiate between the ideals of a good family life and a happy household and the everyday realities of domestic life.

THE VICTORIAN HERITAGE

In retrospect the domestic rituals of the Victorians in their overdecorated homes, attended by slaving servants, may seem distant and exotic. Yet it is striking how many values and habits we have inherited from this culture. We only have to look back on our own upbringing to realize how powerful this cultural influence has been during the twentieth century. Our attitudes toward family life, domestic duties, home, and privacy are still perhaps more influenced by Victorian ideology than we care to admit. So effectively may these notions and cognitive frameworks be internalized that many people take them for granted and find it hard to understand cultures or historical settings where household relations are structured in a different way.

We must also remember that it was the Victorians who collected and organized most of our information on nineteenth-century peasant domestic life and household patterns. "The possession of an entire house is strongly desired by every Englishman; for it throws a sharp and well-defined circle round his family and hearth—the shrine of his sorrows, joys, and meditations," wrote the Registrar General in the introduction to the British census of 1851 (Davidoff 1976:69). He probably had no doubts about how a proper household should be organized.

In Sweden Victorian ideas about home and family stimulated middle-class ambitions to reform and educate the lower classes. As the old social structure of Swedish society crumbled, traditional rules of hierarchy, loyalty, and social control no longer seemed to hold. The rapidly growing working class was seen as a menace to the old social stability. The atmosphere of tension, of clashing values, frightened those at the top. If the old order could not be rebuilt, certainly a new "moral cement" was needed to bind the disintegrating society. One of the answers to this problem was found in the promoting of a good home life. If only the working classes could be domesticated, argued middle-class reformers, if only their unrest and ambitions could be turned inward, toward the home and the family, many problems would be solved. Change was to be moral rather than economic.

Arguments like these were common in late nineteenth-century discussions, where they could be more or less consciously formulated. The virtues of a stable home life were echoed in parliamentary debates, in newspaper articles, and in pamphlets and soon started to spread through channels such as housing and educational reform programs and campaigns for better housekeeping among working-class women. By the turn of the century we find the ideal of the happy nuclear family extolled almost everywhere. It appears in penny novels, in advertisements, in popular oleographs. Even in zoological illustrations the animals appear in family groups according to the Victorian model of father-mother-child rather than in the actual biological pattern.

It would be wrong, however, to talk in terms of a well-planned attack with the explicit goal of pacifying the unruly working class. Many of the social reformers saw themselves as missionaries of "the good life," of modernization and development. They wanted to improve housing, food habits, and child care. Many of them were not aware that their reforming activities had heavy moral overtones.

WORKING-CLASS DOMESTIC LIFE

We find great variation in household patterns among Swedish working-class families at the beginning of this century. Industrialization was late but relatively rapid in Sweden, and thousands of peasants moved to cities and industrial towns in search of work. The household unit for them was an important condition of economic survival. Low wages required that all household members contribute to the domestic economy. Single wage earners could not survive on their own but had to form a family or attach themselves to an existing household (see Hackenberg, Murphy, and Selby, this volume).

Urban working-class household structure was complex, with a high percentage of lodgers, both kin and nonkin. The degree of integration of these lodgers in the household could vary. Some lodgers just rented a room or a bed, while others shared a number of activities with the other household members. The institution of lodgers can be seen as a flexible strategy for maintaining viable household units. It was well suited to this period of massive rural-urban migration. Those who left their parental homes or their spouses and children in search of work could attach themselves to a new unit in town. Kinship and neighborhood links could be important assets in this situation, for a relative or a local family already in town could function as a bridgehead for a new life.

For large sectors of the working class lodgers were indispensable, a way to cut down the cost of living. Lodgers could also contribute to the household economy in other ways. In many families both man and wife had to work outside the home, so a lodger, like an old single woman, could help to look after the children. Lodgers were especially important during the difficult stages in the household cycle when children were too small to contribute to the economy. Once the children had moved away lodgers could again be a source of income for the aging couple. We can view this flexible household organization as an economic necessity during the early stages of industrialization (cf. the discussion in Modell and Hareven 1973).

Another factor that complicated household structure was the low frequency of marriage in some urban and rural working-class settings. Formal church marriages were resisted as symbols of an oppressive culture and the female role of "housekeeper" became an alternative.

The Victorian middle class viewed this seemingly loose family and household structure as a grave problem. The habit of taking in lodgers was opposed on the grounds that it violated the important boundary between family and outside world. The following quotation from a leading figure in the campaign for better working-class housing illustrates this attitude:

> The dwelling is the practical foundation of the home. Without a sound and clean dwelling, where happiness is not destroyed by being forced to take in lodgers, and where health is not damaged by cold and damp, a home life is impossible. From both a moral and sanitary viewpoint the system of lodgers is a canker in the domestic life of the working classes. It produces coarse habits and demoralizes thinking, in a way which no statistics can show. . . .
>
> Finally, it robs the dwelling of the last bit of feeling found in the word *home*, and changes it into a place where men and women sleep like animals next to each other without the hope of a better future. . . .
>
> "Give us better working class housing," a philanthropist once said, "and Stockholm will have a better working-class population within twenty years." (Geijerstam 1894:52)

Statements like this mix social indignation with middle-class fears of sexuality and bodily contact. Obviously, in such working-class homes the two basic virtues of modesty and privacy could not be upheld.

But attitudes toward lodgers also varied among workers. Many working-class wives aspired to a home without lodgers, and a proper parlor was an important ambition for such women. These ideals of working-class respectability were not, however, mere reflections of middle-class values. Working-class family life was anchored in distinct subcultural values and cognitive categories. The housewife considered one silent and well-kept room, where no one was allowed to sleep, well worth the nuisance of an overcrowded kitchen or second room.

Overcrowded lodgings did not provide much opportunity for a family-centered home life. A striking feature of working-class social organization up to the Second World War was the relative unimportance of family togetherness during leisure time. Men spent their free time with other men outside the home, women formed informal neighborhood groups, and children looked after themselves. Again, this was not what middle-class observers could call "a happy home."

FEELING AT HOME

Social life in Sweden in the twentieth century has become more private, more home-centered. The rising standard of living and new ideals of consumption have made home life more important to all social classes. The change in working-class attitudes can be seen in the context of growing anonymity in public life and alienation at work. In a world where the individual feels that he cannot make his voice heard, the domestic arena becomes more important as a microworld with its own rules, its own order and family traditions. Managing one's own household, living on one's own, now stand as important symbols of individual freedom in contemporary society. People who cannot fend for themselves tend to be regarded as second-class citizens. Setting up an independent household is in some ways a ritual statement of independence. In contemporary Sweden it has become the most important rite of passage to adulthood.

If we look at changes in household structure in Sweden in the twentieth century the most striking feature is the increase in small households. In 1890 less than 6 percent of all households were made up of single persons. The average household size was 4.56 persons. In 1976 the size had been reduced to 2.4 persons. In a city like Stockholm the average household size is now 1.8 persons (Gaunt, forthcoming).

Living singly was hardly an alternative in preindustrial society. The household formed the basis of production and reproduction, but it was also a powerful ideological concept. In order to survive, economically and socially, individuals had to attach themselves to a bigger household unit (see Herlihy, this volume). For these reasons kin and nonkin mixed in the same household, as lodgers, servants, or workmates. This solution was common to the old, the unmarried farmhand, the young factory worker, or the middle-class spinster, but the ways in which the persons living under the same roof were or were not integrated into a household unit differed greatly from setting to setting.

CONCLUSION

My examples from three centuries of household history in Sweden illustrate how a basic social unit can take on different cultural shapes over time and in various classes and subcultures. Such a deepened historical perspective can also help us to understand our own notions of family and household.

I have argued for a processual approach that focuses on the flexibility of household units. I have emphasized adaptive strategies rather than form. Such an approach underlines the gap that exists between household ideals and everyday realities in a given society. This tension is evident in the life of seventeenth-century peasants, middle-class Victorians, and contemporary urbanites. Furthermore, ideals of proper family and household life often tend to change more slowly than the actual patterns of household arrangements. We only have to think of the current commercial image that equates the standard consumption unit with the nuclear family. The combination of Mom, Dad, and the two kids appears more frequently in color advertisements than in the population census.

An analysis of changing ideological connotations attached to the household concept may also help us to understand the ways in which state authorities have perceived and tried to influence household organization, from the eighteenth-century Lutheran ideology of the patriarchal house to the family policies of the welfare state. Households have been important for state authorities, but important for different reasons during different periods. I have outlined a striking paradox in government attitudes toward domestic life over the last century. On the one hand the importance of drawing clear boundaries between public and private spheres has been stressed in the public debate and the importance of equating the concepts of home, family, and household has been underlined. On the other hand authorities have seen domestic life as far too important to be left to people themselves: the household walls are penetrated by good advice, counseling, and state regulations.

Connected to this question is the problem of judging household autonomy or dependency in different settings. I have criticized the tendency in some types of historical demography to isolate the household as a unit of analysis; I stress the need to look closer at the ways in which households are integrated into wider socioeconomic networks. This becomes especially important in comparative discussions of households as units of production. We should ask what kinds of infrastructures in the form of systems for pooling and cooperation are needed to make a certain household form or adaptation viable.

The degree of household autonomy and distinctiveness must also be analyzed on a cultural level. What does it mean to be a member of a household or a family in a peasant village, a working-class neighborhood, or a Victorian middle-class home? As I have shown this type of analysis calls for a study of the boundaries separating the household from the outside world or the family from the household unit. Such analysis must include study of the household as an adaptive strategy and a cognitive category as well as a symbolic image.

NOTES

1. Quotations of Swedish recollections of peasant and middle-class family life have been translated from Löfgren 1979 unless otherwise stated.

REFERENCES

Boqvist, Agneta
1978 Den dolda ekonomin: En etnologisk studie av näringsstrukturen i Bollebygd 1850–1950 [The Hidden Economy: An Ethnological Study of the Economic Structure in the Bollebygd region 1850–1950]. Lund: Liber.

Christiansen, Palle Ove
1978 The Household in the Local Setting. A Study of Peasant Stratification. *In* Chance and Change: Social and Economic Studies in Historical Demography in the Baltic Area, ed. D. Gaunt, H. C. Johansen & S. Akerman. Odense: Odense University Press.

Davidoff, Leonore
1979 The Separation of Home and Work? Landladies and Lodgers in Nineteenth- and Twentieth-century England. *In* Fit Work for Women, ed. Sandra Burman. New York: St. Martin's Press.

Davidoff, Leonore, Jean L'Esperance, and Howard Newby
1976 Landscape with Figures: Home and Community in English Society. *In* The Rights and Wrongs of Women, ed. J. Mitchell and A. Oakley. Harmondsworth: Penguin.

Gaunt, David
1977*a* Pre-industrial Economy and Population Structure: The Elements of Variance in Early Modern Sweden. Scandinavian Journal of History 3:183–210.
1977*b* I slottets skugga: Om frälsebönders sociala problem i Borgeby och Löddeköpinge under 1700-talet [In the Shadow of the Manor: On the Social Problems of Tenant Farmers in Borgeby and Löddeköpinge during the 18th Century]. Ale (1977):15–30.
Forthcoming. Familj, hushåll och grannskap sedan 1890-talet i Sverige [Family, Household, and Neighborhood in Sweden since the 1890s].
Geijerstam, Gustaf af
1894 Anteckningar om arbetareförhållandena i Stockholm. Reprint 1973. Lund: Student-litteratur.
Hanssen, Börje
1979/1980 Households, Classes, and Integration Processes in a Scandinavian Village over 300 Years. Ethnologia Europea 11:76–118.
Löfgren, Orvar
1974 Family and Household among Scandinavian Peasants: An Exploratory Essay. Ethnologia Scandinavica (1974):17–52.
1978 The Potato People: Household Economy and Family Patterns among Rural Proletarians in Nineteenth-century Sweden. *In* Chance and Change: Social and Economic Studies in Historical Demography in the Baltic Area, ed. D. Gaunt et al., pp. 95–108. Odense: Odense University Press.
1977 Fångstmän i industrisamhället. En halländsk kustbygds utveckling 1800–1970 [Maritime Hunters in Industrial Society: The Development of a Halland Coastal Community 1800–1970]. Lund: Liber.
1979 Familjemänniskan. *In* J. Frykman and O. Löfgren, Den kultiverade människan, [Civilized Man], pp. 74–130. Lund: Liber.
1981 Historical Perspectives on Scandinavian Peasantries. Annual Review of Anthropology (1980):187–215.
Modell, J., and T. Hareven
1973 Urbanization and the Malleable Household: An Examination of Boarding and Lodging in American Families. Journal of Marriage and the Family 35:467–79.
Netting, Robert McC.
1976 What Alpine Peasants Have in Common: Observations on Communal Tenure in a Swiss Village. Human Ecology (1976):135–46.
Ortner, Sherry
1973 On Key Symbols. American Anthropologist 1975:1338–46.
Stoklund, Bjarne
1981 Peasant Diaries. Ethnologia Europea (1981) 1.
Weber-Kellermann, Ingeborg
1969 Kontinuität und Familienstruktur. *In* Kontinuität, ed. Hermann Bausinger. Berlin: Erich Schmidt.

Index

Designer: UC Press Staff
Compositor: Trend-Western

Text: Palatino
Display: Palatino

www.ingramcontent.com/pod-product-compliance
Ingram Content Group UK Ltd.
Pitfield, Milton Keynes, MK11 3LW, UK
UKHW040413180926
475586UK00002B/57

9 780520 322936